October 11–13, 2012
Calgary, Alberta, Canada

**Association for Computing Machinery**

*Advancing Computing as a Science & Profession*

# SIGITE'12

Proceedings of the ACM

## Special Interest Group for Information Technology Education Conference

*Sponsored by:*
**ACM SIGITE**

*Supported by:*
**Academic Alliance, Piazza, and Mount Royal University**

**Association for Computing Machinery**

*Advancing Computing as a Science & Profession*

**The Association for Computing Machinery**
2 Penn Plaza, Suite 701
New York, New York 10121-0701

**ISBN:** 978-1-4503-1464-0 (Digital)

**ISBN:** 978-1-4503-1923-2 (Print)

Additional copies may be ordered prepaid from:

**ACM Order Department**
PO Box 30777
New York, NY 10087-0777, USA

Phone: 1-800-342-6626 (USA and Canada)
+1-212-626-0500 (Global)
Fax: +1-212-944-1318
E-mail: acmhelp@acm.org
Hours of Operation: 8:30 am – 4:30 pm ET

Printed in the USA

# SIGITE/RIIT 2012 Chair's Welcome

Welcome to Calgary and Mount Royal University!

It is our great pleasure to host the 13th Annual Conference on Information Technology Education and the 1st Annual Research in IT Conference. This year is especially exciting since it introduces the brand new IT Research conference; our aim in this and in future joint SIGITE/RIIT conferences is to provide a venue for showcasing research in information technology along with our traditional focus on teaching IT. Inspired by the new research conference, our joint conference has the theme of *Working Together: Research & Education for IT*.

Over the years, we have found the SIGITE conference to be both a wellspring of ideas to address issues such as the above and a much-needed opportunity to network and bond with fellow IT educators. We hope you find this year's conference as beneficial and rewarding as the many we have attended in the past.

We are truly fortunate this year to have Randy Thompson of Venture Alberta as our keynote speaker. Randy provides a keynote that combines our interest in both IT education and IT research. Integrating his many years of experience at the head of an IT angel investors group, Randy shows us how IT departments in universities can play a key role in commercializing IT research and thereby improve local economies as well as IT education.

SIGITE/RIIT 2012 is truly a team effort, and we would like to acknowledge and thank Dave Armitage as Program Chair for SIGITE. Dave was last year's Sponsorship Chair so he has been deeply involved with the conference organization for over a year. We are also very indebted to Jeffrey Brewer, who had the very difficult task of being the inaugural Program Chair for RIIT, which necessitated not only navigating many uncharted waters at ACM but also organizing reviewers and the conference schedule for both SIGITE and RIIT. We would also like to thank Rob Friedman for his successful efforts as Sponsorship Chair, Mark Stockman for his leadership and guidance as SIGITE Chair, and all of our sponsors for their generous support of this event.

We would also like to thank the many people who worked so hard behind the scenes on the many administrative challenges and needs. These include Bill Paterson as Local Arrangements Chair, Faith-Michael Uzoka as Finance and Registration Chair, April Mosqus at ACM for assistance with overall planning, Lisa Tolles at Sheridan Printing Company for organizing the proceedings, Jeane Vincent at the University of South Florida for the graphic design work on the conference program, and Henry Walker for administering the paper reviewing submission system.

We hope that you will find the conference's program to be both inspiring and thought-provoking and that the conference will provide you with a valuable opportunity to share ideas with other researchers and practitioners from institutions around the world.

**Randy Connolly**
*SIGITE/RIIT '12 Conference Chair*
*Mount Royal University, Canada*

# SIGITE/RIIT 2012 Program Chairs' Message

Being part of something new is always a great experience, and this year's inauguration of the Research in Information Technology (RIIT) conference as a new companion to the more "venerable" SIGITE conference is no exception. The dual conference theme, *Working Together: Research & Education for IT*, emphasizes the increasing synergy between teaching and research in our field. It's a long-standing principle among academics that research should inform our teaching; over years of SIGITE conferences, we've demonstrated the bi-directionality of that relationship, as teaching has often generated the source data and motivation for our research in IT education.

A strong motivation for launching RIIT was the need to recognize "research in IT" as more than a fragmented collection of pursuits in other computing disciplines. We have been watching a body of research develop that is uniquely characteristic of information technology. With a hands-on flavor and stronger connections with industry, it is clearly differentiating itself from research in more traditional computing disciplines, and is deserving of its own conference venue.

We have a selection of exceptionally strong papers this year. Making final choices of papers for presentation was anything but easy, and many quality papers could not be included due to the constraints inherent in a conference schedule. We received a total of 87 paper submissions, 18 of which were classified as RIIT submissions and the rest (69) as SIGITE submissions. Papers received a minimum of three reviews, with approximately 4.6 reviews per paper being the mean. We had a shorter than usual review time available for this year's conferences; a large and enthusiastic group of reviewers – 134 of you! – were instrumental in getting the job done. Each reviewer handled from one to eight papers; the mean was approximately three papers per reviewer. A total of 402 reviews were submitted. Additional recognition and thanks must go to a self-sacrificing subset of reviewers who took on emergency reviews with turnaround times of less than two days.

Of the eighteen paper sessions at the dual conference, four of them feature RIIT papers, while fourteen present SIGITE papers. Nine of the forty-nine papers to be presented represent RIIT submissions; one accepted RIIT paper was withdrawn after notification. While twenty percent of accepted papers coming from RIIT submissions is a respectable number for the first year of the conference, we look forward to building on that in 2013 and beyond. We need to spread the word to our non-IT education colleagues that RIIT is open for business and will be a welcoming venue.

We have some great panel sessions on the conference schedule. At thirty minutes each, you will find concentrated discussions of significant issues by highly qualified panelists. And don't miss Thursday afternoon's opportunity to view the six posters selected for our conferences.

Welcome to RIIT 2012 and SIGITE 2012. Hear about the latest research in our field, meet new colleagues and link up again with old friends. And, of course, start looking forward to SIGITE/RIIT 2013. Thanks for attending!

**Dave Armitage**
*SIGITE'12 Program Chair*
*University of South Florida*

**Jeff Brewer**
*RIIT'12 Program Chair*
*Purdue University*

# Table of Contents

## Keynote Address

## Session 1: Networking and Security
Session Chair: Yin Pan *(Rochester Institute of Technology)*

## Session 2: IT Curriculum (1)
Session Chair: Barry Lunt *(Brigham Young University)*

## Session 3: IT Curriculum (2)
Session Chair: Jeff Brewer *(Purdue University)*

## Session 4: Web Development and HCI
Session Chair: Amber Settle *(DePaul University)*

## Session 5: Networking and Security
Session Chair: Ed Sobiesk *(United States Military Academy)*

## Poster Session

## Session 6: System Administration
Session Chair: Dale Rowe *(Brigham Young University)*

## Panel Session 1

## Session 11: Industry Engagement (1)

Session Chair: Bryan Goda *(University of Washington)*

## Panel Session 3

## Session 12: Industry Engagement (2)

Session Chair: Joseph J. Ekstrom *(Brigham Young University)*

## Session 13: Interesting Topics

Session Chair: Bill Paterson *(Mount Royal University)*

## Session 14: Web Development and HCI

Session Chair: Craig Miller *(DePaul University)*

## Panel Session 4

## Author Index

# SIGITE/RIIT 2012 Conference Organization

**General Chair:**    Randy Connolly, *Mount Royal University, Canada*

**SIGITE Program Chair:**    William D. Armitage, *University of South Florida, USA*

**RIIT Program Chair:**    Jeffrey L. Brewer, *Purdue University, USA*

**Sponsorship Chair:**    Rob Friedman, *University of Washington, Tacoma, USA*

**Local Arrangements Chair:**    Bill Paterson, *Mount Royal University, Canada*

**Local Arrangements Committee:**    Alan Fedoruk, *Mount Royal University, Canada*
Charles Hepler, *Mount Royal University, Canada*
Namrata Khemka, *Mount Royal University, Canada*
Ricardo Hoar, *Mount Royal University, Canada*

**Treasurer & Registration Chair:**    Faith-Michael Uzoka, *Mount Royal University, Canada*

**Steering Committee Chair:**    Mark Stockman, *University of Cincinnati, USA*

**Steering Committee:**    Jim Leone, *Rochester Institute of Technology, USA*
Terry Steinbach, *DePaul University, USA*
Barry Lunt, *Brigham Young University, USA*
Han Reichgelt, *Georgia Southern State University, USA*
Richard Helps, *Brigham Young University, USA*
Diane Delisio, *Miami University of Ohio, USA*
Mihaela Sabin, *University of New Hampshire, USA*
Daniel Benjamin, *American Public University System, USA*
Ken Baker, *University of Cincinnati, USA*
Rick L. Homkes, *Purdue University, USA*

# SIGITE/RIIT 2012 Reviewers

Adnan Ahmad, *Massey University*

Sohaib Ahmed, *Massey University*

Syed Ishtiaque Ahmed, *Cornell University*

Mahir Ali, *University of Sharjah*

Hend Al-Khalifa, *King Saud University*

Fatima Al-Raisi, *Sultan Qaboos University*

Peter Alston, *Edge Hill University*

Jose Antonio Alvarez-Bermejo, *Universidad de Almeria*

William D. Armitage, *University of South Florida*

Alethe Bailey, *Newman University College*

Ken Baker, *University of Cincinnati*

William Barge, *Trine University*

Dianne Bills, *Rochester Institute of Technology*

Michael Black, *University of South Alabama*

Larry Booth, *Clayton State University*

Lynn Braender, *The College of New Jersey*

Wayne Brookes, *University of Technology, Sydney*

William Burkett, *Capella University School of Undergraduate Studies*

Rob Byrd, *Abilene Christian University*

Yu Cai, *Michigan Technological University*

Mario Camilleri, *University of Malta*

Peng-Wen Chen, *Oriental Institute of Technology*

Sam Chung, *University of Washington Tacoma*

Jean Coppola, *Pace University*

Monica Costa, *Instituto Politecnico de Castelo Branco*

Amanda Debler, *DIS AG*

Sonal Dekhane, *Georgia Gwinnett College*

Michele Dijkstra, *Pacific Lutheran University*

Nalaka Edirisinghe, *Temasek Polytechnic*

David Eggert, *University of New Haven*

Abdel Ejnioui, *University of South Florida*

Joseph Ekstrom, *Brigham Young University*

Stefano Federici, *Università di Cagliari*

Alan Fedoruk, *Mount Royal University*

Allan Fowler, *Waiariki Institute of Technology*

Robert Friedman, *University of Washington Tacoma*

Chunming Gao, *Michigan Technological University*

Daniel Garrison, *George Mason University*

Alessio Gaspar, *University of South Florida*

Angela Lemons, *North Carolina A&T State University*

Jim Leone, *Rochester Institute of Technology*

Chengcheng Li, *East Carolina University*

Sergio F. Lopes, *University of Minho*

David Luna, *Escola Superior de Tecnologia De Castelo Branco*

Phil Lunsford, *East Carolina University*

Barry Lunt, *Brigham Young University*

Cynthia Marcello, *SUNY Sullivan*

Kevin McReynolds, *LDS Business College*

Gabriele Meiselwitz, *Towson University*

Jose Metrolho, *Politecnic Institute of Castelo Branco*

Susan Miertschin, *University of Houston*

Trudi Miller, *University of Wisconsin - Stevens Point*

Craig Miller, *DePaul University*

Besim Mustafa, *Edge Hill University*

Rao Nemani, *The College of St. Scholastica*

Yin Pan, *Rochester Institute of Technology*

Bill Paterson, *Mount Royal University*

Sylvia Perez-Hardy, *Rochester Institute of Technology*

Nelson Piedra, *Universidad Técnica Particular de Loja*

Wayne Pollock, *Hillsborough Community College*

James Pomykalski, *Susquehanna University*

Annu Prabhakar, *University of Cincinnati*

Lakshmi Prayaga, *University of West Florida*

Barbara Price, *Georgia Southern University*

Junfeng Qu, *Clayton State University*

Hugo Rehesaar, *Griffith University*

Han Reichgelt, *Southern Polytechnic State University*

Janet Renwick, *University of Arkansas - Fort Smith*

Dale Rowe, *Brigham Young University*

Rick Gee, *Okanagan College*

Kathy Gill, *University of Washington*

Bryan Goda, *University of Washington*

Mingwei Gong, *Mount Royal University*

Prakash Goteti, *Mahindra Satyam*

Marco Aurélio Graciotto Silva, *University of São Paulo*

Ruth Guthrie, *Cal Poly Pomona*

Shekhar H M P, *Education and Research Department, Infosys Technologies Ltd.*

Thomas Hacker, *Purdue University*

Raymond Hansen, *Purdue University*

Richard Helps, *Brigham Young University*

Gregory Hislop, *Drexel University*

Ricardo Hoar, *Mount Royal University*

Edward Holden, *Rochester Institute of Technology*

Arno Hollosi, *Campus 02 University of Applied Sciences*
William Homer, *Core Business Technology Solutions*
Rick Homkes, *Purdue University*
Janet Hughes, *University of Dundee*
Diane Igoche, *Effat University*
Sudharsan Iyengar, *Winona State University*
R. Kent Jackson, *Brigham Young University - Idaho*
Mark Jaeger, *Baker College*
Hetal Jasani, *Northern Kentucky University*
Michael Jonas, *University of New Hampshire at Manchester*
Harshad Joshi, *Indiana University*
Yih-Ruey Juang, *Jinwen University of Science and Technology*
Suraj Juddoo, *Middlesex University*
Shakeel Khoja, *Institute of Business Administration*
Jane Kochanov, *Penn State Harrisburg*
Steven Kollmansberger, *South Puget Sound Community College*
Walter Kuhn, *University of Applied Sciences for Business Administration Zurich*
Deborah LaBelle, *Nazareth College of Rochester*
Mary Last
Kam Fui Lau, *Armstrong Atlantic State University*
Seamus Lawless, *Trinity College Dublin*
Chi Un Lei, *University of Hong Kong*
Rebecca Rutherford, *Southern Polytechnic State University*
Amber Settle, *DePaul University*

Faezeh Seyedarabi, *City University London*
Zaffar Ahmed Shaikh, *Institute of Business Administration, Karachi*
Carlos Silva, *University of Minho*
Suyash Sinha, *Microsoft Corporation*
Edward Sobiesk, *United States Military Academy*
Theresa Steinbach, *DePaul University*
Adriana Steyn, *University of Pretoria*
Mark Stockman, *University of Cincinnati*
Leigh Ann Sudol-DeLyser, *Carnegie Mellon University*
Andrew Suhy, *University of Michigan*
Bob Sweeney, *University of South Alabama*
Maciej Syslo, *Nicolaus Copernicus University*
Sue Talley, *Capella University*
Suleyman Uludag, *University of Michigan - Flint*
Faith-Michael Uzoka, *Mount Royal University*
Jey Veerasamy, *Baker College Online*
Xinli Wang, *Michigan Technological University*
Janice Warner, *Georgian Court University*
Linda Webster, *Westminster College*
Elissa Weeden, *Rochester Institute of Technology*
Glenn Wilson, *University of Southern Maine*
Jenifer Winter, *University of Hawaii*
James Woolen, *Ferris State University*
Daniel Yoas, *Pennsylvania College of Technology*
Dongqing Yuan, *University of Wisconsin - Stout*
Chi Zhang, *Southern Polytechnic State University*
Stephen Zilora, *Rochester Institute of Technology*

# SIGITE/RIIT 2012 Sponsor & Supporters

Sponsor:

Supporters:

MOUNT ROYAL
UNIVERSITY
1910

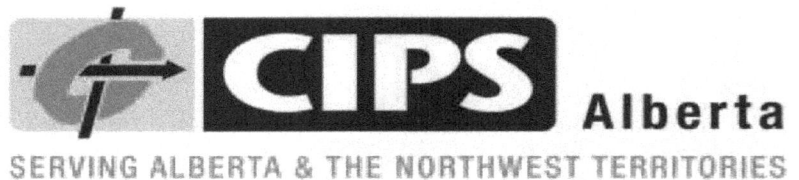

# Why Tenure is not a Private Sector Term: A Look at the Role of Educational Institutions in a Changing World of Commercialization, Investing, and Community Development

Randy Thompson
CEO, Venture Alberta Investor Forum
3553 – 31 Street NW
Calgary, AB, T2L 2K7
403-313-2695
thompson@venturealberta.com

## ABSTRACT

This talk will examine the following topics: why post secondary institutions need to be involved in commercialization, how universities have changed for the better local economies, the difference between incubators and accelerators, and why commercialization times need to shorten inside of academic institutions.

## Categories and Subject Descriptors

K.3.1 [**Computers and Education**]: General.

## General Terms

Management

## Keywords

Commercialization, Investment, Education.

# Planning Organizational Security:
# The Health First Case Study

Susan J. Lincke
University of Wisconsin-Parkside
900 Wood Road
Kenosha WI 53141 USA
+1(708)453-2069

lincke@uwp.edu

## ABSTRACT

Security is important skill for an IT professional, and allows him/her to advance and specialize in their career. We developed an Information Security course with a goal of training students for the ISACA CISA and CISM exams, and having students participate in security planning with not-for-profit organizations. The Health First Case Study enables students to practice security planning with a hypothetical Doctor's office, including risk analysis, business continuity, information security, network security, personnel security, incident response, and physical security. Students use the Small Business Security Workbook, which leads them through the security planning process. The case study also helps students to understand the perspective of the business owner.

## Categories and Subject Descriptors

K.3.2 Information Systems Education; K.6.5 Security and Protection

## General Terms

Security, Management.

## Keywords

Security Planning, IT, Security Workbook, Case Study.

## 1. INTRODUCTION

This NSF-funded project has developed lecture materials and a hypothetical case study, based on a doctor's office, to help students plan security. Students use the Small Business Security Workbook to guide them through the security planning process. They practice with the Health First Case Study, and then optionally work with real organizations, as part of community-based learning.

We developed our Information Security course from professional security materials. These materials are based on ISACA's Certified Information Systems Auditor (CISA) and Certified Information Security Manager (CISM) review manuals [1,2].

These materials discuss security from a high-level, business perspective. This knowledge compliments the Security+ certification, which emphasizes secure computer operations. The CISA/CISM help to train security analysts, while the CompTIA Security+ certifications help to train security administrators [3]. The CISA or CISM focus on aspects covered by the CISSP certification, and thus can serve as a spring board to eventual CISSP certification [4].

This course is an elective for our Computer Science and Management Information Systems majors, and a required course for our graduate Computer Information Systems program. This course is most useful as an upper level undergraduate or a graduate IS/IT/CS program.

We developed this course with a case study, to provide an active-learning or problem-based learning experience. Lu and Wang [5] found that case studies enable student-centered learning, by promoting interactivity between students and faculty, reinforcing educational concepts taught by lecture, and deepening student understanding by building knowledge into students. Students not only learn to apply theoretical knowledge to practical problems, but also to be creative in discovering solutions.

Our case study was meant to provide students real world experience in security planning. Wei et al. [6] found that cases help students transition to the workplace, by exposing students to diverse situations, thereby enhancing adaptation skills to new environments, and increasing students' self confidence in dealing with the world. Students increase their communications skills, which includes listening and persuasion skills.

We did not expect, but found that our case study exposes students to multiple views. Chinowsky and Robinson [7] stress that case studies enable interdisciplinary experience, which students are more likely to encounter in the real world. They stress the importance of using real-world artifacts in the case study. Our case study achieves the interdisciplinary aspect, by enabling students to experience multiple perspectives: the doctors', HIPAA regulation, IT and financial, including through the use of real artifacts: business documents.

We are aware of four sets of case studies relating to security. Dhillon [8] has written a security text that describes a company's basic scenario as an introduction to each chapter. At the end of each chapter is a case study problem, which has students consider specific aspects related to the case study. ISACA also provides graduate-level teaching cases [9,10], which emphasize corporate governance problems related to security management and the COBIT maturity model. However, understanding law, in addition to security technology, is also important for IS security students [11,12]. Schembari has students debate legal case studies, to help them learn about security-related law [12].

In this case study, students plan security for a doctor's office, which must adhere to the U.S. Health Insurance Portability and Accountability Act (HIPAA). Through this law, students understand that security procedures are important, including risk, business continuity, physical security, and personnel security. HIPAA is important in the U.S., because approximately 58% of organizations must adhere to it, and it is representative of regulation that is concerned with state-of-the-art privacy and security [16]. While these teaching materials are freely available, some aspects of the case study will need to be modified for use in other countries to reflect national law. Nearly all of the lecture materials and the Small Business Security Workbook can be used in other countries without modification.

This paper describes an introduction to our course, our IT-related case studies, notes on teaching with the case study, our results, and a conclusion.

# 2. THE INFORMATION SECURITY COURSE MATERIALS

The Health First Case Study can be used for a semester long course. It is one case study in that it addresses one business: a doctor's office. However, it is a collection of case studies, since each case study develops some aspect of the security plan. The case studies can be used as active learning exercises or homework assignments, after each lecture.

Students make important decisions regarding the security planning process. The case study is provided as conversations between the doctor and staff, and an IT person. The Small Business Security Workbook leads students through the security planning process. The Workbook has been tested with real small businesses, via service learning [13]. Other aspects of the full case study investigate secure software development, working with HIPAA [14], and technical network security (including protocol analysis) [15]. The case studies described here are IT-related, and used for security planning.

Each case study is associated with a PowerPoint lecture, which includes sample Workbook tables for a scenario related to a university.

## 2.1 Case Study Exercises

The Health First Case Study addresses seven areas in IT: 1) risk management, 2) business impact analysis and business continuity, 3) information security, 4) network security, 5) physical security, 6) incident response, and 7) personnel security. For each of the case studies described below, the students refer to the lecture and Workbook to complete each exercise. The case study exercises include:

### 2.1.1 Analyzing Risk

This case study is performed after the Risk Management lecture. Students first determine the value of the assets and list the probable threats for the doctor's office. Students work with real business documents, including an Income Statement, Statement of Retained Earnings, and a Balance Sheet. HIPAA jail sentences and financial penalties increase the cost of security breaches, and factor heavily into the risk analysis process. Students then complete the remaining risk analysis steps of: estimate likelihood,

compute expected loss, and treat risk. Table 1 shows a partial result of the treat risk process.

The outcome for the business is a risk analysis plan within the Workbook. Learning outcomes include working with qualitative and quantitative risk analysis, using real business documents.

### 2.1.2 Addressing Business Impact Analysis & Business Continuity

For a Business Impact Analysis (BIA) plan, students first define potential threats that could severely impact the business. Students then define the business recovery objectives, including the Recovery Time Objective and Recovery Point Objective.

Students then allocate a Criticality Classification to each information asset, and define security controls to address the Recovery Time Objective (RTO) and Recovery Point Objective (RPO) for critical services.

The outcome for the business, and the student learning outcomes, is the development of a Business Impact Analysis and the start of a Business Continuity Plan. A complete Business Continuity Plan would include detailed Procedures for Handling, which is not part of the case study.

### 2.1.3 Designing Information Security

The case study has students classify organizational data by Sensitivity (secrecy) and Criticality (reliability). They then discuss how the data should be protected: e.g., for which data classifications should data at rest be encrypted, and how labeled? (See Table 2.) They define organizational roles and define which roles shall have access to which data. With role-based access control, students consider who should be have read/write/execute permissions to the various forms of the Health First database.

**Table 1. Analysis of Risk versus Controls**

| Risk | ALE Score | Control | Cost of Control |
|---|---|---|---|
| Malpractice | $50K | Medical server up | |
| Social Engineering | $25K | Awareness training  HIPAA Adherence | Weekly HIPAA meetings,  Annual training |
| Stolen Information / HIPAA audit | $15K | HIPAA Adherence,  Encrypted disks,  VPN, firewalls, antivirus software,  Audit tech/service | Weekly HIPAA meetings,  Encryption & security technology |

**Table 2. Handling of Sensitive Data**

|  | Confidential | Privileged |
|---|---|---|
| **Access** | Need to know | Need to know |
| **Paper Storage** | Locked cabinet, Locked room if unattended | Locked cabinet Locked room if unattended |
| **Disk Storage** | Server-only storage Password-protected, Encrypted, Hashed | Password-Protected |
| **Labeling & Handling** | 'Confidential' Clean desk, low voice, shut doors | Clean desk |
| **Transmission** | Encrypted | Local only, Encr. |
| **Archive** | Encrypted | |
| **Disposal** | Degauss & damage disks Shred paper | Reformat disks |

### 2.1.4 Planning for Network Security

For this case study, students consider which applications can be stored together on physical or virtual machines, based on access control and Criticality classification. Next, students determine which services are allowed to enter and leave the network, and in which direction those connections should originate. This information is important in configuring the firewall(s). Based on the Criticality and Sensitivity classifications, students then define the required specific controls for each service (e.g., encryption, hashing, anti-virus). Firewalls need to protect the organization's data from both the internet and wireless access!

Finally, students draw a network map for Health First with Microsoft Visio, and color code the different systems according to their Sensitivity Classification. See Figure 1.

The outcome for the business is a network security plan within the Workbook. Learning outcomes include documenting the requirements for a circuit-level firewall, and organizing data by Criticality/Sensitivity classification and role-based access control.

### 2.1.5 Designing Physical Security

The lecture on Physical and Personnel Security are combined, since they are somewhat shorter than other lectures.

For this case study, room classifications are defined for Sensitivity and Criticality, according to room contents. Appropriate room controls are defined for each classification, including procedural and other physical access and availability controls (e.g., locks, fire suppressant, UPS, etc.) See Table 3. Students prepare a map showing room sensitivity and criticality classifications for Health First.

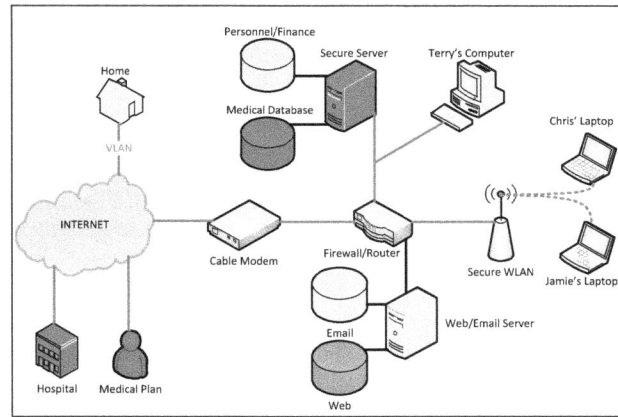

**Figure 1. Color-coded Network Diagram**

**Table 3. Room Classifications**

| Sensitivity Class | Description | Special Treatment (Controls related to Confidentiality) |
|---|---|---|
| Proprietary | Room contains Propriety information storage | N/A |
| Confidential | Room contains Confidential information storage | Workstation monitor has hood. All cabinets remained locked. Room remains locked when not attended. No patients are allowed in these areas. |
| Private | Room contains computer with access to sensitive or confidential data | Laptops are physically secured using cable locking system. Room remains closed when unattended, since locks are not in place. Building remains locked when unattended. All cabinets remained locked. No patients are allowed in these areas. |
| Privileged | Room contains computer with access to sensitive or confidential data but public has access when escorted | Laptops are physically secured using cable locking system. Room remains closed when unattended, since locks are not in place. Building remains locked when unattended. All cabinets remained locked. |
| Public | The public is free to spend time in this room, without escort. | Room remains open. Building remains locked when unattended. No computers or confidential papers left in room. |

The outcome for the business is a physical security plan. The student learning outcomes include a consideration for physical controls for both access and availability.

### 2.1.6 Planning for Incident Response

This lecture reviews six stages of incident response: Preparation, Identification, Containment, Analysis and Eradication, Recovery, and Lessons Learned.

This case study addresses Stage 1 Preparation, which prepares an organization for an incident (i.e., the remaining incident response stages). This case study leads students to define potential incidents, and their detection mechanisms or controls to limit their occurrence. Suggested incidents include hacker intrusion, lost laptop or backup tape, social engineering, and theft of proprietary information.

Students next address what should happen in the remaining incident response stages, including who should be notified, and what actions need to be taken. Students define which procedures need to be developed, without developing full procedures.

The outcome for the business is an Incident Response Plan, including a list of threats and detection mechanisms, and a definition of actions for when incidents occur. Learning outcomes include students developing appropriate responses for each of the incident response stages, and exposure to the breach notification law (valid for most states in the United States).

### 2.1.7 Organizing Personnel Security

The Personnel Security is an advanced case study, which requires students have a good understanding of the full information security picture, since they will be allocating security responsibilities to each employee. The Personnel Security lecture describes personnel security issues dealing with hiring/termination, different forms of security training, and segregation of duties.

This case study problem first defines internal threats from fraud for each employee, and then discusses possible controls for each threat. HIPAA requires that organizations define a Chief Security Officer (CSO). During the case study students review the HIPAA Security Rule to allocate responsibility to the CSO and other employees to ensure adherence to HIPAA. Finally, the Workbook has students define the training and procedures that will enable everyone to complete their security-related responsibilities.

The outcome for the business is a coherent system of security, including allocation of security responsibilities, training, and documentation. Learning outcomes include that students evaluate security from the personnel perspective, consider security as a system, work with security regulation, and review previous exercises.

## 3. NOTES ON TEACHING THE CASE STUDY

The NSF-funded case study materials include PowerPoint lectures, case study, Small Business Security Workbook, and Small Business Requirements Document (with Health First forms). There is also a Small Business Security Workbook Solution, which includes a solution for the full case study.

The lectures have been enhanced to include appropriate example tables from the Small Business Security Workbook, for a University application. These examples help students to observe how tables are properly used, and may provide ideas for their solution (or not!) The lecture notes are made available to students from the course web page during the case study exercise, and they are often referred to.

We teach the case study as an active learning exercise in class, although it could be used as homework. A PowerPoint lecture is given in the first half of a 3-hour class, and the second half is the active learning exercise. For active learning, students are grouped into 3-4 person teams, and each team is provided a computer to edit the Small Business Security Workbook directly on-line. All students should be able to see the display, so computers are selected and manipulated for the best display. The best computers tend to be the ones at the end of a row of tables, providing 3 sides for students to sit, discuss, and observe Workbook use.

The instructor provides a copy per student, of the 2-3 pages of the specific case study exercise (or a link to the specific case study). The beginning of each case study indicates the corresponding section in the Workbook to work with, but is also announced by the instructor. The case study has headings to indicate the conversations for each subsection of the appropriate chapter in the Workbook. The Workbook is retained on the computer, so that students may add to the Workbook each week. This enables students to review previous decisions during case study exercises.

The application of the HIPAA regulation is important for this business case. It is important that the HIPAA lecture (or appropriate alternative regulation lecture) is given before some case study exercises. The HIPAA lecture notes are made available to students when necessary. One hard copy of the HIPAA lecture is provided for each group. The HIPAA lecture copies are distributed at the beginning of appropriate labs, and retained for reference in the teaching lab.

The best way to start the case study is to have students volunteer to read the first part of the case study out loud in front of the whole class. Each role is read by a different student. Most case studies have 4 roles, so there would normally be 4 readers. A benefit is that it starts out the case study with students actively talking, and not silently reading (or being confused). Then the instructor can provide direction for class discussion, and get initial ideas into play before letting the groups go off on their own. Assigning roles in each group has the advantage that students get to play a different role each week, including an IT person, versus a doctor or medical administrator.

While the case study is being actively discussed per group, the instructor may see that some groups are too quiet or heading in the wrong direction. It is advantageous to correct this. Rarely, it may make sense to move people between groups, if some groups are not making sufficient progress or not getting along. At the end of the class, the instructor can ask specific teams for their solutions, particularly if they had brilliant ideas that should be shared, and/or can discuss the solution provided by this case study.

As an active learning exercise, students are given a small amount of credit for participating. If students miss the active learning exercise, they can submit it as homework. Due to time constraints, perfect solutions may not occur during the lab time. However, having students think about the solution, and observe a good solution, helps them to assimilate the material. Often students come up with brilliant ideas, which have been incorporated into the official solution!

## 4. RESULTS

There are two questions when a course is taught: is the teaching effective, and do students appreciate their learning?

The real test of whether the teaching effectively "helps students transition to the workplace", is whether students can work with a community partner on a real project afterwards. After a trial run with the case study, undergraduate students used the Workbook to work with small business management in our community. The instructor led the students for one visit to the community partner if students had IS/IT experience, or participated twice (of 6 visits) if they had no experience. The semester's work was rated highly by the community and students. Of our five community partner organizations that used this Workbook with student guidance, 100% were Very Satisfied with "The Quality of Students' Work". During our last year, students agreed (100%) or strongly agreed (28.6%) with the statement: "I felt that the community project I did through this course benefited the community partner's organization."

To obtain feedback from students about their learning, an independent evaluator performed a qualitative assessment with the students at the end of the course. The consensus on the case study was: "It was a good test drive". "Gave you a guideline for working with your partner". However, there was also a consensus that 'catching on' in the first few labs was difficult.

We also noticed that later labs had higher approval ratings than earlier labs. Our first four labs had an average 78% agreement rate to the statement: "I understood what was expected as part of the case study exercise, and it helped me to learn the material." During the next six labs this rate increased to 87.5%. (In both cases, all remaining students selected "Neither agree nor disagree".) To fix this, we start the case study as a class (and not in separate groups). Volunteers read the case study out loud and discussion begins class-wide. Our initial approval rating then started out higher, with 93% 'agreeing' with the statement: "I understood what was expected as part of the case study exercise, and it helped me to learn the material."

An unexpected benefit noticed by the instructor was that students experience the perspective of the business owner. Students learn that a solution is not just about technology – it is also about the business. Business and technology costs are provided for students to work with, including business financial reports.

## 5. ACKNOWLEDGMENT

The development of the Small Business Security Workbook, lecture materials, and Health First Case Study was funded by the National Science Foundation (NSF) Course, Curriculum and Laboratory Improvement (CCLI) grant 0837574: Information Security: Audit, Case Study, and Service Learning. These materials are available at: www.cs.uwp.edu/staff/lincke/infosec. Any opinions, findings, and conclusions or recommendations expressed in this material are those of the authors and do not necessarily reflect the views of the NSF.

## 6. CONCLUSION

This case study teaches students to plan for security in IT. Students gain practice with the case study, as for a real-world experience. Students learn to work with the Small Business Security Workbook, which they can use in their workplace, after they graduate.

The case study also achieves an interdisciplinary aspect, by enabling students to experience multiple perspectives: the doctors', regulation, IT, and financial. It is effective, in that students can lead real world community partners through security design.

## 7. REFERENCES

[1] ISACA. 2009. *CISA Review Manual 2010*. Arlington Heights IL, DOI=http://www.itgovernance.co.uk/products/1403.

[2] ISACA. 2009. *CISM Review Manual 2010*. Arlington Heights IL. DOI=http://www.itgovernance.co.uk/products/1402.

[3] Farwood. 2012. Security+ Guide to Network Security Fundamentals, 4th Ed. CENGAGE Learning.

[4] Harris, S. 2010. *CISSP All-in-One Exam Guide, 5th Ed.* McGraw-Hill, NY.

[5] Lu, S. and Wang, Y. 2009. "The Research and Practice of Case Teaching Method in Computer Curricula for Undergraduates". *Proc. 2009 4th International Conf. on Computer Science and Education*. IEEE, 1460-1463.

[6] Wei, H., Xin, C., and Ying, H. 2010. "Non-computer Professional IT Education in the MBA Model". *The 5th International Conf. on Computer Science & Education*. IEEE, 612-614.

[7] Chinowsky, P. S., and Robinson, J. 1995. "Facilitating Interdisciplinary Design Education Through Case Histories". *1995 IEEE Frontiers in Education Conf.* IEEE, 4a3.6-4a3-9.

[8] Dhillon, G. 2007. *Principles of Information Systems Security*, John Wiley & Sons, Inc.

[9] ITGI. 2007. *IT Governance Using COBIT® and Val IT: Student Book, 2nd Ed.* IT Governance Institute, **www.isaca.org**, Rolling Meadows, IL.

[10] ISACA. 2010. *Information Security Using the CISM® Review Manual and BMISTM: Caselets.* **www.isaca.org**, Rolling Meadows, IL.

[11] Katerinsky, A., Rao, H. R., and Upadhyaya, S. 2010. "Harsh Realities 101 - Augmenting Information Assurance with Legal Curricula". *Proc. 14th Colloquium for Information Systems Security Education (CISSE)*. **www.cisse.info**.

[12] Schembari, N. P. 2010. "An Active Learning Approach for Coursework in Information Assurance Ethics and Law". *Proc. 14th Colloquium for Information Systems Security Education (CISSE)*. **www.cisse.info**, 1-8.

[13] Burri, T. and Lincke, S. J. "Security planning for small businesses: A service-learning course". *IEEE Frontiers in Education Conference (FIE)*. IEEE. Oct. 12-15, 2011, pp. F1E-1 - F1E-6.

[14] Lincke, S. J. 2012. "The Health First Case Study: Teaching HIPAA Regulation with Security". *Colloquium for Information Systems Security Education (CISSE)*. June 13-15.

[15] Lincke, S. J. 2012. "Network Security: A Case Study". *Midwest Instruction and Computing Symposium*. April 13-14.

[16] *14th Annual CSI Computer Crime and Security Survey Executive Summary*, Computer Security Institute, GoCSI.com, Dec. 2009, p. 2.

# Designing a Masters Program in Cybersecurity and Leadership

Bryan S. Goda     Robert Friedman
University of Washington, Tacoma
Institute of Technology
Tacoma, Washington, USA 98405
godab@uw.edu     rsfit@u.washington.edu

## ABSTRACT

The Master of Cybersecurity and Leadership (MCL) taught at the University of Washington Tacoma is a partnership between the Institute of Technology and the Milgard School of Business. The 10-course graduate level program was initially benchmarked against existing masters programs, surveys of prospective student population were conducted, and an assessment was done on the estimated demand for MCL graduates in the region. The program outcomes were then mapped against the course objectives to insure the correct mix of courses and topics. The program's admission requirements and schedule were then tailored to our expected pool of applicants. The MCL program is proposed to start in January 2013.

This paper discusses the design process and possible ways to reduce risk in the start-up of a new degree program. How a program is marketed to prospective students and what program graduates will do after program completion is just as important as the initial design of the program. Planning for the administration of the program and the assessment process is an important phase of the initial design.

## Categories and Subject Descriptors

K.3.2 [Computers and Education]: Computer and Information Science Education – Information Technology Education.

## General Terms

Degree Programs, Design

## Keywords

Information Technology Education, Cybersecurity

## 1. INTRODUCTION

The University of Washington Tacoma (UWT) was founded in 1990 to meet regional needs for community college transfer students. UWT is set in downtown Tacoma's Union Station neighborhood, a district of historic warehouses. The vision of the University is to provide access to an exceptional university education; provide an interdisciplinary approach to knowledge and discovery in the 21st century; and develop a strong and mutually supportive relationship between the campus and its surrounding communities. The MCL program leverages the resources of the University of Washington's Center for Information Assurance and Cyber Security by extending the reach of the Center's related certification courses to new military populations in the South Sound region of Washington State. By identifying, addressing, and promoting solutions for issues of information assurance and cyber security, MCL will serve as an educational foundation for invention, innovation, and entrepreneurship in the state of Washington, thereby sustaining the vitality of existing and prospective information assurance and cyber security industries.

## 2. PROGRAM DEVELOPMENT

A benchmarking of similar programs concludes that there are no similar programs in Washington State and most of the similar programs are located on the east coast of the US. The University of Maryland, Virginia College, Washington Governor's University, Utica College, and New York University offer online master degrees in cyber security [1,2,3,4,5], while George Washington University, New Jersey Institute of Technology, and American University offer it as part of their resident computer science degree [6,7,8]. The National Defense University offers a Government Information Leadership [9] master's degree, the program most similar to the MCL program.

The Joint Base Lewis McChord (JBLM) and the Naval Bases at Bremerton and Bangor near UWT have a pool of 3000 junior officers who would be attracted to an MCL type program. Many of these officers work in units that specialize in Information Assurance or need better organizational leadership skills. While a masters degree is not required for promotion, a masters degree in cybersecurity and leadership would enhance unit performance. An interest survey was conducted at a National Guard unit specializing in information warfare and the local commanders were interviewed. The feedback was overwhelming support for the startup of a new program. Auburn University has created a master in cybersecurity with a similar officer population at Maxwell Air Force Base [10]. The Institute of Technology at UWT offers BS degrees in Computer Science, Computer Engineering, Information Technology and a graduate program in Computer Science. Students majoring in Information Technology have also shown a keen interest in the MCL program.

The Information Technology field is expected to be one of the top two employment growth areas, with an expected increase in demand of 23% [11]. The I-5 corridor around UWT is home to such tech savvy companies as Microsoft, Amazon, Boeing, Liberty Mutual, Pacific Medical Centers, KPMG, and the Port of Tacoma. Companies are looking for programs that can produce managers and technology leaders who can design, implement, and manage cybersecurity systems. Complex distributed systems operating in a mobile, cloud computing environment demand skilled professionals highly trained in cybersecurity.

On April 27, 2009, in a speech to the National Academy of Sciences, President Obama called for major investments in attracting students to science and engineering, because science is now "more essential for our prosperity, our security, our health, our environment, and our quality of life than it has ever been before." James Gosler, a veteran cyber security specialist who has worked at the CIA, the National Security Agency and the Energy Department, says we do not have enough talented cyber workers coming into the field to support national security objectives. James Gosler and System Administration, Networking and Security Institute (SANS) Research Director Alan Paller estimate that there are only 1,000 highly skilled cyber defense specialists in the U.S., but that the nation needs 20,000 to 30,000 of these skilled workers to meet national computer security needs [12].

## 3. PROGRAM DESIGN

The MCL program will combine coursework in both the cyber security (technical) and leadership (organizational/strategic) areas. It is designed to have students from a wide variety of technical backgrounds. Since UW is certified by the National Security Agency as a Center of Excellence in Information Assurance, this program will help in the continued certification of the university. The MCL will expose students to a Common Body of Knowledge in preparation for the Certified Information Systems Security Professional (CISSP) examination. Upon completion of the program, students should be able meet the program outcomes specified in Table 1.

### Table 1. Program Outcomes for the MCL

| |
|---|
| 1. Be able to identify and critically assess issues and concepts related to the protection of information and information systems. Develop and articulate an organization's strategic direction. |
| 2. Assess an organization's security attributes: confidentiality, integrity, and availability. Understand an organization as complex, interdependent system operating in an ever-changing and uncertain environment. |
| 3. Analyze and evaluate proposed or extant information security policies, practices, and procedures in order to assess potential advantages and disadvantages that might flow from implementing them. Provide leadership so that confidentiality, integrity and availability can be protected. Insure an environment of threat reduction is maintained in an organization. |
| 4. Use risk management principles to assess threats, vulnerabilities, countermeasures and impact contributions to risk in information systems. Perform a risk analysis for an environment. Create a management plan for security in an environment. Analyze and diagnose complex organizational problems, design effective solutions, and implement change. |
| 5. Create policies, strategies and standard operating procedures for securing information and communication systems. Manage people, information, and processes to accomplish organizational goals and objectives. |
| 6. Identify and critically assess the social political, economic, and ethical dimensions of IA and CS in an organizational context. |

The MCL program was designed to accommodate students in the military who are normally working during the day. MCL will consist of ten 4-credit courses of eight week durations. The program is a joint venture of the Institute of Technology and the Milgard School of Business. The Institute of Technology will teach 5 cybersecurity courses and the Milgard School of Business will teach 5 courses from their Masters of Business Administration program. Courses will run 4 hours one night per week, which allows a cohort to complete the program in a calendar year.

Module 1
*Principles of Cyber Security*
Business Communication

Module 2
*Information Assurance / Cybersecurity and Risk Management in Context*
Business Ethics and Social Responsibility

Module 3
*Designing and Executing Information Assurance and Cybersecurity Strategies*
Strategic Management

Module 4
*Network and Internet Security*
Individual and Group Dynamics

Module 5
*Building an Information Risk Management Toolkit*
Organization Change

The modules are designed to build on a student's prior experience in a previous module. Prior to entering Module 1, most students should have experience working in an organizational environment and have taken the recommended background coursework in information technology. In Module 1, students will be exposed to the concepts, strategies and skills related to the life cycle of information assurance. The Principles of Cybersecurity will cover information assurance organizational goals, the threat spectrum, risk, and legal/ethical issues. The Business Communication course promotes the understanding of important communication dynamics and the ability to communicate strategically and professionally in organizations.

Module 2 builds on the introductory material presented in Module 1 and examines risk management involving assessment, analysis and mitigation planning. Students will be able to evaluate polices, practices, and procedures to determine overall advantages and disadvantages from implementation. The Business Ethics course will focus on the ethical and moral challenges facing business managers today. The combination of both of these courses is that our graduates will be able to evaluate alternatives and determine if they conform to ethical standards.

Module 3's courses on designing cybersecurity strategies and strategic management will focus on how to effectively direct an organization's direction. Students will be working on case studies that allow students to apply what they have learned in Modules 1 and 2. Students will be halfway through the program and should be able to appreciate how the cybersecurity and leadership courses complement each other.

Module 4 provides the skills necessary for securing networks, email, and cryptographic methods. The Individual and Group Dynamics course prepares our graduates to assemble the skills, talents, and resources of individuals and groups to solve problems. So we have an electronic network as well as a human network being implemented during the Module 4.

Module 5 is designed to tie the previous 8 courses together so that our graduates will have the necessary tools to develop security architectures. The Organizational Change course will have students apply these concepts to real organizations and assess their own managerial skill as they relate to creating and reacting to change.

Each of the course objectives was mapped to the program outcomes to insure a balanced coverage of topics. Figure 1 shows that balance among the courses.

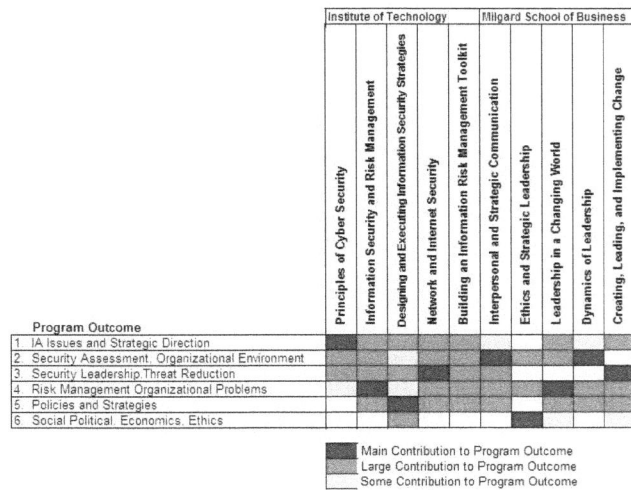

**Figure 1. Program Outcomes Mapped to Courses.**

The student population entering into the MCL program will likely have a wide variety of skills and backgrounds, some not necessarily in a science and technology area. It was determined the admission requirements should be based on the graduate programs of the Milgard School of Business and other cybersecurity graduate programs, and that each entrant should have a grounding in information technology. Admission requirements to the program are:

- Bachelor's Degree from a US Institution or equivalent

- Minimum Grade Point Average of 3.0 on a 4.0 scale

- Competitive scores from the Graduate Record Exam

- Fluency with Information Technology

The potential student pool of applicants will come from the National Guard, alumni of Bachelors of Information Technology and Systems program, and from the enlisted ranks of Joint Base Lewis/McChord. Working professionals in the public, private, and non-profit sectors will be interested in expanding career choices in Information Assurance and Cybersecurity. These individuals desire to learn more about advanced cyber- security concepts, strategies and methods in order to improve their performance in their current job, progress faster in their careers, or transition to a new career field. Table 2 depicts the projected growth of the MCL program.

**Table 2. Projected Growth of MCL Program**

| Year | 1 2013 | 2 2014 | 3 2015 | 4 2016 | 5 2017 |
|------|------|------|------|------|------|
| Students | 24 | 30 | 40 | 50 | 50 |
| Graduates | 21 | 27 | 36 | 45 | 45 |

The quality of the curriculum and the UWT faculty will create a positive reputation for the MCL program, resulting in organic growth over the life of the program. Additionally, despite recent budget constraints and tuition increases, UWT's enrollments continue to increase. This fee-based program will be charging tuition that can be accommodated by the 9-11 GI Bill benefits. This is a relatively unexplored source of enrollment, but the number of potential students and the enthusiasm expressed by JBLM and National Guard Camp Murray officers suggests that there could be significantly positive potential in student enrollments and the revenue base. There is a certain advantage in being a first mover in this direction. Though the proposed MCL program is designed initially for military personnel, it could potentially also attract career-changing college graduates, as indicated by interest from the Healthcare Leadership program at UWT.

The admission process of the MCL program will make effective use of the UWT diversity policy. It will also maintain and enhance the School's existing diversity perspective in its undergraduate and graduate admission processes. Program advertising materials will be used in regional and local newspaper/magazine and academic/education websites. Working with the UWT's Assistant Chancellor for Equity and Diversity, a number of media outlets will help to provide outreach to underrepresented minorities. While maintaining consistency of admission criteria in screening student applications, diversity among the admitted students will ensure a robust and exciting learning environment.

## 4. ADMINISTRATION AND ASSESSMENT

The MCL will require incremental resources in the administration of the program and student advising. This includes (1) co-program directors to oversee the academic program; and (2) one half-time staff person, whose responsibilities will be related to admissions, tracking, maintaining program guidelines, course scheduling, coordinating with the administration and student services staff, students counseling, verifying student requirement fulfillment for graduation and similar tasks. The admission process will be handled by a faculty committee, similar to those in our current MBA and MS-CSS programs. The program directors will be selected from the management faculty of the Milgard School and the ITS faculty in the Institute, and may be compensated in the form of course release or stipend for the additional administrative responsibilities assumed, if necessary. The staffing of the program will be fully supported by the revenue generated by the MCL program and will not require any state funding.

MCL will have an annual online course and program evaluation survey to assess the program. There will also be group discussions to get feedback on the courses and program. Student course evaluations and classroom assessments (peer evaluations) will also be an integral part of the assessment process. Faculty will consider this information and recommend improvements to the program. Faculty teaching MCL courses with an embedded measure of key learning objectives will also discuss results from the prior year, their plans for modifying course assignments based on data and any changes to evaluation criteria used. Additionally, the faculty will discuss what they cover in their MCL courses and how they can better integrate their efforts.

The program leadership will hold focus groups with managers at organizations that employ MCL graduates to garner feedback towards continuous improvement of the program. Similarly, there will be follow-up focus groups with MCL alumni to gather feedback based on their work experience and how well the program prepared them for careers in cybersecurity.

## 5. CONCLUSIONS

The lack of a graduate program in cybersecurity in a technology heavy region fills a need that students, employers, and the community desires. Careful research is required prior to launching a new program, else it is doomed to fail. A graduate program needs to be designed from the top-down, so that the courses support the program outcomes. The administration and assessment of the program have to be considered early-on in the design process, because a new program will evolve and grow as it becomes mature. Cybersecurity is a new area that encompasses several disciplines. Merging leadership skills with technological expertise is an exciting combination with a bright outlook.

This paper proposes a new advancement in the field of Computer Science education by combining the fields of cybersecurity and leadership together into a graduate degree. The idea of a modular design where students will steadily progress into becoming cybersecurity professionals with an acute business sense makes them very attractive to future employers and can further promote cooperation between business schools and technology programs.

## REFERENCES

[1] University of Maryland. Retrieved May 16, 2012 from http://cyber.umd.edu/education/index.html

[2] Virginia College Online Programs. Retrieved May 16, 2012 from http://www.vconline.edu/graduate-degrees-online/cyber-security-degree.cfm

[3] Washington Governor's University. Retrieved May 16 2012 from http://washington.wgu.edu/online_it_degrees/information_security_assurance_degree

[4] Utica College Cyber Security – Intelligence and Forensics. Retrieved May 16, 2012 from http://www.onlineuticacollege.com/programs/masters-cybersecurity.asp

[5] NYU-ePoly Cybersecruity MS. Retrieved May 16, 2012 from http://cs.njit.edu/academics/graduate/mscsp.php

[6] Department of Computer Science, George Washington University. Retrieved May 16, 2012 from http://www.cs.gwu.edu/academics/graduate_programs/master/cybersecurity/program-requirements

[7] Master of Science in Cyber Security and Privacy NJIT. Retrieved May 16, 2012 from http://cs.njit.edu/academics/graduate/mscsp.php

[8] Master of Arts in Intelligence Studies, American Military University. Retrieved May 16, 2012 from http://cs.njit.edu/academics/graduate/mscsp.php

[9] National Defense University Cyber Security Program. Retrieved May 16, 2012 from http://cs.njit.edu/academics/graduate/mscsp.php

[10] Top Career Fields. Retrieved May 16, 2012 from http://www.moneycrashers.com/5-great-career-fields-for-the-future/

[11] Sahinoglu, M., Cybersystems and Information Security Master of Science Program at Auburn University Montgomery. *GSFT International Journal on Computing, Vol 1, No.3,* August 2011. 70-76.

[12] Gjelten, T., Cyber Warrior Shortage Threatens U.S. Security. Retrieved October 6, 2010 from National Public Radio: http://www.npr.org/templates/story/story.php?storyId=128574055s

[13] Petrova, K., Kaskenpalo, P., Philpott, A., Buchan, J., Enbedding Information Security Curricula in Existing Programmes. In *InforSecCD Conference '04,* pages 20-29, Kennesaw GA, USA, 2005. ACM Press.

[14] Bacon, T., Tikekar, R., Experiences With Developing A Computer Security Information Assurance Curriculum, In *Consortium for Computing in Small Colleges,* 2003, 254-267.

[15] Taylor, C., Ednicott-Popovsky, B., Phillips, A., Forensics Education: Assessment and Measures of Excellence. In *Proceedings of the 2ⁿᵈ International Workshop on Systematic Approaches to Digital Forensic Engineering,* Seattle WA, USA, April 10-12, 2007. IEEE Computer Society.

[16] Polson, C., Persyn, J., Cupp, O., Partnership In Progress: A Model for Development of a Homeland Security Graduate Degree Program. *Homeland Security Affairs*, Vol VI., No. 2, May 2010.

# Game-based Forensics Course for First Year Students

Yin Pan, Sumita Mishra, Bo Yuan
and Bill Stackpole
Department of Computing Security
Rochester Institute of Technology
102 Lomb Memorial Drive
Rochester, New York 14623
(585) 475-4645

{yin.pan; sumita.mishra; bo.yuan; bill.stackpole}@ rit.edu

David Schwartz
School of Interactive Games and Media

Rochester Institute of Technology
102 Lomb Memorial Drive
Rochester, New York 14623
(585) 475-5521

disvks@rit.edu

## ABSTRACT

Identifying and attracting talented students to digital forensics programs is a crucial first step to developing professionals in this relatively young field. To respond to these challenges, we propose to develop a fun, entertaining, and yet educational forensics-course suitable for first year students in college, in an effort to identify and attract students to a forensics program.

This paper focuses on the design and development of a game-based forensics course using the game-based learning (GBL) approach building the game *in a real computing environment* that has direct access to actual forensics tools from a forensics machine and the evidence from a suspect machine. Interactive visualizations will be used to help students to understand the intangible and inaccessible abstract concepts such as deleted/hidden/encrypted/over-written digital evidence.

## Categories and Subject Descriptors

K.3.2 [**Computers and Education**]: Computer and Information Science Education – *curriculum, information systems education.*

K.8 [**Computing Milieux**]: Personal Computing – *games.*

## General Terms

Security, Design, Legal Aspects, Experimentation.

## Keywords

Computer Forensics, Game Design, Visualization, Information Assurance, IT education, Curriculum Development.

## 1. INTRODUCTION

Cyber security and forensics is among the most critical areas of national importance in growing need of knowledgeable professionals [17]. According to Bureau of Labor Statistics [2], Private Detectives and Investigators' job outlook for 2010-2020 will grow 21% (the number of jobs in 2010 was 34,700) with the projected main growth in the area digital forensics. In response to the increasing need for advanced studies in the areas of computer and network security and forensics, several security and forensics programs have been developed in the past 10 years [23, 24].

However, since digital forensics is a relatively young field, college freshman, especially the underrepresented groups, do not have sufficient exposure to the subject matter. Therefore, identifying and attracting students with interests, passion, and talent in forensics is crucial to the development of future forensics professionals. It would be ideal to offer an *Introduction to Computer Forensics* course in the freshman year, especially for colleges sharing a common first year experience. However, the main challenge in offering such a course so early in the program is that it requires students to have understanding of advanced concepts in a variety of areas including computer operating systems, file systems, and network traffic analysis. For example, unlike fingerprints, blood samples, and other evidence found at a traditional crime scene, digital evidence, formatted as 0's or 1's, cannot be seen by the naked eye and leaves no actual physical evidence to visually assess for relevance. Recovering digital evidence that may have been deleted/hidden/encrypted/over-written is impossible without an understanding of how operating systems and file systems work. It is therefore difficult for incoming students to grasp forensics concepts and techniques. In addition, computer forensics involves intensive hands-on exercises that require students to follow potentially tedious procedures that demand a long and focused span of attention. Due to these challenges, current forensics courses are often designed for advanced students – junior and seniors – when they are better prepared to absorb advanced abstract concepts and work on intensive investigations.

This paper proposes an innovative idea to overcome these obstacles so that the course can be offered for general education or as an introductory course for a forensics degree. We will use the Game-Based Learning (GBL) approach to attract students and to explore technologies and procedures commonly used in a forensics investigation. A game will be developed *in a real computing environment* that has direct access to actual forensics tools from a forensics machine and the evidence from a suspect machine to allow students to practice using state-of-the-art forensic technologies. Visualizations will be used to help students to understand the intangible and inaccessible abstract concepts such as deleted/hidden/encrypted/over-written digital evidence on various computer systems.

The rest of this paper is organized as follows. In Section 2, the authors introduce the game-based learning approach and visualization technology as well as how to apply these technologies in a forensics course. The game-based forensics course content and forensics game design are detailed in Section 3. In Section 4, the authors present the assessment plan to evaluate the effectiveness of this game-based approach for a forensics course, followed by conclusion and future work in Section 5.

## 2. PREVIOUS WORK

### 2.1 Game-based learning

Game-based learning (GBL) has gained considerable traction since 2003 when James Gee described the impact of game play on cognitive development [12]. It usually utilizes an interesting narrative and competitive exercises to motivate students learning according to specific designed learning objectives [22]. Studies have shown that GBL can engage students with the material and make significantly improvement over those participating in learning with other educational software due to game's feature of inductive reasoning and frequent interactions with content [20, 26].

### 2.2 Visualization

Visualization techniques have just been introduced to security education during the past five years [8]. They are most effective in helping students to understand abstract concepts and protocols, identify patterns, monitor activities and follow complex procedures [18]. Schweitzer [19] defined Interactive classroom visualization (ICV) as a term for visualizations used in the classroom specifically designed to demonstrate concepts such as formal models, algorithms or processes. When applying visualization in teaching forensics concepts in our classroom, we will design forensics ICVs as follows:

- Abstract forensic concepts: visualizations that illustrate a general concept such as deleted data, slack data, stegnography, etc.
- Formal models: visualizations that demonstrate a forensics model such as forensics procedure and chain-of-custody.
- Forensics tools: visualizations that demonstrate how a forensic tool works. For example, the basic Unix file convert and copy utility *dd*, *Autopsy/Sleuthkit* [21], the forensic analysis tools *FTK* from AccessData [11], *EnCase* from Guidance Software [9].
- System concepts: visualizations that illustrate open files, system files such as registry/log/history files, running processes, open connections.

Even though both game-based learning and visualization techniques have been successfully used in geosciences, computer and network security [6] and other fields, based on our knowledge, the use of GBL in forensics education, especially in combination with the visualization technologies in a real computing environment, is a novel idea.

As the current generation of students grows up with computer games and television shows such as Crime Scene Investigation (CSI), the game-based forensics course utilizing visualization will harness their interests, engage and guide them to learn digital forensics concepts and practice forensics techniques in an immersive environment. Students who "play" the game will develop their forensics skills and better understand the challenges with respect to the field. This game-based approach to teaching is an innovative way to help convey knowledge about forensics and should serve to capture the interest of technologically-focused students who may then be more likely to pursue a career protecting our digital assets.

## 3. FORENSICS COURSE DESIGN IN A GAME-BASED ENVIRONMENT

Computer forensics involves understanding specific aspects of digital evidence and following the general forensic procedures of investigation. The field utilizes sophisticated technological tools to appropriately preserve, extract and analyze digital evidence.

This introductory course will be taught in an active learning environment involving classroom activities and in-class hands-on exercises. Visualization techniques are used to create an active learning environment that enables effective teaching of forensics principles and concepts. Specifically, we will develop a digital forensics game that includes graphical visualizations to illustrate fundamental computer forensics concepts, and interactive lab-based forensic investigation activities that allow students to practice gathering, preserving, analyzing, and reporting digital evidence in a fun and real computing environment.

### 3.1 Goal of the forensics course

This undergraduate introductory forensics course is designed to provide students with the ability to identify pertinent digital evidence and employ appropriate tools to gather, preserve, analyze and report admissible evidence in court. The course emphasizes both the fundamental computer forensics procedure and the hands-on experience of utilizing digital forensics technologies needed to uncover illegal activities of computer users.

### 3.2 Course Outcomes

Upon completion of this course, students will be able to

1) Describe and follow basic procedures of incident response.
2) Define fundamental computer forensics concepts and procedures.
3) Apply digital forensic tools to discover, collect and preserve digital evidence.
4) Use Windows and Unix operating systems and file systems to uncover and analyze digital evidence.
5) Identify and utilize appropriate network forensics tools to detect and analyze network intruders.
6) Document and report digital evidence to court.

### 3.3 The digital forensics game design

The digital forensics game will be built on a Windows system that includes 1) visualizations to illustrate fundamental computer forensics concepts, and 2) interactive lab-based forensic investigation modules to allow student practice in gathering, preserving, analyzing and reporting digital evidence. All Windows-based forensics software will be directly installed in the Windows host while Linux/Unix-based software will be accessible through a Linux virtual machine installed as a guest operating system of the Windows host. This game accesses real forensics images and runs actual forensics tools from both the Windows and Linux operating systems with the following features:

- Digital Crime Scene investigations that include several real world white-collar cases such as hacking, fraud, intellectual property theft and espionage. Each case is associated with a level of difficulty to allow students to investigate different cases throughout the course, increasing in difficulty as the competence of the student increases.
- Visualizations for computer forensics concepts and tools. Players can access concepts, procedure and forensics tools using visualizations through tutorials available from the game interface.
- Sound tracks for the narrative, music, and hints, where appropriate.

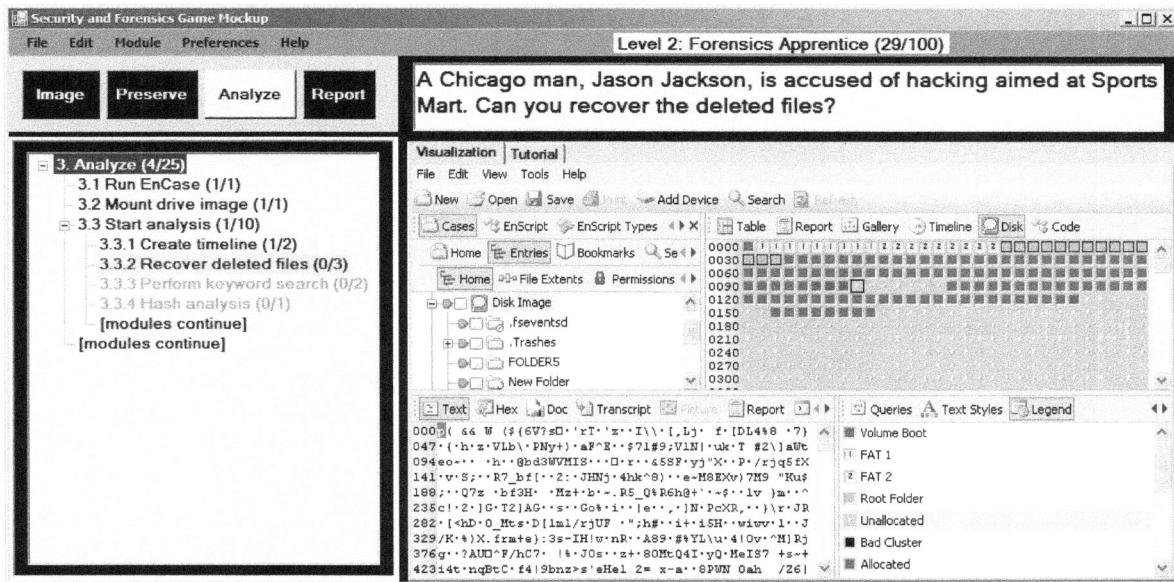

**Figure 1: Mockup of the game, which shows an example session at "Stage 3" (Analyze) of a particular session. The player would now attempt to recover deleted files using EnCase.**

The interface of the proposed game has six main displays, as shown in Figure 1:

- Menu options for running and saving a game, as well as customization and other options.
- A forensics tools and visualizations pane. This is the main panel where students will gain hands-on experiences by running various forensics tools such as *EnCase*, *FTK*, *Autopsy/Sleuthkit*, etc. Visualizations are also shown in this space, Illustrated in Figure 1 is an example disk space with allocated and deleted data visually shown with *EnCase*. The associated tutorials, which may include other visualizations, provide students with immediate help and feedback.
- A sequence of buttons: Image, Preserve, Analyze and Report. By following the four stages of Image→Preserve→Analyze→Report, the proposed game reinforces the core forensics procedure and provides hands-on experience using real forensics tools.
- A detailed set of steps for each module. For example, Figure 1 demonstrates series steps the player would need to attempt as part of the Analyze module. Note that each step indicates achieved points. For example, the current player missed part of the timeline formulation and received partial credit. This panel also keeps a running tally of module points, which the player can continue to improve by repeating previous steps and a running tally of total points for all attempted modules and their steps. As demonstrated in Figure 1, the player might have missed points in previous modules. The game will provide a series of titles as the player finishes more steps.
- A level of difficult for the current case is shown on the top of the pane.
- A narrative to help motivate the players as they progress through the steps. The narratives can also help to motivate student and provide additional explanation of the current step. Different from other simulation games, this game

allows students to practice their skills in a real forensics investigation environment following the appropriate forensics procedure. The proposed interface also facilitates explanations for students with visual and/or auditory disabilities, with the ability to provide audio explanations as well as text captions.

## 3.4 Course Content

Digital forensics is the process of "gathering and analyzing data in a manner as free from distortion or bias as possible to reconstruct data and determine what has happened in the past on a system" as Farmer and Venema defined in 1999 [10]. When a crime is committed today, evidence, especially digital evidence, needs to be collected from the scene. Investigators must follow an appropriate forensics procedure to insure that data is handled in a manner as free from distortion or bias as possible. Digital evidence is defined as the information in binary form that may be relied on in court [3]. Evidence might be persistent, such as data stored in non-volatile storage; for example, magnetic, solid-state, or optical. It might be non-persistent, such as over a transmission medium that has no storage. Evidence might also exist in media that is volatile but only temporarily accessible, such as random access memory on a live system or "weakly" erased disk data. Furthermore, the investigation may involve more than the subject and host machine. It could also involve routers, servers, backup storage devices, and even printers [3, 16].

As indicated in the Department of Defense Cyber Crime Center's training program [7], cyber analysts require knowledge on how network and system intrusions occur, how various logs are created, what comprises electronic evidence, how electronic artifacts are forensically gathered, and also the ability to analyze data to produce comprehensive reports and link analysis charts.

The following table ties the course content with visualization tools and hands-on exercises created in the forensics game.

**Table 1: Course content, visualization and exercises**

| Course Outline | Visualization Built In the Forensics Game | Hands-on Exercises Built In the Forensics Game |
|---|---|---|
| Module 1: Incident response [4, 5, 15] | Link to CSI: Crime Scene Investigation<br><br>Where evidence resides – RAM, hard drive compact disks, floppy disk, logs, tapes, usb, cell-phone, PDAs, ..., etc. | Incident Response Lab (mock crime scene) |
| Module 2: Forensic Essentials and General Procedure [3, 15, 16] | What you should do?<br><br>What you should avoid?<br><br>Type of digital evidences | A game that students will follow the Chain-of-Custody and a correct forensics procedure sequence to receive points.<br><br>Deduct points for any wrong doing actions such as destroying volatile data, altering original media, patching and updating suspect system prior to evidence seizure. |
| Module 3: Volatile data (processes, open files, open ports, memory) acquisition and analysis [27] | Demonstrate the tools to show users who are currently logged on, running processes, open files, open sockets/ports from a live system.<br><br>Dump physical memory and identify readable information such as ip address, *TrueCrypt* keys, passwords from the memory | Collect volatile information from the game system. |
| Module 3: Forensics imaging techniques and tools (*dd*, *encase* and *FTK imager*) [16] | Visually show how *dd* does a bit-to-bit copy from the selected source to destination and also show the difference from cp and dd.<br><br>Visually show other common Imaging formats such as *EnCase* image, E.01 | Hands-on exercise to create bit-by-bit image of a usb or small partition using *dd* and *FTK imager*<br><br>Use *netcat/cryptcat* to transfer data |
| Module 4: Forensics preservation of the image (*md5sum*, *sha1* and *sha2*) [16] | Visually show how hash function such as *MD5*, *sha1*, *sha2* works | Hands-on exercise to create and verify hashes. |
| Module 5: Unix Filesystem and Unix Forensic Techniques [4, 5, 15, 16] | Visually show allocated disk space vs. unallocated (deleted) disk space on the game computer.<br><br>Show a Unix file system EXT2 and EXT3 in a dynamic diagram that links a filename to its inode and the data-blocks associated with this file.<br><br>Show the possible indications for compromised systems<br><br>• Check the passwd and shadow files for new/deleted accounts, for UID=0<br>• Identify wrong doing from history file and user login information<br>• Identify hidden directory<br>• Identify regular files in /dev<br>• Find all SUID/SGID files<br>• Recently modified binaries, recently created files | Examine various compromised Unix/Linux images (including honeypot projects) and identify pertinent evidence with open source *Autopsy*, *Sleuthkit* and *PTK*.<br><br>Have hints built into the game to guide students for the investigation<br><br>• Timeline Creation and analysis<br>• Data recovery / retrieve deleted files<br>• String/key-word search<br>• Hash analysis<br>• Signature analysis<br>• Hidden data (unused partitions, unallocated space, virtual memory)<br>• Check images, emails, internet access |
| Module 6: Steganography [13] | Visually show the image with | Identify images and audio file with secrets |

| | | |
|---|---|---|
| | secrets embedded vs. a clean image. | embedded and extract the secrets from the images |
| Module 6: Windows Filesystems and forensics techniques [4, 5, 15, 16] | Windows FAT filesystem and NTFS filesystem.<br><br>Similar to Unix, show the possible indications for compromised systems<br><br>Display Windows Registry entries that is crucial to forensics investigations | Given compromised Windows images and lead students to analyze the image.<br><br>Have hints built into the game to guide students for the investigation. Besides the list similar to Unix hints, additional considerations are:<br><br>• Hidden data – Slack space<br>• Registry view<br>• Windows recycle bin<br>• IE analysis/Internet history |
| Module 7: Network Forensics Essentials --Determine what happened on a system based on network traffic study [1] | IDS, router and web server logs. Captured network traffic using sniffing tools | Using *wireshark* or *snort* to capture network traffic.<br><br>Post-mortem network analysis using *wireshark* and *NetworkMiner* [36]<br><br>• MAC time analysis<br>• Discover the reconnaissance, exploitation and covert operations<br>• Which vulnerability was exploited<br>• Recover the contents of rootkits<br>• Where it came from<br>• Who (ip addr) did it |
| Module 8: Forensics report and Forensics investigator and expert witness in reality | Video of expert witness in court.<br><br>Invite a forensics professor for a talk and discussion | Play mock court |

As shown in Table 1, when teaching the content the instructor uses the Interactive classroom visualization (ICV) to help students to understand advanced concepts and technologies. The corresponding game-based exercises reinforce the concepts when students are working on these specially designed games. For example, the course starts with a video clip of a crime scene investigation and shows several criminal cases that involve digital evidence stored in various media such as RAM, hard drives, compact disks, floppy disks, logs, tapes, USB drives, cell-phones, PDAs, etc. The incident response principles and procedures are covered in the lecture followed by an interactive, group-based, mock incident response game to tie the incident response principles and procedures to real-world practice. The objective of this particular game is to learn the correct procedure to respond to an incident and to answer questions such as: How to identify evidence to confirm/dispel an incident, where to collect pertinent evidence, and how to collect evidence in a forensically-sound manner. In this incident response game, students work in groups of 3~4 acting as forensics investigators called to a crime scene. A number of crime scene scenarios will be created for this project to allow students to use forensically-sound investigative techniques to 1) evaluate the scene 2) collect important data and information 3) document everything; interviewing personnel as appropriate 4) maintain chain-of-custody, and finally, 5) to write a report documenting their findings and present the report to the class.

The other game-based exercises focus on OS-specific and network forensic tools and techniques. For example, the exercise of creating a forensic image and preserving the integrity of the image with appropriate forensic tools provides students with a comprehensive understanding of the imaging and hashing (data authentication) processes. Analytical exercises focus on how to recover, categorize and analyze data from the contents of captured drive images which include building timelines based on file dates and times, performing keyword searches, and other activities. The labs are designed at varying difficulty levels. Students are able to choose the level of play, beginning at the entry level, and then move on to more advanced levels.

This fun class concludes with a video of an expert witness testifying and discussing the technical and other skills required to act as an expert witness. A forensics investigator will come to the class to discuss the challenges of the profession and the preparations needed to become an investigator.

The next table specifies how each defined learning outcome is covered in our course outline.

**Table 2: Objectives vs. Course Outline**

| Objectives | Lecture material |
|---|---|
| Describe and follow the basic procedure of incident response | Module 1: Incident response |
| Define fundamental computer forensics concepts and procedure. | Module 2: Forensic Essentials and General Procedure |
| Apply digital forensic tools to discover, collect and preserve digital evidence | Module 3: Forensics imaging techniques and tools to collect both volatile data (processes, open files, open ports, memory) and non-volatile data<br><br>Module 4. Forensics preservation of the image |

| Use Windows and Unix operating systems and file systems to uncover and analyze digital evidence. | Module 5: Unix File-system and Unix Forensic Techniques; <br><br> Module 6: Windows File-systems and forensics techniques and Steganography |
|---|---|
| Identify and utilize appropriate network forensics tools to detect and analyze network intruders. | Module 7: Network Forensics Essential |
| Document and report digital evidence to court. | Module 8: Forensics Report |

## 4. COURSE ASSESSMENT

This course will be piloted in 2013. The course assessment will be conducted to measure the effectiveness of the GBL-based Forensics course by assessing gains in student knowledge for each objective for each offering of the GBL modules. The proposed evaluation will focus on directly measuring student learning attributable to the GBL Forensics course. An experimental design will compare the GBL version of the course to an existing, non-GBL version of the course. This will allow us to examine the motivational aspects of the GBL approach along with comparing learning benefits.

## 5. CONCLUSION AND FUTURE WORK

This paper proposed the course design for a fun, entertaining, and yet educational forensics course suitable for first year students in college, in an effort to identify and attract students to a forensics program. The design of the GBL-based course is based on established research about game-based learning, which has been successfully used in geosciences, information security and other fields. Based on our knowledge, use of GBL in forensics education, especially in combination with the visualization technologies in a real computing environment, is a novel idea. We believe that this approach will be most effective in computer forensics and other advanced fields that involve understanding abstract concepts and hands-on practice. The future work includes implementing the game, based on this design, and conducting a thorough assessment to measure the effectiveness of this approach. Also, we plan to apply this GBL approach to other advance course development.

## 6. REFERENCES

[1] Buchanan, W., Introduction to Security and Network Forensics, CRC Press, 2011.

[2] Bureau of Labor Statistics, Occupational Outlook Handbook for Private Detectives and Investigators, http://www.bls.gov/ooh/Protective-Service/Private-detectives-and-investigators.htm, 2012.

[3] Casey, E., Digital Evidence and Computer Crime: Forensic Science, Computers, and the Internet (3rd edition), Elsevier Science & Technology Books, (ISBN-13 9780123742681), 2010.

[4] Carvey, H., Windows Forensics and Incident Recovery,

Addison-Wesley Professional, 2004.

[5] Carvey, H., Windows Registry Forensics, Syngress, 2011.

[6] CyberCiege, http://cisr.nps.edu/cyberciege/.

[7] Department of Defense Cyber Crime Center's training program, www.dc3.mil/dcita/courseDescriptions/cac.php.

[8] Dino Schweitzer, D., Baird, L., Collins, M., Brown, W., and Sherman, M., "GRASP: A Visualization Tool for Teaching Security Protocols", Proceedings of the 10th Colloquium for Information Systems Security Education, 2006.

[9] EnCase, http://www.guidancesoftware.com/forensic.htm.

[10] Farmer, D., and Venena, W., Forensic Discovery, Addison-Wesley Professional Computing Series, 2004.

[11] Forensic Toolkit (FTK), http://accessdata.com/products/computer-forensics/ftk

[12] Gee, J., What Video Games Have to Teach Us About Learning and Literacy, Palgrave Macmillan, NY, 2003.

[13] Katzenbeisser, S., and Petitcolas, F., Information Hiding Techniques for Steganography & Digital Watermarking, Artech House Books, 2000.

[14] Hjelmvik, E., Passive network security analysis with NetworkMiner. Insecure.com, Issue 18, page 18-21, 2008.

[15] Kruse, W., and Heiser, J. Computer Forensics: Incident Response Essentials. Addison-Wesley, Boston, 2002.

[16] Nelson, B., Phillips, A. and Steuart, C., Guide to computer forensics and Investigations, 4th Edition, Course Technology, 2010.

[17] Remarks by President on Securing Our Nation's Cyber Infrastructure, http://www.whitehouse.gov/the-press-office/remarks-president-securing-our-nations-cyber-infrastructure.

[18] Schweitzer, D. and Brown, W., "Using Visualization to Teach Security", Journal of Computing Sciences in Colleges, Volume 24 Issue 5, 2009.

[19] Schweitzer, D. and Brown, W., Interactive Visualization for the Active Learning Classroom, Proceedings of the 38th ACM Technical Symposium on Computer Science Education, SIGSCE 2007.

[20] Sheldon, L., The Multiplayer Classroom: Designing Coursework as a Game, Cengage Learning, 2012.

[21] Sleuthkit, http://www.sleuthkit.org/.

[22] Teed, R., Game-Based Learning, http://serc.carleton.edu/introgeo/games/, 2012

[23] Troell, L., Pan, Y., and Stackpole, B., "Forensic Course Development – One Year Later," Proc. of the SIGITE 2004 conference, Salt Lake CIty, Utah, 2004.

[24] Troell, L., Pan, Y., and Stackpole, B., "Forensic Course Development," Proc. of Conference on Information Technology Curriculum 4. North Carolina, 2003.

[25] Van Eck, R. "Digital game-based learning: It's not just the digital natives who are restless, " EDUCAUSE review, vol. 41, pp16-16, 2006.

[26] Virvou, M., et al., "Combining software games with education: Evaluation of its educations effectiveness, Educational Technology & Society, vol. 8, 54-65, 2005.

[27] Waits, C. Akinyele, J., Nolan, R., and Rogers, L., Computer Forensics: Results of Live Response Inquiry vs. Memory Image Analysis, Carnegie Mellon Technical Review, Cert Program, 2008.

# Influence of Proximity to and Accessibility of School on School Choice of Information Technology Students

Rex P. Bringula
College of Computer Studies and Systems, University of the East
2219 C.M. Recto Avenue, Sampaloc,
Manila, Philippines
(632) 735-54-71 loc 425

rex_bringula@yahoo.com

## ABSTRACT

The study determined the profile, level of school choice, and influence of proximity to and accessibility of school on the level of school choice of Information Technology (IT) students. Descriptive statistics revealed that most of the respondents were male, did not have a home province, lived in Manila and Quezon City, belonged to a middle-income class, belonged to a family with five members, spent almost an hour in going to school, and utilized jeepneys and the Light Railway Transit to reach the school. They lived near their school and they perceived that their school was accessible. The university was their preferred school. Perceived accessibility of school was the only factor found to influence school choice. Thus, the null hypothesis stating that proximity to school and accessibility of the school, singly or in combination, would not influence school choice was partially accepted except. Recommendations and implications were also discussed.

## Categories and Subject Descriptors

K.3.2 [**Computer and Information Science Education**]: Information systems education

## General Terms

Management

## Keywords

Accessibility, Distance, Information Technology Education, Proximity, School choice, Travel time

## 1. INTRODUCTION

One of marketing foci of Philippine Higher Education Institutions is on Information Technology (IT)-related degree programs because of the declining enrollment on the said degree programs. The decline in enrollment in IT degree programs could be attributed to the antisocial image of technology courses, cyclic nature of demand on the degree, and the notion of outsourcing of technology jobs overseas [19]. Also, the situation was aggravated by the fact that few women were attracted to the field of computing [11, 18, 29]. To compete for a handful of students, the

university exerts great marketing efforts to inform students of their competitive advantage over other students from other schools.

The administrators are aware that they should now "get inside the heads of their target markets, assess their needs, modify their offerings to meet those needs, and thereby enhance the perceived quality of the service which they provide" [6, p. 171]. If these important matters are attended urgently, they may be able to attract students to enroll in their schools.

Numerous studies about school choice were conducted and written (e.g., [5, 6, 7, 23]). These varied studies used different factors that might be considered in choosing a school. One of these factors was school location. Location was one of the educational attributes of a school [5, 23] and this was one factor considered in choosing a school in Australia [25], Malaysia [20, 21], Scotland [7], Canada [12], and New Zealand [14]. High school seniors in California (Tillery, 1973 cited in [8]) and Chinese students studying abroad [31] also considered location as a major factor in school choice. Alderman et al. [1] found out that the poor households in Pakistan were very sensitive to proximity in their school choice. Students had the propensity to transfer to other schools because of location [24].

However, location is a generic term. Its discussion has been intertwined with other factors of school choice, such as security or safety of the place, proximity, accessibility, and geographic setting (e.g., urban or rural school setting) of the school. For instance, Warrington (2005 cited in [2]) noted that school location was important to the working-class parents since they were concerned with the following: violence and crime in the area, children traveling alone by public transport after dark, being able to go to school quickly in case of emergency, and the anxiety of children in the family who were attending different schools. In the study of Wang [31], it disclosed that families of young Chinese students studying in Australia considered the safe environment of the school. Chinese people also looked into the hardware components of the school – its appearance, facilities, and location [31].

Furthermore, Dahari and Ya [9] considered location as a very important factor in parents' choice of preschools in Malaysia. They learned that most parents would send their children to schools close to their homes or near their workplaces – about less than three kilometers from their homes or from their workplaces. They also argued that young children should not spend long periods of time in going to school. Perhaps, parents did not choose a distant school for it could affect the attendance of their children [17, 30].

Nevertheless, several studies discussed accessibility, proximity, and school safety and security distinctively. Andre-Bechely [2] investigated how parents managed the issues of time and distance in choosing a public school in an urban California district. In the study of Bell [5], parents gave 102 varied reasons for choosing a school for their children. One of these reasons had to do with logistics which included transportation and cost of getting to school.

Hurtado et al. [16] showed that one of the college choice preferences of students was a school close to their homes. This was also supported by the studies of Theobald [28], Briggs and Wilson [7], and Tatar and Oktay [27]. On the other hand, students would also choose a school that was safe and secured. This was discussed extensively in the studies of Bauch and Goldring [3], Belanger et al. [4], Davis [10], and Srikantanyoo and Gnoth [26].

Literature revealed a wealth of studies on safety and security of schools but very few investigations were done on school choice of IT students and the influence of proximity to and accessibility of a school on their choice of school. In the light of this dearth of studies related to these two factors that could possibly influence school choice of IT students, the present study was conceived.

Toward this aim, the study sought answers to the following questions. 1) What is the profile of the respondents in terms of sex, home province, city address, monthly family income, number of family members, hours spent in going to school, and mode of transportation utilized to go to school? 2) What is the proximity of the respondents' home address to their school? 3) How do the respondents perceive the accessibility of the school? 4) What is the level of school choice of the respondents? 5) Do the proximity to and accessibility of the school, singly or in combination, influence the level of school choice?

## 2. RESEARCH HYPOTHESIS

As used in this study, location of school had two constructs – proximity and accessibility. Proximity to school and accessibility of school served as the independent variables of the study. Proximity to school referred to the nearness of the city home address of the respondents to the school. On the other hand, accessibility of school had two subcomponents. The first component was the time spent in traveling from the home address of the respondents to the school. The second component was the subjective perception on the accessibility of the school with respect to good road conditions, availability of different modes of transportation, convenience of getting to school, and affordability of fare.

Level of school choice was used to mean the degree to which the students preferred to enroll in the university. This served as the dependent variable.

It was hypothesized that proximity to school and accessibility of the school, singly or in combination, would not influence school choice.

## 3. METHODOLOGY

This descriptive design study employed a descriptive survey. The respondents of the study were students of the College of Computer Studies and Systems, University of the East (UE) in Manila. UE is located at the University Belt (UBelt) – the area where 22 universities in Manila are situated. It can be noted that 18 of the 22 universities in the UBelt offer IT-related programs.

A total of 576 freshmen in 15 class sections served as the population of the study. One hundred (100) respondents who participated in the pretest were not included in determining the actual population. Thus, the actual population considered was 476. With the use of Sloven's formula (e = 0.05), a minimum sample of 217 was computed.

Two hundred twenty-seven (227) out of 234 distributed survey forms were retrieved. These were all used in the analysis. The forms were distributed to six randomly selected class sections. Class sections were written on a piece of paper and randomly picked out.

The questionnaire was divided into three sections. The first section gathered information on the demographic data of the respondents, such as name, sex, home province, city address, monthly family income, number of family members, hours spent in going to school, and mode of transportation utilized to go to school. The actual distance of city home address with respect to Manila was determined.

However, it was very difficult to measure the actual distance of the school to the home address (e.g., respondents living within the vicinity of the school). Thus, distance of home address to school was recoded from 1 to 20. The code value "1" (nearest) represented the place of residence living in Manila while the code value "20" represented the place of residence farthest with respect to Manila. Manila was used as the reference point since the university was situated in Manila. Table 1 shows the recoded values.

**Table 1. Distance of Manila to the Different Home Locations**

| From Manila to | Distance (km) | Recoded Value |
|---|---|---|
| Manila | – | 1 (nearest) |
| Pasay City | 5.11 | 2 |
| Navotas | 6.97 | 3 |
| Mandaluyong City | 7.11 | 4 |
| Makati | 7.33 | 5 |
| San Juan | 7.42 | 6 |
| Caloocan City | 7.47 | 7 |
| Malabon City | 7.68 | 8 |
| Quezon City | 9.07 | 9 |
| Valenzuela City | 11.1 | 10 |
| Las Piñas City | 11.2 | 11 |
| Pateros City | 11.7 | 12 |
| Pasig City | 12.5 | 13 |
| Taguig | 13.2 | 14 |
| Parañaque City | 14.0 | 15 |
| Marikina City | 15.4 | 16 |
| Rizal | 20.87 | 17 |
| Muntinlupa City | 24.0 | 18 |
| Cavite | 39.7 | 19 |
| Bulacan | 48.0 | 20 (farthest) |

The second section gathered the perception of the respondents on the accessibility of the school. There were four questions on this section. The respondents could answer from 1 (Disagree) to 5 (Strongly Agree) as shown in Table 2. In Table 3, all questions were found to be valid (factor loading $\geq 0.50$) and reliable ($\alpha \geq 0.70$) [15, 22].

The third part gathered the responses of the respondents on their level of school choice. The respondents could respond from 1 ("Not my preferred school") to 5 ("Highly preferred school"). (See Table 2.)

**Table 2. The 5-Point Scale, Mean Range, and Verbal Interpretation**

| Weight/ Scale | Mean Range | Verbal Interpretation |
|---|---|---|
| 5 | 4.51 – 5.00 | Strongly agree / Highly preferred |
| 4 | 3.51 – 4.50 | Agree / Preferred |
| 3 | 2.51 – 3.50 | Moderately agree / Moderately preferred |
| 2 | 1.51 – 2.50 | Slightly agree / Slightly preferred |
| 1 | 1.00 – 1.50 | Disagree / Not preferred |

**Table 3. Validity and Reliability of Questions on the Perception on Accessibility of the School**

| Questions | Factor loading | Cronbach's alpha (α) |
|---|---|---|
| Roads leading to the school are in good condition. | 0.738 | |
| There are diverse modes of transportation available to get to school. | 0.762 | 0.805 |
| It is convenient to go to school from my place of residence. | 0.863 | |
| Fare to go to school is inexpensive. | 0.822 | |

Frequency counts, percentages, and mean were used to describe the profile of the respondents. Regression analysis was utilized to determine whether proximity to school and accessibility of school influenced school choice. A 5% level of probability with 95% reliability was adopted to determine the degree of significance of the findings.

# 4. RESULTS AND DISCUSSION

## 4.1 Profile of the Respondents and Proximity of their Home Address to their School

Table 4 shows that most of the IT students were male ($f = 163$, 72%), lived in Manila ($f = 87$, 38%) and in Quezon City ($f = 45$, 20%), and spent less than an hour (mean = 54 minutes) to go to school by means of jeepneys ($f = 162$, 71%) or LRT ($f = 76$, 33%). Jeepneys were the most utilized means of transportation in Metro Manila. Meanwhile, LRT provides the fastest and most inexpensive transportation to travel from specific locations in Metro Manila. This shows that most of the respondents were commuting students. Respondents lived near in the university (mean proximity = 7.25).

Meanwhile, most of the respondents belonged to a household of five members and to a middle-income class ($f = 115$, 51%). The university offers IT-related degree programs for about Php40,000 per semester or about USD1,000 (USD 1 = Php 42). This indicates that the income of the family was sufficient — just enough to pay the students' tuition fee and other necessities of the family. In other words, the respondents of the study came from a family whose income had to be spent judiciously.

Conversely, about one-half (49%) of the respondents belonged to a higher-income class. This signifies that the university caters to families from two distinct income classes. This puts the university in a difficult position in terms of tuition fee increase. It should be noted that tuition fee is the major source of funds of the university. While the higher-income class can afford to pay the increase, the lower half cannot afford to pay. Tuition fee increase should be then reasonable if the university wants to retain its students.

**Table 4. Profile of the Respondents**

| Profile | Findings |
|---|---|
| Sex | Most of the respondents were male ($f = 163$, 72%). |
| Home Province | Most of the respondents did not have a home province (Metro Manila settlers) ($f = 83$, 37%). On the other hand, those respondents that came from the provinces were from Rizal ($f = 21$, 9%), Bulacan ($f = 18$, 8%), and Batangas ($f = 10$, 4%). |
| City Address | Most of the respondents were living in Manila ($f = 87$, 38%) and in Quezon City ($f = 45$, 20%). Using the recoded value, most of the respondents lived near the school (mean proximity = 7.25). |
| Monthly Family Income | Most family earned to Php40,000 or less monthly income ($f = 115$, 51%). |
| Number of Family Members | The average number of family member was five. |
| Hours Spent in Going to School | The average time spent to go from home to school was 54 minutes. |
| Mode of Transportation Utilized to Go to School | Jeepneys ($f = 162$, 71%) and Light Railway Transit (LRT) ($f = 76$, 33%) were the most utilized modes of transportation to go to school. |

Table 4 also reveals that most of the respondents were Metro Manila settlers ($f = 83$, 37%). Meanwhile, if the respondents have provincial addresses, then most of them would be from the provinces of Rizal ($f = 21$, 9%), Bulacan ($f = 18$, 8%), or Batangas ($f = 10$, 4%). Rizal and Batangas are part of the CALABARZON region (Region IV-A) while Bulacan is part of Central Luzon (Region III). These are the two closest regions in Metro Manila. Follow-up informal interviews with the respondents showed that the convenience provided by LRT enabled the students from Rizal and Bulacan to travel to the university.

## 4.2 Accessibility of the School, Level of School Choice and Its Predictors

Table 5 shows the perception of the respondents on the accessibility of the school and level of school choice. The respondents gave an "agree" response to show that there were diverse modes of transportation to choose to get to school (mean rating = 3.92). They also perceived that it was convenient to go to school from their place of residence (mean rating = 3.56) and the fare was inexpensive (mean rating = 3.53). Overall, they perceived that the school was accessible (overall mean rating = 3.62, "Agree"). It was also revealed that the university was their "preferred" (mean rating = 4.15) school.

Regression analysis was conducted to determine the influence of proximity to and accessibility of school on the level of school choice of IT students. Table 6 shows that Perceived Accessibility of the School (beta = 0.204, $p$-value < 0.05) influenced school choice of IT students. The predictor has a 2% explanatory power (Adjusted $R^2$ = 0.021). This means that any variation in school choice of IT students is accounted to the respondents' perceived accessibility of school. The result of the regression is unlikely to have arisen from sampling error (F-value = 2.652, p-value < 0.05).

As shown in Table 6, distance of home to school and accessibility in terms of hours spent in going to school did not influence school choice of IT students. This means that it did not matter whether the school was near their home address or far from it. It was also shown previously that respondents would commute for at least 54 minutes by means of public transportation. This may imply that it did not matter if the respondents would spend almost one hour to go to school. They would still choose the university regardless of its distance from their place of residence and the time they would spend in going to school.

**Table 5. Perceptions of the Respondents on the Accessibility of the School and Level of School Choice**

| Perceived Accessibility | Mean | Verbal Interpretation |
|---|---|---|
| Roads leading to UE are in good conditions. | 3.48 | Moderately agree |
| There are diverse modes of transportation available to get to UE. | 3.92 | Agree |
| It is convenient to go to UE from my place of residence. | 3.56 | Agree |
| Fare to go to UE is inexpensive. | 3.53 | Agree |
| **Overall Mean** | **3.62** | **Agree** |
| | | |
| **Level of School Choice** | **4.15** | **Preferred** |

In other words, school choice of IT students was not sensitive to proximity (i.e., distance) and hours spent in going to school. The disparity in the findings of Alderman et al. [1] and Rabovsky [24] can be explained by three key factors. First, unlike in the study of Alderman et al. [1] and Rabovsky [24], the respondents of the study did not belong to poor households. The respondents of the study had the means to pay their transportation. Second, this can also be explained by the home residence of the respondents. It was shown previously that the farthest home residence of the respondents, which is Bulacan (as shown in Table 1), is still relatively near Manila. A forty-eight (48)-kilometer travel became a reasonable distance since the presence of LRT and other modes of transportation made the transportation easy and fast. This was the third key factor.

**Table 6. Regression of Level of School Choice on Proximity to School and Accessibility of School**

| Variables | Beta | p-value |
|---|---|---|
| Proximity – Distance of Home to School | 0.025 | 0.744 |
| Accessibility – Hours Spent in Going to School | 0.072 | 0.384 |
| **Perceived Accessibility of the School** | **0.204** | **0.006** |

*Adjusted $R^2$ = 0.021*
*F-value = 2.652*
*Sig. = 0.05*

Meanwhile, the perceptions of the respondents on the accessibility of the school influenced their school choice. The p-value of 0.006 which was far lower than the 0.05 level of significance showed that the finding was very unlikely to have arisen from sampling

error. Thus, it can be ascertained that the respondents' perception of accessibility of school had an influence on their school choice. This shows that as long as the respondents perceived that the university was accessible, they would choose to study IT in the university.

It can be noted that the perceived accessibility of the school was composed of four subcomponents. These were good road conditions, diverse modes of transportation, convenience of getting from their place of residence, and inexpensive fare. This implies that the university could inform their prospective entrants in these areas of accessibility. The university could include this information in their marketing program.

The strategic location of the university makes it "marketable" for prospective entrants. It is situated in major roads (e.g., España Boulevard and C.M. Recto Avenue) that connect the university to the rest of the other cities in Metro Manila. In the event of heavy traffic condition, there are alternate routes available. It is also highly accessible by means of different modes of transportation like jeepneys and LRT. Since the University is along C.M. Recto Avenue, jeepneys are just passing by at its main gate.

The LRT provided the fastest and the most convenient means of transportation as well as the most inexpensive fare. For Php30 (less than a dollar), students can go from endpoint to endpoint of the LRT for about twenty-five minutes. The accessibility of the university provides a marketing advantage for the university since it covers seven cities in Metro Manila (e.g., Marikina, Quezon City, San Juan, Pasay, Caloocan, Pasig, and Manila). This implies that the university can conduct their marketing in these cities.

However, it can be observed that these four subcomponents are external factors that the university cannot control. For instance, road conditions and fare hikes are very sensitive to local, national or international events. This also implies that the university should collaborate with the local government units about the road infrastructure within the vicinity of the school.

# 5. CONCLUSIONS, LIMITATIONS, AND RECOMMENDATIONS

The results of the study show that among all the factors investigated, only perceived accessibility of school significantly influenced school choice of IT students. Thus, the null hypothesis stating that proximity to school and accessibility of the school, singly or in combination, do not influence school choice is partially accepted.

Based on the findings of the study, the following recommendations are set forth. First, the university should be sensitive to tuition fee increase. If the university wants to retain its lower-income class students, a reasonable tuition fee increase that is affordable to them should be considered. Second, the university could extend its marketing in the areas that the LRT traverses and in Regions III and IV-A. Third, university-local government unit collaboration can be initiated to strengthen roads and streets infrastructure. The university can provide the technical expertise of engineering faculty members while the local government units can materialize their road infrastructure plans.

Lastly, the university can stress the accessibility of the school in terms of good road conditions, different modes of transportation, convenience in getting to the university, and inexpensive fare. Conversely, the university can be proactive by investigating the impact of the changes on road conditions, modes of transportation, fare hikes, and convenience in reaching the university.

The study can be considered a pioneering work in school choice of IT students. Nevertheless, the study acknowledges its limitations for there are still gaps that need to be filled in. First, future studies can investigate the effects of the class schedules of the school on commuting students. For instance, the university has been offering morning (7:30 a.m. to 1 p.m.) and afternoon (1 p.m. to 7 p.m.) classes. No studies have been conducted to determine whether these schedules are convenient to commuting students. In short, future studies can help school administrators formulate policies with regard to class schedule. This will give students sufficient time for curricular, cocurricular, and extracurricular activities. In return, their involvement in these activities can uplift the image of the university.

Second, a study on school choice of parents in terms of proximity and accessibility can be initiated. A comparison of school choice between parents and students in terms of these factors can be investigated. Third, though the university was their "preferred" school, the rank of the school – whether the university was their first, second, third, etc. choice of school among their choices – was unclear. There were anecdotal evidences to show that students could have chosen other expensive schools if they had the means. In other words, students most probably would shortlisted the names of schools where they would apply. Then, from the list, they would choose the school to enroll in.

Third, though it was found out that proximity and accessibility in terms of hours spent did not have a significant influence on school choice of IT students, it is not clear whether the same findings would arise if the study would have been conducted in different geographic locations (e.g., more than 48 kilometers from the school).

Fourth, the findings were limited only to one university. The study can be replicated by the 18 universities in the UBelt to come up with more valid generalizations.

Lastly, data gathering was conducted during the last stage of school choice. School choice is a multi-stage process. Thus, it can be argued that proximity and accessibility might (or might not) influence school choice in the previous stages. Further studies can shed light on this matter.

# 6. ACKNOWLEDGMENTS

The author is greatly thankful to the invaluable help of Vice-Chairman Jaime Bautista, Dr. Ester A. Garcia, Dr. Olivia C. Caoili, Dean Rodany A. Merida, Dr. Socorro R. Villamejor, and to all students who participated in the study.

# 7. REFERENCES

[1] Alderman, H., Orazem, P. F., & Paterno, E. M. 2001. School quality, school cost, and the public/private school choices of low-income households in Pakistan. *The Journal of Human Resources, 36,*2 (Spring 2001), 304–326.

[2] Andre-Bechley, L. 2007. Finding space and managing distance: Public school choice in an urban California district. *Urban Studies, 44,*7 (June 2007), 1355–1376. DOI= http://dx.doi.org/10.1080/00420980701302304.

[3] Bauch, P. A., & Goldring, E. B. 1995. Parent involvement and school responsiveness: Facilitating the home-school connection in schools of choice. *Educational Evaluation and Policy Analysis, 17,*1 (Mar. 1995), 1–21. DOI = http://dx.doi.org/10.3102/01623737017001001.

[4] Belanger, C., Mount, J., & Wilson, M. 2002. Institutional image and retention. *Tertiary Education and Management, 8,*3 (Sep. 2002), 217–230. DOI= http://dx.doi.org/10.1023/A:1016335309885.

[5] Bell, A. C. 2009. All choices created equal? The role of choice sets in the selection of schools. *Peabody Journal of Education, 84,* 2 (April 2009), 191–208. DOI= http://dx.doi.org/10.1080/01619560902810146.

[6] Bosetti, L. 2004. Determinants of school choice: Understanding how parents choose elementary schools in Alberta. *Journal of Education Policy, 19,*4, 387–405. DOI= http://dx.doi.org/10.1080/0268093042000227465.

[7] Briggs, S., & Wilson, A. 2007. Which university? A study of the influence of cost and information factors on Scottish undergraduate choice. *Journal of Higher Education Policy and Management, 29,*1 (Mar. 2007), 57–72. DOI = http://dx.doi.org/10.1080/13600800601175789.

[8] Chapman, D. W. 1981. A model of student college choice. *The Journal of Higher Education, 52,*5 (Sep.-Oct., 1981), 490–505.

[9] Dahari, Z. B., & Ya, M. S. (2011). Factors that influence parents' choice of pre-schools education in Malaysia: An exploratory study. *International Journal of Business and Social Science, 2,*15 (Aug. 2011), 115–128.

[10] Davis, K. 2003. The financial side of choosing a college. *Kiplinger's Financing College, 1,* 187–207.

[11] De Raadt, M. 2004. Searching for tomorrow's programmers. *Issues in Informing Science and Information Technology, 1,* 597–603. Retrieved June 28, 2011,from http://informingscience.org/proceedings/InSITE2004/086raa dt.pdf

[12] Drewes, T., & Michael, C. 2006. How do students choose a university?: An analysis of applications to universities in Ontario, Canada. *Research in Higher Education, 47,*7 (Nov. 2006), 781–800. DOI= http://dx.doi.org/10.1007/s11162-006-9015-6.

[13] Epoc, F. J. 2008. Tuition fee increment and quality of education of selected private secondary schools in Metro Manila. *Luz y Saber, 2,*1, 61–70.

[14] Ford, J. B., Joseph, M., & Joseph, B. 1999. Importance-performance analysis as a strategic tool for service marketers: The case of service quality perceptions of business students in New Zealand and the USA. *The Journal of Services Marketing, 13,*2, 171–186. DOI= http://dx.doi.org/10.1108/08876049910266068.

[15] George, D., & Mallery, P. 2009. *SPSS for Windows step by step: A simple guide and reference 16.0 update 9th edn.* Boston: Pearson Education.

[16] Hurtado, S., Inkelas, K. K., Briggs, C., & Rhee, B.-K. 1997. Differences in college access and choice among racial/ethnic groups: Identifying continuing barriers. *Research in Higher Education, 38,* 1 (Feb. 1997), 43–75. DOI= http://dx.doi.org/10.1023/A:1024948728792.

[17] Kondylis, F., & Manacorda, M. 2012. School proximity and child labor: Evidence from rural Tanzania. *The Journal of Human Resources*, *47*,1 (Winter 2012), 32–63.

[18] Leiviskä, K., & Siponen, M. 2010. Attitudes of sixth form female students toward the IT field. *SIGCAS Computers and Society*, *40*,1 (Mar. 2010), 34–49.

[19] Lenox, T. L., Woratschek, C. R., & Davis, G. A. 2008. Exploring declining CS/IS/IT enrollments. *Information Systems Education Journal*, *6*,44 (Oct. 2008), 1–11. Retrieved June 28, 2011, from http://isedj.org/6/44/

[20] Ming, J. S. K. 2010. Institutional factors influencing students' college choice decision in Malaysia: A conceptual framework. *International Journal of Business and Social Science*, *1*,3 (Dec. 2010), 53–58.

[21] Padlee, S. F., Kamaruddin, A., & Baharun, R. 2010. International students' choice behavior for higher education at Malaysian private universities. *International Journal of Marketing Studies*, *2*,2 (Nov. 2010), 202–211.

[22] Pallant, J. (2001). *SPSS survival manual: A step by step guide to data analysis using SPSS for Windows version 10.* Buckingham: Open University Press.

[23] Parker, R. S., Cook, S., & Pettijohn, C. E. 2007. School choice attributes: Positioning a private school. *Services Marketing Quarterly*, *28*, 4, 21–33. DOI= http://dx.doi.org/10.1300/J396v28n04_02.

[24] Rabovsky, T. 2011. Deconstructing school choice: Problem schools or problem students?. *Public Administration Review*, *17*, 1 (Jan./Feb. 2011), 87–95. DOI= http://dx.doi.org/10.1111/j.1540-6210.2010.02309.x.

[25] Shah, M., & Nair, C. S. 2010. Enrolling in higher education: The perceptions of stakeholders. *Journal of Institutional Research*, *15*, 1, 9–15.

[26] Srikantanyoo, N., & Gnoth, J. 2005. Quality dimensions in international tertiary education: A Thai prospective students' perspective. *The Quality Management Journal*, *12*, 1 (Jan. 2005), 30–40.

[27] Tatar, E., & Oktay, M. 2006. Search, choice and persistence for higher education: A case study in Turkey. *Eurasia Journal of Mathematics, Science and Technology Education*, *2*, 2 (July 2006), 115–129. Retrieved January 29, 2012, from http://www.ejmste.com/022006/d7.pdf.

[28] Theobald, R. 2005. School choice in Colorado Springs: The relationship between parental decisions, location and neighbourhood characteristics. *International Research in Geographical and Environmental Education*, *14*, 2 (May 2005), 92–111.

[29] Tsagala, E., & Kordaki, M. 2007. Critical factors influencing secondary school pupil's decisions to study computing in tertiary education: Gender differences. *Education and Information Technologies*, *12*, 4, 281–295. DOI= http://dx.doi.org/10.1007/s10639-006-9026-0.

[30] Vuri, D. 2010. The effect of availability of school and distance to school on children's time allocation in Ghana. *Labour*, *24* (Dec. 2010), 46–75. DOI= http://dx.doi.org/10.1111/j.1467-9914.2010.00499.x.

[31] Wang, Z. 2007. Key factors that influence recruiting young Chinese students. *International Education Journal*, *8*, 2 (Nov. 2007), 37–48.

# Comparing Achievement of Intended Learning Outcomes in Online Programming Classes with Blended Offerings

Waleed Farag, Ph.D.
Indiana University of Pennsylvania
Computer Science Department
Indiana, PA 15705
+1 (724)357-7995

farag@iup.edu

## ABSTRACT

In the past decade, there has been a noticeable increase in the number of courses/programs offered online by higher education institutions in US and worldwide. This increase makes it necessary to comprehensively study the effectiveness of these offerings to ensure that they yield comparable outcomes to traditional offerings. This research discusses findings of a multi-year, in-depth quantitative study with the objective of assessing the effectiveness of delivering computer programming courses online and analyzing the quality of this delivery mechanism. The paper addresses several aspects of comparing tradition/blended offerings with fully online offerings. Several data sets are used in this study with primarily focus on direct assessments. Specifically, this research measures the Intended Learning Outcomes (ILOs) attained by students enrolled in online programming classes and compares them to the ILOs obtained when teaching the same course in a blended format. Moreover, several other students' success and involvement indicators are measured in both cases and compared. Besides, the paper briefly addresses other indirect assessment findings. The employed data sets have been collected over a number of years (from 2006 till 2011) to enhance the accuracy and implications of the reported statistical findings. Generally, no significant differences were found regarding the attainment of almost all of the ILOs with the exception of one that showed better performance, on average, in the online offerings. On the other hand, blended offerings yielded favorable results that are statistically significant when considering other performance criteria such as withdrawal and failure rates.

## Categories and Subject Descriptors

K.3.2 [**Computers and Educations**]: Computer and Information Science Education - *computer science education, self-assessment.*

## General Terms

Measurement, Performance.

## Keywords

Intended learning outcomes, Performance evaluation of learning, Student's achievements.

## 1. INTRODUCTION

With the availability of current technologies, online delivery of various course contents has become practical; therefore, there have been many recent attempts to deliver programming courses online by a number of institutions. This trend has been welcomed by higher education institutions and students alike. On one hand, the educational institutions see several advantages of online course delivery including increased enrollment, reduced cost and expanded outreach. All of these are very appealing pros for higher education especially in light of the many financial challenges facing higher education in general and public higher education in particular. On the other hand, students positively view online delivery as a flexible way of obtaining college credits. In fact many non-traditional students consider online courses and programs as their only way of finishing their programs or having access to graduate school in order to enhance their professional development.

There is no doubt that the introduction of online delivery has many influential impacts on the IT education and the transfer of knowledge. Many top schools have recently initiated online courses and programs with several of them open to public. A recent example is a joint initiative between Harvard University and Massachusetts Institute of Technology called edX [11]. EdX is a free massively open online course system that allows students from all over the world to take free courses offered by both universities. These are indicative that online delivery is on the rise in both traditional college course offerings and the open education domain. Moreover, such attempts make use of some inherit and powerful features of online delivery such as having no geographical boundaries.

With the wide-spread proliferation of online delivery several important questions emerge which require effective and scientific answers. Is this delivery mechanism effective? Are courses offered online suitable for everyone? What are the impacts of this spread on higher education? These are just some examples but probably the most important question to be answered is: Do these online courses yield comparable Intended Learning Outcomes (ILOs) to traditional offerings? The last question is especially important in the IT field where some students already report difficulties with traditional courses and their contents.

This work discusses a sub-set of the findings of a long-term research study that has the objective of fully investigating the usefulness of delivering introductory computer programming courses online and assessing the quality of such offerings. This paper focuses on presenting the results of direct assessment of the Intended Learning Outcomes (ILOs) of the online course in comparison with the ILOs achieved in blended courses. Appropriately measuring the ILOs of the course provides reliable indicators to the success of the course and to whether students have attained the expected outcomes or not. In addition, several other direct assessment performance metrics are analyzed and compared. The paper also succinctly reports on the findings of other indirect assessment analyses such as the measurement of student perception of online delivery and the comparison of students' satisfaction in both delivery mechanisms. This study employs extensive data sets collected from classes offered over a period of six years. It is believed that the use of such large and extended data has considerably contributed to the reliability and significance of the reported results. A brief review of related work in online delivery of programming contents follows.

There have been many attempts to deliver computer programing courses online and among the pioneer ones was a junior-level programming course described in [14]. That study was concluded by reporting a set of lessons learned. Other recent ones are presented in [1, 7, 12] where the authors have reported on their experience teaching online programming courses and presented suggestions to improve such offerings.

Edwards et al. [4] presented the results of comparing students' perception of pair programming in face-to-face (f2f) and online courses and reported significant difference between the two groups in which students preferred the f2f modality. In [9] a blended design to an Engineering Materials course was introduced and very primitive results showing students' satisfaction were presented. Warren et al. [15] published the results of studying student satisfaction with an online homework generation modules added to an electrical Engineering course. The results of that study addressed only students' perception of the modified course and only provided simple quantitative findings without further analysis of whether these findings are significant or not. The quality of student experience was assessed in [8]. Miles [10] compared students' satisfaction and success in traditional and online classes. That study found no significant difference in students' satisfaction but reported that online students scored significantly lower grades than traditional ones. That study was done over one semester and used very limited sample size. In [3] interesting comparative study of three instruction modalities was presented. Although this research presented some useful findings, the limitation of the study time and sample sizes are of concern.

Although some researchers have considered the importance of assessing online offerings, as described above, many of these studies focused only on using indirect measures of course success such as students' perceptions and satisfaction. However, it is more important to conduct comprehensive studies that directly measure the degree of students' attainment of the course ILOs in order to have more robust view of the success of online courses. The direct assessment of the ILOs, the use of multi-year, diverse data sets, and the in-depth statistical analyses represent the main contributions of this study. Below is a brief description of our study followed by sections reporting on the results of comparing several performance parameters.

## 2. DESCRIPTION OF THE STUDY
The findings presented in this paper are the results from an experimental study that mainly uses direct assessment of a number of performance parameters to compare two groups. The first (control) group data were collected from fourteen different

sections of our first programming course (CS1) which is taken by computer science majors and other related majors. Our CS1 is a conventional introduction to programming that emphasizes functional programming and algorithm design. Topics covered range from introductory ones such as arithmetic operations and decision making then advance to structured data types and recursion. These fourteen sections were taught in the period between 2006 and 2011 where 347 students enrolled in them. The course was offered in a blended format where the f2f component of the course is preserved via weekly class and laboratory sessions. The blended flavor was achieved by moving a number of class activities online including project submission and exams in addition to a comprehensive set of course materials. WebCT was used first then our institution switched to Moodle as the chosen Learning Management system (LMS).

The experimental group data were collected from five sections of the same course taught fully online during 2010 and 2011 and enrolled 104 students. The online course has the same exact course objectives and its contents are identical to the blended course with the exception that there was no f2f interaction between the instructor and students. Rather, all class activities were conducted online. The syllabus of the online course provides a comprehensive coverage of all class policies, expectations and course contents. Large sets of online course materials are posted online in addition to various activities. Course activities include asynchronous ones such as discussion forums in addition to light use of synchronous activities such as chatting. The syllabus also fully describes the set of assessment tools used in such course.

In designing the experiments, special attention has been made to ensure the homogeneity of the study and to exclude extraneous factors. For instance, we tried our best to make sure that course contents, facilitator, and assessment methods are identical in both offerings (the blended and the online ones). The following section presents the methodologies, the analyses and the findings obtained from comparing the ILOs in both groups.

## 3. COMPARING COURSE INTENDED LEARNING OUTCOMES
The course syllabus lists nine learning objectives. These objectives were mapped into four main Intended Learning Outcomes (ILOs) that the student needs to acquire/exhibit upon completion of the course. These outcomes address several categorizes of the Bloom's taxonomy of cognitive levels. Our data analyses will focus on these four main ILOs, mentioned below:

1. Put into practice effective use of an Integrated Development Environment to edit, compile, and run programs (O1).
2. Demonstrate the ability to develop algorithms from problem specification and apply various structured programming techniques to proficiently transform them into programming code (O2).
3. Illustrate the ability to use debugging and testing techniques to locate and fix errors to ensure program correctness (O3).
4. Recognize the proper use of the language's constructs and apply this knowledge in creating effective programs (O4).

Measuring the ILOs is very important because equivalent ILOs in both groups signify that both student populations have acquired comparable knowledge and skills upon completion of the course. As part of ABET -Accreditation Board for Engineering and Technology- accreditation requirements, our department continues, after being accredited, the assessment of its courses. Therefore, a model called EAMU proposed in [5] was adopted by our department in its assessment procedure and is also adopted in this research in order to quantify students' achievement of the ILOs. In our experiments, the above-mentioned four course ILOs were measured by computing the EAMU vector for each outcome. Specifically, for each outcome, a set of course graded activities are selected as a measure for this particular outcome. Each student's achievement in this set is measured to come up with a percent value indicating how well a student attains such an outcome. Then, a number of thresholds were used to differentiate Exemplary (E), Adequate (A), Minimal (M), and Unsatisfactory (U) performance. This procedure is applied to the four outcomes and on every student in the course to derive EAMU vectors for the ILOs. For example, in a blended offering of this course in spring 2011, the computed EAMU vector for the first outcome (O1) is [16, 3, 1, 2] meaning that among the 22 students who passed the course, 16 exhibit exemplary attainment of outcome 1, 3 at the adequate level, one minimal and 2 unsatisfactory. These computed EAMU vectors are analyzed in details in the following sub-sections.

## 3.1 EAMU Vectors as Categorical Data

In this subsection, our statistical analyses [6, 13] deal with the data as categorical ones in which we consider the attainment of an ILO as a categorical variable that can take one of four different values (E, A, M, or U). All computed EAMU vectors for all ILOs in both the online and the blended classes are weighed to form the contingency table shown in Table 1. To statistically analyze the relationship between the control and the experimental groups, the Pearson's chi-square test was used. Results of applying the chi-square test on each of the four studied outcomes are given in Table 2.

**Table 1. Contingency table showing the number of students receiving E, A, M, and U in the two groups**

| Delivery | EAMU | O1_weight | O2_weight | O3_weight | O4_weight |
|---|---|---|---|---|---|
| Blended | E | 192 | 105 | 117 | 45 |
| Blended | A | 31 | 94 | 72 | 139 |
| Blended | M | 11 | 31 | 27 | 44 |
| Blended | U | 19 | 23 | 37 | 25 |
| Online | E | 33 | 22 | 24 | 16 |
| Online | A | 5 | 10 | 9 | 17 |
| Online | M | 3 | 8 | 3 | 8 |
| Online | U | 3 | 4 | 8 | 3 |

**Table 2. Chi-square test results for all four outcomes**

| Outcome | $X^2$ | df | p | odds ratio |
|---|---|---|---|---|
| O1 | 0.54 | 3 | .91 | 1.05 |
| O2 | 3.86 | 3 | .28 | 0.71 |
| O3 | 2.29 | 3 | .52 | 0.72 |
| O4 | 8.58 | 3 | .035 | 0.39 |

Based on the results listed in Table 2 (where: $X^2$ is the chi-square test value, df is the degree of freedom, and p is the 2-sided test significance), the test statistic for Outcome 2 (O2) can be interpreted as follows: there was no significant association between the delivery mechanism and whether or not students can demonstrate the ability to develop algorithms and implement them from problem specifications, $X^2 (3) = 3.86$, $p = 0.28$. This finding was also supported by the computed odds ratio, 0.71, which indicates that the odds of students performing at the exemplary level in the blended class were only 0.71 times if they were taking the online class. It is worth noting that the chi-square test yielded non-significant results also for both outcomes 1 and 3. For outcome 4, there was a significant association between the delivery mechanism and the ability of the students to recognize the proper use of various language's constructs and apply this knowledge in creating effective programs, $X^2 (3) = 8.58$, $p < 0.05$. This finding was also confirmed by the computed odds ratio, 0.39 which indicates that the odds of students performing at the exemplary level in the blended class were 0.39 times if they were taking the online class. To summarize these interested findings, there was no significant difference between the two delivery mechanisms in the first three outcomes (O1–O3) but outcome 4 has significant difference. Interestingly enough, the difference found in O4 indicated that students taking the online class have better chances achieving that outcome than those taking the blended one, see Table 2. It is worth noting that the odds ratio was computed by considering the E values versus all three other levels. Besides, the chi-square test assumptions are fulfilled including that expected frequency constraint in which all cases have only one or two cells with expected values less than 5 which still give acceptable statistical power for the test [6].

## 3.2 Using t-test to Compare ILOs Attainment

In order to confirm the interesting findings in the previous subsection, the obtained EAMU vectors data are analyzed differently in this section. First, all computed EAMU vectors for each delivery method are accumulated to produce a single EAMU vector. The blended course was offered in eight different academic semesters (253 passing students) while the online course was offered five times including two during summer sessions (44 passing students). The accumulated EAMU vectors for each outcome along with the percentage of each level are listed in Table 3 for both delivery methods.

**Table 3. Accumulated EAMU vectors and percentages**

| Outcome | EAMU vectors | %E | %A | %M | %U |
|---|---|---|---|---|---|
| O1-blended | [192 31 11 19] | 76% | 12% | 4% | 8% |
| O1-online | [33 5 3 3] | 75% | 11% | 7% | 7% |
| O2-blended | [105 94 31 23] | 42% | 37% | 12% | 9% |
| O2-online | [22 10 8 4] | 50% | 23% | 18% | 9% |
| O3-blended | [117 72 27 37] | 46% | 28% | 11% | 15% |
| O3-online | [24 9 3 8] | 55% | 20% | 7% | 18% |
| O4-blended | [45 139 44 25] | 18% | 55% | 17% | 10% |
| O4-online | [16 17 8 3] | 36% | 39% | 18% | 7% |

The percentages in Table 3 show comparable values for corresponding EAMU levels in both mechanisms with the exception of O4 where online class has 36% for E level compared to 18% in the blended one. To further investigate these preliminary trends and verify their statistical significance, the following analyses were performed. For each semester in which the course was offered, an overall EAMU vector is computed for each outcome. Then, each EAMU vector is transformed to a scalar value that indicates the degree of achievement of this outcome in this offering. The transformation is accomplished by using a proposed weighted sum formula, see equation 1, that places increasingly higher weights on good performance (A and E) while penalizes marginal and unsatisfactory performance by assigning them diminished weight values. The formula is normalized to the number of students (N) in the offering to produce a comparable scale. For each semester, we have a value that expresses the degree of attainment of an outcome and we would like to compare the average of these values for blended offerings with the average for the online offerings. A straightforward statistical method is to use the Independent Samples t-Test provided that the data satisfy the parametric test assumptions. To test the normality and homogeneity of variance assumptions the Shapiro-Wilk and Levene's tests are used and the results are listed in Table 4.

$$\text{Outcome}(i) = \frac{1}{N}(0.55E + 0.25A + 0.15M + 0.05U) \quad (1)$$

**Table 4. Results of parametric assumptions tests**

| Outcome overall | Shapiro-Wilk | | | Levene Statistic | | | |
|---|---|---|---|---|---|---|---|
| | Stat | df | Sig. | Stat | df1 | df2 | Sig. |
| O1-blended | 0.96 | 8 | .78 | 0.60 | 1 | 11 | .46 |
| O1-online | 0.81 | 5 | .09 | | | | |
| O2-blended | 0.98 | 8 | .98 | 1.13 | 1 | 11 | .31 |
| O2-online | 0.94 | 5 | .66 | | | | |
| O3-blended | 0.91 | 8 | .32 | 2.82 | 1 | 11 | .12 |
| O3-online | 0.93 | 5 | .62 | | | | |
| O4-blended | 0.92 | 8 | .45 | 0.86 | 1 | 11 | .37 |
| O4-online | 0.96 | 5 | .82 | | | | |

Given that all significant values (p) are larger than 0.05 for both tests in Table 4, one can conclude that the data conform to the parametric assumptions and the independent samples t-test can be used. The detailed results of all t-tests along with descriptive statistics and the computed effect sizes are listed in Table 5 (where: M is the mean, SE is the standard error, t is t-test value and r is the effect size). For outcome 1, on average, students in the online class scored slightly higher in achieving the ILO (O1) (M = 0.463, SE = 0.02) than students taking the blended class (M = 0.455, SE = 0.01). This difference was NOT significant t(11) = - 0.37, p > 0.05. Moreover, the effect size (r) is 0.11 which represents a small effect. Similar conclusions can be drawn for both O2 and O3 based on the fact that the t-test produces non-significant results for both outcomes. On the other hand, the t-test yields a significant difference between the two groups for outcome 4. One can conclude that for outcome 4, on average, students in the online class scored higher in achieving the ILO

(O4) (M = 0.330, SE = 0.007) than students taking the blended class (M = 0.266, SE = 0.008). This difference was significant t(11) = -5.59, p < 0.001. Moreover, the effect size (r) is 0.86 which represents a very large effect. These obtained results are in conformance with the ones in section 3.1 where the first three outcomes have no significant differences between the two groups while the last outcome (O4) gives a statistically significant higher average in the online class.

**Table 5. Results of independent samples t-test comparisons**

| Outcome overall | Descriptive values | | Independent t-test | | | |
|---|---|---|---|---|---|---|
| | M | SE | t | df | Sig. | r |
| O1-blended | 0.455 | 0.010 | -0.37 | 11 | .72 | .11 |
| O1-online | 0.463 | 0.021 | | | | |
| O2-blended | 0.346 | 0.012 | -0.96 | 11 | .36 | .28 |
| O2-online | 0.371 | 0.027 | | | | |
| O3-blended | 0.347 | 0.013 | -1.02 | 11 | .33 | .29 |
| O3-online | 0.375 | 0.029 | | | | |
| O4-blended | 0.266 | 0.008 | -5.59 | 11 | .000 | .86 |
| O4-online | 0.330 | 0.007 | | | | |

## 3.3 MANOVA Analysis of ILOs

In the previous two subsections, the analyses were performed on each outcome individually as a single dependent variable which gave us conclusions about each outcome separately. In order to also consider the correlations that might exist between the studied four dependent variables, Multivariate Analysis of Variance (MANOVA) [13] is used here. First, we need to check if the data satisfy the MANOVA test assumptions.

1. Test of normality: Shapiro-Wilk tests were used for each one of the outcomes individually and all yielded normally distributed data, see Table 4.

2. Homogeneity of variances was also confirmed by Levene's test results for all four outcomes, see Table 4.

3. Homogeneity of covariance matrices were tested using Box's test that gives non-significant result M = 18.85 with p = .43, i.e., the assumption is tenable.

Running MANOVA on the four outcomes simultaneously produces between-subject effects test results and significant values identical to the ones obtained in Table 5. Using the Pillai's Trace, there was a significant effect of the delivery mechanism on the collective attainment of the course ILOs, V = 0.79, F(4, 8) = 7.59, p < .01. The MANOVA test was followed by discriminant analysis to investigate the nature of the relationship between the four dependent variables. The discriminant analysis revealed only one discriminant function which significantly discriminant both groups. According to [2], higher correlational coefficient value indicates that this variable contributes the most to group separation. This is obvious by examining the values of the canonical variate correlation coefficients in the structure matrix (0.06, 0.15, 0.16, 0.87 for O1, O2, O3, and O4 respectively). Outcome 4 has a corresponding variate value of 0.87 while other outcomes have very small values. One can conclude that the significance of the MANOVA test was mainly the result of the effect produced by the O4 variable while the other lower values in the structure matrix confirm the previous findings that all other outcomes did not differ significantly across the studied groups.

# 4. SUCCESS AND INVOLVEMENT

Although measuring and comparing the ILOs in the previous section gives a reliable indicator to the effectiveness of the course, it also helpful to assess other students' success and involvement criteria. Therefore, in this section, a number of student-related performance criteria are measured and compared across both delivery mechanisms. First, the chances of receiving the highest grade (A), a failure grade (F), and withdrawing from the course (W) are first assessed using simple descriptive statistics then the chi-square test is used to verify whether the observed differences are statistically significant or not. Moreover, statistical comparison of the overall class grade percentage is presented. Lastly, student involvements are also analyzed by measuring and comparing the unitization of online resources.

## 4.1 Analysis of Chances of Receiving Grade A

The following analysis focuses on comparing grade A rates in both delivery mechanisms. For the blended class, the percentage of A students (the number of students received A grade to the total number of students passed the class: 81/253) is 32% while the corresponding percentage for the online class (21/44) is 48%. It is clear that the rate of receiving A is higher in online classes compared to the blended ones. To ensure the significance of that observation, the chi-square test is used yielding NO significant association between the delivery mechanism and whether or not students can receive a final grade of A in the class $X^2 (3) = 4.72$, p = 0.19. The computed odds ratio is 1.94.

## 4.2 Chances of Failing the Class

For the blended course, the percentage of failure (the number of students received F grade to the total number of students completed the class: 43/296) is 15%. This percentage (22/66) is 33% for the online class which is obviously much higher (around twice) than the corresponding percentage in the blended course. Chi-square test also confirmed that there was a significant association between the delivery mechanism and failure rates in the class $X^2 (4) = 16.95$, p < 0.01. This finding was also supported by the computed odds ratio, 2.94 which indicates that the odds of students failing the online class were 2.94 times if they were taking the blended class.

## 4.3 Chances of Withdrawing from the Class

The withdrawal ratio is defined here as the number of students who withdrew from the class to the total number of students who enrolled in the class. For the blended class, the withdrawal percentage from class (51/347) is 15%. In other words, 85% of the students initially enrolled in the class have completed the class and received a final grade. For the online class, the withdrawal percentage (38/104) is 37% which is a much higher rate compared to the blended case. Again, chi-square test was used and it was found that there was a significant association between the delivery mechanism and whether or not students withdraw from the class $X^2 (1) = 24.1$, p < 0.001. This conclusion was also confirmed by the odds ratio, 3.34, indicating that the odds of withdrawal from the online class were 3.34 times the blended case.

## 4.4 Comparing Overall Percentage Grade

This analysis focuses on comparing the average overall percentage grade in the blended course with the corresponding percentage for the online one. Such a comparison gives us better understanding of whether the delivery mechanism has a role affecting the average overall percentage grade for all students in the class. The null hypothesis states that the distribution of final grade percentages is the same across categories of class delivery. Although the data have homogenous variance, the data for both cases are not normal; the Shapiro-Wilk test produced significant results. Figure 1 also shows a distribution with apparent negative skewness and kurtosis. Thus, the Mann-Whitney non parametric test is used to compare both averages and yielded non-significant difference. To summarize the test outcome, students final grade percentages in the blended class (Median = 83.21) did not differ significantly from those enrolled in the online class (Median = 89.35), U = 4663.00, z = -1.72, ns: p > 0.05, r = -0.10. This was also obvious in the close values of the average final grades in the blended and the online class, 82.53 and 85.14 respectively.

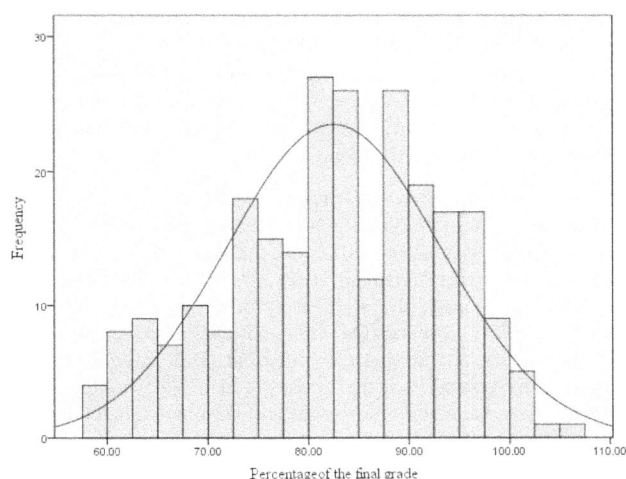

**Figure 1. Distribution of percentage grades in blended courses**

## 4.5 Analysis of Resources Utilization

In this subsection, we use the frequency of utilization of course online resources as a rough indicator to the involvement of the student then compare the computed values across both delivery methods. Our research hypothesis states that students enrolled in the online class will utilize the online class contents much more than those enrolled in the blended class. As expected students in the online class have higher access frequency to course online materials (M = 1343) while the corresponding mean for the blended students is (M = 637). Applying the Levene's test found that the variance is not homogeneous; therefore, Mann-Whitney, a non-parametric test, was used yielding the following. There was a highly significant difference between the utilization of online contents between students taking the online class (Median = 1388.00) and those taking the blended class (Median = 606.00), U= 297,z = -4.48, p < 0.001. The obtained effect size (r) was -0.48 which represents a large effect that accounts for around 25% of the variance. It is worth noting that the online contents used are exactly the same in both classes. This finding supports our research hypothesis mentioned-above. Thus, one can conclude that the nature of the online class stimulates students to more frequently utilize the online contents compared to other offerings.

## 5. INDIRECT ASSESSMENT

In addition to the direct assessment analyses reported in sections 3 and 4, the study also measures and statistically compares students' perception and satisfaction of online delivery with blended one. Due to space limitation, the details of indirect assessment analyses are not discussed here but generally comparable satisfaction levels were found. Moreover, very interesting correlations between various perception-related factors were spotted.

## 6. CONCLUSIONS

In spite of the rapid spread use of online courses, it is believed that there is a gap in the literature of the assessment of online programming courses. This paper is a trial to fill this gap and to comprehensively assess the effectiveness of online delivery in comparison with blended offerings. The results presented in this paper focused on direct assessment of such offerings which is definitely a more important factor in determining the effectiveness of these offerings than indirect assessment techniques used by the majority of other studies. This paper used more than 450 samples (students) and such data were collected over a period of six years. The longevity of the study in addition to the used sample sizes are some of its positive features. In addition, we consider that the main contribution of this paper is the measuring and comparison of the Intended Learning Outcomes (ILOs) as the prime determining factor of effectiveness.

All three statistical tests (chi-square, t-test- and MANOVA) used to compare the four studied ILOs yielded identical findings where there was no significant difference between the blended and online delivery mechanism in attaining the first three outcomes. Interestingly enough, the significant difference revealed by all tests for the last outcome (O4) indicted that online students have higher chances of attaining this outcome. This finding might be explained by considering that most students who completed the online classes were very motivated and serious students and thus have higher chances of attaining some of the ILOs.

With respect to other success and involvement indicators, there was no significant effect of the delivery mechanism on the chances of students receiving A as final course grades and on the distribution of the percentage of final grades. On the other hand, statistically significant differences were reported for both failure and withdrawal chances in which the blended offering has a positive role in reducing these ratios compared to the online offering. Moreover, it was found that there is a significant difference in the frequency of utilizing online resources between the two groups in which online students have used them more frequently. The last finding can be attributed to the nature of the online environment which stimulated the students to better unitize the available materials and be active contributors to the learning process.

## 7. REFERENCES

[1] Armitage, W., Boyer, N., Langevin. S., and Gaspar, A. 2009. Rapid conversion of an IT degree program to online delivery: impact, problems, solutions and challenges. In *Proceedings of the SIGITE Conference on information technology education* (Fairfax, Virginia, October 22 - 24, 2009). ITE '09. ACM, New York, NY, 100-107. DOI= http://doi.acm.org/10.1145/1631728.1631758.

[2] Bray, J. and Maxwell, S. 1985. *Multivariate Analysis of Variance*, volume 54, Sage, Newbury Park, CA.

[3] Caldwell, E. 2006. Comparative study of three instructional modalities in a computer programming course: Traditional instruction, web-based instruction and online instruction. Doctoral Thesis. UMI Order No. AAI3227694, University of North Carolina at Greensboro.

[4] Edwards, R. Stewart, J., and Ferati, M. 2010. Assessing the effectiveness of distributed pair programming for an online informatics curriculum. *ACM Inroads* 1, 1 (Mar 2010), 48-54. DOI= http://doi.acm.org/10.1145/1721933.1721951.

[5] Estell, J. 2007. Streamlining the assessment process with the faculty course assessment report, *Workshop in the 37th ASEE/IEEE Frontiers in Education Conference* (Milwaukee, WI, October 10 - 3, 2007), IEEE, W1A-1. DOI= http://doi.ieeecomputersociety.org/10.1109/FIE.2007.4418236.

[6] Field, A. 2009. *Discover Statistics Using SPSS*. SAGE Publications Ltd, London, UK.

[7] Karsten, R. Kaparthi, S., and Roth, R. 2005. Teaching programming via the Web: A time-tested methodology, *J. College Teaching Methods & Styles,* 1, 3, 73-79.

[8] Kist. A. and Wandel, A. 2011. Performance evaluation of online learning tools, In *Proceedings of the 41st ASEE/IEEE Frontiers in Education Conference* (Rapid City, SD, October 12 - 15, 2011), IEEE, T1C-1-T1C2. DOI= http://doi.ieeecomputersociety.org/10.1109/FIE.2011.6143077.

[9] Masad, L. and Griffin, R. 2011. Effectiveness of multiple curriculum delivery methods on students' learning, In *Proceedings of the IEEE Global Engineering Education Conference*, (Rapid City, SD, April 4 - 6, 2011), EDUCON '11. IEEE, 850-852. DOI= http://doi.ieeecomputersociety.org/10.1109/EDUCON.2011.5773243.

[10] Miles, G. 2011. Comparison of satisfaction and success of traditional and online students in an introductory computer literacy course in a small liberal arts university, *J. Computing Sciences in Colleges*, 27, 2 (December 2011), 206-212.

[11] MIT-edX 2012. Retrieved May 21, 2012 from http://web.mit.edu/press/2012/mit-harvard-edx-announcement.html.

[12] Romanowski, C., Raj, R. and Ramkumar. S. 2011. Successful practices for online computing, engineering, and technology courses, In *Proceedings of the 41st ASEE/IEEE Frontiers in Education Conference* (Rapid City, SD, October 12 - 15, 2011), IEEE, T1C-1-T1C6. DOI= http://doi.ieeecomputersociety.org/10.1109/FIE.2011.6143092.

[13] Tabachnick, B. and Fidell, L. 2007. *Using Multivariate Statistics*. Pearson – Allyn and Bacon, Boston, MA.

[14] Thomas, R. 2000. Experiences Teaching C++ Online, *J. Computing Sciences in Colleges* 15, 5, 214-222.

[15] Warren, S., Tare, B. and Bennett, A. 2008. Lessons learned from the application of online homework generation modules in a signals and systems course, In *Proceedings of the 38th ASEE/IEEE Frontiers in Education Conference* (Saratoga Springs, NY, October 22 - 25, 2008), IEEE, T4B-17-T4B-22. DOI= http://doi.ieeecomputersociety.org/10.1109/FIE.2008.4720500.

# Experience with a Cross-Disciplinary Aggregated Glossary of Technical Terms

Joseph J. Ekstrom
Brigham Young University
Provo, UT
jekstrom@byu.edu

## ABSTRACT

A glossary typically provides a binding of terminology to concepts specific to a particular document or specialty. What would an aggregation of these concept descriptions reveal about how specialists in various fields use terminology? In particular would it help students and educators understand how terminology is used by specialists with whom they need to communicate? This paper provides a status report on an effort to find out. Starting with *ISO/IEC 24765: Systems and software engineering vocabulary* which aggregated the glossaries from 120 standards, we have created a database of 131 glossaries gathered from various sources. Though only 4% of terms have 3 or more concept descriptions, some have 10 or more. Initial analysis indicates that such a glossary can provide useful insights into potential areas of miscommunication. Simple exposure to the diversity of concepts associated with a given term will help sensitize people to the issues.

## Categories and Subject Descriptors

H. Information Systems     H.4 INFORMATION SYSTEMS APPLICATIONS     H.4.3 Communications Applications

## General Terms

Management, Documentation, Human Factors, Standardization

## Keywords

Glossaries, sevocab, vocabulary, miscommunication

## 1. INTRODUCTION

Accurate human communication can be a problem in many contexts. Who hasn't been frustrated by strong-willed participants dominating a meeting with a long, loud discussion that turns out to be "violent agreement" about a concept but a lack of agreement about terminology? The lack of effective communication often comes from nuanced differences in the meaning assigned by the participants to a few terms or phrases. There is a fascinating chapter in *A Framework for Understanding System Engineering* [1] called "System engineers are from Mars, software engineers are from Venus". It starts with the following example:

"When told to 'secure' a building it has been related that,

- The Navy issues a purchase order for the building.

- The Air Force locks the doors and turns on the alarm system.
- The Army evacuates the personnel, then locks the doors and turns on the alarm system.
- The Marines assault the building using ground troops and air support, and then deploy squads in and around the building checking the credentials of all who aspire to enter the building.

This example illustrates a subtle communications problem. When one hears unknown words, such as in a foreign language, the failure to communicate is obvious. However, when one hears words that sound correct in the context, the failure to communicate is not realized and sometimes produces serious consequences." [2]

The chapter goes on to analyze the communication issues between Systems and Software Engineers in the context of origins and history. The goal is to help software and systems engineers communicate better. The final resolution is "Active listening is a well-established technique for bridging communications problems and sharing meaning."[3] One cannot help but agree with this statement. As educators, we need to sensitize our students to this issue so that they can participate in cross-disciplinary teams effectively. However, might we not provide some tools to help sensitize students to the issues and possibly provide some indication of where the miscommunication might occur?

Technical terminology is designed to help avoid communication problems; in fact there is an entire discipline devoted to terminology that attempts to accurately represent concepts with appropriate terminology [4]. The focus of Terminology as a discipline is given a concept -> associate an appropriate term (which can be a short phrase). This contrasts with dictionary building (Lexicography) which given a word -> analyzes word usage to create a definition.[5] [1]. Since specialized terminology is bound to concepts in the creation of a typical glossary, there might be a higher probability that the same concept is bound to multiple different terms, but even worse, the same term can be bound to two different concepts by different terminologists in different domains. This corresponds to equivalent descriptive prose being attached to different terms, and multiple descriptions associated with a single term. Tools to help in analysis of the first correspondence is a research project in natural language

---

[1] Since Terminology management as a discipline creates concept descriptions and then binds them to terms, the term *concept description* will be used rather than the term *definition* which seems to imply the Lexicographical approach.

processing. The second can be addressed by simply listing all available descriptions associated with a term.

IT professionals spend much of their time in a world with more potential communications problems than just those between Software and Systems engineers. IT people must deal with the business management context, the system and software engineering context, and the various user communities that are stakeholders in the systems and services. Each of these communities has their own conceptual context and associated terminology - terminology which is specialized to allow the individual community to communicate efficiently. What does this efficiency do to our ability to communicate across disciplines? Is it possible to provide IT people with the tools to analyze terminology of another discipline with which they need to communicate?

Our common experience demonstrates that there are communications issues. Popular humor successfully exploits these issues. Consider *The IT Crowd*, [6] this popular British sitcom is based on stereotypical behavior of IT departments. There is humor in miscommunication; however, it is not funny when a project fails because of a misunderstanding. Are there disciplines that will have particular difficulty communicating with each other? Is there a way to know ahead of time the conflicts that might arise in a particular meeting? One approach to find out is to create an aggregation of terms from multiple disciplines and analyze the resulting data. This paper presents an initial analysis of specialized terminology collected from various sources. Starting with *ISO/IEC 24765: Systems and software engineering vocabulary* [7] which aggregated the glossaries from 120 standards, we have created a database of 131 glossaries gathered from various sources. Initial analysis indicates that such a glossary can provide interesting insights into potential areas of miscommunication.

## 2. A GLOSSARY AGGREGATION PROTOTYPE

Many of us have participated in discussions that were resolved only after all of the participants agreed to a common vocabulary. That is, we had to agree to a "glossary of terms" in order to communicate. Teams always seem to develop a set of acronyms and terms specific to the team. Is there a way to know ahead of time where miscommunication is likely in order to accelerate the vocabulary normalization phase of teambuilding? As was noted in [2], this problem has been recognized at the boundary of Systems and Software Engineering. As a result an aggregated glossary was created, ISO/IEC 24765.[7] There is also an associated web site, sevocab [8]. From the perspective of an IT educator this aggregation of glossaries from standards was incomplete. The term *enterprise architecture* returns 0 hits on a search of this glossary! However, the term *system* has 8 concept descriptions and the word *system* occurs 625 times in term phrases and descriptions. In reading the 8 concept descriptions I found several conflicts in term usage of different standards. The idea of this kind of utility was very intriguing; however, the user interface of *sevocab* [8] didn't provide the access I wanted. The only way to get a listing of the terms in the glossary was to download the entire ISO/IEC 24765 standard [7]. The search interface of *sevocab* is great for checking for a specific term, but the interface does not allow one to browse the terms and explore their relationships. I was curious whether one could use this data

to flag potential areas of miscommunication. Thus began my personal glossary aggregation prototype.

### 2.1 Data Acquisition
The initial task was to download the text of ISO/IEC 24765 and parse it into a normalized form. The form chosen was an in-memory python 'dict' data structure. The initial approach has been to construct a custom parser in python to handle the idiosyncrasies of the individual glossaries. As with any ad-hoc parser, there were syntax issues. For example, an integer enclosed in parentheses indicates a concept description is starting. However, it sometimes means a reference to another description for the term in sevocab[8]. This was detected only after reading many terms, since 85% of the terms have a single concept description. This approached worked fine for initial exploration of the text. Python code is a very effective query language, but it isn't that useful if you don't know python or have access to the text. A more generally accessible approach was needed.

### 2.2 Web Access
After the initial analysis it was clear that comparing concept descriptions was a reasonable approach to sensitize one to potential miscommunication issues. When colleagues learned what I was doing, several asked for access to the data for their own research. Their first question was "what is the link?" It became very clear that web access was required for the work to be useful to anyone but the author and his students. We decided that we would use Django [9] to build a prototype web site.

Django's built-in data modeling and automatic object-relational mapping features make it a good choice for prototyping web displays of data objects. SQLite was chosen as the relational database technology since the dataset is relatively small and it is installed along with Django. The automatically generated Django admin site provided general access to the data. All that was required was to provide a script to load the data and to generate the UI. Django also makes it very simple to map customized URLs to page generation code.

### 2.3 User Interface
The first problem I encountered with the SEvocab interface was the inability to list the terms and browse their definitions. After implementing a simple list of terms where each term was a link to a URL that was displayed in an adjacent frame, we found that we needed additional meta-information to know which term to display. Single concept terms were not our first interest so we added an indicator of how many concepts were associated with the term. This was helpful, but paging through a list of 5500 names became tedious. We added additional sorts on the term list. Sorting high to low on the number of associated concepts associated is the most useful if one is searching for terms with potential misunderstanding. We are currently experimenting with the prototype, adding glossaries, and adding features as the needs emerge.

### 2.4 Lessons Learned
The first lesson that has emerged is that we need a more formal methodology for normalizing the data found in the glossaries. We also need to retain all of the information in the original glossary. Ad-hoc parsers written by multiple authors leads to inconsistency in the storage of concepts. Our initial work with SEvocab had *concepts, notes, see also,* and *synonym* fields associated with the terms. Using those as optional attributes in the database seemed

like the obvious answer. However, other glossaries have had other annotation fields: *scope notes*, *comments*, *alias*, and some others. It is impractical to add an attribute every time a glossary includes another annotation.. Since the database was already defined, the individual doing the import is at liberty to bind these additional fields wherever they choose. *Scope notes* can be mapped to *notes*, but is an *alias* the same as a synonym? It also became apparent that the names applied to these extra attributes carried some semantics to the authors of the text. *Notes* and *comments* may not be the same abstract entity.

We also found that it is very inconvenient to keep track of parsers, especially when the tendency is to modify an existing parser to build the next one. Even with source code control, some way to bind parser code to versions of the imported glossary is necessary. We need to formalize this process.

Another problem is the ability to review the performance of a parser before the data from the glossary is imported into the database. It has become apparent to us that we should parse into a normalized text format and use a common import script to load the data into the database. This provides a human-readable audit on the parser and avoids bugs in the code that stores the data elements in the database. In some other projects, we have found that it is better to define an XML schema to store the normalized text. This allows a human audit of the normalized glossary and also allows analysis using an XML database tool to explore each glossary independently.

Finally, we can aggregate this data for research purposes; however, most glossaries are copyrighted. There is no problem as long as we use the tools for academic research against the imported text, since that is easily justified as fair use. However, in order to make the tools generally available, we must deal with the permission issues.

To summarize, the next generation of glossary aggregation tools will:

1. Provide a model for optional attributes that retains the naming from the original glossary.

2. Stores imported glossaries in a normalized XML format to provide a human readable audit and edit.

3. Use a common import script that accepts only the normalized XML format to load the persistent store behind the tools.

4. Display copyright information and respect all copyright laws.

## 3. ANALYSIS

As was described above, the initial site provides an alphabetical list of the terms; clicking on the term brings up all of the descriptions for that term. Since 85% of all of the terms have a single description, the most useful sort of the list of terms is in high to low order by number of descriptions as in Table 2. There are currently 5545 terms aggregated from the 131 distinct glossaries. Table 1 lists the distribution of definitions associated with a term. Over 85% of the terms have only one concept description. However, 1.4% have 5 or more. These terms tend to be some of the most used and therefore more likely to be candidates for miscommunication. Table 2 lists the Top 10 terms for number of concept descriptions. Actually there are 11 since there is a 6 way tie for the last slot. Appendix A contains a list of all the terms that are described 5 or more ways.

**Table 1**

Term Frequencies

| Term Counts | Frequency | % of Terms | Aggregate % |
|---|---|---|---|
| 1 | 4757 | 85.79% | 85.79% |
| 2 | 495 | 8.93% | 94.72% |
| 3 | 152 | 2.74% | 97.46% |
| 4 | 61 | 1.10% | 98.56% |
| 5 | 28 | 0.50% | 99.06% |
| 6 | 20 | 0.36% | 99.42% |
| 7 | 14 | 0.25% | 99.68% |
| 8 | 7 | 0.13% | 99.80% |
| 9 | 6 | 0.11% | 99.91% |
| 10 | 3 | 0.05% | 99.96% |
| 11 | 0 | 0.00% | 99.96% |
| 12 | 0 | 0.00% | 99.96% |
| 13 | 1 | 0.02% | 99.98% |
| 14 | 1 | 0.02% | 100.00% |

**Table 2**

Top 10 Terms

| 1 | CONSTRAINT | 14 |
|---|---|---|
| 2 | PROCESS | 13 |
| 3 | ENTITY | 10 |
| 4 | MEASURE | 10 |
| 5 | FUNCTION | 10 |
| 6 | BASELINE | 9 |
| 7 | IMPLEMENTATION | 9 |
| 8 | INPUT | 9 |
| 9 | ACTIVITY | 9 |
| 10 | SYSTEM | 9 |
| 11 | INTERFACE | 9 |

If our hypothesis holds, analysis of terms that are bound to multiple concepts with be the most confusing. Let us consider the term *constraint*. In the current data set, this term is the most described, with 14 associated concepts. The system engineering concepts (1) (2) and (3) use the terms limitation, restriction, and statement; these are more intuitive meanings. Concept description (7) is more information management oriented. (4) and (5) indicate that a constraint is a rule; these both come from a conceptual modeling context. (11) comes from the Project Management Body of Knowledge and provides a very formal notion of constraints on an overall project. It is clear that this

## CONSTRAINT

(1) - a limitation or implied requirement that constrains the design solution or implementation of the systems engineering process and is not changeable by the enterprise. (IEEE 1220-2005 IEEE Standard for the Application and Management of the Systems Engineering Process, 3.1.5)

(2) - a restriction on software life cycle process (SLCP) development. (IEEE 1074-2006 IEEE Standard for Developing a Software Project Life Cycle Process, Annex E)

(3) - a statement that expresses measurable bounds for an element or function of the system

(4) - a rule that specifies a valid condition of data (IEEE 1320.2-1998 [R2004] IEEE Standard for Conceptual Modeling Language Syntax and Semantics for IDEF1X97 (IDEFobject), 3.1.41)

(5) - a rule that specifies a valid condition of data

(6) - a responsibility that is a statement of facts that are required to be true in order for the constraint to be met (IEEE 1320.2-1998 [R2004] IEEE Standard for Conceptual Modeling Language Syntax and Semantics for IDEF1X97 (IDEFobject), 3.1.41)

(7) - a restriction on the value of an attribute or the existence of any object based on the value or existence of one or more others (ISO/IEC 15474-1:2002 Information technology -- CDIF framework -- Part 1: Overview, 4.2)

(8) - a responsibility that is a statement of facts that are required to be true in order for the constraint to be met

(9) - an externally imposed limitation on system requirements, design, or implementation or on the process used to develop or modify a system (IEEE 1362-1998 [R2007] IEEE Guide for Information Technology-System Definition -Concept of Operation Document, 3.5)

(10) - an externally imposed limitation on system requirements, design, or implementation or on the process used to develop or modify a system

(11) - [Input]. the state, quality, or sense of being restricted to a given course of action or inaction. An applicable restriction or limitation, either internal or external to a project, which will affect the performance of the project or a process. For example, a schedule constraint is any limitation or restraint placed on the project schedule that affects when a schedule activity can be scheduled and is usually in the form of fixed imposed dates. (A Guide to the Project Management Body of Knowledge [PMBOK[R] Guide] -- Fourth Edition)

(12) - a statement that expresses measurable bounds for an element or function of the system (IEEE 1233-1998 [R2002] IEEE Guide for Developing System Requirements Specifications, 3.4)

(13) - A semantic condition or restriction. Certain constraints are predefined in the UML, others can be user defined. Constraints are one of three extensibility mechanisms in UML. (http://sparxsystems.com/uml_tool_guide/glossary_of_terms/glossaryof terms.htm)

(14) - A rule or condition that applies to some element. It is often modeled as a pre- or post- condition. (http://sparxsystems.com/uml_tool_guide/glossary_of_terms/glossaryof terms.htm)

Note: That is, a constraint is a factor that is imposed on the solution by force or compulsion and may limit or modify the design changes.

See also: software life cycle process (SLCP) , tagged value, stereotype

term, used in a multidisciplinary context, could be misunderstood by some parties trained to use the term in a specialized way. Simply displaying this list of alternative concepts associated with the term could sensitize the participants to potential misunderstandings. We have tried this approach informally and it does seem to smooth the initial process of building a common base of communication.

## 4. SUMMARY

In this paper we have reported our experience with aggregating some publicly available glossaries and using the resulting aggregated glossary to look for potential miscommunication issues by comparing the different meanings associated with the terms. We described the prototype tool set and indicated the weaknesses of the implementation. We provided a descriptive analysis of the current database consisting of over 5500 terms from 131 distinct glossaries.

The initial results have been promising enough that we will continue the effort to aggregate more glossaries and improve the data import toolset along with the analysis and visualization. We believe that this effort will provide educators with tools to improve students understanding of the communications issues in teams, especially those consisting of members from diverse disciplines.

Appendix A lists the terms most likely to be misunderstood based upon the number of associated meanings. Try the experiment with your students. Search for a common term from the list in http://www.computer.org/sevocab see if simply showing them multiple definitions for terms they think they know doesn't help them understand why miscommunication is so common.

We solicit help from the community to locate and obtain access to relevant glossaries. We will be making the normalized XML format available soon.

## 5. ACKNOWLEDGMENTS

Our thanks to the IEEE Computer Society for the work to aggregate SEvocab and the inspiration it provided to explore the potential of aggregated glossaries further.

## 6. REFERENCES

[1] Kasser, Joseph E., *A Framework for Understanding Systems Engineering,* The Right Requirement, Ltd. 50 Crane Way, Cranfield, Bedfordshire, MK43 OHH, England. ISBN:1-4196-7315-7

[2] Ibid. p. 9-1

[3] Ibid. pp. 9-17

[4] Cabre, M. Teresa, 1999. *Terminology: Theory, methods and applications*, John Benjamins North America Philadelphia, PA, USA

[5] Ibid. p 37

[6] BBC Channel 4, *The IT Crowd* , http://www.channel4.com/programmes/the-it-crowd/ ,(retrieved July 2012)

[7] ISO/IEC 24765, *http://pascal.*computer.org/sev_display/24765-2010.pdf, (retrieved July 2012)

[8] ISO/IEC 24765 (SEvocab), *h*ttp://www.computer.org/*sevoc*ab

[9] Django, www.djangoproject.com

[10] SQLite, http://www.sqlite.org/

# Appendix A

## Terms with 5 or more Concept Descriptions

| | | | | | | |
|---|---|---|---|---|---|---|
| 1 | CONSTRAINT | 14 | 40 | BUFFER | 6 | |
| 2 | PROCESS | 13 | 41 | OPERATOR | 6 | |
| 3 | ENTITY | 10 | 42 | COMPONENT | 6 | |
| 4 | MEASURE | 10 | 43 | DOCUMENTATION | 6 | |
| 5 | FUNCTION | 10 | 44 | FRAMEWORK | 6 | |
| 6 | BASELINE | 9 | 45 | RELATIONSHIP | 6 | |
| 7 | IMPLEMENTATION | 9 | 46 | OBJECT | 6 | |
| 8 | INPUT | 9 | 47 | LINK | 6 | |
| 9 | ACTIVITY | 9 | 48 | CUSTOMER | 6 | |
| 10 | SYSTEM | 9 | 49 | VIEW | 6 | |
| 11 | INTERFACE | 9 | 50 | VALUE | 6 | |
| 12 | RISK | 8 | 51 | BRANCH | 6 | |
| 13 | SEGMENT | 8 | 52 | VALIDATION | 6 | |
| 14 | NODE | 8 | 53 | PROGRAM | 5 | |
| 15 | ATTRIBUTE | 8 | 54 | ASSET | 5 | |
| 16 | MODEL | 8 | 55 | METHODOLOGY | 5 | |
| 17 | PROCEDURE | 8 | 56 | SCENARIO | 5 | |
| 18 | OPERATION | 8 | 57 | TESTABILITY | 5 | |
| 19 | RISK MANAGEMENT | 7 | 58 | PATCH | 5 | |
| 20 | ARCHITECTURE | 7 | 59 | END USER | 5 | |
| 21 | STAKEHOLDER | 7 | 60 | ENVIRONMENT | 5 | |
| 22 | CONFIGURATION ITEM (CI) | 7 | 61 | QUALITY ASSURANCE (QA) | 5 | |
| 23 | REQUIREMENT | 7 | 62 | BUYER | 5 | |
| 24 | VERIFICATION | 7 | 63 | METAMODEL | 5 | |
| 25 | DOCUMENT | 7 | 64 | STANDARD | 5 | |
| 26 | OUTPUT | 7 | 65 | CASE | 5 | |
| 27 | DESIGN | 7 | 66 | VERSION | 5 | |
| 28 | MEASUREMENT | 7 | 67 | RELEASE | 5 | |
| 29 | USER | 7 | 68 | EVENT | 5 | |
| 30 | CONTROL | 7 | 69 | MAINTAINABILITY | 5 | |
| 31 | QUALITY | 7 | 70 | SIMULATION | 5 | |
| 32 | AUDIT | 7 | 71 | DUMP | 5 | |
| 33 | PREVENTIVE MAINTENANCE | 6 | 72 | ERROR | 5 | |
| 34 | SUPPLIER | 6 | 73 | DATABASE | 5 | |
| 35 | CALL | 6 | 74 | ROLE | 5 | |
| 36 | TASK | 6 | 75 | MODULE | 5 | |
| 37 | PROJECT | 6 | 76 | STATE | 5 | |
| 38 | PRODUCT | 6 | 77 | PM | 5 | |
| 39 | REQUEST FOR PROPOSAL (RFP) | 6 | 78 | CONFIGURATION | 5 | |

# Learning by Design: Making the Case for a Teaching Strategy to Teach Information Systems Courses

Dr. Malak T. Al-Nory
Effat University
PO Box 34689 Jeddah 21478
Saudi Arabia
+966 2 636 4300 Ext 2325
malnory@effatuniversity.edu.sa

Dr. Diane A. Igoche
Effat University
PO Box 34689 Jeddah 21478
Saudi Arabia
+966 2 636 4300 Ext 2327
digoche@effatuniversity.edu.sa

## ABSTRACT
Teaching Information Systems in the undergraduate level requires certain skills to integrate theory with practice. One of the most effective teaching pedagogies is "Learning by Design" in which learners are fully engaged in the construction and the execution of the course activities. In the experience presented in this paper, "Learning by Design" helped students of Information Systems to understand very complex Decision Support Systems concepts. Students studied the typical academic advising process and developed a decision support tool for effective academic advising to support institutional planning and optimized resource allocation. Analysis of students' performance and assessment evidence shows students understanding of course concepts. The successful transfer of knowledge from the theory base of the course to the completion of the final course project will make a case for the use of Learning by Design as a teaching tool in an Information Systems course.

## Categories and Subject Descriptors
H.0 [**Information Systems-General**]: *Effective Teaching Strategies for Information Systems Courses*. K.3.0 [**Computers and Education**]: *Information Systems Education*.

## General Terms
Human Factors.

## Keywords
Learning by Design, Constructionism, Information Systems, Complex Concepts.

## 1. INTRODUCTION
The 21st century classroom has evolved from the instructor centered classroom with the restriction of four walls and the teacher solely relaying information to the learners. The traditional classroom is becoming a notion of the past. The learner is encouraged to take an active role in the learning process. Learners are engaged in their learning and assume responsibility for the building of knowledge. The introduction of this teaching and learning style does not change the fact that complex concepts are

Permission to make digital or hard copies of all or part of this work for personal or classroom use is granted without fee provided that copies are not made or distributed for profit or commercial advantage and that copies bear this notice and the full citation on the first page. To copy otherwise, or republish, to post on servers or to redistribute to lists, requires prior specific permission and/or a fee.
*SIGITE'12,* October 11–13, 2012, Calgary, Alberta, Canada.
Copyright 2012 ACM 978-1-4503-1464-0/12/10...$15.00.

being relayed to the students for comprehension. The instructor or facilitator must guide the students in understanding these complex concepts in order to truly build knowledge that is applicable to real world problem solving.

There are many teaching strategies and educational methods that can be employed to aid the instructor in guiding students on the path of building meaningful knowledge. This paper posits the use of a teaching strategy that encourages the learner to understand complex concepts via the design and creation of solutions to real world Information Systems/Information Technology problems. The paper explores Seymour Papert's Constructionism Theory; a theory that was conceived from Piaget Constructivist Theory [1], and finally suggests a learner-centered teaching method applicable to teaching the complex concepts in an information systems course. The theory of Constructionism suggests that learners will understand complex concepts by engaging in the design of an artifact, which will aid in the comprehension of the complex concept. Learning by Design was birth from Constructionism, and it has been tested in both pre and post secondary education [2][3]. The authors will make a case for the use of Learning by Design as a teaching strategy for information systems courses.

### 1.1 An Overview of Constructionism Learning Theory
The instruction of information systems courses at the baccalaureate level involves teaching complex topics to students with little to no industry experience. The successful learning outcomes of these novice learners are seen through the application of these complex concepts to real world problems. Parker, LaRouge and Trimmer [4], Magnani and Montesi [5], call for the competent information systems professional that will bridge the gap between theory and practice in the field. The preparation of these graduates will be done by assisting learners in using the complex concepts learned to solve real world problems [6]. Learning theories that position the learner to engage in real world problem solving, would be most favorable for the IS students learning experience.

Papert [7] posits the idea that knowledge is constructed in the mind of the learner; these building blocks of knowledge are successfully created when learners are engaged in the construction of artifacts related to the complex concept taught in a course. The application of Constructionism in an IS course is encouraged because it is one of the learning theories that sees an important role in affect [7]. The Constructivist Learning Theory supports Constructionism [8]; the former suggests that knowledge is built by the learner and the latter further emphasizes the specific construction of external artifacts that are shared by learners.

Although learners can construct and present knowledge or meanings without producing artifacts, the processes of construction are more evident when learners produce through reflection and interaction with other learners [9].

## 1.2 Learning by Design: Constructionism in the Information Systems Course

Constructionism encourages building knowledge blocks by creating external artifacts. The concept of Learning by Design is an extension of the Constructionism Theory. Learning by Design highlights the value of learning through creating or participating in the design of an external artifact. The introduction of a teaching strategy that emphasizes the learning process and the outcome encourages learners to construct knowledge that is meaningful. Incorporating Learning by Design in a course will encourage learners to efficiently grasp complex concepts from the design experience. The learners will be engaged in the learning process as they sojourn through designing and solving a real world problem applicable to the complex concepts. The Learning by Design process will encourage question posing as learners reflect on the design of the artifact.

A course that mirrors the Learning by Design process should engage the following components:

- Authenticity: tasks that are assigned to students should be based on real world problems and applications.

- Multiple contexts for design activities: Design activities should be as unstructured and similar to real world experiences.

- A balance of constrained, scaffolded challenges with open-ended design tasks

- Rich, varied feedback for designers: Learners should receive effective and frequent feedback from facilitators as this will motivate students.

- Discussion and collaboration: Learners should be allowed to collaborate with other learners. This creates a richer environment for learning.

- Reflection: Learners should reflect on feedback, the design process and their final product. These reflections can be captured in journals or presentations. The reflection process helps with the transfer of knowledge and the creation of knowledge.

## 2. RESEARCH

The participants in the experience were the students in a university level course called "Decision Support Systems" offered by the Information Systems Department and taught by the first author during the spring semester of 2011. The students were given the chance to work in groups. The students formed three groups among themselves. The course specific objectives aimed to give the students adequate knowledge to (a) explain what a Decision Support System (DSS) is, how it is used, who are the personnel involved in creating and using such systems, and their organizational and societal implications, (b) describe the process of building a DSS, and explain the factors that contribute to their success, (c) describe the types of DSS, including their components, applications, strengths and weaknesses; and (d) to design and implement simple DSS of various types.

## 2.1 Case Design

The case was designed using the "backward design" process. In such design process, the instructional designer should "identify desired results", "determine acceptable evidence", and "plan learning experiences and instruction" as consecutive but iterative design stages. Figure 1 below shows the three stages of Backward Design. The process starts with determining what is worthy to be learned by identifying the goals of the curriculum and the essential questions. In the second stage, the designer gathers assessment evidence to evaluate student understanding compared to the identified desired results in the first stage. In the third stage, the designer identifies learning activities and resources to facilitate the student learning experience [10].

**Figure 1. Backward Design stages.**

Designing technology curriculum such as Information Systems curriculum following the "backward design" process is very advantageous for many reasons; we list two of these in the following.

1. In the traditional design, the assessments are created after the delivery of the lessons to evaluate the student learning, making assessment an activity after the fact in which the students are tested to report achievement levels; while in the backward design, assessment is a way of enduring learning specifically with complex concepts such as concepts taught in a Decision Support Systems course.
2. Technology courses usually involve practical and theoretical concepts that need to be taught for students to attain the course objectives. The balance between the amount of theory versus practical activities and tutorials is very important. However, faculty members usually plan the activities ahead of time (typically before the semester starts) leaving very little flexibility to tailor the activities to students' needs at the time the course is delivered.

Using the "backward design" framework and the course objectives above as the goals for Stage 1, the course instructor designed the following "assessment evidence" as Stage 2 of the "backward design".

*Assessment Evidence 1 (Phase 1)*
Students work in groups to research how DSS technologies are used in academic advising. This assessment aimed to set a theoretical background about the decision-making process, Decision Support Systems and models. The specification of the domain as academic advising aimed to synthesize a focus point in the research. At the end of this phase students were asked to present their research to the other groups during class meetings.

*Assessment Evidence 2 (Phase 2)*
Students interviewed academic personnel in the university to research the academic advising process and decision points in the process, and the models used. This assessment aimed to familiarize the students with a real-world decision making process and the use of Decision Support Systems and models in practice. Again students had to share their work with the other groups during class meetings.

*Assessment Evidence 3 (Phase 3)*
This assessment is the most important and motivating for the use of cognitive skills. Students had to implement a simple decision support model, tool, or system to support academic advising in their university. At the end of this phase each group of students had to prepare a report on the tool they created and peer-evaluate each other final projects to assess the level of success in solving the problem using forms provided by the instructor.

The third stage of Backward Design framework entails designing the learning activities. Students were introduced to Visual Basic Application (VBA) programming language as a possible tool to implement DSS [11] but the instructor did not require the use of the tool in the project. Two of the groups decided to use the tool and familiarized themselves using supplemental resources. The third group decided to solve the problem without programming with VBA. The group decided to conduct additional research and interviews to improve the currently used models.

## 2.2 Application of the Constructionist Learning Theory in an IS Course
The following points describe how the Constructionist Learning Theory was applied to the delivery of the course described in the case.

1. Presentation of rubrics which define expectations: In this Decision Support Systems project, expectations were defined with the students. Students received rubrics that acted as guides for embarking on the design of their projects.
2. Dialogue on interpretation of the assignment: Learners were allowed a session with the Instructor to relay questions about the assigned project. The students also had the opportunity to post questions related to the project on the course management system used at Effat University.
3. Learner Collaboration and Exploration of multiple strategies for tackling the assignment: Learners formed teams, as this aided the brainstorming process.
4. Presentation of work: Due to the academic calendar, students were given a deadline to complete the design of their projects. The students were asked to present their artifacts to the instructor and fellow students for discussion, review and assessment.
5. Learners working with professionals in the outside world: Students were not given this opportunity but it is encouraged in the students' capstone project, that they involve the knowledge of an outside party as a technical advisor. In the experience of the researchers, this has created an environment for real world problem solving.

## 2.3 Research Methodology
The basic hypotheses for the design of the above described intervention are:

1. We can improve the student learning experience of complex Information Systems concepts using Learning by Design.
2. Students can be motivated by Learning by Design supported curriculum, to develop the assigned learning activities.

The current research constitutes basically of a simple case study. The research approach is based on the Learning by Design framework supported by instructional design using the backward design model. The research data collected include the analysis of students' performance and assessment evidence.

## 3. RESEARCH FINDINGS
### 3.1 Students Designs
In Learning by Design, the learning outcomes are assessed by the final product design. The following is a summary of the final designs submitted by students. We list parts of the student work for space limitations.

*Assessment Evidence 1 Outcome*
Students concluded that "with the advancements in technology and the inclusion of it in assisting most of the academic institution processes, the academic advisors and the students are exposed to a variety of opportunities, enhancements, problems, and choices. Almost all universities and academic institutions around the world use some type of automated advising systems. Typically such systems utilize Student Information Systems or a Data Warehouse to provide information to faculty members and advisors seamlessly, without using cumbersome interfaces associated with the campus transaction processing systems or enterprise resource planning systems. These systems however lack major important features to facilitate effective academic advising. A second category of academic advising systems mostly developed internally by universities to provide true decision support for students and advisors by processing specific student information and producing customized advice for that particular student. Some commercial products allow students to run "What if" scenario planning and get a real-time advising support. The system provides advisors and students with customized advising reports on their progress in their current major or a different major, and experiment with future courses and grades to see how this would affect their progress towards the degree."

*Assessment Evidence 2 Outcome*
Below is a summary of the student findings in this phase.

"The academic department in their university has to make significant decisions to prepare the semester plan for students and to offer courses accordingly for the following semester. The decision making process for the given problem has the following three phases:
1. A four year plan for each academic department is pre-outlined, which has the courses required to be taken and credits to be completed as graduation requirements. As a result, courses for pre-registration of the next semester are proposed. Pre-registration is not effective without the approval of the student's advisor.

2. During registration at the beginning of semester, the proposed plan for semester is checked. If student has passed courses and prerequisites, the courses are added to the suggested courses to be opened that semester. If the student has incomplete course(s), her pre-plan has to be revised.

3. The courses are opened based on the number of students for a course or the course being required for expected graduating student(s)."

*Assessment Evidence 3 Outcome:*
While the outcome in assessment evidence 1 and 2 of the three groups was similar to large degree, the outcome from assessment evidence 3 was notably differentiable. The first group of students designed a spread-sheet based tool built using VBA scripts to aid the advisors in preparing pre-registration plans for students and the department in projecting the demand on each course and making decision on which courses should be offered each semester such that the resources are optimally allocated. The papers provided by the students were very detailed explaining the proposed tool. The following is a summary of the description of the first group proposed tool.

"The tool aims to semi-automate the decision-making process and solves decision problems for the academic department. It would enable to enter student information efficiently and easily. The tool gives summarized information to aid in offering courses every semester. It allows making calculations for decision-making, for example calculating the GPA, credits completed, remaining courses, number of pre-registered students for each course, etc. Designing an Excel-based DSS and combining it with VBA is the appropriate solution because Excel provides a great variety of functions for decision-making in a much easy-to-use way, for example, Excel charts can be inserted to display results. Information is currently saved mostly in Excel files, thus the proposed tool does not require much change or transfer of data"

The students developed the tool and attached screen prints of their work to their paper.

The second group of students implemented a spread-sheet based tool and a simulation model to be integrated with the student information system database. The tool is accompanied by an advising manual to educate the users and complement the tool functions. The group partially implemented and integrated the tool. The third group implemented a web-based application to solve the problem in similar fashion to the first group.

## 3.2 Analysis of Course Learning Outcomes

The analysis we conduct in this section looks at the set of intended learning outcomes achieved by each group. We use the scores that students achieved in the final project components as an indicator to assess the learning outcomes. The set of learning outcomes directly contribute to the course objectives indicated in Stage 1. The learning outcomes in the list below were discussed, finalized, and accepted by the students in the form of the final project rubric.

(a) Students learn to analyze a decision-making process and identify a problem (cognitive domain of learning);
(b) Students propose an appropriate solution for the problem (cognitive domain of learning);
(c) Students provide a detailed plan on the solution and implementation (cognitive domain of learning);

(d) Students learn about DSS types, technologies, models implemented (knowledge domain of learning);
(e) Student communicate their findings about DSS in a professional manner (communication and interpersonal domains of learning);

Table 1 below maps the assessment evidence described in the previous section to the learning outcomes above. The purpose of creating such mapping is to ensure that assessment evidence actually cover all learning outcomes as indicated in the table. Table 2 shows the scores achieved by the different students groups in the final project components.

**Table 1. Mapping Assessment Evidence to Learning Outcomes**

| Learning Outcomes/ Assessment Evidence | (a) | (b) | (c) | (d) | (e) |
|---|---|---|---|---|---|
| Assessment Evidence 1 *Research how DSS technologies are used in academic advising* | | | | √ | √ |
| Assessment Evidence 2 *Interview academic personnel in the university* | √ | | | √ | √ |
| Assessment Evidence 3 *Implement a simple decision support model* | | √ | √ | | √ |

**Table 2. Groups Achievement of Learning Outcomes**

| Learning Outcomes/ Assessment Evidence | (a) | (b) | (c) | (d) | (e) | Total |
|---|---|---|---|---|---|---|
| | 22.5 | 25 | 22.5 | 20 | 10 | 100 |
| Group 1 | 20 | 25 | 22.5 | 17 | 10 | 94.5 |
| Group 2 | 22.5 | 25 | 15 | 20 | 10 | 92.5 |
| Group 3 | 19 | 20 | 22.5 | 18 | 10 | 89.5 |
| Average | 20.5 (91.1%) | 23.3 (93.2%) | 20 (88.9%) | 18.3 (92.5%) | 10 (100%) | - |

The University and the Information Systems Department requires a minimum of 75% of learning outcome to be achieved in the average class. The scores in the table above indicate that the students have achieved high percentages of learning outcomes. Even in comparison to students average scores in other courses the results achieved in this intervention are considered impressive. Since the assessment design, implementation, and scoring are all done by the instructor, it is possible that the evaluation of the learning outcomes is not significantly precise, however, the comparison of the level of achievement occurred in this course (overall of 93%) was higher than the levels achieved in other courses taught by the same instructor.

## 4. CONCLUSION

The Information Systems field requires graduates that have a theoretical and technical grasp of concepts from database design, system analysis and administration, to decision support system design and support. It is important that educators take advantage of instructional strategies that encourage students to construct meaningful knowledge from the course material while being able to transfer this knowledge to the design of end products that solve real world problems.

The authors of this paper will continue to use Learning by Design as a teaching strategy for the information systems courses at their University. The authors hope to add to the literature on teaching strategies in the Information Systems field and encourage other educators to consider this teaching tool as an effective means of preparing competent graduates.

# 5. REFERENCES

[1] Orey, M. 2001. Emerging perspectives on learning, teaching, and technology. Retrieved May 11th, 2012 from http://projects.coe.uga.edu/epltt.

[2] Bhattacharya, K. and Han, S. 2001. Piaget and cognitive development. In M. Orey (Ed.), Emerging perspectives on learning, teaching, and technology. Retrieved May 11th, 2012, from http://projects.coe.uga.edu/epltt.

[3] Parker, K.R., LeRouge, C., and Trimmer, K. 2005. Alternative instructional strategies in an IS curriculum. Journal of Information Technology Education, 4, 43-60. Link

[4] Crawford, M. 2001. Contextual teaching and learning: Strategies for creating constructivist classrooms. Connections 11 (6), 1-2, 6. Retrieved May 11th, 2012, fromhttp://www.cord.org/pdf/LayoutforWeb.pdf.

[5] Magnani, M., and Montesi, D. 2006. A unified approach to structured and XML data modeling and manipulation. Data Knowledge Engineering. 59(1): 25-62.

[6] Martin, A. 2004. Addressing the Gap between Theory and Practice: IT Project Design, Journal of Information Technology Theory and Application. 6 (2) 5. Retrieved May 11th2012 from http://aisel.aisnet.org/jitta/vol6/iss2/5

[7] Papert, S. 1980. Mindstorms: Children, Computers, and Powerful Ideas. New York: Basic Books.

[8] Piaget, J.1953. The origin of intelligence in the child. New Fetter Lane, New York: Routledge & Kegan Paul.

[9] Wiggins, G and McTighe, J. 2005 Understanding by Design. Expanded 2nd Edition. (Upper Saddle River, NJ/Alexandria, VA: Pearson Education/Association for Supervision & Curriculum Development.

[10] M. Seref, R. Ahuja, and W. Winston. 2007. Developing Spreadsheet-based Decision Support Systems, Dynamic Ideas.

[11] Fessakis G., Dimitracopoulou A., and Tatsis K. 2008. Supporting "Learning by Design" Activities Using Group Blogs, Journal of Educational Technology and Society. 11(4). Pp.199-212.

# Developing and Improving Interdisciplinary Health Information Technology Certificate Programs

Chi Zhang, Han Reichgelt, Becky Rutherfoord, Bob Brown and Andy Ju An Wang
Department of Information Technology
Southern Polytechnic State University
Marietta GA 30060
+1 (678) 915-7399
{chizhang, hreichge, brutherf, bbrown, jwang} @spsu.edu

## ABSTRACT

Health Information technology (HIT) professionals are in increasing demand as healthcare providers need help in the adoption and meaningful use of electronic health record (EHR) systems while the HIT industry needs workforce skilled in HIT and EHR development. To respond to this increasing demand, the School of Computing and Software Engineering at Southern Polytechnic State University designed and implemented a series of HIT educational programs. An overview of HIT workforce development initiatives and major HIT and health information management (HIM) educational resources are provided. The paper summarizes our experience in the HIT curriculum development and student feedback. Future improvement for the programs is also discussed.

## Categories and Subject Descriptors

K.3.2. [Computers and Education]: Computer and Information Science Education *Curriculum*

## General Terms

Design

## Keywords

Health Information Technology (HIT), Health Information Management (HIM), Curriculum Development, Curriculum Design, Curriculum Assessment, Program Accreditation

## 1. INTRODUCTION

Health Information technology (HIT) professionals are in increasing demand as healthcare providers need help in the adoption and meaningful use of electronic health record (EHR) systems while the HIT industry needs workforce skilled in HIT and EHR development. According to Bureau of Labor Statistics, the demand for personnel in medical records and health information technology for the 10-year timeframe between 2010 and 2020 will increase by 21%. The average growth rate for all occupations is 14 percent [3]. Additionally, Atlanta is often referred to as the healthcare IT capital of the U.S. with more than 200 HIT companies in the state of Georgia, the majority in Atlanta [10].

In light of this, the School of Computing and Software Engineering at Southern Polytechnic State University started an effort in health information technology in 2010 to (1) design and implement a series of educational programs, including professional development courses, certificate programs, and degree courses; (2) conduct research into the issues that healthcare providers and hospitals face in selecting, implementing, and integrating HIT systems; and (3) conduct research and develop tools to strengthen the privacy and security of health information, and help people understand their rights and the resources available to safeguard their persona health data.

Currently, we have a concentration in HIT in our program of Bachelor of Science in Information Technology (BSIT) and a graduate certificate program in Health Information Technology, which can be taken either as a stand-alone certificate or as part of our Master of Science in IT. Additionally, in partnership with Consort Institute and Southern Polytechnic State University Continuing Education Center, an Accelerated Training in Health Information Technology (ATHIT) program is being offered for individuals seeking a new career in HIT field. In this paper, we will share our experience in the program curriculum and course development, course evaluation, student feedback, and future improvement for the programs.

## 2. CURRICULUM DEVELOPMENT

One of the key elements essential for "meaningful use" of HIT as legislated in the American Recovery and Reinvestment Act (ARRA) on February 17, 2009 and Title XIII of ARRA – Health Information Technology for Economic and Clinical Health (HITECH) Act was a new workforce of HIT professionals who will be able to help healthcare providers implement electronic health record systems to improve healthcare quality, safety, and cost-effectiveness. Of the $118 millions allocated for the Office of National Coordinator for Health Information Technology (ONC) for workforce development, as of 2011 a total of $116 millions has been awarded to the HIT workforce development programs [11].

The goal of ONC HIT workforce development is to provide specialized HIT training to new health IT professionals in the 12 ONC workforce roles. The community college consortia programs focus on training students for the six professional roles: practice workflow and information management redesign specialists, clinician/practitioner consultants, implementation support specialists, implementation managers, technical/software support, and trainers. The program of assistance for university-based training focuses on establishing or expanding the university level health IT training programs for health IT professional roles: Clinician or public health leaders, Health information management and exchange specialists, Health information privacy and security specialists, Research and development scientists, Programmers and software engineers, and Health IT sub-specialists.

Taking the ONC workforce roles, our student population and existing courses into consideration, as well as in collaboration with health IT experts and professionals, we identified and developed five courses for students with an IT background to focus on training for the eight health IT workforce roles as shown in Table 1. Our current five required HIT courses can be completed in two semesters:

(1) Foundations of Health Information Technology
(2) Clinical Workflow Process: Analysis & Redesign
(3) EHR Systems & Applications
(4) Health Information Security & Privacy
(5) System Acquisition & Integration

**Table 1. Roles Prepared and HIT Courses**

| Workforce Roles | Courses |
|---|---|
| Practice workflow and information management redesign specialists | (1), (2), (3) |
| Clinician/practitioner consultants | (1), (2), (3), (4), (5) |
| Implementation support specialists | (1), (2), (3), (4), (5) |
| Implementation managers | (1), (2), (3), (5) |
| Technical/software support | (1), (2), (3) |
| Trainers | (1), (2), (3), (5) |
| Health Information Privacy and Security Specialist | (1), (2), (3), (4) |
| Programmers and Software Engineer | (1), (2), (3), (4) |

We are to offer the training for " Health Information Privacy and Security Specialist" and "Programmers and Software Engineers" roles with a relatively short-term training because (1) we are a computing school that has extensive programming and software engineering courses; (2) we already offer an array of information security and privacy related courses for our information assurance and security concentration; and (3) we conduct information assurance research, and health information privacy and identity management in particular, from our CAE/IAE (Center for Academic Excellence in Information Assurance Education).

When developing our HIT programs, we not only considered the policies, regulations, grant opportunities, along with input from local HIT industry experts, our own expertise and student population, but also major HIT organizations and their programs, HIT professional certifications and program accreditation standards as well.

As a product of the workforce development programs, ONC develops and provides HIT workforce development curriculum components [12] online at http://www.onc-ntdc.org/. Our courses have covered 15 out of 20 ONC curriculum components as shown in Table 2.

**Table 2. Mapping ONC Curriculum Requirements**

| ONC Curriculum Components | Covered in Course(s) |
|---|---|
| - Introduction to Healthcare and Public Health in the US<br>- The Culture of Healthcare<br>- History of Health Information Technology in the U.S Health Management Information Systems<br>- Public Health IT<br>- Professionalism/Customer Service in the Health Environment | (1) |
| - Fundamentals of Health Workflow Process Analysis & Redesign<br>- Quality Improvement<br>- Special Topics on Vendor-Specific Systems | (2) |
| - Working with Health IT Systems<br>- Configuring Electronic Health Records | (1), (3) |
| - Planning, Management and Leadership for Health IT<br>- Introduction to Project Management<br>- Working in Teams | (5) and existing courses |
| - Introduction to Information and Computer Science | existing course |
| - Terminology in Health Care and Public Health Settings<br>- Installation and Maintenance of Health IT Systems<br>- Networking and Health Information Exchange<br>- Usability and Human Factors<br>- Training and Instructional Design | future courses |

Two major health information management and health IT organizations are AHIMA and HIMSS. AHIMA (American Health Information Management Association), as the health information management professional association, plays an important role in educating medical records professionals. AHIMA provides educational resources and programs, guiding and developing curriculum, and administers certifications such as Registered Health Information Technician (RHIT), Registered Health Information Administrator (RHIA), Certified in Healthcare Privacy and Security (CHPS), among others [1]. CAHIIM (Commission on Accreditation for Health Informatics and Information Management Education) sponsored by AHIMA accredits associate and baccalaureate degree programs in health information management, and masters' degree programs in the health informatics and health information management professions [4]. Individuals seeking entry-level professional credentials: RHIT or RHIA must graduate from a CAHIIM-accredited program [5].

HIMSS (Healthcare Information and Management Systems Society) promotes optimal use of information technology and management systems for better healthcare. HIMSS provides professional development opportunities for healthcare information and management systems professionals. CPHIMS is a well-respected professional certification program administered by HIMSS. Information required by the CPHIMS is divided into 3 areas: General, Systems, and Administration, which is further divided into General (Healthcare & Technology Environments), Systems (Analysis; Design; Selection, Implementation, Support, & Maintenance; Testing & Evaluation; Privacy & Security), and Administration (Leadership & Management) [6]`.

As AHIMA and HIMSS are the leading organizations for identifying HIT and HIM professionals' credentials and competencies, we examined both CPHIMS and AHIMA curriculum competencies and knowledge clusters [2] and mapped them with our course components, as shown in Table 3 and 4. The AHIMA curriculum competencies and knowledge cluster are identified based on revised Bloom's Taxonomy – remembering, understanding, applying, analyzing, evaluating, and creating [9]. AHIMA has specified that the content will be introduced and reinforced in the curriculum and may occur in more than one course in the program.

**Table 3. Mapping AHIMA Curriculum Requirements**

| HIM Competencies (student learning outcomes) | Knowledge Clusters | Covered in course(s) |
|---|---|---|
| Health Data Management | Health data structure, content, and acquisition; Healthcare information requirements and standards; Clinical classification systems; reimbursement methodologies | (1), (2), (3) |
| Health Statistics, Biomedical research, and quality management | Healthcare statistics and research; quality management and performance improvement | (1), (2) |
| Health services organization and delivery | Healthcare delivery systems; Healthcare Privacy, Confidentiality, Legal, and Ethical Issues | (1), (4) |
| Information technology and systems | Information and communication technologies; information systems; data security | (1), (4) |
| Organization and management | Human resource management; strategic planning and organizational development | (5) |

**Table 4. Mapping CPHIMS Curriculum Requirements**

| CPHIMS Competencies | Knowledge Clusters | Covered in course(s) |
|---|---|---|
| General | Healthcare & Technology Environments | (1), (2), (3) |
| Systems | Analysis; Design; Selection, Implementation, Support, & Maintenance; Testing & Evaluation; Privacy & Security | (2), (3), (4), (5) |
| Administration | Leadership & Management | (1), (5) |

## 3. COURSE DESIGN

The individual courses are designed with reference to the ONC HIT workforce curriculum development program together with pedagogical models for effective teaching and learning experience.

For example, Fink's Integrated Course Design model was used to refine the course Clinical Workflow Process: Analysis and Redesign. Integrated Course Design methodology [8] is used for improving the design and delivery of the course in order to enhance student learning. The methodology was centered on Fink's taxonomy of significant learning, namely foundational knowledge, application, integration, human dimension, caring, and learning how to learn, as shown in Figure 1. It is believed that significant learning is achieved

through in-depth situational analysis, effective teaching and learning activities correlated to the course objectives and appropriate feedback and assessment procedures. The course was designed to engage students, enhance student learning and prepare them to meet the needs of healthcare organizations and HIT development.

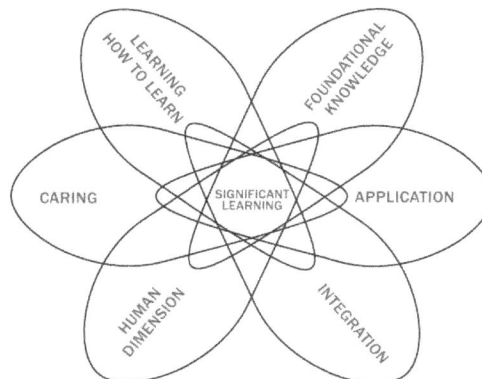

**Figure 1. Fink's Taxonomy in Course Design [7]**

The use of Fink's Integrated Course Design model with the objectives of Clinical Process and Workflow course led to teaching, learning, and assessment activities designed using problem-based learning strategy. The foundational material was taught using lectures, case scenario videos and assigned reading and was assessed using multiple-choice quizzes and short answer questions. Students applied the foundational material in case studies that were evaluated through rubrics to ensure that students' work met expectations for each assignment. The material was integrated as the student used additional knowledge and tools in increasingly complex assignments through the semester. The human dimension was addressed in discussion topics that required the student to develop and support positions based on course material and literature reviews. Caring about the course material was encouraged through guest speakers including medical and health IT professionals and through a required clinic visit. The learning how to learn skills were developed through the use of a variety of sources of information and the application of the skills in case studies. Table 5 illustrates the course design using Fink's model. The case studies and clinic visit project were well received by the students; as one student commented "the real world assignments were effective. I enjoyed applying the concepts to real world projects."

**Table 5. Using Fink's ICD Model for HIT Course Design**

| Fink's Taxonomy | Teaching and Learning Activities | Assessment |
|---|---|---|
| Foundational Material | Lectures and assigned reading | Multiple-choice and short answer quizzes |
| Application | Case Studies | Assignment rubrics |
| Integration | Increasingly complex case studies requiring use of tools discussed in lectures | Assignment rubrics |
| Human Dimension | Discussion topics that required positions supported by research | Discussion rubrics |
| Caring | Guest lectures by Medical and IT professionals; Case study requiring clinic visit | Student report and clinic surveys |

| Learning to Learn | Discussions and case studies requiring use of a variety of sources of information and the application of the skills | Report and research paper rubrics |
|---|---|---|

In addition to learning material delivery, hands-on exercises with electronic health record (EHR) systems are integrated into the courses. The dean and the department chair helped secure a range of EHR systems such as CPSI, NeuMD, and eClinicalWorks, as well open source software such as VistA CPRS by Department of Veteran Affairs, openEMR, and AHIMA Virtual Lab to support students in these various HIT programs. These commercial and open source systems provide students the opportunities with the hospital and ambulatory EHR and practice management systems.

# 4. PROGRAM AND COURSE ASSESSMENT

To meet ABET requirement for our accredited BSIT program, we include the HIT courses in the curriculum assessment. Instructor reflection and student feedback are collected at the end of each semester when the courses are offered, and curriculum assessment is conducted regularly. Most of the HIT courses have been developed with distance learning as well as classroom delivery in mind, which will make entirely online HIT programs available in the near future.

To enhance effective teaching and student learning, we consider the following aspects when delivering our HIT courses. First, we tie course material to real-world issues by introducing students to current information in the fields from major HIT online portals, academic publications, and professional organizations. We also integrate real-world issues and research into course material. Secondly, we keep current with the teaching content, engage the classroom with a variety of media, provide prompt and constructive feedback, and encourage active learning. Thirdly, we invite guest speakers to classes for students to have opportunities to meet with healthcare professionals and HIT industry experts and establish connections with local HIT companies. Students are also provided with information of professional training webinars, certification training and HIT job fair information. Lastly, we involve students in HIT research. Two graduate students published their class research papers in regional academic conferences in 2012.

Students reported that they had learned a lot from the HIT courses and satisfied with their learning experience. The student with a published paper in the discipline wrote "I feel very lucky to have you support my paper in such a way that no one else before has. The final revision you gave me is stellar and needs no additional tweaking in my opinion. I can say that I am very happy with it." Another student expressed his gratitude for the guest presentation: "Thank you for organizing this event! The guest speaker delivered a great presentation. It was both informative and inspirational, and included extremely valuable career advice - that can be applied to any student, not just Health IT. In fact, the audience consisted of many Computer Science students and even faculty. I truly believe that such guest speakers are very important component in preparing students to real world of IT."

# 5. FUTURE IMPROVEMENT

## 5.1 Expansion of HIT Programs

Our various HIT programs are designed to provide students studying IT and IT professionals with sufficient knowledge of the healthcare industry, the peculiarities of HIT and EHRs to enable them to assist providers and hospitals in the selection and implementation of EHRs and other HIT systems. The future goals of this effort also include (1) providing CIOs of hospitals who have a thorough understanding of the healthcare sector but who may lack a formal background or in-depth training in a specific area of HIT, with the knowledge and skills to manage the HIT in their organizations more effectively; (2) providing healthcare providers with technical competency to implement EHRs with certified EHR technology and tools for building health information exchange capacity; (3) combining business intelligence and data mining with healthcare data to provide high-level decision support in medical information management; and (4) providing certification and compliance testing services both to organizations that build and market HIT systems, and to healthcare providers and hospitals who have implemented HIT systems, including EHRs and Health Information Exchange (HIE) systems.

To prepare individuals qualified to serve in specific health IT professional roles requiring university-level training in addition to the skilled professionals for a career in HIT requiring short-term training, we will be considering how to expand the curriculum in our current certificate programs with more courses and knowledge clusters, such as Terminology in Health Care and Public Health Settings, Mobile Health Development, Quality Improvement, Health Information Exchange, and Practicum in Health Information Technology, to name a few. We are also considering collaborating with other academic programs at our school to integrate different course modules into new courses targeting different groups of students.

## 5.2 Accreditation Consideration

Further curriculum effort also focuses on measurement of the course evaluation results, application to online and international students, and development of a learning portfolio for the course and certificate programs.

The Commission on Accreditation for Health Informatics and Information Management (CAHIIM) is an independent accrediting organization establishing and enforcing quality Accreditation Standards for Health Informatics and Health Information Management (HIM) educational programs.

We are revising our programs to meet CAHIIM Candidacy requirements for both our undergraduate and graduate certificate programs – the standards For Health Informatics - Master's Degree Education; and the Standards for Health Information Management (HIM) Education.

# 6. CONCLUSION

While one would normally expect IT students are able to independently develop sufficient knowledge of an application domain, the structure of the health care industry in the United States is complex, leading us to the conclusion that we needed to introduce a series of courses to prepare students for careers in Health Information Technology.

We have developed our curriculum with careful consideration to the workforce roles for university based education set out by the ONC. Course organization and content development have been guided by the work of AHIMA and HIMSS. All of this has been done within the framework of continuous assessment and improvement required by ABET, our program accrediting agency.

Our programs were introduced relatively recently, and it is therefore too early to make any definitive statements on the success of our program. However, a number of our graduates have found employment either with health care providers or with health information technology vendors, and we believe that one of the reasons for their success have been the programs that we designed to help them development a greater understanding of the health care sector and the way in which it uses IT. As the sector becomes convinced of the value of well educated HIT professionals, the need for such professionals will continue to grow, and we believe that our programs in this area help the nation address this human resource development need.

# 7. REFERENCES

[1] AHIMA (American Health Information Management Association), accessed on May 30, 2012 from http://www.ahima.org

[2] AHIMA (American Health Information Management Association) curriculum competencies and knowledge clusters for health information management (HIM) education, 2011. http://www.ahima.org/schools/FacResources/CAHIIM_2011 _BS_Curriculum_Requirements_final.pdf

[3] Bureau of Labor Statistics Occupational Outlook Handbook, 2012. Accessed on May 28, 2012 from http://www.bls.gov/ooh/healthcare/medical-records-and-health-information-technicians.htm

[4] CAHIIM (Commission on Accreditation for Health Informatics and Information Management Education), accessed on May 30, 2012 from http://www.cahiim.org

[5] CAHIIM (Commission on Accreditation for Health Informatics and Information Management Education) Accreditation Standards, 2012. Accessed on May 28, 2912 from http://www.cahiim.org/accredstnds.html

[6] CPHIMS (Certified Professional in Healthcare Information and Management Systems), accessed on May 30, 2012 from http://www.himss.org/ASP/certification_cphims.asp

[7] Fallahi, C. (2011). Using Fink's taxonomy in course design. *APS Observer,* 24(7), 39-41.

[8] Fink, D. (2003). Creating Significant Learning Experiences: An Integrated Approach to Designing College Courses. *Jossey-Bass.*

[9] Krathwohl, D. R., 2002. A Revision of Bloom's Taxonomy: An Overview. *THEORY INTO PRACTICE, Volume 41, Number 4,* Autumn 2002. Accessed on May 28, 2012 from http://www.unco.edu/cetl/sir/stating_outcome/documents/Kr athwohl.pdf

[10] Metro Atlanta Chamber report, report of Health IT, 2012. Accessed on May 28, 2012 from http://www.metroatlantachamber.com/content/IntPage.aspx? Id=328&SId=9&

[11] ONC (Office of National Coordinator for Health Information Technology) Health IT Workforce Development Program, 2011. Accessed on May 28, 2012 from http://healthit.hhs.gov/portal/server.pt?open=512&objID=14 32&mode=2

[12] ONC (Office of National Coordinator for Health Information Technology) Health IT workforce development curriculum components, accessed on May 30, 2012 from http://www.onc-ntdc.org/.

# Analysis and Extraction of Sentence-Level Paraphrase Sub-Corpus in CS Education

Faisal Alvi, El-Sayed M. El-Alfy, Wasfi G. Al-Khatib, Radwan E. Abdel-Aal
College of Computer Sciences and Engineering
King Fahd University of Petroleum and Minerals
Dhahran 31261, Saudi Arabia
{alvif, alfy, wasfi, radwan} @kfupm.edu.sa

## ABSTRACT

Since the advent of the Internet, plagiarism has become a widespread problem in student submissions. Paraphrasing is one of the several types of plagiarism employed by students to mask the original source. In this work, we construct a sub-corpus of paraphrased sentences by extracting all lightly and heavily revised sentences from the Corpus of Plagiarized Short Answers, using modified criteria for sentences. We then apply document similarity measures on this sub-corpus and derive some interesting features of this sub-corpus. Our findings suggest that this sub-corpus is more suited for testing paraphrase detection techniques by providing sentence-level paraphrasing samples instead of the file-level classification provided in the original corpus. Additional sentence samples may also be added to this sub-corpus to achieve variety and scale.

## Categories and Subject Descriptors

I.2.7 [**Natural Language Processing**]: Language Parsing and Understanding

## General Terms

Experimentation

## Keywords

plagiarism, paraphrasing, similarity measures

## 1. INTRODUCTION

Plagiarism in colleges and universities is on the rise according to a recent report [1] by the Pew Research Center. Earlier, Maurer et al. [2] have analyzed several surveys carried out at leading universities detailing quantitative estimates of students engaging in plagiarism. Students may attempt several types of plagiarism including, but not limited to, direct copy, modification and paraphrasing. Zahrani et al. [3] have proposed a classification of plagiarism types which includes, among others, paraphrasing, summarization, copy-paste and idea-based plagiarism.

According to the Merriam-Webster Dictionary [4], paraphrasing is defined as "*a restatement of a text, passage, or work giving the meaning in another form*". From the stated definition, it is clear that the restatement of a text in different words is paraphrasing, however the extent to which words must be altered in order for a text to be considered a paraphrase is not strictly defined. Therefore, in the context of plagiarism detection, we consider two texts as paraphrased versions of each other if they are semantically equivalent but may not be syntactically identical. By semantic equivalence we imply that the essential information conveyed by the two texts is the same, however they may differ in at least one or more words. An identical approach has previously been adopted in the Microsoft Research Paraphrase Corpus [5] which is a collection of 5801 sentence pairs extracted from news sources and judged as paraphrased or not by human evaluators.

Another collection of plagiarized documents is the Corpus of Plagiarized Short Answers [6]. These short answers are written by students in answer to five computer science tasks; hence it is a valuable resource for investigating paraphrasing patterns in computer science education. There are several other corpora available, e.g., the PAN PC-09 [7] corpus; however these may not be useful for evaluating academic plagiarism due to automatic content generation as well as being not related to education.

In this work, we extract paraphrased sentence pairs from the Corpus of Plagiarized Short Answers using a slightly modified scheme adapted to sentences. We call this collection a 'Sub-corpus of Paraphrased Sentences' since this collection is a subset of the original corpus. We then apply document similarity measures to this sub-corpus and derive some interesting features of this sub-corpus. This sub-corpus can be used for testing paraphrasing detection techniques in student work in computer science education. Additional samples can also be added to this sub-corpus to achieve scale and variety.

The rest of the paper is organized as follows: Section 2 describes an analysis of the file-level classification of the original corpus and the methodology of building the sentence-level sub-corpus. Section 3 describes the contents of the sub-corpus, its limitations and ways to extend it. Section 4 describes an application of document similarity measures to this sub-corpus and states some features extracted from this sub-corpus. Section 5 concludes the paper and provides directions for future work.

| Task | Original | Light Revision | Heavy Revision |
|------|----------|----------------|----------------|
| A | It is intended to help reuse existing code with little or no modification. | It was intended to allow existing code to be used again with minimal or no alteration. | The peropos of inheritance in object oriented programming is to minimize the reuse of existing code without modification. |
| B | A page that is linked to by many pages with high PageRank receives a high rank itself. | ...if a webpage is linked to others that have a high ranking, then it too will receive a high rank. | The algorithm basically works like a popularity contest - if your site is linked to by popular websites, then your site is considered more popular. |
| C | The order in which the terms appear in the document is lost in the vector space representation. | and the order that the terms appear in the document is not represented in the vector space model. | the order of words does not matter |
| D | It is often used to compute posterior probabilities given observations. | The theorem is often used when we have observations and wish to compute posterior probabilities | It is mainly used to calculate the probability of one event's outcome given that the previous event has happened |
| E | The method takes much less time than naive methods | This is a much quicker method than other more naive method | The advantage being the less time consumption in comparison to other amateur methods |

Table 1: Lightly and Heavily Revised Sentence Examples from the Corpus of Plagiarised Short Answers [6]

## 2. CORPUS ANALYSIS

The Corpus of Plagiarised Short Answers [6] is a collection of short responses of 200–300 words that have been plagiarized by students according to the predefined instructions. It consists of a total of 95 responses to five tasks in total, with each task having 19 responses. Each response is plagiarized according to a level classified as (1) Cut or Near-copy, (2) Light Revision, (3) Heavy Revision, and (4) Non-plagiarized based on the original source which is also provided. Although the size of the corpus is small, it is a very useful resource for researchers since,

- the answers are written by human respondents in contrast to automatically generated corpora,

- being at the student level, the corpus simulates actual writing styles of students (for example, inclusion of typographical errors), and

- the tasks are related to computer science in particular and technology-related areas, in general.

Each of the 95 plagiarized files in the corpus contains a response and is classified according to the four levels mentioned above. However, a file-level classification gives little insight into which parts of the file are exactly copied, revised or are completely non-plagiarized. Hence, we conducted a sentence-level comparison by comparing each sentence of every response with each sentence in the original file of the corresponding task. Each sentence was then labeled as cut/near-copy, lightly revised, heavily revised or non-plagiarized.

### 2.1 Methodology

Each task in the original corpus was assigned to an evaluator, with the evaluator himself being an instructor in computer science or computer engineering. The evaluators conducted the sentence-level evaluation by first determining sentence boundaries.

#### 2.1.1 Sentence Boundaries

The evaluators adopted the following criteria for identifying sentence boundaries in the original corpus for the purpose of sentence-level comparison:

1. A period or dot ('.') is considered as a boundary between two sentences, except in case of abbreviations (for example i.e.).

2. In case of numbered lists, each list item is considered as a sentence even though it may be a phrase or part of a larger sentence. In such cases a comma, semicolon or a colon is considered as a sentence boundary. For example the phrase '*The vector space model has the following limitations:*' was considered as a sentence, although it ends with a colon.

3. Technical texts written using English alphabet but not in English language (such as short computer programs appearing in Task A, or mathematical formulae in Task D) are treated as one sentence in their entirety, although they may span multiple lines.

#### 2.1.2 Sentence Classification

The evaluators compared each sentence in the 19 files with each sentence in the original file and classified these as one of the four types: (a) cut or near-copy, (b) lightly revised, (c) heavily revised or (d) non-plagiarised according to the following criteria:

1. **Cut or Near-Copy**: A target sentence is considered as a near-copy of a source sentence if the two sentences contain exactly the same words and in the same order. Sentences were also considered near-copy if they differed in non-significant parts of speech, for example articles (such as replacing 'a' by 'the'), and in some cases prepositions.

2. **Lightly Revised**: A target sentence is considered as a lightly revised version of a source sentence if the two

| Sentence Type | Task A (File Type) | | | | Task B (File Type) | | | | Task C (File Type) | | | | Task D (File Type) | | | | Task E (File Type) | | | |
|---|---|---|---|---|---|---|---|---|---|---|---|---|---|---|---|---|---|---|---|---|
| | C | L | H | N | C | L | H | N | C | L | H | N | C | L | H | N | C | L | H | N |
| C | 28 | 13 | 1 | 0 | 11 | 10 | 2 | 0 | 21 | 22 | 13 | 0 | 33 | 13 | 22 | 0 | 54 | 9 | 3 | 0 |
| L | 7 | 17 | 21 | 0 | 0 | 14 | 2 | 1 | 2 | 32 | 30 | 1 | 6 | 36 | 17 | 0 | 0 | 23 | 14 | 2 |
| H | 0 | 3 | 10 | 2 | 1 | 0 | 22 | 22 | 0 | 1 | 19 | 1 | 1 | 7 | 6 | 2 | 0 | 3 | 15 | 1 |
| N | 4 | 3 | 8 | 101 | 24 | 0 | 6 | 58 | 14 | 7 | 8 | 56 | 22 | 8 | 13 | 43 | 13 | 5 | 7 | 71 |

**Table 2: Sentence classification according to file types, where C=Cut/Near-Copy, L=Light, H=Heavy and N=Non-Plagiarised)**

sentences differ in a few words, however the information conveyed by the two sentences is almost the same. For example, in Table 1 (Task C), the word 'lost' is replaced by 'not represented' in the lightly revised version.

3. **Heavily Revised**: A target sentence is considered as a heavily revised version of a source sentence if the two sentences differ in a significant number of words and/or their order, however the essential information conveyed by the two sentences is the same. The idea of what constitutes as essential information of the sentence is left to the evaluator and hence this may differ from one evaluator to another.

4. **Non-plagiarised**: A target sentence is considered as a non-plagiarised sentence if it did not match all source sentences in the number and order of words. Furthermore, the information conveyed by the non-plagiarised sentence also did not match that of any sentence in the source file.

Some sentences were considered borderline by the evaluators especially between the lightly revised and the heavily revised categories. In this case a second evaluator reviewed all of these classifications and reassigned sentence categories in order to be consistent. Table 1 lists a sample of lightly and heavily revised sentences from each task. The levels of sentence classification proposed here are similar to the file level classifications of the actual corpus, however they are at the sentence level and give us a finer level of similarity as compared to a file-level classification.

## 2.2 Results

Table 2 shows the actual number of sentences categorized by file-type and sentence type for each task. It may be observed from this table, that each sentence type appears in almost all file types. For example, we find that for Task A, the number of cut or near-copy sentences in each file-type were found as follows (Table 2, Row 1):

- 28 cut sentences in 'Cut' files,
- 13 cut sentences in 'Light Revision' files,
- 1 cut sentence in 'Heavy Revision' files, and
- 0 cut sentences in 'Non-plagiarised' files.

Hence we may infer that each file-type may contain more than one type of sentence. Furthermore, we also observe that for some tasks, file-types of a particular category may not contain a majority of that sentence-type. For example, for task C, the Heavy Revision files contain a total of 19 heavily revised sentences which is much less than 50% of the total number of all sentence types.

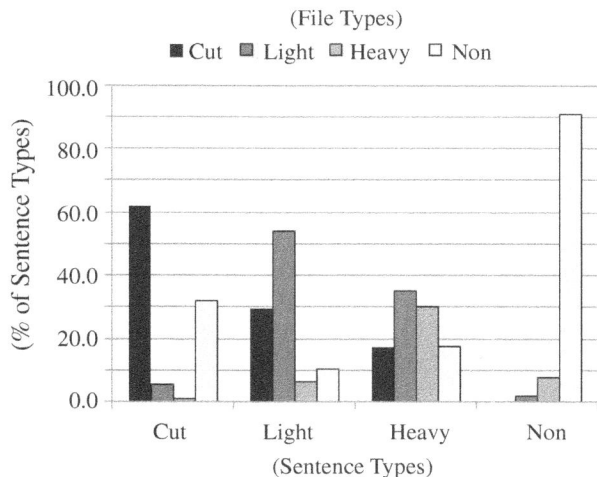

**Figure 1: Cumulative Sentence Classifications**

Figure 1 shows the percentage of sentence types in each file type for all tasks. From this figure, it can be observed that on average, for all tasks:

1. The non-plagiarised files contain the highest relative percentage of non-plagiarised sentences. Furthermore, there are very few cut, lightly revised and heavily revised sentences in this category.

2. The heavy revision files contain a mix of heavily revised and lightly revised sentences as a majority of the marked sentences. They also contain some cut and non-plagiarised sentence types.

3. The light revision files contain a significant number of cut or near-copy sentences, suggesting that the participants in the original corpus creation considered a near-copy to be a light revision.

4. The cut file category contains the highest relative percentage of cut sentences. Moreover, this category also contains some percentage of non-plagiarised sentences.

The above observations suggest that the file categories of cut, light revision, heavy revision and non-plagiarised each may not contain a majority of the corresponding sentence types. Rather, we observe that for some categories (light and heavy), there is a mix of both sentence types with significant number of other sentence types. These findings suggest that it would be worthwhile to ignore file-level markings and compare sentence pairs on their own.

# 3. SUB-CORPUS OF PARAPHRASED SENTENCES

For the purposes of paraphrase detection, we may consider only the revised sentences (i.e., lightly and heavily revised sentences only) for comparison, as these are modified versions of the original sentences. Hence, we suggest to create a 'Sub-Corpus of Paraphrased Sentences'. This sub-corpus is a subset of the Corpus of Plagiarised Short Answers [6] with each file corresponding to a sentence from the original file and the corresponding revised (i.e., lightly and heavily revised) sentences only.

## 3.1 Description

The sub-corpus consists of a total of 101 files, with each file corresponding to an original sentence from each task. The number of sentences from the original files for each task is as follows:

- Task A: 14 original sentences,
- Task B: 24 original sentences,
- Task C: 16 original sentences,
- Task D: 19 original sentences,
- Task E: 28 original sentences.

Each file contains the original sentence taken from the original file marked by an 'O:', followed by all lightly revised sentences marked as 'L1, L2, L3...:', and heavily revised sentences marked as 'H1, H2, H3...:'. Figure 2 shows a sample file from the sub-corpus.

## 3.2 Limitations

Although the sub-corpus contains carefully evaluated sentences, the evaluation is not exactly defined. There may always be some sentences which may be judged as lightly revised by some evaluators and as heavily revised by others. However, for the purpose of paraphrase detection this fine distinction may not matter, as we are interested in the collection of all revised sentences.

Another shortcoming of the corpus is the evaluation of a sentence that is the result of sentence joining. In particular, if in the original corpus, two sentences S1 and S2 are joined together to form a larger revised sentence, it may be difficult for an evaluator to determine whether S1 or S2 forms the central piece of information in the newly formed sentence. In this case an evaluator may consider the newly formed sentence to be a lightly or a heavily revised version of S1, S2 or both. Similarly, in case of sentence splitting, an evaluator may link two or more shorter, split sentences as revised versions of an original larger sentence; however the split sentences may contain partial information from the source sentence only.

## 3.3 Extension

The sub-corpus is a small and selected version of the original Corpus of Plagiarised Short Answers. Since the size of the original corpus is small [6], therefore the size of the sub-corpus is even smaller.

One way to achieve an extension in the size of the sub-corpus is to compare all sentence pairs in all files across the entire corpus. This may add to the size of the corpus by including sentence pairs that have not been intentionally plagiarised, but are similar versions of each other due to topic similarity. For example, it is possible that two non-plagiarised sentences in two different files may be somewhat

```
TaskE_SentenceJ.txt

O: Programming, in this sense, means finding an
acceptable plan of action, an algorithm.

L1: Programming means finding a plan of action.

H1: This leads to the concept of programming being
a helper in finding an acceptable plan of action,
which can also be termed as an algorithm.
```

**Figure 2: A Sample File in the Sub-corpus (a subset of the Corpus of Plagiarised Short Answers [6])**

similar to each other due to choice of words or the information contained. However, since the non-plagiarised sentences were not plagiarised in the first place, any similarity found between two non-plagiarised sentences would be purely coincidental. The resulting collection would then more appropriately be called 'Sub-corpus of Similar Sentences'.

# 4. SIMILARITY MEASURES

Clough and Stevenson [6] have given similarity measures for the original corpus based on $N$-gram overlap and longest common subsequence. Chong et Al. [8] have applied natural language processing techniques to the Corpus of Plagiarised Short Answers with the objective of distinguishing between file categories. For the proposed sub-corpus, we apply $N$-gram and longest common subsequence based similarity measures to extract some properties of the sentences.

## 4.1 N-gram Similarity

$N$-gram based similarity measures [9], [10] can be used to evaluate similarity between two documents. However $N$-gram based containment measures [11], especially for higher values of $N$ are more suited to document similarity as opposed to similarity measures for sentences. We choose a value of $N = 1$ (unigram) for sentence comparisons due to their shorter length. Furthermore, we normalize all common unigrams by the the length of the original and the revised sentences as follows:

$$c_1(O, R) = \frac{|S(O) \cap S(R)|}{|S(O)|} \quad (1)$$

$$c_2(R, O) = \frac{|S(O) \cap S(R)|}{|S(R)|} \quad (2)$$

where $O$ = original sentence, $R$ = revised sentence, and $S(O)$, $S(R)$ represent the number of unigrams in original and revised sentences, respectively.

We then evaluate the measure ($c_1$, $c_2$) as an ordered pair for each sentence in each task. Here $c_1$ represents the containment measure normalized w.r.t. original sentence and $c_2$ represents the containment measure normalized w.r.t. the revised sentence. For example, the sentence H1: *This leads to...* shown in Figure 2 has ($c_1$, $c_2$) = (0.846, 0.480) = (84.6%, 48.0%).

Figure 3 shows a plot of ($c_1$, $c_2$) for each sentence type for Task E. Here, heavily revised sentences are represented by a triangle ($\triangle$) and the lightly revised sentences by a box ($\square$). It can be seen that most of the heavily revised sen-

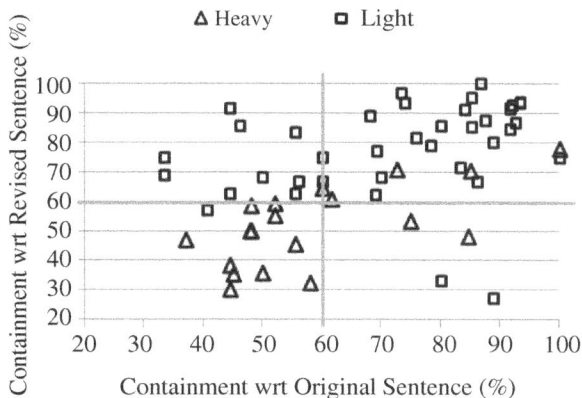

**Figure 3: Containment Measures for Task E**

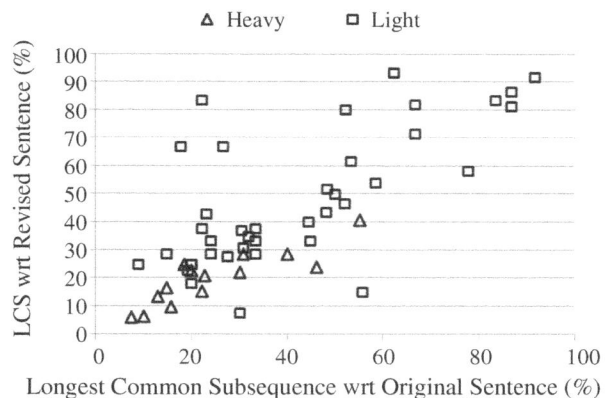

**Figure 4: Longest Common Subsequence for Task E**

tences lie in the lower left part of the graph, i.e., $(c_1, c_2)$ for heavily revised sentences is less than or equal to $(60\%, 60\%)$, where the point $(60\%, 60\%)$ represents a possible dividing point between lightly revised and heavily revised sentences. Likewise, most of the lightly revised sentences have $(c_1, c_2)$ greater than $(60\%, 60\%)$.

Sentences in the lower right part of the graph in Figure 3 represent sentences for which the value of $c_1$ is higher than 60% while that of $c_2$ is lower than 60%. These sentences may have been paraphrased in a way such that the length of the revised sentence is greater than the length of the original sentence. This could be due to sentence joining or insertion of new information into the sentence. Likewise, sentences in the upper right part of the graph may represent sentence splitting, deletion or summarization.

It may be relevant to mention here that the value of $(60\%, 60\%)$ simply presents a threshold separating most of the lightly revised sentences from most of the heavily revised sentences for Task E only. Similarity measures for other tasks may produce similar results albeit with different threshold values.

## 4.2 Longest Common Subsequence

Another measure of document similarity is the longest common subsequence similarity (lcss) measure. We computed the length of the longest common subsequence for each sentence pair in Task E. Similar to $N$-gram similarity, we normalized this length with the original and revised sentence lengths. The result is plotted in a graph in Fig. 4 which shows $(l_1, l_2)$, where

$$l_1 = length(lcs)/length(original) \qquad (3)$$
$$l_2 = length(lcs)/length(revised) \qquad (4)$$

The results are similar to those Fig 3, however, the heavily revised sentences cluster for a lower value of $(l_1, l_2)$. These results confirm our observations presented earlier.

## 4.3 Observations and Discussion

From the graphs in Figure 3 and 4, we observe that most of the highly revised sentences have a lower containment value with respect to both the original and the revised sentences as compared to the lightly revised sentences. We also note that some sentences may have a higher containment

measure with respect to the original sentence as compared to the revised sentence suggesting sentence splitting, summarization or deletion. A similar observation can be made for sentence joining, expansion or insertion. For example, the sentence 'H1: *This leads to...*' represents an example of addition of information since $(c_1, c_2) = (0.84, 0.48)$.

In addition to the above, we note a very basic but important observation: That both lightly and heavily revised sentences have some degree of overlap with respect to the original sentences. One possible reason for this could be that in Computer Science Education in particular (and technical education in general), technical terms cannot be revised or replaced. For example a student cannot replace 'Dynamic Programming' with 'Movable Planning' or 'recursive algorithm' with 'repetitive method'. Hence, we may expect some degree of string overlap in student work in CS Education which may prompt for the use of appropriate methods in detecting similarity in academic work. Another possible explanation for this overlap could be use of unsophisticated revision methods by students. This issue requires further investigation by analyzing student responses as well as by increasing the size of the sub-corpus. Although these findings have been stated in the context of Task E, they can be generalized by including results from other tasks.

## 5. CONCLUSION AND FUTURE WORK

In this work we constructed a sub-corpus of paraphrased sentences by extracting all lightly and heavily revised sentences from the Corpus of Plagiarised Short Answers. One of our findings was that our sentence-level similarity evaluation offers a finer level of similarity as compared to the file-level categorization of the original corpus. We also applied document similarity-based measures to observe containment patterns of this sub-corpus.

Several directions of future work can be undertaken. A basic application of this sub-corpus could be testing of paraphrase detection techniques, especially in student work. In order to achieve this, the size of the sub-corpus could be increased by adding further sentences from within and outside of the original corpus to include both scale and variety. Moreover, the sub-corpus can also be used to analyze patterns of plagiarism within student work in Computer Science in particular, and technology related areas in general.

# 6. ACKNOWLEDGMENTS

The authors would like to acknowledge the support provided by the Deanship of Scientific Research at King Fahd University of Petroleum & Minerals (KFUPM) under Research Grant RG-113.

# 7. REFERENCES

[1] K. Parker, A. Lenhart, and K. Moore, "The Digital Revolution and Higher Education," tech. rep., Pew Research Center, August 2011.

[2] H. Maurer, F. Kappe, and B. Zaka, "Plagiarism - A Survey," *Journal of Universal Computer Science*, vol. 12, no. 8, pp. 1050–1084, 2006.

[3] S. Alzahrani, N. Salim, and A. Abraham, "Understanding Plagiarism Linguistic Patterns, Textual Features, and Detection Methods," *IEEE Transactions on Systems, Man, and Cybernetics, Part C*, vol. 42, no. 2, pp. 133–149, 2012.

[4] Merriam Websters Dictionary, *Definition of Paraphrase*. Retrieved June 1, 2012. URL: www.merriam-webster.com/dictionary/paraphrase.

[5] W. B. Dolan and C. Brockett, "Automatically Constructing a Corpus of Sentential Paraphrases," in *Third International Workshop on Paraphrasing (IWP2005)*, Asia Federation of Natural Language Processing, 2005.

[6] P. Clough and M. Stevenson, "Developing a Corpus of Plagiarised Short Answers," *Language Resources and Evaluation*, vol. 45, no. 1, pp. 5–24, 2011.

[7] M. Potthast, B. Stein, A. Barrón-Cedeño, and P. Rosso, "An Evaluation Framework for Plagiarism Detection," in *23rd International Conference on Computational Linguistics (COLING 10)*, pp. 997–1005, Aug. 2010.

[8] M. Chong, L. Specia, and R. Mitkov, "Using Natural Language Processing for Automatic Detection of Plagiarism," in *Proceedings of the 4th International Plagiarism Conference (IPC-2010)*.

[9] S. Brin, J. Davis, and H. Garcia-Molina, "Copy Detection Mechanisms for Digital Documents," in *Proceedings of the 1995 ACM SIGMOD International Conference on Management of Data*, pp. 398–409, 1995.

[10] C. Lyon, J. Malcolm, and B. Dickerson, "Detecting Short Passages of Similar Text in Large Document Collections," in *Proceedings of the 2001 Conference on Empirical Methods in Natural Language Processing*, pp. 118–125, 2001.

[11] A. Z. Broder, "On the Resemblance and Containment of Documents," in *In Compression and Complexity of Sequences*, pp. 21–29, IEEE Computer Society, 1997.

# A Holistic and Pragmatic Approach to Teaching Web Accessibility in an Undergraduate Web Design Course

Ye Diana Wang
Applied Information Technology Department
George Mason University
10900 University Blvd. MS 4F5
Manassas, VA 20110, USA
1-703-993-9288
ywangm@gmu.edu

## ABSTRACT

Web accessibility is a fundamental instrument to support the shift towards an inclusive cyberspace and a socially responsible society, and higher education plays an essential role in this effort. This paper fills the gap of lacking literature by reporting an undergraduate Web design course that adopts a holistic and pragmatic approach to teaching Web accessibility and presenting the specific accessibility topics and techniques that are appropriate for the course scope and its assessment strategies. It is hoped that the instructional approach presented in the paper will prove beneficial to instructors facing similar demands and challenges in computing programs.

## Categories and Subject Descriptors

K3.2 [**Computers and Education**]: Computer and Information Science Education – *Information Systems Education*

## General Terms

Design, Human Factors, Legal Aspects

## Keywords

Web Design, Accessibility, Web Accessibility Education, Pedagogy, People with Disabilities

## 1. INTRODUCTION

Since its inception in the early 1990s, the World Wide Web and the number of people and businesses using it have been growing at a stunning rate. The resources, products, and services that are built upon the Web have become fundamental tools in people's daily lives. Parallel to the growth of Web, the demand for accessible websites and content is continuously increasing, with no signs of slowing down. According to the 2011 World Report on Disability produced by the World Health Organization (WHO) and the World Bank [20], more than one billion people around the world live with disabilities. In the United States, approximately 20% of individuals above the age of 18 have some disability [6].

As people with disabilities, the largest minority group in society, need to use the Web and participate in the information revolution as much as anyone else, issues surrounding Web accessibility are as crucial as ever.

The Web Accessibility Initiative (WAI) defines Web accessibility as the ability for people with disabilities to use the Web. More specifically, "Web accessibility means that people with disabilities can perceive, understand, navigate, and interact with the Web, and that they can contribute to the Web" [10]. More and more people start to look beyond the merely physical access to buildings and focus on providing access to cyberspace by people with disabilities. Worldwide there is an ever-increasing recognition of the necessity of Web accessibility in the public sector, in the corporate world, in government, and at academic institutions. The reasons for making the Web accessible to people with accessibilities are multifold:

*Ethical Reasons:* Frankly, it's the right thing to do. From the perspective of the disabled, having access to the information and resources on the Web is a matter of basic human rights. When it comes to using the Web, they should not be left discouraged or desperate. It should be noted that universal access was actually the exact driving force for Sir Timothy Berners-Lee, inventor of the World Wide Web, to found the World Wide Web Consortium (W3C) in 1994. He stated, "the power of the Web is in its universality. Access by everyone regardless of disability is an essential aspect" [19].

*Legal Reasons:* Many countries have established legislation to specifically protect access to the Web by people with disabilities and regulate the accessibility practices of both educational and non-educational organizations. For instance, in the United States, three pieces of federal legislation—Americans with Disabilities Act of 1990, Section 504, and Section 508 of the 1973 Rehabilitation Act—require federal agencies and non-federal organizations that receive federal funds to provide disabled individuals with equal educational opportunities and make their electronic and information technology, including Web-based information or applications, accessible [16]. These civil rights acts and legislation all send a clear message and legally mandate that people should have equal access to the information and services provided on the Web.

*Pedagogical Reasons:* The IT2008 Model Curriculum approved and published by ACM makes it mandatory that accessibility topics must be covered in any four-year programs in Information Technology under both the Human Computer Interaction (HCI)

and Web Development categories [3]. In addition, one of ABET's main criteria for accrediting applied science programs is whether the graduates can demonstrate "an understanding of professional and ethical responsibility" [1].

*Technical Reasons:* Complying with usability standards encourages compatibility and interoperability in browsers and operating platforms [15], and therefore, can improve the availability of Web content for not only people with disabilities but also the majority of users who are increasingly accessing the Web using mobile devices or emerging technologies. As a result, Web designers who are technically competent in dealing with accessibility issues and creating standard-compliant websites are more employable in the current market place than those who are not.

As the general awareness of the necessity of Web accessibility continues to expand, there is a high demand towards knowledge and practice in accessible Web design. This paper presents our efforts to meet this demand by teaching Web accessibility in an undergraduate Web design course. The rest of the paper is organized as follows. First, the context for this paper is discussed in terms of the challenges of improving Web accessibility, followed by a literature review of other curricula for accessibility and Web design in higher education. The next two sections describe our holistic and pragmatic approach to Web accessibility education and provide the implementation details and instructional strategies. The last section discusses the results of the course and concludes with possible directions for future research.

## 2. BACKGROUND

### 2.1 Challenges of Improving Web Accessibility

Despite widespread attention to the issue, Web accessibility continues to be a major problem. A majority of existing websites are far from satisfactory and suffer from accessibility problems, which make it difficult or even impossible to work with the assistive technologies used by people with disabilities. Assistive technologies, such as screen readers or voice browsers, are supposed to help and promote greater independence for their users. However, if the websites are made impossible for these devices and technologies to operate properly, they become barriers.

One of the latest large-scale studies, based on the evaluation of over 23,000 Web pages at over 180 universities in the United States, reported that most higher education websites still lack basic accessibility features [9]. The Summary Scores ranged from as low as 29% (pages implemented with form-related accessibility features) to 62% (pages implemented with image-related accessibility features). It was disappointing to find out that even ALT text for images, a minimum requirement for Web accessibility, was not fully implemented on almost 40% of the Web pages. Although we cannot draw global conclusions, the aforementioned results can be used as an indicator that Web accessibility still has a long way to go.

There are a number of special challenges and issues for improving Web accessibility and resolving the current situation. Firstly, the disabled have remained an invisible minority, and their needs are often considered secondary to security or design aesthetics in a given Web development project. Without appreciating the social importance of accessibility, Web designers and developers can hardly be motivated to "burden" their design with accessibility limitations. The more serious issues are the lack of training and education among Web designers and developers about how to implement technical adaptations in their Web design and the lack of knowledge about how people with disabilities use the Web [8, 18]. A survey of some popular textbooks on Web design has revealed that accessibility topics do not receive much coverage and discussion in depth [15].

### 2.2 Web Accessibility Education

The inclusion of Web accessibility education in computing programs, such as Computer Science and Information Technology, is crucial to overcoming the current challenges to promoting Web accessibility. It is these educational entities that are training the next generation of Web designers, software developers, systems analysts, and IT project managers, so they are in a unique position to provide Web accessibility education to students and to instruct students in creating websites that are accessible to a wide audience. Accessibility education is also very important to address the special needs of people with disabilities not only in schools, but also in society, by educating the students of these needs and stimulating the students' desire to promote accessibility in their professional practice [8].

In general, literature on teaching Web accessibility in higher education and related work is lacking and limited, and almost all have been reported as conference papers. Some focus on incorporating accessibility topics into four-year undergraduate curricula [11, 18], postgraduate courses [14], or short introductory courses [4, 8]; however, they do not provide specific techniques and implementation guidelines for teaching the topic. The rest of the works aim to provide practical knowledge on Web accessibility education in a classroom setting and present some technical details; however, they are mostly outdated [3, 7, 12, 13, 15] except one [2]. Version 1.0 of the Web Content Accessibility Guidelines (WCAG) was made a formal recommendation by the WAI in 1999, and a lot has changed since then. Version 2.0 of WCAG was published in December of 2008, and it is a major departure from WCAG 1.0 for its testable nature and using "a different language, a different structure and a different rationale" [2]. Therefore, pedagogical knowledge and evidence that reflect new Web technologies and standards are currently in a great need.

## 3. A HOLISTIC AND PRAGMATIC APPROACH TO TEACHING WEB ACCESSIBILITY

In response to the demand towards knowledge and practice in accessible Web design and the call for the inclusion of accessibility into education, this author has taken an improved approach to teaching Web accessibility in an undergraduate Web design course. Compared to some previous approaches that have either spread accessibility coverage into several courses or appended accessibility discussion as a single lecture at the end of the course, the current approach encompasses some significant features and improved strategies:

Firstly, the approach is holistic in the sense that accessibility topics are broken into a series of lectures throughout the course and introduced along with the entire Web development process, from designing the website, constructing various multimedia components, to testing and publishing the website. Each lecture is presented from the perspective of how to create functional and attractive websites with accessible multimedia components (e.g., text, forms, images, video, audio, animation, etc.), so various accessibility features and techniques related to different types of Web content are covered in a comprehensive matter. The approach also supports all major types of disability, including visual, auditory, physical, cognitive, and neurological disability, in order to provide students with a full understanding of the different needs of people with disabilities.

From the instructor's perspective, such a holistic approach is feasible and makes Web accessibility requirements potentially easier to understand and apply by students. The instructor does not need to be an expert in the accessibility field to teach the course or significantly modify the course scope and structure; accessibility topics can be seamlessly embedded into each lecture with little overhead. From the student's perspective, accessibility is seen as an integral part of the website development process, rather than something extra to be added at the end of the process. Keeping accessibility in mind encourages students to make better design decisions along the way and seek optimal methods to ultimately achieve Web accessibility. When accessibility is a goal from the beginning, it is also much easier to implement technically. As with most technology and products, retrofitting is difficult and costly and may even lead students to the wrong conclusions that accessibility is always difficult to achieve and may not be worth the effort [15]. Therefore, taking a holistic approach to teaching Web accessibility is essential.

The second significant feature of the approach is its pragmatic nature. Accessibility is not just a collection of theoretical concepts and principles. Besides discussing the importance of Web accessibility and the policies and standards behind it, the majority of the instructional efforts focus on operationalizing accessibility in Web design through live demonstrations, hands-on exercises, and technical implementations. Many specific techniques related to XHTML, CSS, and multimedia authoring tools are pertinent to the context of Web accessibility and covered in the course. The teaching of these techniques can not only keep students engaged but also enhance their Web design skills in general. In addition, embedding practical usability and accessibility techniques enables instructors to include accessibility requirements into development projects and testable exam questions. Such a pragmatic approach provides students with the opportunities to learn the particular techniques for creating accessible websites, to practice in implementing the techniques, and more importantly, to understand the difference that these techniques can make in improving Web accessibility and meeting the needs of the people with disabilities.

## 4. COURSE DETAILS

The course, Multimedia and Web Design, is one of the three-credit-hour core courses in our BSIT (Bachelor of Science in Information Technology) program, and it is required for all IT majors and open to students of other majors who have an interest in Web design. It is a standard lecture/lab course of 15 weeks and usually taken by IT students in their first or second year of study, before taking any higher-level or concentration courses. By teaching accessibility topics early in an introductory-level Web design course, we can educate not only the students who will become Web developers but also the students who will play other roles in a computing profession. This helps ensure the impact of Web accessibility education is as wide as possible and create a general awareness of the surrounding issues among students.

## 4.1 Objectives

There are two primary objectives for this course: the first one, which should be mostly accomplished through the lecture session, is to introduce students to the concepts and principles for designing and developing a functional, accessible, and attractive website with graphical interface and multimedia components; the second objective, which should be mostly accomplished through the lab session, is to provide students with hands-on experience in the use of tools (e.g., Adobe Dreamweaver, Photoshop, and Flash) for developing websites and multimedia products.

## 4.2 Textbooks and Supplemental Material

The current textbooks used for the lecture and the lab section are Web Design: Introductory [17] and The Web Collection CS5 Revealed [5], respectively. The books are widely used in Web design courses that cover Adobe Creative Suite software; however, similar to other popular textbooks on the topic, there is a lack of sufficient coverage on accessibility issues and techniques.

As a supplement to the textbooks, many of the excellent resources found on the Web are put to use, such as a resource page, which is made available on the Blackboard course site and regularly updated to provide references (e.g., a customizable quick reference to WCAG 2.0 at the W3C website), product documentations (e.g., Adobe Accessibility Resource Center), tools (e.g., validation services, free-download of assistive technologies), and techniques (e.g., tutorial articles at the WebAIM website). The lecture slides have also been developed, either partially or entirely, based on these resources.

## 4.3 Topics

An outline of the lecture topics and some specific accessibility topics and techniques that are appropriate for each lecture are provided below. It is not meant to be the definitive solution, but an example of how Web accessibility topics can be integrated into a Web design course despite its limited class time and the introductory scope. In practice, many important techniques are demonstrated and performed by the instructor during the lecture, and the students continue to practice these techniques using the Adobe authoring tools during the lab session that immediately follows.

*Lecture 1: Introduction to Web Design and Multimedia*

- Function and purpose of the W3C and the WAI
- Importance of Web accessibility and valid XHTML
- Social responsibilities of various Web design roles
- Adobe Dreamweaver Accessibility: e.g., Accessibility Preferences options

*Lecture 2: Web Development Process I: Information Design*

- Conduct user needs assessment
- Create liquid design with relative width
- Home/underling pages: e.g., consistent navigation
- Splash page: e.g., provide link to skip or turn off music
- Accessibility guidelines for naming files and folders

*Lecture 3: Web Development Process II: Interaction Design and Presentation Design*

- User-based and user-controlled navigation
- Types of navigational elements
  - Hyperlinks: e.g., indicate in link text when the **target** attribute is used

- o Image links: e.g., combine adjacent image and text links for the same resource
- o Image maps: e.g., provide an alt attribute for each hot spot
- o Navigation menus/bars/tabs: e.g., indicate current location
- o Frames: e.g., provide a title attribute for each frame
- o Site map, breadcrumb trials, search function
- Accessibility guidelines for navigation design
- Basic Web design principles: balance and proximity; contrast and focus; unity and visual identity
- Tools and techniques for creating visual consistency

*Lecture 4: Writing for Multimedia Web and Typography*

- Web writing
  - o Accuracy and currency
  - o Scannability: e.g., use ol, ul and dl tags for lists or groups of links; use em and strong tags instead of b and i tags for boldface and italics for highlighting purposes
  - o Organization: e.g., provide a descriptive top-level page heading; provide a page title using the title tag
- Typography
  - o Fontface: e.g., present text in sans serif font
  - o Font size: e.g., use relative-length units
  - o Text block: e.g., avoid fully justified text; avoid chunks of italic or uppercase text
  - o Accessibility issues with converting text to graphical typography
- Use CSS for typography: e.g., leading, tracking, kerning

*Lecture 5: Color and Graphics*

- Accessibility guidelines for use of color and contrast
  - o e.g., use complementary colors to create contrast
- Web-safe colors and their hexadecimal values
- Accessibility guidelines for scanning
- Web-usable graphic types and optimization
- Accessibility guidelines and techniques for graphics
  - o e.g., use alt attributes on img tags; when to use null alt attributes
  - o e.g., avoid the use of text in raster images
  - o Accessible ways to add background image, side bar, and favicon

*Lecture 6: Animation & Interactivity*

- Accessibility guidelines for multimedia
  - o e.g., provide text equivalents (long description, transcripts, captions) for multimedia elements
  - o e.g., use the accessibility attributes of the object tag when embedding into a Web page
- Accessibility guidelines for Web-based forms
  - o e.g., use the label or title tags to identify form controls
  - o e.g., use the fieldset and legend tags to provide a description for groups of form controls
- Adobe Flash Accessibility: e.g., Accessibility Panel

*Lecture 7: Audio and Video*

- Accessibility guidelines for audio and video
  - o e.g., apply audio descriptions or alternatives to video
- Accessibility techniques for embedding audio and video into a Web page

*Lecture 8: Web Accessibility*

- Barriers and assistive technologies

- Initiatives and regulations
  - o WAI and WCAG 2.0
  - o Section 508 and other US laws on Web accessibility
- Types of disabilities and Adaptations in Web design
  - o Visual: e.g., blindness, low vision, color blindness
    - Adaptations in Web design
    - Adobe Photoshop Accessibility: e.g., Soft Proof features
  - o Auditory: e.g., deaf, hard-of-hearing
    - captioning tools
  - o Physical: e.g., paralysis, poor motor skills
    - Adaptations in Web design
  - o Cognitive: e.g., learning disabilities, dyslexia
    - Readability tests of Web content
  - o Neurological: e.g., seizures
    - Adaptations in Web design
- More accessibility techniques
  - o Skip links
  - o PDF files
  - o Tables: e.g., use the caption tag and summary attribute to describe the table; use the scope attribute to associate header cells and data cells
  - o Access keys and tab index
  - o Use CSS to hide text
- Accessibility statement
- Accessibility validation services and tools

*Lecture 9: Copyright & Fair Use*

- Creative Commons licenses and accessibility

*Lecture 10: Designing Static and Dynamic Web Sites*

- Provide client-side validation and alert

*Lecture 11: Testing, Publishing, Marketing & Maintaining a Web Site*

- Examine a sample website consisting of bad accessibility practices
- Use Adobe Dreamweaver validation reports
- Use W3C markup validation service
- Target Audience Testing

## 4.4 Lecture 1 and Lecture 8

The instructor needs to pay particular attention to the first and the eighth lectures. As most students have not been familiar with or given any thought to the issue prior taking to the course, it is necessary to point out the need for creating accessible websites with multimedia components to the students at the very first class meeting. In addition to explaining the purpose of the WAI, the importance of Web accessibility, and the social responsibilities of various Web design roles, the instructor can provide an overview of some built-in accessibility features of Adobe Dreamweaver and conclude the class by preparing the students with the expectation that they will learn about Web design from an accessibility perspective and more techniques will be covered in the remaining courses and evaluated through the required course deliverables.

Lecture 8 is also of particular importance because it is entirely dedicated to the topics of Web accessibility and aims to give a concentrated treatment of the various adaptations in Web design to accommodate different types of disabilities. The instructor usually starts the class with a short video provided at the WebAIM website, in which six students with various disabilities share some of their experience with the Web and accessibility. By watching the video, the students are able to see some assistive technologies in action, gain a sense of empathy for the disabled students of their age in the video, and have a deeper understanding of why it is crucial to create accessible websites. As a result, the students are motivated to learn about more accessibility techniques and apply the techniques in their Web design. By the time of Lecture 8, students should have been introduced to a variety of accessibility techniques and tips related to different types of Web content, so the focus of the lecture is also on implementing the accessibility features that are required in the course projects (e.g., skip links). At the end of the lecture, the instructor demonstrates a validation service (e.g., WAVE) or a testing tool (e.g., Vischeck) using a sample website and then discusses the results, which contain warnings, errors, and some other information.

## 4.5 Assessment

Assessment of student performance is an essential part of any course and can effectively reinforce learning. In the course, final grades are based on lab assignments (25%), lecture quizzes (5%), midterm and final exams (30%), and projects (40%). All assessment items are provided with rubrics for clarifying the grading criteria and aim to evaluate the students' mastery of skills and knowledge in Web design and accessibility from different angles.

There are a total of twelve weekly lab assignments, of which three require Adobe Dreamweaver, four require Adobe Flash, four require Adobe Photoshop, and the last one requires the integration of all three pieces of software. These lab assignments allow the students to put the lecture content into practice by exercising the development techniques covered in the lecture and using the accessibility features and tools that are built into the Adobe software. They are excellent preparation for both the written exam questions and the hands-on projects.

The five in-class quizzes are similar to the midterm and final exams in terms of format, which are rather traditional and mostly multiple-choice, true-false, and short-answer questions. Approximately 20% of the questions are specifically related to accessibility and aim to assess students' theoretical understanding of the accessibility topics embedded into each lecture.

The course assigns five projects, which span the entire semester and are targeted at the common goal of designing and building a functional and accessible website with attractive graphical interfaces and multimedia components. Project 1 requires students to review two existing websites, draw two flowcharts, and critique each site's design and structure. The two websites must be of the same company type, either (1) Defense Contractor, (2) Government, or (3) Non-Profit, as these companies are usually required to comply with Section 508 and their websites are more accessible than those of private companies. By reviewing these existing websites, students can use what they have observed from the websites, either best practices or lessons learned, to help them design their own website in the following projects. Project 2 requires students to make the "blueprint" of their website by creating a flowchart and a storyboard for each of the minimum twelve Web pages required. Project 3 and Project 4 focus on the creation of an animation commercial using Adobe Flash and a graphical logo using Adobe Photoshop, which will be embedded in the final website. And lastly, Project 5 is about implementing the website using Adobe Dreamweaver and publishing it from the university Web server. The specific focus, grading weight, and accessibility-related requirements for each project are summarized in Table 1:

**Table 1. Accessibility-related requirements in projects**

| Project | Accessibility-Related Requirements |
|---|---|
| Project 1 (5%): Review | • Understand the selected company type and its legal/social responsibilities for accessibility<br>• Describe and discuss the accessibility of the selected websites in the Review section |
| Project 2 (10%): Storyboards | • Use the same company type that is selected in Project 1<br>• Design a simple navigational path of the website and document it in the flowchart<br>• Design the various aspects (e.g., file name, text, user interaction, hyperlink, font, color) of the website according to accessibility guidelines and document it in the storyboards |
| Project 3 (10%): Animation Commercial | • Create an animation commercial with the Flash Accessibility Panel activated<br>• Select the "Make Movie/Object Accessible" option on movie or individual objects<br>• Provide an alternative equivalent in the Name and Description fields<br>• Place text within the button symbol<br>• Ensure no component of the content flashes more than three times in any 1-second period |
| Project 4 (5%): Graphical Logo | • Save the logo in a Web-usable graphics format<br>• Create sufficient color contrast<br>• Test CUD-compliance by using the Photoshop color-blindness soft proofing features<br>• Write a narrative and explain how the logo meets accessibility guidelines |
| Project 5 (10%): Multimedia Website | • Use of frames is not permitted<br>• Provide a title on each Web page both in the body as an <h1> heading and in the <title> tag<br>• Create a Site Map that consists of hyperlinks<br>• Insert a visible Skip Link on each Web page<br>• Use alt attributes on all images<br>• Use title attributes on all non-text objects<br>• Home page passes the WAVE accessibility validator<br>• Home page passes the W3C markup validator |

## 5. CONCLUSIONS

Web accessibility is a fundamental instrument in supporting the shift towards an inclusive cyberspace and a socially responsible society, and higher education plays an essential role in this effort. This paper fills the gap of lacking literature by reporting the undergraduate Web design course entitled "Multimedia and Web Design", which adopts a holistic and pragmatic approach to teaching Web accessibility, and presenting the specific accessibility topics and techniques that are appropriate for the course scope and its assessment strategies. It is hoped that the instructional approach presented in the paper will prove beneficial to instructors facing similar demands and challenges in computing programs.

The course has been successful in terms of the accomplishment of the course objectives. Students who have successfully completed the course can not only acquire solid skills for creating a functional and accessible website with attractive graphical interfaces and multimedia components using Adobe Web authoring tools, but also gain a deep appreciation for keeping accessibility in mind throughout the development process. The websites and multimedia products created by the students as part of the course projects or lab assignments are mostly usable and meet the accessibly requirements. The majority of the students have also answered the questions related to accessibility correctly in the exams and quizzes. In the past few years in which the course has been offered, some students have expressed their appreciation of the coverage of accessibility issues and the way they have been taught. One written testimonial from a graduated student, who is now a Web developer, states as follows:

*"Everything that I have learned in your class has been implemented into my work everyday. Especially 508 compliance, that one is very important, even more now than ever. In my first deliverable, I only had 1 minor error in compliance, which this company thought was amazing, typically most developers have several errors or bugs in their programming. I told them I was taught right."*

In addition to continuously improving the course curriculum with more Web accessibility techniques and keeping it updated with the latest development in Web technologies and standards (e.g., WAI-ARIA), future efforts will focus on creating a distance education section of the course for online delivery. Other areas of prospective exploration may include some instructional methods that have been previously reported as effective, such as student participation in service-learning partnerships [12] or the direct use of assistive technologies [8].

# 6. REFERENCES

[1] ABET. 2011. *Criteria for Accrediting Applied Science Programs*. Retrieved April 10, 2012, from http://www.abet.org/uploadedFiles/Accreditation/Accreditation_Process/Accreditation_Documents/Current/asac-criteria-2012-2013.pdf

[2] Alonso, F., Fuertes, J. L., González, Á. L., and Martínez, L. 2010. On the testability of WCAG 2.0 for beginners. In *Proceedings of the International Cross-Disciplinary Conference on Web Accessibility*.

[3] Association for Computing Machinery (ACM). 2008. *Information Technology 2008 Curriculum Guidelines for Undergraduate Degree Programs in Information Technology*. Retrieved April 10, 2012, from http://www.acm.org//education/curricula/IT2008%20Curriculum.pdf

[4] Benavídez, C., Fuertes, J.L., Gutiérrez, E., and Martínez, L. 2006. Teaching Web Accessibility with "Contramano" and Hera. *Lecture Notes in Computer Science*, 341-348.

[5] Bishop, S., Shuman, J.K and Reding, E.E. 2011. *The Web Collection CS5 Revealed*. Cengage, Boston, MA.

[6] Centers for Disease Control and Prevention (CDC). 2009. *How Many People have Disability?* Retrieved April 22, 2012, from http://www.cdc.gov/ncbddd/documents/Disability%20tip%20sheet%20_PHPa_1.pdf

[7] Cohen, R., Fairley, A., Gerry, D. and Lima, G. 2005. Accessibility in introductory computer science. In *Proceedings of the 36th SIGCSE Technical Symposium on Computer Science Education*, 17-21.

[8] Freire, A.P., Fortes, R.P.M, Paiva, D.M.B., Turine, M.A.S. 2007. Using Screen Readers to Reinforce Web Accessibility Education. In *Proceedings of the 12th ACM Annual SIGCSE Conference on Innovation and Technology in Computer Science Education* . New York, NY. ACM Press, 82-86.

[9] Gunderson, J. 2011. The status of web accessibility in higher education. In *Proceedings of 26th Annual International Technology & Persons with Disabilities Conference*, San Diego, CA, USA, March 14-19, 2011. CSUN.

[10] Henry, S.L. 2005. *Introduction to Web Accessibility*. Retrieved April 22, 2012, from http://www.w3.org/WAI/intro/accessibility.php

[11] Lazar, J. 2002. Integrating accessibility into the information systems curriculum. In *Proceedings of the International Association for Computer Information Systems*, 373–379.

[12] Lazar, J. 2003 Improving Web accessibility through service-learning partnerships. *Information Systems Education Journal*, *1*, 33.

[13] Ludi, S. 2002. Access for everyone: Introducing accessibility issues to students in internet programming courses. In *Proceedings of 32nd ASEE/IEEE Frontiers in Education Conference*, S1C-7—9.

[14] Ortner, D., Batusic, M. and Miesenberger, K. 2004. Postgraduate course on accessible design. In K. Klaus, K. Miesenberger, W. Zagler and D. Burger (eds). *Computers Helping People with Special Needs*. Berlin Heidelberg: Springer-Verlag, 183-186.

[15] Rosmaita, B.J. Accessibility first! A new approach to web design. In *SIGCSE '06: Proceedings of the 37th SIGCSE technical symposium on Computer science education*. New York, NY, USA. ACM Press, 270–274.

[16] Seale, J.K. 2006. *E-Learning and Disability in Higher Education*. Routledge, New York, NY.

[17] Shelly, G.B. and Campbell, J. T. 2012. *Web Design: Introductory*. Cengage, Boston, MA.

[18] Waller, A., Hanson, V., and Sloan, D. 2009. Including accessibility within and beyond undergraduate computing courses. In *Proceedings of the 11th international ACM SIGACCESS conference on Computers and accessibility (ASSETS '09)*. New York, NY, USA. ACM Press, 155-162.

[19] Web Accessibility Initiative (WAI). 2012. *Web Accessibility Initiative Home*. Retrieved April 22, 2012, from http://www.w3.org/WAI/

[20] World Health Organization. 2011. *World Report on Disability*. Retrieved April 22, 2012, from http://whqlibdoc.who.int/publications/2011/9789240685215_eng.pdf

# Introducing Mobile Widgets Development in an Advanced Web Technologies Course

Hend S. Al-Khalifa and Afnan A. Al-Subaihin
Information Technology Department
College of Computer and Information Sciences
King Saud University
Riyadh, Saudi Arabia
{hendk/aalsubaihin}@ksu.edu.sa

## ABSTRACT

Mobile Widgets are mobile applications built using standard web technologies. Due to their increasing popularity and the potential they hold as the new frontier of mobile applications development, IT students need to have the essential knowledge to develop and deploy mobile widgets. To address this demand in knowledge, this paper presents our experience in improving the curriculum of an advanced web technologies course to incorporate a portion about mobile widgets development. We also report the students' feedback obtained after exposing them to the technology along with our final remarks.

## Categories and Subject Descriptors

K.3.2[**Computer and Information Science Education**]: Computer science education.

## General Terms

Design, Experimentation, Human Factors.

## Keywords

Mobile, Web Design, Mobile Widgets, PhoneGap.

## 1. INTRODUCTION

Web development is an essential pillar in the ACM Information Technology curriculum [1]. During the past couple of years, teaching web development has moved from introducing students to the basics of building simple static pages to the development of more advanced fully fledged web-applications that target different platforms.

Currently, as the discipline of mobile web development has become an essential skill in any web developer arsenal; an increased need to teach IT students the basics of mobile-based application development and how to package and distribute them as widgets became a necessity.

Mobile widgets are packaged interactive applications designed to provide certain functions. They can be developed using standard web technologies such as HTML, CSS, JavaScript and XML, and require some kind of runtime environment in order to operate.

To build a mobile widget based on standardized web technologies, developers normally consult the W3C website directly [2]; however, the case is somewhat different for undergraduate students. Students usually get overwhelmed by the amount of detailed technical specifications provided by the W3C website. On the other hand, there are not enough educational resources available for teaching the development of cross-platform mobile widgets in an easy way. Not to mention that a major challenge pertaining mobile widgets development is the ability to develop a widget that is cross-platform [3], i.e. the problem of mobile widget runtime fragmentation.

Furthermore, to the best of our knowledge, there have been no significant published work that guide instructors on how to teach these concepts. All these challenges must be overcome in order to devise the best approach to introduce IT students to mobile widgets development. Therefore, in this paper we present our experience in introducing IT students studying web and multimedia track to mobile widget development. We will start by giving a short background and discussing the motivation behind mobile widgets development. Then, we will briefly present the content of the advanced web technologies course and how we improved it by including the topic of widgets development to the mobile web module. Finally, we conclude the paper by reporting the students' evaluation of the module.

## 2. MOTIVATION AND BACKGROUND

As mobile users increase in numbers, their demand to access the web increases as well. And since mobile phones need special considerations for design and development, most web application providers need to provide mobile versions of their services, not to mention the newly introduced category of web applications that are specifically tailored for mobile users which was facilitated by the remarkable advancements in the capability of web scripting and markup languages to access the resources of the local device, including mobile-specific features such as location services.

However, mobile phones are known for their limited, unreliable and sometimes slow internet connection, which introduces a drawback when implementing a web application aimed at mobile phones. A solution would be implementing the application as a native application targeted for the specific operating system of the device. Although the usage of the manufacturer's development kit may offer the programmer more control over the device-specific features; this will cost programmers effort and time to use and familiarize themselves with a proprietary mobile applications development platform that is usually only related to a specific operating system, thus, the application loses its interoperability.

Mobile Widgets lend themselves as a great solution for developing, packaging and distributing mobile applications that are based on web technologies, which are already well-known by thousands of web developers; especially as new web technologies are now equipped with the ability to access some crucial device-specific features such as the local storage and GPS services.

The World Wide Web Consortium (W3C) defines mobile widgets as "an interactive single purpose application for displaying and/or updating local data or data on the Web, packaged in a way to allow a single download and installation on a user's machine or mobile device."[2] Simply put, a mobile widget is the set of HTML, JavaScript, CSS and other resources (such as image files) needed to display the web application which is compressed using a typical file archiving tool. The folder must also contain a manifest file to provide some metadata about the widget. The W3C proposes the .wgt extension for this compressed folder.

As the W3C provided global standards for mobile widgets, their great potential as the next era of mobile applications development was getting attention. This is due to the fact that mobile widgets will unify the development technologies and runtime requirements of mobile applications.

A group of 24 mobile network operators was formed under the name of Wholesale Applications Community (WAC) in order to realize the goal of having an open standard mobile application development platform. The WAC now boasts more than 60 full members including network operators, device and network equipment manufacturers [4]. WAC currently provides the software development kits, APIs and runtime environments that will enable W3C-compliant mobile widgets and is regarded the industry's standard for mobile widgets.

Executing mobile widgets requires specific software support in the device's operating system. The system contains a widget engine, which is not entirely different from a web browser that acts as a runtime environment for the mobile widget [5]. The widget engine, enables the system to instantiate a widget and enables users to manage their inventory of widgets [6].

The only obstacle that hinders the teaching process of building mobile widgets is the current obscurity of widgets runtime environments. While there are quite a few environments that enable running WAC-compliant widgets in their own sandbox, abiding by these environments standards and surrounding interface, makes the student questions the difference between packaging the widget and making it available through these environments and simply making the widget a mobile application hosted on the web and accessible via mobile browsers. Furthermore, these runtime environments stand in the way of enabling mobile widgets to be truly platform-independent. The need for a specific engine to run widgets started when widgets were regarded as small utilities similar to desktop widgets which naturally need their own sandbox to run. However, as mobile widgets converge towards being the new alternative for mobile native applications, they need to be supported by the mobile operating system in order for them to fulfill their potential and replace mobile-specific native applications.

The major, currently available, runtime environments for mobile widgets are proprietary software of providers who also offer their own widget development environment and SDKs. Most of these platforms are compliant with the WAC widget specifications. And to the best of our knowledge, there are no runtime environment that supports all (or at least) most common mobile platforms.

These platforms include OBIGO [7] which provides a WAC-compliant SDK and the 'OBIGO Web Runtime' application which will run the widget on the mobile phone. Opera Widgets is a WAC-ready widget runtime environment that is only targeted for Android mobile phones which also provides an Eclipse plug-in to enable the developer to package the widget as a .wgt file [8]. Vodafone, a

telecommunications company, offers developers the ability to develop mobile applications using the WAC specification and run it using its own Applications platform called 360 Apps [9].

In order to bridge the gap created by the fragmentation in mobile widgets runtime environments, we have tried to simplify the students entry-level into this area by providing a clear how-to guide into mobile widgets development using available technologies. Next we will give an overview about the course that implements our approach and discuss the improvements made.

## 3. COURSE DESCRIPTION
Advanced web technologies course taught as a core course in the web and multimedia track at the Information Technology Department, College of Computer and Information Sciences, King Saud University, is a 3-hours credit course offered in the sixth level (i.e. Third year) of the IT program. As a prerequisite to the course, the students are required to complete the web applications course, where they learn about the principles of web design and development using basic web technologies including HTML, Java Script, CSS and PHP.

The advanced web technologies course exposes the students to many advanced web technologies delivered in a module based teaching style. This style encompasses the use of mini-projects that the students are required to solve after the end of each module to insure better understanding of the presented technologies.

Basically, the course covers the following modules:

- XML Technologies.
- Rich Internet Applications using (Ajax, JSON, HTML 5 and CSS3).
- Java Web Technologies (i.e. JSP, Servlets, Java Beans, etc.)
- Web services, Web APIs and Mashups.
- Cloud Computing.
- Mobile Web Design and Development.

The course has been offered for more than two semesters [10]. In each semester, the content of the course is revised and enhanced to reflect the recent advancement in the web domain. Among the enhanced modules is the Mobile Web Design and Development module. Prior to this module the students are exposed to the new features of HTML 5 and CSS3 in general, and during the mobile web module these technologies are tailored toward mobile development. In principle, this module equips the students with the appropriate skills and techniques to build mobile websites.

In previous installments of the course, the students were only exposed to the design and development of mobile websites. This semester we improved the module to offer the necessary technical skills to develop mobile widgets.

## 4. COURSE IMPROVEMENTS
To simplify the students learning, we started in the lecture by giving the students the essential theoretical and technical aspects needed to create mobile widgets. This includes: web technologies involved in building mobile widgets and tools used to package and deploy them. This, in addition to their background in designing web applications in general, and mobile website design best practices, shall equip the student with the necessary elements to design a mobile widget.

The lab complements the lecture by asking the students to create a simple mobile website based on the technical specification explained in the lecture. The students were given our College full website version (http://ccis.ksu.edu.sa) and were asked to convert it into a mobile friendly website.

The tasks required for achieving this mini-project was as follows:

1- Analyze the College of Computer and Information Sciences (CCIS) website and determine what pages and functions will be added to the mobile version.

2- Design the clickstream and wireframes of the mobile website.

3- Implement the mobile website using HTML 5, CSS 3 and JavaScript, at the same time take into consideration mobile web best practices [11].

Finally, the students are required to wrap the website as a widget following these steps:

1- Create a directory and place inside it all HTML, CSS, JavaScript and images files of the mobile website.

2- Prepare the manifest file. This is an XML configuration file that must reside at the root of the widget and named "config.xml", an example is shown in Figure 1.

3- Zip all files using any compression program.

After the last step, the students will get a zipped file containing their mobile website. To deploy it as a widget there are two options:

1- Changing the extension of the zipped file from .zip/.rar to .wgt and running the package using Opera Widgets Runtime environment. This requires installing the Opera Widgets app in the mobile phone for testing. This will introduce a problem since Opera Widgets are not available for all mobile operating systems.

2- Using PhoneGap online builder (https://build.phonegap.com/) to wrap the mobile website under the disguise of a native application for every known mobile operating system. Hence, it can run without the need for any third party runtime environment. In this option, the students need only to create an account in the service and upload their zipped file so that PhoneGap builder can produce different packages for different mobile platforms (see figure 2).

```
<widget
xmlns="http://www.w3.org/ns/widgets"
height="200" width="200">
  <name short="website">Application
Name</name>
  <description>
    This is a simple website application.
  </description>
  <author        href="http://example.com/"
email="me@example.com">
    Someone
  </author>
  <icon src="website.png"/>
  <content src="index.html"/>
</widget>
```

Figure 2: A sample manifest file

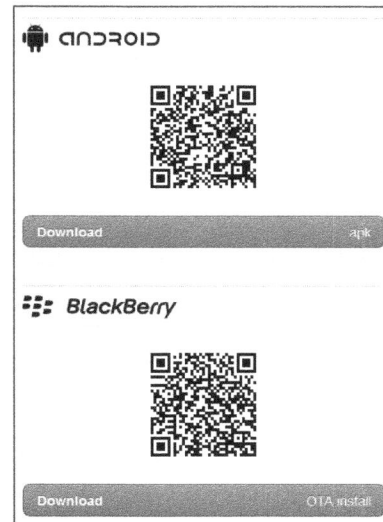

Figure 3: Deployment options offered freely by PhoneGap service, the student can either scan the QR code or download the widget directly

Figure 3 shows the result of developing the college website as a widget after following the previous steps and using PhoneGap for deployment.

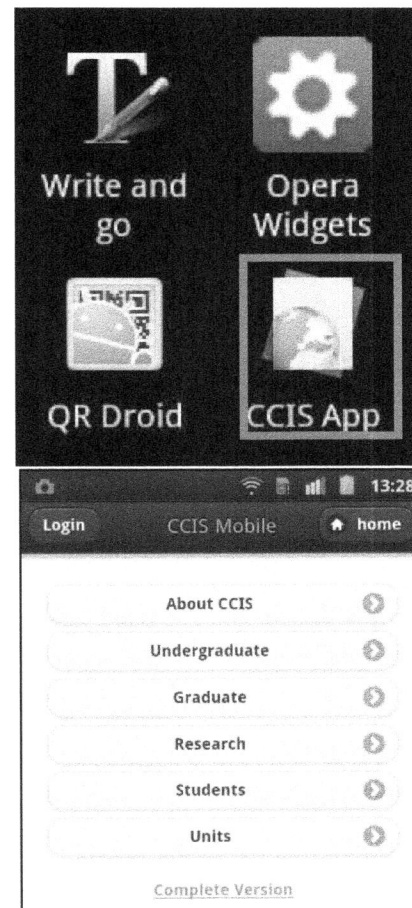

Figure 1: A Screenshot of a Samsung phone running "CCIS Application" widget; the top is the app icon and the bottom is the running application

## 5. STUDENTS' FEEDBACK

Teaching students to build mobile widgets was received quite successfully and was met with excitement by the students. This is attributed to the fact that, via building mobile widgets, the students learn to leverage their past experience in building mobile web applications into building something akin of a native mobile application, which are presently trendy and are receiving much interest in the web developers' community.

Upon gathering students' feedback to measure the Course Learning Outcomes (CLOs), the students answered the question of whether they think they met the goals of each module of the course using a five-point Likert scale.

The mobile web development module with the following objective "*Design, develop and evaluate Mobile websites based on recommended best practices*" garnered a relatively high positive feedback from the students, as 41.6% answered that they strongly achieved the objectives of this module and 52.7% answered that they have simply achieved the goal, as shown in Figure 4.

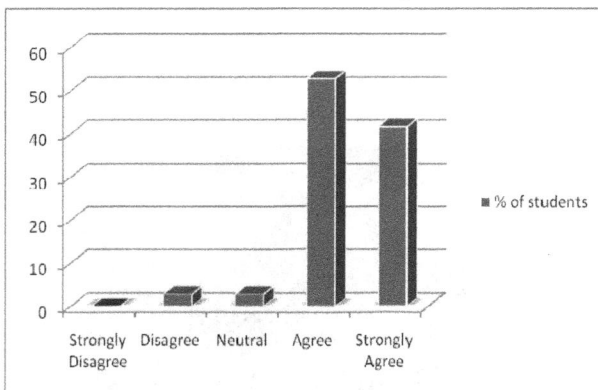

**Figure 4: Students answer to meeting the goals of the Mobile Web development module**

## 6. CONCLUSION

In this paper we presented our experience in introducing undergraduate IT students majoring in web technologies with the skills needed for building mobile widgets. The approach we have followed did not overwhelm the students with the technical details pertaining to such a technology. In fact, the teaching process followed a simple approach of using readily available services and tools. The approach also assumes that the students have prior knowledge of basic web applications development and teach them to leverage this knowledge by first introducing them to best practices in building mobile web applications, and then, on how to package them into mobile widgets.

After introducing this topic, the students' feedback was very encouraging and met with much excitement from their side. This positive feedback will encourage us to consider future improvements to the module to cope with the evolving nature of the web.

## 7. ACKNOWLEDGMENT

This work is partially supported by a grant from the Excellence Center for Learning and Teaching, King Saud University.

## 8. REFERENCES

[1] IT Curriculum 2008, "Information Technology 2008 Curriculum Guidelines for Undergraduate Degree Programs in Information Technology", Retrieved July 23, 2012 from http://www.acm.org/education/curricula/IT2008%20Curriculum.pdf/view

[2] "Requirement For Standardizing Widgets." [Online]. Available: http://www.w3.org/TR/widgets-reqs/. [Accessed: 31-May-2012].

[3] B. Zhang, T. Xu, W. Wang, and X. Jia, "Research and implementation of cross-platform development of mobile widget," in Communication Software and Networks (ICCSN), 2011 IEEE 3rd International Conference on, 2011, pp. 146 –150.

[4] "WAC History - Developer Website." [Online]. Available: http://www.wacapps.net/history. [Accessed: 31-May-2012].

[5] C. Kaar, "An introduction to widgets with particular emphasis on mobile widgets," Computing, Oct, 2007.

[6] P. Mendes, M. Caceres, and B. Dwolatzky, "A review of the widget landscape and incompatibilities between widget engines," in AFRICON, 2009. AFRICON '09., 2009, pp. 1 –6.

[7] "Obigo." [Online]. Available: http://obigo.com/solution/widget-sdk.html. [Accessed: 31-May-2012].

[8] "Opera releases WAC-ready widget runtime for Android." [Online]. Available: http://www.opera.com/press/releases/2010/12/22/. [Accessed: 31-May-2012].

[9] "Publishing apps to the Vodafone 360 Shop through JIL.org | Mobile Apps Developer | Vodafone." [Online]. Available: https://developer.vodafone.com/blog/2010/04/08/publishing-apps-to-the-vodafone-360-shop-through-jilorg/. [Accessed: 31-May-2012].

[10] H. S. Al-Khalifa and N. I. Al-Rajebah, "Integrating mobile web development into IT curriculum," in Proceedings of the 2011 conference on Information technology education, New York, NY, USA, 2011, pp. 87–90.

[11] "Mobile Web Best Practices 1.0." [Online]. Available: http://www.w3.org/TR/mobile-bp/. [Accessed: 31-May-2012].

# Metonymic Errors in a Web Development Course

Craig S. Miller
DePaul University
243 S. Wabash Ave.
Chicago, IL USA
cmiller@cs.depaul.edu

## ABSTRACT

This paper investigates a class of database access errors that occur in the context of a web development course. While the use of an Object-Relational Mapping (ORM) simplifies database access, students still demonstrate reference errors such as mistakenly referring to the whole object rather than an attribute value that is a part of the object. Metonymy, a rhetorical device used in human communication, offers an interpretation to these errors. A study is presented where student answers are reported and analyzed in this context. Findings indicate the prevalence of reference errors and offer instructional strategies for addressing them.

## Categories and Subject Descriptors

K.3.2 [**Computers and Education**]: Computer and Information Science Education

## General Terms

Design, Human Factors, Languages

## Keywords

programming errors, web development, metonymy

## 1. INTRODUCTION

The IT program at our university offers a sequence of web development courses whose goals include teaching students the architecture of a web application and the programming fundamentals for connecting the components of the architecture. This emphasis on architecture in IT coursework is supported by findings in previous work. For example, in interviews of IT employers, knowledge of software architecture and the need to integrate existing components to solve a problem were commonly cited as critical competencies for

IT careers [8]. The importance of these competencies is consistent with recent articles promoting architecture [1, 9] and the need to compose systems from working components [5].

The model-view-controller (MVC) architecture provides an exemplary use of architecture in web development. By presenting web development as separate components, students learn how data models, controller logic and display templates (views) relate to each other. The emphasis on architecture motivated the choice of Ruby on Rails [2] as the development framework used in the web courses discussed in this paper. The Rails framework provides a clean separation of the MVC components, each residing in its own folder in the file structure. An additional benefit is that the framework provides automatic scaffold generation for quickly building a working web application. Most relevant for this paper, the Rails framework makes use of an Object-Relation Mapping (ORM) for its data model component.

Use of an ORM in introductory web development courses has several advantages. First, it abstracts away the details of SQL queries and replaces it with the syntax and object-based notation consistent with the framework's programming language. Second, it provides a practical context for teaching or reviewing object-based programming. Finally, it permits database-independent development. Students can develop an application with one database knowing that deployment can use a different database with little or no changes to the application.

The first advantage is particularly important for emphasizing architecture since the use of an ORM allows the course to focus on the role of the database with respect to the rest of the application, rather than dwelling on the details of the database.

Despite the benefits of using an ORM, application development still presents challenges for students learning to develop software applications. Successfully accessing content requires precise references to data objects and their properties. As we will see, students encounter difficulties specifying the correct referent, whether for display in a view or for integration with other components in an application.

These reference errors are the focus of this paper. The thesis is that a major insight to many of these errors involves understanding that humans can automatically resolve ambiguous references whereas computer systems—whether through an ORM, SQL or other notations—require exact specification of the referent. More specifically, the paper draws upon the rhetorical device of metonymy to explain a class of reference errors observed among students. As we will see, student work is often more consistent with their experience in everyday communication than what is required for producing correct code.

Previous analysis has already identified metonymy as a unifying account for a broad range of programming errors [7]. In this sense, the analysis and study presented in this paper complement previous work identifying common misconceptions that produce student errors. Like the analysis in this paper, some of these misconceptions originate from human language [3]. However, these previously studied misconceptions are generally based on words that have different meanings in everyday communication than they do in programming languages (e.g. *if* or *while*).

This paper examines the potential role of metonymy in the context of application development and data access. The goal is to explain errors, predict when they are likely to occur and suggest teaching strategies for addressing the errors. The next section explains metonymy and its relevance to programming. The following section then presents metonymy in the context of database access using an ORM with the goal of identifying when it occurs. This analysis leads to an empirical study that reveals student responses consistent with the analysis. Finally, we use the analysis to recommend possible approaches for teaching.

## 2. METONYMY AND PROGRAMMING

Metonymy is a rhetorical device used to reference an item by stating another item associated with it. For example, consider this sentence: the host opened the wine to be served with the meal. People have little difficulty understanding that it was not the wine that was actually opened. Rather, the host opened the bottle containing the wine. Here the stated referent (wine) actually refers to its container (bottle). Humans readily use metonymy in everyday communication and quickly resolve the referent with little to no conscious awareness of the needed inference (for an extensive review of metonymy in everyday communication, see Lakoff and Johnson [6]). As will be discussed, computer programming languages generally do not resolve intended referents in this way. As a consequence, the practice of using metonymy in everyday communication may be an impediment for successfully learning how to specify precise referents in computing.

Use of metonymy is particularly common when the goal is to contrast against another possible referent. For example, our host may have two bottles of wine to choose from: a Bordeaux and a Burgundy[1]. If the goal is to emphasize the choice between the two wines, we may state, "The host opened the Burgundy to be served with the meal." Explicitly mentioning the bottle does not improve communication since both wines come in a bottle and listeners effortlessly infer that it is the bottle (of Burgundy wine) being opened. Figure 1 illustrates the use of metonymy for this example. It indicates that specifying the type of wine indicates which bottle should be opened. The bottle itself is not explicitly referenced since it does not have the distinguishing qualities relevant for the choice.

---

[1] Referring to a wine by its region is yet another example of metonymy. Here the reference to Burgundy (or Bordeaux) is not a reference to a region in France, but to the wine that comes from that region.

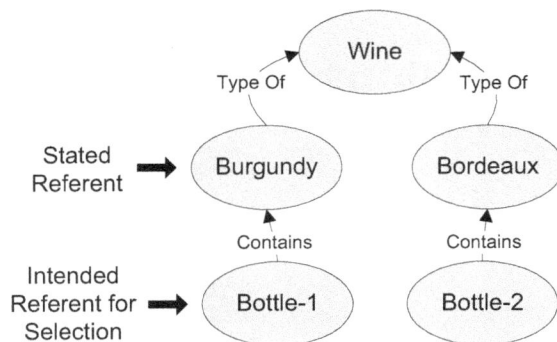

Figure 1: Metonymy selects the referent.

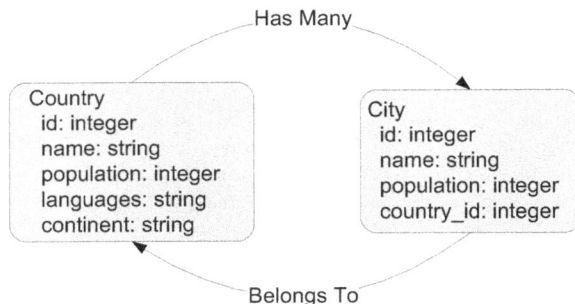

Figure 2: Example models with Rails' relations.

While everyday language permits flexible expression using metonymy, it cannot usually be applied in the context of programming and application development. Previous work [7] surveys common programming errors where metonymy provides some insight. These errors may involve arrays, objects, and linked lists. For example, when referencing a value in an array, a student may mistakenly reference the index to that value, perhaps in the context of swapping array values.

In this paper, the focus is on metonymic errors in the context of ORM access. Even though ORM offers a simplified method for accessing a database, it nevertheless requires precise references to objects (database rows or records) and properties (database columns or fields). As we will see, metonymy suggests a natural tendency for humans (particularly novice developers) to reference an object instead of a property in specific cases (or vice versa). In the next section, ORM terminology is reviewed and a working example is developed.

## 3. ORM EXAMPLE

Before we present any errors, let us first review database access in the context of the Rails' ORM, Active Record. For the rest of the paper, examples are based on two schema models presented in Figure 2.

The Country model and the City model are adequate to explain student errors and develop exercises for studying them. In addition to a few attributes (e.g. name, population, languages), both models have a primary key (id), which Active Record provides by default. Also note that city has a foreign key (country_id). This foreign key provides the basis of a relationship between the two models. Using Active

Record terminology, we say that a City *belongs to* a Country and that a Country *has many* Cities.

Once the models are specified and the relationships declared, Active Record provides object-oriented access to the database by automatically defining classes and methods for the models. Class methods selectively query records from the database:

```
france_country = Country.find_by_name('France')
london_city  = City.find_by_name('London')

all_city_objects = City.all
some_objects = City.where('population > 1000')
```

The assigned variable names document what the methods return. In the examples above, the Ruby on Rails framework dynamically defines methods such as `find_by_name`, which are based on the model's properties.

Given an object (record) from the database, instance methods[2] can be called with them:

```
france_city_objects = france_country.cities
uk_country_object = london_city.country
```

Finally, attribute values can be assigned to an object, which can then be saved to the database:

```
new_country = Country.new
new_country.name = 'Fredonia'
new_country.population = 12000
new_country.save
```

Even though Active Record simplifies database access using object-based notation, student developers are still required to correctly state the intended referent. For example, if the goal is to list a country, more precisely, the name of the country, the reference must explicitly reference the name property with the country object:

```
new_country.name
```

However, given the prevalence of metonymy in human languages, students may be tempted to simply indicate the object:

```
new_country
```

Other circumstances may call for simply referencing the object (representing the entire database record), perhaps to gain access to other fields associated with it. Considering the use of metonymy, students may be inclined to simply indicate the name (a string) since it is the name that clearly distinguishes it from other country objects. Figure 3 provides a working example that is structurally similar to the wine example. As the figure indicates, `Obj-1` and `Obj-2` are usefully identified by their 'name' property. However, simply providing the name attribute will not be sufficient if the application requires a reference to the object.

In the next section, we review actual student work in the context of the analysis presented here.

---

[2]Technically all object-based references are method calls in Ruby even if they seem like properties. Parentheses are optional for method calls in Ruby.

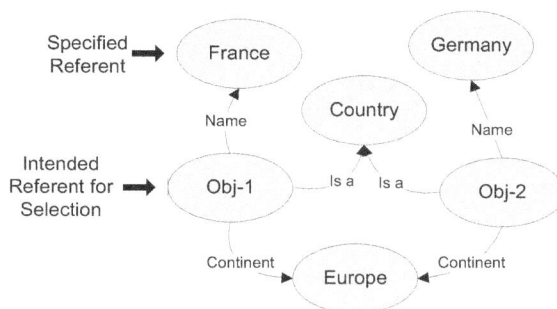

**Figure 3: Reference error.**

## 4. STUDY OF STUDENT WORK

An exercise with ORM questions was developed to assess student ability to access database content using the Rails ORM, Active Record. The exercise presented the schema shown in Figure 2. The exercise also presented a few working examples similar to those presented in the previous section.

The first two questions (presented with answers below) ask students to provide expressions that require an explicit reference to the **name** property:

- The country name with id 5.
  *Answer: Country.find(5).name*

- The population of the city of Toronto.
  *Answer: City.find_by_name('Toronto').population*

While there are many correct answers for each question, all correct answers require an explicit reference to the **name** property. However, as previously discussed, students may (mistakenly) just reference the object. For example, for the first question, they may omit the name reference and thus just provide the object: *Country.find(5)*. For the second question, they may mistakenly omit the name reference when matching the city name: *City.Toronto.population*. Consistent with the use of metonymy, an identifying property (e.g. name) can be interchanged with the referent itself.

The last two questions in the exercise were expressly developed to explore how students specify referents. Both questions ask students to delete an object from an array:

- Assume that `country_list` is an array of Country objects. Provide ruby code that uses the remove method to delete the country named 'France' from the array.
  *Answer:*
  *country_obj = Country.find_by_name('France')*
  *country_list.remove(country_obj)*

- Provide the Ruby code that uses the remove method to delete the country whose continent is 'Europe'. For this example, you may assume that there is only one country from Europe in the table.
  *Answer:*
  *country_obj = Country.find_by_continent('Europe')*
  *country_list.remove(country_obj)*

The answers to both questions are structurally identical. However, the first requires use of the name property and the second requires the use of the continent property. Since the name property is commonly used to identify the object, we hypothesize that it is more likely to be used in place of the object itself.

Given the scope of the paper, the analysis focuses on the four questions (first two questions and last two questions) just discussed. However, all the questions to the exercise are provided in the appendix.

## 4.1 Method

The ORM questions were offered as an exercise in a second web development course at a large university. While the exercise was offered to all students, students actively chose to participate in the study by submitting their answers in a sealed envelop to the instructor, which were then turned over to the study's investigator. Seventeen students (14 male, 3 female) submitted their answers for analysis. The average age was 25 and the average number of prior programming courses was 3.

## 4.2 Results

Results focus on student answers to the previously discussed questions (the first two questions and the last two questions in the exercise). These questions directly address metonymic usage. While the other questions may also involve metonymy-based errors, they are more difficult to analyze since they require more complex answers. Furthermore, students responded to fewer of them (students provided answers for only 66% of these questions).

Student responses are categorized by whether they successfully referenced the needed property in their answers. In this section, student answers are presented without interpretation. The next section discusses the answers in the context of metonymy.

- **The country name with id 5** (question 1). A correct answer accesses the country object and then references the name attribute. Of the 17 responses, 9 students produced an answer that did not resolve to the name attribute, compared to 5 students who explicitly referenced the name attribute. The remaining 3 students did not produce an answer that could be interpreted as belonging to either group.

- **The population of the city of Toronto.** (question 2). A correct answer selects the City object by matching the city name to the name property. 7 students explicitly referenced the name property, including 3 with fully correct answers. 8 responses did not explicitly use the name property anywhere in their answers. 1 student did not provide an answer and 1 student provided an unfinished answer (missing a closing parenthesis).

For the last two questions (questions 8 and 9), 16 of the 17 students had answers that could be classified into one of the three categories.

- **Just property.** The answer just provides the property value to indicate what should be deleted.
  Examples:
  ```
  country_list.remove('France') or
  country_list.remove('Europe')
  ```
  For question 8 (remove object using the name property), 8 students provided an answer in this category. For question 9 (remove object using the continent property), 2 students provided an answer in this category.

Table 1: Frequency counts for last two questions

| Remove by Name (Q 8) | Remove by Continent (Q 9) | | |
|---|---|---|---|
| | Just property | Match property | No answer |
| Just property | 2 | 2 | 4 |
| Match property | 0 | 4 | 0 |
| No answer | 0 | 0 | 4 |

- **Match property** (correct approach). The answer matches the property value to its attribute to select the country object that should be deleted.
  Example:
  ```
  country_list.remove(
      Country.find_by_continent('Europe'))
  ```
  For question 8 (remove object using the name property), 4 students provided an answer in this category. For question 9 (remove object using the continent property), 6 students provided an answer in this category.

- **No answer.** No answer is provided.
  For question 8 (remove object using the name property), 4 students provided no answer. For question 9 (remove object using the continent property), 8 students provided no answer.

Table 1 presents the frequencies of how each student responded to both questions. For example, 2 students (upper-right cell) referenced just the property ("France" for question 8 and "Europe" for question 9) for both questions 8 and 9. Four students (center cell) correctly matched the properties to access the object for removal. Note that no students correctly matched the property for question 8 but then just used the property for question 9. The difference in student responses for the two questions will be further discussed in the next section.

Figure 4 summarizes the frequency of observed reference errors for each question as a percentage of student answers ($N = 17$ and includes blank answers). The error bars indicate 95% confidence intervals[3]. The lower end of the confidence intervals for questions 1, 2 and 8 set minimal expectations for this population of students and indicate that at least a quarter of the student answers have problems specifying the correct referent. In the next section, the reference errors will be discussed in the context of metonymy.

## 4.3 Discussion

The results indicate that a substantive number of student programming errors for ORM access involve problems specifying the correct referent. Here those errors are analyzed in the context of metonymic expression.

For question 1, most students (9 of 17) provided the whole object (entity representing the full database record) when the question asked for the name. Consistent with metonymy, the name and the object itself can be used interchangeably in common language (e.g. "France" and the country of France). With this experience, students may be inclined to reference the whole object in place of just the name property.

---

[3]The confidence intervals are calculated using the Clopper and Pearson exact method [4], which does not require an *a priori* estimation of the proportion.

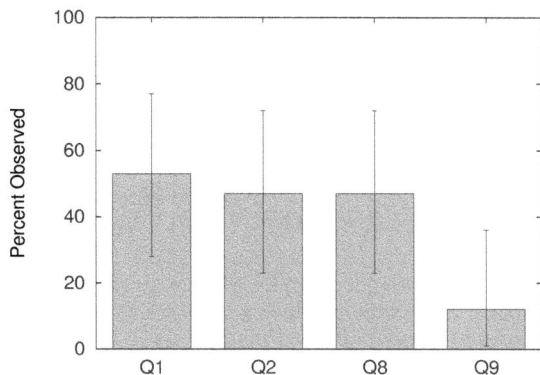

**Figure 4: Observed reference errors by questions.**

For question 2, many students (8 of 17) did not compare the string "Toronto" to the **name** property for identifying the needed city object. Instead, and consistent with metonymic expression, they used the name "Toronto" as a proxy for the city itself. Similarly, for question 8, most students used the country name "France" in place of the country object with the name of "France."

In contrast to question 8, relatively fewer students committed reference errors for question 9. Even though the correct answers for question 8 and question 9 are structurally identical, fewer students just used a string when the object is required. Use of metonymy in common language explains the discrepancy. For question 9, the identifying property is the continent "Europe." Since the continent name is not normally adequate to identify a particular country, common language usually does not permit reference to a continent as a means for identifying a country. In this way, students are more likely to think of the continent as a property of the country and not the country itself.

While use of metonymy offers an explanation for student answers, results do not conclusively indicate that metonymy accounts for the difference in responses between question 8 and 9. First, it is possible that the relative order of questions 8 and 9 account for differences in responses. Student experience with a prior question could influence how they answer a subsequent question. Second, despite the structural similarity of question 8 and 9, they are not phrased identically. Different phrasing could lead to different answers. Finally, given the small sample size, the difference between question 8 and question 9 is not statistically reliable. These shortcomings could be addressed with further study using a larger sample and controlling for order and question presentation.

Study findings are also subject to the student population. Diverse populations may yield varying frequencies of reference errors. In particular, students who are just beginning to learn programming may commit more reference errors than observed here. Given this study's population with an average of three courses (1 year on a quarter system) of prior programming experience, we can expect reference errors in at least a quarter of the student answers (lower limit of the confidence interval) for similar questions for students with less programming experience. Of course, additional studies could further clarify prevalence of reference errors among various populations.

## 5. IMPLICATIONS

Despite noted limitations in the study, the findings demonstrate student difficulties in correctly specifying a referent in the context of data access. An immediate practical consequence is that it calls attention to the commonality of these mistakes. Instructors can accordingly alert students to these pitfalls and providing supporting examples.

Our understanding of metonymy in human communication provides a framework for identifying the errors and categorizing them. By knowing where these errors occur, we can develop questions that evaluate student progress towards addressing them. It also opens an avenue of inquiry for exploring possible teaching strategies. For example, it might be helpful to teach students about metonymy in everyday language and contrast it with what is required for application development, where correct referents cannot be automatically inferred.

Theoretical analysis based on metonymy also indicates that non-identifying properties may produce fewer reference errors. The study's results provide preliminary empirical evidence that supports this analysis. If so, instructors may want to use examples and problems with non-identifying properties before they present those with identifying properties. In any case, additional studies could explore such instructional strategies and evaluate their effectiveness. Such work may draw upon established strategies for identifying misconceptions and addressing them [3].

Finally the work identifies a critical competence that has broad applicability in computing. Not limited to programming, correct referent specification is needed wherever application development or configuration calls for explicit representations consisting of entities and properties. Computing systems will not be able to automate referent resolution in the near future. To do so would require an explicit domain model and full understanding of natural language. Until then, the ability to precisely and literally specify a referent remains critical for many areas of computing.

## 6. ACKNOWLEDGMENTS

Thanks to John Rogers, who allowed the study to be conducted in his web development class.

## 7. REFERENCES

[1] S. J. Andriole and E. Roberts. Point/counterpoint: Technology curriculum for the early 21st century. *Commun. ACM*, 51(7):27–32, July 2008.

[2] M. Bachle and P. Kirchberg. Ruby on rails. *Software, IEEE*, 24(6):105 –108, nov.-dec. 2007.

[3] M. Clancy. Misconceptions and attitudes that interfere with learning to program. In S. Fincher and M. Petre, editors, *Computer science education research*, pages 85–100. Taylor and Francis Group, London, 2004.

[4] C. Clopper and E. Pearson. The use of confidence or fiducial limits illustrated in the case of the binomial. *Biometrika*, 26(4):404–413, 1934.

[5] J. J. Ekstrom and B. Lunt. Education at the seams: preparing students to stitch systems together; curriculum and issues for 4-year it programs. In *Proceedings of the 4th conference on Information technology curriculum*, CITC4 '03, pages 196–200, New York, NY, USA, 2003. ACM.

[6] G. Lakoff and M. Johnson. *Metaphors We Live By*. The University of Chicago Press, Chicago, IL, 1980.

[7] C. S. Miller. Metonymy and student programming errors. Technical Report 20, DePaul University, 2012.

[8] C. S. Miller and L. Dettori. Employers' perspectives on IT learning outcomes. In *Proceedings of the 9th ACM SIGITE conference on Information technology education*, SIGITE '08, pages 213–218, New York, NY, USA, 2008. ACM.

[9] K. A. Morneau and S. Talley. Architecture: an emerging core competence for it professionals. In *Proceedings of the 8th ACM SIGITE conference on Information technology education*, SIGITE '07, pages 9–12, New York, NY, USA, 2007. ACM.

# APPENDIX

## A. EXERCISE QUESTIONS

*The following questions were those used for the student exercise and whose answers were analyzed for the study. In addition to the questions below, the students were presented with the Country and City models presented in Figure 2. The exercise also provided several examples that access data based on the models.*

For the following items, provide the ruby code that produces the following:

1. The country name with id 5.

2. The population of the city of Toronto.

3. The country name where Timbuktu is located.

4. The number of cities listed for France.

5. A listing of all of the cities in Canada.

6. Create a new city record for Saskatoon (population: 190657) and have it indicate that it belongs to the Canada record.

7. Assume that `@my_country` is a Country object. Using template view code, produce a table that lists all of the cities and their populations that belong to `@my_country`.

Ruby has a remove method that allows an object to be deleted from an array of objects. For example if `word_list` has the contents `['cat', 'dog', 'cow', 'horse']`, then `word_list.remove('dog')` would delete the string 'dog' from the array. That is, the contents of `word_list` would then be `['cat', 'cow', 'horse']`.

8. Assume that `country_list` is an array of Country objects. Provide ruby code that uses the remove method to delete the country named 'France' from the array.

9. Provide the ruby code that uses the remove method to delete the country whose continent is 'Europe'. For this example, you may assume that there is only one country from Europe in the table.

# Using Student Professional Development Planning to Inform Program Review

**Anita Girton**
Pennsylvania College
of Technology
One College Ave
Williamsport, PA 17701
570-326-3761

agirton@pct.edu

**Dr. Sandra Gorka**
Pennsylvania College
of Technology
One College Ave
Williamsport, PA 17701
570-326-3761

sgorka@pct.edu

**Dr. Jacob Miller**
Pennsylvania College
of Technology
One College Ave
Williamsport, PA 17701
570-326-3761

jmiller3@pct.edu

**Daniel Yoas**
Pennsylvania College
of Technology
One College Ave
Williamsport, PA 17701
570-326-3761

dyoas@pct.edu

## ABSTRACT
*Development and modification of academic programs is enhanced by incorporating input from the stakeholders of the program. This paper discusses the process used by an Information Assurance and Security (IAS) program to obtain input from students during their final year of the program. Students evaluated job advertisements and information assurance curriculum recommendations and compared their findings to the IAS program. Students provided recommendations on how to better facilitate student learning. Faculty plans on using the student work and recommendations as input to the Academic Review Process during the upcoming year.*

## Categories and Subject Descriptors
K.3.0 [**Computing Milieux**]: Computers and Education, General.
K.3.2 [**Computer and Information Science Education**]: Self-assessment..

## General Terms
Management, Measurement, Documentation, Security.

## Keywords
Outcome Assessment, Curriculum, Information Assurance Education, Academic Program Review, Accreditation.

## 1. INTRODUCTION
Traditionally programs use a variety of assessment methods to determine if the outcomes described within a program and the results of the teaching efforts are the same. These assessments include testing, labs, and homework. As differences are found a program may be adjusted to address the shortfall. Previous work has been studied to help define and improve the evaluation process [4].

When completing an academic program review or assessment, it is also helpful to obtain input from the stakeholders of the program. This includes items like general surveys conducted after

students have graduated [3]. But this is only part of the information regarding a student's perception of their education. In particular, it is helpful to obtain student input about their learning prior to leaving the program. For example, student input can be used to modify the program in an effort to increase student interest, improve student learning, and address student career goals.

Penn College requires all IAS students to enroll in IAS492A and IAS492B – IAS Seminar. IAS Seminar is a pair of 1-credit courses taken during the fall and spring semesters of the student's last year of enrollment. IAS Seminar was designed so that faculty can assist students in making the transition from being a student to being in the workforce. Goals include exploring the job market, developing a resume, assessing their own skills and creating a professional development plan.

Students enrolled in IAS492B in spring 2012 as part of identifying the needs for respective professional develop plans were assigned the task completing a program review of the current IAS program. They reviewed the current job market and Information Assurance curricular recommendations, the program's goals and the course student learning outcomes. Once their review was complete, students compiled a collection of recommendations that can be used to assist faculty in their upcoming Academic Program Review.

This paper addresses the process of this student review (Section 2), the benefits gained by both the students and faculty (Section 3) and a conclusion (Section 4).

## 2. PROCESS
During their review, the students developed a collection of job skills and academic skills and combined them to obtain an expected SKILL SET. Once the skill set was developed, students compared this skill set to the IAS program goals and the student learning outcomes from required course syllabi in order to develop a gap analysis. They also determined the extent to which they are comfortable with the content of the skill set. The students used their comfort level to develop a gap analysis between the skill set and their understanding of it. Finally, the students developed a collection of recommendations that would increase student understanding and retention of the material.

As students gathered information they used a high degree of collaboration taking time to discuss and gather information in small groups and as a full class. All student work was documented in a collection of Google Docs documents. Each student as well as all faculty teaching IAS courses had access to these documents.

## 2.1 Developing the Skill Set

The class started with a discussion of the importance of self-evaluation within the aspects of the jobs they were likely to hold. Faculty then spent a few classes answering questions about the process used to develop a program and to evaluate various resources appropriate to their degree. Students used this information to begin the first process and would then bring questions about documentation and evaluation back to faculty in later classes.

The task was to develop a collection of IAS skills that should be developed within an IAS program. Since our students were about to graduate from our IAS program that was based on the NSA's NSTISSI 4011 (National Training Standard for Information Systems Security (INFOSEC) Professionals) [1] and CNSSI 4016 (National information Assurance Training Standard for Risk Analysts) [2], students were asked to develop the skill set based on these two training standards. Students were also asked to conduct a review of the current job requirements for IT positions with five years of experience. A set of common knowledge skills for current jobs were then incorporated into the documentation.

Students were split into a total of three groups for this activity. One group concentrated on finding a collection of current job advertisements and extracting the skills expected by employers. A second group evaluated NSTISSI 4011 [1] to extract a list of skills related to INFOSEC Professionals. The third group evaluated CNSSI 4016 [2] to extract a list of skills related to Risk Analysts. Each group updated the collaboration documents with the skills they determined were important under their assigned framework.

## 2.2 Skill Set to Program Gap Analysis

After students determined the skill set based on their job search and review of NSTISSI 4011 [1] and CNSSI 4016 [2], they compared their skill set with the program goals of the IAS program. Without seeing the original mapping created by the faculty at the time the program was designed, the students developed their own mapping between the determined skill set and the program goals. The student's mapping and the original faculty mapping were close. Differences between them will be evaluated during the next program review. Their mapping indicated that all items in the knowledge skills they found were covered by at least one of the program goals.

Students also compared the program goals to the student learning outcomes of the courses required in the IAS program. Any differences in this document will also be evaluated at the next program review. Their mapping also indicated that the required courses sufficiently covered the program goals. At this point, students determined that the IAS program was designed to deliver all of the items in their knowledge skill set.

## 2.3 Skill Set to Security Experience Gap Analysis

In this step, each student was asked to identify the skill level they have retained from previous classwork. The students decided to use "comfort" level as their gauge of understanding the material. The students jointly developed a rubric ranging from 1 – 5 to determine their comfort level with each item, 1 being low comfort level and 5 being high. Once all students completed this activity, they computed the average comfort level of all of the students. For each identified skill, students needed to determine three things.

The first was their individual comfort level with the skill. The second was the course and student learning outcomes where they expected to learn that skill. The third was the assignments that they felt supported them learning that skill.

Students reviewed the results and selected a threshold of understanding that they decided was too low. The students discussed each of the "weak skills" that fell below the threshold. During their discussion of the weak skills, they were able to reference the course and outcome combinations and even assignments that addressed the weak skills. After discussing each of these weak skills, students documented their discussion.

Their documentation began to include some of their recommendations. Additionally, some of the discussions ended with "I remember that now". This generated additional debate as students reminded each other about assignments and work efforts that others had forgotten. In these cases recommendations were revised as the students were able to remember what knowledge skills they had covered in classes.

## 2.4 Student Recommendations

At this point the students were ready to formalize their recommendations. Most of their recommendations had to do with providing an alternative delivery method for the material. Some examples include:

- Role playing interviews for case studies rather than printed information from interviews.

- More time to work on specific auditing techniques either in-class or under supervision rather than working on their own.

- Greater opportunity to audit live systems.

- Different opportunities for collaboration. (Interestingly enough, in some cases they wanted more collaboration and in other cases they wanted less collaboration.)

- Generally they wanted more independent work including homework assignments and labs.

- Generally they wanted more challenging assignments.

Faculty did discuss some of the constraints and limitations that affect our ability to implement some of their recommendations. In many cases faculty concurred with the recommendations as being desirable, but that constraints on the program made many of the recommendations impractical at this time.

## 3. BENEFITS

This process provided benefits to both students and faculty. The purpose of a program review through a self-study is recognized as a necessity for improving a program [3, 4]. In our case we wanted to see what the stakeholder's (our student's) impression were of that system since perceptions are frequently different based on perspective (e.g. faculty versus student).

## 3.1 Student Benefits

This process provided students with the opportunity to develop a solid understanding of what they learned throughout their IAS program. It provided them with a final review of what they learned and provided many of them with a higher level of self-confidence.

Students also developed a good understanding about what perspective employers want an appreciation for cooperation in a large group process, and the amount of knowledge they had gained over their four year education. This coupled with a better understanding of their own skills, allowed them to create a professional development plan that will help them attain their career goals.

This process also allowed students to apply skills they learned in prior courses in different situations. For example, one of the previous courses discussed the process of auditing IT systems for compliance. Students were able to apply the auditing process to an academic program. Another previous course discussed issues of security awareness, training and education including creating assessments for trainings that they developed. Some of their recommendations included alternative methods of assessing student learning.

At the end of the semester the students put together a formal presentation that summarized their work, provided comments about the program, and identified areas of improvement that should be considered in future changes to the IAS program.

## 3.2 Faculty Benefits

Faculty gained insight into the types of jobs our students are seeking. In previous years, the majoring of our students were interested in jobs that were government or government-related. This process indicated that a larger percentage of our students are showing more interest in private sector jobs.

This process provided faculty with an indirect assessment of student learning and verification that the students are able to recognize how their knowledge skills can be applied to future job skills. The skill areas identified by the students as deficient (weak skills) have provided faculty a better understanding of areas where the educational process can be improved. Faculty realize that in many cases these weaknesses are a function of student perception and changes need to be considered in this context.

The process also provided an assessment of the entire curriculum by one of our major stakeholders. Faculty intend to use the results of this assessment as input into our Academic Program Review process.

## 4. CONCLUSION

Students enrolled in the IAS Seminar class for the spring 2012 semester completed an assessment of the entire curriculum in which they were enrolled. The process used by the students provided them with a solid understanding of both what they learned throughout their education and what they still need to learn as they enter the workforce.

Students indicated that the main deficiency within the program was in the delivery style of parts of the program. They provided recommendations for alternative delivery and assessment methods for various courses and student learning outcomes. Students determined that there were no deficiencies in program intent or implementation.

The IAS faculty are about to embark on the Academic Program Review process during the upcoming academic year. Faculty intend to use the student recommendations as part of the review process to evaluate the program and to inform recommendations for curriculum modifications.

## 5. ACKNOWLEDGMENTS

Our thanks to the students enrolled in Penn College's IAS492B for their efforts in preparing and presenting their research and recommendations.

## 6. REFERENCES

[1] *National Training Standard For Information Systems Security (Infosec) Professionals.* 1994; Available from: www.cnss.gov/Assets/pdf/nstissi_4011.pdf.

[2] *National Information Assurance Training Standard For Risk Analysts.* 2005; Available from: www.cnss.gov/Assets/pdf/CNSSI-4016.PDF.

[3] Aasheim, C., A. Gowan, and H. Reichgelt, *An IT program assessment process*, in *Proceedings of the 8th ACM SIGITE conference on Information technology education*. 2007, ACM: Destin, Florida, USA. p. 161-166.

[4] Matveev, A.G., N.F. Veltri, H.W. Webb, and E.G. Zapatero, *Curriculum mapping as a tool for continuous improvement of IS curriculum.* Journal of Information Systems Education, 2011. **22**(1): p. 31+.

# Risks, Rewards and Raising Awareness: Training a Cyber Workforce Using Student Red Teams

Kellie Kercher
Brigham Young University
Information Technology Program
Provo, UT, 84602
1 (801) 422 6051

kkercher@somethingk.com

Dale C. Rowe Ph.D.
Brigham Young University
Information Technology Program
Provo, UT, 84602
1 (801) 422 6051

dale_rowe@byu.edu

## ABSTRACT
In this paper we discuss how a research-orientated student red-team provides free security assessments to organizations within the community. Such activities provide students with valuable skills and knowledge in dealing with real-world security issues. We present our approach to implementing such a team as a permanent fixture within our IT program's Cyber Security Research Lab and discuss the mutual benefits that such an offering presents.

## Categories and Subject Descriptors
K3.0 [**Computers and Education**]: General

C.2.0 [**Computer-Communication Networks**]: General --- Security and Protection

## General Terms
Experimentation, Security.

## Keywords
Information assurance and security, Cyber security, IT research, Red team, Blue team, Cyber challenge, Real-world experience, Education, Collaboration.

## 1. INTRODUCTION
Providing students with practical hands-on experience can reinforce key knowledge areas and provide skill development [2, 3, 5, 7]. Typically this has been provided in the form of classroom laboratory sessions where students are given an objective that can involve research, analysis, configuration, troubleshooting, testing or other technical skills to be used in forming a solution. As students develop their skillset they are encouraged to find their own solutions rather than be given a predefined sequence of steps.

This last year, the Information Technology program at BYU has created a Cyber Security Research Lab (CSRL) to provide a mentoring environment for student research, educational enrichment and community service. The purpose of the CSRL is to provide an optimal environment for students to study and engage in a variety of cutting edge research activities. Students in the CSRL may take the opportunity to qualify for the CSRL Red Team and participate in real-world penetration tests for third parties.

Due to attractiveness of cyber security research, there is currently more interest than can be funded. While efforts are underway to solicit additional funding, we have implemented a selection process for students to join CSRL research projects. The CSRL encourages volunteer-based participation in a personal research project from any interested individuals. Volunteers who demonstrate dedication in their work and maintain a satisfactory grade in their coursework may be offered a paid research assistant (RA) position. The availability of RA positions is dependent on:

- Funding
- Number of research projects
- Number of graduate students

The objective is to place a graduate student on each major project who will act as a 'team-lead' for the undergraduates he or she may be assigned. Full-time graduate students hold RA positions within the CSRL and are encouraged to mentor an undergraduate student throughout their degree. This helps ensure the longevity and continuity of projects. Current research projects include:

- Securing SCADA & Critical Infrastructure
- Open-Source Cyber Intelligence Frameworks
- Multi-User Computer Aided Applications Security
- Exploit Discovery
- Defense-in-Depth Multi-Point Anomaly Detection

The lab not only is a foundation for research but it also reaches out to the community. The CSRL Red Team provides volunteer vulnerability assessment services to local organizations and businesses. The CSRL Red Team applies their skills to discover and verify threats to a specific network along with developing new penetrating methodologies and security techniques. This service has been an astounding success and has helped build strong relationships with various companies along with providing exposure to both the CSRL and IT program.

CSRL research assistants with an interest in vulnerability assessment may be invited to the CSRL Red Team. An invitation to the red team is viewed as a prestigious opportunity (akin to the athletics team of IT) and comes with several benefits. These will be discussed later in this paper.

## 2. MENTORING ENVIRONMENT
One of the key aspects of the CSRL environment is faculty-to-student and student-to-student peer mentorship. CSRL participants are required to meet with a professor on a biweekly basis (although this may be more frequent if required). The biweekly meeting is designed to review research, share ideas, provide encouragement, advise, and set future goals. Between

these meetings there is a CSRL team meeting. In a team meeting, students and faculty meet for 30-60 minutes to discuss research projects, upcoming events and resolve any research impediments or obstacles. This meeting begins with a round-table one-minute summary of each project allowing participants to keep track of other projects.

Student-to-student peer mentorship provides a more personal environment for learning. This helps students become acclimatized more quickly to a research environment and helps ensure the longevity of research projects. Each new student that is accepted into CSRL will be paired with a more experienced research student (typically a senior or graduate RA). Although all new CSRL participants receive initial mentoring in this manner, graduate students or project team-leads are assigned a permanent mentee. The mentee continues the research of their mentor, allowing the laboratory to have continuing research and deeper investigation in cutting edge topics.

In addition to research project, this mentoring approach extends to reach-out initiatives and has proven beneficial in red team vulnerability assessments. Due to the high-risk and sensitive nature of red-team assessments, a faculty member provides constant supervision in an advisory role and organizes students into pairs. This is designed to place less experienced students with a senior student mentor. Red team methodologies and skill sets are passed along with fresh ideas from new members. For each assessment one student is assigned the role of 'team lead'. This role is not based on experience, but aims to provide each student with the opportunity to manage a penetration test.

Due to schedules and other constraints on students, a student may be paired with the faculty advisor during an engagement when an odd number of students are present. We have found that in all types of mentorships, not only is knowledge and expertise transmitted from the mentor to the mentee, but the mentee frequently has uninhibited ideas and approaches that may not have been considered by their mentor.

## 3. ORGANIZATION AND PLANNING

The objective of the CSRL Red Team is to provide a free penetration-test service to local organizations. Penetration tests differ substantially from blue-team activities which are common in the form of inter-collegiate cyber-defense. Blue-team activities are typically lower risk involving tasks such as service/server hardening and forensic activities [9, 10]. In contrast, red-team activities focus on finding and verifying through exploitation vulnerabilities to penetrate system defenses.

The CSRL Red Team itself typically comprises 5 students with a faculty advisor. The selection process for admission is quite stringent. Only CSRL research assistants are eligible to apply and must demonstrate knowledge in a needed technical area. Initially the candidate is interviewed by the CSRL director and subsequently by 2 or 3 senior team members. While technical ability is part of the interview process, the emphasis is placed on the students understanding of ethical and moral issues. Red-team members are required to be exemplary in their conduct. They absolutely must not use their skills to 'show off', share any information on client vulnerabilities or attempt to test any system without written authorization and the approval of the CSRL director. Applicants may also have to demonstrate their knowledge against vulnerable virtual systems as part of this process.

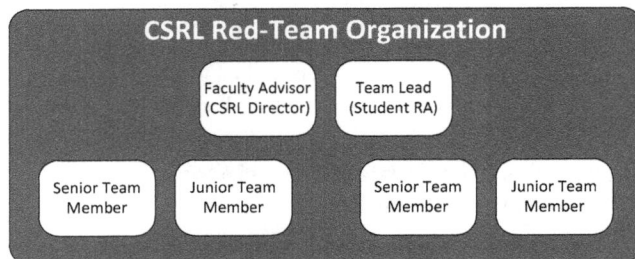

**Figure 2 - Red Team Organization**

Successful applicants join the red team as junior members and are mentored by a senior member during penetration tests. Each member receives two embroidered shirts bearing the CSRL logo and the text 'Red Team' in red-block writing. One shirt is a casual design to help promote awareness of the team whereas the other is more formal for client meetings or a discussion topic in job interviews. Naturally team members are not obliged to wear these however they have attracted significant interest from younger students in the program!

Preparing for an engagement takes a significant amount of time and effort, and follows the same policies and steps as many reputable security-assessment businesses. Team-members create draft proposals including contractual terms, rules of engagement and scope. This is a key learning-activity in the process and helps

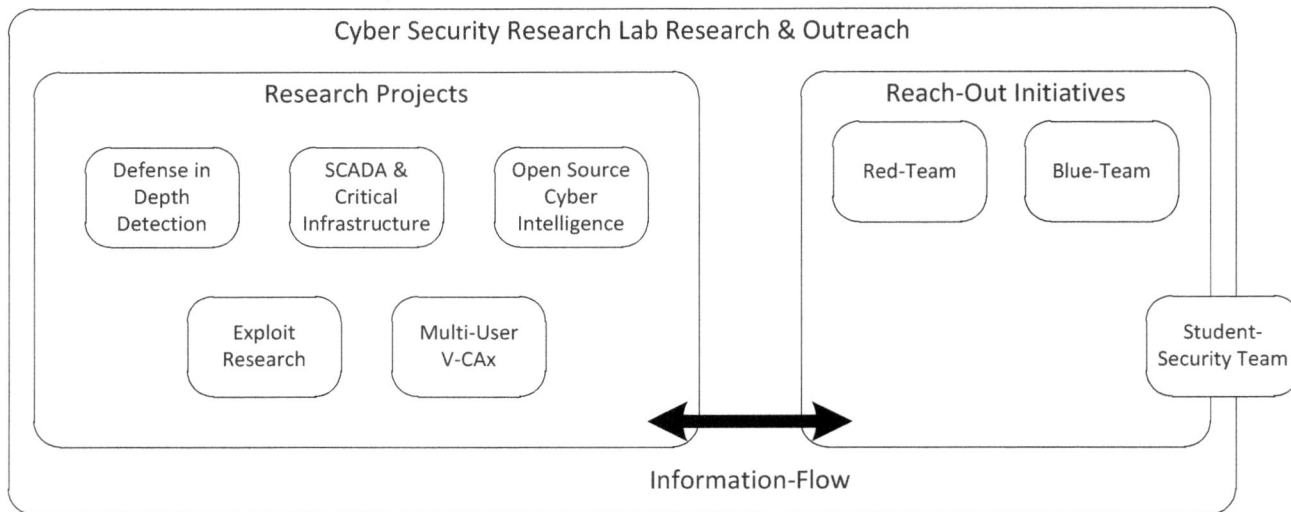

**Figure 1 - CSRL Research and Outreach**

participants to understand the significance of these documents. In a typical engagement the sequence of preparatory events is:

1. Client expresses interest in an assessment

2. Team holds initial meeting with client's responsible and authorizing managers to discuss objectives, select dates and explain process.

3. Team prepares draft contract, rules of engagement, scope and permission memo.

4. CSRL Faculty Director reviews documentation and forwards to client.

5. Client reviews/edits documentation. Return to step 3 until all parties are in agreement then proceed to step 6.

6. Dates are reviewed and set. All documentation is signed and witnessed except for the permission memo.

7. 24 hours before engagement, the permission memo is signed. Point-of-contact information is exchanged between red-team and client.

To expedite the initial process, the team created an engagement template which is completed for each client and contains all agreement of terms. This documentation includes the objectives, the hardware to be used and the scope of the investigation and is customized by the team for each proposal. After faculty review, this is then passed to the client. The proposal undergoes an iterative drafting process. Each time the document is returned to the red-team the document version is incremented and previous versions are archived. When both parties are satisfied, the document is signed in the presence of witnesses. This becomes a contract that binds both parties. If followed, it protects both sides from possible legal ramifications. In the final twenty-four hours before the test, a permission memo is signed by the faculty advisor, team lead and client responsible managers who are permitted to authorize the test. The memo references the previously signed documentation and is used as the final green-flag for testing to proceed on schedule.

The University Office of Information Technology's Security Team is copied on all correspondence to (a) ensure coordination with potential alerts from the campus intrusion detection systems and (b) gain approval to use the campus network during the engagement. A senior security analyst from this team also signs the permission memo as a record of this approval.

The red team efforts are not allowed to persist past designated time slots. This discussion and agreement is critical. We have found in some instances, the client has peak hours of operation and needs to ensure that their servers are not being tampered during these times.

It should be clearly identified from what location the testing will take place. An early mistake made in preparing for an engagement resulted in the team planning to travel to the customer's site on the test day only to find out the night before the customer was expecting (but had not explicitly specified) a remote test of external internet-facing systems!

One issue that had to be addressed early was the use of personal equipment during a penetration test. When the creation of the team was being considered it was decided that any computers and equipment used in a penetration test must belong to the University. This is primarily due to the need of securely wiping all gathered data during a test. It was also desirable to have a network image for the re-imaging of systems on-demand. The image is a dual-boot Windows 7 x64/Backtrack 5R2 with over 50 additional penetration-testing tools installed on the Windows environment. An additional Backtrack 5R2 virtual machine is maintained pre-configured on network storage and copied to each system after imaging.

The CSRL gained approval to purchase several systems for student research and penetration tests. Dual purposing the systems in this manner meant that network storage had to be configured to backup student research prior to an engagement.

Key criteria for the systems included:

- Portable (laptop)
- Multi-core 64 bit processor
- CUDA/OpenCL supporting video card
- Min 8Gb RAM for multiple VM's
- Excellent thermal dissipation for brute-forcing without CPU/Graphics throttling

In particular the final requirement led to looking towards high-end gaming laptops capable of maintaining near 100% CPU and video load.

In total, 6 laptops were purchased in the following configurations:

Alienware M14x (Quantity 4)

- Intel Core i7 2760QM Quad Core 2.4GHz
- 8Gb RAM
- GeForce GTX550 Graphics
- 500Gb HDD

Alienware M17xR3 (Pentest Server)

- Intel Core i7 2760QM Quad Core 2.4GHz
- 16Gb RAM
- GeForce GTX580M
- 256Gb SSD and 720Gb HDD

Dell Latitude E6420 XFR (Quantity 1)

- UL1604 Certified Ruggedized Laptop
- Intel Core i7-2620M Dual Core 2.7GHz
- 8Gb RAM
- NVidia Quattro NVS 4200M
- 128Gb SSD

**Figure 3 - Red-Team Laptop**

The latter system is used to facilitate field research and access to Industrial Control Systems (ICS). This hardware is equipped with multiple I/O devices, an internal GPS and waterproof keyboard. The team is currently in discussions with several organizations to perform testing of SCADA systems and software is currently being customized to support this.

These systems are 'checked out' to red-team members on a renewable 3-month basis. This equipment has unsurprisingly attracted attention throughout the IT program from other students and an excellent marketing activity for the CSRL! It also provides an extra incentive to accept an RA wage which is typically 10-30% lower than is offered by off-campus employment.

As a final step of preparation, a private red-team only accessible file-share and secure wiki are created on the pentest server designated laptop. These collaborative tools are designed to facilitate information sharing during the test and report-writing after the test. These tools are discussed further in the next section.

# 4. TESTING METHODOLOGY

To date, all tests have been against internet-facing systems from on-campus. In these engagements, all testing must be carried out from a single physical location. Should the team wish to travel to the customer's site (for example, to carry out a man-in-the-middle attack) they must coordinate this with the client's point-of-contact (PoC) and gain approval from the PoC and CSRL director. All client representatives and an Office of IT (OIT) security analyst are invited to be present during testing as their schedules permit.

The tests begin with a review of customer agreements along with delegation of assignments and teams. Mentioned beforehand, mentorship is used between senior red team members and inexperienced members to ensure skills are developed and knowledge is passed on.

The test involves multiple steps. The team first performs foot-printing reconnaissance on the target using available information from the public domain. This information-gathering exercise takes place up to one week before the scheduled test date and includes manual legitimate browsing of the client's website, information in search engines, DNS/Whois records and social networks. The team is not permitted to mislead the client or misrepresent themselves during this phase. They must not conduct port scans, or attempt to circumvent any security measure.

In the second phase the team begins fingerprinting reconnaissance. This typically involved port scanning and takes place strictly within the scheduled periods defined in the permission memo. If explicitly in scope, the team may also begin engaging in social engineering techniques to discover information on the target systems. Information obtained in this phase is correlated with foot-printing reconnaissance to generate network topology diagrams, detailed service enumeration and any other information that may assist in formulating an attack. If the target is a webserver, it is browsed using a local proxy server to gain understanding of its implementation and possible weaknesses. They may also use automated tools to enumerate websites on the same server. No exploitation attempt is made at this stage.

As the reconnaissance phases complete, the team meets to share their findings and assign tasks for vulnerability assessment. The team brainstorms all possible vulnerability points and lists these such as:

- SAMBA Service on host xxx.xxx.xxx.xxx
- SSHv1 supported on host yyy.yyy.yyy.yyy
- Joomla site at http://sitename/dirname
- /admin page on https://sitename
- GET request used to login to site http://sitename
- LDAP listening on xxx.xxx.xxx.xxx

- SQL in http://sitename/qwerty.php
- MySQL listening on yyy.yyy.yyy.yyy

This information is recorded in a private team-wiki that is on an internal network accessible only by the team. In addition to potential vulnerabilities, there are wiki pages with pre-built tables to store usernames, password hashes, passwords, websites and any log files discovered. The private network file share is used to store related information, logs and outputs as well as scans, screenshots and any other relevant documentation.

Additionally automated vulnerability assessment tools are used in this phase such as Nessus, Openvas, VEGA, Nikto and MySqlI. Each discovered vulnerability is classified on the wiki as 'probably exploitable', 'maybe exploitable' or 'probably not exploitable'. In addition they are given the tags 'easy', 'medium' or 'hard' depending on the amount of time and difficulty the finder believes it will take to successfully exploit.

In the exploitation phase, the team attempts to verify vulnerabilities by using exploitation methods. Vulnerabilities are attempted based on their difficulty and probability. The wiki is used to store information on exploitation attempts to minimize wasted repetition later in the engagement. During the engagement, the team holds a meeting every two hours to share findings, assign tasks, brainstorming attacks and set goals. A meeting is brought forward when there are any significant findings (such as a successful exploit that can be used to launch attacks deeper into the scoped network).

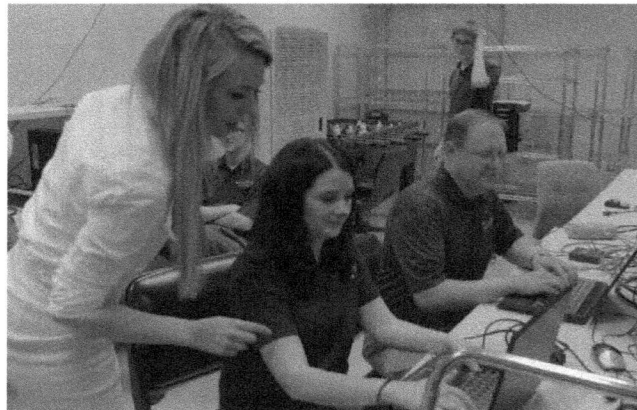

**Figure 4 - Student Red Team Engagement**

After the test has concluded, a final debrief and presentation is given to the client. The presentation is informal; its purpose is to convey results, suggest mitigation steps for high-risk confirmed vulnerabilities and retrieve feedback from the customer. A professional report will be written including all the results, findings and suggestions and passed to the customer at a later date (the goal is to provide this within two weeks of test completion). This will allow the company to have a hard copy of the assessment along with possible security improvement ideas for their network. It has been noted that some client organizations do not always have the know-how to correct vulnerabilities; it would be beneficial to incorporate a blue team to follow up on the red team actions. This concept is further discussed later on in the paper.

## 5. STUDENT IMPACT[1]

The Cyber Security Research Laboratory provides multiple educational opportunities. One of the main priorities for each student is to participate in personal security research. Students can appreciate and learn more on topics of interest in security. This research can be more specific than classroom instruction. In addition, CSRL researchers on the red-team are asked to apply their knowledge in real world penetration tests. This gives valuable experience and exposure to the students, most likely opening more employment offers.

From a student perspective, this CSRL facility has greatly improved my penetration skills. I joined the laboratory after taking a great interest in the information security and assurance class offered within the IT curriculum. I had very little experience with penetration testing outside of the material taught in this class. During the tests, I was teamed with other students to learn and shadow their techniques and expertise. The mentoring within the CSRL was the greatest teaching asset.

The penetration tests the CSRL takes part in are very different from a traditional course lab assignment. In an assigned lab, there is always a solution and an exploit to find. In a company penetration test, there may or may not be a vulnerability to find. This mirrors what professional's experience. The frustration from the test only encourages students to be more creative in their exploits. Solutions vary greatly from different clients, providing real involvement with current security problems rather than theorized problems in a closed lab environment. Some class labs have been passed down throughout the term of the course and may be outdated. The red team offers hands-on learning in client situations with current security issues.

The CSRL has changed my schooling experience. The skill set I have gained from my participation has increased the confidence I have in my abilities. I am an active contributor in the assessments and in the process of attempting to exploit the target I have gained a greater knowledge on how to strengthen and protect a system.

## 6. BENEFITS

Typically red-team activities are seen as high-risk engagements due to their efforts to bypass security countermeasures and gain access to services and systems in illegitimate ways. For this reason, the cost of a penetration test is usually significant, requiring highly trained and certified professionals with many years of experience. It is commonly said that it takes a minimum of 5 years for a graduate to become a cyber-specialist. We believe that with a strong curriculum in place and extra-curricular opportunities such as red-teaming, this time can be dramatically reduced. Recruiters in this industry have indicated their support of this and we hope to publish future works further indicating the benefits of these activities [4]. If successful this could help to address the current skill shortage in a shorter timeframe [1].

The Cyber Security Research Lab offers local companies free network vulnerability assessments. That is to say that there is no financial charge required at this stage. Given the benefit to students and the perceived increased risk in allowing a student team this level of systems access, it is seen as a mutually beneficial endeavor. In reality, organizations benefit from a penetration test team with classroom training to a similar level of common penetration testing certificates, such as those offered by the SANS (System Administration, Networking and Security)

---

[1] This section has been written in the first person as it relates my personal experiences.

institute. The faculty advisor also maintains current security and penetration testing certificates.

The benefit to the community is also significant. Organizations can gain understanding about potential risks along with advice on how to mitigate them (thus improving their overall security posture), while increasing the skills and knowledge of an imminently graduating cyber-workforce.

By connecting research and red-team exercises in this manner, we have also discovered several new research avenues that would not have otherwise been considered. One client, for example, used a document-based NOSQL database. This genre of database by its nature is not vulnerable to SQL injection attacks. However there are other command-injection attacks that may provide an alternate means of access. This is a method of information sharing that actually maintains sensitivity. The benefits of sharing information for cyber-security have been deemed valuable in previous studies [6, 8].

In summary the benefits of red-teaming consist of:

- Valuable skill development and respect for penetration test pre-requisite planning

- Shorter field-time for graduates to become self-sufficient in helping to address the current skill shortage

- Improved security posture for clients at no financial cost

- Key information sharing between research and red-team efforts

## 7. CONCLUSIONS AND FUTURE PLANS

Red team penetration tests have been performed successfully on numerous organizations. The information brought forward from the tests has brought to the attention possible security threats. It is felt that this is a great learning experience and service; however it can be improved. After performing initial tests, there is evidence that some of the companies asking for security assessments may not have the knowledge to respond to all found security concerns. The CSRL is currently preparing to introduce a blue team. This team would follow up after the red team's assessment. The blue team would physically go on site or be granted remote access in order to assist the company. The objective of this new group would be to assist such organizations with correcting discovered vulnerabilities through training and working with the organizations full-time staff.

With both teams operating in this way, organizations would be able to request a penetration test from the red team. Following the investigation, the blue team can be called upon to advise in mitigation procedures. The blue team can also be alert for additional security issues found in the local environment that were not detectable in the test. To assess the effectiveness of these new countermeasures, a final test can be requested and performed by the red team. This opportunity for students will provide knowledge in not only penetration practices but in the physical implementation of correcting and fortifying measures.

There have been found possible problems with the document reporting process in place for the vulnerability testing. These issues are based on (a) the time taken to produce a report, and (b) the effectiveness of current joint record-sharing methods. Google offers a service where users can create and collaborate on a live document together called Google Docs. This service provides a friendly user interface and controls with much improved availability. However, Google is in the public domain on servers outside of the CSRL's control; the confidentiality of private information from clients cannot be guaranteed. This has led to the development of a new research project within the CSRL into collaborative tools for security and vulnerability assessments. This research, in addition to reporting templates will allow the reports to be completed within the two week goal.

A further related project is the establishment of a Student Security Team (SST) as a cross-disciplinary endeavor between different computing programs at the university. In part driven by the success of the red-team, this project recognizes the benefit of working collaboratively to establish pre-approved support teams for on-campus security incidents. The SST is in effect, an incident-response service to the University and has been initiated from the campus IT department.

Students from Computer Science will work with on-campus developers in verifying and inspecting code for a variety of vulnerabilities. Information Technology students will provide red-team (penetration testing) and blue-team (hardening & incident response) services as well as a secure sandbox environment for threat analysis. Information Systems students will provide forensic data analysis and may assist in gathering evidence suitable for prosecution. Teams will frequently work together tackling various aspects of the same event.

Unlike the red-team which is supervised by an IT faculty member, the SST is managed by the OIT security manager. There is no formal commitment of availability or service-level agreement from supporting programs. Involvement is voluntary on a case-by-case basis. The advantages of involvement for both students and OIT are however, quite significant. As well as the obvious benefits of experience for students and resources for OIT, the project seeks to promote bridge-building across three disciplines. This collaborative engagement will help to promote understanding, respect and teamwork between these programs in a security context.

**Figure 5 – BYU CSRL Red Team (April 2012)**

In conclusion, we have found that the CSRL Red Team is an excellent opportunity to provide an enriching experience for students and at the same time, offer a needed public service. Students appreciate and benefit from working with a client in a professional vulnerability test. Clients often express surprise at the professionalism and capabilities of the team. Added to these benefits is the information flow between CSRL research and the red team activities. From time to time, the team discovers new technologies or implementations where the security research is lacking. The CSRL is a growing facility that has already helped many students and the local community. With suitable funding we hope to expand this initiative and continue to promote an exceptional and enriching environment.

# 8. ACKNOWLEDGMENTS
Although we cannot reference our clients in publications, we wish to express our sincere heartfelt thanks and gratitude for their willingness to 'go first' in such a high-risk endeavor.

# 9. REFERENCES
[1] Cybersecurity experts needed to meet growing demand: 2012. *http://www.washingtonpost.com/business/economy/cybersecu rity-experts-needed-to-meet-growing-demand/2012/05/29/gJQAtev1yU_story.html*. Accessed: 2012-05-05.

[2] Ma, J. and Nickerson, J.V. 2006. Hands-on, simulated, and remote laboratories: A comparative literature review. *Acm Computing Surveys*. 38, 3 (2006), 7.

[3] Nersessian, N.J. 1989. Conceptual change in science and in science education. *Synthese*. 80, 1 (1989), 163-183.

[4] Rowe, D.C. et al. 2012. Cyber-Security, IAS and the Cyber Warrior. *The Colloquium for Information Systems Security Education* (Lake Buena Vista, Fl, 2012).

[5] Rowe, D.C. et al. 2011. The Role of Cyber Security in Information Technology. *ACM SIGITE 2011* (New York, 2011).

[6] Sandhu, R. et al. 2010. Towards Secure Information Sharing models for community Cyber Security. *Collaborative Computing: Networking, Applications and Worksharing (CollaborateCom), 2010 6th International Conference on* (2010), 1-6.

[7] Stohr-Hunt, P.M. 1996. An Analysis of Frequency of Hands-On Experience and Science Achievement. *Journal of Research in Science Teaching*. 33, 1 (1996), 101-109.

[8] White, G.B. and DiCenso, D.J. 2005. Information Sharing Needs for National Security. *System Sciences, 2005. HICSS '05. The 38th Annual Hawaii International Conference on* (2005), 125c-125c.

[9] White, G.B. and Williams, D. 2005. Collegiate Cyber Defense Competitions. *Ninth Colloquium for Information Systems Security Education*. The ISSA Journal.

[10] White, G.B. and Williams, D. 2006. The National Collegiate Cyber Defense Competition. *Tenth Colloquium for Information Systems Security Education*.

# Green IT: Serving Multiple Purposes

Susan J. Lincke
University of Wisconsin-Parkside
900 Wood Road, Kenosha WI 53141 USA
+1(708)453-2069

lincke@uwp.edu

## ABSTRACT

Data centers require 40 times the energy requirements of a regular office. Projections show that IT growth will continue to increase, with annual network growth at 45%. Increased energy demand in IT is growing rapidly as the world becomes more industrialized. Increasing energy demands results in an increase in both costs and global warming. To be competitive and a good world citizen means reducing IT energy costs.

This poster discusses teaching materials to prepare the educator and the student in this relevant topic. Teaching this subject helps to achieve five ABET program goals, including ethics and local/global impact. It also enables students to experiment with electricity, graphs, and a lab report.

## Categories and Subject Descriptors

K.3.2 [**Computers & Education**]: Computer & I.S. Education: Accreditation, IS Education.

B.8.0 [**Hardware**]: Performance and Reliability – General.

K.6.4 [**Computing Milieux**]: Mgmt of Computing & Info. Systems

## General Terms

Performance, Economics, Management

## Keywords

Education, Green IT, Energy efficiency.

## 1. INTRODUCTION

Green IT is in its infancy, but there are two good reasons to start teaching it now: energy efficiency (cost containment) and global warming. However a third benefit is that this topic helps to achieve ABET program goals, including: a) apply knowledge of computing and math; e) understand professional, ethical, legal, security, social issues; f) communicate effectively; g) analyze local/global impact of computing; h) continuing professional development.

This module has been introduced into a Computer Architecture course. The topic included a lecture, an exercise with Kill-a-Watt [1], a homework assignment, and an extra-credit assignment. The Kill-a-Watt exercise had students measuring the volts, amps, watts, frequency (etc.) to contrast a desktop with a laptop computer. They entered the results into an Excel

spreadsheet, and produced a graph. The spreadsheet was available on line for them, and included automatic equations to calculate expected annual electrical costs and greenhouse gas emissions. Thus, the active learning objectives gave them experience with electricity measurement and Microsoft Excel.

The homework assignment was to write a paper that included a nontechnical and technical component, which included a set of references, including professional (e.g., ACM/IEEE) papers. The first section required an introduction to the ethical or social (including business) and local/global impacts of their technical topic. The technical topic could be in one of 5 areas: 1) data center efficiency; 2-3) Computer and network efficiency; 4) Smart grid/Smart home; 5) Green IT lifecycle (procurement, disposal).

Students also gave a presentation on their topic. Although the topics were not coordinated, with a small class there was little overlap in the presentations. The written and presentation assignment addresses four ABET program goals: e) professional/social/ethical, f) communicate effectively, g) analyze local/global impact of society, and h) continuing professional development.

The lecture first introduced the reasons for green efficiency, to give students ideas of topics they could write on. One excellent source for this is Hot, Flat, and Crowded [2], by Thomas L. Friedman (author of *The World is Flat*). This well-researched book covers the expected growth of energy consumption, the problem of global warming, the potential technological directions and political issues.

One of the most impressive issues Friedman discusses is that a few years ago there were two energy hogs: America and Europe. Now with India and China emerging, there are four. As these heavily-populated nations and other regions further develop, there will be the equivalent of 9 Americas consuming fossil fuel power. Friedman shows how this growth affects five major issues: energy and natural resources, petrodictatorship, climate change, energy poverty, and biodiversity loss [2]. While many of the topics can be categorized as 'liberal' politics, 'conservative' issues are also raised, since oil production helps to fund Muslim extremists, and desert war conditions requires massive air conditioning, leading to trucking of petrol across unfriendly terrain. These issues are discussed in the lecture to emphasize the importance of the topic.

The lecture then demonstrates the power usage of a number of recent processors [3] and the recent and projected energy usage statistics [4, 6]. To sum up projections, computers have become more energy efficient, but demand is increasing. For example, network traffic volume is expected to increase 190 times between 2006 and 2026 [6]. Then the lecture discusses how computers and networking devices can be made more efficient, through dynamic power scaling, including adaptive rates, and low power idle [4,5].

It is estimated that up to 40% of data center costs are for air conditioning [7]. This can be reduced using an air economizer, which uses colder outside air to assist in air conditioning. Chillers are tubes which carry colder (e.g., ocean) water to where they are needed, and improving airflow can also reduce costs. Also, running the room temperature higher but within computer specifications may be useful if leakage does not result in greater energy loss [8]. Alternatively, turning some computers off during slow periods and selecting Energy Star (efficient) computers can reduce electrical costs, as well as server consolidation through virtualization. Green actions also include using computers longer, recycling, and reselling the computers. In the future, the smart grid will influence electrical use.

To prepare students for the active learning lab, the lecture reviews Ohm's law, and definitions for voltage, current, and resistance. Then the instructor shows how to calculate kilowatt hours, greenhouse gas emissions, and electrical costs, producing annual statistics, using the downloadable Excel spreadsheet. The following two equations show how to calculate kilowatt hours, and pounds of carbon dioxide, as a function of kilowatt hours [9]:

$$KWhour = [Watt * 24 \text{ (hrs/day)} * 365 \text{ (days/year)}]/1K \qquad (1)$$

$$Pound_{C02} = 1.75 * KWhour \qquad (2)$$

The technical aspects of the lecture and active learning lab address ABET program goal: a) apply knowledge of computing and math.

An extra credit assignment is for students to select a lab, and work with the Kill-a-Watts to estimate annual electrical costs and greenhouse gas emissions. They can contrast two techniques, such as using more efficient computers or turning off computers/monitors at night, and show the difference in costs and emissions.

Lecture and spreadsheet materials are available by contacting the author. Students appeared to enjoy the assignments and the presentations were very interesting to all.

## 2. REFERENCES

[1] SmartHome. 2012. Kill-a-Watt. DOI= http://www.smarthome.com/9034/Kill-A-Watt-P4400/p.aspx.

[2] Friedman, T. L. 2008. *Hot, Flat, and Crowded, Release 2.0*, PICADOR, New York NY, DOI= http://www.picadorusa.com.

[3] Patterson, D. A., and Hennessy, J. L. 2009. *Computer Organization and Design, 4th Ed.*, Morgan Kaufmann, 403.

[4] Bolla, R., Bruschi, R., and Lombardo, C. 2011. "State of the Art of Existing Standards for the Evaluation of Network Performance and Energy Consumption", *2011 International Symposium on Performance Evaluation of Computer & Telecommunication Systems (SPECTS 2011)*, 62-68.

[5] Bolla, R., Bruschi, R., Christensen, K., Cuchietti, F., and Singh, S. 2011. The Potential Impact of Green Technologies in Next Generation Wireline Networks: Is there room for Energy Saving Optimization? *IEEE Communications Magazine*, Aug. 2011, 80-86.

[6] Sato, K. 2010. Optical Technologies that Enable Green Networks, *12th International Conf. on Transparent Optical Networks (ICTON 2010)*, 1-4.

[7] Ahuja, N., Rego, C., Ahuja, S., Warner. M., and Docca, A. 2011. Data Center Efficiency with Higher Ambient Temperatures and Optimzed Cooling Control, *27th IEEE Semi-Therm Symposium*, 105-109.

[8] Patterson, M. K. 2008. The Effect of Data Center Temperature on Energy Efficiency, *11th Intersociety Conf. on Thermal and Thermomechanical Phenomena in Electronic Systems (ITHERM 2008)*, 1167-1174.

[9] DeGunther, R. 2008. *Home Energy Efficiency for Dummies*. John Wiley & Sons.

# Assisting Students with Disabilities in Distance Education: An Exploratory Study into Their Experiences

Ye Diana Wang
Applied Information Technology Department
George Mason University
10900 University Blvd. MS 4F5
Manassas, VA 20110, USA
1-703-993-9288
ywangm@gmu.edu

Gabrielle Webster
New Century College
George Mason University
4400 University Dr.
Fairfax, VA 22030, USA
1-281-761-4466
gwebste2@masonlive.gmu.edu

## ABSTRACT

The escalation in DE presents both opportunities and challenges to students with disabilities. For students with disabilities, DE technology can help them read when they cannot see and learn when they have the desire to study. However, when the proper care is not taken in the development of these technological resources and tools, DE courses can be inaccessible to these students. The current study seeks to investigate how to assist students with disabilities in DE environments, and ultimately, to improve the role that technology plays in the distance education of students with disabilities in the higher education arena.

## Categories and Subject Descriptors

K3.1 [**Computers and Education**]: Computer Uses in Education
– *Distance Learning*

## General Terms

Human Factors

## Keywords

Distance Education, Accessibility, People with Disabilities, Higher Education

## 1. SIGNIFICANCE AND RELEVANCE

Distance Education (DE) is proliferating with no signs of slowing down, especially in the higher education arena. The number of students taking at least one online course in the fall of 2011 has surpassed 6.1 million; online enrollment accounted for nearly one-third of the total enrollment in higher education [4]. The escalation in DE presents both opportunities and challenges to students with disabilities. The percentage distribution of students with disabilities enrolled in postsecondary institutions during the 2007–2008 year was 10.8% at the undergraduate level and 7.6% at the graduate level [2]. According to Roberts et al. [3], of the respondents who indicated that they had participated in an online course, 46% stated that their disability did have a negative impact on their ability to succeed in an online setting.

The purpose of this study is to investigate how to assist students with disabilities in distance learning environments. The study is significant because it places emphasis on two research areas; namely, distance education and accessibility, which are often disconnected in the literature. This disconnect puts the entire academic community at a disadvantage as instructors lack the knowledge of how to meet the needs of all of their students. Insight gained and improvements made as a result of this study will not just aid the disabled, but also contribute to the universal design of DE and learning management systems and instructional tools that can be used by all; including those students who have disabilities, are learning in a second language or simply have unique learning styles.

## 2. CONTENT

This poster session outlines a study that aims to gain insight into the current status of students with disabilities who have taken or plan to take DE courses at a four-year university and their online educational experiences. To guide the study, the following research questions are pursued:

1) How many students with one or more documented disabilities have taken or plan to take DE courses at their current university?

2) What have been their overall experiences in taking DE courses and using DE tools?

3) What specific implications can be generated to direct the implementation of accessibility features and enhancements in DE courses?

The study consists of two phases:

1) In Phase 1, a comprehensive literature search for publications on DE and disabilities released in the last five years (from 2007 onwards) is conducted, as a continuation to Kinash and Crichton[1]'s efforts of a classification of relevant literature between 2000 and 2006. Based on these publications, a literature review of previous research investigating disabled students' needs and experiences with DE is performed.

2) In Phase 2, a university-wide survey is conducted to gain insight into the current status of students with disabilities who have taken or plan to take DE courses at a four-year university and their online educational experiences. A web-based survey is developed and distributed to students who have identified themselves as having one or more

documented disabilities with the Office of Disability Services. The data collected through the survey is analyzed using statistical software.

The outcomes of this study are three-fold. Firstly, a classification of more than 50 publications on DE and disabilities released in the last five years is constructed based on four categories; namely didactic, description, opinion, and research. Secondly, the results generated from the survey can answer the important research questions outlined previously and will be beneficial to our understanding of how to assist students with disabilities in DE environments. The data collected from the survey is also expected to provide useful information needed by other university entities, such as the Office of Disability Services, the Office of Distance Education, the Assistive Technology Initiative (ATI) Office, etc. Thirdly, the specific implications and techniques learned as a result of the study will be used by the authors and guide their implementation of accessibility features and enhancements in an existing DE course. This study will establish a basis for further investigation.

Advancing accessibility in DE can improve the learning experience of students with a wide variety of barriers, such as: knowing English as a second language or with physical or mental limitations. It is hoped that the results from this study will decrease the number of barriers in technology based educational resources for the disabled while increasing the overall accessibility of distance education programs to the student body.

## 3. REFERENCES

[1] Kinash, S., & Crichton, S. 2007. Supporting the disabled student. In M. G. Moore (Ed.), *Handbook of distance education* (2nd ed.), pp. 193-204. New York, NY: Routledge.

[2] National Center for Education Statistics (NCES). 2011. *Digest of Education Statistics*. Retrieved March 15, 2012, from http://nces.ed.gov/programs/digest/d09/tables/dt09_231.asp

[3] Roberts, J.B., Crittenden, L.A., & Crittenden, J.C. 2011. Students with disabilities and online learning: A cross-institutional study of perceived satisfaction with accessibility compliance and services. *The Internet and Higher Education, 14*(4), 242-250.

[4] The Sloan Consortium. 2011. *Going the Distance - Online Education in the United States*. Retrieved February 25, 2012, from http://sloanconsortium.org/publications/survey/going_distance_2011

# Desktop as a Service Proof of Concept

Andrew Eaves
University of Cincinnati
2160 McMicken Circle
Cincinnati, OH 45221-0002
1-419-889-2421
eavesaj@mail.uc.edu

Mark Stockman
University of Cincinnati
2160 McMicken Circle
Cincinnati, OH 45221-0002
1-513-556-4227
stockmma@ucmail.uc.edu

## ABSTRACT

Desktop as a Service is an idea that has taken root in enterprises today, but has not reached consumers. In order to show this, a proof of concept lab was constructed. The proof of concept lab that the authors devised shows that this idea is viable. The lab uses a virtual desktop infrastructure environment. The environment uses VMWare's View solution on top of their hypervisor and virtualization management server. These solutions provide the backbone of the environment that is used to access desktops from mobile devices anywhere and anytime. The desktops provided are persistent which allows users to keep their settings and data in a single location.

## Categories and Subject Descriptors

K.6.4 [**Management of Computing and Information Systems**]: System Management

## General Terms

Management, Performance, Design.

## Keywords

Operating Systems, Service, Virtual Desktop Infrastructure.

## 1. Significance and Relevance

The market for mobile devices is large and highly in demand. As mobile devices become more readily available, consumers gain more freedom with where they use their devices. Consumers want access to their desktop and their data whenever possible. The solution that the authors came up with uses a full virtual desktop infrastructure environment. The solution is to use a VDI environment to offer customers a persistent, highly available desktop that can be accessed from all of their mobile devices. This is significant because right now there are no services that are available that offer those services. The idea is to take the burden off of the customer by removing the tedious upkeep that they must regularly go through. Desktop as a Service, or DaaS, is used in enterprises for a similar reason. The employees no longer have to worry about maintaining a PC since the operating system would be centrally managed. The idea is to reduce complexity by centralizing management which leads to a more productive and efficient IT organization.

This is significant because as the times change consumers are looking for different, innovative solutions to their problems. One problem that consumers have is that they have to regularly maintain their data and hardware. Consumer DaaS would provide a turnkey solution for consumers looking for a simpler computer experience.

The reason for the proof of concept lab was to show that the idea is feasible. There is little to no documentation of DaaS that uses persistent desktops. The small setup of the lab showed that the idea is feasible if you maximize the number of virtual machines that the hardware can maintain.

## 2. Content

The poster would be a way to show how we set up a small virtual desktop infrastructure in order to prove the concept of DaaS. The poster would show the basic structure of the VDI environment. This would show hardware specifications that the system was built on. It would show the MacPro, as the server, and the Dell workstation that was used to run all of the necessary components. Also, it would show the software components that were used to create the VDI environment. The setup used the VMWare View solution which consists of the ESXi hypervisor, the vCenter Server, and the VMWare View components. There will be a diagram that shows the level at which the software components are situated. The components will all have a separate description explaining their purpose in the VDI environment. The disadvantages and advantages to DaaS will be in a table for comparison. Some of the disadvantages that will be shown are that there can be lag issues, data security issues, and licensing issues. The poster will compare the differences between Commercial and Enterprise DaaS. One difference is that Commercial DaaS looks to provide a space for users to do as they please with a single, persistent interface while Enterprise DaaS looks to provide a workspace managed by the business.

There will also be a handout with information to allow the audience to recreate the setup for themselves. The information will be in a data flow detailing what occurs in each step.

# Real-world Testing:
# Using FOSS for Software Development Courses

Evelyn Brannock
Georgia Gwinnett College
1000 University Center Lane
Lawrenceville, Georgia 30043
678-939-9007
ebrannoc@ggc.edu

Nannette Napier
Georgia Gwinnett College
1000 University Center Lane
Lawrenceville, Georgia 30043
678-524-1511
nnapier@ggc.edu

## ABSTRACT

We designed a self-contained learning module on testing and free and open source software (FOSS) for a junior-level software engineering course. In this three-part module, students first learned software quality assurance concepts, and then used JUnit to create unit tests for their code. After being familiar with JUnit from a user perspective, students were required to investigate a defect reported in the JUnit code. Students were required to reproduce the problem, write test cases, and outline an approach for fixing the problem. In this pilot study, we conducted pre and post surveys of students' knowledge of and interest in FOSS. In the poster, visual data will be presented summarizing the results obtained.

## Categories and Subject Descriptors

K.3.2 [**Computers and Information Science Education**]: Computer science education – *curriculum*

## General Terms

Experimentation

## Keywords:

Open Source, testing.

## 1. INTRODUCTION

Students are frequently motivated by real-world projects where their efforts can positively impact a client or broader user community [1-3]. For software development students, free and open source software (FOSS) projects provide an opportunity for authentic learning characterized by high relevance, ill-defined problems, and complex tasks [4]. Through active participation in an open source community, students can gain experience with large and complex codebases, learn a variety of software tools, and better understand the code behind the products they actually use. Seeking these benefits, some instructors have incorporated open source projects in capstone software engineering courses [5, 6].

Unfortunately, there are some challenges to getting started with FOSS development such as overcoming limited skills of faculty and students, identifying appropriate projects, and defining assignments that fit within the constraints of an academic semester. To address these challenges, we designed a self-contained learning module on testing and FOSS which required minimal pre-requisite knowledge of students. The module was used as part of a junior-level software engineering course.

## 2. CONTENT

Software Development I (SD I) requires a software quality module as a portion of its curriculum. Historically, the authors' software quality module consisted of two important components. The first (portion I) covered the important concepts such as non-execution based testing (walkthroughs and inspections), execution based testing (test plans and test cases), black-box testing and glass box testing, unit testing, integration testing, regression testing, writing test cases and plans and quality metrics. The second part (portion II) introduced the students to hands-on test-driven development that would use these concepts via the JUnit framework, a free and open source software (FOSS) automated testing tool that can be used with the Eclipse IDE. To learn how to use JUnit, the students were provided some pre-written Java classes, including a domain model class, a user view interface class, and a controller class and were asked to provide proper scripts to verify that all of the classes were individually valid, that they passed integration testing together, and all tests (according to the test data given) passed successfully. Any errors found were reported via a bug report and modifications required due to those errors were made. After comprehending the usefulness and efficacy of JUnit, a new exciting piece (portion III) was added to help the students to familiarize themselves with a "real-world" testing scenario by acting as contributors, in the course, to the JUnit FOSS community. They were now familiar with the operation of the JUnit software as a tester; they were challenged to contribute to the quality of JUnit's framework as a tester and bug fixer.

Their first directive as a tester and bug fixer for this actual, widely-used product was to read about the JUnit FOSS community to determine how an issue is reported, and to document the material an excellent, effective issue report should include. Then the students were assigned a REAL issue in JUnit (found at https://github.com/KentBeck/junit/issues). They were expected to determine if the issues was a bug or feature request, the date reported, and if it had been assigned. The next step was to reproduce the bug in their own environment. They were given a little more additional information than the issue report gave, such as the fact that the instructor could reproduce the problem, and the exact version of JUnit to use to replicate the issue. The students were required to provide a minimum of two new additional test cases, one that provided correct results and one that provided incorrect results. The students were challenged to improve the original bug report, as the instructor purposefully chose an issue that omitted vital information (such as the operating system utilized and the exact version of JUnit.) A last requirement was to outline the approach for coding a successful solution for this issue including, after the fix is made, how their fix would be committed to the JUnit repository.

Fifteen students successfully completed the module, and were surveyed using pre and post tools. In the poster, visual data will be presented summarizing the results obtained. More than fifty percent of the students, in the pre and post assessments of the SD I course, recognized they had a high level of interest, and it was relevant to their career path. Interestingly, nine students in the pre-survey strongly agreed that "I like the mix of theoretical learning combined with hands-on application of the subject matter" as compared to only four in the post-survey. Also, data detailing the student's attitudes and acceptance of portion I of the module that addressed learning to use JUnit in an exercise and the portion II of the module that involved the students taking part in the development (in the quality assurance stage) of JUnit, as well as a comparison of the two portions, will be presented. The third prong of the module (portion III) in which the students were exposed to a

FOSS did appear to be more frustrating and difficult for the students. This was confirmed by anecdotal statements such as "for the FOSS testing project homework I would make sure that there

are at least some concrete answers instead of having the questions require looking through hundreds of posts...", "a lot more thought goes into creating software than just coding", and "I really enjoyed the FOSS except that it was so unstructured I felt lost, which is very real world experience, but not at all satisfying...".

# 3. REFERENCES

[1] Pinkett, R.D., *Strategies for motivating minorities to engage computers*, in *Carenegie Mellon Symposium on Minorities and Computer Science*1999, MIT Media Laboratory.

[2] Schwartz, D., et al., *Towards the development of flexibly adaptive instructional design*, in *Instructional-design theories and models: a new paradigm of instructional theory*, C. Reigeluth, Editor 1999, Erlbaum: Mahwah, NJ. p. 183-213.

[3] Preston, J.A., *Utilizing authentic, real-world projects in information technology education*. SIGITE Newsl., 2005. **2**(1): p. 1-10.

[4] Reeves, T.C., J. Herrington, and R. Oliver. *Authentic activities and online learning*. in *Higher Education Research and Development Society of Australasia*. 2002. Perth, Australia.

[5] Morelli, R.A., et al., *Revitalizing Computing Education by Building Free and Open Source Software for Humanity*. Communications of the ACM, 2009. **52**(8): p. 67-75.

[6] Marmorstein, R., *Open source contribution as an effective software engineering class project*, in *Proceedings of the 16th annual joint conference on Innovation and technology in computer science education*2011, ACM: Darmstadt, Germany. p. 268-272.

# Cloud Computing Performance Benchmarking and Virtual Machine Launch Time

Dylan Steinmetz
Michigan Tech University
Houghton, MI 49931
dtsteinm@mtu.edu

Brian W. Perrault
School of Technology
Michigan Tech University
Houghton, MI 49931
bwperrau@mtu.edu

Ross Nordeen
School of Technology
Michigan Tech University
Houghton, MI 49931
rjnordee@mtu.edu

Jacob Wilson
School of Technology
Michigan Tech University
Houghton, MI 49931
jdwilson@mtu.edu

Xinli Wang[*]
School of Technology
Michigan Tech University
Houghton, MI 49931
xinlwang@mtu.edu

## ABSTRACT

This research is to study the performance of cloud computing platforms in the perspective of information technology (IT) management. Two separate test clouds of Eucalyptus and OpenStack were established on identical hardware. The BYTE UNIX benchmark suite was employed to conduct various performance tests on both clouds. While the OpenStack cloud out performed Eucalyptus considerably in the larger size copy test, the Eucalyptus cloud performed better than the OpenStack in the tests of serial excel and serial shell scripts. Scripts were written to compute the amount of time that was needed for the clouds to launch a virtual machine (VM) in two different ways. On average, it took a shorter time to launch a VM instance in both clouds when several VMs were created simultaneously than that when they were created one by one, the results showed a variation with different numbers of VMs that were launched concurrently.

## Categories and Subject Descriptors

H.4 [**Information Systems Applications**]: Miscellaneous;
H.3.4 [**Information Systems**]: Systems and Software—
*Performance evaluation (efficiency and effectiveness)*

## General Terms

Experimentation

## Keywords

Cloud computing, Performance, Eucalyptus, Open Stack

## 1. INTRODUCTION

Eucalyptus [5, 4, 3] and OpenStack [6] are two fast developing cloud computing platforms that can be used to build private and public clouds. This research aims to provide IT

[*]Corresponding author: Phone: 906-487-1873

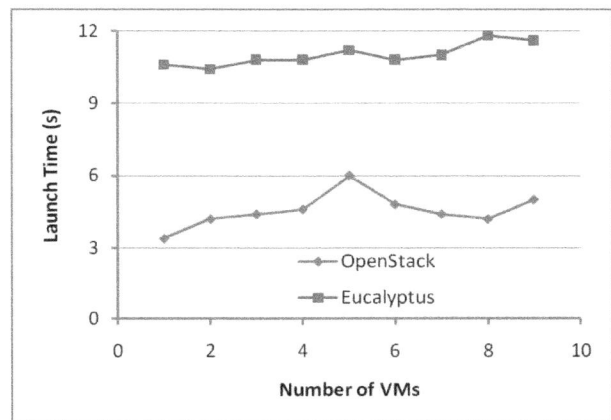

Figure 1: VM serial launch time. X-axis: the number of VMs that were running at the end of the current VM launch; Y-axis: the average time in seconds taken by the operation of a VM launch.

professionals and system administrators with an easy to understand comparison of these two platforms with industry standard test results for virtualization and resource management issues.

## 2. METHODOLOGY

Two separate test clouds of Eucalyptus and OpenStack were built on identical hardware. Each of the clouds was made with two computers. One was a DELL T4400 with 2 GB of RAM and 1 hyper threaded 64-bit Pentium 4 and the other was a DELL T410 16 core 12 GB RAM tower server. A Cisco 2600 Series Router was used for routing. A Brocade Fast Iron Edge GS 648P-POE switch was used for switching on the internal network.

Scripts were written to compute the amount of time that it takes the cloud to procure resources for launching a VM instance. We define this amount of time as *VM launch time* or *VM start time*. The BYTE UNIX benchmark suite [1]

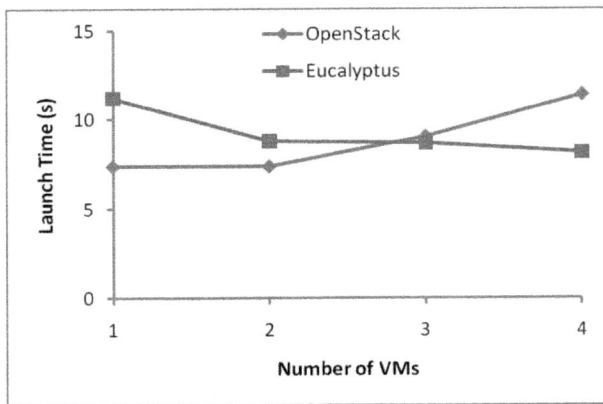

Figure 2: VM parallel launch time. X-axis: number of VMs launched with each command; Y-axis: the average time to launch each VM.

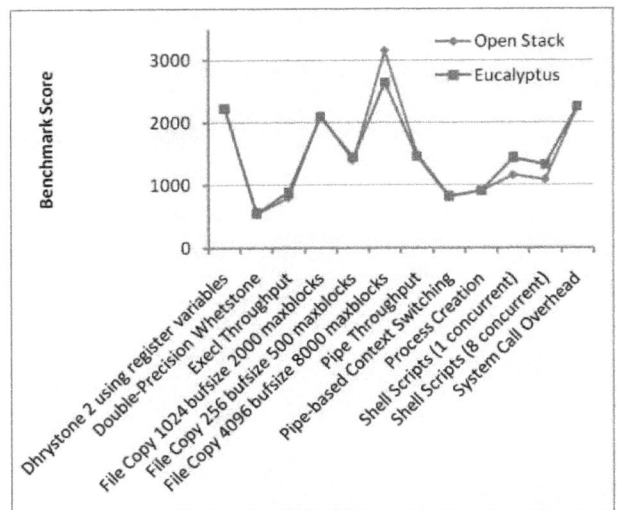

Figure 3: Benchmark comparison. X-axis: the benchmarks; Y-axis: the benchmark scores for each cloud.

was employed to conduct multiple performance measures on both the Eucalyptus cloud and the OpenStack cloud.

## 3. RESULTS AND DISCUSSIONS

### 3.1 VM launch time

There are two ways to launch VMs in a cloud environment. The VMs can be launched in serial, one at a time in succession, or in parallel, several VMs being launched at the same time. The serial VM launches showed a drastic difference in the time taken for a VM to start (Fig. 1). On average the VM launch time was 10-12 seconds in the Eucalyptus cloud, while it was between 3.5-6 seconds in the Open Stack cloud.

Parallel VM launches were done by using one command to simultaneously launch several images at one time. As shown in Figure 2, for launching one or two VMs the Eucalyptus cloud was slower than the OpenStack. While launching three or more VMs simultaneously, the Eucalyptus cloud is faster than OpenStack. In addition, the individual VM launch time decreases with the increase of the number of VMs launched with one command in the Eucalyptus cloud, while the opposite trend holds in the OpenStack cloud. This is mainly due Eucalyptus not resending the image for multiple instances. On the other hand, the OpenStack management system handles each VM instance as if it was being launched individually.

### 3.2 VM performance benchmarking results

Figure 3 shows the the benchmarking results of VM performance in both clouds. The Eucalyptus cloud out performed OpenStack slightly in the tests of serial excel and serial shell scripts, while the OpenStack cloud performed considerably better than Eucalyptus in the larger file copy test. Especially, in the "file copy 4096 buffer size 8000 max blocks" test, the OpenStack cloud out performed more than 16% over Eucalyptus.

In addition, by running the benchmarks on the traditional hardware stack on our computer node and in our cloud environment on a single instance utilizing 16 cores, we saw a 4% gain in the OpenStack cloud and a 15% gain in the Eucalyptus cloud. This result suggests that the cloud computing

management system exploits the computing resources on the same hardware stack better than the bare-metal system.

### 3.3 Interface

For the interface comparison we looked at how easy it was to administer, setup and use the clouds. We also looked at how well they were documented. The Right Scale cloud management interface [2] was integrated into the Eucalyptus cloud, while the OpenStack's Horizon was integrated into the OpenStack cloud. Compared with Right Scale, the OpenStack's Horizon has a relatively poor interface in terms of easiness for resource management and system administration. For example, the Right Scale would allow us to integrate a private cloud into a public cloud through its user friendly interface. This feature has not been implemented in the Horizon.

## 4. REFERENCES

[1] byte-unixbench: A Unix benchmark suite. http://code.google.com/p/byte-unixbench/. Retrieved May 31, 2012.
[2] Right scale cloud management. http://www.rightscale.com/. Retrieved June 1, 2012.
[3] Eucalyptus. http://www.eucalyptus.com/. Retrieved May 29, 2012.
[4] Eucalyptus. The open source cloud platform. http://open.eucalyptus.com/. Retrieved May 29, 2012.
[5] D. Nurmi, R. Wolski, C. Grzegorczyk, G. Obertelli, S. Soman, L. Youseff, and D. Zagorodnov. The Eucalyptus open-source cloud-computing system. In *CCGRID '09: Proceedings of the 2009 9th IEEE/ACM International Symposium on Cluster Computing and the Grid*, pages 124–131, Washington, DC, USA, 2009. IEEE Computer Society.
[6] openstack. Open source software for building private and public clouds. http://openstack.org/. Retrieved May 29, 2012.

# Identifying the Link between Project Management Standards and Practices in IT Education and the Industry Expectations and Requirements

**Faith-Michael E. Uzoka**
Department of Computer Science and Information Systems
Mount Royal University, Calgary, AB, Canada
+1-403-440-6674
fuzoka@mtroyal.ca

**Anthony Chima**
Financial Planning & Analysis
Suncor Energy Inc
Calgary, AB, Canada
+1-403- 471-6788
a.chima@shaw.ca

**Kalen Gibb**
Library
Mount Royal University, Calgary, AB, Canada
+1-403- 440-8516.
kgibb@mtroyal.ca

**Jody Johnson**
Department of Computer Science and Information Systems
Mount Royal University, Calgary, AB, Canada
+1- 403- 827-4509
jjohn939@mymru.ca

## ABSTRACT

Is current university-level education in IT project management meeting industry needs and expectations? The purpose of this project overview poster is to highlight a research plan to identify critical IT project management participation skills that are required of graduates of computer information systems and other information technology programs. The results of the survey, examining the critical project management skills from the point of view of actual project managers will be used to inform and create an industry focused project management course and provide new insight into contextual factors affecting IT project success.

## Categories and Subject Descriptors

K [**Computing Milieux**]: Management of Computing and Information Systems – *Project and people Management*

## General Terms

Management

## Keywords

IT Project, IT Education, quality assurance, critical success factors, skills.

## 1. INTRODUCTION

This poster presents a research project initiated in June 2012 and fully underway during SIGITE 2012. The poster is meant to highlight our project to determine whether current university-level education in IT project management is meeting industry needs and expectations.

Today's organizational growth comes with more complexities in business and technical processes (including management of IT projects). These complexities are worsened by shortage of skilled project management personnel needed for IT project implementation in most industries. Consulting firms are increasingly demanding hi-tech IT skilled persons, while most companies have outsourced their IT departments due to shortage of in-house skills to manage the technology required to meet the needs of their complex processes. Forward-looking and focused

enterprises attempt to tie their vision to a technology forecast. This leads to IT skills requirement forecast and skills/ competencies gap analysis. Based on the gaps identified, organizations attempt to develop IT training programs to meet future growth prospects.

To what extent therefore does a university IT graduate fit into this scenario? How adequate are university IT Project Management programs in preparing students to fill the skills gap needed to meet the growing industry complexities? Universities generally train graduates in project management based on a general framework provided in project management texts. While this provides some requisite project management skills, it might be deficient in terms of entry level project participation skills. An informal interaction with employers of IT graduates tends to indicate that the skills acquired in project management courses may be inadequate in preparing graduates with entry level project participation skills. The purpose of this research is to identify critical IT project management participation skills that are required of graduates of computer information systems and other information technology programs. We also would want to determine if the critical skills are generic or industry specific.

By examining the critical project management skills from the point of view of actual project managers, the intent is to inform the creation of an industry focused project management course as part of a course development plan by the principal investigator at Mount Royal University.

## 2. BRIEF REVIEW OF LITERATURE

The literature reviewed for this initiative sought to determine the criteria for successful project management outcomes as well as the characteristics of an effective project manager, specifically in IT projects, but also in a broader project management context.

Al-Ahmad et al. [1] created a taxonomy to categorize what they found to be the root causes of IT project failure. In addition, they highlight several project failure points including: poor roles definition, lack of effective project management skills and technology. On the flip side, Belassi and Tukel [2] created a critical success factor classification schema for evaluating project performance. They focused specifically on the interaction of a number of factor groupings including the project manager and the team members. The critical success factors utilized in our questionnaire were based on works of [1, 2] and from interactions with industry operatives. The critical success factors are related to the following: the project, project manager, project team, organization, environment, project governance, risk management, reasons for project, consultant selection, reward selection, technology selection and change management.

Parker and Skitmore [3] examined the role of project manager turnover during the project lifecycle. They performed a web-based survey to: "find the reasons for project management turnover; examine the extent to which project management turnover is associated with a particular phase of the project life cycle; and investigate the effects of project management turnover on project performance" (p.206). They note that "recruitment and selection of project managers have been long-running problems" (p.207). Additionally, the demographics section of the survey developed in [3] highlighted the relationship between the project manager's role and an emphasis on the educational background requirement for the project manager role.

Smith [4] defines 40 root causes of troubled projects in six categories, each of which contains an element of project management failure with "poor and unimaginative project management" (p.112) as one of the seven key causes of project failure. In our questionnaire, the causes of project failure were identified based on the works of [1 and 4] and from interactions with practicing project managers. The following causes of failure were identified: lack of needed resources including time, lack of expertise (identified as critical), lack of governance model, lack of stakeholder support, wrong technology choice, product maturity, unexpected expectations from customers, and wrong choice of partners/contractors.

# 3. METHODOLOGY
## 3.1 Sampling
Recruitment for this study is from IT project managers and other top level employees, who are directly (or indirectly) responsible for IT projects in corporate organizations. We are utilizing purposive sampling that targets 30 (out of about 60) Calgary based companies (in different industries) listed on the Toronto Stock Exchange (TSX). We are also sampling an additional 30 (small and medium) companies that are not listed on the TSX. We would be distributing questionnaires to an average of three persons from each of the sampled TSX listed companies and two from each of the non-listed ones (total sample = 150). The survey combines both online and paper methods. We expect a response rate of at least 25%. We would strive to obtain at least 30 responses (statistical minimum).

## 3.2 Instrument and Measures
The instrument for data collection in this study is the questionnaire. The questionnaire is divided into three sections. Section A deals with demographic information, while Section B extensively covers project success factors. Section C provides a free form writing space for the respondent to indicate the critical skills required of an entry level project participant.

## 3.3 Data Analysis
Demographic information obtained from the survey would be analyzed using descriptive statistics. Correlation analysis would be conducted to determine the relationship between demographic variables and IT project success factors, while regression analysis would be used in determining the individual levels of impact of the various project success factors on the actual project success. Mean and ranking order analysis would be applied in analyzing project risk and project close out variables. Qualitative analysis (content analysis) would be employed in determining the critical skills based on responses in Section C of the questionnaire.

# 4. CONCLUSION
IT project participants (irrespective of their level on the project) are required to have some minimum skills and knowledge in IT project management. This study is expected to analyze IT project management skills set required by the industry to participate meaningfully in IT projects, identify the skills acquired by new IT graduates, perform gap analysis of skills acquired to skills required, and identify what needs to be done to bring the skills acquired by the graduates to a level where they can participate meaningfully in IT project management of various industries. The results of this study would:

a. Help university professors of IT project management in structuring the IT project management curriculum to meet the requirements of the industry;

b. Lead to new relationships between the university and the industry in tailoring the teaching/learning of IT project management to the needs of the industry;

c. Help eliminate or reduce industry cost of retraining university graduates of IT project management as new entrants to project management; and,

d. Increase the university-industry consultation with a view to reviewing and understanding industry future needs, thereby making IT project management curriculum and teaching dynamic enough to meet the changing and challenging technology needs of the industry.

# 5. REFERENCES
[1]  Al-Ahmad, W., Al-Fagih, K., Khanfar, K., Alsamara, K., Abuleil, S. and Abu-Salem, H. 2009. A Taxonomy of an IT Project Failure: Root Causes. *Int. Mgmt. Rev.* 5, 1.(Jun. 2009) 93-104, 106.

[2]  Belassi, W. and Tukel, O.I. 1996. A new framework for determining critical success/failure factors in projects. *Int. J. Proj. Mgmt.* 14,3, (Jun. 1996), 141-151.

[3]  Parker, K and Skitmore, M. 2005. Project management turnover: cause and effects on project performance. *Int. J. Proj. Mgmt.* 23, (Apr. 2005), 205-214. DOI=10.1016/j.ijproman.2004.10.004.

[4]  Smith, J. 2002. The 40 root causes of troubled IT projects. *Comp. & Cont. Eng. J.* 13,3. (Jun. 2002,) 109-112. DOI=10.1049/ccej:20020

# Partnering with Industry to Deliver a Senior Level Course in the Bachelor of Computer Information Systems Degree Program

Ruben Yumol, Ph. D.
Mount Royal University
4825 Mount Royal Gate SW
Calgary, AB T3E 6K6
(403) 440 - 6028

ryumol@mtroyal.ca

Fahad Zaidi, BCIS
Mount Royal University
4825 Mount Royal Gate SW
Calgary, AB T3E 6K6
(403) 690 - 9946

fahad.a.zaidi@gmail.com

## ABSTRACT

The senior level course titled Information Systems Organization in the Bachelor of Computer Information System Program at Mount Royal University was designed to have an industry based project component. This paper describes the implementation of this project as well as the comments and perspectives of the instructor, the industry partners, and the students. The students' perspective is written by the co-author who took this course last winter.

## Categories and Subject Descriptors

This paper is in the broad class of **Education – Experience Reports**. It addresses the topic of **Systems Administration and Maintenance**. It is also in the general topic of **Industry-Education Relationships**.

## General Terms: Management.

## Keywords

Project Governance, Systems Development Life Cycle, Industry Exposure.

## 1. INTRODUCTION

The Bachelor of Computer Information Systems (BCIS) program at Mount Royal University (MRU) is a new degree with roots in the older Applied Bachelor degree in Computer Information Systems and Business (CISB). When the new degree was being developed, it was felt that there should be a senior level course that would somehow provide an integrative perspective of what CIS is all about. This course looks at how organizations manage and use Information Systems/Information Technology as an integral part in the achievement of its strategic goals. Its topics include Information as a Strategic Resource, IS/IT Strategic Planning, Project Governance, IS/IT Security, and Ethics, Society and the Green Initiative.

The students taking this course would have already taken a Systems Analysis course and most of them have taken the Project Management / Quality Assurance course. These two courses have exposed the students to Project Management and the entire Systems Development Life Cycle. In addition, all students would have had at least one 4 month work term.

To fully develop the course, the developers needed input from industry professionals and consulted the BCIS Advisory Committee.

## 2. COURSE DEVELOPMENT

The BCIS program has an Advisory Committee composed of IS/IT professionals in Calgary, Alberta. These professionals are high ranking IT personnel within their own organizations, some of them serving as Chief Information Officers (CIO) or Chief Technology Officers (CTO) or heads of the Project Management Office (PMO). During the course development, the developers presented their ideas to the Advisory Committee and sought their advice as to what this course should focus on. During the discussion, the committee members emphasized that this course should concentrate on the management, governance and organizational aspects of the IS/IT function rather than on the specific and technical aspects of IS/IT administration. In addition, they also recommended that there should be a strong industry component through real world case analysis.

These recommendations were in line with what the developers were thinking, thereby strengthening their belief that they were on the right track. In addition, one of the innovations that the developers were thinking of implementing was to have an industry based project where the students are exposed to how an IT/IS department functions within the organization. The strong recommendation by the Advisory Committee to have an industry component gave the developers the incentive to pursue this innovative learning activity for this course.

## 3. INDUSTRY BASED PROJECT

The industry based project was conceived very early in the course development. It was felt that because it was a senior level course, there should be some kind of project. The developers felt that the project would be different from the normal projects that the students have during their studies at MRU. It was at this time, that the industry based project was conceived.

The developers felt that the scope of the study should be limited. After some discussion, one area of study would be looking at a particular technology that has been or is being implemented in the partners' organization, learning how the technology was implemented by studying the IT development life cycle. Another area of study would be project governance, how the IT/IS department manages their portfolio of projects.

Implementing the project presented a challenge. On one hand, we will require the cooperation of our industry partners. The main concern that faced the developers would be the expectations of the partners, that is, what would they receive in return for their cooperation, since they will be using their resources to host the students. On the other hand, we are sending students to our partners. These are not consultants and should not be expected to provide any recommendations but only to learn how an IS/IT organization functions. The students' role would be to learn and be exposed to how large organizations manage IT projects. They will not be involved with the projects themselves but rather act as observers and learn from the experiences of our partners.

When the Advisory Committee recommended that the course have an industry component, the developers then presented the idea of the industry based project as described. The committee agreed that this was a good idea and that we should pursue it. In addition, the committee mentioned that they do not have any expectation from the students except that they learn from their exposure to a real IS/IT organization. They were willing to provide a learning environment to our students. In the end, the developers were able to get five organizations that will partner with us and provide our students with projects.

## 3.1 Preparing for the Industry Based Project

Once our industry partners were identified, the next step was for the instructor of the course to meet with the contact person or persons of each partner organization. The main purpose of the meeting is to identify the specific project and provide an overview of the project. Because the partner organizations are large corporations, they have a number of ongoing projects. The instructor and the contact persons discuss these candidate projects and eventually decide on a specific project that will best provide the students with a good learning environment. It should be pointed out that during these discussions, no details of the project were provided. Only the general concept of the project was discussed. This was deliberately done by the instructor.

When the course was conceptualized, the course developers felt that the students should take ownership of the industry based project. Hence, by not discussing the details of the project, the instructor can only provide a general description of the project and let the students fill in the details as they conduct their studies.

After the interviews, the instructor prepared a write-up of the project that provided the description of the project and the contact information of the project contact. In most of the projects, the person who will be the main contact of the students is different from the initial contact persons. The instructor did not interview the project contacts.

We will comment on this approach by the instructor later in the paper.

The projects that the students were involved in were:

1. The Digital Railway, the convergence of engineering and Information Technology in railway operations
2. Managing the Internal IT services to support delivery of services to the clients of a consulting firm.
3. Project Governance of multiple province wide projects in the health care industry
4. Enhancing Information Systems to accommodate required business changes for a major pipeline company.
5. Project Governance of the In-Cab Device Replacement Project for a large bulk trucking service provider.

## 3.2 Project Set-up and Mechanics

There were 20 students registered in the course. The students were divided into 5 groups (or project teams) of 4 each. In addition to the instructor, three other faculty members volunteered to be faculty advisers to the project teams. Each project team and their faculty adviser were provided with the project description and contact information.

The project team first met with the faculty adviser to discuss expectations from the project team as well as identify the adviser's role in the project. It was left to the adviser as to how involved he would be in the project.

The project team initiated the initial meeting with the project contact. During this meeting, the scope and details of the project was provided to the students as well as the expectations of the project team. In addition, some project teams and the instructor were asked to sign a non-disclosure / confidentiality agreement. This agreement is important to the industry study since the students will be exposed to and report on confidential information.

How the project team conducted the project varied from project to project. Some project teams met periodically with industry partners while others met for a few times and then communicated via telephone or email whenever necessary. It was stressed on the project team that they should abide by the constraints of their contact persons since many of these are quite busy. They were also advised that they should conduct themselves in a professional and ethical manner.

Each project team was required to provide a bi-weekly report to the instructor and faculty advisers updating them of the progress of the project. The purpose of the report is to enable the instructor and advisers to assess if the project is going well as planned or an intervention is required.

Overall, the projects all ran smoothly. In our opinion, because our partners knew that they will provide a learning experience and industry exposure to the students is the major reason why the projects were successful. In addition, our students acted in a professional manner whenever they were dealing with our industry partners and this also contributed to the success of the projects.

## 3.3 Project Windup

At the end of the semester, the students had two class activities. First, they presented in class the results of their study. I asked the students to invite their contact persons to their presentations. Unfortunately, because of timing, none of our industry partners was able to make the presentation. Nonetheless, at least one group actually went back to their organization and presented their work there.

The project teams also submitted a final report. I have asked the project teams to provide a copy to their contacts in order that they can comment and confirm that the information that the students have written are correct and complies to any non-disclosure agreement that was signed.

Although the presentations and reports were well done and in a professional manner, the instructor felt that there is room for improvement. Some recommendations will be discussed later in the paper.

## 4. ASSESSMENT OF THE INDUSTRY BASED PROJECT

Our students found this project to be a true educational experience. Many of the students mentioned informally that the project allowed them to have a much larger view of IS/IT organizations than their work term experience and that this industry exposure enhanced their desire to continue on with their IS/IT careers. Many of them witnessed leading edge technology being used to support the organization and many of the students benefited from this experience. Thus, our students felt that this was a good course and that the industry project was a major learning experience.

## 5. INDUSTRY PERSPECTIVE

After the course was over, the instructor requested the advisory committee for a meeting with the project contacts to obtain their feedback on the project as well as get suggestions on how to improve the project. Subsequently, the instructor met with three of the project contacts. The following describes the results of these interviews.

### 5.1 Industry Partners' Perspective

Overall, there is a consensus that the industry based project was a good exercise for the students. It enabled the students to get exposure to real life situation and to see how an IT/IS department functions. In addition, it allowed students to interact with practicing industry professionals. On the other hand, the project contacts were enthusiastic in meeting the students and showcasing their own IT careers. They felt that by interacting with the students, they are able to show not only how IS/IT fit into the organization as a whole, but also show the different careers in IS/IT. As one of the project contacts said, "I wish we had something like this when I was a student."

The project contacts found our students to be quite professional and fairly knowledgeable in project management and the Systems Development Life Cycle. Since the project looks at how IT was implemented in an organization or at project governance as practiced in industry, they felt that this background knowledge was very important for this project. In addition, they felt that the students were quite adept at interviewing and gathering data. Our industry partners treated the students as they would their own

employees and welcomed them into the organization. This fostered an open discussion between the project team and the project contacts.

Because the projects involved the implementation of some kind of IT or IS in an organization, the project contacts felt that it is important that the project teams have an understanding of project management particularly as it relates to systems development. In addition, the project teams should have a good understanding of the entire Systems Development Life Cycle.

Some stated that once the students felt at ease, often the question went beyond the scope of the project and into IT/IS careers and the project contacts were willing to discuss their careers with the students. They felt that this was as important as the project.

## 6. RECOMMENDATIONS FOR IMPROVEMENT

This is the first time that this course was offered in the BCIS program. As such, it is expected that the course will undergo an evolutionary process every time it is offered during the first few years. Although the course was developed in prior semesters, nonetheless, there was developmental work still happening while it was being offered. This was particularly true of the industry based project. The course developers had conceptualized the project. However, the implementation of this concept required the instructor to make a number of ad hoc decisions with regards to the project itself. It is in this area that there are recommendations for improvement. These recommendations come from the instructor, the faculty advisers, from the industry partners, and more importantly, from the students themselves. Our students recognized that they were the "experimental" class and therefore a number of them came out with suggestions to make the course and the project better.

Some of the areas that can be considered for improvement include:

1. Interview the project contact in addition to the partner contact

   A number of the project teams felt they were going in "blind" because the project descriptions were general rather than specific. In addition, some of the project contacts did not really have a clear idea of what the project hopes to accomplish. This resulted in some awkward initial meeting situations.

   By interviewing the project contacts, the instructor can then provide the project contact with the objectives of the project, the project outcomes, and identify and clarify what was expected from them. Furthermore, the project contact can provide more details about the project to give the students some idea of what the project is about.

2. Our industry partners recommended that there should be a defined number of meetings (3 or 4) rather than just leaving this open. In this way, clearer agenda can be created for each meeting and help the project contacts prepare for the meeting and other activities. It was also

suggested that perhaps one of the meetings could be devoted to discussing IS/IT career questions and concerns of the students

3. Hand out the Final Report Requirements before the students go to the first meeting

This semester, the final report requirements were handed out during the last 3 weeks of classes. Some of the requirements, such as a functional organizational chart, were not expected by the project teams and this resulted in them scrambling to meet this requirement. Had they known this from the beginning, they could easily gather this information.

In addition, it was felt that if the project team has an idea of what will be required, they could then focus their data gathering better, particularly during the first few meetings.

These are valid suggestions. However, its downside is that the project teams gather information to meet the requirements and possibly miss all the wealth of other information that provided the depth of knowledge and level of experience that the students received from the project.

Perhaps, this issue can be addressed in other ways such as in #1 above and also by creating an initial meeting guideline that identify what information should be gathered in the first few meetings.

4. Our industry partners suggested that there should be more written reports that the project contacts can review. But more important is that these reports should have due dates identified at the beginning so that the project teams and the project contacts are well aware of the milestones.

For example, require the project team to submit a write-up of the first meeting with confirmation from the project contact

In line with the idea that the students are the drivers of the project, the only report required from the project teams was the final report and presentation. Although this was initially welcomed by the students, it actually became quite a burden to the students towards the end of the term. This was particularly true when the draft of the report was presented to the project contacts and there were some misinterpretations that were found. Thus, the project team had a very short time to gather the correct information and incorporate these into their documents.

Had a write-up been required at the beginning and confirmed by the project contact, then the misinterpretations will be caught earlier.

In addition to this, perhaps an interim report sometime near midterm would also help the ease the workload at the end and allow our project contacts to review and confirm the information that the project team has gathered.

Although the unstructured approach looks good, nonetheless, these suggestions imply that somehow, there is a need for some structure in the project. As one of the faculty advisers commented, we are still working with under 25 year old students with some industry experience. They still will need guidance.

5. Draft of the Final Report should be due earlier than the last week of classes

The Final Report was due on the last day of classes, normally after the presentations were done. And the Final Report is the only written report that was expected from the project teams. This was part of the loose structured approach for the project.

What happened though is that the project teams did not really start working on the final report early enough to allow the project contacts to review and comment on their report. As a result, the last week of classes became quite hectic with students trying to get their contact's comments in a short time and finalize their reports.

It was suggested that the draft of the final report be set earlier, such as three weeks before the end of the term. This will allow the project contacts to review the report and provide comments and still allow time for the project teams to finalize their reports.

Again, this suggestion identified the need to provide some structure to the project and guidance to the project teams.

6. Bi-Weekly Report Requirements should be improved

As previously mentioned, the project teams submitted a status report every two weeks. In most instances, these reports contained a chronicle of the activities undertaken by the project team during the previous two weeks and hence were not taken seriously by the students.

It was suggested that these reports should contain more substance for it to have more meaning for the students. Perhaps, it should be a reflection paper on the activities that were undertaken as well as on the information that was gathered. This would encourage the student to do more critical thinking about the project.

# 7. STUDENT PERSPECTIVE

This course was taken by mostly third and fourth year students in the Bachelor of Computer Information Systems program at Mount Royal University. This portion on the paper will discuss the benefits and appealing aspects of the course from a student's perspective.

## 7.1 Student's Perspective of the course

One of the main benefits was the opportunity to learn Information Systems Organizations (ISO) concepts after completing several work terms. The reason being is that, students obtain jobs that are entry level and as a result, they do not get exposure to some of the high level concepts covered in this course. Students enroll in this course after completing courses in Systems Analysis, Project Management, Programming, Networking, Database Management Systems, and Web Development. This allows them to take the next step and understand the importance of aligning the technical goals with a company's organizational objectives.

By far, the most beneficial and appealing aspect of the course for students is the Industry Based Project. This allows students to gain exposures to other local companies. Although the students have a little bit of experience, their exposure is still limited to only those companies that they have worked for. This course allows them to not only learn about the company that they have been assigned but also the companies that their peers have been assigned since every group presents their report at the end of the semester. This allows students a chance to see IT concepts such as IT Governance, PMO, Outsourcing, and others in the real world. Programming and other technical concepts can be covered in courses via assignments and exercises but the other high level IT concepts are not. This is why this course is important in giving the students a full understanding of the IT industry and how IT departments within companies are structured.

The three main aspects of the course are interrelated with each other, which is another benefit for the students. The students learn about the concepts in class, then read case studies relating to the topics being covered, and then discuss these topics with the company that they have been assigned to. For example, one of the topics the course focuses on is the gap between IT and Business units and how the CIO, CTO, or another high-level employee must see the need to bring this gap together. The group that was assigned to a local IT consulting firm, known as Ideaca, chose to focus on this aspect for their industry-based project. The students were able to learn from Ideaca that the company introduced a new group called Application Infrastructure to address this very need. Ideaca wanted their internal IT staff to also interact with the external clients to bridge the gaps between IT and other business units. This was the main focus of the students' report and a main topic covered in the course. By doing so, the students saw the concept being applied in the real world and its benefits as opposed to only learning it in the classroom.

The students that take part in this course are required to do one mandatory work term as part of their degree. What makes this course different than the work term is that most students will have done their work term before entering the course and the knowledge and experience gained through the industry based project is on a much higher level than a typical work term. As previously mentioned, the course covers topics that an entry level student will not be exposed to during his or her work term with a company.

The students had no expectation when meeting with the client so there was no pressure on the student. This created a very welcoming environment for the students. The students were simply there to gain an understanding of a certain project the company was working on or a certain aspect of the company they were interested in. As mentioned earlier, this was a great opportunity for students to network with professionals in their field that they had not previously worked with. The project itself is initiated by the professor but the details are left for the student. This allows students to use project management concepts learned earlier and apply them to a real world project with an external company. Overall, the students were very pleased with the result of this project since it is a great opportunity to learn about a company that otherwise is not possible.

## 7.2 Suggestions for improvement

From a student's perspective, the reason the bi-weekly reports component was a failure is because each one was not worth any marks. As a whole, the reports are worth a few percent but the student's did not receive them back with a grade on them. This made students less motivated to complete them on time and keep them up to date. In the future, we would suggest to make them worth one mark and hand them back with a mark attached to them.

## 8. CONCLUSION

The industry based project is a critical component of the Information Systems Organization course. Based on the reactions of the students, it was the major learning experience that made the course unique. There was a lot of effort used to implement this component but this effort was well worth it. Our experience has shown that industry based projects augment classroom instruction well and provide students with exposure to the real world. We will continue to use industry based projects for this course and perhaps other courses as well.

Nonetheless, for the next offering of this course, the industry based project will be tweaked based on the suggestions above as well as the suggestions of our industry partners. It is hoped that by doing this, the project and the course will improve.

## 9. ACKNOWLEDGMENTS

The success of this industry based project can be attributed to a number of stakeholders. First of all, the role of the Advisory Committee is central. They provided guidance in the course material development, the encouragement to incorporate the industry based project into the course and provide projects for the students.

Secondly, the project contacts from industry who took time off from their busy schedules to work with our students and accommodate them. They provided the key learning experience. In addition, they also provided feedback on their experience and suggestions for improvement.

Thirdly, the three colleagues who volunteered their time to help supervise a project team and provide guidance to the project team.

Lastly, to the students themselves as they have accepted their role as the "experimental" class. They approached this whole industry based project as a true learning experience and as such made this industry based project a meaningful experience in the pursuit of their future and their careers.

# IT Service Management Education in Tanzania: An Organizational and Grassroots-Level Perspective

Jyri Kemppainen
University of Eastern Finland
P.O.Box 111
Joensuu, 80110, Finland
+358 44 999 7000
jyri.kemppainen@uef.fi

Matti Tedre
Stockholm University, DSV
Forum 100
16440 Kista, Sweden
+46 701 453 714
matti.tedre@acm.org

Erkki Sutinen
University of Eastern Finland
P.O.Box 111
Joensuu, 80110, Finland
+358 13 251 7923
erkki.sutinen@uef.fi

## ABSTRACT

Technology transfer from developed countries to developing ones is not a straightforward process. This is due to the expertise required for utilizing technology. Literature shows that education and transfer of expertise are necessary for technology transfer, but implementation of locally relevant education is a demanding process. Development of IT students' expertise requires adequate ICT facilities, but the effects of organizational support, human capacity, and the relevance of curriculum to the local context are crucial factors in IT service management education. This paper is based on fourteen years of experience in a Tanzanian university, and it shows the importance of the topics above for IT education in general. This paper also presents a two-tier approach to education of IT service management professionals: In that approach specific contextual factors of IT education complement generic perspectives of IT support.

## Categories and Subject Descriptors

K.3.2 [Computer and Information Science Education]: Curriculum

## General Terms

Management, Design, Experimentation.

## Keywords

ICT for development, ICT4D, IT education, IT curriculum development. IT service management, developing countries

## 1. INTRODUCTION

For decades various kinds of information systems and networks have played a central role in the organizations of developed countries [9,23]. Especially the use of information and communication technology (ICT) has spread to most areas of society. Computerization of society has been a fast process, and today ICT in its various forms creates an economic and productive backbone in the developed world. ICT plays a central role in terms of productivity as well as quality of production [4,7].

Due to the extensive diffusion of technology in developed countries' economies, development aid donors have, for a number of years, considered technology transfer to be a key element in development assistance to developing countries (e.g. [25,26,33]. Despite the criticism towards technology transfer in general, today

the focus of technology transfer has turned towards ICT, as its importance to various types of development is often emphasized [13,18,30]. Unfortunately, as historical accounts from a number of developing countries show, the impact of transferred technology on the economies of developing countries has often been insignificant despite sustained technology transfer efforts [15,25,26,28].

Technology can be seen as a tool towards a given purpose (e.g. [25,31,33]). Functional technology simplifies operations and improves productivity and quality. The precondition to functional use of technology in an environment has been summarized as follows: *"the precondition for embedding ... technology successfully in the local environment is the proper training and orientation of local experts, who can operate, maintain and repair the technology without reference to donor sources"* [40]. In addition, it has been argued that the sustainability of new technology (when transferred to developing countries) requires the involvement of beneficiaries and their capacity building for managing change [27].

Hence, functional ICT, or successful ICT transfer, calls for information technology (IT) education that graduates local IT professionals who are competent in IT service management (ITSM) in a given context. This perspective is crucial for the relevance of IT education even beyond the context of developing countries.

### 1.1 Role of Education in ICT Transfer

The above-mentioned preconditions of technology transfer—appropriate training and orientation of local experts—seem to be rarely met when transferring high technology, such as ICT, from developed countries to developing countries [3]. The most challenging aspect of the technology transfer process is the need for local expertise to use and maintain the new technical solutions (e.g. [19,40]). In this light, the main question regarding technology transfer turns out to be "How can technology be transferred in a way that its users gain a sense of ownership of technology?" People should be able to use the new technology to solve problems they define in their own communities [6,33,41]. It has been shown that acceptance or rejection of a new technology depends on actual needs that the users perceive, users' previous knowledge about the technology, observability of the benefits of technology, and the relative advantage, compatibility, trialability, and low experienced complexity of the new technology [24].

The traditional response to the expertise-related challenges of successful technology transfer has been formal education [37]. For example, individuals from developing countries have been sent to study abroad in developed countries (e.g. [39]), and educational programs and curricula from developed countries have been transferred to educational institutions in developing countries [3,11]. In spite of the advantages, both methods also have well-known disadvantages: the competences that are needed in developed countries are not always useful in a developing country (e.g. [32]). In addition, graduates of developing countries' own institutions have often been professionally trained for developed countries' labor markets only, which frequently results in them searching for job opportunities abroad [14]. As education abroad as well as imported curricula both face a number of disadvantages, there is a need for a different approach to the expertise-related challenge.

## 1.2  ICT Infrastructure in IT Education

Research reports indicate that successful transfer of ICT from one context to another requires simultaneous transfer of knowledge and skills [6]. However, one can hardly transfer IT knowledge and skills without having ICT infrastructure that facilitates the learning process of IT knowledge and skills. The ICT infrastructure of the school can serve as a real-life learning milieu that ITSM education requires due to its inherent orientation towards practical problems. Learning the skill set that IT professionals should have requires that students use IT in practice. Development of local expertise requires and benefits from a heavy emphasis on practical training [19,40,42].

Therefore, successful IT education requires well-functioning ICT infrastructure that can facilitate learning of IT skills. However, several studies show that the construction of ICT infrastructure in the context of a developing country—including its educational institutions—is challenging due to the lack of local IT expertise (e.g. [6,18,28,40]). Those studies argue that in addition to challenges during the planning and implementation phases of ICT projects, the local stakeholders and beneficiaries of ICT projects are rarely able to operate, maintain, and repair the infrastructure without outside support.

In addition, it has been argued that IT professionals who work in a developing country context need more profound knowledge about the factors affecting technology than IT professionals who work in a developed country do [19,35]. Without broad and fundamental knowledge about complete technical systems, IT professionals in developing countries cannot ensure that the ICT infrastructure fulfills its purpose (which is to provide services for its users at an acceptable level). East Africa currently has a shortage of IT professionals who can design, implement, and maintain IT systems of organizations (e.g. [19,22]).

The two concerns above form a vicious circle: Education of competent ITSM staff requires robust ICT infrastructure that can facilitate practical learning—but building, maintaining, and repairing ICT infrastructure requires competent ITSM staff. In addition, implementing ICT-facilitated IT education is an expensive undertaking. The price tag is particularly relevant in developing countries, where financial resources are scarce and ICT is expensive.

Our efforts to break the vicious circle in a Tanzanian university have given rise to the core question of this study: *"What are the salient features of well-functioning ITSM in a higher education institution in Tanzania?"* Answers to that question must take into account the complete economic, social, cultural, technical, and environmental context of developing countries.

In order to answer that question, we took a systemic view of ITSM requirements in Tanzania. Section 2 presents the research approach and methodological underpinnings for constructing that systemic view. Section 3 presents, from practical and organizational perspectives, the elements that ITSM education in our target country must take into account. Section 4 presents conclusions and our recommendations for ITSM programs in similar developing country contexts.

This paper introduces a two-tier approach to ITSM education. The approach complements the generic IT support viewpoints with aspects that determine educational requirements in a specific context of education. Hence, our approach helps educational experts and administrative personnel to match ITSM education with the expectations of IT in their own educational context.

## 2.  RESEARCH APPROACH AND METHODOLOGICAL STANDPOINTS

This research study is a part of a curriculum development process towards a new contextualized Master's Degree program in IT at Iringa University College, Tanzania. That M.Sc. program specializes in ITSM, and is designed from the local perspective, for local job markets, and for local organizational needs. The first milestone of this process is to identify and develop the course selection, course contents, and pedagogical approach for a Master's Degree curriculum in ITSM. In addition to the ACM/IEEE curricula recommendations for IT [16], increasing the local relevance of such curriculum requires three to six supporting topics, depending on the context of education.

The quality of IT education depends on a large number of contextual factors [19,30]. Hence, a broad systemic understanding of the educational context creates a foundation for improvement of IT education. For this paper, we analyzed relevant literature, international curricula recommendations, such as ACM curricula guidelines, as well as our personal learning process during our work in the past fourteen years in Tanzania. The foundation of this research is in our own extensive work in a Tanzanian university, where we gained experience of various IT positions on all levels ranging from ITSM to IT education, such as IT support person, IT instructor, IT manager, IT advisor, IT director, adjunct professor, associate professor, and professor. We recorded our experiences in research diaries, project reports, email exchanges, work calendars, to-do lists, meeting minutes, research studies, and other documents. That data set consisted of roughly 9000 pages of records. In addition to our own documentation, our data sources include IT coverage in Tanzanian media, visits to educational institutions and IT project sites, and a great number of informal discussions with people who have been involved in IT work in developing countries as teachers, administrators, or project workers. This paper omits deeper data analysis and presentation, and the paper focuses on broad guidelines instead.

The research was based on the action research approach and was exploratory by nature [12]. Our work followed the action research pattern of continuous learning through experiences when working in the organization. Typical of the action research framework, our practical actions were based on our existing knowledge, our successes and failures were analyzed post-hoc, and through reflection those new experiences led us to merge former and newly obtained knowledge together. This learning process gradually developed our expertise in the research area. During the process, we used qualitative and quantitative methods of data collection as well as data analysis. In addition, our modus operandi informally followed the design research approach, as we cyclically planned, observed, designed, prototyped, and tested numerous IT solutions based on initiatives and feedback by teachers, students, and administrative personnel of our college [20].

# 3. A TWO TIER APPROACH TO IT SERVICE MANAGEMENT EDUCATION

The goal of ITSM is to manage the ICT infrastructure that delivers the ICT services of an organization, and to guarantee continuous operation of ICT services because many vital functions of organizations depend on those services [1,5,7]. This dependency means that prediction and prevention of possible incidents that might hinder operation of ICT services play a key role in IT professionals' work. In order to fulfill its purpose, ITSM has to be well organized, follow transparent and predictable practices, and employ appropriate IT professionals. These requirements concerning ITSM call for a systematic approach from the people who are involved in the construction of an organization's ICT services.

This section introduces a two-tier approach to ITSM education. The approach is derived from our learning process in a Tanzanian university and it is supported by analyses of relevant literature. The approach systemizes the findings of the learning process, i.e., the salient features of well-functioning ITSM in a higher education institution in a developing country. The first tier, or the inner sphere, identifies the generic factors that influence the management of IT services of an organization, and their mutual interplay. The second tier, or the outer sphere, positions the generic scheme in the context where ITSM is learnt and taught, i.e., the educational context.

## 3.1 Tier 1: ICT Services of an Organization

An organization that recognizes the importance of ICT services in its operations normally describes its understanding about the role of ICT services for its operations in its ICT policy [1,5,34]. In addition, an ICT policy should define the governance and management structure for maintenance, operation, development, and implementation of ICT services. Therefore, the ICT policy creates the foundation for all use of ICT in the organization.

Practical implementation of an ICT policy depends on ITSM practices of the organization. For example, ITSM practices described in ITIL (2011 and 2007 editions) calls ICT policy by the name *IT Service Strategy* [1,8]. ITIL divides the management of ICT services to a number of phases: *service design*, *service transition*, and *service operation* [1,5,8].. Each phase is directed by *continual adjustment and change*. After implementation, when ICT services run on the service operation stage, those services are said to be at the phase called *continual service improvement*. From an educational perspective, ITIL fits well a problem-based learning process that aims at improving ICT services according to the goals of the organization.

Unfortunately, structured and well-organized practices for ITSM—such as those described in ITIL—are rarely achieved in organizations of developing countries, [1,11,18,21,36,38,42]. The reasons vary, but the most common challenges are related to the lack of a proper ICT policy and the low level of IT professionalism. Weaknesses in these two areas easily lead to improvised "ad hoc" implementations and inadequate maintenance procedures of ICT services. Even more, those IT professionals who try to improve the situation may face resistance due to disagreement with co-workers about the role of ICT in the operations of the organization. Therefore, IT professionals often

have to start from attitude changes towards a situation where the significance of ICT as a tool for the success of organization is recognized. This work necessitates various kinds of advocacy skills, for which IT professionals are rarely trained. Educational programs do include topics that are aimed at the management of an IT project's life cycle but they hardly ever include leadership or management aspects where continuation of IT services plays a key role [16,17].

Our research indicates that IT professionals should recognize the role of organizational support as a key factor for developing the ICT services of that organization. It is difficult for IT professionals to design, implement, operate, and maintain ICT infrastructure appropriately without strong organizational and managerial support. In addition, ITSM work is impossible unless the leaders are willing to invest on ICT equipment, spare parts, and human capital. This means that ITSM education should address the necessary advocacy skills. IT professionals must know how to understandably present and justify ICT requirements of organization, and how to assume an active role in discussions that concern the ICT services of organization.

In addition to organizational support, employing experienced IT professionals can be a challenge for the organization's management [6,18,29,39]. For example, at our college it has been a decade-long process to educate and commit an adequate number of IT professionals. The most difficult challenge has been the lack of well-educated and experienced IT professionals who are committed to settle in a rural educational institution. This is a special issue for ITSM because its vacancies are normally full time posts, which gives few opportunities for extra earnings. For example, it has been a common practice in our college that educators teach part-time in other educational institutions during their normal working hours. This kind of arrangement is not possible for ITSM staff due to their heavy workload.

Technical requirements set another cornerstone for reliable ICT services [18,32]. ICT infrastructure that consists of a large number of ICT devices requires continuous maintenance to function reliably. Maintenance of ICT equipment requires adequate work force, appropriate tools, and experience of good practices of ITSM. This is a challenge to ITSM because inadequately educated IT workers may ignore the importance of maintenance work to the continuation of ICT services and they are rarely able to do preventive maintenance [6,18,29,39]. The role of preventive maintenance is especially important in developing countries where procurement and delivery of spare parts can take a long time. In practice, ITSM cannot organize preventive maintenance without the capacity of IT professionals to anticipate incidents that may cause ICT equipment to malfunction and fail. For example, only through experience will an IT professional start to notice atypical sounds which may indicate an imminent hard drive or fan failure—both of which may harm ICT services, lead to loss of data, and cause a long disruption in services [18]. IT graduates' capacity to do contextually appropriate preventive maintenance is a goal that IT education must address, and for that goal adequate laboratory resources for problem-based learning are essential.

Figure 1 brings together the factors that affect ICT services in a higher education institution through ITSM. In addition, the figure presents interplay between the factors and uses the systemic approach of ITIL in terms of ITSM. The factors are identified in our research and also reported in various literature sources [1,2,5,10,12,20,23,32,35,37,38]. Although the factors have been

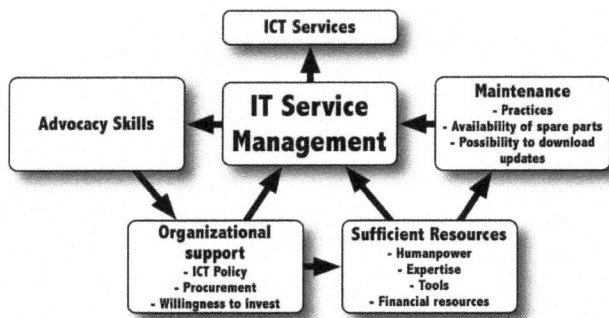

**Figure 1. Context of IT service management**

identified in a developing country context, they are generic to any context.

## 3.2 Tier 2: Context of IT Service Management Education

The context of ITSM (Figure 1) sets the scene and determines the structure of the ITSM curriculum, but that is not sufficient for high quality of ITSM education. ITSM must also be appropriately integrated into its broad educational context. Figure 2 summarizes a number of contextual factors that affect the quality of ITSM education. Those factors are collected from a number of sources [1,2,5,10,14,16,20,23,32,35]. Many of the aspects are straightforwardly justified. For instance, it is obvious that without financial, administrative, and academic resources, IT education cannot meet international standards. Still, resources alone do not guarantee contextually relevant ITSM education.

Our ITSM perspective to IT education differs from related educational approaches that are found in the literature. For example, Selinger's model considers the challenges of applying ICT to education—in general, not only to IT education—in developing countries [38]. Her generic approach hence differs from the more specialized approach of ITSM. ITSM education takes place in a particular context, and issues such as curriculum contents, its practical implementation, and organizational support need to be adjusted to the competences that are required from and expected of an IT professional in that very context. However, the design of relevant IT education needs both approaches.

In an analysis of the context of ITSM education, organizational support can be considered to be the crucial element underlying all other factors, since organizational stakeholders are strongly involved in employing teachers, choosing students, developing curricula, and organizing facilities for the IT program. In addition, the quality of education services benefits from broad collaboration networks.

Besides the organizational stakeholders, other elements of human capacity also have to be recognized. The quality of education depends on teachers' professionalism and on a sufficient number of teachers in relation to the student body. Curriculum designers also have to consider the balance between designing the IT curriculum to the needs of surrounding society and designing the IT curriculum to meet international standards. In addition to organizational and curricular considerations, training responsible professionals is impossible without talented and motivated students.

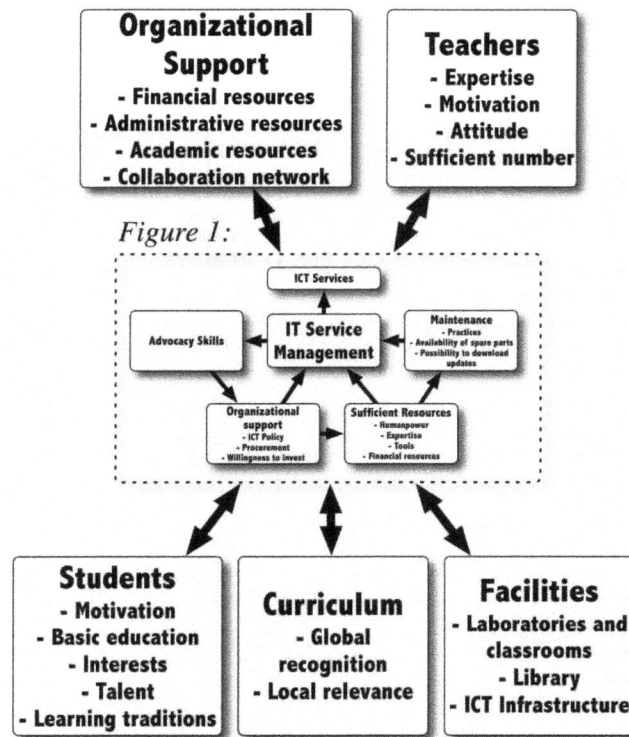

**Figure 2. Context of IT service management education**

It is also logical from the ITSM perspective that up-to-date facilities, such as classrooms, laboratories, library, and ICT infrastructure are valued as crucial elements to the quality of IT education. Facilities and rest of the learning environment must be well aligned with the curriculum and pedagogical approach, and facilities must support them. There again, curriculum and pedagogy are aligned with the educational goals of the educational institution.

The two tiers presented above must intertwine together when ITSM education is developed in a certain context. For example, *humanpower* is presented as a contextual factor of ITSM in Figure 1. Firstly, in that regard, the teacher must gain enough understanding about the issue. This relates the *humanpower* factor to the *teachers* aspect in Figure 2. Secondly, the teacher has to consider the students' backgrounds to facilitate students in a particular context. This adds the second aspect in Figure 2 (*students*) to the interplay. Thirdly, the teacher has to adapt the content of education to reflect the local job markets but also general professional qualifications. This adds the third aspect in Figure 2 (*curriculum*) to the interplay. Finally, education requires facilities, such as a library or simulation equipment to extend the students' views regarding the *humanpower* factor. In addition, a collaboration network is often a useful resource in all phases.

Similarly, the two tiers intertwine when students are educated about *advocacy skills* (Figure 1) as a contextual factor of ITSM. Firstly, in the two-tier approach, in addition to understanding about internationally recognized management practices and leadership styles, teachers must have appropriate understanding about their organizational role and position in the local context. This way the *advocacy skills* in Figure 1 relate to the *teachers* aspect in Figure 2. Secondly, the teacher has to combine those two notions to locally relevant knowledge and take students' pre-understanding into account. This way the pedagogy and course contents are culturally relevant, and meet global and local requirements. In this sense, three aspects in Figure 2—*teachers, curriculum,* and *students*—are tightly interrelated. Finally, the education aims at training ITSM graduates who are able to apply management procedures and leadership skills in the local context. This way the interplay between the tiers returns to the *advocacy skills* factor in Figure 1.

# 4. CONCLUSIONS

ICT services play a key role in everyday operations of organizations today. Hence, the importance of the quality of ICT services has increased. A central factor behind the quality of ICT services is a reliable ICT infrastructure that fulfills the organization's requirements. Organizations' dependency on ICT services has changed organizations' view on IT professionals' expertise and their formal education.

Research literature shows that adequate ICT infrastructure in educational institutions is essential for developing IT students' expertise to an adequate level. In addition, research literature describes a number of specific challenges related to the construction of ICT infrastructure in the developing country context. IT education everywhere has to find a balance between international recognition and local relevance. International recognition of ICT education is normally achieved when the curriculum covers a sufficient number of elements in some internationally recognized IT curriculum such as ACM/IEEE IT 2008. Locally relevant aspects of education are more challenging to discover, and they always require deep understanding and careful consideration of the local environment and circumstances.

Our analysis of aspects of ITSM found that the role of organizational support is essential for the quality of ICT services. This emphasis highlights the contextually relevant advocacy work within the organization as a vital element in the work of IT professionals. This means that management, leadership, and communication skills are a vital part of IT professionals' expertise when management of ICT services in an organization is considered.

Based on the analysis of our 14 years of experience of teaching and IT work in the Tanzanian IT sector, we have compiled an approach to ITSM education that takes into account the local realities. Our approach to IT education assists one to overcome the discrepancy between IT graduates' educational and working milieus. In most cases, IT students in Tanzania have not had transparent access to those types of ICT infrastructure that they should be building in their work. To solve this dilemma, our approach pays particular attention to pragmatic issues, which in most cases determine the success of ICT transfer between developed and developing countries.

Our approach consists of two tiers. The inner tier (Fig. 1) is the ITSM curriculum, which is based on the ITSM core knowledge, identified from the literature and on our analysis of experiences in the Tanzanian IT sector. The outer tier (Fig. 2) shows how factors related to the broader educational context need to be taken into account when designing the ITSM curriculum in a given environment. The two tiers interact with each other in order to guarantee a balance between the inner tier—representing the universal or general curriculum—and the outer one, representing the particular or specific expectations set for the curriculum.

Our approach to ITSM education serves as the foundation of a corresponding Master's program. However, as a product of an action research study, it suffers from the limitations set by a particular research environment. Therefore, its accountability requires continuous and close work with the relevant stakeholders.

Our approach proposes a new viewpoint to ITSM education beyond its original setting—even to the development of ITSM education in developed countries. That is because enhancing ITSM education with systemic and contextual viewpoints can make the profession more challenging and thus increase its attraction among prospective students.

# 5. ACKNOWLEDGMENTS

This research was funded by the Academy of Finland grants #128577 and #132572.

# 6. REFERENCES

[1] Adams, S., Cartlidge, A., Hanna, A., Range, S., Sowerby, J., and Windebank, J. 2009. *ITIL V3 Foundation Handbook*. TSO Information and Publishing Solutions. London, UK.

[2] Andersson, A. and Grönlund, Å. 2009. A conceptual framework for e-learning in developing countries: A critical review of research challenges. *The Electronic Journal on Information Systems in Developing Countries*, 38(8). 1-16.

[3] Bass, J. and Heeks, R. 2011. Changing Computing Curricula in African Universities: Evaluating Progress and Challenges via Design-Reality Gap Analysis. *The Electronic Journal on Information Systems in Developing Countries*, 48(5). 1-29.

[4] Bennet, S., McRobb, S., and Farmer, R. 2002. *Object-Oriented Systems Analysis And Design Using UML*, 2nd ed. McGraw-Hill Education. Berkshire, UK.

[5] Bon, J., Pieper, M., and Veen, A. (Eds.). 2006. *Foundations of IT Service Management Based on ITIL*, 2nd ed. Van Haren Publishing.

[6] Brewer, E., Demmer, M., Ho, M., Honicky, R., Pal, J., Plauche, M., and Surana, S. 2006. The Challenges of Technology Research for Developing Regions. *IEEE pervasive Computing*, 5(2). 15-23.

[7] Brooks, P. 2006. *Metrics for IT Service management*. ITSMF-NL. Van Haren Publishing.

[8] Cabinet Office. 2011. *ITIL Service Strategy*. The Stationery Office. London, UK.

[9] Castells, M. 2001. *The Internet Galaxy: Reflections on the Internet, Business, and Society*. Oxford University Press. Oxford, UK.

[10] Coate, K. 2009. "Curriculum," in *The Routledge International Handbook of Higher education*. pp. 77-99. Routledge.. New York, USA.

[11] Drew, E. and Foster, F. (Eds.). 1994., *Reports from Ireland, Ethiopia, Nigeria, and Tanzania*. The United Nations University. Tokyo, Japan.

[12] Greenwood, D. and Levin, M. 2007. *Introduction to Action Research, Social Research for Social Change*, 2nd ed. Sage Publications, Inc.

[13] Heeks, R. 2008. ICT4D 2.0: The next phase of applying ICT for international development. *Computer*, 41(6). 26-33.

[14] Hoffer, J., George, J., and Valacich, J. 2002. *Modern Systems Analysis & Design*, 3rd ed. Pearson Education Inc. New.

[15] Human Development Report 2011. 2011. The United Nations Development Programme, New York. Retrieved April 23, 2012, from United Nations development programme: http://hdr.undp.org/en/media/HDR_2011_EN_Complete.pdf.

[16] Information Technology 2008. 2008. Curriculum Guidelines for Undergraduate Degree Programs in Information Technology. Association for Computing Machinery (ACM) and IEEE Computer Society. Retrieved April 20, 2012, from ACM: http://www.acm.org/education/curricula/IT2008 Curriculum.pdf.

[17] Jarnan, R. 2011. Progress in Introducing ITIL into an Information Systems Curriculum. In *AMCIS 2011 Proceedings*, Detroit, 2011. Retrieved April 24, 2012, from AIS Electronic Library: http://aisel.aisnet.org/amcis-2011_submissions/396.

[18] Kemppainen, J. 2007. *Building ICT Facilities for Education in a Developing Country. Analysis of an ICT Project at Tumaini University/Iringa University College 2000-2004.* Master's Thesis. Department of Computer Science and Statistics, University of Joensuu. Joensuu, Finland.

[19] Kemppainen, J., Tedre, M., and Sutinen, E. 2012. A Tanzanian Perspective of the Technical Aspects of IT Service Management Education. *Journal of Information Technology Education: Research*, vol. 11, pp. 103-124, 2012. Retrieved April 24, 2012, from http://www.jite.org/documents/Vol11/JITEv11p103-124Kemppainen1061.pdf.

[20] Laurel, B. (Ed.). 2003. *Design Research: Methods and Perspectives.* The MIT Press. Cambridge, USA.

[21] Nfuka, E., Rusu, L., Johannesson, P., and Mutagahywa, B. 2008. The State of IT Governance in Organizations from the Public Sector in a Developing Country. In *42nd Hawaii International Conference on System Sciences.*

[22] Picot, A., Reichwald, R., and Wigand, R. 2008. *Information, Organization and Management.* Springer-Verlag. Heidelberg, Germany.

[23] Rogers, E. 2003. *Diffusion of Innovations,* 5th ed. New York, USA: Free Press.

[24] Sachs, J. 2008. *Common Wealth: Economics for a Crowded Planet.* New York, USA: The Penguin Press.

[25] Sachs, J. 2005. *The End of Poverty: Economic Possibilities For Our Time.* Penguin Group. New York, USA.

[26] Sallis, E. 2002. *Total Quality Management in Education,* 3rd ed. Kogan Page Ltd. London, UK.

[27] Smillie, I. 2000. *Mastering the Machine Revisited: Poverty, Aid and Technology.* Practical Action Publishing. Warwickshire, UK.

[28] Surana, S., Patra, R., Nedevschi, S., Ramos, M., Subramanian, L., Ben-David, Y., and Brewer, E. 2008. Beyond Pilots: Keeping Rural Wireless Networks Alive. In *5th USENIX Symposium on Networked Systems Design and Implementation,* 119–132.

[29] Swantz, M-L. 1989. *Transfer of Technology as an Intercultural Process.* Finnish Anthropological Society. Helsinki, Finland.

[30] Tedre, M., Apiola, M., and Cronje, J. 2011. Towards a Systemic View of Educational Technology in Developing Regions. In *Africon 2011 Conference.* Livingstone, Zambia.

[31] Tedre, M., Bangu, N., and Nyagava, S. 2009. Contextualized IT Education in Tanzania: Beyond Standard IT Curricula. *Journal of Information Technology Education*, 8(1). 101-124.

[32] Tedre, M., Kemppainen, J., and Nkumbuke, F. 2011. What IT Professionals Should Know About IT Work in Developing Countries. In *IST-Africa Conference*, Gaborone, Botswana.

[33] Tedre, M., Ngumbuke, F., Bangu, N., and Sutinen, E. 2009. Implementing a Contextualized IT curriculum: ambitions and Ambiguities. In *Proceedings of the 8th Koli Calling Conference*, Lieksa, Finland.

[34] The International Organization for Standardization (ISO) and the International Electrotechnical Commission. 2011. *Information technology - Service management.* International Standard ISO/IEC 20000-1. Retrieved April 23, 2012, from ISO: http://www.iso.org/iso/iso_catalogue/catalogue_tc/catalogue_detail.htm?csnumber=51986

[35] The Task Force on Higher Education in Developing Countries. 2000. Higher Education in developing Countries, Peril and Promise. The World Bank, The United Nations Educational, Scientific and Cultural Organization, and The International Bank for Reconstruction and Development. New York, USA.

[36] Torero, M. and Braun, J. (Eds.). 2006., *Information and Communication Technologies for Development and Poverty Reduction.* International Food Policy Research Institute. The John Hopkins Universtity Press. Baltimore, USA.

[37] Tumaini University/Iringa University College. 2005. *IPSP project's file,* 2001-2004. Iringa, Tanzania.

[38] Unwin, T. (Ed.). 2009. *Information and Communication Technology for Development.* Cambridge University Press. Cambridge, UK.

[39] Vesisenaho, M. 2007. *Developing University-level Introductory ICT Education in Tanzania: a Contextual Approach.* Doctoral Thesis. Department of Computer Science and Statistics, University of Joensuu. Joensuu, Finland.

[40] Vesisenaho, M. and Dillon, P. 2009. Information and communication technology education contextualized in a cultural ecological view of learning. In *Proceedings of Frontiers in Education Conference.*

[41] World Summit on the Information Society (WSIS). 2003. *Geneva Plan of Action.* Retrieved April 24, 2012, from WSIS: http://www.itu.int/dms_pub/itu-s/md/03/wsis/doc/S03-WSIS-DOC-0005!PDF-E.pdf.

[42] Zaku, A. 1989. Developing Engineers: Some reflections on University Education in Developing Countries. *IEEE Review*, 35(6). 229-232.

# Multi-perspective Survey of the Relevance of the Revised Bloom's Taxonomy to an Introduction to Linux Course

Gregory K. Johnson
Polk State College
3425 Winter Lake Rd
Lakeland, FL 33803-9715
863-669-2839
gjohnson@polk.edu

William D. Armitage
University of South Florida Lakeland
3433 Winter Lake Road
Lakeland, FL 33803-9807
863-667-7091
armitage@poly.usf.edu

Alessio Gaspar
University of South Florida Lakeland
3433 Winter Lake Road
Lakeland, FL 33803-9807
863-667-7088
alessio@poly.usf.edu

Naomi Boyer
Polk State College
999 Avenue H. NE
Winter Haven, FL 33881
863-298-6854
NBoyer@polk.edu

Cliff Bennett
Polk State College
3425 Winter Lake Rd
Lakeland, FL 33803-9715
863-669-2837
cbennett@polk.edu

## ABSTRACT

Equipping students with higher-order thinking skills as part of a program in information technology is no trivial aim. Course creation must always have this goal in mind. In particular, learning activities and assessments must be designed to teach, encourage the use of, and assess success in achieving this goal beyond merely teaching facts, methods and techniques. In this paper, we examine the degree to which we were able to assess higher-order thinking skills in students enrolled in the first course of an online Linux system administration curriculum. To assist other educators contemplating similar efforts, we briefly describe methods used to classify quiz and assignment items using the Revised Bloom Taxonomy (RBT) and discuss results from a survey administered to students who completed the course. Lessons learned throughout the process are described.

## Categories and Subject Descriptors

K.3.2 [**Computers and Education**]: Computer and Information Science Education – *computer science education, curriculum, information systems education.*

## Keywords

Revised Bloom's Taxonomy, Linux system administration, online learning.

## 1. INTRODUCTION

The need for qualified Linux technicians and system administrators prompted our two institutions, Polk State College (formerly Polk Community College) and University of South Florida in Lakeland (formerly USF Polytechnic), to collaboratively build an NSF-funded online program in Linux

System Administration to prepare advanced technicians with technical, higher order thinking, and problem-solving skills [1]. Linux specialists and educators constructed each course with an emphasis on higher-order thinking skills, as defined in the Revised Bloom's Taxonomy (RBT) [2].

Following the first three offerings of the initial course in the curriculum, we conducted a preliminary assessment of our success in integrating higher order thinking skills. Building on earlier efforts described in a previous paper [1], our team used RBT as a standard to assess the assignments and quizzes in the course. Additionally, students in the course completed exit surveys that requested demographic and pedagogical information, and specifically asked students to assess the degree to which the course helped them acquire higher-order thinking skills in Linux Administration.

Since enrollment in these courses was low, the number of students on which this work is based is necessarily low. The authors feel, however, that the information garnered from these surveys reveals worthwhile characteristics that have proven useful in improving the curriculum and may also provide guidance for educators interested in developing higher-order thinking skills as part of an online course.

Section 2 of this paper briefly reviews the Revised Bloom's Taxonomy (RBT) and its history in computing education. Section 3 summarizes efforts (fully described in an earlier paper [1]) to classify quiz and assignment items using RBT. Section 4 presents student exit survey results, including student characteristics and implications for the degree of success in imparting higher-order thinking skills in this content area. Section 5 presents our conclusions and advice, while Section 6 describes future work. Sections 7 and 8 provide acknowledgments of support and references from the literature.

## 2. REVISED BLOOM'S TAXONOMY

### 2.1 Overview

Bloom's Revised Taxonomy (RBT) represents an update from the initial taxonomy created in 1956 by a team of educators to define, measure, and categorize learning objectives and academic standards [2]. RBT was a necessary update that incorporated new understanding of learning research, cognitive science and pedagogy. In subsequent years since the updates, RBT has become a standard tool of reference for educators or anyone interested in learning in the cognitive domain. The new taxonomy defines six overlapping levels of thinking skills, including:

1. *Remembering,* accounting for the student's ability to recall or retrieve basic information from long term memory,

2. *Understanding,* tasking students with communicating meaning from the presented content by explaining or summarizing,

3. *Applying,* assessing whether the student can use his or her learning in a new way or can complete or implement a procedure,

4. *Analyzing,* requiring students to compare, contrast, and break a concept into its component parts and determine how the parts relate to each other and to the whole,

5. *Evaluating,* requiring learners to assess worth or value and justify a recommendation, and

6. *Creating,* assessing students' ability to produce, reassemble, or generate a new product or idea [2].

Levels 1-3 are recognized as lower-order thinking skills, while levels 4-6 are considered higher-order thinking skills.

## 2.2 Application to Computing Education

Both the original and revised Bloom taxonomies were designed for K-12 education. While they were generalized to higher education, the topics used to illustrate them in defining publications suggest their use in various computing disciplines might require adaptation, e.g. nutrition, Macbeth, mathematics, parliamentary acts, volcanoes, and report writing [2]. Consequently, a significant amount of computing education research literature has been devoted to investigating how these taxonomies apply to computing disciplines. However, most of this research was focused on the original taxonomy and emphasized its application to programming. For instance, many studies have been devoted to mapping Bloom levels to programming tasks. The consensus groups Bloom levels in three consecutive pairs, 1-2 / 3-4 / 5-6, which are then used to teach the whole programming skillset [7]. Having such a sequential progression in the pedagogy of programming benefits students, especially when compared to the "natural tendency" of instructors to teach the entire programming skillset in one offering and expect students to start by writing entire programs [4][6][7]. Bloom's taxonomies not only reflect the dependence of higher level cognitive processes on lower-level skills but also suggest a scaffolding approach for teaching the easiest skills to students until they are ready to progress to more difficult tasks [6]. This pedagogical insight also influenced the creation of improved assessment tools that assign better grades to students able to produce responses that reflect higher level cognitive skills [5].

These studies illustrate the overall relevance of Bloom's taxonomies; however, the literature also warns about the difficulties in applying them. RBT "is a valuable tool which could enable analysis and discussion of programming assessments if it could be interpreted consistently" [11]. Assigning appropriate Bloom levels to a given assessment is not a trivial task [9] and has led to the development of improved faculty training tools [8]. In some situations, ambiguity led investigators to suggest defining a computing education specific taxonomy instead [10]. The

consensus is that Bloom's taxonomies are helpful but present a serious challenge when applied to programming. This paper addresses a similar challenge for system administration.

## 3. ITEM CLASSIFICATION USING RBT

This section summarizes previous work [1] our team used to establish a "RBT profile" of our first Linux course offering.

## 3.1 Methodology

An interdisciplinary team of four faculty members—two from information technology, one instructional specialist, and one education faculty—examined quiz items and assignments designed for an Introduction to Linux System Administration course taught at Polk State College. Each assessment item was examined to determine its placement on Bloom's Revised Taxonomy.

Each team member first reviewed each assessment item and assigned an RBT level individually. The team then met as a group to discuss differences in taxonomy categorization and resolved differences through active discussions, research and extensive analysis of the assessment item. A review of the lesson content itself was frequently needed to determine whether it and the assessment item were so closely aligned that students would only require remembering skills to answer, thus warranting the lowest RBT ranking for the item. Group meetings were also used to develop consistent standards as they emerged from the collaborative process.

A stepwise process was gradually defined from team meetings:

1. Review each quiz question at least twice independently.

2. Identify the main verb associated with the cognitive process the student must employ to answer.

3. Assume the intended verb based on the context of the quiz question, if the verb is missing.

4. Select the verb that requires the highest level of cognitive skill if multiple verbs are used in the assessment item.

5. Review RBT and determine the best category that fits the chosen verb for each quiz question.

6. Consult the lesson content that supports the assessment question to determine whether lesson context explicitly contains the expected responses. If content and question are closely matched, then the question is rated at RBT level 1 (remembering) or level 2 (understanding) depending on perceived cognitive demand.

7. Compare researchers' RBT categorizations and note differences. Then determine best RBT level for each disputed assessment item after debate and analysis.

The process was time-intensive but necessary, as the team found that classification decisions were frequently non-trivial, and that significant discussions and debates among assessment team members were needed to classify many items.

Table 1 illustrates some examples of categorization of assessment items found in the course.

Table 1. Sample Classified Assessment Items

| RBT Level | Item Text |
|---|---|
| Remembering | Your IP address is 200.45.23.1, and the subnet mask is 255.255.255.0. What do these two sets of numbers tell you about the network and the host? |
| Applying | You are employed as an entry level Linux Admin for EZfactory that deploys Windows PCs throughout the company. Recently, Ubuntu 10.043 was added to each system as a virtual OS via Virtualbox. Unfortunately, dozens of employees have expressed frustration when attempting to access mobile devices such as USB drives on their virtual OS. Your supervisor asked you to create a technical document that details the procedures for mounting / unmounting a USB drive in Virtualbox on a Windows 7 host machine. Additionally, he wants you to use simple language that anyone can understand in your write-up and to include common problems users may encounter while attempting to mount / unmount drives and how these problems may be addressed. |
| Evaluating | You are the Linux administrator for a medium-sized firm and are responsible for maintaining four servers and 100 desktop computers and portables. After a stormy meeting in which the CEO demanded a reduction in the IT budget, the Chief Information Officer approached you for a special project.<br><br>He wants you to explore the use of Ubuntu Linux as a standard OS across the company but does not want immediate drastic changes to the core Windows-based configuration. Instead, he wants you to draft a report detailing three options he could explore to introduce Linux to all employees without disrupting their current installations and programs. He specifically wants to know the advantages and disadvantages of each option, the feasibility of a Linux rollout with minimal downtime, and your recommendation for the best choice. |

Table 2. RBT Levels of Quiz vs. Assignment Items

| RBT Level | % of Quiz Items | % of Assignment Items |
|---|---|---|
| 1. Remembering | 99% (99) | 28.2% (11) |
| 2. Understanding | 1% (1) | 33.3% (13) |
| 3. Applying | 0% (0) | 7.7% (3) |
| 4. Analyzing | 0% (0) | 23.1% (9) |
| 5. Evaluating | 0% (0) | 5.1% (2) |
| 6. Creating | 0% (0) | 0% (0) |
| Could Not Classify | 0% (0) | 2.6% (1) |

## 3.2 Assessment Distribution in RBT Levels

The classification process revealed significant differences in the RBT level of quiz items versus assignment items. Table 2 shows the distribution across RBT levels of each type of assessment.

The team noted the difficulties in designing computer-graded quiz questions that would require the use of higher-order thinking skills. In fact, *all* quiz items examined were classified as requiring only lower-level thinking skills. Indeed, all but one were classified at the lowest level – *remembering*.

Assignment items, in contrast, were constructed as essay or short answer questions, allowing greater opportunities for exercising higher-order skills.

The team found that creating assessment items with high RBT levels was challenging. Beyond the issue of assessment grading (automated or human), our classification experience found many cases in which assignment items attempting to assess higher-order thinking skills were an outcome of a flawed and debatable process in their creation. We concluded that the task of designing assessments demanding higher-level thinking skills is difficult, and intent does not easily translate into accomplishment.

## 4. STUDENT EXIT SURVEY

In each of three recent offerings of the course (all during fall of 2011), students were surveyed at the conclusion of the course. The number of students in each class was 6, 9 and 5, respectively, for a total population of 20 students. The low number of cases limits the depth of analyses that can be performed, but items of interest can still be found in demographics and student reports of learning activities in which they engaged. Students were also asked to rate the degree to which the learning activities supplied in the course helped them develop higher-order thinking skills as defined in the RBT. Surveys for the three offerings of the course were identical, so we combined the survey results into one dataset for analysis.

## 4.1 Selected Student Demographics

The students in the three offerings of the course were enrolled in an open access community/state college setting in either the AS degree program or high school dual-enrollment students in a Computer Network Engineering program (Linux concentration). Most enrollees were male, but two of twenty were female students. Sixty-five percent were full-time students (no outside employment), while five were employed full-time and two part-time. Seventy percent of students had no IT work experience; the remaining thirty percent were split evenly between students with some IT experience and students with significant (more than five years) IT experience. The mean age of students in the course was 27.1 years, with a range from 16 to 45 years. Students reported a current course load from 1 to 7 courses with the mean being 3.65 courses.

The implication from these results is that the students taking this course vary widely with minimal homogeneity. The five full-time employed students were probably able to take the course due to its online delivery mode. Students reported expending a reasonable amount of effort taking this course. The mean number of hours spent each week on the course was 6.8, with a minimum of 4 hours and a maximum of 12.

## 4.2 Learning Activities

To impart higher-order thinking skills to students in this course, learning activities were made available. Students were surveyed as to their use of each. Learning activities included:

- **Reading assignments**. 90% of students rated this activity "somewhat useful" or "very useful."

- **Watching videos**. 90% of students rated this activity "somewhat useful" or "very useful."

- **Discussion forum participation**. 70% of students rated this activity "somewhat useful" or "very useful."

- **Taking non-graded practice quizzes**. 35% of students rated this activity "somewhat useful" or "very useful."

- **Working on non-graded practice assignments**. 35% of students also rated this activity "somewhat useful" or "very useful."

Reading assignments, watching videos and participation in discussions are fairly standard techniques, but the provision of non-graded quizzes and assignments is less typical.

## 4.3 Development of RBT Skills

The survey used six questions meant to establish the students' perception on how learning activities supported the development of higher-order thinking skills. These were written with the preamble "Indicate how much the learning activities in this course helped you develop the following skills," followed by the RBT skill name (i.e., remembering), and ending with an example of the use of that skill. Students were asked to select among the following options: "No learning activities helped me develop this skill," "few did," "somewhat, some did," and "many did."

**RBT Level 1:** *Remembering*. This level, the lowest in Bloom's hierarchy, is typified by verbs such as "define," "list," match," "quote," and "recite." Student responses suggest this skill was well served by the course, as shown in Figure 1.

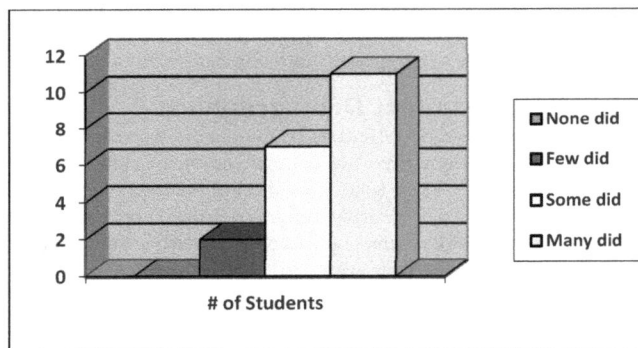

Figure 1. Activities Useful in Developing *Remembering* Skill

**RBT Level 2:** *Understanding*. This level is typified by verbs such as "discuss," "interpret," restate", and "summarize." Student responses shown in Figure 2 suggest that this skill was also well served by the course, although not quite as well as RBT Level 1 (understanding).

**RBT Level 3:** *Applying*. This level is typified by verbs such as "manipulate," "demonstrate," "compute," and "apply." Here we begin to see a significant decline in the number of learning activities students found useful in developing this skill. Student responses shown in Figure 3 show a clear shift from "many" activities to "some."

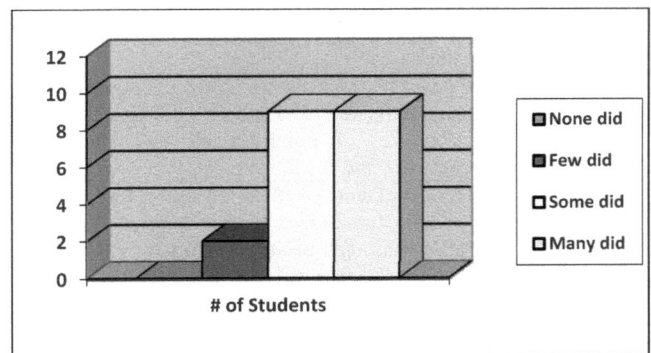

Figure 2. Activities Useful in Developing *Understanding* Skill

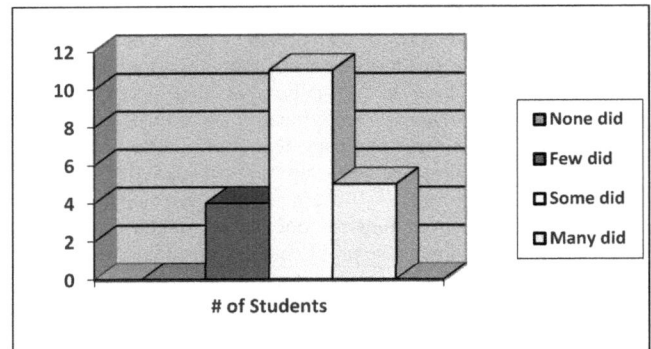

Figure 3. Activities Useful in Developing *Applying* Skill

**RBT Level 4:** *Analyzing*. This level is typified by verbs such as "contrast," "differentiate," "infer," and "analyze." Here we see further erosion in the number of learning activities students found useful in developing this skill. We also observe, for the first time, a significant number of students indicating that "no learning activities helped me develop this skill." This may be due to some activities being inherently low-level on the RBT scale.

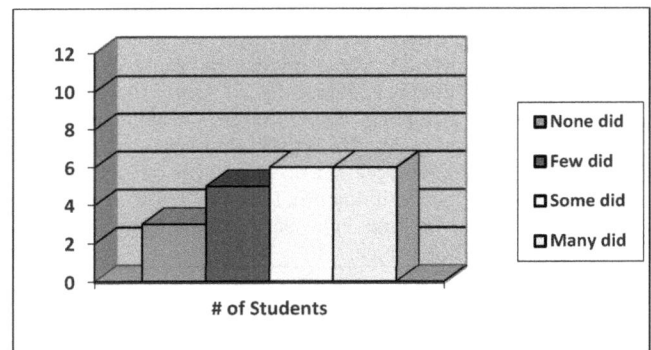

Figure 4. Activities Useful in Developing *Analyzing* Skill

**RBT Level 5:** *Evaluating*. This level is typified by verbs such as "assess," "deduce," "recommend," and "evaluate." In Figure 5, we see some "recovery" in the number of learning activities students found useful in developing this skill compared to the previous RBT level. We also see more heterogeneity in student responses; some reporting that no activities helped develop their ability to evaluate, while a larger number indicated many did.

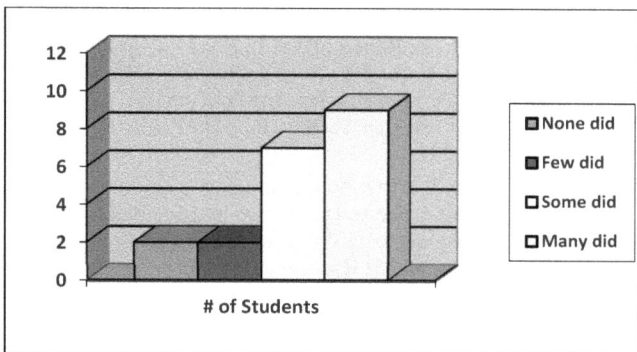

Figure 5. Activities Useful in Developing *Evaluating* Skill

**RBT Level 6: *Creating*.** This level is typified by verbs such as "construct," "originate," "propose," and "create." In Figure 6, we might see the presence of two groups of students with differing views on creativity, and what activities might prompt it. Nine students indicated none or few activities helped, while ten students felt some or many were of use.

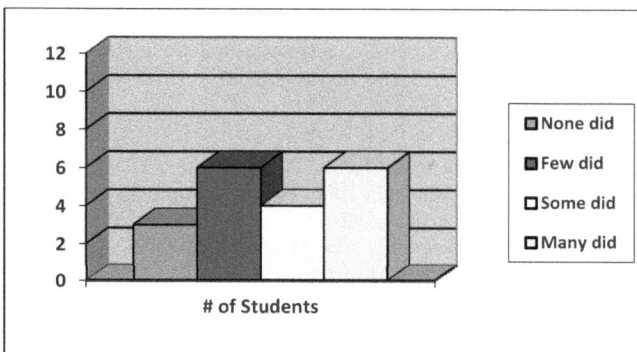

Figure 6. Activities Useful in Developing *Creating* Skill

**Comparing RBT Levels**. Figure 7 compares RBT levels using the number of students who felt that "some" or "many" learning activities in the course helped develop the skill.

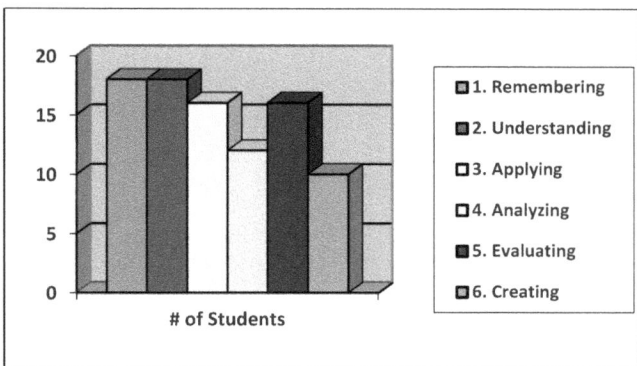

Figure 7. Comparison of RBT Levels

In general, students reported that they found the learning activities in the course useful in developing thinking skills, from a high of 18 of 20 students at the lower end of the RBT scale, to a low of 10 students for *creating*, the highest Bloom level. Within the limitation of the low N of our dataset, and given the natural variance in any group of students, we might cautiously conclude that learning activities provided in the course were successful in their aim of assisting the development of thinking skills, if only in students' estimation.

## 5. Discussion

Creating a course or program that will yield student graduates possessing higher-order thinking skills, as enumerated in the Revised Bloom's Taxonomy, is achievable, but requires an approach focused on learning activities that will prompt such thinking in a wide range of students. Such activities cannot be mere "add-ons," but must be designed into the structure of the course from the start.

While provision of learning activities and other materials that encourage higher-order thinking can be challenging, measuring the degree to which students possess these skills through quizzes and assignments can be even more difficult. We found that simply rating each quiz and assignment item to its perceived RBT level was a time-consuming and sometimes contentious process. We also found many cases in which a quiz or assignment item that might be seen as an excellent assessment of high-level thinking skills, e.g. a troubleshooting situation, was rendered trivial by a sufficiently analogous example being discussed during lectures. Instructors often evaluate the question "out of context" thus ranking it based on the cognitive processes required to solve it with only elementary knowledge. This view is inappropriate when students might leverage an analogy with a strongly similar problem or simply remember previous discussions.

While our findings suggest a predominance of lower level thinking skills, it is important to note that the course studied in this work is the *initial* course in the program sequence, and therefore more elementary and less challenging than later courses these students will undertake. We expect that materials and assessment items for the advanced courses will be inherently more adaptable to higher RBT levels.

## 6. Future Work

The authors plan to extend the work addressed in this paper in multiple ways.

We will continue to gather data from future offerings of this initial course, increasing the number of students in the dataset, and enabling more in-depth analysis.

We will integrate metrics of student performance in the course into the dataset, which will provide us with more data points to judge whether the course is accomplishing its aim of imparting higher-order thinking skills to students. Additional student surveys will also assist with this task.

As data is collected from offerings of more advanced courses in the program sequence, we will assess whether the higher level knowledge addressed in those courses enables more attention to higher-order thinking skills and makes assessment of success in that effort more practical.

We found that computer-graded quiz items were almost uniformly at the lowest RBT level. Consequently, we will explore creative ways to design computer-graded assessment items that rank higher on RBT and encourage higher-order thinking.

## 3. ACKNOWLEDGMENTS

This material is based in part upon work supported by the National Science Foundation under award #0802551 Any opinions, findings, and conclusions or recommendations expressed in this publication are those of the author(s) and do not necessarily reflect the views of the National Science Foundation.

## 4. REFERENCES

[1] G. Johnson, A. Gaspar, N. Boyer, C. Bennett, W. Armitage. 2012. Applying the revised bloom taxonomy of the cognitive domain to Linux system administration assignments. *CCSC-SE – 26th Annual Consortium for Computing Sciences in Colleges*. Southeastern Conference, November 2-3 2012, Southern Polytechnic State University, Marietta, GA. In cooperation with SIGCSE & ACM http://www.ccscse.org/

[2] Anderson, L.W., Krathwohl, D.R., Airasian, P.W., Cruikshank, K.A., Mayer, R.E., Pintrich, P.R., Raths, J., Wittrock,M.C. (Eds.) 2001. *A taxonomy for learning and teaching and assessing: a revision of bloom's taxonomy of educational objectives*. Addison Wesley Longman.

[3] Airasian, P.W. and H. Miranda. 2002. The role of assessment in the revised taxonomy. *Theory into Practice*, 41(4), 249-254.

[4] Buck, D. and Stucki, D.J. 2001. JKarelRobot: a case study in supporting levels of cognitive development in the computer science curriculum. In *Proceedings of the thirty-second SIGCSE technical symposium on Computer Science Education* (SIGCSE '01). ACM, New York, NY, 16-20. DOI=10.1145/364447.364529 http://doi.acm.org/10.1145/364447.364529

[5] Lister, R. and Leaney, J. 2003. Introductory programming, criterion-referencing, and bloom. In *Proceedings of the 34th SIGCSE technical symposium on Computer science education* (SIGCSE '03). ACM, New York, NY, USA, 143-147. DOI=10.1145/611892.611954 http://doi.acm.org/10.1145/611892.611954

[6] Lister, R. and Leaney, J. 2003. First year programming: let all the flowers bloom. In *Proceedings of the fifth Australasian conference on computing education* - Volume 20 (ACE '03), T. Greening and R. Lister (Eds.), Vol. 20. Australian Computer Society, Inc., Darlinghurst, Australia, 221-230.

[7] Oliver, D., Dobele, T., Greber, M. and Roberts, T. 2004. This course has a Bloom Rating of 3.9. In *Proceedings of the Sixth Australasian Conference on Computing Education - Volume 30* (ACE '04), R. Lister and A. Young (Eds.), Vol. 30. Australian Computer Society, Inc., Darlinghurst, Australia, 227-231.

[8] Gluga, R., Kay, J., Lister, R., Kleitman, S., and Lever, T. 2012. Over-confidence and confusion in using bloom for programming fundamentals assessment. In *Proceedings of the 43rd ACM technical symposium on Computer Science Education* (SIGCSE '12). ACM, New York, NY, 147-152. DOI=10.1145/2157136.2157181 http://doi.acm.org/10.1145/2157136.2157181

[9] Shuhidan, S., Hamilton, M., and D'Souza, D. 2009. A taxonomic study of novice programming summative assessment. In *Proceedings of the Eleventh Australasian Conference on Computing Education* - Volume 95 (ACE '09), M. Hamilton and T. Clear (Eds.), Vol. 95. Australian Computer Society, Inc., Darlinghurst, Australia, 147-156.

[10] Fuller, U., Johnson, C.G., Ahoniemi, T., Cukierman, D., Hernán-Losada, I., Jackova, J., Lahtinen, E., Lewis, T.L., Thompson, D.M., Riedesel, C., and Thompson, E. 2007. Developing a computer science-specific learning taxonomy. *SIGCSE Bulletin,* 39, 4 (December 2007), 152-170. DOI=10.1145/1345375.1345438 http://doi.acm.org/10.1145/1345375.1345438

[11] Thompson, E., Luxton-Reilly, A., Jacqueline Whalley, J., Hu, M., and Robbins, P. 2008. Bloom's taxonomy for CS assessment. In *Proceedings of the tenth conference on Australasian computing education* - Volume 78 (ACE '08), Simon Hamilton and Margaret Hamilton (Eds.), Vol. 78. Australian Computer Society, Inc., Darlinghurst, Australia, 155-161.

# Panel: Capstone Experiences for Information Technology

Gregory W. Hislop
Drexel University
3141 Chestnut St.
Philadelphia, PA
19104
011-215-895-2179
hislop@drexel.edu

Joseph J. Ekstrom
Brigham Young
University
Provo, UT 84602
011-801-422-1839
jekstrom@byu.edu

Heidi J. C. Ellis
Western New England
University
1215 Wilbraham Rd.
Springfield, MA 01119
011-413-782-1748
ellis@wne.edu

Sandra Gorka
Pennsylvania College
of Technology
One College Ave
Williamsport, PA
011-570-329-3761
sgorka@pct.edu

## SUMMARY

The integrative capstone experience is central to the advanced level of a four-year IT degree program as defined by the IT 2008 Curriculum Guidelines [1]. The general requirements for this experience include that students work in teams of 4-8 on a real-world project. This project should be sufficiently complex to require a team effort over many weeks. However, the implementation of the integrative capstone experience can vary widely from a design course without external clients, to projects that have real clients to professional internships and co-operative education experiences. Courses may also vary based on length, evaluation approach, process and deliverables, and instructor role.

The goal of this panel is to discuss best practices for capstone experiences for BSIT degree programs. The panel will contrast varied implementations of IT integrative capstone experiences to provide a starting point for discussion. Each panelist will briefly describe their institution's capstone experience, discuss the benefits and drawbacks to their implementation, share issues and ideas they have for improving the capstone, and discuss student opinions of the capstone. A minimum of 35 minutes will be set aside for audience interactions. Questions for discussion will include:

- How are BSIT projects different from capstone projects for other computing disciplines?
- What process and products are appropriate for a BSIT capstone?
- How important are external clients for capstone projects?
- How should individual vs. team contribution be evaluated?

## Categories and Subject Descriptors

K.3.2 [**Computers and Education**]: Computer and Information Science Education – *Computer Science Education.*

## General Terms

Human Factors.

## Keywords

Information technology education, capstone projects, team projects

## 1. GREGORY HISLOP

Drexel University is a medium sized research university with 12,000 full-time undergraduates and about 16,000 total students. Drexel is known for technological and professional education and for extensive co-operative education. There is a full range of computing degree programs including IT, IS, CS, CE, and SE. All these degrees are co-op oriented and the typical student follows a five year program that includes three co-ops of six months each.

Drexel has quarter terms and capstone design for the BSIT has been structured two ways in recent years. Initially, the capstone was a single term team project followed by a two term team project. More recently, this approach has been replaced with an integrated three term team project sequence (totaling about 33 weeks).

The capstone has been taught with combined sections that mix IT, IS, and SE students. Teams may contain a mix of majors, although students often choose to work within their major. Given this mix of majors, projects tend to be software centric, and there has been some faculty discussion as to whether IT majors should be encouraged to consider a broader range of projects. External clients are not required, but students often use projects connected to co-op experiences. The College is moving in the direction of requiring more client participation. As in many colleges, the tension between team experiences and individual grading is a concern.

## 2. JOSEPH EKSTROM

Brigham Young University is a private university of 33,000 students located in Provo Utah. The IT program is one of 6 programs in the School of Technology. The School is part of the Ira A. Fulton College of Engineering and Technology. The IT program offers an undergraduate IT degree and an MS in Technology with an IT emphasis. The undergraduate program was accredited by CAC of ABET in 2005 and 2011.

The integrated capstone experience consists of a sequence of two courses and a required work experience. The first course is a 2 hour project initiation, requirements, and preliminary design experience during the fall semester. The second course is a 3 hour project implementation, test, and documentation course taught during the winter semester. In addition, students are required to document at least 200 hours of work in a professional IT position. Since most of our students have part-time employment in IT after their sophomore year, this requirement is almost never a problem.

The 2-course sequence is done on a single project as part of a team formed early in the first course. The projects are proposed to the students during the first two weeks of the first course. During the 2011-2012 sequence 30 projects were proposed, 20 were presented to the students and 5 were chosen by the students to be implemented. The projects were originated by business entities, other entities in the University, students, and this year by one of the faculty. Students select their top 3 choices and a short paragraph explaining their motivation. The faculty then form teams and assign faculty coaches.

Working with their "customer" the teams complete a project life cycle through presentation of the project deliverables to the Industrial Advisory board. The last 2 years' teams have competed and placed in the top 10 nationally in Microsoft's Imagine Cup. Projects included an automatic scaling infrastructure for provisioning Infrastructure as a Service environments, a test environment for using streaming video goggles to assist hearing impaired children in watching an ASL translation at the same time as participating in other activities (i.e. a planetarium), and a cloud based management system for dairy farms. Grading is based on individual assignments and group performance, including coach and peer evaluation of all participants.

## 3. HEIDI ELLIS

Western New England University (WNE) is a small university located in Springfield Massachusetts with approximately 2500 full-time undergraduates. The Computer Science and Information Technology department is located in the College of Arts and Sciences. WNE has had a Bachelor's of Science in Information Technology since 2006.

The integrative capstone experience at WNE is accomplished via a required 3-credit internship which is a natural fit to WNE's emphasis on learning outside of the classroom. The internship requires students to work a minimum of 150 hours typically over 10-15 weeks. Students usually complete internships during their junior or senior year or the summer between junior and senior year and students may be paid for their effort. There is strong support from local industries and most students are placed into an internship with ease. Many students are hired by the companies in which they intern.

Grading is based on a combination of internship supervisor evaluation, student logs, and a paper. Students are required to identify learning goals and outcomes specific to the internship in which they are participating before starting the internship. These goals and objectives are set in consultation with both the industry supervisor and the faculty overseer. The student must also identify a tentative paper title. Grading is flexible, however the majority of the weight of grading (typically 60-80%) is placed on the internship supervisor evaluation.

## 3. SANDRA GORKA

Pennsylvania College of Technology (Penn College), a special mission affiliate of Penn State, is committed to applied technology education. Located in Williamsport Pennsylvania, Penn College attracts the second-highest enrollment in the Penn State system. Penn College has nearly 6,000 students enrolled in associate- and bachelor-degree programs relating to more than 100 different career areas. Penn College offers students hands-on instruction and access to the latest equipment, leading to excellent graduate placement and "degrees that work". The IT program is located in the School of Business and Computer Technologies and has students in several concentrations.

The Information Technology programs at Penn College are designed in such a way that all IT students take courses within the core information technologies at the beginning of their curriculum. Once this foundation is developed, students take courses that develop depth within their area of specialization such as application development or networking. Prior to taking their capstone course, they take a specialized 3-credit "pre-capstone" course within their area of concentration. This course develops project design, planning and budgeting within their concentration.

During their capstone semester, students are required to propose a project of their own design. The project must go through an approval process where the faculty member verifies that it meets the depth and breadth of IT. The depth requirement ensures that the project is not trivial in nature and includes aspects of project planning, time management, system analysis and design, and adherence to accepted standards. The breadth requirement ensures that the project includes integrated aspects of databases, programming, networking, web technologies, security, documentation and support. Additionally, projects must incorporate some aspect of IT of which the student is unfamiliar. The students are expected to complete independent research in this area and then integrate the knowledge into their project.

## 4. REFERENCES

[1] Lunt, et. al., "Information Technology 2008 - Curriculum Guidelines for Undergraduate Degree Programs in Information Technology," ACM/IEEE, Nov. 2008.

# Best Practices in Teaching Information Technology Development

Amber Settle (moderator)
DePaul University
Chicago, IL 60604

(312) 362-5324

asettle@cdm.depaul.edu

Deborah LaBelle
Nazareth College
Rochester, NY 14618

(585) 389-2563

dlabell1@naz.edu

Hazem Said
University of Cincinnati
Cincinnati, OH 45221

(513) 556-4874

saidhm@ucmail.uc.edu

Sheila S. Sicilia
Onondaga Community College
Syracuse, NY 13215

(315) 498-7218

sicilias@sunyocc.edu

## ABSTRACT

Programming is one of the most fundamental and central topics in the information technology curriculum. Because of its importance it is crucial to understand how to effectively teach development students. In this panel we share best practices for teaching programming to a variety of populations, including freshman, non-majors, and community college students. Various pedagogical approaches including pair programming, studio-based instruction, peer instruction, active learning, cooperative learning, project-based pedagogy, high-impact education practices, and CS Unplugged type activities are included.

## Categories and Subject Descriptors

K.3.2 [**Computers and Education**]: Computer and Information Science Education

## General Terms

Human Factors, Languages.

## Keywords

Best practices, programming, development, CS1, high-impact practices, project-based pedagogy, CS Unplugged.

## 1. OVERVIEW

One of the most fundamental topics in the computing curriculum is programming, and it is often the case that the first experience students have with computing is a programming course. The information technology discipline holds programming as fundamental, making it one of the pillars of the model curriculum [6]. An article discussing the development of the curriculum notes that "as with any computing professional, the IT graduate must develop the skill to program" [4, p. 354].

Because of its importance to the information technology curriculum, understanding the best ways to teach programming is crucial for faculty. In this panel we discuss best practices for teaching students to program, including techniques that are most effective in a first programming course, practical ways to implement high-impact educational practices in the context of programming classes, teaching non-majors cutting edge technology, and non-traditional activities for community college students. The discussion will include relevant pedagogies such as pair programming, studio-based instruction, peer instruction, active learning, cooperative learning, project-based pedagogy, high-impact education practices, and CS Unplugged type activities.

## 2. AMBER SETTLE: TEACHING CS1

A programming course is often the first experience that students have with computing, and as such, it is one of the most widely studied courses in the curriculum. In the past decade a variety of novel approaches to the CS1 classroom have been developed and studied, including pair programming, peer instruction, student-generated content, studio-based instruction, active learning, and cooperative learning. Each provides a way to approach the CS1 course in a novel way, by restructuring student interaction and reframing the interaction between faculty and students.

While they all differ in their details and the ways in which they have been shown to be effective, these approaches share some commonalities that illustrate best practices for the CS1 classroom, including: make the classroom dynamic, increase student-to-student interaction, encourage reflection, reduce isolation, and encourage a cooperative classroom environment. The connections between various novel CS1 pedagogies will be discussed to provide instructors with best practices that can be used in conjunction with or independent of other teaching techniques.

## 3. DEBORAH LABELLE: HIGH-IMPACT PRACTICES FOR PROGRAMMING

High-impact educational practices (HIPs) applied to a liberal education have shown to increase student success in all disciplines [7]. The IT student may take part in high-impact practices such as capstone projects and internships during junior and senior year [6]. Therefore, these practices are more likely experienced as summative rather than formative activities. Research suggests that students engage in multiple HIPs in lower-level courses for optimal success [1].

Opportunities for programming students to engage in HIPs such as service learning, community-based learning and collaborative learning projects are hidden in plain view on a typical college campus. As I walk around my small campus I look for development projects. There's a green house that needs a plants database with a web interface, there's a student taking volleyball stats on paper, and there's the sociology students using a 21-page paper survey to gather information about homelessness. How does the geology teacher keep track of his baby-jar collection of sand?

I work out the project expectations with my colleagues in these other disciplines, to try to ensure that the projects will have as much benefit for the recipients as for the students working on them [3]. The projects are designed to start in the classroom, and run well beyond the semester. My students volunteer to continue working on the projects on their own time. They become committed to the user and along the way they develop better programming skills and gain an understanding of how to use their skills to help others.

## 4. HAZEM SAID: PROJECT-BASED PEDAGOGY FOR NON-MAJORS

Cutting-edge courses such as those teaching iPhone development are particularly good attractors for non-majors. Teaching those populations development techniques can be challenging, but using project-based pedagogy can be helpful. Project-based methodology keeps the students engaged and focused on problem solving and enable students to relate development to their field of study.

In this context students are asked to develop four applications at an institution on the quarter system. Students spend two to three weeks on each application, and learning is done within the class time. Weekly journals are used to offer opportunities for the students to reflect on the challenges they are facing and offer the instructor an opportunity to provide context to the activities of the previous week and to adjust the pace, contents and challenges as the class proceeds. A group project is used for the final assignment. Students work in groups where they select an idea and work on developing the application for that idea. Class time is used for group work with the instructor consulting as necessary. As an important piece of the course, students are offered opportunities for extra credit or resubmitting the projects so they can focus on understanding the technology without a negative impact on their grade.

## 5. SHEILA S. SICILIA: CS UNPLUGGED IN THE COMMUNITY COLLEGE

Community colleges have a very diverse student body, in terms of age, past experience, and college preparedness. Many of our

students have not had good academic experiences in the past and are potentially "at-risk" for failure in college. Various studies have suggested that a factor for many of these students is a mismatch between the students' learning styles and traditional teaching methods [8]. Many of our students are "concrete-active" "tactual" or "kinesthetic" learners [5]. The study of computer programming, however, involves understanding logical processes that are not easy to see or touch.

Community college students respond positively to activities that model the processes in a way that is more tactual or kinesthetic. For instance, an activity called "The Living CPU" can be used to explain how the CPU processes machine code. We walk through running a short program at the binary opcode level, by acting out the parts of a simplified CPU, with a simplified instruction set. Students are assigned roles, such as ALU, Control Unit, Program Counter, Memory manager, etc. I draw grids for the memory on the whiteboard, as well as areas for the program counter and registers. The "program" that we execute is about 24 bytes long. These activities can be seen as a type of CS Unplugged activity for a community-college population [2].

## 6. REFERENCES

[1] Brownell, J. E., & Swaner, L. E. 2010. Five High-Impact Practices. Washington DC: AAC&U.

[2] CS Unplugged, http://csunplugged.org/, accessed May 2012.

[3] Connolly R. 2012. Is There Service in Computing Service Learning? In *Proceedings of the 43rd SIGCSE Technical Symposium on Computer Science Education* (Raleigh, North Carolina, February/March 2012).

[4] Ekstrom, J.J., Gorka, S., Kamali, R., Lawson, E., Lunt, B., Miller, J. and Reichgelt, H. 2006. The Information Technology Model Curriculum. *Journal of Information Technology Education*, 5.

[5] Honigsfeld, A. and Dunn, R. 2009. Learning-Style Responsive Approaches for Teaching Typically Performing and At-Risk Adolescents. *Clearing House*, 82(5), 220-224.

[6] Information Technology 2008. Curriculum Guidelines for Undergraduate Degree Programs in Information Technology. Association for Computing Machinery and IEEE Computer Society. http://www.acm.org//education/curricula/IT2008%20Curriculum.pdf, accessed May 2012.

[7] G.D. Kuh. 2008. High-Impact Educational Practices: What They Are, Who Has Access to Them, and Why They Matter, *Association of American Colleges and Universities*.

[8] Schroeder, C. C. 1993. New students--new learning styles. *Change*, 25(5), 21.

# MOBILE: A MOBile Instructional Laboratory Environment for Hands-on Information Technology Education

Paul Wagner
wagnerpj@uwec.edu

Chris Johnson
johnch@uwec.edu

University of Wisconsin, Eau Claire
Eau Claire, WI, USA

## ABSTRACT

We present MOBILE, a software system providing ad-hoc and hands-on learning environments for information technology education. Using MOBILE, instructors can hold workshops on any available computers, even in restricted lab settings or using participant computers. Features supported by this software include the ability to build and configure a workshop session on any desired information technology topic, creation and management of that session on top of any existing network, distribution and configuration of additional operating systems and applications, and the inclusion of auxiliary content relevant to the session. In this discussion paper, we describe the MOBILE infrastructure and explore an actual workflow for an instructor using it to teach a workshop on computer security. We have successfully piloted the system to conduct four highly-rated workshops at technology education conferences.

## Categories and Subject Descriptors

K.3.2 [**Computer and Information Science Education**]: Computer science education

## Keywords

hands-on learning, ad-hoc laboratories, workshops

## 1. INTRODUCTION

Educators face a tremendous question as they plan for workshops and outreaches: what is the best way to present the material? Most would agree that a hands-on, active learning approach engages students and has a greater educational impact. However, in information technology, active learning often means a computer is involved, and the prospect of setting up a lab full of computers is intimidating to many and time-consuming for all. Perhaps the venue is a school in which the lab machines are locked down and whose IT staff is not interested in installing new software.

Or perhaps the workshop is at a conference, and the lab is an amalgamation of machines assembled a few hours before the presentation. Maybe participants are bringing their own machines. Whatever the hardware infrastructure may be, creating a successful hands-on learning environment to teach information technology means addressing the problem of unknown and heterogeneous client machines. As a solution, we present MOBILE, a mobile interactive learning environment for information technology education. MOBILE is a software system that homogenizes a diverse information technology learning environment without burdening IT staff or permanently altering the client machines.

This project was born out of the frustration of the authors, who've been frequent instructors of and participants in workshops at conferences and schools. More than 50% of the workshops we've attended have been plagued with hardware and software issues, including a) limited lab space due to high demand from concurrent conference sessions, b) limited physical access to host site machines, and c) restricted software privileges on host site machines. These issues led to the prototyping of a software infrastructure that runs on top of a diverse set of machines, including participants' personal computers, without modifying them in any way. This prototype was used to successfully deliver four large-scale and highly-rated computer security workshops at computer science education conferences. MOBILE is a generalization of this prototype, such that it can be used to administer an ad-hoc laboratory for almost any information technology topic.

MOBILE solves the challenges of using machines outside of the instructor's control by providing a baseline operating system, a customization of Ubuntu Linux, which participants boot into from a portable storage device. Layered on top of this system is a communication utility the instructor uses to dynamically share files with participants. Linux is not suitable for every workshop, and for this reason, the MOBILE system may be populated with virtual machine images preconfigured by the instructor. With a little advanced preparation of the MOBILE system, an instructor may expect uniform software configurations and focus on delivering content instead of providing technical support during a workshop.

In this paper, we describe the MOBILE project in detail. We discuss in Section 2 relevant related work, in Section 3 its software architecture, in Section 4 our experiences in successfully using it to conduct several workshops, and in Section 5 our future plans for MOBILE.

## 2. RELATED WORK

Our development of MOBILE as an instructional tool builds on two main ideas: a) that laboratory-based learning is a valuable component in information technology education and b) that the administrative challenges instructors face in physical laboratories can be overcome. Work related to ours addresses these two points.

### 2.1 Active learning

Laboratory experiences complement the passive learning that comes from reading and listening to lectures, and no one questions their educational value. Nersessian [20] states that "hands-on experience is at the heart of science learning." However, it's not as clear what form the laboratory experience should take. Corter et al. [11] explore the question of whether remote, web-based labs can be as effective as hands-on labs. While the authors find that students can learn as much in remote labs as they can in hands-on labs, students strongly favored hands-on labs, ranking physical presence as the most important factor in effective lab experiences. Participants in the study commented that the inability to ask questions and clarify instructions was a major concern for remote labs.

Kumar [18] investigated the influence of labs on retention in a computer science program. His work contrasts open labs, which consist of exercises students complete on their own time, with closed labs, which are scheduled and structured. Switching to closed labs had no impact on retention in the study, but the assessment indicates that closed labs have a positive impact on student learning, especially in the first part of a course.

These studies, a few among many [24, 6, 19], strongly suggest that hands-on labs serve a crucial role in education. Despite the complications and cost of setting up a physical laboratory, the social and communication benefits are significant.

### 2.2 Lab Administration

Administering a lab full of machines has become a much simpler task in recent years, thanks largely to better software tools [14]. We discuss several aspects of configuring and maintaining a lab that are relevant to our project.

#### 2.2.1 Efficiency

The improved efficiency of configuring and maintaining a lab has mostly been a result of virtualization. Virtualization decouples the notion of a computer from discrete physical hardware; it is the "logical representation of a computer in software." [16]. There are many reasons virtualization is becoming increasingly popular, including reduced costs, improved hardware resource utilization, and lower energy consumption through the use of thin clients.

Educators have reported frequently the merits of virtualization in laboratory settings [9, 3, 24]. Van Aardt and Mossom [23] summarize the well-known dangers of running a physical laboratory: high cost, hardware failures, operating system (OS) breakage, and significant instructor time spent reimaging the systems for each new project. After switching to a virtual environment, they reduced the time to reimage their labs to just a few minutes.

The MOBILE project strives for efficiency in a slightly different way. Its intended purpose is to serve presenters offering workshops away from their home environment, such as at other schools or conferences. In such settings, the presenter has little control over the machines, which may not have the necessary software installed to conduct the workshop. MOBILE provides a baseline OS to run on the hardware that is available, turning a heterogeneous lab into a homogeneous one.

We note that while virtualization is a feature directly supported by MOBILE, the MOBILE OS itself runs on a real machine, not a virtual one. Participants boot into it from a portable storage device. We chose this approach in order to have complete software independence from the native machines, on which no guest accounts or virtual machine managers are needed.

#### 2.2.2 Flexibility

Many researchers have reported on ways to assemble labs for special purposes, like teaching networking or computer security [24, 15, 10, 7]. Often such labs have been designed to work under tight budgets [12, 13], and nearly all of them employ virtualization to reduce costs and allow script-driven maintenance. From an instructional perspective, it is important that labs remain general purpose—one lab, virtual or physical, may serve many purposes [3, 9, 4].

MOBILE has its origins in a software infrastructure for conducting workshops on computer security. However, MOBILE is an intentional repurposing and abstraction of this first project and has been designed to meet the needs of any software-driven lab.

Several curricula have been published that support physically portable labs [22, 5]. One of MOBILE's primary goals is to allow presenters to conduct labs on the road, at other schools or conferences where the presenters may have little control over host machines.

A project similar to ours is CPVM [8]. Butler et al. designed CPVM to provide a completely portable and predictable development environment for their students and for faculty away from their offices. By design, their environment is restricted in size and builds off a processor-emulation layer. Users still need access to host machine software. With MOBILE, we offer a full computing environment that runs directly on the hardware without requiring user accounts.

#### 2.2.3 Sandboxing

To learn, students need to have freedom to break things [13]. One of the features of virtualization most widely reported in recent years is the ability to create sandboxed environments [17, 4]. Users custom-build virtual machines configured for a particular purpose; these self-contained images do not interfere with other images or endanger the user's native operating system and personal files. MOBILE similarly protects the workshop participant's machine by imposing an instructor-configured baseline OS atop the client hardware.

## 3. DESCRIPTION

### 3.1 Architecture

#### 3.1.1 Overall architecture

MOBILE is designed with two major goals: a) to provide a standard yet flexible hands-on instructional environment using a heterogeneous set of computers brought by workshop participants or provided by a hosting venue and b) to protect those various systems from any harm. The environment is launched by booting MOBILE from either a system's hard disk or, more likely, an external storage device. Booting from an external device allows MOBILE to use a system's processor and memory without reading from or writing to any internal hard drives, thereby protecting the computers from configuration or data modification.

Booting MOBILE directly from USB devices is possible on Windows or Linux systems. With the aid of an auxiliary boot CD, MOBILE can be booted into indirectly on Macintosh systems. The foundation of MOBILE is a modified version of Ubuntu Linux that provides a standard base platform for the instructional environment as well as additional functionality for managing workshops and interacting with participants.

Suppose an instructor wishes to construct an educational workshop or outreach on some topic. In MOBILE, we call the software configuration for the event a *session*. For example, one may develop sessions for workshops on computer security, CS1 software development, or mobile application development.

The instructor first sets up a base installation of the MOBILE environment. Then, the instructor configures the session by installing any necessary application software that either runs directly on top of MOBILE or on top of a virtualization layer included in MOBILE and based on the opensource Oracle Virtual Box product [21]. The instructor may not want to teach in an Ubuntu Linux environment; this virtualization layer allows other operating systems to be used. Virtual machine images and application software for any operating system can be included, subject to licensing rights.

Next, educational materials such as slides, lab exercises, papers, and so on can be loaded. The virtual images, plus any application software, plus any instructional materials, are considered to be *content*, which is distributed to each participant along with the base MOBILE platform.

Once the session is configured by the instructor, the instructor clones onto other storage devices as many copies as necessary for the number of participants in their instructional setting.

The overall architecture of MOBILE is shown in Figure 1.

### 3.1.2 Networking

During a MOBILE session it will almost always be useful for the instructor computer and all participant computers to be networked together. This allows the addition of educational communication features such as "hand-raising," chat between participants and the instructor, and screen captures, which MOBILE supports through another opensource web conferencing software package called Big Blue Button [1]. Networking also allows for interaction between participants (e.g., gathering information from remote machines in a computer security cyberwar exercise), as well as between a given participant and the instructor (e.g., remote instructor examination and/or testing of each participant-written mobile application).

A base networking layer is considered to be outside of the scope of MOBILE per se, so if the session demands networking, an existing network must be present and all participating systems must be able to access this network.

In the case of a session which demands isolation (e.g., a cyberwar exercise), an isolated network can be created in a variety of ways, such as by using a switch and network

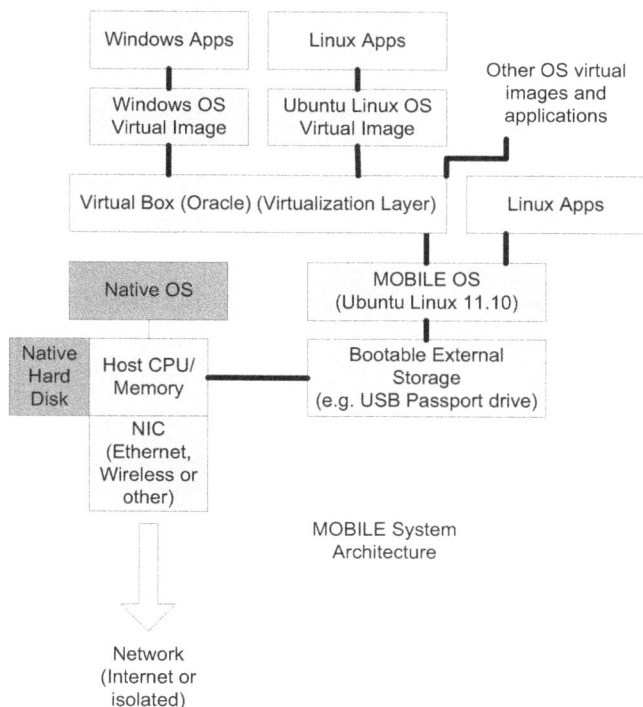

Figure 1: MOBILE System Architecture. MOBILE runs atop host hardware but provides a flexible and homogeneous software layer for lab instructors running hands-on workshops.

cables, or by using a session-specific wireless access point which can be accessed by each participant computer.

## 3.2 Workflow

### 3.2.1 Session Preparation

As noted in Section 3.1, the instructor must set up a number of layers for a MOBILE session. These layers are discussed in more detail below, and a summary of the steps is shown in Figure 2.

First, the base MOBILE platform must be created. This is done by downloading the alternate install version of the current Ubuntu Linux release. This version is necessary so that the actual installation can be run with a custom installer configuration file provided by the MOBILE developers, which customizes the installation to provide the MOBILE base and adds some necessary base applications (e.g. the Virtual Box virtualization layer).

Second, content specific to the given session must be created and added to the MOBILE content area. This includes virtual operating system images, which in turn must have any necessary applications installed as well. Such virtual operating system images can be created by the instructor, or obtained from virtualization repositories such as Jumpbox [2].

Third, the instructor needs to either clone enough copies of the session for each participant onto portable read-write media such as a USB disk, or make the MOBILE session available for download. Utilities for cloning and updating MOBILE environments are included in the platform.

PRE-WORKSHOP CHECKLIST

1. On base machine, install Ubuntu Linux from alternate installer using MOBILE's custom installer configuration file.

2. Prepare on base machine workshop content, including virtual machine images, slides, and supplementary software.

3. Clone base machine on to portable storage devices or to a downloadable system image.

4. Distribute clones to attendees.

**Figure 2: A summary of the steps an instructor must complete to administer a MOBILE-based workshop.**

Fourth, the instructor needs to distribute the cloned MOBILE platform to each participant, which can be done easily just prior to the session itself if cloned drives are used. If a downloadable system image is created, the participants are responsible for downloading MOBILE to a portable storage device before the workshop.

It should be noted that both distribution options have advantages in certain situations. While the former option of making physical clones is more time-consuming for the instructor, it ensures that each participant will have the system ready to go when the session starts. The latter option of making a downloadable image is easier for the instructor, but may be time-consuming for each workshop participant depending on the size of the image and the local network bandwidth, and it is of course essential that each participant complete this step before the session.

### 3.2.2 Session Process

As a networked MOBILE session begins, the instructor first boots the MOBILE environment and runs a utility called the *presenter* to establish a session. Each participant then boots their MOBILE environment and runs a utility called the *announcer,* which allows the participant to specify the name of the desired session and announces their participation in that session. The instructor's presenter window shows the participants as they connect to the session, which then enables further communication and interaction.

MOBILE supports several additional actions during the session. First, MOBILE supports the copying of files from the instructor to each participant system (e.g., a modified set of slides or an updated lab exercise), though this is limited in practice by the size of the files and the network bandwidth (e.g., copying an updated client OS image to thirty participants would not be feasible in most situations.) Second, MOBILE supports the remote execution of scripted commands on a participant system. This can be used for actions such as the automated installation of a software package on

**Figure 3: Screen snapshot of the MOBILE system from the instructor's point of view.**

the client systems in order to guarantee a certain configuration, or the remote execution of commands on the participant system to check that system's status or change the system's configuration to a known state.

It is also possible to further customize a session environment. For example, in a cyberwar exercise, you may want to have other host systems in the network act as possible targets and track how each participating system meets a certain set of session requirements (e.g., keeping up a specified set of software services). While we have proven the concept by making such customizations in specific sessions, generalizing support for such customization is part of our future work.

At this point, a workshop can proceed, with participants working individually in their MOBILE environment, but communicating with the instructor and other participants as needed as the workshop progresses.

## 4. RESULTS

We have used a prototype version of MOBILE in computer security workshops for technology instructors at the annual ACM SIGCSE conference in the years 2005, 2006, 2007, and 2009. Each workshop consisted of two stages: the first focused on information gathering and vulnerability assessment, and the second on system hardening and a small cyber-defense exercise which involved a period of system hardening followed by a period of scripted attacks from the workshop organizers. The workshops contained a total of seven exercises.

The first three years' workshops used team-provided notebook computers and a wired/switched network, while the last year's workshops used participant-provided notebooks. We provided two virtual machine images—a Windows image and a Linux image, both further configured with various security tools. Participants learned about and practiced using the tools during the workshops, and they then applied their overall knowledge in the final cyber-defense exercise. We further enhanced the environment by adding additional target systems to the network to provide different levels of secured systems for participants to investigate, and we added additional software utility support for tracking the availability of services on each participant team as well as for scoring the overall exercise.

Each exercise consisted of two parts. The first was a more

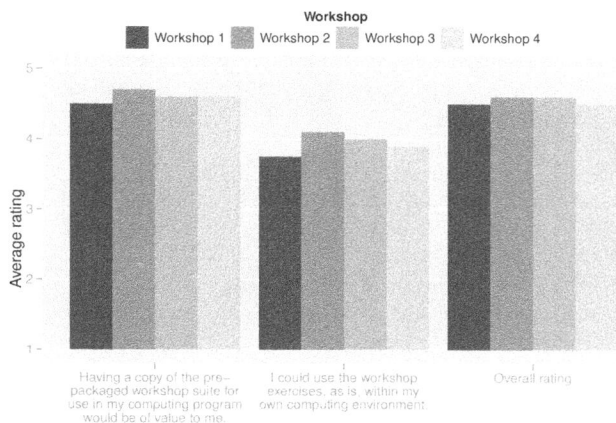

**Figure 4: Peer assessment of four workshops on computer security conducted with MOBILE framework.**

traditional lecture based on slides relevant to one computer security topic such as information gathering or system hardening as well as sample Linux and Windows security tools that were useful for that topic. The second was a hands-on exercise, where participants were given a lab sheet with several focused questions, leading them to practice with the relevant tools. The exercises involved a combination of tool usage local to each participant's system, as well as tool usage across the session network which interacted with the target systems and/or other participants. The MOBILE environment supported these hands-on exercises very well.

We had no system failures during these four workshops, though we discovered issues with individual participant machines due to their lack of sufficient main memory or other resources. Precisely identifying participant system resource needs is part of our continuing work.

Our research team has also created several other session scenarios as examples for future workshop and general use. These scenarios include CS1 software development using Java and Eclipse, mobile application development using the Android platform, and teaching graphics exercises using GLUT and OpenGL. A body of images supporting common session scenarios will be made available in a repository to support and encourage easy usage of the MOBILE system.

Overall, we have found that the MOBILE system enables hands-on CS workshops in a flexible yet stable environment. Preliminary usage shows that MOBILE can meet the goals and deal with the problems that originally led to this project.

### 4.1 Assessment

We have not yet directly assessed the effectiveness and usability of the MOBILE system. However, our assessment of the computer security workshops using the MOBILE prototype was very positive and provides initial evidence of its usefulness. A chart of selected evaluation questions and scores is shown in Figure 4. Overall evaluation of the workshops certainly includes evaluation of the content and instruction as well as the MOBILE platform. However, we feel that the positive response to the question asking if the workshop participants want to use our presentation tools does give initial evidence of the quality of our prototype system. An area of future work is indicated by the need to make the system more usable for the average information technology instructor.

We are ready to begin giving dissemination workshops with a full version of the MOBILE system starting in the summer of 2012. We plan for specific assessment of 1) overall effectiveness of MOBILE system in delivering quality hands-on information technology education to instructors, and 2) the usability of the MOBILE system in preparing, distributing and delivering educational materials to workshop participants. Focused assessment in these areas will better evaluate the quality, usability, and overall usefulness of the MOBILE system.

## 5. FUTURE WORK

While we have accomplished much, there is much more to do as well. Our immediate focus involves the following.

First, we will further develop the MOBILE system functionality and interface, with an emphasis on increasing the usability of the system. Ease of use is key for gaining wider usage of the MOBILE system. Further assessment of usability enhancements is essential and will be done as the interface is finalized. Providing an application programming interface or other means of customizing session functionality is a priority improvement as this as this allows better fit of a given topical session to many possible desired workshop environments and instructor goals.

Second, we plan for further dissemination through faculty workshops starting summer 2012. The dissemination workshops will also be used to find additional use cases which feed back into our development cycle. While we have found many possible uses and several potential development paths for the MOBILE system, we want to get more feedback on the best ways of making the MOBILE system useful to information technology instructors.

Third, we plan for specific assessment as noted above. While the initial evidence of usefulness is promising, we need to verify that the MOBILE system provides useful functionality in a package that is usable by the average information technology instructor. Assessing both functionality and usability are necessary to accomplish this goal.

Fourth, we are working to release, distribute, and support the MOBILE system as an open-source project, which will make the system available to all to use, modify, and enhance. We are also working to develop a community of users that can carry on development of this system after our research work ends.

Fifth, there are potentially other directions for the MOBILE system. Future hands-on information technology education will likely be occurring in the cloud or in some kind of virtual laboratories, and we will examine how the MOBILE system might fit with these new directions as well.

## 6. ACKNOWLEDGMENTS

This material is based upon work supported by the National Science Foundation under Grant No. DUE-0817295. We also acknowledge the design and development work performed by entire MOBILE team, including Tom Paine, Jamison Schmidt, Jason Wudi, and numerous student developers.

## 7. REFERENCES

[1] Big blue button. http://www.bigbluebutton.org.

[2] Jumpbox. http://www.jumpbox.com.

[3] Sam Abbott-McCune, A. J. Newtson, Jeffrey Girard, and Bryan S. Goda. Developing a reconfigurable network lab. In *Proceedings of the 9th ACM SIGITE conference on Information technology education*, SIGITE '08, pages 255–258, New York, NY, USA, 2008. ACM.

[4] Joel C. Adams and W. David Laverell. Configuring a multi-course lab for system-level projects. In *Proceedings of the 36th SIGCSE technical symposium on Computer science education*, SIGCSE '05, pages 525–529, New York, NY, USA, 2005. ACM.

[5] Monica Anderson, David Touretzky, and Chutima Boonthum-Denecke. ARTSI robotics roadshow-in-a-box: turnkey solution for providing robotics workshops to middle and high school students. In *Proceedings of the 43rd ACM technical symposium on Computer Science Education*, SIGCSE '12, pages 661–661, New York, NY, USA, 2012. ACM.

[6] Yuichiro Anzai and Herbert A Simon. The theory of learning by doing. *Psychological Review*, 86(2):124–140, 1979.

[7] William I. Bullers, Jr., Stephen Burd, and Alessandro F. Seazzu. Virtual machines - an idea whose time has returned: application to network, security, and database courses. In *Proceedings of the 37th SIGCSE technical symposium on Computer science education*, SIGCSE '06, pages 102–106, New York, NY, USA, 2006. ACM.

[8] Ralph Butler, Chrisila C. Pettey, and Zach Lowry. Cpvm: customizable portable virtual machines. In *Proceedings of the 44th annual Southeast regional conference*, ACM-SE 44, pages 616–619, New York, NY, USA, 2006. ACM.

[9] Xiaojun Cao, Yang Wang, Adrian Caciula, and Yichuan Wang. Developing a multifunctional network laboratory for teaching and research. In *Proceedings of the 10th ACM conference on SIG-information technology education*, SIGITE '09, pages 155–160, New York, NY, USA, 2009. ACM.

[10] Jean-Samuel Chenard, Zeljko Zilic, and Milos Prokic. A laboratory setup and teaching methodology for wireless and mobile embedded systems. *IEEE Trans. Education*, 51(3):378–384, 2008.

[11] James E. Corter, Jeffrey V. Nickerson, Sven K. Esche, Constantin Chassapis, Seongah Im, and Jing Ma. Constructing reality: A study of remote, hands-on, and simulated laboratories. *ACM Transactions on Computer-Human Interaction*, 14(2), 2007.

[12] Steve R. Cosgrove. Bringing together a low-cost networking learning environment. In *Proceedings of the 2011 conference on Information technology education*, SIGITE '11, pages 101–106, New York, NY, USA, 2011. ACM.

[13] Crystal Edge and John Stamey. Security education on a budget: getting the most "bang for the buck" with limited time and resources. In *2010 Information Security Curriculum Development Conference*, InfoSecCD '10, pages 29–35, New York, NY, USA, 2010. ACM.

[14] Alessio Gaspar, Sarah Langevin, William Armitage, R. Sekar, and T. Daniels. The role of virtualization in computing education. In *Proceedings of the 39th SIGCSE technical symposium on Computer science education*, SIGCSE '08, pages 131–132, New York, NY, USA, 2008. ACM.

[15] Bruce Hartpence. Teaching wireless security for results. In *Proceedings of the 6th conference on Information technology education*, SIGITE '05, pages 89–93, New York, NY, USA, 2005. ACM.

[16] IBM. Virtualization in education. http://www-07.ibm.com/solutions/in/education/download/Virtualization%20in%20Education.pdf.

[17] Kirk L. Kroeker. The evolution of virtualization. *Communications of the ACM*, 52(3):18–20, March 2009.

[18] Amruth Kumar. The effect of closed labs in computer science I: An assessment. *Journal of Computing Sciences in Colleges*, 18:40–48, 2003.

[19] Jean Lave and Etiette Wenger. *Situated Learning: Legitimate Peripheral Participation*. Cambridge University Press, New York, 1991.

[20] Nancy J. Nersessian. Conceptual change in science and science education. *History, Philosophy, and Science Teaching*, pages 133–148, 1991.

[21] Oracle. Virtualbox. http://www.virtualbox.org.

[22] Kai Qian and Chia-Tien Dan Lo. A novel embedded system curriculum with portable hands-on labs in a box. In *Proceedings of the 48th Annual Southeast Regional Conference*, ACM SE '10, pages 53:1–53:4, New York, NY, USA, 2010. ACM.

[23] Albert van Aardt and Mike Mossom. Using virtualization in teaching in a software laboratory. In *Proceedings of the 22nd Annual Conference of the NACCQ*, Napier, New Zealand, 2009.

[24] Michael G. Wabiszewski, Jr., Todd R. Andel, Barry E. Mullins, and Ryan W. Thomas. Enhancing realistic hands-on network training in a virtual environment. In *Proceedings of the 2009 Spring Simulation Multiconference*, SpringSim '09, pages 69:1–69:8, San Diego, CA, USA, 2009. Society for Computer Simulation International.

# Use of a Mobile Application to Promote Scientific Discovery Learning: Students' Perceptions towards and Practical Adoption of a Mobile Application

Sunmi Seol
San Francisco State University
1600 Holloway Avenue
San Francisco, CA 94132
+1 650 644 6049

smseol@mail.sfsu.edu

Aaron Sharp
Seeds of Empowerment
P.O BOX 19536
Palo Alto, CA 94309
+1 650 704 6034

aasharp@gmail.com

Paul Kim
Stanford University
520 Galvez Mall #3084
Stanford, CA 94305
+1 650 723 7729

phkim@stanford.edu

## ABSTRACT

This paper examines what students think about the use of a mobile application as a learning support tool and describes how a mobile application helps students improve scientific discovery learning outside of school. To meet the needs of conveniently saving and retrieving student's learning, the customized mobile application eBookMaker was developed for our two studies. This application enables students to quickly create mobile documents offering media-rich functionalities. Thirty-two fourth- and fifth- grade students in a public school participated in the studies. Each student was given an Android-powered Motorola smart phone pre-loaded with eBookMaker. In the first study, students were asked to make a mobile document about what they learned in class and fill out a survey form for their feedback about the use of a mobile application. In the second study, students were required to individually explore the scientific phenomena from their daily life, record their investigations, and create mobile documents using eBookMaker for two weeks outside of school. Based on the findings from these two studies, we can suppose that students have a positive attitude (80% of the students replied that they were mostly satisfied with a mobile application, eBookMaker) towards the use of a mobile application as an educational tool. Furthermore, a majority of students (86%) could figure out their own topics, search relevant information from a variety of sources (i.e. Textbooks or websites), and come to their own conclusion, which is a basic scientific discovery learning process, and even 24% of the students could design an experiment, conduct the experiment and draw a conclusion from the experiment, which is a more advanced scientific discovery learning process.

## Categories and Subject Descriptors

K.3.2 [Computers and Education]: Computer and Information Science Education –Curriculum

## General Terms

Documentation, experimentation, design

## Keywords

Mobile application, scientific discovery learning, mobile document, constructivism

## 1. INTRODUCTION

Today, one of the widely accepted claims in science education community is a constructivist idea that discovery learning is the best way to gain deep and lasting understanding of scientific phenomena and procedures for young children [2]. Constructivism claims that knowledge is actively constructed by the student, not passively delivered by the instructor or absorbed from textbooks and lectures. Each student will develop his or her own knowledge because the construction builds recursively on knowledge that the student already has [5]. Scientific discovery learning can be defined as a highly self directed and constructivist form of learning according to de Jong and Van Joolingen [14], which may refer to the instructional model that engages learners in the learning process through discovery. Thus, offering the opportunity to directly explore scientific phenomena to the student may be a practical approach to promote student learning in science education.

Many studies have pointed out the distinct benefits of mobile devices as educational tools ([3, 4, 9, 15]). The rapid advances (i.e., increase in processing power, memory, and connectivity) in information and communication technology (ICT) have made mobile devices more interactive and media-rich than before [12], offering a fun and engaging context to learners. Moreover, mobile devices require less infrastructure and electricity, which may give educational advantages over traditional computers [8]. In particular, the affordances of mobile phones can present a valuable opportunity to re-integrate student self-investigation into the discovery learning both inside of and outside of school. More specifically, students are already actively using their mobile phones ([1, 6, 10, 11]), so there is an opportunity to apply mobile phones into the real learning environment as a way to promote scientific discovery learning. Considering the current trend toward the consolidation of open-source mobile operating system platforms [1] and that mobile phone ownership among children has increased by 68% in the past five years [7], this is the perfect time to take advantage of these benefits of mobile devices [13]. Therefore, use of mobile devices (or mobile learning) may play an essential role in promoting student learning, in particular scientific discovery learning offering the opportunity to directly explore the scientific phenomena in the real world.

This paper introduces the use of a mobile application "eBookMaker" as a learning support tool in science education.

This application enables students to summarize their previous learning and share their summaries with peers in real time. Students can freely add images to their mobile document from the image gallery on the mobile phone or take a picture of their surroundings. Moreover, students can add their voices to give more detailed explanations about their mobile documents. Created mobile documents can also be shared with other students using Bluetooth, which is an open wireless technology standard for exchanging data over short distances. These features of eBookMaker may provide a particularly effective means of promoting student scientific discovery learning both inside of and outside of school.

The remainder of the paper is organized as follows. Section 2 describes basic functionalities of eBookMaker and section 3 describes purposes, participants, and procedures of two studies. And section 4 discusses the results from the studies and finally section 5 outlines brief conclusion and direction for future studies.

## 2. EBOOKMAKER

The customized mobile application eBookMaker was developed by a developer at Stanford University. eBookMaker, an android based mobile application, enables students to create their own mobile documents. This application was designed to help students add images and sounds as well as texts. There are two reasons to develop the application on the Android platform. First, Android is an open-source platform, which enables everyone to freely and conveniently develop mobile applications, upload them to their own mobile devices, and share them with other people. By simplifying the complicated steps to publish mobile applications, amateur developers can design and develop mobile application for their own research. Second, Android based mobile applications can be readily installed on any wireless Android devices unlike iPhone or iPad.

Figure 1 shows the main functionalities of eBookMaker. Upon opening the eBookMaker application, students can create a new mobile document that is a summary of what they learned in class (Figure 1a). This application provides students with three functions: create (edit), read, and send or receive (Figure 1b). After making a mobile document, students can edit and add new contents to it (Figure 1c). The application allows students to take pictures or download images from the embedded image gallery on the phone, and insert the images into the pages of their mobile documents (Figure 1d). Students can also record audio or insert audio files in the same way (Figure 1e). After students have finished creating a mobile document, it is automatically uploaded to the mobile document library of eBookMaker on the phone and then students can read any mobile documents of the library (Figure 1a and Figure 1f). Moreover, students can send (Figure 1g) and receive (Figure 1h) their mobile documents to their peers using Bluetooth technology, a local communication network (Figure 1g). All functionalities of this application are not difficult, a 15-minute overview on how to use this application would be introduced to the students and they can perform the task of creating their own mobile documents.

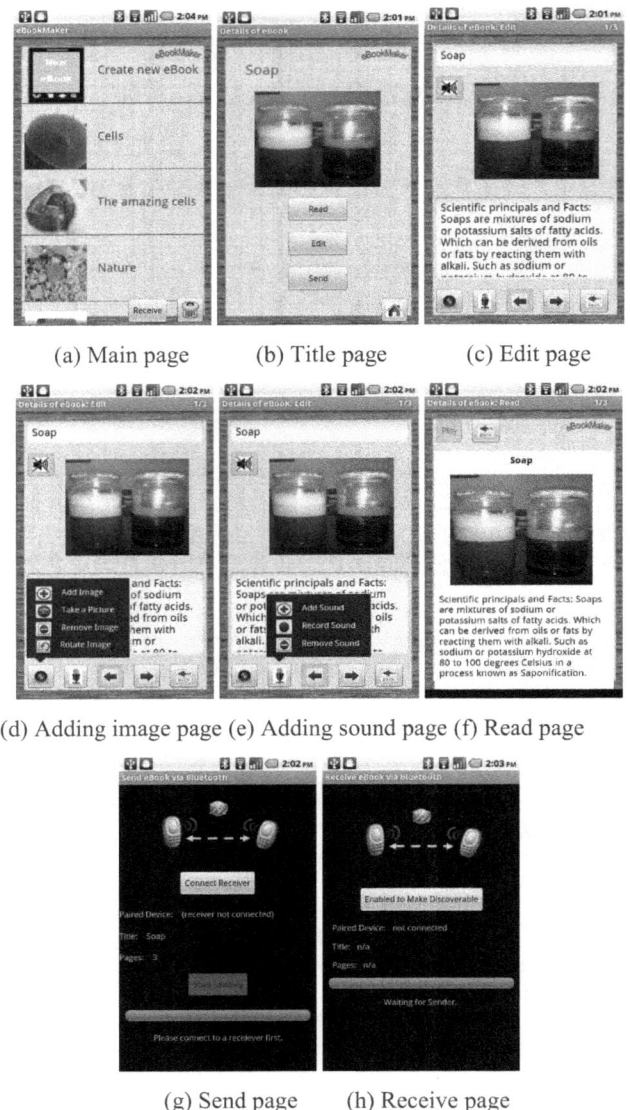

(a) Main page    (b) Title page    (c) Edit page

(d) Adding image page (e) Adding sound page (f) Read page

(g) Send page    (h) Receive page

**Figure 1. Basic functionalities of eBookMaker**

## 3. STUDY I & STUDY II

### 3.1 Purpose

The purpose of the first study was to investigate students' perception of the use of a mobile application, eBookMaker, as a learning support tool in a classroom setting. The purpose of the second study was to examine if the use of a mobile application has a positive effect on improving students' individual scientific discovery learning in their daily life.

### 3.2 Participants

The participants in these studies were 32 fourth- and fifth graders (16 female, 50%) from a public school in California. The class was a hybrid composed of 14 high-achieving fourth grade students and 18 fifth grade students.

### 3.3 Method: Study I

Each student received one Motorola Android smart phone preloaded with the eBookMaker application regardless of whether or not he or she already owned a phone. The students would listened to a 15-minute explanation of the application's basic functionality as well as what they are supposed to perform during the activity session. Figure

2 shows photographs of the students completing each of the required activities during the activity session. Students typed what they summarized based on their previous learning (Figure 2a), took a picture of materials that are related to their prior learning (Figure 2b), and recorded an audio explanation about their summary (Figure 2c). After creating a mobile document, students read the newly created mobile document (Figure 2d), shared them with their peers (Figure 2e), and then completed a survey that asked what they thought about using a mobile application in their learning process (Figure 2f).

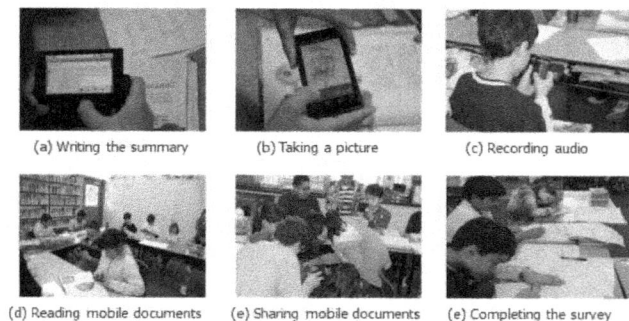

(a) Writing the summary
(b) Taking a picture
(c) Recording audio
(d) Reading mobile documents
(e) Sharing mobile documents
(e) Completing the survey

**Figure 2. The entire procedure of study I**

## 3.4 Method: Study II

All students have experienced how to use a mobile application, eBookMaker, to create a mobile document about their previous learning through study I. One month later, they took part in the second study using the same mobile application. Unlike the first study, they were asked to individually explore the scientific phenomena from their daily life using the mobile application, eBookMaker. All activities the students participated in during study II are shown in Figure 3. First, students were asked to share their thoughts about scientific phenomena that can be discovered from their daily life, and the instructor encouraged them to decide and select their own topics (Figure 3a). At that time, the instructor gave several examples to the students in order to help them figure out their own selection. At this point, the instructor let the students decide their topics of discovery scientific phenomena and explore how to use various functionalities offered by the mobile application, eBookMaker (Figure 3b). For the next two weeks, students were required to explore everyday life, discovery scientific phenomena, and figure out what is happening in the real world based on their topics. After two weeks, students got together and presented their own discoveries using a document camera (Figure 3c). Each student was given 90 seconds to report the topic of their investigation, how they chose to explore the scientific phenomena, the most interesting thing they had learned in the discovery learning process, and the conclusion on the findings of their own investigation (Figure 3c).

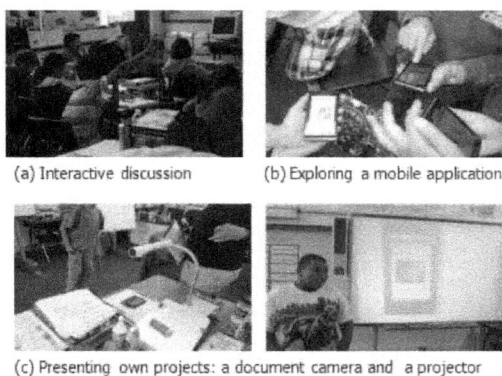

(a) Interactive discussion
(b) Exploring a mobile application
(c) Presenting own projects: a document camera and a projector

**Figure 3. The entire procedure of study II**

## 4. RESULTS & DISCUSSION

### 4.1 Students' Perceptions

#### 4.1.1 Overall Student Satisfaction

After completing the required actions, students were asked to indicate how satisfied they were with the use of eBookMaker on a four-point Likert scale: Very satisfied, mostly satisfied, somewhat satisfied and not satisfied. As shown in Figure 4 below, 67% of respondents were very satisfied and 0% of students replied that they were not satisfied.

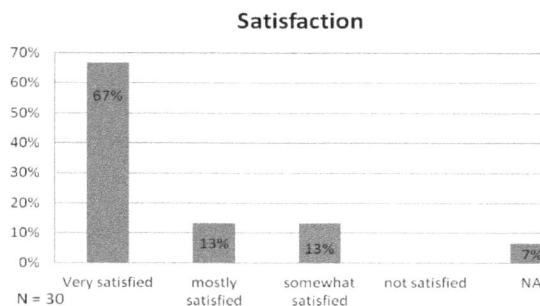

**Figure 4. Student satisfaction with the use of eBookMaker**

#### 4.1.2 Student Perception of the Use of eBookMaker

In order to evaluate student perception of the use of eBookMaker in depth, the following questions were offered to the students:

*(Q1) What do you like about eBookMaker?*

*(Q2) What do you not like about eBookMaker?*

*(Q3) How does eBookMaker help you learn?*

*(Q4) What features do you want to add to eBookMaker?*

*(Q5) What was the best thing about eBookMaker?*

Students' responses to each of these questions are discussed in the sections that follow.

*Q1. What do you like about eBookMaker?*

Students' responses to Q1 were coded and then categorized into six response types, which are displayed in Figure 5. 67% of the students replied that they liked to make their own documents with eBookMaker. For example, one student responded, "What I liked about this application is that using my imagination to write a story." Another mentioned, " I like that I can record my voice and take pictures."

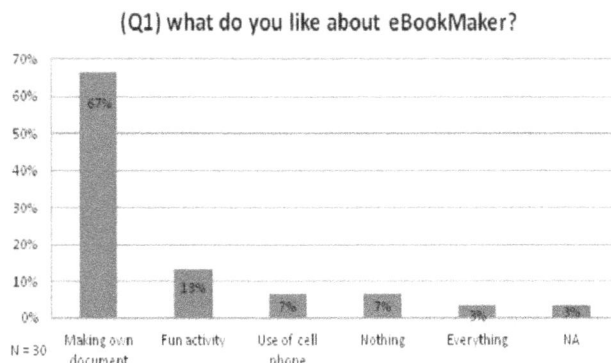

**Figure 5. What students liked about eBookMaker**

*Q2. What do you not like about eBookMaker?*

Students' responses to Q2 were coded and categorized into five types, which are displayed in Figure 6. A majority of students (70%) replied, "Nothing." 13% of students indicated they experienced technical problems: long loading time and accidental data loss. Another responded, "I don't want others read my story." In addition, 7% of students said that it is difficult to type with the small keyboard.

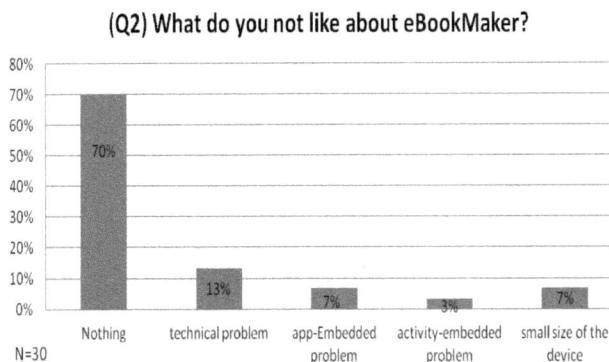

**Figure 6. What student did not like about eBookMaker**

*Q3. How does eBookMaker help you learn?*

Students' responses to Q3 were coded and categorized into five response types, which are displayed in Figure 7. 57% of students responded that eBookMaker enabled them to learn by writing their own summary about what they learned. Moreover, 20% of students indicated that reading others' documents helped them learn. In addition, remembering facts and looking at pictures that were collected as ways to learn with eBookMaker. Lastly, only one student (3%) replied that eBookMaker didn't help him to learn.

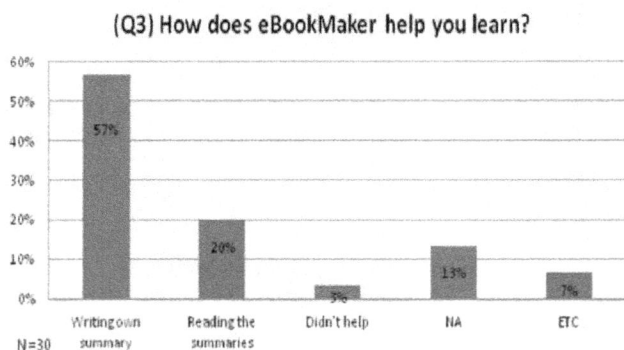

**Figure 7. What students thoughts they could learn with eBookMaker**

*Q4. What features do you want to add to eBookMaker?*

Students' responses to this question were coded and categorized into two types, which are shown in Figure 8. 77% of students responded that there is nothing to be added to eBookMaker. One student said, "Nothing. It is really perfect by itself." The rest of students (23%) gave a variety of responses: spell checker, dictionary, music, video, and more bright colors.

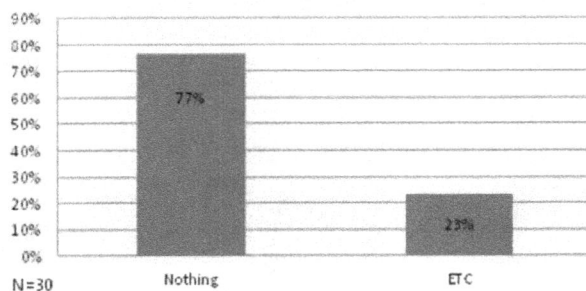

**Figure 8. What features students wanted to add to eBookMaker**

*Q5. What was the best thing about eBookMaker?*

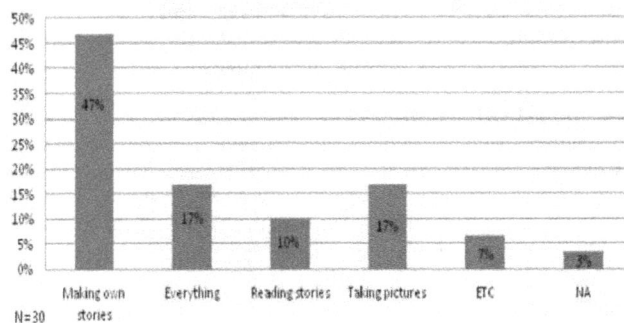

**Figure 9. What students liked best about eBookMaker**

Lastly, their responses to this question were coded and categorized into six types, which are displayed in Figure 9. Similar to Q1, 47% of students replied they liked to make their own stories. For example, one student responded, "It was so awesome and fun. It can help me write better." 17% of the students responded that they loved everything about eBookMaker. Besides these responses, reading stories, taking pictures, and voice recording were also mentioned as the best thing about eBookMaker.

## 4.2 Practical Adoption

In the study II, 29 of the 32 students had completed the task and submitted their scientific mobile documents. The collected students' mobile documents average 4.48 pages, 3.73 pictures and 352.17 words. More detailed evaluations about the collected mobile documents will be described in the following sections.

### 4.2.1 Types of Images Used in Mobile Document

The images collected from student-created mobile document came from a variety of sources, including photos of images from their computer screen (Figure 10a), photos of images from textbooks (Figure 10b), photos of their own drawings (Figure 10c), downloaded images from the internet onto their phones (Figure 10d), and photos taken in a real environment with the mobile application (Figure 10e). This information may demonstrate that students with a mobile application can freely collect any images from their surroundings that are related to their own topics.

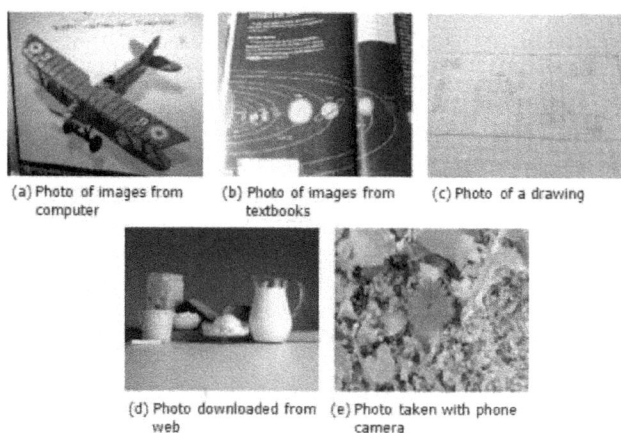

(a) Photo of images from computer  (b) Photo of images from textbooks  (c) Photo of a drawing

(d) Photo downloaded from web  (e) Photo taken with phone camera

**Figure 10. Types of images used in student-created mobile documents**

### 4.2.2 Research Method Used in Mobile Document

The collected student-created mobile documents were categorized into three types of research method based on how to explore scientific phenomena and conclude from their investigations (See Figure 11). Method I is to collect information relating to their research topics and summarize their collections. Method II is to gather information regarding their chosen topics and conclude from their investigations in their own words. Method III is to come up with a question, design the experiment, conduct the experiment, analyze the results from the experiment and conclude based on their findings.

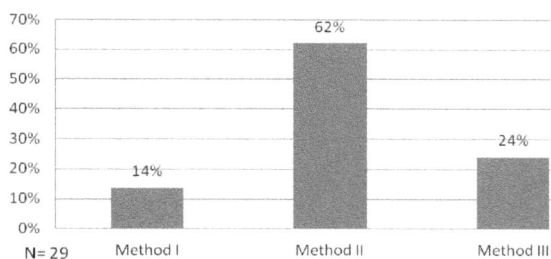

**Research method used in mobile documents**

**Figure 11. Research methods used in mobile documents**

A majority of students (86%) collect information regarding their topics, analyze their collections and conclude based on them. Furthermore, 24% of the students designed the experiment to investigate their topics, and conducted the expriment, which is typical learning process in discovery learning. Figure 12 demonstrate one student's mobile document using Method III. This student researched relevant information about soap (Figure 12a) and designed his/her own experiement about what will happen with and without soap (Figure 12b) and concluded in his/her own words (Figure 12c). While conducting the experiment, he/she took a picture of the experiment and add it to the mobile document (Figure 12a). The findings from this study suggest that various functionailits of the mobile application, eBookMaker, stimulate students to actively explore scientific phenomena in everyday life and figure out what it is through discovery and even experimentation.

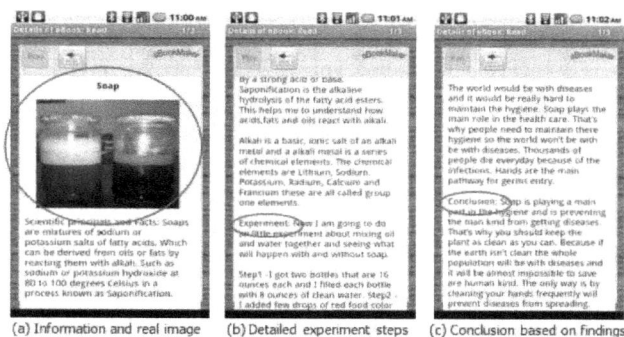

(a) Information and real image  (b) Detailed experiment steps  (c) Conclusion based on findings

**Figure 12. Mobile document using Method III**

## 5. CONCLUSION & FUTURE STUDY

This paper describes what students think about the use of a mobile application, in particular eBookMaker, for their learning and how the use of a mobile application affects scientific discovery learning outside of school. Preliminary findings from the study I indicated that 67% of students were very satisfied with the use of a mobile application, eBookMaker, in their learning process. Also, a majority of the students (77%) responded that they learned by writing summary what they have learned and reading others' summaries. These results can suppose that students see the positive benefits of using a mobile application in the learning environment. Furthermore, the study II demonstrated that students experienced the scientific discovery learning process with a mobile application by coming up with their own research question, designing the experiment, and drawing conclusion in their own words. To summarize, it can be said that the use of a mobile application in the learning process helps students build logical and scientific argumentation skill. Furthermore, the obtained findings from this study suggest that mobile publishing can be a new learning competency of the 21st century.

Based on these positive findings about the use of a mobile application in the learning environment, we will design science curriculum using a mobile application and apply that to more learning settings in the next studies.

## 6. ACKNOWLEDGMENTS

We would like to thank the teacher, Claudia Olaciregui, and her 32 students at Ellis elementary school for taking part in these two studies. We also thank Belle Wang for her advices and suggestions. This work has been sponsored by the National Science Foundation grant (NSF#0832380, Programmable Open Mobile Internet) and the POMI research team at Stanford University.

## 7. REFERENCES

[1] C. Shuler. 2009. "Pockets of Potential: Using Mobile Technologies to Promote Children's learning," New York: The Joan Ganz Cooney Center at Sesame Workshop.

[2] D. Klahr & M. Nigam. 2004. "The Equivalence of Learning Paths in Early Science Instruction," Psychological Science, Vol. 15, 660-667.

[3] G. M. Chinnery. 2006. "Emerging technologies going to the MALL: mobile assisted language learning," Language Learning & Technology, vol. 10, 9-16.

[4]  J. Sandberg, M. Maris, & K. de Geus. 2011. "Mobile English Learning: An evidence-based study with fifth graders," *Computers & Education*, vol. 57, 1334-1347.

[5]  M. Ben-Ari. 2001. "Constructivism in Computer Science Education," *Jl. Of Computers in Mathematics and Science Teaching*. Vol. 20, 45-73.

[6]  M. Gilroy. 2004. "Invasion of the Classroom Cell Phones," *The Hispanic Outlook in Higher Education*, 56-60.

[7]  Mediamark Research & Intelligence. 2010. "Kids Intelligence," MRI report.

[8]  R. Dodds & C. Y. 2005. "Cell Phones and PDA's Hit K-6," *Education Digest*, Vol. 70, 52-53.

[9]  R. D. Pea & H. Maldonado. 2006. "WILD for learning: Interacting through new computing devices anytime, anywhere," Cambridge handbook of the learning sciences, 427-442.

[10] R. Mulye & K. Westberg. 2009. "Mobile phone clickers in the classroom: experiences from a large introductory marketing class," The World University's Forum. Vol. 2, 109-121.

[11] S. L. Cheung. 2008. "Using Mobile Phone Messaging as a Response Medium in Classroom Experiments," *The Journal of Economic Education*, Vol. 39, 51-67.

[12] S. Seol, A. Karimi, P. Kim, A. Goyal, B. Dodson, & M. Lam. 2011. "Pocketschool interactive Learning Ad-hoc Network," In *proceedings of International Conference e-Education, Entertainment and e-Management (ICEEE)*, 70-75.

[13] S. Seol, A. Sharp, & P. Kim. 2011. "Stanford Mobile Inquiry-based Learning Environment (SMILE): using mobile phones to promote student inquires in the elementary classroom," In *Proceedings of the 2011 International Conference on Frontiers in Education: Computer Science & Computer Engineering*, 270-276.

[14] T. de. Jong & W. R. Van. Joolingen. 1998. "Scientific discovery learning with computer simulations of conceptual domains," *Review of Educational Research*, Vol. 68, 179-202.

[15] T. J. Franklin. 2011. "The Mobile School: Digital Communities Created by Mobile Learners," *Bringing Schools into the 21st Century*, 187-203.

# Identifying Measures to Foster Teachers' Competence for Personal Learning Environment Conceived Teaching Scenarios: A Delphi Study

Zaffar Ahmed Shaikh
Faculty of Computer Science
Institute of Business Administration, Karachi
Karachi, Sindh, Pakistan
(92) 333-7113817
zashaikh@iba.edu.pk

Shakeel Ahmed Khoja
Faculty of Computer Science
Institute of Business Administration, Karachi
Karachi, Sindh, Pakistan
(92) 333-2108984
skhoja@iba.edu.pk

## ABSTRACT

Personal learning environment (PLE) is a learner centered and controlled environment where learner constructs knowledge socially and collaboratively with the help of knowledgeable peers, mentors, and teachers. Teacher, being the most knowledgeable other in this environment, has to develop a strong and multifunctional association between the learner and the PLE. However, in real world scenarios, this is not the case as teachers' current competencies are not sufficiently developed to provide desired results. A major reason for this inefficiency is the unawareness of the required roles that a teacher has to play in such environments. Our study is aimed at identifying measures to foster teachers' competence in PLE conceived teaching scenarios. We used the modified version of policy-Delphi in which we worked with 34 international experts who are either associated with PLEs in one of the four dimensions: teachers, researchers, designers, or practitioners. These experts reviewed a 10-item teachers' PLE competency developing measures list, which we developed through an exhaustive literature review. As per Delphi procedure, the consensus on measures list was achieved in three rounds. During the process, participants collaboratively modified measures list at length and extended list from 10 items to 16 items. Based on the findings, we argue that institutional support is of prime importance to improve teachers' PLE competence.

## Categories and Subject Descriptors

K.3.1 [**Computing Milieux**]: Computers and Education: Computer Uses in Education – *collaborative learning, computer-assisted instruction, computer-managed instruction.*

## General Terms

Management, Performance, Design, Human Factors.

## Keywords

Teachers' PLE competence, personalization, personalized learning, personal learning environment, PLE, policy-Delphi.

## 1. INTRODUCTION

Nowadays, it has been widely accepted within education and research community that teachers need to be meticulously competent not only in subject matter, but also emotionally intelligent in handling classroom related issues, technologically advanced in instructional and pedagogy related competencies, and should be knowledgeable regarding personalized learning and PLE conception [1][2][3].

Latest research findings regarding teachers' competencies for Web 2.0, social software and advanced learning technologies context dispense many roles to teachers (other than their compulsory instructional and pedagogy related roles): planner of collaborative learning environment, constructor of learners' learning plans, learning advisor, guide, and promoter of learners' autonomy, confidence, and effectiveness [4][5][6][7].

In response to these developments, Shaikh [8] argues that competencies required of todays' teachers for these changed learner-driven and –controlled scenarios should be reviewed strategically, carefully, and thoroughly in order to inform and transform todays' teachers for upcoming risks and opportunities. Therefore, we decided to involve the real stakeholders – the PLE community – to sort out this matter. The aim was to identify measures which can be integrated or applied to any teacher training module in order to develop teachers' emotional and professional competence for PLE conception teaching scenarios. However, while extracting the literature on this subject matter, we found that, prior to this study, only a few researchers (e.g., Downes [6], Shaikh [8], Alvarez, et al. [9], Aragon [10], Minocha, et al. [11], Selvi [12]) have examined teachers' PLE competences. In addition, to-date, the literature has not measured nor verified teachers' capabilities for satisfying such competences [1][13]. Moreover, we also found that most of teachers' characteristics and competences regarding personalizing of learners' learning experiences have not yet been documented to-date. Thus, we deemed fit to use teachers' PLE competency developing model (developed by Shaikh [8]) as a guiding reference for this study. The study was guided by the following research questions:

1. To what extent, are todays' teachers capable of assuming the suggested new competencies?

2. Which measures need to be taken to develop teachers' PLE competence that empower them to become entrenched in these new fields of learning?

For this study, we relied on the definition of competence proposed by McLagen [14] as "an area of knowledge or skill which is critical to the production of key outputs."

The contribution of this paper is as follows: Research background is subject of Section 2, where relationships between 21st century learners and Web 2.0, personalization of learning and PLE, and applicability of Delphi in finding teachers' PLE competencies, have been discussed. Research method is described in Section 3, while the analysis of data is carried out in Section 4. Section 5 portrays the results of study, which is followed by discussion on results in Section 6. Conclusion is the subject of Section 8.

## 2. RESEARCH BACKGROUND

Adapting learning that is learner-driven, self-directed, facilitated by experts and co-planned with other learners, and based on the needs and challenges of the individual learner is termed as personalized learning [15][16]. McLoughlin [17] argues that Web 2.0 plays a significant role in personalizing learning; "it enable learners to learn the way they deem fit and offer them greater flexibility and choice of options to personalize their learning." While reaffirming this statement, Chatti [18] argues that Web 2.0 applications (such as social networking, social bookmarking, wikis, blogs, mashups, webinars, and podcasts) are more intuitive, personalizable, and have built-in support to learn. These Web 2.0 applications enable the various aspects of learning such as content, mode of delivery, and access to be offered to learners, so that they can manage technology according to personal preferences [17][18].

Personal learning environment (PLE) is a learner centered and controlled environment where learner (exploiting the potential of Web 2.0 tools) constructs his knowledge socially and collaboratively with the help of knowledgeable peers, mentors, and teachers [19]. PLE provides a platform to collect and process information, connect people, and thus create value or knowledge [20]. Recent work at the crossroads of personalization of learning experiences and PLEs (e.g., McLoughlin [17], Compen, et al. [21], Pearson, et al. [22]) focuses on how to guide 21st century learners in developing their personalized learning spaces that enable them to mashup their heterogeneous learning resources at one place, allow them to interact socially with online learner communities, and share content through social media [23].

Dam, et al. [24] argue that teachers can create powerful motivational and creative force in learners by inducting personalization in their pedagogies. Arenas [25], and Attwell [26] suggest that augmenting learners' cognition with personalized learning approaches should not be the only objective of improving teachers' competencies, but they should also be empowered to familiarize learners with how to exploit PLEs for learning. Downes [6] argues that conceptualizing PLEs to learners require teachers to be behavioral scientists, psychologists, designers, planners, guides, and managers. Gaston [27] realizes that such changed phenomena increases the load on teachers' professional responsibilities at work. They are expected to possess diverse set of competencies while performing many roles efficiently and effectively in order to be successful [28].

The above mentioned literature review suggests teachers' required PLE competence against five categories. Shaikh [8] have divided teachers' PLE roles into planning and design (P&D), instruction and learning (I&L), communication and interaction (C&I), management and administration (M&A), and use of technology (UoT) competences. This study seeks to identify teachers' PLE competency developing measures in order to cultivate teachers' PLE competence against these categories. To achieve this objective, we deemed fit to use modified-policy Delphi method of group consensus.

### 2.1 Using Delphi to Identify Measures to Cultivate Teachers' PLE Competence

Delphi study is a technique of eliciting collective expertise for forecasting or measuring policymaking opinion of a group of geographically dispersed domain experts without being holding a face-to-face meeting. In order to reach a consensus or gain a stability in Delphi participants' opinions, often a multiple-round probe is carried out [29]. Many variations of Delphis – called modified Delphi methods – have been developed and used recently [30]. Ranking-type Delphis rank probed items on participants' votes [31]. Rating-type Delphis usually assign weights to likert-type scale options and thereby rank items. These days modified-policy Delphi techniques have been very popular among the research community [32][33]. These techniques have been used successfully in situations when the objective of study is not only to get consensus in participants' viewpoints, but when stable results would also be considered in order to understand clearly the researched phenomena [30][33].

In the area of educational and learning technologies, many researchers have successfully used Delphi technique. The researchers (e.g., Shaikh [30], Holden [34], Pollard [35]) used it for forecasting future events and research trends. Brill et al. [36] and Yang [37] drew consensus on vague problems through this technique. In order to gain a better understanding of current practices and perceived obstacles, the researchers (e.g., Herring [38], Cramers, et al. [39], Williams, et al. [40]) deemed Delphi method useful. The selection of Delphi for this study was based on the facts that: (a) to-date, teacher communities keep only some knowledge about PLEs, personalization, and personalized learning teaching approaches; (b) since the field is considered new (so far) and the current situation is vague, many teachers and educational technology experts are still unaware of their roles and required PLE competence; and (c) many researchers desire to value the opinion of domain experts and ask them to inform the rest of community the importance of teachers' roles and competence for teaching through PLE conception [6][8][17][26].

## 3. METHODOLOGY

This online Delphi took place asynchronously during a 7-weeks duration. Acknowledging the many distinguished features of Delphis and the nature of the problem in hand, we used its policy Delphi version. Typical for this Delphi was a heterogeneous response group. There was no face-to-face interaction, and participants reacted anonymously. We provided previous round feedback to each participant with due justification and need for proceeding to the next round. Conclusions were reached by majority consensus over probed measures.

### 3.1 Literature Survey for the Design of Questionnaire

In order to design a questionnaire instrument for probe, we reviewed a wide range of research material published between 2006 and 2011. Below we outline, which bibliographic resources we used as literature, the criteria we used for their selection, and the method we applied to carry out the review. We started our literature review with a check on ACM, IEEE, CUDOS,

EBSCOhost, ICYT (Science and Technology), ISOC (Social Sciences and Humanities), JStor, and ScienceDirect databases. These sources mostly contain articles from online journals, educational and magazine reports, conference proceedings, series, compilations, monographs, etc.

We developed a 10-item teachers' PLE competency developing measures synopsis to be used as first-round questionnaire (FQ) – duly verified through pilot testing by a team of three local domain experts – for debate. The literature review was guided by two theme questions listed in Introduction section. We reviewed studies which highlighted the need for faculty development in the context of personalization of learning, personalized learning instructional methodologies, and PLEs. Studies that highlighted teachers' roles and competence for online, distance, face-to-face, and blended learning environments were also covered.

## 3.2 Selection of Experts

We paid particular attention to search representative experts in teaching, research, and professional community that interests in PLEs. Thus, to explore the variety of views, a broad range of expertise for experts was pursued. We selected internationally reputed experts whose reputation was derived either from academic publications or professional record of achievements. At the start of study, only 36 participants returned filled demographic survey forms out of a total of 54 (who agreed to participate in response to Delphi invitation to 150 potential experts). However, in the third round, the number reduced to 34, as two participants could not return their responses in due time. Of the 34 participants, eight had an academic background as teachers, six were PLE researchers at the doctoral level, other six were PLE designers and or developers, and remaining 14 members introduced themselves as PLE practitioners or eLearning experts working as staff members or executives in commercial enterprises. Participants included both males and females (males=19, ratio=56 percent, and females=15, ratio=44 percent). There were six participants (two males and four females) with at least doctorate and or more advanced level qualifications.

## 3.3 Procedure of Conduct of Study

We (the first author of this study) personally invited to the attendees of *The PLE Conference 2011* for participating in this Delphi. Another formal invitation was sent to widespread international PLE community through personalized emails, tweets, website entries, Facebook, and blog posts.

The study started with an introduction of Delphi studies, intended purpose of the study, explanation of the modified methodology, commitment of time and feedback required from participants, and results' expectation by the researchers. We started the study by emailing FQ to 36 participants. This study lasted for three rounds until it achieved either some level of consensus or stability in participants' opinions during the online discussion. Many participants expressed their personal opinions in open-ended questions. After each round, we provided participants the synopsis of new and old discussion topics. Participants' agreement with the synopsis depicted the actual representation of the debate. Afterwards, we aggregated the results in a concluding report.

## 4. DATA ANALYSIS

From the second round onward, each participant was provided with the synopsis of previous round discussion and was asked to compare each of his or her response with that of panel mean value for that measure. Based on this review, we allowed participants to either change their previous round responses with panel mean values if they are satisfied with the panel point of view or retain their previous response(s) and justify their difference from panel opinion properly. We show in Table 1 the analysis of one of the probed measures during Delphi's last two-rounds.

**Table 1: Analysis of one of teachers' PLE competency developing measures**

| Measures | Round | Analysis | | | HD |
|---|---|---|---|---|---|
| | | R | M | IQR | |
| One way to motivate teachers to adopt the roles described is through workshops and pilot testing in order to prove them the benefits of PLEs. | 2nd | 3 | 3.9 | 1.5 | Yes |
| | 3rd | 4 | 4.2 | 0.5 | |

The following abbreviations are applicable: R=Individual Rating; M=Panel Mean; IQR=Consensus level; HD=Highly Desirable

The analysis shows that during the third round of Delphi the measure achieved not only high-consensus, but was also designated to highly desirability measure status.

We sought participants' responses for acceptance of teachers' PLE competency developing measures on 5-1 likert type scale. The 25 to 75 percent interquartile range (IQR) was used to determine participants' consensus. We relied on three consensus levels: high-consensus (H→IQR<=0.5), moderate-consensus (M→0.5<=IQR<=1.0), and low-consensus (L→1.0<=IQR<=1.5). We assumed consensus is achieved when an IQR of 1.0 or less has attained on most of the statements. Delphi participants were also asked to designate highly crucial measures as highly desirable (HD) measures.

Delphi studies are mainly aimed at drawing high consensus. Kenis [33] argues that the facilitators should be well-off at applying consensus results appropriately. Thus, we combined measure acceptance ratings, consensus ratings, and desirability ratings to generate a final status for a measure. Acceptance ratings were assigned unbiased weights (from +2 to -2), consensus ratings were assigned biased weights (H=0, M=-1, L=-2), and HD measures were assigned a weight of 1.

## 5. RESULTS

Table 2 shows teachers' PLE competency developing measures ranked on descending order of desirability rating (column 4). We witnessed participants' personal approach to every measure. They shared their work experiences, everyday life observations, explorative thoughts, and tried to learn through collaborative sharing of ideas. The consensus developing process (column 3) shows moderate to high convergence (IQR<=1.0) in most of the statements; thus, we terminated the study at this stage and collected results. The results have been calculated using the formula explained in Section 4. The final status (column 5) shows the acceptance status of measures. Thus, the statements that gained *strongly accept* or *accept* status were termed as the results of this study.

**Table 2: Showing Teachers' PLE competency developing measures**

| Measures | Agre-ement | Conse-nsus | Desir-ability | Final Status |
|---|---|---|---|---|
| 1. Dissemination of exemplary practices, support in the first uses of technology in class | A | H | HD | Strongly Accept |
| 2. Management should provide reinforcement to teachers that put into practice these new roles. | A | H | HD | Strongly Accept |
| 3. Organize workshops and pilot testing to prove them the benefits of PLEs. | A | H | HD | Strongly Accept |
| 4. Teacher training programs should include courses that emphasize personalized learning principles and participation. | A | H | HD | Accept |
| 5. Have teachers learn in environments similar to those we expect our students to learn in. | A | H | HD | Strongly Accept |
| 6. Teachers should emphasize more on contextual use of tools and technologies in their pedagogies. | A | M | HD | Accept |
| 7. For new teachers, the focus should be on giving instructional or learning designer training rather than the traditional instructional skills focusing on the presentation. | A | H | HD | Strongly Accept |
| 8. Planning and Design competency (P&D) should recognize peer sharing or exchange. | SA | H | D | Strongly Accept |
| 9. Courses that include building and managing PLEs need be offered at a regular basis. | SA | M | D | Accept |
| 10. Faculty evaluation modules include questions on teachers' personalized learning approaches. | A | H | D | Accept |
| 11. Expand face to face and virtual networking with learning leaders or missionaries. | A | H | D | Accept |
| 12. Constructivism and Connectionism model methodologies can improve teachers' PLE skills. | A | H | D | Accept |
| 13. Incorporate into individual goal setting each year. One new thing to learn or try per term or something like that. | A | H | D | Accept |
| 14. Teachers need to become involved with PLE skills. They will then develop and entrenched. | A | H | D | Accept |
| 15. Release time for course development if more than incremental change is desired | A | H | D | Accept |
| 16. Incorporate these skills set within teacher training and in service training. | SA | M | D | Accept |
| 17. *Teachers who adopt personalized learning in their pedagogies should be rewarded.* | *A* | *M* | *D* | *Undecided* |

The following abbreviations are applicable: SA=Strongly Agree/Accept=2; A=Agree/Accept=1; U=Undecided=0; DA=Disagree/Reject=-1; SD=Strongly Disagree/Reject=-2; H=High-consensus=0; M=Moderate-consensus=-1; L=Low-consensus=-2

# 6. DISCUSSION

Here, we discuss on the measures which achieved *strongly accept* or *accept* status. During the three round process, participants extended the 10-statement measures list to 17 statements. However, only 16 measures were accepted by this study. Seventeenth measure (see Table 2) scored only zero marks; thus it gained an *undecided* measure status (as formula reveals: A=1 M=-1 D=0, 1+(-1)+0=0→undecided).

Proposed measures' list correspond to teachers' five core PLE competences, and covers aspects of teachers' training and development. The measures put emphasis on teachers' required skills for performing PLE roles. Participants showed a strong desire for enhancing teachers' PLE competence about how to use personalized learning skills in the classroom, how to think differently and innovatively, and how to get improved teachers' current teaching skills while benefitting from PLE research. Thus, we suggest that teacher training modules should include training sessions which train teachers on how to design course material that is based on personalized learning instructional approaches. Participants also unanimously agreed on exploiting the constructionism and connectionism models of learning (learning together, learning through circles, reciprocal learning).

Evaluating the effectiveness and efficiency of teachers' pedagogics in a classroom, it is suggested that teachers' evaluation modules should include questions that measure students' opinion for teachers' personalized learning instructional approaches. This Delphi suggests that teachers should be skilled in instructional or learning design, context analyzing, planning, and programming in order to be able to design curriculum that would comply with personalized learning instructional requirements. Participants accept the need of a PLE-driven curriculum that incorporate teachers' personalized learning instructional practices, and regular offering of courses that require students to build PLEs. Management support is also termed critical for teaching through PLE conception scenarios. Participants' suggest teachers' personalized learning efforts should be acknowledged by the management. Teachers' may be rewarded honorariums, promotions, praises, etc.

Recognizing the extra efforts that teachers put on adopting personalized learning instructional approaches, this Delphi proposes measures about how to increase PLE competence of teachers. Participants suggest teachers' should increase their PLE competence by practicing on PLE roles and skills. Teachers' trainers should work on one PLE role or competency at a time, and move on to other activity after that. Teachers who have earned a considerable reputation in PLE practices should arrange workshops and seminars for other teachers. Recognizing the fact that Delphi participants put emphasis on teachers' professional development, task compensations as well as teachers' involvement in decision-making activities regarding teaching through PLE conception scenarios should inform administrator practice in developing effective learning programs.

# 7. CONCLUSIONS

This study proposes measures to develop teachers' competence for teaching through PLE conception. In the end of study, Delphi participants developed consensus for 16 PLE competency developing measures for teachers.

The findings of this study contribute and clarify to the growing body of research on teachers' competence for PLE conception teaching scenarios. The results suggest that apart from teachers skills and competences, the nature and complexity of the tasks that teachers deal with in learning environments have been the key issues that need to be considered. It is reasonable to assume that the 34 Delphi experts belonged to teaching, research, and PLE industry serve as the random sample of the field. Their viewpoints are equally valuable to managers, teachers, researchers, and policy makers interested in PLEs. Thus, it is imperative that management heed the perceptions of these individuals.

In order to get the benefit from this study, we recommend applying these PLE competency developing measures in teacher training and development programs. Based on the findings, it is argued that support is extremely important for developing teachers' PLE competence. Teachers need management support, compensation for extra time spent on curriculum development, and acknowledgement of their efforts. This study suggests teachers to be involved with proposed skills and accentuate on contextual use of technologies to their pedagogies; they will then develop and become entrenched in these new fields of learning.

## 7.1 Acknowledgements

We would like to extend our gratitude to the participants of this Delphi who made this project possible.

## 8. REFERENCES

[1] Struyven, K., and Meyst, M. D. 2010. Competence-based teacher education: illusion or reality? an assessment of the implementation status in Flanders from teachers' and students' points of view. *TEACH TEACH EDUC.* 26 (2010), 1495-1510.

[2] Volman, M. 2005. A variety of roles for a new type of teacher. educational technology and the teaching profession. *TEACH TEACH EDUC.* 21 (2005) 15–31.

[3] Brien, D. L., and Webb, J. 2008. The Australian postgraduate writing network: developing a collaborative learning environment for higher degree students and their supervisors. In D. Orr, P. A. Danaher, G. Danaher, and R.E. Harreveld (Eds.), Lifelong learning: reflecting on successes and framing futures. Keynote and refereed papers from the *5th International Lifelong Learning Conference* (Rockhampton: Central Queensland University Press), 79–84.

[4] British Columbia. 2010. *A Vision for 21st Century Education.* Premier's Technology Council 1600 - 800 Robson Street Vancouver, British Columbia.

[5] Committee of Inquiry into the Changing Learner Experience. 2009. *Higher education in a Web 2.0 world.* Bristol: JISC.

[6] Downes, S. 2010. New Technology Supporting Informal Learning. *J. Emerging Technologies in Web Intelligence.* 2 (1), 27-33.

[7] Klamma, R., Chatti, M. A., Duval, E., Hummel, H., Hvannberg, E. H., and Kravcik, M. 2007. Social software for life-long learning. *EDUC TECHNOL SOC.* 10 (3), 72-83.

[8] Shaikh, Z. A., and Khoja, S. A. 2012. Role of Teacher in Personal Learning Environments. *Digital Education Review.* 21, 22-32

[9] Alvarez, I., Guasch, T. and Espasa, A. 2009. University teacher roles and competencies in online learning environments: a theoretical analysis of teaching and learning practices. *EUR J TEACH EDUC.*32(3), 321- 336 DOI= http://dx.doi.org/10.1080/02619760802624104

[10] Aragon, R. and Johnson, D. 2002. Emerging roles and competencies for training in e-learning environments. *Advances in Developing Human Resources* 4 (4), 424- 439.

[11] Minocha, S., Schroeder, A. and Schneider, C. 2011. Role of the educator in social software initiatives in further and higher education: a conceptualization and research agenda. *BRIT J EDUC TECHNOL.* 42, DOI= 10.1111/j.1467-8535.2010.01131.x

[12] Selvi, K. 2010. Teachers' competencies. *Cultura. International Journal of Philosophy of Culture and Axiology.* 7 (1), 167-175.

[13] Lee, M. J. W. 2005. New tools for online collaboration: Blogs, wikis, RSS and podcasting. *Training and Development in Australia.* 32 (5), 17-20.

[14] McLagen, P. 1983. Models for excellence. *American Society for Training and Development.* Washington, DC.

[15] Häkkinen, P., and Hämäläinen, R. 2011. Shared and personal learning spaces: challenges for pedagogical design. *INTERNET HIGH EDUC.* DOI= http://dx.doi.org/10.1016/j.iheduc.2011.09.001

[16] Riecken, D. 2000. guest ed. Personalized views of personalization (special section). *COMMUN ACM.* 43, 8 (Aug. 2000).

[17] McLoughlin, C. and Lee, M. J. W. 2010. Personalized and self-regulated learning in the Web 2.0 era: international exemplars of innovative pedagogy using social software. *AUSTRALAS J EDUC TEC.*26 (1), 28-43.

[18] Chatti, M. A. 2011. LMS vs. PLE. Mohamed Amine Chatti's ongoing research on Knowledge and Learning http://mohamedaminechatti.blogspot.com/2010/03/lms-vs-ple.html

[19] Harmelen, M. V. 2006. Personal Learning Environments. In *Proceedings of the Sixth IEEE International Conference on Advanced Learning Technologies* (Washington, DC, USA, 2006). ICALT '06. IEEE Computer Society, 815-816

[20] Compen, R. T., Edirisingha, P., and Mobbs, R. 2008. Building Web 2.0-Based Personal Learning Environments: A Conceptual Framework," In *Proc. EDEN Research Workshop 2008.*

[21] Dolog, P., Henze, N., Nejdl, W., and Sintek, M. 2004. Personalization in distributed eLearning environments. In *Proc. of WWW2004 — The Thirteenth International World Wide Web Conference.* (May 2004).

[22] Pearson, E., Gkatzidou, S., and Green, S. 2009. A proposal for an Adaptable Personal Learning Environment to support learners needs and preferences. In *Same places, different spaces. Proceedings ascilite Auckland 2009.*

[23] Liber, O., and Johnson, M. 2008. Personal Learning Environments. *INTERACT LEARN ENVIR*.16 (1), 1-2, DOI= http://dx.doi.org/10.1080/10494820701772645

[24] Dam, K. V., Schipper, M., and Runhaar, P. 2010. Developing a competency-based framework for teachers' entrepreneurial behavior. *TEACH TEACH EDUC*. 26:4 (May 2010), 965-971.

[25] Arenas, E. 2008. Personal learning environments: implications and challenges. In D. Orr, P. A. Danaher, G. Danaher, and R.E. Harreveld (Eds.), Lifelong learning: reflecting on successes and framing futures. Keynote and refereed papers from the *5th International Lifelong Learning Conference (*Rockhampton: Central Queensland University Press), 54–59.

[26] Attwell, G. 2007. The personal learning environments - the future of eLearning? eLearning Papers, 2 (1). http://www.elearningeuropa.info/files/media/media11561.pdf

[27] Gaston, J. 2006. Reaching and teaching the digital natives. *Library Hi Tech News*, 23 (3), 12-13.

[28] Larike H., Bronkhorst, Paulien C., Meijer, Koster, B., Jan D., Vermunt, and Avalos, B. 2011. Teacher professional development in Teaching and Teacher Education over ten years. *TEACH TEACH EDUC*. 27 (2011), 10-20

[29] Delbecq, A. L., Van de Ven, A. H., and Gustafson, D. H. 1975. Group techniques for program planning: a guide to nominal group and Delphi processes, Glenview, IL: Scott, Foresman.

[30] Shaikh, Z. A. and Khoja, S. A. 2011. Role of ICT in shaping the future of Pakistani higher education system. *TURK ONLINE J EDUC T*. 10 (1), 149-161, ISSN: 1303 – 6521, Jan 2011, http://www.tojet.net/articles/10116.pdf

[31] Stewart, J. 2001. Is the Delphi technique a qualitative method? *Medical Education*. 35 (10), 922-923.

[32] Linstone, H. A., and Turoff, M. 1975. The Delphi method: techniques and applications, Reading, MA, USA: Addison-Wesley.

[33] Kenis, D. G. A. 1995. *Improving group decisions: designing and testing techniques for group decision support systems applying Delphi*. Doctoral Dissertation, University of Utrecht, The Netherlands. 20-34.

[34] Holden, M. C., and Wedman, J. F. 1993. Future issues of computer-mediated communication: the results of a Delphi Study. *ETR&D-EDUC TECH RES*. 41 (4), 5-24.

[35] Pollard, C., and Pollard, R. 2004. Research priorities in educational technology: A Delphi study. *Journal of Research on Technology in Education*. 37 (2), 145-160.

[36] Brill, J. M., Bishop, M. J., and Walker, A. E. 2006. The competencies and characteristics required of an effective project manager: A web-based Delphi study. *ETR&D-EDUC TECH RES*. 54 (2), 115-140.

[37] Yang, Y. N. 2000. Convergence on the guidelines for designing a Web-based art-teacher education curriculum: a Delphi study. *Paper presented at the Annual meeting of the American Educational Research Association*.

[38] Herring, M. C. 2004. Development of constructivist-based distance learning environments: a knowledge base for K-12 teachers. *The Quarterly Review of Distance Education*. 5 (4), 231-242.

[39] Kramer, B. S., Walker, A. E., and Brill, J. M. 2007. The underutilization of information and communication technology-assisted collaborative project-based learning among international educators: A Delphi study. *ETR&D-EDUC TECH RES*. 55, 527-543.

[40] Williams, D. L., Boone, R., and Kingsley, K. L. 2004. Teacher beliefs about educational software: a Delphi study. *Journal of Research on Technology in Education*. 36 (3), 213-229.

# Turning the Tables: Learning from Students about Teaching CS1

Amber Settle
DePaul University
243 S. Wabash Avenue
Chicago, IL 60604
(312) 362-5324

asettle@cdm.depaul.edu

## ABSTRACT

Programming has a central role in the computing curriculum, and introductory programming classes have been extensively studied in the computer science education literature. However, most of the studies focus on the effectiveness of various pedagogical approaches on student learning and engagement, and relative little attention is paid to faculty development. The gap in the literature puts CS1 faculty interested in effectively implementing innovative pedagogical approaches in a difficult situation. This article argues that taking a behaviorist approach to the CS1 classroom can provide much-needed feedback. Students provide instructors with one of the best sources of information about effective programming instruction, both with respect to pedagogical approaches and with respect to less formal issues such as classroom management, student-faculty interactions, and course policies. Faculty who choose to listen and learn from the comments made by their CS1 students will find a wealth of information to guide them in their development as instructors.

## Categories and Subject Descriptors

K.3.2 [**Computers and Education**]: Computer and Information Science Education

## General Terms

Human Factors, Languages

## Keywords

Faculty development, CS1, programming, students, pedagogy, behaviorism

## 1. INTRODUCTION

One of the most fundamental topics in the computer science curriculum is programming, and it is often the case that the first experience students have with computing is a programming course. There have been some recent efforts to expand the notion of computing beyond programming, including a push to include computational thinking [28] into undergraduate and K-12 curricula. Some authors who hold the position that computer science is more than programming believe that equating

programming and computer science narrows the field and drives away students [11]. Others argue that programming is a more advanced skill, akin to proof construction in mathematics or literary analysis in English, and that foundational ideas and terminology need to be conveyed to students first [19]. But it is clear that programming remains a crucial part of computer science. It was identified as an essential skill that must be mastered by anyone studying computer science [10] and remains crucial in the general and tier-1 courses in the Computing Curriculum 2013 strawman document [9]. The information technology discipline also holds programming as fundamental, making it one of the pillars of the model curriculum [15]. An article discussing the development of the curriculum notes that "as with any computing professional, the IT graduate must develop the skill to program" [12, p. 354]. Courses in which students learn to program are not in danger of disappearing from the computing curriculum.

Because of their important role in computing, introductory programming classes have been extensively studied. Nearly every computing education conference contains at least one paper, panel, or poster in which the topic is a programming course, tool, or pedagogical approach, with work about CS1 courses appearing most commonly. For a variety of reasons these articles typically focus on student learning, on student engagement, or on both. The biggest reason that introductory programming courses are so widely studied is that, as stated before, students are most likely to have their first experience with computer science be a programming course and that the experience in the first course often has a strong impact on students' persistence in the major. For example, one study found that when students perceive the pace and workload in introductory classes to be too heavy, especially in relation to their experience level, they are unlikely to pursue the computer science major [3]. For a field that experiences periodic and dramatic enrollment fluctuations [17], understanding the best way to teach students in their first class is important and worthy of deep study. Many of the pedagogical approaches to teaching programming, including collaborative and collaborative learning, active learning, peer instruction, peer assessment, studio-based instruction, and team-based learning, provide useful tools for instructors. These approaches and selected findings about them are summarized in the next section.

However, significantly less attention is paid to faculty development with respect to teaching CS1 courses. Faculty attending computing education conferences certainly have many opportunities to learn about the latest pedagogical approaches and the effectiveness of such approaches. Further, the instructor's role in the CS1 classroom is discussed in nearly every paper focused on a particular pedagogical approach, and some studies have considered the impact of the instructor in the CS1 classroom [22]. But articles about faculty development for the CS1 classroom are difficult to find, and this phenomenon is not limited to the computing discipline. In her work, Adams noted "most teachers are not taught how to teach and most universities do not expect other than time-honored teaching strategies from their faculty members" [1, p. 3]. Often the only regular feedback that CS1 instructors receive about their teaching is information from student course evaluations [1]. While student teaching evaluations have been widely studied in many disciplines, the focus of this work is typically on the correlation between student learning and course evaluations [8]. Other problems with student course evaluations are the necessity of delivering the information after the conclusion of the course, which does not allow for adaptive change, and the issue that "many course evaluation instruments are poorly designed or carelessly administered" [1, p. 3].

A wealth of information on pedagogical approaches to CS1 courses may have the ironic effect of putting instructors in a difficult position. The most motivated of them may choose to adopt a novel pedagogical approach, but implementation and evaluation of the effectiveness of the changes can be challenging and time-consuming. However, a look at faculty development in other disciplines provides a fruitful approach [1]. The thesis of this article is that it is productive to take a behaviorist approach to faculty development in CS1 courses. Behaviorism "assumes that the classroom environment is rich in a series of reciprocal cues, actions, and reactions between the teacher and learner" [1, p. 6]. By carefully observing the clues that CS1 students provide, faculty can learn a great deal about effective implementation of novel pedagogical approaches to teaching programming.

In the remainder of this paper we show how pedagogical approaches that are widely studied in the computing education literature can be reinforced and augmented using information gleaned from student comments. Students in the CS1 classroom provide instructors with one of the best sources of information about the effective delivery of programming instruction, resulting in approaches that mirror many of those studied in the computing education literature. They also provide information about less formal approaches, informing instructors about productive ways of handling student-faculty interactions. The contention here is that faculty who choose to listen and learn from the comments made by their CS1 students will find a wealth of information to guide them in improving their teaching techniques.

## 2. EXAMINING THE CS1 LITERATURE

The thesis here is that careful analysis of student comments provides insight echoing that which can be found in the literature, which necessitates a review some of the previous work on CS1 pedagogy. Note, however, that this section should not be considered an exhaustive review of the CS1 literature. Instead, it focuses on pedagogical approaches that have been developed or modified, and in some cases widely studied, in the past 5-10 years. The intention is to provide an overview of recent trends in CS1 education. The approaches to student interaction found in the literature discussed are then summarized to find common ideas and themes.

## 2.1 Pedagogical Techniques in CS1

One of the most widely studied techniques employed in the CS1 classroom is pair programming. In pair programming two people work side-by-side to develop code. One is the driver who is responsible for designing and typing the code. The other is the navigator who has responsibility for observing the driver in order to detect errors and offer ideas in solving a problem. The pair switches roles at regular intervals [25]. Compared with students who work alone, students who use pair programming in introductory courses are more confident and more likely to remain in a computing-related major [23]. Pair programming results in significant improvement in individual programming skill, particularly for students with lower SAT scores [6]. Multiple studies have also found that students who use pair programming in a CS1 course are more likely to complete the course [6, 23]. In a systematic literature review of seventy-four papers, fourteen compatibility factors that can impact the effectiveness of pair programming as a pedagogical technique were identified [25]. The review found that students' satisfaction was higher using pair programming than when working solo, and that it was effective in improving students' grades on assignments [25]. Lacking from the literature was studies on pair compatibility factors [25]. The importance of pair compatibility is echoed in a study of first-year students' impressions of pair programming [27]. The authors conducted semi-structured interviews with students who had used pair programming in their CS1 course and then moved to solo programming in CS2. Students reported that solo programming was more frustrating and pair programming was a good way to learn to program and prepared them well for solo programming, although scheduling is an issue in a course using pair programming [27].

A CS1 technique adopted from science pedagogy is peer instruction [26]. In this approach students answer multiple choice questions typically using hand-held remote devices (clickers), discuss the questions with their peers, and then answer the questions again. Peer instruction has been widely used in physics education for over 20 years and has been shown to be effective in improving performance on conceptual questions, but only recently have researchers considered how the technique can be adapted for the CS1 classroom [26]. One interesting suggestion to come out of the work is: "It is important to inform students about your choice of pedagogy, and explain to them the benefits of using it." [26, p. 345]. A particularly interesting article is one that arose out of an experiment to replicate a study in biology that found students who discussed questions with their peers were better able to answer a second, conceptually-related question [24]. It should be noted that this work was done in the context of upper-level computing courses.

Another approach to facilitating student interactions is to allow students to generate content. Typically the format of this content is exam-style questions with corresponding solutions. The questions are typically peer-reviewed and are used for drill-and-practice sessions [20]. They may also be rated by students as part of the peer-review process. There are a large number of systems that have been designed to support student-generated content [21]. These systems support contributing student pedagogies as well as peer assessment [21]. It has been shown that the act of question-generation has a positive impact on performance in related exam questions, although correlations between activity and exam performance can be explained by the level of student ability in the context of the course [20]. The authors suggest that a more sophisticated analysis of the relationship between the activities supported by the technology and the impact of the interventions be performed [20].

Another new approach in the CS1 literature is the use of studio-based instruction. In a studio-based curriculum, students are given complex and meaningful problems for which they have to construct computational solutions, and they present their solutions and justifications to the entire class for feedback. The critiques provided by their classmates are used to make appropriate modifications [14]. Proponents of a studio-based approach to the computing classroom argue that like other design sciences, metrics of success and stopping criteria for computer science projects are often unclear. This results in an iterative approach to computing projects, which lends itself to a studio-based approach [7]. Some universities have modified entire degree programs to center on a studio-based approach or applied the technique to gaming or other computing curricula [7]. One interesting adaptation of the studio-based approach is the pedagogical code review, which is modeled after the code inspection process used in the software industry [14]. In this review, students individually review code and then come together as a group to log issues with the code. The researchers on this study found no learning differences between a class using a traditional approach and a pedagogical code review approach, but they did find that student self-efficacy decreased more in the traditional course and that peer learning increased in the studio-based course [14]. An article reviewing studio-based approaches to computing curricula has noted that comparative studies between studio-based learning and other pedagogies remain sparse and that using studio-based learning as a driver for class lectures might be a productive area for exploration [7].

Many novel approaches to the CS1 classroom employ mixed pedagogical methods. There is a large body of work that suggests that active learning is more effective than lecturing, and one study found that student-generated active-learning exercises were an effective addition to the classroom [13]. The study found that students reported feeling significantly more attentive in class where active learning was used, and that there was no significant difference between satisfaction with student- and instructor-generated activities [13]. Cooperative learning has been used in a wide variety of subjects over many years, and some computer science educators have considered the use of specific roles for students to focus their attention on key concepts [4]. The authors of this particular study found that the benefits of cooperative learning outweighed any losses in learning due to reduced lecture time [4]. Peer-led team learning is a collaborative and active-learning technique that identifies certain students as peer leaders whose role it is to mentor and lead other students in creative problem solving [5]. In a quantitative study, the researchers showed marked and statistically significant improvements in student performance in a large-sized introductory computer science course [5]. Team-based learning has been used extensively in medicine since the 1980s, and a four-year study of team-based learning in a CS1 course found that it reduced attrition and improved student success [18]. Tools to promote active learning and collaboration in programming classes have also been developed. The Java Wiki Integrated Development Environment (JavaWIDE)is a particularly promising system that

has been shown to promote active learning and collaboration in a heterogeneous set of teaching and learning environments [16].

Finally there is a study that considered the computer science classroom in general, and not just CS1 classes, that is of interest. Barker and Garvin-Doxas conducted an ethnographic research project in which they analyzed the learning environment in a selection of computer science classrooms at a large, research university in the United States [2]. Several of the classes were CS1, but the study included other computer science classes. They found that many of the approaches taken in the classrooms by instructors generated an impersonal environment that resulted in guarded behavior and the creation and maintenance of an informal hierarchy that enforced competitive rather than cooperative behavior [2]. They concluded with a case study demonstrating ways instructors can reduce the guarded and competitive behavior in students, including learning and using student names in order to decrease the distance between the instructor and students [2].

## 2.2 Commonalities

Although the pedagogical approaches surveyed in the previous section vary significantly in the details, there are some commonalities that exist with respect to student engagement:

1. **Make the classroom dynamic**: Pair programming, peer instruction, and the studio-based classroom all move the student from a passive observer into an active role. All of the pedagogical techniques discussed in this section are student-focused, which also contributes to a dynamic classroom for students.

2. **Increase student-to-student interaction**: Pair programming, peer instruction, peer-led team learning, and studio-based learning all require that students have significant interaction with each other, and this interaction is a significant contributor to the benefit of the approaches.

3. **Reduce isolation**: Students attribute some of the success of pair programming to their ability to rely on, and in some cases teach, other students. Techniques like pair programming, studio-based learning, collaborative learning, and peer instruction allow students to see that their classmates have many of the same issues that they do learning to program. These techniques also counteract the common misconception that computing is a field where most work occurs in isolation from other people.

4. **Encourage a cooperative classroom environment**: Many of the student-focused pedagogies include some form of cooperative learning, including pair programming, peer instruction, and studio-based learning. The ethnographic study of computer science classrooms suggests that this can be enhanced by specific instructor behaviors that reduce the distance between students and faculty, such as learning and using student names.

All of the techniques described in this section take a student-focused approach to teaching programming, and many of the techniques have been well-studied either in the context of computing or in related disciplines. However, short of adopting a technique and designing a formal experiment, faculty who wish to use a novel pedagogical approach lack a way of evaluating their implementation. In the next section a behaviorist lens is applied to the commonalities found in the literature on CS1 pedagogy, demonstrating that student feedback can provide suggestions consistent with quantitative and qualitative studies on CS1 pedagogy.

## 3. LESSONS FROM STUDENTS

Student feedback can provide valuable information for CS1 faculty, both about the benefit of various pedagogical techniques as well as productive approaches for classroom management, contact with students, and ways to encourage student learning.

### 3.1 Background

The author has taught various introductory programming classes at the university level since 1993, but the information provided here is taken from courses taught in approximately the past five years. During that time the author worked as a professor at DePaul University. DePaul University is the largest Catholic institution of higher education in the United States, and all introductory programming courses are a part of the curriculum in the College of Computing and Digital Media (CDM). The student comments referenced here are taken primarily from CSC 241: Introduction to Computer Science I and CSC 242: Introduction to Computer Science II. The language taught in CSC 241/242 is Python. The population for CSC 241/242 consists only of undergraduates, and during the time in question, restricted to computer science majors or minors. All student comments are taken from private e-mails or from an anonymous survey conducted by a graduate researcher working with the instructor.

### 3.2 Student Comments

This section provides examples of CS1 student feedback and illustrates how that information can help instructors in evaluating their use of particular pedagogical approaches.

#### 3.2.1 Dynamic Classroom

One of the most important ways that faculty can create a dynamic classroom is by encouraging student enthusiasm. Students who are excited about what they are learning will help to inspire other students to learn. Instructors who show students that they are excited about the material can make their students enthusiastic. The following rave was sent by a student in response to some help provided on an assignment in CSC 242:

> GUIs and I are in love again thanks to your help today!

Students who express love about the material are willing to work harder and create a positive atmosphere for their classmates. This particular student regularly makes comments in class about how interesting computer science is, which provides a positive impression of the course for his peers in the classroom.

Another important approach to cultivating a dynamic classroom is managing student frustration. Students taking their first programming class need to remain positive even while they are struggling to learn difficult concepts. The following quote illustrates an important attitude the instructor should take with respect to student frustration:

> Then I'll be able to explain my hatred for said problem before class, and we can attempt to get me to love it.

This student had indicated at the end of a class session that he hated one of the homework problems, a situation that needed to be remedied. By working with the student, an instructor can transform frustration into something more positive which will allow the student to remain engaged.

Another important consideration in CS1 courses is the interaction with non-majors. The focus of introductory computing courses is often on preparing majors for future classes, but non-majors can be an important audience. The following quote is from a student in CSC 241:

> The subject fascinates me and I would have loved to have majored in it, but my parents were very insistent on my going into the physical sciences.

Non-majors can provide a remarkable enthusiasm and different perspective on the material in CS1. Instructors need to be respectful of the contribution that non-majors can make in the classroom and encourage them to the same extent that they encourage students majoring in a computing field.

#### 3.2.2 Student Interaction

Although it is shown in the literature on CS1 that student-to-student interaction has significant benefits for learning, it should be noted that students are not always pleased to be required to interact with other students. In the CSC 241 course a portion of class time is spent on a series of peer instruction activities. Students were surveyed about their reaction to the project in the Winter quarter 2012, and in response to the question "what did you like least about taking part in this project?" a student made the following comment:

> I didn't like some of the questions, and I don't like talking to people.

Although this feedback on the surface is negative, that is likely because it pushed the student beyond her comfort zone. Challenging students to move beyond computing stereotypes is not always comfortable for them, but it can be worth it. An instructor who is attuned to negative attitudes about novel pedagogical techniques can improve student impressions of the approaches, for example by mentioning the benefits of the activities.

#### 3.2.3 Reduce Isolation

One of the most significant issues that students in a first programming course face is the adjustment to college. Provided with more independence than many of them have previously experienced, it is all too easy for them to develop poor study habits and a disregard for the importance of class attendance. Attendance during the freshman year, and particularly in classes for the major, is important for a student to avoid a sense of isolation. While taking attendance can be troublesome for various reasons, it may be sufficient to make students understand that you value their input, as illustrated by this comment from a freshman in her second quarter of Python who was going to miss a class:

> I know not everyone sends you e-mails about absences as this is college now, but it's important to me that you know I'm not ditching.

This student was not always active in the classroom, but she clearly internalized the message that her attendance was expected. She also formed close bonds with several of her classmates, in no small part because of her regular attendance.

Student isolation can be exacerbated by a lack of connection with an instructor. The following note came from a former Python student:

> *I was wondering if you knew Java and would you mind me asking questions about it because I have a really hard assignment and I'm a little lost.*

While it is encouraging that the student felt a strong enough connection with a former instructor to ask for help on material beyond the class, it is discouraging that he did not feel comfortable talking with his Java instructor about the questions. Poor communication between the Java instructor and the student resulted in the instructor losing valuable opportunities to reinforce the information provided in the classroom.

### 3.2.4 Cooperative Environment

A large part of ensuring that there is a cooperative environment in the classroom is reducing the distance between faculty and students. Students who are comfortable asking a question, which is at its heart a display of ignorance, will be able to make more progress with the material. The following segment from an e-mail indicates several important things about this process:

> *So I typed out this long letter with a question, only to figure out the answer myself while typing it. BUT I thought you might find it humorous or want to use it as an example or whatever, so I'm sending it to you anyways.*

This was part of a lengthy exchange with the student about a homework assignment in which he consistently began to formulate a question and in the process of doing so discovered the answer to his own question. Students in the CS1 courses are encouraged to apply the "one-hour rule" in which they should ask a question after one hour of concentrated work without progress on an issue. They are also specifically told that sending a question and then retracting it if they discover the answer on their own is fine and often occurs. That the student did this and then wanted to share his thought process is particularly revealing because it indicates a feeling of connection and two-way dialog with the instructor.

### 3.2.5 Multiple Approaches

Often the approaches taken to improve the atmosphere and learning in the introductory computing classroom cannot be separated. Using students' names is one approach to decreasing the distance between the students and instructor, but another is to allow the students to use the instructor's first name. The following segment of an e-mail from a former Python student illustrates this:

> *Ok, I'll try to call you Amber! I find it weird when [other student] reminisces about "Amber's class." I have to think about what she is talking about. I think it seems strange to me just because she is so young. [...] I wouldn't call another professor by their first name, but I also don't think I've ever sent another professor more than 1 (maybe 2) emails.*

As this quote illustrates, not all students are comfortable with using a faculty member's first name, but doing so conveys equality. The student remarking on the relative ages of all people involved highlights this. A cooperative atmosphere extends past the boundaries of the classroom, as is illustrated by the student's comment about a lack of contact with other faculty outside of class. And, finally, the students in question clearly continue to interact after the conclusion of the quarter, which demonstrates that the bonds they formed during the class remain.

## 4. CONCLUSION

The CS1 classroom is one of the most studied environments in computing education. A host of researchers have shown that innovative pedagogical techniques such as pair programming, peer instruction, and studio-based instruction have promise to improve student learning and engagement. Many of these approaches share common features, such as making the classroom dynamic, increasing student-to-student interaction, reducing isolation, and producing a cooperative learning atmosphere. But faculty who wish to adopt these approaches or otherwise improve their CS1 classroom have few formal approaches for professional development. Student evaluations can provide feedback, but it is typically not formative and comes after the fact. This article makes the case that faculty wishing to adopt new strategies in the CS1 classroom can use a behaviorist approach in their evaluation of their implementation. Student comments often echo the recommendations seen in the CS1 literature and can provide faculty with constant feedback throughout the quarter. The feedback is not always positive, since students exposed to new pedagogical approaches may be forced past their comfort zone, but it can be used to gauge in a less formal way whether the interventions the instructor is making are having the intended effect. Faculty who closely listen to their students may find that they are able to learn about teaching programming from the CS1 learners themselves.

## 5. ACKNOWLEDGMENTS

Thanks to Randy Connolly for an idea that eventually became this article and to André Berthiaume for his feedback on an earlier draft of this work.

## 6. REFERENCES

[1] Adams, P. 2008. The Role of Scholarship of Teaching in Faculty Development: Exploring an Inquiry-based Model. *International Journal for the Scholarship of Teaching and Learning*, 3:1.

[2] Barker, L.J. and Garvin-Doxas, K. 2004. Making Visible the Behaviors that Influence Learning Environment: A Qualitative Exploration of Computer Science Classrooms. *Computer Science Education*, 14:2, pp. 119-145.

[3] Barker, L.J., McDowell, C., and Kalahar, K. 2009. Exploring Factors that Influence Computer Science Introductory Course Students to Persist in the Major. In *Proceedings of the 40th SIGCSE Technical Symposium on Computer Science Education* (Chattanooga, Tennessee, March 2009).

[4] Beck, L.L. and Chizhik, A.W. 2008. An Experimental Study of Cooperative Learning in CS1. In *Proceedings of*

the 39th *SIGCSE Technical Symposium on Computer Science Education* (Portland, Oregon, March 2008).

[5] Biggers, M., Yilmaz, T., and Sweat, M. 2009. Using Collaborative, Modified Peer Led Team Learning To Improve Student Success and Retention in Intro CS. In *Proceedings of the 40th SIGCSE Technical Symposium on Computer Science Education* (Chattanooga, Tennessee, March 2009).

[6] Braught, G., Eby, L.M., and Wahls, T. 2008. The Effects of Pair-Programming on Individual Programming Skill. In *Proceedings of the 39th SIGCSE Technical Symposium on Computer Science Education* (Portland, Oregon, March 2008).

[7] Carter, A.S. and C.D. Hundhausen. 2011. A Review of Studio-Based Learning in Computer Science. *Journal of Computing Sciences in Colleges*, 27:1, pp. 105-111.

[8] Clayson, D.E. 2009. Student Evaluations of Teaching: Are They Related to What Students Learn?: A Meta-Analysis and Review of the Literature. *Journal of Marketing Education*, 31:16, pp. 16 – 30.

[9] *Computer Science Curricula 2013: Strawman Draft.* February 2012. The Joint Task Force on Computing Curricula, Association for Computing Machinery, IEEE-Computer Society, CS2013 Steering Committee, accessed May 2012.

[10] *Computer Science Curricula 2001.* December 15, 2001. The Joint Task Force on Computing Curricula, Association for Computing Machinery and IEEE Computer Society, accessed May 2012.

[11] Denning, P.J. and McGettrick, A. 2005. Recentering Computer Science. *Communications of the ACM*, 51:8, pp. 15-19.

[12] Ekstrom, J.J., Gorka, S., Kamali, R., Lawson, E., Lunt, B., Miller, J. and Reichgelt, H. 2006. The Information Technology Model Curriculum. Journal of Information Technology Education, 5.

[13] Gehringer, E.F. and Miller, C.S. 2009. Student-Generated Active-Learning Exercises. . In *Proceedings of the 40th SIGCSE Technical Symposium on Computer Science Education* (Chattanooga, Tennessee, March 2009).

[14] Hundhausen, C., Agrawal, A., Fairbrother, D., and Trevisan, M. 2010. Does Studio-Based Instruction Work in CS 1? An Empirical Comparison with a Traditional Approach. In *Proceedings of the 41st SIGCSE Technical Symposium on Computer Science Education* (Milwaukee, Wisconsin, March 2010).

[15] Information Technology 2008. Curriculum Guidelines for Undergraduate Degree Programs in Information Technology. Association for Computing Machinery and IEEE Computer Society. http://www.acm.org//education/curricula/IT2008%20Curriculum.pdf, accessed May 2012.

[16] Jenkins, J., Brannock, E., Cooper, T., Dekhane, S., Hall, M., and Nyugen, M. 2012. Perspectives on Active Learning and Collaboration: JavaWIDE in the Classroom. In *Proceedings of the 43rd SIGCSE Technical Symposium on Computer Science Education* (Raleigh, North Carolina, February/March 2012).

[17] Kumar, D. 2011. Ready for a third peak? In *ACM Inroads*, 2:3, September 2011.

[18] Lasserre, P. and Szostak, C. 2011. Effects of Team-Based Learning on a CS1 Course. In *Proceedings of the 16th Annual Conference on Innovation and Technology in Computer Science Education* (Darmstadt, Germany, June 2011).

[19] Lu, J.J. and Fletcher, G. H. L. 2009. Thinking about Computational Thinking. In *Proceedings of the 40th SIGCSE Technical Symposium on Computer Science Education* (Chattanooga, Tennessee, March 2009).

[20] Luxton-Rielly, A., Bertinshaw, D., Denny, P., Plimmer, B., and Sheehan, R. 2012. The Impact of Question Generation Activities on Performance. In *Proceedings of the 43rd SIGCSE Technical Symposium on Computer Science Education* (Raleigh, North Carolina, February/March 2012).

[21] Luxton-Rielly, A. 2009. A systematic review of tools that support peer assessment. *Computer Science Education*, 19:4, pp. 209-232.

[22] McCauley, R., Starr, C., Pharr, W. Stalvey, R., and Pothering, G. 2006. Is CS1 Better with the Same Lecture and Lab Instructor? *Inroads*, 38:2, pp. 54 – 60.

[23] McDowell, C. Werner, L, Bullock H.E., and Fernald, J. 2006. Pair Programming Improve Student Retention, Confidence, and Program Quality. *Communications of the ACM*, 49:8, pp. 90-95.

[24] Porter, L., Bailey Lee, C., Simon, B., and Zingaro, D. 2011. Peer Instruction: Do Students Really Learn from Peer Discussion in Computing? In *Proceedings of the 7th International Workshop on Computing Education Research* (Providence, Rhode Island, August 2011).

[25] Salleh, N., Mendes, E., Grundy, J.C. Empirical Studies of Pair Programming for CS/SE Teaching in Higher Education: A Systematic Literature Review. 2011. *IEEE Transactions on Software Engineering*, 37:4, pp. 509-525.

[26] Simon, B., Kohanfars, M. Lee, J., Tamayo, K. and Cutts, Q. 2010. Experience Report: Peer Instruction in Introductory Computing. In *Proceedings of the 41st SIGCSE Technical Symposium on Computer Science Education* (Milwaukee, Wisconsin, March 2010).

[27] Simon, B. and Hanks, B. 2008. First-Year Students' Impressions of Pair Programming in CS1. *ACM Journal on Educational Resources in Computing*, 7:4.

[28] Wing, J. 2006. Computational Thinking. *Communications of the ACM*, 49:3, pp. 33-35.

# Engaging Undergraduate Programming Students: Experiences using Lego Mindstorms NXT

Collette Gavan
Edge Hill University
St Helens Road
Ormskirk, Lancashire, L39 4QP, UK.
(+44)1695 657633

gavanc@edgehill.ac.uk

Dr Mark Anderson
Edge Hill University
St Helens Road
Ormskirk, Lancashire, L39 4QP, UK.
(+44)1695 657634

mark.anderson@edgehill.ac.uk

## ABSTRACT

In this paper, the experiences gained in adopting an approach to first year undergraduate programming classes which attempts to engage the students in problem-solving and teamworking activities are discussed. Both have a significant role to contribute in the development of employability skills. The approach taken makes use of Alice to introduce programming concepts and Lego Mindstorms NXT kits to develop Java programming skills. The module assessments combine individual and team-based components, encouraging the students to engage with their peers in order to solve the challenges they are set. This paper reports on the results achieved by the students on the module over a four year period which correlates to the introduction of the changes to the module design. The paper also considers the views of the students gathered from anonymous module evaluation forms.

## Categories and Subject Descriptors

K.3.2 [**Computer and Information Science Education**]: Computer science education

## General Terms

Design, Experimentation, Human Factors, Theory.

## Keywords

Programming, student engagement, teaching.

## 1. INTRODUCTION

The teaching of programming to first year undergraduate students has, for a long time, been a problematic area [8]. Students often struggle with both the conceptual ideas along with the syntax of the language being taught [1,20,19]. In many respects, the move towards teaching using an object-oriented language, such as Java or C++, has served to amplify these issues [19,24]. Unlike procedural programming, in which the students would concentrate on the development of algorithms and syntactic correctness of the code that they are being asked to develop, the object-oriented paradigm introduces further complexity in its level of abstraction. Following this, students are required to model the relevant features of a "world" which their program is to implement. Whilst it is possible to teach procedural programming to students

in the first instance and then move on to the object-oriented paradigm at a later point in a programme [19], the students may then face confusion as the methods they follow to design and implement their code will change.

In an attempt to address this barrier to learning, there have been a number of approaches which have been adopted to assist student understanding of programming concepts. Some approaches have focused on the development of specialized programming environments in which students develop their code [3,10,16]. Alongside assisting students to develop code, often by providing visualisation which demonstrates the structure of the program which has been developed (an example of this is BlueJ to teach Java programming), the creation of a specialized teaching environment removes some of the complexity of a standard Integrated Development Environment (IDE) from novice programmers. The outcome of this is that students still need to encounter these IDEs at a later point in their academic studies.

However, in conjunction with the development of the practical skills associated with the teaching of programming there is also an increased focus to develop employability skills amongst students [6,11]. Whilst the employment figures for graduates may be high, there is no indication whether graduates are fully benefitting from the abilities that they have developed through their degree programmes. Indeed, there have been predictions that graduates may face periods of unemployment, or of employment in positions which are not relevant to their chosen degree paths [21]. However, the issues involved when developing work-related practices within degree programmes are highly complex [13,25].

This paper presents an approach taken to teaching introductory programming to first year undergraduate students and reports on the experiences from the module. The module has been designed not only to engage the students with the underpinning concepts of programming, but also to develop both an understanding of the object-oriented paradigm and assist the students in developing their employability skills in terms of problem-solving and team working. The module design has evolved over the previous four years, and the paper reflects upon the changes that have been introduced and the impact which these have had upon the student experience.

## 2. EMPLOYABILITY SKILLS

There is a well held view that, alongside the teaching of academic subjects, the "focus for university is to...[prepare] students for life beyond the disciplines" [12]. A traditional view presented by Barrie (2006) identifies the key attributes a graduate would possess [2]. The focus of these abilities relates to the academic values and concepts that have been long-established within the higher education sector and include academic inquiry, academic rigour, the generation of ideas, and the development of learning skills. It could be argued, however, that these attributes would define a highly generic skill set. However, it has also been argued that these skills form the basis of the skill set sought by employers [22]. A question would then arise concerning the relevance of the skills developed through a degree programme to the careers of those who graduate from those programme. A degree may deliver the high level skills to satisfy these attributes, but may not meet the more specific requirements of the potential employers.

A key distinction of experiential learning as opposed to other learning theories is that it is based on an ongoing process of learning [9]; the forming and reforming of concepts through practice and experience. In this respect there is a close alignment with the HE sector reforms which also focus on education [22]. The importance of experiential learning was echoed by Winter and Maisch (1996) when reporting upon the experiences from the Accreditation and Support for Specified Expertise and Training (ASSET) programme [23]. This programme made use of a competence-based model of education for students in two subject areas, and found that the students were able to develop levels of professional understanding through the experience which they gained whilst on the programme. Furthermore experiential learning has been advocated as an appropriate means of teaching problem-solving to students [17]. It has been argued that experiential learning, through the implementation of Problem Based Learning (PBL), should be a pedagogy which is adopted centrally to the higher education curricula [18].

Instilling experiential learning will commence the ongoing process for graduates to enter the workplace and continue their development through further learning [15]. This notion is supported by the work of Teichler and Kehm (1995) who identify that there is an ongoing rise in the development of lifelong learning processes [21], with the suggested implication that the role a university should adopt is that of preparing the graduates for self development during their careers and not to have a focus of attempting to produce the finished article. This is strongly supported by the findings of Mason and Williams (2003) who found, when surveyed, that the vast majority of employers did not expect a graduate employee to be "work-ready"[13]. In this regard, new employees were expected to undertake additional training to meet the needs of their job. However, the findings also revealed that the role of most training programmes the graduates had completed was to teach the technicalities of the roles, for example how to use software packages or equipment, and not the transferrable skills, such as communication skills. The implication here is that employers would expect graduates to already be in possession of those skills on joining a company.

## 3. MODULE DESIGN
In designing the first year module to introduce programming concepts to first year undergraduate students, the course needed to address the issues relating to both the employability requirements and also the "fear factor" which is often faced by students when presented with modules in such subjects. The module would make use of the Java programming language. The module runs over two semesters (26 weeks) and is taken by all students who enter the undergraduate Computing and Web Systems Development programmes on offer at Edge Hill University in the United Kingdom. The result is that the module has a cohort size of 50-90 students every year, and that there can be no assumption

made about the level of programming experience that the students have on joining the module. The students are typically in classes of 20-25 students and will attend two 2 hour laboratory sessions each week. Additional support is offered to the students through a mentoring scheme in which second year students are available to assist the first years once a week in a laboratory with their programming problems to offer guidance and advice.

The structure of assessment within the module enables module tutors to quickly identify any areas of the subject which may require reinforcement, although the module generally adopts a Problem-Based Learning approach. As such, the students are required to complete two sets of individual portfolio work to develop skills in specific topics within the subject, and also complete two team-based projects within the module to supplement and extend the skills developed through the portfolios. The portfolio elements of assessment are compulsory elements which the students must pass in order to pass the module, regardless of whether a passing grade has been achieved in the other components of the module assessment.

## 3.1 Developing Employability Skills
The development of employability skills within the curriculum is focused on the team assessments which the students are required to perform. In these assessments, the students are guided in developing their problem-solving skills and in forming effective teams. In doing so, the students develop team norms by which the members of the team will operate, which are essential for effective team operation [14].

Students working within teams will experience a structured environment with a clearly defined role in a project [4,7]. The structure offers immediate access to a support network which may provide support at a number of different levels, both academic and otherwise. Indeed, most teams will also consist of students who possess different levels of experience or knowledge, therefore providing an invaluable resource to the network for members of the team. The teams also nominate a team leader, and assign roles to the team members (although it is important to note that all team members must perform programming tasks on the project). To aid team interaction, the teams are provided with online tools through the institutional Virtual Learning Environment (VLE) which enables the team to communicate and delegate tasks when they are away from the campus.

## 4. LANGUAGES AND ENVIRONMENTS
To introduce students to the concepts of programming and build both their skills and confidence in terms of problem solving, the modules makes use of two programming environments. The Alice programming environment[1] is used to introduce students to the key constructs of programming, such as sequence, selection and iteration. Given that there can be no assumption made about the previous programming experience of the students, Alice offers two significant benefits for teaching introductory programming. Firstly it makes use of a drag-and-drop interface with code presented in a Java style. This enables students to focus on enhancing their problem solving skills without the necessity of learning language syntax simultaneously. Students are also able to view their code in a style which looks like Java code, and so become aware of the syntax implicitly such as the use of blocks

---

[1] http://www.alice.org/

| | A | B | C | D | Fail | Pass rate (%) | No Students | Mean | SD |
|---|---|---|---|---|---|---|---|---|---|
| 2008/09 | 10% | 28% | 44% | 16% | 2% | 94% | 50 | 57.34% | 11.27 |
| 2009/10 | 11% | 21% | 27% | 36% | 5% | 90.32% | 62 | 53.61% | 12.61 |
| 2010/11 | 20% | 43% | 12% | 21% | 1% | 96% | 81 | 59.83% | 12.56 |
| 2011/12 | 48% | 21% | 14% | 1% | 13% | 84% | 86 | 61.72% | 20.64 |

and semi-colons related to the development of Java code. The second key advantage of using Alice is based in its adoption of an object-oriented paradigm. Within Alice, students place objects into a virtual world and interact with those objects by sending messages to the object concerned. Students create objects by selecting the appropriate class from the Alice Class Library. The visualization of these concepts has proven extremely useful when introducing object-orientation to students. One set of portfolio exercises, one formative team exercise and one summative team exercise are undertaken by the students in this section of the module.

In the second section of the module the students move towards programming in Java using the Eclipse IDE. Within this section of the module, the students also complete a set of portfolio exercises along with a team exercise. As an initial component of the portfolio, the students are required to develop their own tutorial guide for Eclipse to help them explore the IDE prior to performing the Java-based tasks.

Following the portfolio, the team task which the students are required to complete has introduced the use of Lego Mindstorms NXT robotics kits into the programming curriculum. In order to program the robots, the students use leJOS NXJ[2] with the relevant plugin for Eclipse. This enables the robots to be programmed using Java running under a customized Java Virtual Machine on the NXT control brick. In the coursework groups of 3 or 4 students are required to solve a number of problems and, in order to do so, the students must design their robot, design their coding solution for each problem, build the robot and program the device for each problem, or level, that has been set. Prior to the introduction of the Lego Mindstorms robots, students were required to develop a game using Java. This remains as an option to students although, as shall be discussed in this paper, the students have been enthused and fully engaged in developing their programming skills through the final team-based project.

## 5. MODULE RESULTS ANALYSIS

Table 1, shown above, contains the overall module results from the introductory programming module for four iterations. The letter grades relate to percentage scores achieved by the students where

- A = 70-100%
- B = 60-69%
- C = 50-59%
- D = 40-49%

---

[2] http://lejos.sourceforge.net/index.php

These grade boundaries correlate to degree classifications in the UK. A student is required to attain 40% or greater to pass the module. The Mean column shows the mean student mark achieved within the module in that academic year.

The results which are shown for 2011/12 are those which have been produced prior to the reassessment period, and hence the module pass rate appears lower in this year than in previous years.

It should also be noted that the 2008/09 module results represent the structure of the module prior to the introduction of Lego Mindstorms into the module curriculum. In that academic year, the students were required to implement a game in Java using the skills which they had acquired throughout the earlier stages of the module. The structure of the module, however, remained the same and the students completed the final assessment in small teams. These results are included to represent a baseline from which the effect of introducing robotics as a mechanism for engagement can be judged. However, it is acknowledged that the results achieved by the students in that academic year were impressive, with a high pass rate and a normal distribution of student grades on the module.

The use of the NXT kits was first introduced into the curriculum in 2009/10. In this academic year, all students were required to make use of the robots for their final programming coursework. However, the department only had a limited number of kits for the students to use. Difficulties were also experienced in the laboratory environment when installing and using the software to program the robots. The teaching team addressed these problems by providing the students with caddies with the Eclipse and leJOS software installed so the students could attempt the programming tasks. The students were also provided with pre-built robots, and so selected the robot which they wished to use to attempt the challenges. The results for this year represent the issues which the students faced, with little change in the overall results profile of the cohort.

In the following academic year 2010/11, the Module Leader amended the module to continue the experiment to evaluate the impact of using the Mindstorms NXTs to teach programming. In this year, the use of the robots was optional. The student teams were able to select between a coursework to program the NXT robots, or alternatively to write a game in Java using Swing. The significant difference in experience which the students gained when using the NXTs was that the teams had to design and build their own robots, and so had greater access to kits which they could use. The teaching team observed a difference in behavior between the students using the NXTs and the students writing the game. Those teams using the robots were on campus and in the laboratories far more frequently, staying until late in the evening and demonstrating high levels of engagement. The module results for this academic year also demonstrate a changed profile of results. The number of students gaining an 'A' or 'B' grade increased significantly, and the overall pass rate and average module result also improved. Furthermore when examining the individual coursework results, it is clear that those students who worked with the Mindstorms for their final coursework achieved improved grades over their previous coursework submissions in the module. In comparison, those students who undertook the game development task achieved results that were broadly in line, or slightly lower, than their previous grades in the module.

In the current academic year 2011/12 the use of the Mindstorms has been extended so that the majority of students would work in teams to design, build and program their own devices to resolve the challenges they were set. A small number of students (8) who had not engaged in earlier teamwork exercises, either out of choice or for personal reasons, were set an alternative programming coursework. Each team was allocated their own kit and was given a brief introduction to programming using leJOS. Again, the teaching team noted high levels of engagement with the teams using the NXT devices. This has been reflected in the results profile for the module. The innovation and creativity which the students have demonstrated has led to over two-thirds of the students achieving an 'A' or 'B' grade. It is also noted that the average grade on the module has increased significantly. If the results for the courseworks in 2011/12 are examined in further detail (Figure 1 below), then there can be seen to a significant change in the pattern of results gained by the students across each of the assessments. The portfolio exercises (shown in gold) and the Alice team exercise (shown in blue) both represent a skewed normal distribution. However, the assessment which engages the students using the NXTs inverts these results. A high proportion of the students achieved grades of 'A' or above (which represents marks of 70% or higher). It is also interesting to note that there is only one team of three students (out of 77 students) who used the NXTs for their coursework who are currently classified as not passing the module. The remaining 8 students who have currently not passed the module consist of those who attempted the game writing coursework. As stated earlier, the reassessment period for this module has not concluded, so it is expected by the authors that the number of students passing the module should increase.

# 6. STUDENT EXPERIENCE

Whilst it is important to acknowledge the statistical evidence of the improvements that have been achieved by adopting the NXTs in the teaching of programming, the student experience is also a major factor in judging the success of this approach. Each module at Edge Hill University concludes with the students completing an evaluation form which is submitted anonymously and enables the students to express their thoughts regarding the module which they have completed. Each student in the cohort completes an evaluation form which gathers both qualitative and quantitative data relating to the student experience on the module. The results presented in this paper relate to the 2010/11 and 2011/12 academic years which reflect the experiences of the students from the broader introduction of the Lego Mindstorms NXTs into the curriculum.

Broadly, the students in 2010/11 reported that they enjoyed the module and benefitted from the design of the course, describing the course as "stimulating" and "fun and interesting". The use of Alice to introduce programming concepts was identified by a number of students as having a positive impact upon their experiences, with one student stating that they

"Enjoyed using Alice, especially the game coursework."

In many respects, this comment demonstrates not only the benefit of using Alice, but also the value felt by the students in relation to the teamwork elements. Indeed, this is supported by further student comments, such as

"Lots of variety in coursework, and individual/group exercises were good."

In terms of building employability skills, the development of teamworking skills are significant so the identification of these elements of assessment as having a positive impact on the student experience were particularly pleasing.

When referring to the use of the NXT kits, students who made use of the kits were unanimous in their response "Programming using Eclipse and the robots"

Or more simply,

"ROBOTS!!!"

This demonstrated the beneficial effect on their engagement in determining the good aspects of the module. Within this cohort, the issues that were generally raised concerning the module were that the students felt they wanted more lectures and tutorials in Java, and that they wanted to spend more time in the module programming in Java.

The issues raised in 2010/11 were addressed for the subsequent academic year by introducing lecture classes to introduce fundamental concepts to the students, whilst retaining the core PBL elements of the assessments, and moving the transition point from Alice to Java to two weeks earlier in the module.

In comparison to the previous cohort, the 2011/12 evaluations reveal that the students appreciated the wider adoption of the NXT kits as a means of developing their programming skills. They report that "getting to work with the robots" was "interesting" and "fun". The students again identified the introduction to programming using Alice, with comments such as

"I like the way that I came here with very little knowledge in programming. Alice was a great way to start learning."

However, of particular interest were the comments which indicated that the students felt benefit from the activities which assist them to develop broader skills to assist them in the workplace, such as teamworking

"Enjoyed working in groups. Helped me to see problems from different perspectives and tackle them differently",

and enhanced problem-solving skills

"Changed my opinion of tackling unfamiliar computer problems and programming overall".

**Figure 1: 2011/12 Module coursework results profile**

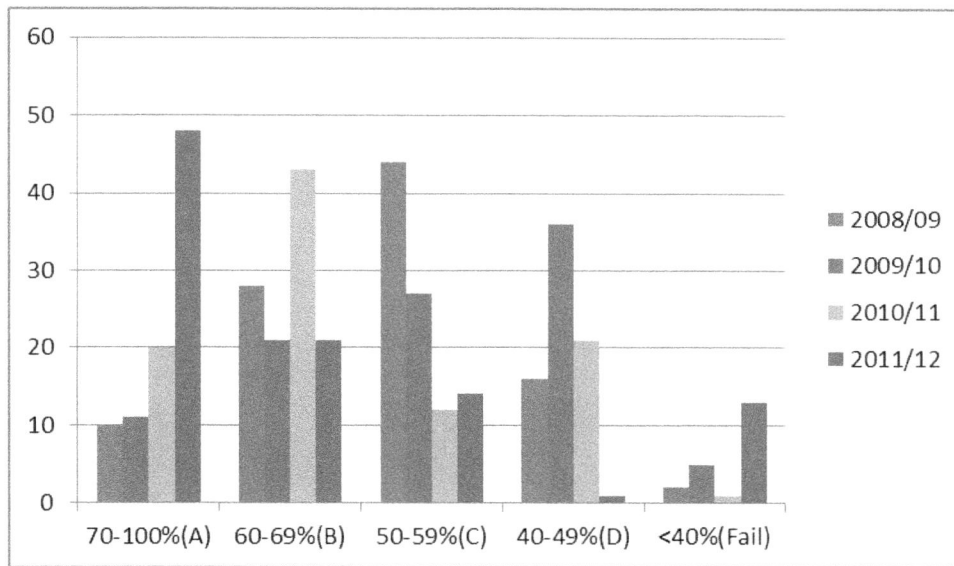

The improvements suggested by this cohort centered around the inclusion of reflective blogs to enhance academic skills, and the provision of longer tutorial sessions to provide further opportunity for team building. These amendments to the module shall be considered for implementation in the 2012/13 academic year.

## 7. CONCLUSIONS

The introduction of the Lego Mindstorms robots into the first year programming course, accompanied by an introduction to the fundamental concepts through the use of Alice, have had a demonstrable effect on the engagement and results of the students on the module. Where students would be fearful of programming exercises and maintain an attitude of "just doing enough" to be able to pass the module, both the Alice and Mindstorms team assessments have led to students wishing to extend their skill sets beyond those that are taught in the course and push themselves to produce work which far exceeds the requirements of the course. This is reflected in both the assessment results and the student evaluations. The module results show a marked improvement in the assignments where the students collaborate and develop their skills using the NXT kits. The module evaluations provide feedback which demonstrates that the activities within the module resulted in a stimulating and engaging challenge for the students, but also that the students felt their teamworking and problem-solving skills had developed through the courseworks. Indeed, the interest and excitement which has been generated through these changes to the module have led to further changes in the curriculum.

Modules have been introduced in the second and third years which explore the development of robots, maintaining a focus on programming, for students to further enhance their problem-solving skills. These modules have proven to be extremely popular, with module registrations increasing five-fold over the three years that the modules have been running. The second change to the curriculum has been the introduction of a new route within the Computing suite of programmes which specializes in the development of programming skills. The route, Application

Development, followed a significant number of requests from students for further modules and opportunities to develop their programming knowledge. This is in stark contrast to the Computing programmes of four or more years ago at Edge Hill University when students would try to avoid programming modules if they could. Both of these developments have resulted in increased creativity and inspiration by the students to develop innovative software using new and emerging technologies, such as the Microsoft Kinect camera, where use of the SDKs are not currently taught within the curriculum.

In terms of addressing employability skills, then the changes in the curriculum that have been driven by the model of teaching programming introduced in the first year programming module and discussed in this paper have brought significant and tangible changes to the behavior and interaction of the student cohort. This is reflected in the students' ability to work within teams, to negotiate during teamwork, to engage with external clients during projects, and in designing solutions to problems which may lie outside of the topics covered within the modules that they have studied. Students are actively interested in developments across the broad spectrum of Computing subjects, and are bringing ideas for external visitors, workshops and the introduction of technologies to the departmental staff.

## 8. ACKNOWLEDGMENTS

Our thanks to the Computing students at Edge Hill University for participating in this study.

## 9. REFERENCES

[1] Azemi, A. 1995. Teaching Computer Programming Courses in a Computer Laboratory Environment. FIE '95 Proceedings of the Frontiers in Education Conference on 1995. Volume 1.

[2] Barrie, S.C. 2006. Understanding what we mean by the generic attributes of graduates. Higher Education 51: 215-241

[3] Cavus, N, Uzunboylu, H. and Ibrahim, D. 2006. Using the Moodle Learning Management System and GREWPtool

Collaborative Tool for Teaching a Programming Language. Presented at Creating the Future 4th FAE International Symposium, University of Lefke, 30 Nov – 1 Dec, Lefke, Cyprus.

[4] Delamont, S. (2001). 'The marriage analogy: personal and positional relationships in PhD supervision'. Presented at the Higher Education Close Up Conference 2, Lancaster University, 16-18 July 2001. Available at http://www.leeds.ac.uk/educol/documents/00001732.doc (accessed 8 May 2009)

[5] Enzai, N.I.M., Kar, S.A.C., Husni, H. and Ahmed, N. 2011. Harnessing Creativity in Teaching and Learning Introductory Programming. In Proceedings of 2011 IEEE Student Conference on Research and Development. Putrajaya, Selangor, Malaysia

[6] Fincher, S. 1999. What are we doing when we teach programming? 29th ASEE/IEEE Frontiers in Education Conference, 1999.

[7] Finlay, I. (2002) 'Online support and learning: a study of part-time students on a doctoral programme'. Available at http://www.leeds.ac.uk/educol/documents/00002314.htm (accessed on 8 May 2009).

[8] Kelleher, C. and Pausch, R. (2005) Lowering the Barriers to Programming::A Taxonomy of Programming Environments and Languages For Novice Programmers. ACM Computer Survey, 37 (2), pp. 83–137.

[9] Kolb, D.A. 1984. Experiential Learning: experience as the source of learning and development. New Jersey: Prentice Hall

[10] Kuljis, J. 2004. Orienting the Teaching of an Introductory Object-Oriented Programming to Meet the Learning Objective. Proceedings of the 26th International Conference on Information Technology Interfaces

[11] Lin, C.H. and Liu, E.Z.F. 2012. The Effect of Reflective Strategies on Students' Problem Solving in Robotics Learning. In Proceedings of Fourth IEEE International Conference on Digital Game and Intelligent Toy Enhanced Learning, Takamatsu, Kagawa, Japan.

[12] Matthew, R.G.S. and Pritchard, J. 2009. Hard and Soft – A Useful Way of Thinking about Disciplines? In Kreber, C. (ed) The university and its disciplines: teaching and learning within and beyond disciplinary boundaries. Taylor and Francis.

[13] Mason, G. And Williams, G. 2003. How much does higher education enhance the employability of graduates?. Summary report to HEFCE. Available online http://www.hefce.ac.uk/pubs/rdreports/2003/rd13_03/rd13_0 3sum.pdf [Accessed 21/12/11]

[14] Mayo, E. 1945. The social problems of an industrial civilisation. Cambridge, MA: Harvard University Press.

[15] Raelin, J.A. 2008 Work-based learning: bridging knowledge and action in the workplace. San Francisco: Wiley

[16] Satratzemi, M., Xinogalos, S. and Dagdilelis, V. (2003) An Environment for Teaching Object-Oriented Programming: ObjectKarel. Proceedings of the Third IEEE International Conference on Advanced Learning Technologies (ICALT '03). Athens, Greece.

[17] Saunders, M. And Machell, J. 2000. Understanding emerging trends in higher education curricula and work connections. Higher Education Policy. Pergamon. Pp. 1-16

[18] Savin-Baden, M. 2000. Problem-based Learning in Higher Education: untold stories. Open University Press.

[19] Sheard, J. and Hagan, D. 1997. Experiences with Teaching Object-oriented Concepts to Introductory Programming Students using C++. Proceedings of the Technology of Object-Oriented Languages and Systems (TOOLS'97).

[20] Sobrinho, W.T. and Goncalves, R.S. 2011. Study of Robotics Singularities using LEGO Mindstorms Kit.. Proceedings of 2011 IEEE IX Latin American and IEEE Colombian Conference on Automatic Control and Industry Applications (LARC), 1-4 Oct, Bogota, Columbia.

[21] Teichler, U. And Kehm, B.M. 1995. Towards a New Understanding of the Relationships between Higher Education and Employment. European Journal of Education 30(2). Pp 115-132.

[22] Universities UK Response to the Higher Education White Paper (online). Available at http://www.universitiesuk.ac.uk/Publications/Documents/Res ponseToTheHigherEducationWhitePaper.pdf [Accessed 21/12/11]

[23] Winter, R. and Maisch, M. 1996. Professional Competence and Higher Education: The ASSET Programme. London: The Falmer Press.

[24] Xiaohui, G. and Yaguan, Q. 2010. The Exploration of Teaching about Java Programming. Proceedings of The International Conference on E-Business and E-Government, ICEE 2010, 7-9 May 2010, Guangzhou, China.

[25] Yorke, M. and Knight, P.T. 2006. Embedding employability into the curriculum. Learning and employability series 1. The Higher Education Academy. Avaliable online http://www.heacademy.ac.uk/resources/detail/employability/ Embedding_employability_into_the_curriculum [Accessed 22/12/11]

# A Feasibility Study on using Clustering Algorithms in Programming Education Research

Marzieh Ahmadzadeh
School of Computer Engineering & IT
Shiraz University of Technology
Shiraz, Iran
ahmadzadeh@sutech.ac.ir

Elham Mahmoudabadi
School of Computer Engineering & IT
Amirkabir University of Technology
Tehran, Iran
mahmoudabadi@aut.ac.ir

## ABSTRACT

Designing an experiment for programming education research, in which collecting and interpreting a large number of qualitative data about programmers is required, needs careful consideration in order to validate the experiment. When it comes to finding a pattern in the programming behaviour of a specific group of programmers (e,g. novice, intermediate or expert programmers), one of the critical issues is the selection of similar participants who can be placed in one group. In this study we were interested in finding a method that could shorten the path to finding participants. Therefore, the use of clustering algorithms to group similar participants was put to test in order to investigate the effectiveness and feasibility of this approach. The clustering algorithms that were used for this study were K-means and DBSCAN. The results showed that the use of these algorithms, for the mentioned purpose, is feasible and that both algorithms can identify similar participants and place them in the same group while participants who are not similar to others, and therefore are not the correct subject of the study, are recognised.

## Categories and Subject Descriptors

D.1.5 [**Object-oriented Programming**], D.2.5 [**Testing and Debugging**]: *Code inspections and walk-throughs.*

## General Terms

Algorithms, Measurement, Experimentation.

## Keywords

Program Comprehension, Experiment, Clustering Algorithm, K-means, DBSCAN, Computer Science Education.

## 1. INTRODUCTION

Most programming research, including program comprehension research, is by nature experimental [1, 4, 7, 11] where several issues must be taken into consideration to maintain the validity of the experiment. The first issue is the choice of participants, subjects who should have the qualities that the experiment is based on. For example, when novice programmers are the subjects of the study, a researcher must pay attention to choose participants who fit the definition of novice in a novice programmers' group

category. Likewise, when expert programming ability is studied, one should think about what makes a programmer an expert.

The second issue is the method by which data is collected. Again, in this kind of research in which programmers' behaviour is studied, data gathering is done by methods such as observation, interviews, data logs, and so on. These methods of data gathering are qualitative which require one to analyse the data qualitatively. Among the huge amount of data collected by these approaches are always large amounts of data which are not significantly important to the analysis. These can be identified by the analyser in the process of interpreting the collected data. This, however, is a time consuming job.

The third issue is that the process of interpreting the collected data is subjective, therefore, if the amount of collected data is huge, and consequently the number of analysers is more than one, it will likely lead to inconsistent results.

The issues mentioned above motivated us to develop a method which helps us in many ways. This included: selecting the right participants by filtering potential subjects by various metrics, which were defined by us; and, reducing the amount of qualitative data collected in the experiment to lead us to focus on more important data to eventually assist us in having more consistent data analysis.

The solution to these problems, offered by us, is the use of clustering algorithms. In this research we chose two clustering algorithms, K-means[12] and DBSCAN[6]. We studied the feasibility of using these algorithms in order to categorize the right participants in the same group to be further analysed qualitatively. Therefore, two issues have been tested in this research: a) does this method (the use of clustering algorithms) of data summarization work for this kind of research (i.e. programming research); and, b) which algorithm is more appropriate and shows better results.

The K-means and DBSCAN algorithms were chosen as an instance of centre-based and density-based clustering algorithms respectively. Since this was a feasibility study, other algorithms were not tested in this experiment.

The organization of this paper is as follows: a review of literature is given in the next section; the third section presents the two clustering algorithms that are used for this research; in the fourth section the experiment and its results are addressed; and finally, the last section discusses the conclusion of this study.

## 2. RELATED WORKS

Two types of research are related to the current study. The first group is concerned with learning to program and the second group focuses on the application of data mining algorithms including clustering algorithms. Our research is concerned with the application of clustering algorithms in program learning research.

Research concerning learning to program has spanned nearly four decades with an endless variety of approaches. The broad range of research in this field consists of proposing a cognitive framework to explain the process of learning to program and comprehension to developing tools to assist teaching [5] or measuring a tool's feedback on programmers' motivation to program. As an instance, in 1979 Schneiderman and Mayer [12] proposed a cognitive framework to explain programmers' behaviours when they were composing, debugging and modifying a source code. The participants were selected from the range of novices to expert programmers. One of the most recent studies concentrates on how different feedback from a tool impacts the motivation of programming and introduces a tool that was designed for this purpose[8].

The application of data mining algorithms, including clustering, has been broad. For example, to analyse a log file in order to get information for debugging the program, the K-means algorithm has been used [9]. In other research, text-mining was used to extract functionality of a system from a textual requirement [3]. To produce initial data for evaluation of plagiarism detection a variant of K-means (i.e. bisecting K-means) was used [10].

Investigating the literature reveals no research in which the technique of clustering, in order to study the process in which students comprehend or develop a program, was used. Therefore, this research was developed to act as a feasibility test on using these techniques to make this type of study easier.

# 3. CLUSTERING ALGORITHM

One way to summarize a large amount of data is to use clustering techniques to group data in a meaningful way so that the objects inside the groups, or clusters, have the most similarities while objects in different groups have the most differences.

Two types of clustering algorithms are available: nested and partitioned. A nested clustering algorithm creates overlapped clusters while a partitioned clustering algorithm creates non-overlapping clusters. For programming research, in which differences between groups of programmers is required, the second type of clustering algorithm is more appropriate. For this research we considered two partitioned algorithms called K-means and DBSCAN, which will be explained in the next two subsections. These algorithms were chosen as representatives of two types of portioned clustering algorithms i.e. center-based and density-based.

## 3.1 K-means Algorithm

This algorithm is a center-based clustering algorithm in which a most representative point (object) for one cluster is chosen and the distance between the representative point and all other points (or objects) are computed. Since one can choose K clusters, this algorithm is called K-means. This means that K representative objects (i.e. centroid or medoid) are selected. Each object is then assigned to the closest centroid and therefore, the related cluster. In the next step, the center point is updated according to the objects that have been assigned to the cluster. For the newly created centroid, the new members of the cluster are computed again. This process is repeated until the centroids do not change. At this point the members of each K cluster are known [12].

## 3.2 DBSCAN Algorithm

This algorithm is among the group of algorithms that are based on density. This means that a cluster is a dense part of the objects which are surrounded by a low density collection of data. In this algorithm, any two objects that are close enough within a pre-specified distance (epsilon) are assigned to one cluster. A cluster is formed if it exceeds the specified minimum number of objects (minpoint). The number of clusters, therefore, is estimated by the density distribution of the objects. Thus, the distance and the number of objects required to form a cluster are the two parameters needed for this algorithm. The algorithm starts from a random point and computes the epsilon-neighbourhood of that point. If the number of these points exceeds minpoint, a cluster is formed otherwise, the point is introduced as a noise. This process is repeated until all points of data are labeled [6].

# 4. EXPERIMENT

To investigate whether or not clustering algorithms can help in grouping similar programmers correctly, to be further studied qualitatively, an experiment was designed with 7 participants who are called A, B, C, D, E, F and G for ease of use. Since this was a qualitative research, the low number of participants was not an issue. All seven programmers were novice students who had recently learned object-oriented topics, finished their first semester and achieved almost similar marks. This means that we selected students who had the same efficiency in our classes. Some of these students had some prior experience in programming and high interest in this job while others had no experience and less interest. The summary of the information that we had from these students can be seen in Table I. Since exam marks and the degree of interest were very close it seems reasonable that students with programming experience cluster together against others. We kept in mind that the ability in programming is not the same as the ability in program comprehension [1]. The marks show their programming ability only. Therefore, programming marks might not be an indicator of other abilities such as program comprehension. In this experiment, we were interested in grouping the students based on their program comprehension ability therefore, an experiment that put their program comprehension ability to test was designed.

**Table I. Participants' Information**

| Student ID | Mark out of 40 | Experience | Interest |
|------------|----------------|------------|----------|
| A | 33 | No | Very High |
| B | 30.25 | No | High |
| C | 30.5 | Yes | Very High |
| D | 29.5 | No | High |
| E | 35.5 | Yes | Very High |
| F | 37.5 | Yes | Very High |
| G | 36 | No | Moderate |

It might be asked why we needed to rank novices when the majority of studies compare novices with experts, for which clear metrics are available. The answer to this question is clear. It is observed frequently, by lecturers, that explaining the same concepts to students does not result in the same performance by them while, when students are encouraged to do pair programming, the overall performance improves. We wanted to see how one student's approach in a group was different from his/her peers that could affect performance, which was not possible otherwise. In other words, we wanted to find the differences between the processes in which problems are solved by different groups of novices in order to get a better understanding of their program comprehension differences. We can then take advantage of these findings to improve our teaching.

In this study two similar experiments were designed. The experiments ran in two phases in which participants read the given program specifications and completed the given code in order to get a full working code. We chose to have two experiments since we wanted to evaluate the results from the first experiment by the results from the second experiment. If the results achieved from the second experiment matched the results from the first, we could assert that this method was working.

While students were carrying out the given task, their actions were logged by a screen recorder software called Camtasia and later translated into an *activity code*. For example, defining an instance variable, running the program, switching from one class to another, moving the mouse, defining a class, typing *static* in a method signature, waiting, and all other activities that were observed were given a unique activity code. For the kind of problem that was given, 86 distinct activity codes were defined. Some of these activities were ones that we expected based on the task that was given (for example defining an instance variable) and others were recognised by actions that were observed from the captured video. For each participant, therefore, a series of the activity codes, sorted by the time of occurrence, were inserted into a table in a database which included a total of 4278 records. Then K-means and DBSCAN clustering algorithms developed in Weka [2] software were applied to the data. The same process was repeated for the second experiment and the results were compared.

## 4.1 Clustering by K-Means Algorithm

This experiment was repeated three times, each time with a different number of clusters i.e. two, three and four clusters. In these experiments, during which we were looking for participants who showed similar patterns in comprehending the given program and completing the task of programming, a proper number of clusters were numbers for which more than one member could be assigned to. This meant that clusters with one member were not desired. Therefore, it did not make sense to have more than four clusters because most of the clusters would definitely include only one participant. We were not sure about four clusters therefore, we had to put them in the test.

As can be seen from Table II, when two clusters were chosen, four out of seven participants (i.e. A, B and E, F) stayed in the same group in each of the experiments and three other participants resided in different groups. If we have a second look at Table I, this grouping makes sense since both A and B had no experience and E and F had some experience.

Although the participants' exam marks were close, A and B had closer marks. The same was true for E and F. Participant C had a similarity with A and B (i.e. marks) and a similarity with E and F (i.e. experience) which meant there was no perfect match between those groups. Without looking at the process of program comprehension we did not know in which group participant C should reside. K-means algorithm put this participant in the same group as E and F and the same group as A and B for the first and second experiments respectively. This was also true for participant G. However, the story was different

for participant D which seemed more similar to A and B in terms of marks and experience but had been grouped with different clusters each time.

**Table II. K-Means Clustering Results**

|  |  | Code 1 | Code 2 |
|---|---|---|---|
| **2 Clusters** | C1 | A, B, G | E, F, D, G |
|  | C2 | E, F, D, C | A, B, C |
| **3 Clusters** | C1 | E, F, C | E, F, D, G |
|  | C2 | A, B, D | C |
|  | C3 | G | A, B |
| **4 Clusters** | C1 | E, F, C | E, F, D, G |
|  | C2 | D | C |
|  | C3 | G | A |
|  | C4 | A,B | B |

A clustering was carried out with the same algorithm and three clusters. Again, A and B stayed in the same group and E and F were in another group while other participants were grouped differently in both experiments.

Executing a clustering algorithm with four clusters did not make sense since in the second experiment most of the clusters included only one member. This was not desired for the kind of research we were conducting.

As a result of these clusterings, the right participants for program comprehension were A and B versus E and F. To validate these results we needed to do clustering with another clustering algorithm, which is seen in the next subsection.

## 4.2 Clustering by DBSCAN Algorithm

As explained previously, the DBSCAN algorithm does not input the number of clusters instead, it calculates it by itself. The number of clusters is computed by the *minpoint* and *epsilon* that is provided in this algorithm. We set the minpoint to 6 for all the clustering that we ran, which means the numbers in each cluster could not be less than 6. This was not a problem because for one participant we had more than 6 records of data. For example, for participant F we had 342 records of data for one experiment only. We assigned different values to epsilon to receive the number of clusters that we desired to enable us to compare the results with K-means clustering. For example, to have two clusters epsilon was set to 1.1 and 0.9 for the first and second experiments respectively. This number was 0.9 and 0.8 for three clusters and 0.7 and 0.66 for four clusters in the first and second experiment respectively.

**Table III. DBSCAN Clustering Results**

|  |  | Code 1 | Code 2 |
|---|---|---|---|
| **2 Clusters** | C1 | A, B, G | E, F, D, G |
|  | C2 | E, F, D, C | A, B, C |
| **3 Clusters** | C1 | A,B | A,B |
|  | C2 | G | E, F, D, G |
|  | C3 | E, F, C, D | C |
| **4 Clusters** | C1 | E, F | E, F, D, G |
|  | C2 | D | C |
|  | C3 | G | A |
|  | C4 | A,B | B |

As seen from Table III, when the algorithm clustered data into two groups, it put participants A and B in the same group and participants E and F in the same group in both experiments. The results were not as consistent for other participants. The same was true when the algorithm clustered the data into three groups. Again, grouping data into four clusters was not valid for our research since most of the clusters in the second experiment included only one element of data.

The significant point of the experiment was that the results achieved from this algorithm perfectly matched the results achieved from K-means when data were grouped into two clusters. This was true even when four clusters were formed. The results of clustering for three groups were the same for both algorithms in the second experiment only. But we concluded for sure that both algorithms put A and B together and E and F together.

# 5. CONCLUSION

In this research we aimed to find the right participants to be studied against each other. We proposed to use one of the clustering algorithms. We could have used one algorithm like K-means or DBSCAN, but our results needed to be validated. Two approaches were available for us to validate a clustering, an internal and an external approach. In an external approach there should be some external information available that could validate the clustering. The only information available was a student's programming marks and prior experience in programming. The results suggest that participant E and F could be grouped and studied against participants A and B. If we look at their programming marks and their prior experience as an external metric, we see that these results are valid (see Table I). To validate this clustering internally, we used two clustering algorithms instead of one, to see if the results matched. It can be seen from Tables II and III that similar groupings can be extracted from the result.

In this research, the first question that was answered was that it is possible to use clustering algorithms to group programmers in order to study their behaviour. This was seen by the consistent results that were achieved from running two clustering algorithms. What was not observed was a perfect grouping. However, if two or more elements of data were similar they were put in the same group. This helped the researcher to summarize the data. For example, in this research we found out that group A and B should be studied against group E and F while others did not match with the rest of the participants and therefore could be excluded from the study.

The second question that was answered was that both K-means and DBSCAN were reliable enough to be used for this kind of research.

Two issues need further consideration. The first issue is related to the similar clusters themselves. We need to find out what makes A and B vs. E and F so similar that each of the algorithms puts them in the same group. If this is discovered, the validity of these groupings will be accepted more. The second issue relates to the participants who are placed in different groups each time. It should be explored as to what makes these participants similar to some participants in one execution of the clustering and different in another execution of the clustering. However, this is not related to programming research but is related to performance difference of clustering algorithms.

At this point we can summarize our data and choose the right participants for further study, which involves the understanding of the process of program comprehension of different programmers. From this point qualitative data analysis starts. One opportunity for further work is to investigate the feasibility of analysing the codes that are clustered by those algorithms automatically. If this happens, the process of analysis of these kinds of research becomes very simple.

As mentioned earlier, the two clustering algorithms that were chosen for this experiment are just an example of centre-based and density-based algorithms. Other algorithms, including hierarchical clustering algorithms, can also be tested for different applications in program comprehension research.

# 6. ACKNOWLEDGMENTS

This research was supported by Shiraz University of Technology, grant number 90-EE-1.

# 7. REFERENCES

[1] M. Ahmadzadeh, D. Elliman, and C. Higgins, "An Analysis of Patterns of Debugging Among Novice Computer Science Students," in *ITiCSE '05: ACM SIGCSE Annual Conference on Innovation and Technology in Computer Science Education*, Lisbon, Portugal, 2005.

[2] R. R. Bouckaert, E. Frank, M. A. Hall, G. Holmes, B. Pfahringer, P. Reutemann, and I. H.Witten, "WEKA— Experiences with a Java Open-Source Project," *Journal of Machine Learning Research*, vol. 11, pp. 2533-2541, 2010.

[3] A. Casamayor, D. Godoy, and M. Campo, "Functional grouping of natural language requirements for assistance in architectural software design," *Know.-Based Syst.*, vol. 30, pp. 78-86, 2012.

[4] R. W. Collins, A. R. Hevner, G. H. Walton, and R. C. Linger, "The impacts of function extraction technology on program comprehension: A controlled experiment,," *Inf. Softw. Technol.*, vol. 50, pp. 1165-1179, 2008.

[5] W. Dann and S. Cooper, "Education: Alice 3: concrete to abstract," *Commun. ACM*, vol. 52, pp. 27-29, 2009.

[6] M. Ester, H. P. Kriegel, J. Sander, and X. Xu, "A density-based algorithm for discovering clusters in large spatial databases with noise," in *the Second International Conference on Knowledge Discovery and Data Mining*, 1996, pp. 226-231.

[7] A. Karahasanovic, A. Levine, and R. Thomas, "Comprehension strategies and difficulties in maintaining object-oriented systems: an exploratory study," *Journal of Systems and Software*, vol. 80, pp. 1541-1559, 2007.

[8] M. J. Lee and A. J. Ko, "Personifying programming tool feedback improves novice programmers' learning," presented at the Proceedings of the seventh international

workshop on Computing education research, Providence, Rhode Island, USA, 2011.

[9]     A. Oliner, A. Ganapathi, and W. Xu, "Advances and Challenges in Log Analysis," *Queue,* vol. 9, pp. 30-40, 2011.

[10]    M. Potthast, B. Stein, A. Barr, n-Cede, and P. Rosso, "An evaluation framework for plagiarism detection," presented at the Proceedings of the 23rd International

Conference on Computational Linguistics: Posters, Beijing, China, 2010.

[11]    B. Shneiderman and R. Mayer, "Syntactic/Semantic Interactions in Programmer Behavior: A Model and Experimental Results," *International Journal of Computer and Informtion Sciences,* vol. 8, pp. 219-238, 1979.

[12]    P. N. Tan, M. Steinbach, and V. Kumar, *Introduction to Data Mining*: Addison-Wesley, 2006.

# Building a Cloud Based Systems Lab

Joey Alexander
University of Cincinnati - CECH
Cincinnati, Ohio 45221
513.556.4227
alexanj8@mail.uc.edu

Aaron Dick
University of Cincinnati
Cincinnati, Ohio 45221
513.556.4227
dickab@mail.uc.edu

Jonathan Hacker
University of Cincinnati
Cincinnati, Ohio 45221
513.556.4227
hackerjh@mail.uc.edu

Damen Hicks
University of Cincinnati
Cincinnati, Ohio 45221
513.556.4227
hicksdi@mail.uc.edu

Mark Stockman
University of Cincinnati
Cincinnati, Ohio 45221
513.556.4227
mark.stockman@uc.edu

## ABSTRACT
The system administration lab at the University of Cincinnati consists of 24 high-end desktop PCs, each loaded with client virtualization software. The lab is limited to 24 students per class and does not offer remote access to the virtual machines. The students must either wait for open lab hours or purchase their own high-end systems to work on their schoolwork. To expand the number of classes taught and enable remote access to the lab, the authors created a Microsoft-based private cloud accessible from any computer on the university's network. VPN entry to the network allows students to login to the system using a web browser to access their VM's from anywhere in the world.

## Categories and Subject Descriptors
K.3.2 [Computers in Education]: Computer and Information Science Education.

## General Terms
Management, Performance, Design, Reliability, Experimentation.

## Keywords
System Administration, Networking, Virtualization, Capacity Planning, Cloud Computing.

## 1. INTRODUCTION
The current lab stores template VM's locally on each lab system. Students make copies of these templates then load them on client virtualization software, such as VMware Workstation. Past publications describe this setup [6]. Currently, when a student needs to work on their lab outside of the scheduled class time he/she needs to copy the needed VM's to a portable storage device to use on their own computer system. This requires the student to have a virtualization capable system.

The use of a private cloud makes the manual process of copying VM's unnecessary while also granting remote access to the lab. Additionally, systems administration and networking classes would be able to be scheduled in other computer labs in addition to or in lieu of the expensive systems administration lab. Ideas and implementations of cloud-based solutions for such a lab environment are not new [1, 5, 7].

This paper, however, outlines the creation of a private cloud using Microsoft software, for which many academic institutions have site licenses available. Microsoft provides some documentation to assist in setting up such an environment [2, 3, 4]

## 2. METHODS
The project's goal was to move the current networking/system administration computer lab to a remote solution that could be accessed from anywhere. The current lab has 24 client computers and a handful of servers for management purposes. The lab contains a domain controller to provide authentication and local profile support for each of the client computers. The student must sit at the same computer each time to continue working on their assigned lab work since storage of the large virtual machines is all local to each system.

The internal lab network is isolated from the university's network with a firewall. The firewall prevents any unwanted network services implemented in the IT classes from disrupting the university network. Figure 1 shows the current infrastructure of the lab.

The private cloud must provide all of the existing functionality of the systems administration lab and allow for remote access to the lab resources. The authors determined that the system should be able to handle 100 concurrent users (3 classes of 24 students and approximately 30 students working remotely). The authors chose to use all Microsoft software due to the university's Enterprise License Agreement with Microsoft. Specifically Microsoft's Hyper-V and System Center Virtual Machine Manager 2008 R2 (SCVMM) were used to achieve the remote access and virtual machine creation abilities required by students and professors.

The proof of concept consisted of 10 servers (4 Hyper-V hosts and 6 support/management servers). Each of the Hyper-V hosts contains a quad-core Intel processor and 8-16 GB or RAM. One of the servers was used to host System Center Operations

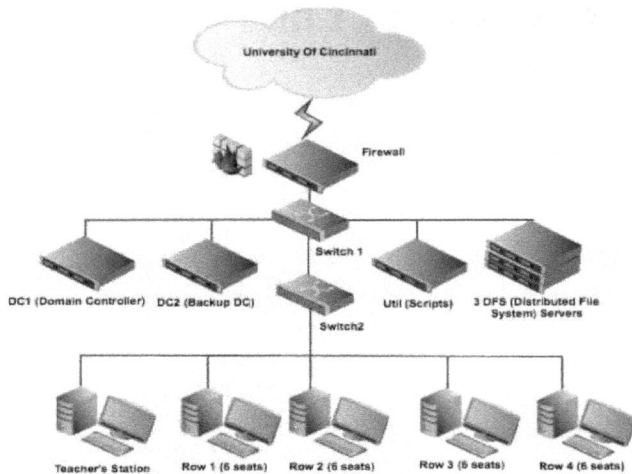

**Figure 1. Current Lab Infrastructure**

Manager (SCOM) to allow prediction analytics. The limited number of viable Hyper-V hosts makes the installation of SCOM necessary to determine the required hardware to scale the environment to a production level.

## 2.1 Hyper-V
Hyper-V is Microsoft's hypervisor solution that allows the guest operating system to share hardware resources with multiple VM's. Hyper-V is available on any server running Microsoft Windows Server 2008 R2 that contains a virtualization capable processor. Hyper-V is installed using the Role Management Console within the Server OS.

In the proof of concept, Microsoft Windows Server Core 2008 R2 with Hyper-V enabled was used to minimize the resources used by the host OS and maximize the resources available to the private cloud.

## 2.2 System Center Virtual Machine Manager
System Center Virtual Machine Manager (SCVMM) is a centralized management console that provides fine-grained access control and functionality for the Hyper-V hosts. SCVMM manages all aspects of the private cloud including all Hyper-V hosts and virtual machines.

SCVMM has several components that can be installed on a number of various servers in the environment. The authors installed the Administration components, database, and Self Service web portal on different servers to prevent overloading a single server. Once the SCVMM Administration console has been installed and setup, Hyper-V hosts can be added. SCVMM will automatically deploy and install the administration client on all managed hosts. As part of this deployment Hyper-V will be enabled on the host if it is not already. Hosts should then be added to different Host groups with SCVMM to provide organization and permission control to individual hosts.

Microsoft packages a self-service web portal with SCVMM. This Self Service portal allows users to interact with the cloud environment from a web browser. The portal sits on a web server running IIS and uses web form authentication against the domain controller. Within SCVMM the administrator must create Self-Service User groups and members must be members of one of those groups to login to the Self Service portal. Each of the Self-Service User groups is completely independent of each other

making it ideal for the systems administration lab replacement. Each class is setup as an individual User group and the templates required for each class are assigned to the group. When the students log into the portal, he/she can view their VM's and create new VM's based on the templates available to the User group. From the Self-Service Portal the student has complete control over the VM's and can connect to the console of the VM.

## 2.3 Forefront Threat Management Gateway
To isolate the private cloud from the university's network, a dedicated server was setup running Microsoft's Forefront Threat Management Gateway (FTMG). FTMG is Microsoft's firewall solution that can filter traffic based on protocol, source and destination IP. This allows the filtering of all harmful network services leaving the network such as DHCP and DNS while allowing safe traffic such as HTTP. The firewall ensures that any network service setup within the private cloud does not leak out and corrupt the services running on the university's network. Since the self-service portal is hosted within the private cloud, a web listener was setup within FTMG that listens for HTTP requests on the external interface and forwards those requests to the appropriate web server.

## 3. RESULTS
The result was a fully functional private cloud. The authors achieved the deliverables of replicating the original network lab functionality while adding remote access. The authors achieved central administration and capacity planning with SCVMM and SCOM. The Forefront firewall was configured to properly limit ingress and egress traffic, while providing better bandwidth management than the current physical network (cached updates/patches as well as everyday web pages). Figure 2 shows the diagram of the cloud-based solution.

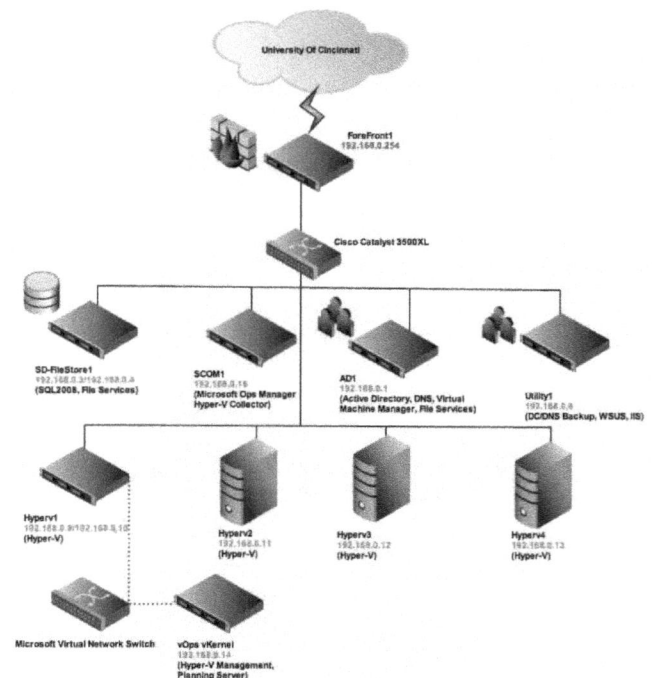

**Figure 2. Cloud Based Lab Infrastructure**

# 4. DISCUSSION

While the authors provided a fully functional private cloud, it was not able to scale to the capacity that would reflect production. This limitation was expected, but the system provided important usability metrics for its scale. The scale of a production environment system will have a similar up-front cost to creating a physical lab. This cost will be less over the long term than the current environment.

The physical lab currently requires replacement of thirty high-end desktops every three years, each desktop costing around $2,500 (price dependent on economy/market) plus licensing. With this cloud solution, configuration virtual hosts would not require powerful CPU, RAM or disk. The system will just need enough RAM to scale to the program's needs. The authors estimate 512MB of RAM per virtual machine and at least two VM's per student on average. This metric puts equates to 50GB (512MB * 100 users) of RAM for the goal of 100 concurrent users.

It is recommended to use a minimum of two servers for redundancy. Using three servers with 25 GB of RAM each can save money. This will allow for one server to be down (for repair or maintenance) and still provide 100 percent uptime. At the time of writing this article, an HP server with 25GB of RAM lists at $5,500 (this price would be lower with academic pricing). The cost comparison for a physical lab is $75,000 (assuming $2,500 per desktop without licensing) to $16,500 for 3 servers for the cloud solution. The difference in this money would go to implementing a shared storage solution.

In addition to this up-front cost comparison, server hardware is designed to last longer than desktops and will not need to be replaced as often. New hardware will only need to be added to scale to meet the demands of the student/class.

# 5. REFERENCES

[1] Li, P., Toderick, L. W., & Lunsford, P. J. 2009. Experiencing Virtual Computing Lab in Information Technology Education. In *ACM-SIGITE: Proceedings of the 10th ACM Conference on Information Technology Education.* Fairfax, Virginia.

[2] Microsoft.com. "Private Cloud Planning Guide for Service Delivery." Private Cloud Planning Guide for Service Delivery. Microsoft.com, 13 Oct. 2011. Web. 13 Oct. 2011. <http://social.technet.microsoft.com/wiki/contents/articles/private-cloud-planning-guide-for-service-delivery.aspx>.

[3] Microsoft.com. "Microsoft Windows Server | Hyper-V | Virtualization | Virtual Server | HyperV Workload Performance." Windows Server 2008 R2 with Hyper-V. Microsoft.com. Web. 13 Oct. 2011. <http://www.microsoft.com/en-us/server-cloud/windows-server/hyper-v.aspx>.

[4] Microsoft.com. "Hyper-V Cloud Fast Track Architecture Brief - Private Cloud Architecture Blog - Site Home - TechNet Blogs." TechNet Blogs - TechNet Blogs. Microsoft.com, 10 Feb. 2011. Web. 13 Oct. 2011. <http://blogs.technet.com/b/privatecloud/archive/2011/02/10/hyper-v-cloud-fast-track-architecture-brief.aspx>.

[5] Stackpole, B., Koppe, J., Haskell, T., Guay, L., & Pan, Y. Decentralized virtualization in systems administration education. 2008. In *ACM-SIGITE: Proceedings of the 9th ACM Conference on Information Technology Education.* Cincinnati, OH.

[6] Stockman, M., Nyland, J., & Weed, W. 2005. Centrally Stored and Delivered Virtual Machines in the Networking/System Administration Lab. Association for Computing Machinery. In *Special Interest Group for Information Technology Education (ACM/SIGITE) Summer 2005 Newsletter,* Vol. 2 Number 2. ACM, New York, NY.

[7] Stockman, M. 2011. Remotely Accessible Systems for the Computing Sciences Disciplines. In *Internet-Based Remote Laboratories: Scalable E-Learning Tools for Engineering and Science Disciplines*, Azad, A., Auer, M., & Harward, J. Eds. IGI Global Publishing, Hershey, PA, 380-396.

# IPv6 Certification and Course Development

Mr. John Pickard
East Carolina University
Greenville, NC
011-252-328-9646
pickardj@ecu.edu

John Spence
Nephos6, Inc.
Raleigh, NC
011-425-247-0520
spence@nephos6.com

Dr. Phil Lunsford
East Carolina University
Greenville, NC
011-252-328-9670
lunsfordp@ecu.edu

## ABSTRACT
The need to train IT professionals, especially network engineers, in the use of Internet Protocol version 6 (IPv6) continues to grow as adoption of IPv6 continues to rise. The adoption of IPv6 is driven by the IPv4 address space depletion, the proliferation of managed devices, the proliferation of mobile wireless devices, and government initiatives. An undergraduate stand-alone course in IPv6 is discussed including previous experiences starting in 2006. The current IPv6 course offering, based on a partnership with Nephos6 Inc. as the pilot of the first Nephos6 Academy, is reviewed including course topics, laboratory environment, and certification. The current course is delivered totally online and includes extensive remote-laboratory exercises, and has objectives that align with the IPv6 Forum Certified Engineer (Silver) objectives.

## Categories and Subject Descriptors
K.3.2 [**Computers and Education**]: Computer and Information Science Education – *computer science education, curriculum, information systems education.*

## General Terms
Documentation, Performance, Design

## Keywords
Certification, Course Development, Distance Education, Industry Collaboration, Internet, IPv6

## 1. INTRODUCTION
At the time of this writing, World IPv6 Launch Day, June 6, 2012 is only days away. First defined in January of 1995 by RFC1752, the "next generation" IP protocol, IPv6, has been around now for almost a generation. Yet seventeen years later, leaders in IP technology such as Cisco, Microsoft, Akamai, and Free Telecom are gathering forces to encourage organizations around the world to "launch" IPv6. For the past decade it has looked as if IPv6 would never become fully adopted and that IPv4, with features such as network address translation (NAT), carrier grade NAT (CGN), and classless inter-domain routing (CIDR), could continue to provide the world with the address space needed.

However, this perspective is now changing as organizations and governments come realize that IPv4 cannot sustain the future demands of Internet connectivity. The transition to IPv6 is going to finally become a reality.

## 2. THE NEED FOR IPV6 IN EDUCATION
A 2010 IPv6 Curricula Studies survey funded by the European Commission found that IPv6 training and studies at universities were not rigorous enough and were not providing students with the IPv6 knowledge or skills necessary to have any critical impact [15]. One of the results of this finding was the launching of the IPv6 Education Certification Logo Program in 2010 by the IPv6 Forum [17]. The IPv6 Forum sees colleges and universities playing a key role as part of this program in accelerating the adoption and integration of IPv6 in the Education Curriculum Worldwide. The program has received laudatory comments of support from industry and government leaders from around the world, a few of which are listed here:

"We believe IPv6 Training will be quite necessary for the whole Internet industry and its users. There is huge demand in China, where IPv6 Internet is now considered as a national strategy." states Liu Dong, Chair China IPv6 Council [17].

"Future Internet will be managed by current students and engineers in industry. It is highly required to provide IPv6 education to make them improve their knowledge and skill in IPv6 technology." states Viho Cesar, Ipv6 Ready Logo Regional Officer, IPv6 Forum Fellow, France [17].

"The IPv6 Curriculum study has abundantly demonstrated that hands-on IPv6 skills and field experience are dearly missing. Achieving parity between IPv4 and IPv6 deployment, quality expertise is the one pillar to focus on. This program is very welcome as it takes on this task globally." states Jacques Babot, IPv6 Team leader, European Commission [17].

## 3. DRIVERS OF IPV6 ADOPTION
### 3.1 IPv4 Address Space Depletion
In February of 2011 the Internet Addressing and Numbers Authority (IANA) allocated the final five /8 IPv4 address blocks to the five Internet Regional Internet Registries (RIRs). Now that these final allocations have been made, each RIR will continue to make allocations according to their own established policies until no more IPv4 addresses remain. For one RIR this event has already taken place. The Asia Pacific network Information Centre (APNIC) [20] exhausted its remaining IPv4 address space in April of 2011 [20]. According to the IPv6 Forum web site, the other four registries are projected to exhaust their remaining space by 2014, with the European registry, RIPE NNC expected to run out next sometime in late 2012 [14].

## 3.2 Proliferation of Managed Devices

Service providers and enterprise networks have a vast number of devices that must be addressed for management purposes. Typically the RFC 1918 private IPv4 address space was used for management of these devices. However, the number of managed devices on these networks has grown to the point that the IPv4 private address space is not large enough to support all devices that need to be managed. Examples include the deployment of residential broadband access such as Verizon's FiOS, and the significant numbers of devices deployed by large Multiple Systems Operators (MSOs), such as COMCAST and Time Warner Cable. The entire RFC1918 private address space only yields 16,846,847 unique addresses. COMCAST alone has more than 50 million set-top boxes deployed to customers. With each set top box requiring 2 IP addresses, one for management and one for customer connections, 100 million addresses are needed [8]. A request to the North American Regional Registry (ARIN) to increase the size of the private address space was rejected forcing organizations use public IPv4 space to manage their devices [23].

## 3.3 Proliferation of Mobile Wireless Devices

Cisco Systems, the world's largest network equipment maker, has predicted an 18-fold increase in global mobile data traffic by 2016 due in part to the projected rapid growth in mobile devices connected to the Internet. Cisco further believes that the number of mobile Internet connected devices will exceed 10 billion by 2016 [3].

According to analysts at International Data Corporation (IDC), the worldwide mobile worker population will reach 1.19 billion in 2013—34.9 percent of the global workforce. Employees around the world are increasingly mobile and want to use their favorite smart phones and other mobile devices, such as tablets and e-readers, for both work and personal purposes [19].

This proliferation of connected mobile devices, is forcing service providers and network owners to migrate to the new IPv6 Internet addressing scheme, resulting in an increase of IPv6 traffic across carrier and enterprise networks [2].

## 3.4 Proliferation of Smart Devices

The term, Internet of Things, was used by Mark Weiser in the 1990's in a Scientific American article to refer to the interconnection between everyday devices or objects over a network [4]. Today the term is used to describe the point at which there are more "things" connected to the Internet than people. Examples of such "things" are radio frequency identification devices (RFID) tags, smart sensors and actuators, and machine-to-machine communication devices. In 2008, Atmel, Cisco, Intel, SAP, and Sun Microsystems, along with other companies, founded the IP for Smart Objects (IPSO) corporate alliance. This alliance promotes the implementation and use of IP for low-powered devices such as radio sensors, electricity meters, and other smart objects. Additionally, the Internet Engineering Task Force (IETF) has set up the IPv6 over Low Power Wireless Area Networks (6LoWPAN) working group to address issues related to supporting IPv6 over the 802.15.4 wireless communication standard [11].

## 3.5 Government Initiatives

In September of 2010, the United States Office of the Federal Chief Information Officer issued a memorandum to all chief information officers of executive departments and agencies that detailed the federal government's commitment to the timely operational deployment and use of IPv6. The memorandum mandated that all United States executive agencies shall upgrade public/external facing servers and services to operationally use native IPv6 by the end of fiscal year 2012 [16].

Cisco Systems outlines in their 2010 white paper, "The Role of Government in IPv6 Adoption", the national strategies and initiatives established by governments around the world to encourage the transition to IPv6 [7].

- The European Commission – i2010 initiative, an action plan to see IPv6 widely adopted in Europe by 2010 [7].

- Peoples Republic of China – Next Generation Internet Project (CNGI), a five year plan to corner a significant proportion of the Internet by implementing IPv6 early. CNGI showcased its IPv6 network infrastructure at the 2008 Beijing Olympics [7].

- Hong Kong – The government established an IPv6-Enabled Government E-Service system in 2010 so that all 231 government websites can be accessed through IPv6 [7].

- Australia – A government strategy for agencies to implement IPv6 capable hardware and software platforms by 2012 and to operate dual-stack IPv6/v4 environments by 2012 [7].

## 4. CURRENT STATE AND TRENDS IN IPV6 ADOPTION

Statistics are showing that IPv6 adoption rates are rapidly increasing. According to the Global IPv6 Deployment Progress Report from Hurricane Electric, 85% of Top Level Domains (TLDs) now have IPv6 name servers and there are now more than 3,230,264 registered domains with IPv6 AAAA records, and 5682 registered IPv6 Autonomous Systems (AS). The number of tunnel broker accounts at Hurricane Electric has tripled in less than 2 years, growing from 100,000 in October of 2010 to 300,000 in May of 2012 [18].

In Akamai's "The State of the Internet" 4th Quarter, 2011 report, growth of autonomous systems in the global IPv6 routing table during the fourth quarters of 2009, 2010, and 2011 grew at the rate of 11%, 13.7%, and 5.7% respectively [1].

Since 2008 Google has collected statistics measuring the availability of IPv6 connectivity among Google users. Their "IPv6 Statistics" site shows the percentage of Google users who are able to connect to Google.com in 2012 using IPv6, although still below 1%, has tripled from the previous year [12].

## 5. PREVIOUS EXPERIENCES DELIVERING IPV6 SPECIAL TOPICS CLASS

The Information Computer Technology (ICT) program at East Carolina University (ECU) offered its first IPv6 Special Topics as a pilot course during the summer semester of 2006. Due to student demand, the course has since been offered every other year as an elective summer course. Feedback obtained from the students through Student Opinion of Instruction Surveys (SOISs) and from industry partners has lead to the following areas of improvement for the course.

- The remote lab environment needs a more user-friendly graphical interface and an easier scheduling system. It should also have the capability for session sharing to allow for real-time collaboration between students and instructors.

- The curriculum should be certified by a recognized body and should map to an industry certification, preferably one that is also globally recognized.

- The class should include more synchronous "lecture" sessions in addition to more asynchronous recorded presentations for students to watch or download to mobile devices.

- More labs are needed to cover the course topics and the content of the labs should go into more depth.

- An industry partner is needed to guide the curriculum, provide advice on keeping course content current, provide internship and employment opportunities to students, and training for instructors.

The following sections of this paper describe how each of these improvements were implemented to create a new course based on IPv6 Forum certified curriculum, and designed to provide students with practical expertise and hands-on knowledge deploying IPv6.

## 6. IPV6 FOUNDATIONS COURSE
### 6.1 Working With An Industry Partner
Working with the Nephos6 Academy Program [12] in early 2012 we developed an IPv6 Foundations course that addressed each of the areas of improvement identified in our pilot course. The Nephos6 Academy provided ECU with curriculum certified by the IPv6 Forum that prepares students for the IPv6 Forum Certified Engineer (Silver) Exam [15]. Nephos6 additionally provided 10 labs modified to work on standard NETLAB+ pod topologies [22].

ECU is the pilot school in the Nephos6 Academy and was the first University to offer this course. The academy program is designed to introduce students to IPv6 and Cloud technologies and equip them with technical skills that compliment their chosen fields of study. The partnership with the Nephos6 Academy was instrumental in the successful development and offering of this course.

### 6.2 Class Delivery
The class was as a five week distance-education special topics class during the summer of 2012 to 28 students. Online synchronous lecture sessions were conducted by the instructor four nights each week using Saba Centra web conferencing software that allowed students to join the lecture session live or view a recoding later. Asynchronous presentations were recorded by the instructor using Tegrity lecture capture software that is integrated with Blackboard. The software allowed the instructor to record presentations for students to view directly from the Blackboard web site or to be downloaded as a video file or podcast. A remote lab environment using NDG Lab Netlab+ provided students with 24/7 access to lab equipment [22].

### 6.3 Class Prerequisites
To maximize student success in the class, students must be familiar with Cisco IOS and basic networking concepts such as the OSI model, DNS, DHCP, IP addressing, and subnetting. For this course we required students to have completed the Cisco Networking Academy CCNA Routing course, or hold a current network certification such as Network + or CCNA as a prerequisite.

### 6.4 Course Topics
The topics for the course were mapped to the IPv6 Forum Certified Engineer (Silver) objectives. The curriculum used is IPv6 Forum Certified Curriculum (Silver) and provided as part of the Nephos6 Academy Program. The following topic areas were covered in the course:

- IPv6 Address Architecture and Scheme – IPv6 addresses, extension headers, Stateless Automatic Address Configuration (SLAAC), ICMPv6, and Default Address Selection (DAS).

- IPv6 Services – DHCPv6 and DNS.

- OS IPv6 Configuration – Windows 7 and Linux.

- IPv6 Device Configuration – Cisco IOS.

- Introduction to Routing – Static Routes, OSPFv3, and EIGRP for IPv6.

- Translation Mechanisms – Dual-Stack and NPTv6.

- Introduction to Tunneling - Manual Tunnels, ISATAP and 6to4 Tunnels.

### 6.5 Remote Lab Environment
Hands-on lab experience for the students was an essential element of this course. In the literature there are numerous examples showing that lab experience plays a critical role in student learning [5, 6, 10, 24, 25, 29].

Because this course was taught completely distance education, the labs had to be either remote or simulation. Literature shows that simulation software can limit student curiosity and experimentation [13]. Therefore, to allow students the fullest possible learning experience and maximum opportunities for experimentation the remote lab option was chosen.

The remote lab solution used for the course was the NETLAB+ server appliance by Network Development Group (NDG) [22]. NETLAB+ enables academic institutions to host physical lab equipment on the Internet for distance learning. NDG currently supports twelve courses offered by the Cisco Networking Academy, virtualization programs offered by the VMware IT Academy Program [26], and storage courses offered by the EMC Academic Alliance [9].

The lab equipment was physically located on the ECU campus and is shown in Fig. 1. Through the NETLAB+ system the lab resources could be scheduled, automated, and accessed remotely 24/7 by the students over the Internet through a web browser. The TCP Ports required to access the equipment are port 80 for the NETLAB+ web interface and TCP port 2201 for the remote equipment access.

Students can log into the remote lab environment through a web interface from any PC and browser connected to the Internet using the username and password provided by the instructor. Once logged in the student uses the Scheduler to schedule lab time on an available "pod". Students can schedule reservations in advance for any day or time that is not already reserved by another student. The maximum duration of a reservation can be set by the instructor. At the end of a student lab reservation the Netlab+ server performs the following actions: (1) archive the final device configurations and command logs under the student's account; (2) reset all equipment back to a pre-defined state; and (3) return any unused time back to the Scheduler for another student to use.

Fig. 1: The Netlab+ server, six Cisco 1941 routers, and the ESXi servers.

## 6.6 Remote Lab Topology

Six Cisco 1941 routers were grouped into two "pods" with identical topologies, as shown in Fig. 2. Each of the two "pods" consisted of three Cisco 1941 routers running IOS release 15.2, two Windows 7 virtual machines, and two Linux CentOS virtual machines. The virtual machines were implemented in VMware using ESXi version 4.1 and managed through a VMware vCenter server [27]. The routers and virtual machines connect to the Netlab+ server appliance through an isolated control network. Because traffic on the two "pods" is isolated by the control network, both "pods" can be in use simultaneously by students without conflict.

The specific topology used was designed by ECU and the Nephos6 Academy to match existing "cookie-cutter" Cisco Networking Academy topologies that are supported by default in the NETLAB+ server appliance. This design makes it seamless for any academic institution that is currently using NETLAB+ to support Cisco Network Academy courses to implement the labs on any of the following NETLAB+ Topologies: Multi-purpose Academy POD; Cuatro Router POD; and Basic Router POD version 2 [22].

Using this topology the students completed the ten labs detailed in the next section as part of the IPv6 Foundations course. Each lab was designed to take a student about an hour to complete and integrates extensive use of the Wireshark protocol analyzer so students could see, visually, the operation of the IPv6 protocol.

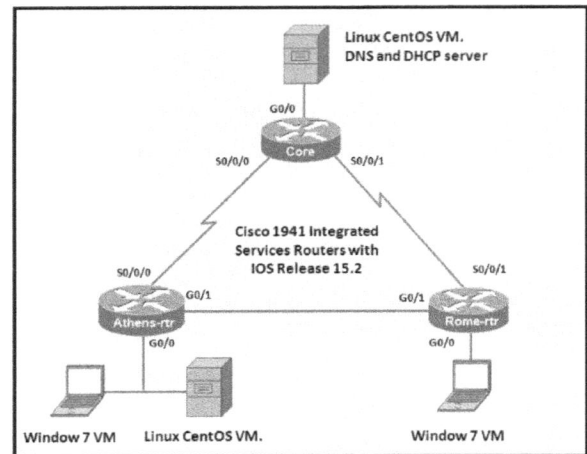

Fig. 2: The lab topology used for the course lab exercises.

## 6.7 Lab Exercise Details

Each student completed ten labs during the course on the Netlab+ remote lab environment. Final configurations and session logs were automatically saved by the Netlab+ server and were used by the instructor to verify lab completion. Students were encouraged to go beyond the scope of the labs and experiment with various IPv6 configurations and investigate IPv6 packets with Wireshark captures. By the end of the course the 28 students in the class logged 334 hours in the lab environment.

### Lab 1: IPv6 Hosts configuration

In this lab the students first verify the network is fully converged with IPv4 before configuring IPv6 on the network devices. Next they examine the data structures using the Wireshark protocol analyzer. The learning objectives for this lab are: (1) validate the lab environment and device configurations as a baseline; (2) configure and verify IPv6 operation on Linux; (3) configure and verify IPv6 operation on Windows7; (4) observe IPv6 header and packet format of actual packets on the wire.

### Lab 2: IPv6 on Cisco IOS configuration

This lab begins with all devices configured for IPv4 and fully converged. Linux and Windows hosts are set to IPv4 and IPv6 default configurations. IPv6 static address and default gateways are then configured on the hosts. Next, IPv6 routing, interface addresses, and static routes are configured on the routers. Students use appropriate "show" commands to verify IPv6 operation and configuration on the routers. The learning objectives for this lab are: (1) validate route configuration; (2) understand IPv6 configuration on Cisco routers; (3) understand static IPv6 routes and importance of link-local addresses.

### Lab 3: Neighbor Discovery and SLAAC

The network in this lab begins as a dual-stacked environment. Static IPv4 and IPv6 routes are configured and IPv6 Router Advertisements (RAs) are disabled at this point. Students use Wireshark to capture and analyze IPv6 Neighbor Discovery (ND) packets from the hosts and routers. Next, Stateless Address Auto Configuration (SLAAC) is enabled on the router LAN interfaces so RAs will be sent. Students again use Wireshark to capture and analyze the RA packets send by the routes. The students also observe the protocol configurations, IPv6 neighbor cache, and routing tables of the Linux and Windows hosts. The learning objectives for this lab are: (1) understand ND and SLAAC concepts and configuration; (2) use and understand Cisco, Linux, and Windows Neighbor Discovery Protocol (NDP) commands and appropriate "show" commands; (3) understand the various IPv6 address types.

## Lab 4: DHCPv6

In this lab the routers are dual-stacked and hosts are set to auto-configure IPv4 and IPv6 addresses. The Linux Core server is acting as a DHCPv6 server. A second DHCPv6 server is configured on the Athens LAN Linux server. Students observe default IPv6 SLAAC operation with Wireshark. Next, students change the NDP configuration on the Athens router so that LAN hosts will use DHCPv6. Students capture and analyze RA and Router Solicitation (RS) packets with Wireshark. The students also use Windows and Linux commands to observe the protocol configurations, IPv6 neighbor cache, and routing tables. The learning objectives for this lab are: (1) observe and understand the interplay between RA and RS packets in the operation of DHCPv6; (2) configure hosts and routers to support a fully converged DHCPv6 environment; (3) identify various NDP packets and their functions in the DHCPv6 process.

## Lab 5: OSPFv3

This lab begins with a dual-stacked network using static routes for both IPv4 and IPv6 convergence. Students implement multi-area OSPFv3 and use Cisco IOS show and debug commands to observe the OSPFv3 neighboring process. The learning objectives for this lab are: (1) understand the basic steps to configuring OSPFv3 on a Cisco router; (2) understand the operation OSPFv3 uses to form neighbor relationships; (3) understand the purpose and configuration of OSPFv3 summarization; (4) understand the purpose and configuration of OSPFv3 interface cost metrics.

## Lab 6: EIGRP for IPv6

The lab begins with the network in a dual-stacked state with static routes. Students implement EIGRP for IPv6 and use Cisco IOS show and debug commands to observe the EIGRP for IPv6 neighboring process. The learning objectives for this lab are: (1) understand the basic steps to configuring OSPFv3 on a Cisco router; (2) understand the operation EIGRP for IPv6 uses to form neighbor relationships; (3) understand the purpose and configuration of EIGRP for IPv6 redistribution between Autonomous Systems (ASs); (4) understand the purpose and configuration of EIGRP for IPv6 routing preferences using the administrative distance.

## Lab 7: DNS

In this lab students perform AAAA queries and add new AAAA records over both IPv4 and IPv6 connections. Students use Wireshark to capture and analyze DNS traffic on the network. The learning objectives for this lab are: (1) understanding the hierarchical nature of DNS and the impact that has on the IPv6 deployment; (2) verify the sending of DNS queries occurs as expected, and under what conditions this process varies; (3) observe Destination Address Selection (DAS) at work.

## Lab 8: ISATAP

The ISATAP lab allows an IPv6 host located within an IPv4-only enterprise network environment to obtain IPv6 services by tunneling the IPv6 packets inside IPv4 packets to the target IPv6-enabled device. Students configure ISATAP on a workstation to obtain limited IPv6 connectivity, then, configure an ISATAP router on the Core to provide more robust IPv6 services to the ISATAP enabled workstations. Wireshark is used to capture and observe ISATAP packets on the network. The learning objectives

for this lab are: (1) describe the most common use for ISATAP technology; (2) Observe and understand Windows 7 default ISATAP behavior (3) understand the limitations of using link-local-only ISATAP implementations; (4) configure an ISATAP router and understand its role in ISATAP operations.

## Lab 9: Manual IPv6-in-IPv4Tunnels

This lab begins with the network running IPv4 and network convergence provided by OSPF. IPv6 is then enabled to dual-stack the network and two IPv6-in-IPv4 manual tunnels are configured. Finally, students configure OSPFv3 to route IPv6 packets between the isolated IPv6 networks across the IPv4 core. The learning objectives for this lab are: (1) understand manual IPv6-in-IPv4 tunnel encapsulation and addressing semantics; (2) recognize the scaling limitations of manual tunnels; (3) understand the concepts of virtual interfaces and virtual point-to-point links.

## Lab 10: 6to4 Automatic Tunnels

The network will begin as an IPv4 only network. Then the Rome-pc will be configured for IPv6 only while the Athens-pc will be dual-stacked. The two site routers will be dual-stacked and 6to4 tunnels configured. Students will send ICMP packets from the dual-stacked Athens-pc across the IPv4 only core to the Rome-pc using the 6to4 tunnel. The learning objectives for this lab are: (1) understand automatic 6to4 tunnels, specifically the 6to4 encapsulation and addressing semantics; (2) recognize the scaling benefits of 6to4 automatic tunnels versus manual tunneling; (3) observe and understand the traffic flow from a 6to4 site to another 6to4 site and a native IPv6 site.

## 6.8 Nephos6 Academy Program

The Nephos6 IT Academy Program is an important component of Nephos6 education programs. The academic institutions that agree to participate in the Nephos6 IT Academy Program are business alliances of Nephos6 with an objective of delivering educational services to their students at high quality standards.

Eligibility to become a Nephos6 Academy is open to accredited, degree-granting higher education institutions worldwide offering 2- or 4- year college programs and technical schools offering accredited degrees through distance education programs [21].

## 6.9 Future Plans

We are currently working with the Nephos6 Academy to create an advanced IPv6 topics class that will cover topics such as ISIS, MP-BGP, MPLS, IPv6 Multicast, and Mobile IPv6 and an IPv6 Security class. These classes will follow a similar format to the IPv6 Foundations course using the Netlab+ remote lab environment and with curriculum that will map to IPv6 Forum certifications.

We are also working with the Nephos6 Academy to grow the network of colleges and universities participating in the academy. We freely offer our experiences and knowledge to other institutions interested in incorporating IPv6 into their curriculum.

## 7. GLOBAL RECOGNIZED IPV6 CERTIFICATION

We place a high value in our courses mapping to industry recognized certification. The curriculum in our IPv6 Foundations class maps to the IPv6 Forum Certified Engineer (Silver).

The IPv6 Forum launched the IPv6 Education Certification Logo Program in 2010 with the intent of acceleration, adoption, and integration of IPv6 in the education curriculum worldwide. The program defines and certifies courses, engineers and trainers with Silver and Gold Logo levels and requires IPv6 implementation on the web site of the education program.

## 8. CONCLUSION

It is vital that our ICT program provides the knowledge and hands-on skills our students will need in tomorrow's information society. We view close relationships with our industry partners as a key component to this objective. The IPv6 Fundamentals class is a case study in the successful collaboration between industry and education.

## 9. REFERENCES

[1] Akamai. 2011. The State of the Internet 4th Quarter 2011 Report. Retrieved June 01, 2012 from http://www.akamai.com/stateoftheinternet/

[2] Anonymous. 2011. NetLogic Microsystems Begins Volume Shipments for its Industry-Leading IPv6 Knowledge-based Processors. *Business Wire*. Retrieved June 01, 2012 from http://search.proquest.com/docview/885565733?accountid=1 0639

[3] Anonymous. 2011. Cisco Forecasts Broadband Explosion; Others See Problems. *Telecommunications Reports, 77*(12), 23-23.

[4] Atzori, L., Iera, A., Morabito, G. 2010. The Internet of Things: A survey. *Computer Networks*. 54(15), 2787-2805. doi: 10.1016/j.comnet.2010.05.010

[5] Brustoloni, C. 2006. Laboratory experiments for network security instruction. J. Educ. Resour. Comput., 6(4), 5. doi: 10.1145/1248453.1248458

[6] Cao, X., Wang, Y., Caciula, A., & Wang, Y. 2009. Developing a multifunctional network laboratory for teaching and research. Paper presented at the Proceedings of the 10th ACM conference on SIG-information technology education, Fairfax, Virginia, USA.

[7] Cisco.com. 2010. The Role of Government in IPv6 Adoption Retrieved May 30, 2012 from http:www.cisco.com/go/ipv6

[8] Durand, A. 2007. IPv6@Comcast: Managing 100+ Million IP Addresses. Retrieved May 29, 2012 from http://meetings .ripe.net/ripe-54/presentations/IPv6_management.pdf

[9] EMC. 2012. EMC Academic Alliance Retrieved 1 June, 2012, from https://education.emc.com/academicalliance/default.asp

[10] Fabrega, L., Massaguer, J., Jove, T., Merida, D. 2002. *A virtual network laboratory for learning IP networking.* Paper presented at the Proceedings of the 7th annual conference on Innovation and technology in computer science education, Aarhus, Denmark.

[11] Florkemeier, C., Mattern, F. 2010. From the Internet of Computers to the Internet of Things. *Informatik-Spektrum,* 33(2), 107-121. Retrieved June 1, 2012 from http://www.us.inf.ethz.ch/publ

[12] Google. 2012. Google IPv6 Statistics Retrieved 1 June, 2012, from http://www.google.com/ipv6/statistics.html#

[13] Hamza, M. K., Alhalabi, B., Hsu, S., Larrondo-Petrie, M. M., & Marcovitz, D. M. 2003. Remote Labs. Computers in the Schools, 19(3-4), 171-190. doi: 10.1300/J025v19v03_14

[14] IPv6Forum. 2012. IPv4 Exhaustion Counter Retrieved 1 June, 2012, from http://www.ipv6forum.com/

[15] IPv6forum. 2012. IPv6 Forum Education Certification Logo Program. Retrieved May 28, 2012 from http://www.ipvforum.com/ipv6_education

[16] Kundra, V. 2010. Memorandum for Chief Information Officers of Executive Departments and Agencies. Retrieved May 15, 2012 from www.cio.gov

[17] Ladid, L. 2010. The IPv6 Forum Launches the IPv6 Education Certification Logo Program. http://www.reuters.com/article/2010/09/06/idUS89980+06-Sep-2010+MW20100906

[18] Leber, M. 2012. Global IPv6 Deployment Progress Report: Hurricane Electric

[19] Mamzellis, C. 2011. Are You Ready for the Explosion in Mobile Devices. Retrieved May 31, 2012 from http://blog.quickcomm.com/Quickcomm-Telecom-Expense-Management-Blog/bid/64809/Are-You-Ready-for-the-Explosion-in-Mobile-Devices.

[20] Marsan, C. D. 2011. APNIC makes final IPv4 adddress delegations to existing network operators; holds reserve for start-ups. Network World.

[21] Nephos6. 2012. Nephos6 Academy Program, from http://www.nephos6.com/services/education/academy.php

[22] Network Development Group. 2012. NETLAB+ Product Overview. Retrieved 1 June, 2012, from http://www.netdevgroup.com/products/

[23] Popociviu, C., Dini, P. 2006. IPv6 as a Practical Solution to Network Management Challenges. Computing in the Global Information Technology. Computing in the Global information Technology, 2006 ICCGI06 International Multi-Conference. doi: 10.1109/ICCGI.2006.42

[24] Sarkar, N. I. 2006. Teaching computer networking fundamentals using practical laboratory exercises. Education, IEEE Transactions on, 49(2), 285-291. doi: 10.1109/te.2006.873967

[25] Sloan, J. D., & Schlindwein, C. 2004. TCP/IP laboratory exercises for use with a remotely accessible networking laboratory. J. Comput. Small Coll., 19(3), 68-78.

[26] VMware. 2012. VMware IT Academy Program Retrieved 1 June, 2012, from http://www.vmware.com/partners/programs/vap/

[27] VMware. 2012. VMware vCenter Server Retrieved 1 June, 2012, from http://www.vmware.com/products/vcenter-server/overview.html

[28] Weiser, M. 1991. The Computer for the 21st Century. Scientific American, 265(9), 66-75

[29] Wong, K., Wolf, T., Gorinsky, S., & Turner, J. 2007. Teaching experiences with a virtual network laboratory. *SIGCSE Bull., 39*(1), 481-485. doi: 10.1145/1227504.1227473

# Meeting MDG 2: Can IT Save Us?

**Charles M. Snow**
George Mason University
Volgenau School of Engineering
Department of Applied Information Technology
10900 University Boulevard
Manassas, VA 20110
csnow@gmu.edu

**Khondkar R. Islam**
George Mason University
Volgenau School of Engineering
Department of Applied Information Technology
10900 University Boulevard
Manassas, VA 20110
kislam2@gmu.edu

## ABSTRACT

While there continues to be rapid growth in the deployment of IT-based teaching technology in the developed world, there is a much greater need to find an effective means of using such technology to reach millions of underserved children in the developing world. This paper briefly looks at the problem, the technology, and how the latter may mitigate the former.

## Categories and Subject Descriptors

H.4.3 [**Information Systems**]: Information Systems Applications

## General Terms

Design, Performance

## Keywords

Distance education, millennium development goals, LMS

## 1. INTRODUCTION

In 2000, the United Nations published its eight Millennium Development Goals (MDG). The objectives were intended to set a course toward establishing a more equitable and peaceful world by the year 2015. The second of the eight goals is to ensure "...that, by 2015, children everywhere, boys and girls alike, will be able to complete a full course of primary schooling" [19]. Since the establishment of the MDGs, there has been a noted improvement in access to primary education: primary school enrollment rose globally from 82% of all primary school aged children in 1990 to 89% in 2008 [2]. This leaves approximately 67 million children not in school, 32 million of them in sub-Saharan Africa [19]. To be able to teach those 32 million children, there is an estimated shortage of over one million instructors, if MDG 2 is to be met [7]. Moreover, the global distribution of these 'underserved' children shows they are found in countries of the developing world (see Figure 1).

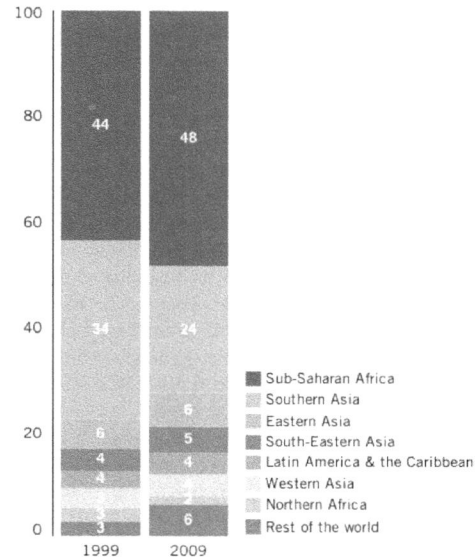

Figure 1: **Distribution of out-of-school children by region, 1999 and 2009 (Percentage)** [19]

There are several facets to the challenge of meeting MDG2. One is the sheer number of students. Another is the location of these students: over half are in areas not characterized by widely available technology. Worldwide, smartphones now account for about 30% of all mobile phones sold, up from 11% in 2008 [4], and shipments are expected to more than double from 2011 (494 million units) to over one billion units shipped in 2015 [16]. It will still be some time before smartphone users dominate the target student market. Further, the United Nations Educational, Scientific and Cultural Organization (UNESCO), the World Bank, and others have a longer-running campaign, Education For All (EFA) begun in 1990, that requires education to continue to be universally available beyond primary school [3]. The potential audience to be reached in that case extends into billions of students.

Can the use of IT-supported instruction help to overcome these challenges and advance progress toward MDG2 and EFA?

## 2. IT IN EDUCATION

IT-supported instruction, where it is most widely deployed in the developed countries, tends to cast IT in three roles: (1) networks for communication, usually the public Internet, (2) storage for content (text, slide presentations, audio, video), and, (3) assessment of student performance. The evolutionary trend has been to merge into large Learning Management Systems (LMS) components using combinations of these roles to provide students with a single portal to one or more courses.

Early tools were relatively primitive, given that processor, memory, disk and network bandwidth were all relatively expensive. Teaching tools, as with other applications, have grown in complexity and sophistication, as the technology needed to support them has plummeted in cost.

Large LMS products available today, e.g., Blackboard [5], Moodle [9], Sakai [11], or Instructure's Canvas [6], provide a set of tools that allow students to interact with instructors, teaching assistants, course content, and with each other. Canvas is designed to be cloud-based, so requires infrastructure beyond a simple hosted web-based service. Some LMS-supported services can require significant network capacity, e.g., live synchronous presentations and video content.

It is tempting to wonder how large a 'class' one could teach using such tools. Stanford University, perhaps unintentionally, performed an experiment that demonstrated how large a class might be. In fall, 2011, it offered three courses online;[1] prospective students – whether of the university or not – could take the course (including doing assignments, quizzes, exams) and, if successful, receive a certificate confirming successful completion. Only registered Stanford students would receive credit for the course. The university reports that "...356,000 people from 190 countries expressed interest in one or more of the first three classes offered, and approximately 43,000 successfully completed a course" [12].

Could one, then, scale up the approach taken by Stanford – and now provided through Coursera (providing courses from three universities in addition to Stanford) – to accommodate the millions of underserved children in sub-Saharan Africa and south Asia?

## 3. A DIFFERENT APPROACH

The short answer is no, as the tools used to participate in the Stanford courses requires both network infrastructure and user end-point technology not available to children in these locations. To meet the challenges of reaching millions of underserved children, an approach quite different from that used successfully in the developed countries will be needed.

For those areas that have some regularity of electrical service, access to data networks, if there are any, remains limited. Figure 2 illustrates the problem: lighter shaded countries have fewest Internet hosts, darker have more.

The technology that will become increasingly available is data over mobile networks to smartphones [13]. The corollary to this trend in platform evolution is that content delivery will be increasingly demanded over wireless networks. Currently the only widely available such technology is Enhanced Data rates for GSM Evolution (EDGE), which typically can provide a data rate of 100 Kbps. This capacity is too low to support media-rich content, though is adequate for non-demanding audio (like voice).

More limiting, though, is that not every student will have access to any device able to access content: the number of

---

[1]They were: Introduction to Artificial Intelligence, Machine Learning, and, Introduction to Databases

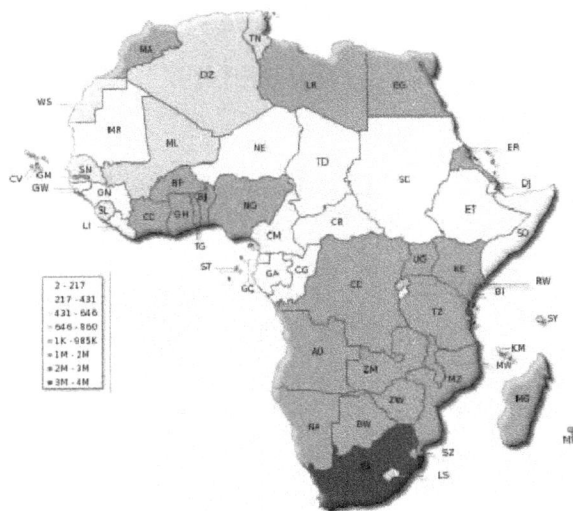

Figure 2: Distribution of Internet hosts across Africa; lighter shaded have fewest, darker shaded have most [8]

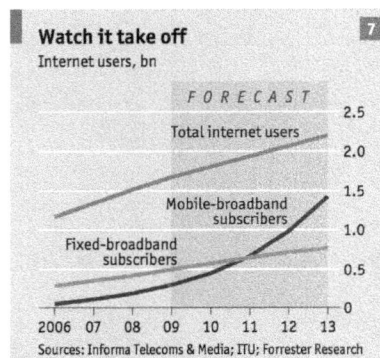

Figure 3: Projected growth of Internet use: wired vs. wireless worldwide. [1]

smartphone users in the developing countries, while growing, remains comparatively small.

IT-tool developers in the developed countries look at newer features that can be implemented to enhance and accelerate the student experience, more than how to provide a reduced-capability version suitable for use in the developing world.

If the way these tools are used in the developed world will not prove useful in the developing world, then a different way of using the technology needs to be pursued.

## 4. GOING FORWARD

It is reasonable to assume that the communication and computing devices that will become widely deployed in developing countries will be smartphones. IT-supported teaching tools, in order to be effective, will need to be tailored to that platform. Whereas students in developed countries will find it convenient to have mobile access to course material, it will be the *only* access for a large number of students. And given projections of wireless network growth, world-

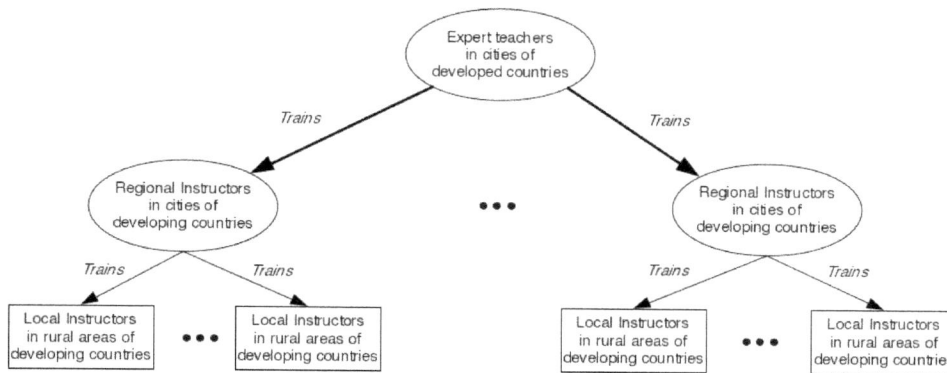

**Figure 4: Three-tier training model. Links between layers are of progressively lower capacity from root toward leaves.**

wide, Internet-capable mobile phones and smartphones are the instruction delivery platform of the future; see Figure 3.

Apart from smartphones, the tablet computing device is a newcomer to this arena. The particular role of tablets in IT-supported teaching is still being determined in developed countries. Their use in teaching in developing countries would seem to remain further in the future.

The cost of tablets is a factor in their deployment in developing countries, as is their reliance on fast data networks. However, Nicholas Negroponte, of One Laptop per Child, has introduced a $75 tablet and suggested an imaginative accommodation to limited network capability in developing countries: tablets are pre-loaded with software and data, and air-dropped to villages. The goal is, initially anyway, only to have children teach themselves how to read using these devices that need no electricity (solar powered) and no network (data preloaded) [18]. The recent introduction of the 'Raspberry Pi' computer [10], a $25 linux machine, may also prove popular, but no suitable products have yet been demonstrated.

Use of some structure of network is largely viewed as essential for instruction. A solution tailored to the peculiarities of these regions is essential, as the kind of infrastructure supporting networks – as deployed in developed countries – largely does not exist in these countries, and is not ever going to, as wireless technology will become ubiquitous in place of wired. Hardware that can be expected to be widely available in developing countries, predominantly EDGE-capable mobile phones, needs to play a major role in providing access to content. The rise in dominance of the Android OS [14] on mobile smartphones keeps them ore cost effective for use in developing countries. Mozilla's recent introduction of an OS for smartphones [17] may provide competition and stimulate further the use of smartphones as the end-point computing device of choice.

A model for scalable and reliable distribution of content, from distributed local sources needs to be put in place. A model proposed by one of the authors is intended to provide a set of characteristics suited to this particular application setting [15]. It is designed to provide access to course resources in a way that is more cost-effective, reliable and efficient, by allowing course material, in fragments of variable size, to be scattered across multiple servers. The servers are organized into a hierarchical P2P network supporting dynamic membership of nodes, automated search for, and

retrieval of, material irrespective of where in the network the fragments are located. Where possible, this architecture makes use of multicast to reduce redundant network traffic; generally this will be a multicast overlay on more available unicast connections.

There can be expected to be greater demand for course material. The Stanford exercise demonstrates that there is tremendous demand for content of quality. It will be vital to have a network infrastructure able to make such content widely available.

While smartphone deployment will be widespread in developing countries, it is not realistic to expect each student to have a smartphone for the foreseeable future. Apart, then, from a network architecture tuned to the needs of developing countries, the style of instruction using distance teaching tools will also have to be adapted to the realities of these countries.

One proposed alternative relies on using a layered hierarchy, as seen in Figure 4.

In this model, expert instructors in the developed world (or elsewhere) teach regional instructors located in urban areas closer to the students to be reached, using network and instructional tools available to both instructor groups. These instructors, in turn, interact with a number of other instructors closer still to the students, whether in smaller urban areas or remote villages, again, using technology available to both groups. This generalizes to as many levels as are needed to provide instruction, with each successive layer of the hierarchy having fewer technological capabilities on which to rely. The actual children students are not, particularly, the target of this model since there is not adequate network capacity, nor enough available devices, to provide each child with direct instruction via IT-supported tools.

## 5. CONCLUSIONS

This paper has briefly looked at one of the largest education challenges facing the world today, the educating of an additional 60 million primary-school aged children scattered across some of the most poverty-stricken, least developed parts of the world. The question examined was whether a powerful tool for educating, as we imagine IT-supported teaching resources to be, can 'save' us by making it possible to reach these children.

By and large the answer is no if we try to deploy the technology in the way it is used in developed countries. But it *may* be effective at meeting this challenge if deployed in a way that better fits the reality of the students' situation, using a three (or more) tiered model where reliance on technological advancement decreases as one heads towards leaf nodes in the tree, and if one has a network architecture for content delivery that works with communications realities in these countries.

Work on these two fronts is on-going, and it is hoped that early prototypes may be ready for small-scale deployment within a few years. We are roughly three years away from the 2015 deadline for MDG2.

## 6. REFERENCES

[1] Mobile marvels: A special report on telecoms in emerging markets. *The Economist*, September 26 2009.

[2] Global targets, local ingenuity. *The Economist*, September 22 2010.

[3] *The EFA movement | Education | United Nations Educational, Scientific and Cultural Organization*, 2011 (accessed June, 2012). http://www.unesco.org/new/en/education/themes/leading-the-international-agenda/education-for-all/the-efa-movement.

[4] *100 Million Club – Top smartphone facts and figures in 2011 | VisionMobile*, 2012 (accessed June, 2012). http://www.visionmobile.com/blog/2012/02/infographic-100-million-club-top-smartphone-facts-and-figures-in-2011.

[5] *Blackboard | Technology Built for Education*, 2012 (accessed June, 2012). http://www.blackboard.com.

[6] *Canvas LMS, the new, open learning management system | Instructure*, 2012 (accessed June, 2012). http://www.instructure.com.

[7] *Education | ONE*, 2012 (accessed June, 2012). http://www.one.org/c/us/issuebrief/93.

[8] *Internet hosts by country - Thematic Map - Africa*, 2012 (accessed June, 2012). http://www.indexmundi.com/map/?t=0&v=81000&r=af&l=en.

[9] *Moodle.org: open-source community-based tools for learning*, 2012 (accessed June, 2012). http://www.moodle.org.

[10] *Raspberry Pi | An ARM GNU/Linux box for $25. Take a byte!*, 2012 (accessed June, 2012). http://www.raspberrypi.org/quick-start-guide.

[11] *Sakai Project | collaboration and learning – for educators by educators*, 2012 (accessed June, 2012). http://www.sakaiproject.org.

[12] *Stanford offers more free online classes for the world*, March 6 2012 (accessed June, 2012). http://news.stanford.edu/news/2012/march/online-courses-mitchell-030612.html.

[13] J. Bertolucci. *Smartphone Sales Boom – Who Needs A Laptop?*, 04 Feb 2012 (accessed July, 2012). http://www.pcworld.com/article/249313/smartphone_sales_boom_who_needs_a_laptop.html.

[14] IDC. *Android- and iOS-Powered Smartphones Expand Their Share of the Market in the First Quarter, According to IDC*, 24 May 2012 (accessed July, 2012). http://www.idc.com/getdoc.jsp?containerId=prUS23503312.

[15] K. Islam. *A Cost-Effective Distributed Architecture to Enable DE over Emerging Wireless Technologies*. Ph. D. thesis, in preparation, 2012.

[16] R. T. Llamas and W. Stofega. *Worldwide Smartphone 2012-2016 Forecast and Analysis*. March 2012.

[17] Mozilla. *Mozilla Gains Global Support For a Firefox Mobile OS | The Mozilla Blog*, 2012 (accessed July, 2012). http://blog.mozilla.org/blog/2012/07/02/firefox-mobile-os.

[18] I. Thomson. *Negroponte plans tablet airdrops to teach kids to read*, November 2 2011 (accessed June, 2012). http://www.theregister.co.uk/2011/11/02/negroponte_tablet_airdrops.

[19] UN. The millennium development goals report 2011. Technical report, New York, 2011.

# Integrating Mobile Storage into Database Systems Courses

Qusay H. Mahmoud, Shaun Zanin, Thanh Ngo
School of Computer Science
University of Guelph, Guelph, ON, N1G 2W1 Canada
{qmahmoud,szanin,tngo01}@uoguelph.ca

## ABSTRACT

The proliferation of smartphones and tablet computers is the newest paradigm shift occurring in the field of computing education. Mobile devices create serious resource and performance constraints that developers must keep in mind when creating applications for these platforms. In order to ensure that future developers have the knowledge required to create quality software solutions, academic institutions must seek to integrate mobile devices into their curricula. This paper presents an approach to integrate mobile application development in database systems courses, in the form of a short module designed to cover the approaches for persistent storage available on mobile devices. The Centre for Mobile Education and Research (CMER) has developed material, released as part of the CMER Academic Kit, including hands-on labs and assignments that instructors can freely download and integrate into their courses.

## Categories and Subject Descriptors

[**Computing Milieux**]: Computer and Information Science Education – *computer science education, curriculum, human factors, literacy.*

## General Terms

Experimentation, Human Factors, Design, Documentation.

## Keywords

Database courses, mobile application development.

## 1. INTRODUCTION

Most computing curricula offer, at minimum, a single course covering database theory and its practical use. Topics covered include different types of database systems, relational algebra and calculus, and query languages such as SQL. While providing an excellent introduction to the subject, these courses are starting to become deficient in their ability to prepare students for industry positions. The primary cause of this is the lack of integration of mobile devices, which have unique limitations, and the variety of methods of accessing data from such devices, presenting a barrier that many instructors are unwilling to challenge.

As technology advances, computing programs must constantly update their courses as well to use the latest tools and technology in order to better prepare students for the industry. One approach instructors have found to be effective in teaching database courses is via practical coursework [10]. An example of a common approach to proving students with hands-on learning experience is to have them work on a project in which they develop an application, either stand-alone or Web-based, that interacts with the most commonly available database system [2, 3, 4, 5]. Not only do students gain a better understanding of the concepts they have learned in class by applying them into the project, but they have also gained experience working with tools that are being used in the industry [9]. Another approach that is gaining popularity is the idea of integrating mobile devices, such as smartphones or tablets, and mobile application development, into the classroom in order to increase student participation and interest [6, 7, 8, 9]. For example, mobile devices could be used by students to interact with their instructor during a lecture, by answering questions during class as seen in [9]. Many students have a smartphone which they use for phone calls, email, Web browsing and day planner. Many of the applications that they use on their devices focus on the social side of computing – instant messaging, social networking sites, Twitter, etc; gaming is also becoming more popular [11]. The continuing trend of users preferring portable devices, such as laptops, over stationary ones, applies to students as well [10]. This means that more of them are buying wireless laptop and tablet computers.

Many academic computing labs, however, are still mainly composed of cabled desktop computers, or terminals connected to a large server. This represents a huge gap in terms of the technology which most students are most likely to use on a day-to-day basis. While learning how to develop applications on larger systems is very important, it nonetheless creates a disconnect between the real world and the academic 'ivory tower'. To overcome this barrier, there is a need to integrate small mobile computing devices into computer courses, while still maintaining the core computing concepts, and development knowledge required for targeting traditional systems. A course whose material covers databases would be an effective place to integrate this new knowledge. Storage on mobile devices relies on many different components, both local and remote. This provides an instructor with a unified platform from which they could demonstrate core ideas, rather than worrying about students having to learn a new language or operating system API in order to complete their project.

The rest of this paper is organized as follows. Section 2 provides ideas for enhancing the learning experience through mobile devices. Section 3 presents an overview of a selection of mobile devices and their storage features. Section 4 presents some examples, from CMER Academic Kit, to be used in a database course. Finally, Section 5 concludes the paper and offers ideas for future work.

## 2. MOBILE DEVICES AND LEARNING

Mobile devices, such as smartphones and tablet computers are becoming widely used on university campuses. The rapid increase is partially the result of mobile devices becoming increasingly sophisticated over time (as per Moore's law). Some of the major advancements include the integration of technologies such as advanced, standards compliant web browsers, enhanced multimedia codecs and players, and applications with high-bandwidth real-time traffic, such as video conferencing.

Similar to how there are several platforms for desktop environments such as Windows and Unix, there are also many platforms for mobile devices, including Java ME, BlackBerry OS, Windows Phone Mobile, iOS, Android, and others. This heterogeneous mobile world requires the examination of the storage options which exist on these systems. Of interest to instructors is that each platform, in many cases, has produced slightly different results for the same problem set; examining these existing options provides an excellent way for students to see the different approaches available for information management. In addition, student developers are required to take many more factors into account, such as limited memory, increased latency in accessing storage, limited CPU power, etc. Creating applications for mobile devices teaches students some of the fundamental programming approaches which are used in developing embedded systems.

Mobile devices can also be used to enhance the learning experience which students undergo in the course. Often, the instructor can make or break a student's experience in a course. Their skill, ability, charisma, etc., can drastically change how students perceive the topic which is being taught. An interactive mode of presentation during the instructor's lectures can help establish a rapport with the class. Mobile devices in the classroom, literally, can, help facilitate this. An example would be an interactive question/answer quiz for bonus marks in the classroom. An instructor could give students an assignment to develop this application at the beginning of the course, which the students would then use in-class, later in the module, order to answer bonus questions (a program running on a server could receive the student's responses). This is only one example of how mobile devices enhance teaching, not only through new technical concepts and techniques, but they can

be used to make a course entertaining and offer an enriching learning experience.

There have been practical examples of using mobile devices in a classroom, in order to enhance students' knowledge of the material. One approach is to create a segment of the course which requires students to develop an app in order to participate. A practical example of this has already been implemented, with successful results [6,7]. Students were required to develop a client in order to retrieve a detailed table of term marks over the course of the term. Students were given a specification of how to invoke and utilize the service, and how the results would be formatted upon return. This made it a relatively simple task for them to implement a client in order to access their marks, and also provided them with a sense of satisfaction since they had implemented a practical project with real world results.

## 3. STORAGE ON MOBILE DEVICES

Most standalone and Web applications utilize some form of database system for managing various amounts of data in a structured environment. For mobile clients, the use of databases doesn't necessarily change but the type of database does. There are many opportunities for an instructor willing to explore the integration of mobile devices within a database systems course. Each of the mobile platforms (e.g. BlackBerry, Android, iOS, and others) have several options available to allow interaction with local and remote database systems in order to store and retrieve data on the device. Examples of local databases include Personal Information Management (PIM) data such as contacts and address book entries, or remotely accessible ones, such as a user's score in an online game.

In this section we provide an overview of the various options available for storing data on mobile devices, and in particular on BlackBerry, Android, and iOS devices.

### 3.1 HTML5

HTML5 has become a great way for developers to build cross-platform mobile applications using standard Web technologies. HTML5 applications for mobile devices usually cannot access the file system on a device directly, without some kind of an API bridge between JavaScript and Native API calls. It does, however, give an option for long-term storage: the *localStorage* API. The localStorage object stores a key-value pair, using strings. Usually, a developer would not be able to store more complex data types, such as objects, in this. However, it is possible using the JSON.stringify() method to store data. This method converts the object into a string that retains a hierarchical format, and saves the values of all member variables in an object. It is important to note that there is a size limit of approximately 5 megabytes for the localStorage object. The second kind of storage which is available to HTML5 applications is the IndexedDB, which provides an implementation of a relational database to the app. It is currently only implemented in Mozilla/Netscape-based. It provides a JavaScript API, which is constructed so that it can have a query-based language framework constructed over it.

One area that developers must be aware of the HTML5 standard is that different platforms use engines to implement the HTML5 standard. Like the IndexedDB example listed above, devices might not always share the same feature set. However, three of the major device platforms use the WebKit framework. These include BlackBerry, Android, and iOS. Developers targeting the Windows Phone 7 should investigate the performance differences between WebKit and Microsoft's Trident framework.

Different implementations of WebKit can have large performance discrepancies between the different mobile platforms. As an example, consider the different implementations of WebKit present on Chrome for Android and Safari for iOS. While using the same rendering engine, Android was significantly faster on some of the industry-standard benchmarks, such as the WebKit's SunSpider [13].

## 3.2 SQLite

SQLite is one of the most popular storage options available on the market today. It is a versatile library which encapsulates SQL functionality, but stores it in a local file, rather than a remotely hosted database. It allows for databases up to a terabyte in size, and permits strings and blobs of up to a gigabyte [12]. It is written in ANSI C, and permits full database functionality, all encapsulated in one source file, which allows for easy integration with any project; it is also a cross-platform library.

Many popular applications use SQLite to store everything from user profiles to configuration settings. It is also well suited for testing and development purposes as well. Given its popularity on multiple platforms, it is important that students be given exposure to it on at least one mobile platform, especially if instructors want to prepare them for work outside of academia.

Beyond mobile devices, SQLite offers another side benefit to database course instructors: a safe testing platform for student projects. Rather than make students set up their own SQL server, host one, or risk a production server which hosts other services, SQLite offers a realistic way to teach students SQL with both minimal setup and risk. SQLite conforms, for the most part, with the SQL92 standard [12], ensuring that students will learn the fundamentals of writing queries for database access.

## 3.3 Cloud Storage

The label "cloud storage" is a broad collection of different web services. These include Apple's iCloud, Google Drive, Dropbox, and many others. Services like these provide an excellent opportunity for any course instructor to provide students with a set of unique problems in assignments and projects. While these "cloud storage solutions" provide a

huge amount of easily accessible space, the latency for accessing these resources is comparatively very high versus local access. Programming assignments which emphasize asynchronous calls to remote databases could easily be developed on this play form.

There are many options available for cloud storage; it can be very overwhelming to pick just one to focus on for mobile development. Two services in particular standout as great choices in the context of a module in a larger academic course: Amazon S3 and Dropbox. Amazon S3 is a widely used service, and provides many features and functionalities for a developer to choose from. The knowledge students would gain from projects based on the utilization of S3 would be immediately applicable for real-world scenarios. In addition, there are Linux distributions, such as Ubuntu Cloud, which provide system API calls that easily authenticate with these services. Dropbox is a well-known service that many students currently use. It provides a very good, easy-to-use web API that is deployable in a matter of hours with mobile devices. For a database systems course, either would be a valid focus; the choice would be a result of what the instructor wanted to focus on.

## 3.4 Device-Specific Storage

The storage options discussed in the previous subsections are supported by all mobile platforms, including BlackBerry, Android, and iOS; however, it is important for instructors and students alike to take note of some of the variations which exist across the implementations of these features on each platform.

BlackBerry devices support the storage options mentioned above, but also provide certain features which enhance their functionality. In addition, BlackBerry devices provide access to a private and shared file system. Research in Motion has released a unique tool in the WebWorks package, a framework which is compatible with both the BB7 and QNX-based Playbook and upcoming BlackBerry 10 devices, that allows for an HTML5 application to go beyond just being a web tool to becoming an application which is able to take advantage of a full range of native device capabilities. It does this by hosting the site locally and packaging it as a separate, stand-alone application. This reduces the run-time required for loading and executing HTML5 based applications. This enhancement of the already-powerful HTML5 standard (as discussed earlier) gives instructors even more options to use in their courses. Lastly, the QNX kernel (on which the PlayBook and BlackBerry 10 devices are based) is largely POSIX compliant; popular database servers may be able to be compiled to run natively on a mobile device.

On Android, several options are available for storing data on Android-powered devices, including: Shared Preferences: a lightweight mechanism for storing primitive data (such as strings) in key-value pairs, essentially acting as a lightweight hash table which persists between application runs. Private and shared directories for regular file I/O are available; of more interest to instructors would be features such as the SQLite database, allowing application-specific relational databases to be used to store records locally. Network IO is also present; both server sockets and client sockets are available. Like the BlackBerry, Android has support for HTML5 built into its native widget system. Using a WebView widget, a developer can quickly integrate web content into their application. However, it is better suited to remote content, and requires a small amount of setup by the developer manually. Android does allow the passing of Java objects to an HTML5 application however, giving access to a rich API, which can be called from a web interface.

On iOS devices, developers have several options for storage. The first is called "Core Data," which is a data modeling framework that uses object-oriented Cocoa Touch applications that are based on Model View Controller (MVC) design pattern. It provides a general-purpose data management solution for handling data from any application. The core data library uses a built-in SQLite engine present in iOS. Developers of iOS applications can also use XML files to store an application's settings and user preferences. A parser is provided as part of the standard platform API to be used for storing and retrieving objects. In addition to XML, the default Safari browser is compliant with many of the HTML5 APIs, including the localStorage object mentioned earlier.

## 4. TEACHING MODULE

Course instructors today often find it difficult to effectively integrate all the material they would like to teach into their courses. Finding a balance between pure theory and practical application of these ideas to real world scenarios can also be hard to achieve. To this end, one of the objectives of the Centre for Mobile Education and Research (CMER) is to help course instructors integrate mobile devices and mobile application development into their courses, by providing modular resources which instructors can use in lectures, hands-on labs, assignments, and projects. They are designed to be applicable to the real world, featuring the most important aspects of the latest technologies, while focusing on open standards which have backward (and forward) compatibility. The materials which CMER provides also let students work with specific mobile operating systems, giving course instructors a chance to expose students to some of the technologies they will have to use in an applied setting.

The CMER Academic Kit [1] provides instructor and student resources in the form of slides, hands-on labs, and ideas for assignments and projects. Concrete teaching modules for integrating mobile devices and mobile application development into courses such as software engineering, databases, and game development are also provided.

The teaching module for a database systems course is designed to be used for two to three week sessions, and provides the instructor with lecture slides, hands-on labs, assignments and project ideas. The process of integrating a teaching module into a core course accomplishes two goals: the key focus of the course doesn't change, and it adds greater flexibility to the course by exposing students to different and currently existing technologies which are used in enterprise development today.

Database systems is a core course in the computing curriculum that should cover topics such as the relational model, SQL, transactions, and designing and building database-driven applications. In the mobile context, this is mainly accomplished through the lab and assignment packages which are included in the CMER Academic Kit. They can be used as a single standalone example in a course, or they can be integrated together into a cohesive whole which can be used by course instructors to provide students with a range of database and storage-related activities on mobile devices. Examples of some o the materials contained within the CMER Academic Kit for the database course are as follows.

The "Review and Assessment App," shown in Figure 1, provide students with a great example of how to use the HTML5 localStorage object to make locally persistent data using only a webpage and JavaScript. It makes use of the localStorage to store a structures object by converting it to the JSON file format and placing it in the localStorage object as a string. It restores the object for viewing by the user later when they want to enter data into the form template which they created. This application would be an excellent "homework" problem or lab exercise. It provides students not only with an example that can be easily understood, but also goes over some of the pitfalls which developers must remember when using JavaScript objects with the HTML5 system; an example being techniques to restore data into an already existing object which has methods, using the hash-like array addressing which is available in JavaScript.

**Figure 1: A snapshot of the Review and Assessment app**

In addition to the above, many unique challenges this form of storage incurs, learning how to synchronize data across different machines efficiently and ensuring that all the versions of a particular file are, consistently, accessible on different devices would be a great skill for students to have when they get into industry. The unique characteristics of databases on mobile devices are an important area for course instructors to cover during a module such as this one. Programming labs, which emphasize asynchronous, optimized approaches to database request, could easily be developed. A sample is provided in CMER's educational module, available at http://cmer.uoguelph.ca/kit.html.

**Figure 2: An example of the Dropbox lab exercise**

Another example is the Dropbox access application, as shown in Figure 2, allowing users to view their folders on a Dropbox account. This original example is setup to poll a directory for its contents every time the user changes from one to the next. The students' job is to optimize the amount of bandwidth being used and to reduce application latency. The solution which the students are required to create maps just a directory and caches the results. When the user goes back to a directory which they have already viewed previously, it presents them the contents of the directory, but using the information which has been cached rather than making another request to the server. In addition, the students are required to implement a refreshing feature, where after x minutes, the cache is marked as invalid and the directory is retrieved from the user's account the next time the user opens it. Keeping track of which folders have been cached could be implemented using the SQLite functionality present on Android. Examples such as this provide the students with the practical, hands-on approach mentioned earlier, while introducing them to database concepts and good programming practices.

## 5. CONCLUSION AND FUTURE WORK

This paper brings to light the possible ways in which to integrate mobile devices and mobile application development into a database course. Our reasoning for doing so are that students become more engaged in the learning process with the inclusion of mobile devices. The approach introduced is supported by a module containing hands on labs and sample assignments. These labs are geared for all levels of students.

The authors encourage all course instructors who are teaching database-related courses to begin to integrate mobile devices into their courses. Experience in this growing field will be extremely important for the next generation of software developers, either in industry or academia. All of the samples discussed here are available at: http://cmer.uoguelph.ca/kit.html.

## 6. ACKNOWLEDGMENT

The Centre for Mobile Education and Research (CMER) is funded in part by Research In Motion.

## 7. REFERENCES

[1] Mahmoud, Q.H., Ngo, T., Niazi, R., Popowicz, P., Sydoryshyn, R., Wilks, M., and Dietz, D.: An Academic kit for Integrating Mobile Devices into the CS Curriculum. Proceedings of the 14th Annual ACM SIGCSE Conference on Innovation and Technology in CS Education, Paris, France, July 2009, pp. 40-44.

[2] Moore, M., Binkerd, C., Fant, S.: Teaching Web-Based Database Application Development - an Inexpensive Approach: Journal of Computing Sciences in Colleges, Vol. 17, No. 4, March 2002, pp. 58 – 63.

[3] Teaching Databases at Southampton University: http://www.ics.heacademy.ac.uk/events/presentations/300_thomas.pdf. Accessed on March 9, 2009.

[4] Bi, Y., Beidler, J.: Teaching Database Systems With Web Applications Team Projects: Journal of Computing Sciences in Colleges, Vol. 23, No. 3, January 2008, pp. 82 – 88.

[5] Ramakrishna, M.V.: A Learning by Doing Model for Teaching Advanced Databases: Proceedings of the Australasian conference on Computing education, Melbourne, Australia, 2000, pp. 203-207.

[6] Mahmoud, Q.H., and Dyer, A.: Integrating BlackBerry Wireless Devices into Computing Programming and Literacy Courses: Proc. of the 45th Annual Southeast Conference, Winston-Salem, NC, USA, March 2007, pp. 495-500.

[7] Mahmoud, Q.H., "Integrating Mobile Devices into the Computer Science Curriculum". The 38th Annual Frontiers in Education Conference (FIE 2008), Saratoga Springs, NY, USA, October 22-25, 2008., pp. S3E-17-S3E-22.

[8] BlackBerry Wireless Devices in Computer Science Education: http://cmer.cis.uoguelph.ca/pubs/CMER-white-paper.pdf. Accessed on March 9, 2009.

[9] Csete, J., Wong, Y.H., Vogel, D.: Mobile Devices In and Out of the Classroom. Proc. of World Conference on Educational Multimedia, Hypermedia and Telecommunications 2004, Chesapeake, VA, USA, pp. 4729-4736.

[10] Schonfeld, Erick: Forrester Predicts Tablets will Outsell Netbooks by 2012, Desktops by 2012: http://techcrunch.com/2010/06/17/forrester-tablets-outsell-netbooks/. Accessed July 30, 2012.

[11] ComScore Press Release, April 2012. http://www.comscore.com/Press_Events/Press_Releases/2012/4/European_Mobile_Gaming_Gets_Social. Accessed on July 30, 2012.

[12] SQLite, http://www.sqlite.org/features.html. Accessed on August 2, 2012.

[13] Nickinson, Phil Chrome vs. Safari - Galaxy Nexus vs. iPhone 4S, Feb 09 2012. http://www.androidcentral.com/chrome-vs-safari-galaxy-nexus-vs-iphone-4s?style_mobile=0. Accessed on August 2nd, 2012.

# Multi-faceted Support for MOOC in Programming

Arto Vihavainen, Matti Luukkainen and Jaakko Kurhila
University of Helsinki
Department of Computer Science
P.O. Box 68 (Gustaf Hällströmin katu 2b)
Fi-00014 University of Helsinki
{ avihavai, mluukkai, kurhila }@cs.helsinki.fi

## ABSTRACT

Many massive open online courses (MOOC) have been tremendously popular, causing a stir in academic institutions. The most successful courses have reached tens of thousands of participants. In our MOOC on introductory programming, we aimed to improve distinctive challenges that concern most of the open online courses: allowing and requiring the participants to be more active in their online learning ("flipped-classroom"), demanding them to go deeper than typical CS1 course, and added incentives for participant retention by treating the course as a formal entrance exam to CS/IT degree. Our Extreme Apprenticeship (XA) method for programming education appeared to be successful in an online environment as well.

## Categories and Subject Descriptors

K.3.2 [**Computers and Education**]: Computer and Information Science Education *Computer Science Education*

## General Terms

Experimentation, Management

## Keywords

mooc, programming, extreme apprenticeship, automatic assessment service, formal acknowledgement

## 1. INTRODUCTION

In IT education, use of technology to support learning has evolved naturally. Most of the university level programming courses are hybrid courses offering both online materials and local lectures. Purely online courses in science and engineering are more rare, even though it has been said that they have "tremendous potential", yet "limited success to date" [14].

Reasons for limited success might lie in the fact that programming is a complex skill that requires rigorous practice [13]. Therefore, it has been stated that it is hard work

to create purely online courses in the domain [7]. However, it has become apparent that the times are changing: "tremendous potential" has recently started to become more and more evident as freely available online courses, so-called MOOCs (massive open online courses) have gained momentum.

MOOCs are originally defined to "integrate the connectivity of social networking, the facilitation of an acknowledged expert in a field of study, and a collection of freely accessible online resources" [10]. As the word *massive* implies, MOOCs need to be inherently scalable. Moreover, they may share "conventions of an ordinary course, such as a predefined timeline and weekly topics for consideration", but typically should carry "no fees, no prerequisites other than Internet access and interest, no predefined expectations for participation, and no formal accreditation" [10].

Some prominent MOOCs, such as various classes from Stanford University, edX, Coursera and Udacity, have attracted tens of thousands of participants. Even though the retention rates may be very low [15], huge popularity in starting students shows that the time is ripe for MOOCs [6]. Courses in computer science and engineering can help to attract students into the field. In addition, easy-to-start web-based programming environments such as Codecademy allow people to get a taste of power of programming with a minimal initial threshold.

This paper presents *yet another MOOC* in introductory programming, and describes how we purposefully employed sophisticated pedagogical, technical and structural support to benefit our MOOC.

## 2. NOT YET ANOTHER MOOC

We claim that our MOOC is worth the effort in three important and distinctive areas: (1) the pedagogical method called Extreme Apprenticeship (XA) behind it has been particularly suitable for programming education [16, 9]. (2) Scaffolding of students' tasks using a purpose-built assessment solution and material combined with XA is especially suitable for self-study. (3) By coupling formal educational structures to support engagement to the course, we have been able to make the course more lucrative, yet more demanding and rewarding than many typical CS1 courses reported in current literary.

Contrary to the definition of a MOOC above, we deliberately wanted to reverse "no predefined expectations for participation, and no formal accreditation" to "clear reasons for participation, and clear formal accreditation".

## 2.1 Pedagogical approach: XA

The Extreme Apprenticeship (XA) method is based on Cognitive Apprenticeship [4, 5] and emphasizes guiding the students' working process and actual activity over "being taught". Core values in XA are [16]:

- The craft can only be mastered by actually practicing it, as long as it is necessary. In order to be able to practise the craft, the students need meaningful activities, i.e. exercises.
- Continuous feedback between the learner and the advisor. The learner needs confirmation that tells her that she is progressing *and* to a desired direction. Therefore, the advisor must be aware of the successes and challenges of the learner throughout the course.

We have completely left out lectures and focused on providing high-quality learning material, exercises, and enough XA lab guidance in our recent CS1 courses. In XA labs the students are scaffolded by course advisors as they work on the exercises. Scaffolding refers to supporting students in a way that they are not given direct answers, rather, just pushed into a direction to discover the answers themselves.

An important factor is that XA is as "genuine" as possible. Therefore, learning to program starts with installing industry-strength programming tools; we use NetBeans as our IDE of choice as it is freely available and provides good debugging and testing capabilities. Using recognized tools emphasizes that the learners are on a path to become true professionals.

The results of applying XA have been impressive in the context of our university, as the drop-out rate, pass rate and grade distribution are all improving [16]. Every student practices with dozens of simple exercises already during the first week, and continues working on more demanding exercises throughout the course. Scaffolding is built into the exercises and material, which makes it easier for the student to proceed to a favorable direction. An important factor is that learning achievements are made visible to the student, thus boosting the motivation to continue.

## 2.2 Test My Code (TMC)

XA is by definition direct one-on-one interaction between the student and the advisor. Although XA can be scaled to hundreds of students with the use of efficient resource and personnel allocation [9], it is evident that XA can benefit from automated tools. In order to allow advisors to focus their time to actual scaffolding tasks, we have crafted a scalable automatic assessment solution that allows building scaffolding into programming exercises, provides full bookkeeping within several simultaneous courses, and has course management functionality.

Test My Code (TMC) is a bundle that contains several parts: a NetBeans programming environment plugin that integrates seamlessly to the normal programming workflow, a scalable assessment server that can be deployed to cloud environments, and a purpose-built domain-specific language (DSL) that is used by the course staff for building exercises with built-in scaffolding messages. More specific tests are crafted using unit tests, which means that there are practically no limits on what can be tested.

As new exercises are released, the TMC NetBeans plugin downloads them as programming projects into the IDE. Each project contains exercise-specific tests and, in some cases, code that is given as a starting point for the exercise.

Contrary to most of the automatic assessment systems [8], students can test their solutions locally using the programming environment and receive direct scaffolding inside the IDE. Tests are quick to run and can be executed as often as the student wishes. Students are also able to see the source code of the tests. However, if we do not want to expose the tests to students, TMC also supports creating *hidden tests* that are only available on the assessment server.

We use TMC in our on-campus CS1 courses. However, as TMC offers bookkeeping and scaffolding, it was only natural to open our course in a completely online form as a MOOC. When comparing our MOOC with our on-campus CS1 course, MOOC participants do not have live one-to-one advisors guiding them. Other than that, our MOOC is exactly the same as the on-campus course.

## 2.3 Extending incentives for participation

We wanted to give the option for formal acknowledgement for participants working through our CS1 course as our university students do. This was done in two parts; (1) we provided five partial exams for students in K-12 institutions that were graded at our university, and (2) we offered a full admission to CS/IT degree program for a top-tier university to every high-performing student of the course.

The track for applying to the computer science department required the ability and motivation to complete most of the exercises, to pass a monitored programming exam and an interview conducted by the faculty of our department, and to be eligible for university-level education (e.g. finishing or finished secondary education).

From our perspective, admitting the top-performers can be seen as a "win-win-win-situation". As they have participated in the course, exam and the interview, we know that (1) they are able to perform in a university level course, (2) they have tried programming and noticed that they want to study computer science, and (3) they have a "flying start" to their studies as they have already finished CS1 with very high marks.

## 3. COURSE ORGANIZATION

With the introduction of XA our CS1 "staff" has become relatively large. We have around 20 persons associated with the course, almost all of them students, so it has been only natural to have a set of well-defined roles, responsibilities, and practises.

### 3.1 Course Personnel

As XA is a form of apprenticeship education, the "pyramid" of the stakeholders is essential in organizing the course: there are *masters* (tenured teachers working also as advisors) that are on the top of the pyramid, crafting material and exercises, coordinating and controlling the operation; *journeymen* (paid advisors that contribute to exercises and help the students with explicit responsibilities); *apprentices* (unpaid advisors among fellow students with limited responsibilities); and finally, *students* of the course (potential apprentices of future courses)

Working as an apprentice is a part of our non-mandatory CS studies, that focuses on the importance of "soft skills" and coaching. Apprentices receive credit that is relative to the amount of advising done, typically between 1 and 3 credits[1]. Using the apprenticeship system allows us to provide teaching and coaching experience for many of the students, as well as give them responsibility. Giving formal credits for the apprentice work is an important incentive, and it enables us to establish an understanding of what is required from the otherwise unpaid advisors.

The journeymen are selected for each course instance using an open call. Usually, they have previous teaching experience or have been working as apprentices in the past CS1 courses. In addition to the extra responsibility and income, it is important that the journeymen proceed in their own studies as they serve as role models for students and apprentices.

## 3.2 Working Process

Because of the rapid feedback cycle in XA labs, our course content and working process is elastic; whenever we notice something that can be improved, we act as soon as possible. Typically, we improve the material weekly, and the material is at least partially rewritten during each course.

The material and exercises are developed by masters with help from journeymen. As developing new exercises includes creating tests that scaffold students, it is important that new exercises are tested thoroughly before publishing them to the course population. To verify the thoroughness of the tests, we have created a "Alpha-Beta-Open" release cycle for verifying that the content is ready for MOOC release.

"Alpha-Beta-Open" means that prior to releasing the material to MOOC participants, the material is tested in required lengths by the journeymen and masters, and gradually released to the apprentices. Each member of the teaching staff, be it an apprentice, journeyman or a master, works as an *alpha-tester* before the release to our CS1 course. Alpha-testers work out the material and exercises and seek out possible issues. The issues are gathered in a helpdesk-like ticketing system that is processed by the journeymen and masters.

Once alpha-testing is finished and the found issues are resolved, the material is released to our CS1 course. The course is set up using XA so that the students work on the exercises in XA labs under guidance from advisors. This provides us another feedback point for improvement. Essentially the students in the university course are the *beta-testers*. Once enough students (over 10) in our CS1 have done the exercises without noticeable problems, the exercises and material are published to MOOC participants.

If problems are noticed after the exercises are published to the public, fixing them is still relatively easy. Updated material is easily republished, and TMC has built-in functionality that can automatically update the students' exercises to contain the latest fixes.

## 4. EXERCISE MATERIAL

As most of the introductory programming books and lecture materials are centered around language constructs and fail to present actual working process [12], we have created our own material. Our material is built around the exercises and emphasizes the actual working process using worked examples [3] and process recordings [2]. Both worked examples and process recordings emphasize *how* a program is crafted

using stepwise subtask division: one must always start small to grow big.

Our semester-length Java CS1 course covers topics typical to most programming courses: assignment, expressions, terminal input and output, basic control structures, classes, objects, arrays and strings as well as object-oriented programming features such as interfaces, inheritance and polymorphism. File I/O, exceptions and GUIs are also covered, and essential features of Java API, such as lists, maps, and sets, receive tons of practise.

Best programming practises are emphasized as well; use of meaningful variable and method names, refactoring existing code into smaller methods, using the single responsibility principle, and using automated tests. Basic algorithmics, such as sorting and searching, are also covered.

It is expected that students in XA-based courses use most of the time they devote to the course in active solving of programming exercises; individual effort plays the key role. In order to provide support for the students' working process, scaffolding the exercises is required.

## 4.1 Scaffolding in Exercises

Exercises form the core of our course: there are a total of 170 exercises that are split into a total of 373 tasks. Learning objectives are embedded into the exercises, and the material is built around the exercises to maximize scaffolding. The learning material is constructed so that new topics are immediately applicable to following exercises.

Most of the exercises are composed of small incremental tasks that together form bigger programs. Incremental tasks imitate a typical problem solving process. Students explicitly practise programming, but are constantly influenced by the written out thought process behind the pre-performed subtask division. Exercises are intentionally written out to be as informative as possible, and often contain sample input/output descriptions or code snippets with expected outputs that provide further support for verifying correctness of the program. This allows the student to confirm that she is proceeding to the correct direction.

In addition to the structural support from the material, students receive scaffolding from TMC. Exercise-specific tests are built in a way that gives direct support to the incremental nature of the exercises. Tests are structured so that the students can focus on progressing in small steps even within a single task.

Typical tasks may require implementing a class, writing method bodies that correspond to given signatures, and verifying that method outputs are correct for a set of inputs. Typically, the working process continues with an increment, e.g. by forming another class that perhaps uses the previously implemented class. In a way the students' workflow reminds the workflow in Test Driven Development [1] except that the tests are often readily given to student[2]. A clear metalevel motivation to the incremental style is to guide students to a similar working process that good professional programmers use: progress in small steps and after each step ensure that what you did works correctly.

Our experiments indicate that the incremental "scaffolded" process backed with tests works reasonably well. However, there is one challenge we still need to solve: with the introduction of TMC, some students have started to rely too

---

[1]In our system one credit generally corresponds to 20-30 hours of work

[2]We also have exercises where the students must create unit tests.

much on the tests, and do not write spontaneous main-programs of their own for testing. Creating small test programs for trials and debugging is extremely important since if a test fails, the corrective actions are not always trivial despite the fact that TMC tests provide rather good diagnostic messages.

After the students have been honing their skills with the scaffolded exercises, scaffolding is faded and students work on more open assignments. Open assignments let the students to design the internal program structure freely, but still provide support e.g. by defining the UI in a relatively strict manner. Depending on the learning objective of the exercise, it may be split into required functionalities providing additional scaffolding.

Open assignments are intentionally complex enough so that programming a solution to a single class will cause chaos, but simple enough so that using an "implement a single requirement, refactor if needed" -approach will end up with a nice object design. They usually describe a well-known domain (e.g. airport, airplanes), that helps students to grasp and design initial domain objects.

Although the majority of the exercises are scaffolded, each week contains open exercises as well. Having non-scaffolded open exercises in the course is of importance since our goal is that every student should be capable of performing elementary program design and problem solving independently.

# 5. SAMPLE EXERCISE

When students are learning to program, it is important that they are shown the process of creating a program step by step. The following Movie recommender -exercise is an example of a scaffolded exercise that supports the student in crafting a working movie recommender. The exercise has been inspired by the personalized book recommendation system presented as one of the nifty assignments in SIGCSE 2011 [11].

In addition to the following description, the description contained small program snippets that could be used for verifying the program functionality at specific stages, as well as reflective narratives. We have omitted them and other details such as packages due to article size constraints.

---

**Movie Recommender**

In October 2006, a corporation called Netflix promised 1 million dollars to the person or the group that would be able to create a program, that is 10% better at making personalized movie recommendations than their existing program. The competition was finished in Sept. 2009 (http://www.netflixprize.com) – unfortunately we did not win.

In this exercise, we build a program for recommending movies. The application can recommend movies based on overall and personal ratings. First we will create necessary domain objects, and then start crafting a database for storing ratings. Once we can store and retrieve ratings, we will build the actual recommender.

**Task 1: Person and Movie** Create classes Person and Movie. Both classes must have a public constructor that takes a name as a parameter, and a public method getName() that returns the name. In addition, create a toString()-method for both classes that returns the name that was received in the constructor, and override the existing equals- and hashCode-methods.

**Task 2: Rating** Create an enum-type class Rating that has the following values: terrible (-5), bad (-3), not seen (0), neutral (1), good (3), awesome (5).The class must have a public method called getValue() that returns a specific int-value.

**Task 3: RatingDatabase (1)** Create a RatingDatabase class. It should provide the following public methods: addRating(Movie movie, Rating rating) that adds a rating to the given movie, movieRatings() that returns movie specific ratings as Map<Movie, List<Rating>>, and getRatings(Movie movie) that returns the ratings for the given movie as a list.

**Task 4: RatingDatabase (2)** Add the following public methods to the class RatingDatabase. Method addRating(Person person, Movie movie, Rating rating) adds a new rating to the given movie done by the person, getPersonRatings(Person person) returns all ratings made by the given person as Map<Movie, Rating>, getRating(Person person, Movie movie) returns the rating for the movie by a given person. If no such rating exists, return rating *not seen*. Method getRaters() returns a list of persons that have added ratings. Each person may rate a specific movie only once; existing ratings are overwritten.

The functionality implemented in the previous task must not break.

**Task 5: MovieComparator** Create a MovieComparator class that implements interface Comparator<Movie>. The class should receive a Map<Movie, List<Rating>> as a constructor parameter, and should allow sorting movies based on their rating averages in descending order.

**Task 6: Recommender (1)** Create a MovieRecommender class that takes RatingDatabase as a constructor parameter. Add a public method recommendMovie(Person person) that recommends a movie to a person. At this point, recommend only the movie that has the highest average rating, and has not yet been seen by the given person. If no such movie exists, return null.

**Task 7: PersonComparator** Create a class PersonComparator that implements the interface Comparator<Person>. The comparator takes Map<Person, Integer> as a constructor parameter, and must allow sorting persons based on the map value in descending order.

**Task 8: Recommender (2)** When the system contains movie ratings from persons, we have knowledge on their movie taste. Extend the method recommendMovie(Person person) so that it gives a personalized recommendation if a person has rated movies. If the person has not given any ratings, the recommender should recommend a movie based on rating average.

Personalized ratings should be based on the similarity of ratings by a person when compared to other raters. Let us consider an example with 3 persons; Tom, Dick and Harry. Tom has rated movie A good (3), movie B terrible (-5). Dick has rated movie B terrible (-5), and movie C good (3). Harry has rated movie B good (3) and movie C good (3). The person-wise similarities are calculated based on the similarities of given movie ratings.

If Tom wants to have a movie recommended to him, we calculate the similarity of each person in relation to Tom. Similarity of Tom and Dick is 25 (-5 * -5), as they both have seen movie B and given it the rating terrible. The similarity of Tom and Harry is -15 (-5 * 3) as they also have both seen the movie B – Harry rated it good. As the similarity between Tom and Dick is higher, movies rated as good or excellent by Dick should be recommended to Tom.

Implement the described functionality.

---

The movie recommender exercise above is done towards the end of the course, as it contains object design, use of maps and lists, and requires basic algorithmic thinking. The exercise was one of five larger exercises in the week where it was released.

# 6. CRAFTING TESTS

Creating pedagogically sound tests for the exercises requires both expertise and experience. As none of the required classes or packages usually exist in the exercise base that is downloaded by TMC, scaffolding needs to be built starting from nothing. We start scaffolding by helping with the very basic properties, e.g. does a required package exist, does a required class exist, is the class public and so on. Once a class is known to exist, the next step is to start verifying the existence of required methods with sensible visibility settings followed by working on the basic functionality of the methods, one by one.

TMC provides a DSL for creating scaffolding for basic properties very easily. In addition to the basic verification and scaffolding, we have created lots of tests for exercise-specific scaffolding; roughly over 1300 tests with over 4000 messages were crafted during the MOOC experiment.

Additional scaffolding is done via rigorous use of reflection. In the movie recommender exercise students are corraled into the right direction with questions like "what happens if the person has not rated a movie?" and "are you sure that the movie comparator produces results in correct order?". Each task has usually several tests that guide the students' working process as well as the student towards a more proper solution.

The testing of open exercises is usually done with a mixture of reflection and input-output testing. Reflection is used to verify consistent object design, for example in specific domain-related problems one may verify that the student has crafted classes that resemble assumed domain objects. Actual functionality testing is done using black-box input-output -testing where most of the possible execution paths as well as error cases are tested.

Testing is not always easy. For example one of our GUI-related exercises requires that the student draws a smiley that looks similar to an example image using only 5 rectangles. Actual testing requires mocking the Java's Graphics-object to verify the number of used rectangles, and approximating distance from the drawn image to an existing image using a %-match ratio needed for acceptance. We also had interactive GUI exercises; one of the more demanding ones scaffolded the students in building the classic snake game from scratch.

Crafting scaffolding into the exercises was considered rewarding by the course personnel. Even though some of them had experience from the industry, there was still lots to learn. It was essential that the staff was good at playing the "what could the student do next that would make the provided scaffolding break up?" -game. We feel that this was only possible due to the presence in local XA labs.

# 7. DATA FROM THE MOOC

We had a total of 417 registered participants in our MOOC using basic word-of-mouth advertising and contacting K-12 institutions. The low number of participants when compared to more established MOOC providers such as Udacity and Coursera can be partially explained by our relatively small language area; we offered the course in our native language with K-12 institutions specifically in mind.

When registering to the course, one did not need to fill in any personal details; we only required desired nickname and a contact email-address. Out of the 417 registered, 405 started working on the exercises and made at least a hello-world application. During our initial survey three weeks into the course, 67 students had indicated that they were applying for full admission – majority of the participants were on to "check out this new MOOC thing".

MOOC drop-out rates are typically very high, and hard

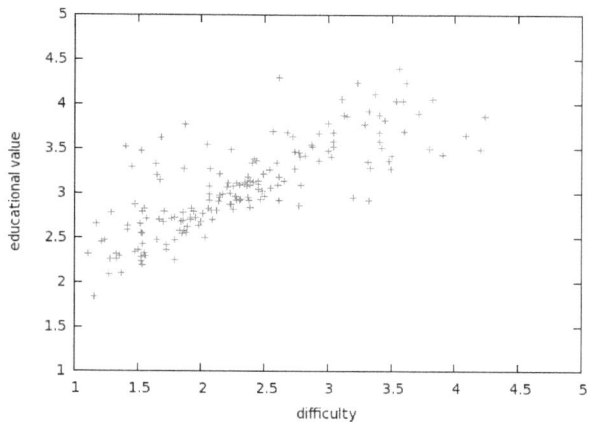

Figure 1: Participant feedback on exercise difficulty plotted against educational value.

figures that could be used for comparison are hard to come by. During our semester-length MOOC where 405 participants programmed at least one program, 329 participants did over programming 20 tasks, 256 continued to program over 50 tasks, and 187 over 100 tasks. After 6 weeks one third of the participants were still actively programming. A bit under 100 participants did over 80% of the tasks, and 70 participants finished over 90% of the tasks.

During the course we gathered voluntary feedback. The participants could provide numeric feedback on the difficulty (1 = easy, 5 = hard) and educational value (1 = low, 5 = high) for each exercise directly from TMC. The students also had an option for adding direct verbal feedback. Only 3 of the exercises had an average difficulty over 4; all of them were at least partially in the wrong place.

We observe a clear correlation between the difficulty and educational value of our exercises, see Figure 1. Our goal was to have each week start easy and early, to addict the students, and build the exercises so that the students could work in their zone of proximal development [16, 17].

In addition to the built-in feedback mechanism, we had setup a IRC channel that served as the main peer-support forum. Because of the clear timeline in the course, it proved to be a solid support channel throughout our MOOC. Our course page provided a web-interface for IRC access, and during the MOOC, we estimated roughly 250 individual participants. Several faculty members were also present – this is only natural given that they wanted to receive feedback and see how the course unfolds.

Most active hours were during the evenings. The IRC activity was relatively low on Saturday, even though Saturdays and Sundays are not typically schooldays/workdays in Finland. High activity on Sundays can be explained by the fact that the submission deadlines for participants were set for Sundays nights. We observed small peaks in the early Wednesdays of the early course. At a further inspection, this was due to our visible, live scoreboard for every nickname for the completed exercises: some participants started to compete on who finishes the exercise set the fastest. This effect was very prominent in the IRC channel in the early stages of the course, as the tasks were relatively straightforward for more experienced participants, but faded away as the course progressed.

# 8. CONCLUSIONS AND FUTURE WORK

We described how we offered our CS1 free for everybody as a MOOC using sophisticated pedagogical, technical and structural support. The initial feedback from the course participants has been fruitful, and we have been able to witness and gather several completely unsolicited, truly spontaneous testimonials among the flow of the IRC discussions (translated by the authors):

*I must praise a bit before I continue. It's been a really good idea to organize this course! I've never programmed before, but have always been interested in programming. Starting to learn programming was made really easy*

*I've learned more about programming on mooc than ever before*

*After mooc one starts to understand why object-oriented programming was invented*

*Right now I just want to quit my work and get back to studying*

*This is the most in-depth programming course that I've ever had .. absolutely merciless*

The first comment was given early in the course and is in line with the "start early, start small" -view. The second and third comments were given mid-way through the course when the participants had been doing object-oriented programming for a few weeks. Scaffolded exercises where the problem had been divided into smaller tasks provided support, conveyed the working process, and described how problems should be solved using object-oriented programming. The second and fifth comment displays that people with existing programming background were also able to learn new things.

Fourth comment indicates the motivation boost that one receives from solving the exercises, and the last comment puts the demand-level of our approach into words: "absolutely merciless".

Our initial experiments have been successful: we have been able to create a model and tools for crafting a MOOC from our CS1 course, and have been able to provide the course for free for everyone. Our MOOC has not been a watered down version of our internal course, which may have increased the observed drop-out rates.

To our understanding, the drop-out rates have been similar to other offered MOOCs. In the fall of 2012, we have 41 starting "MOOC students", which provides an interesting chance of monitoring how they relate to the students admitted in a normal way. We are also investigating reasons on why participants have dropped out midway through the course, and are performing data-analysis on the solutions crafted by the MOOC participants.

As our national K-12 curriculum does not include IT related studies, many of the students miss the opportunity to learn programming. We provide support for basic programming education to any K-12 -school free of charge. The formally acknowledged MOOC approach with partial exams does not demand actual programming knowledge from teachers or the school faculty, and due to the nationwide technology programme any school has computers required for the course. Additionally, majority of the students have computers at home.

# 9. REFERENCES

[1] K. Beck. *Test Driven Development: By Example.* Addison-Wesley, 2002.

[2] J. Bennedsen and M. E. Caspersen. Reflections on the teaching of programming. chapter Exposing the Programming Process, pages 6–16. Springer-Verlag, Berlin, Heidelberg, 2008.

[3] M. E. Caspersen and J. Bennedsen. Instructional design of a programming course: a learning theoretic approach. In *ICER '07: Proceedings of the third international workshop on Computing education research*, pages 111–122. ACM, 2007.

[4] A. Collins, J. Brown, and S. Newman. Cognitive apprenticeship: Teaching the craft of reading, writing and mathematics. In *Knowing, Learning and Instruction: Essays in honor of Robert Glaser.* Hillside, 1989.

[5] A. Collins, J. S. Brown, and A. Holum. Cognitive apprenticeship: making thinking visible. *American Educator*, 6:38–46, 1991.

[6] A. Fox and D. Patterson. Crossing the software education chasm. *Commn. ACM*, 55(5):44–49, May 2012.

[7] J. Gal-Ezer, T. Vilner, and E. Zur. The professor on your pc: a virtual cs1 course. In *Proceedings of the 14th annual ACM SIGCSE conference on Innovation and technology in computer science education*, ITiCSE '09, pages 191–195, New York, NY, USA, 2009. ACM.

[8] P. Ihantola, T. Ahoniemi, V. Karavirta, and O. Seppälä. Review of recent systems for automatic assessment of programming assignments. In *Proc. of the 10th Koli Calling Int. Conf. on Computing Education Research*, Koli Calling '10, pages 86–93, New York, NY, USA, 2010. ACM.

[9] J. Kurhila and A. Vihavainen. Management, structures and tools to scale up personal advising in large programming courses. In *Proceedings of the SIGITE '11*. ACM, 2011.

[10] A. McAuley, B. Stewart, G. Siemens, and D. Cormier. The mooc model for digital practice. 2012.

[11] N. Parlante, J. Zelenski, K. Schwarz, D. Feinberg, M. Craig, S. Hansen, M. Scott, and D. J. Malan. Nifty assignments. In *Proceedings of the 42nd ACM technical symposium on Computer science education*, SIGCSE '11, pages 491–492, New York, NY, USA, 2011. ACM.

[12] A. Robins, J. Rountree, and N. Rountree. Learning and teaching programming: A review and discussion. *Computer Science Education*, 13:137–172, 2003.

[13] H. Roumani. Design guidelines for the lab component of objects-first cs1. In *SIGCSE '02: Proceedings of the 33rd SIGCSE technical symposium on Computer science education*, pages 222–226. ACM, 2002.

[14] J. Subhlok, O. Johnson, V. Subramaniam, R. Vilalta, and C. Yun. Tablet pc video based hybrid coursework in computer science: report from a pilot project. *SIGCSE Bull.*, 39(1):74–78, Mar. 2007.

[15] S. Thrun and D. Evans. Georgia tech talk quoted in computing education blog, 2012.

[16] A. Vihavainen, M. Paksula, and M. Luukkainen. Extreme apprenticeship method in teaching programming for beginners. In *SIGCSE '11: Proceedings of the 42nd SIGCSE technical symposium on Computer science education*, 2011.

[17] L. S. Vygotsky. *Mind in Society: The Development of Higher Psychological Processes.* Harvard University Press, Cambridge, MA, 1978.

# A Modified Team-Based Learning Methodology for Effective Delivery of an Introductory Programming Course

Ashraf Elnagar
Department of Computer Science
University of Sharjah
Sharjah, UAE
ashraf@sharjah.ac.ae

Mahir S. Ali
Department of Computer Science
University of Sharjah
Sharjah, UAE
mahirali@sharjah.ac.ae

## ABSTRACT

This paper sheds the light on an attempt to use a pedagogy integrating Team-Based Learning (TBL) for effective learning and hands-on experience in an introductory programming course. We have adopted a modified version of TBL to study its effect on students learning and to examine how teams intra- and inter-team active interactions influence students' learning and grades. Therefore, the objectives of this work is to evaluate whether the proposed modified TBL methodology would or would not improve students' experience of in-class engagement and their attitude about the value of using teams for learning, compared with experiences students would have had in the traditional lecture format. We refer to this method as LTBL, Lectures and Team-Based Learning, since we added a short but essential teaching component. To explore the effectiveness of this learning pedagogy, we evaluated students' level of engagement and attitudes toward achieving course outcomes and the value of teamwork over four semesters. Our findings demonstrated that LTBL has a positive effect on the success rate and the achievement of learning outcomes.

## Categories and Subject Descriptors

K.3.1 [**Computers and Education**]: Computer uses in Education - Collaborative learning.; K.3.2 [**Computers and Education**]: Computer and Information Science Education - Computer science Education.; D.1.4 [**Programming languages**]: structured programming

## General Terms

Case study, interactive learning

## Keywords

Introductory programming course, Team-Based Learning

## 1. INTRODUCTION

Experimenting with new and different methods in teaching the first programming course is not a new phenomenon [12, 8, 1, 7, 5]. For decades, computer science and other related IT departments have struggled to find a solution to the high drop rates or/and unacceptable level of failures and low grades of their students taking the first programming course[14, 4]. A paradigm shift in teaching CS courses, regardless of the language being taught, is needed it to correct this situation and hopefully improves the students' retention, improves their performance, and also attracts larger numbers to the IT discipline related majors. Adaptation of a variation of method called Team Based Learning, TBL, may be the answer. TBL is a teaching method proposed for and implemented by some medical schools[3, 13, 19, 6, 12, 15] and then migrated to a few IT departments. The implementation of TBL in programming courses has been reported in a number of publications [10, 11, 18]. Simply put, TBL is a method that replaces passive learning by active learning, where instead of the normal form of students listening to an instructor introducing a new concept, they become active participants in learning the new concept themselves. TBL has three phases: students reading the materials scheduled for each class prior to coming to the class (pre-class preparation), testing their understanding of the material, and finally applying the concept learned. The class time is used for group discussions and short tests and quizzes. The tests' results are used as feedback to the students as well as the instructor on the level of understanding of the assigned topic. The feedback from the quizzes can then be used to justify either explaining the topic further or move on to the next topic. This method does not reduce the load and the effort of the instructor; on the contrary it requires him/her to prepare the lectures in a different way which involves greater effort than the straight forward passive lecture format, such as making the material of the next class available to the students prior to coming to class using any online software (such as the Blackboard or Moodle). This method also requires more time for marking. As an extension to TBL, Modified Team Based Learning (MTBL) is a method that has also been developed which, like TBL, requires the students to prepare the materials prior to coming to class, but unlike the classical TBL, MTBL requires the students to have individual self-assessment test for each assigned concept, discussion of the learned issues by the students and if necessary the instructor's involvement for clarification of difficult or not understood topics, followed by a group discussion and finally, the group re-take the same quiz [16]. For our CS1 course, which has a hybrid of science and engineering majors, the classical TBL was customized to include some formal lectures. We named it Lecture and Team Based Learning (LTBL). Just like TBL and MTBL, we still require the students to be prepared prior to attending classes but instead of allocating the whole class time for group discussion and testing, we allocate some classes for lectures only when we feel that the material requires further but formal explanation using the classical teaching method. However, most classes begin by giving a short lecture of the assigned topic(s) followed by group discussion and finally a short quiz. Based on the result of the quiz, the next upcoming class will be decided upon whether, it would all be a regular lecture, a discussion and a quiz lecture, or to move on to a new topic. This paper reports on our finding of using LBTL for 3 semesters and on the feedback we got from the students. We begin by a brief introduction to the methodology of TBL, MTBL, and LTBL. This paper is organized in the following sections. Section 2 describes the modified team-based learning methodology with details on course structure, team formation, and assessment criteria. The analysis and the findings of using LTBL are reported in Section 3 addressing both students' performance and evaluation of LTBL effectiveness. The work is concluded in Section 4.

## 2. MODIFIED TEAM-BASED LEARNING

### 2.1 Course structure

The course (programming 1) is a 4-credit course, which is offered over a 16-week period and consists of two parts: lectures and practical sessions. Each week students are expected to attend three hours in a classroom and a two-hour practical session in a laboratory. Attendance is mandatory in both parts. The course is a multi-section and several instructors are involved in teaching the lectures as well as the lab sessions, all under the supervision of the course coordinator. The course is a required course for CS majors as well as engineering and some science majors. In the traditional model, the course was taught using lectures, homework assignments, and practical exercises (during the lab sessions). Students were encouraged to revise the material and contact teaching assistants and instructors for help whenever required. Online material was made available in addition to several programming exercises. Quizzes and one or two exams were conducted throughout the semester to assess students' comprehension of the course content. The course also has a final exam, which consists of two parts, the first part is a practical exam conducted in a laboratory where students are given programming problems and required to implement them and submit their solutions during a two-hour exam period. The second part, which is conducted a week after, is a traditional written exam. The grade is determined by the lab exercises, homework assignments, quizzes, and the two final exams. It was reported over the past years (in the course assessment report) that the performance of the students in general is under-satisfactory and therefore several of the course outcomes were not satisfied. Course average used to be in the "D+" range. In Spring 2011, we decided to depart from the traditional teaching and learning model to the team-based model. However, requiring and expecting the students to read and prepare for the classes on their own would pose another obstacle. This is because of two main reasons; First, our students are not prepared for this move

especially immediately after leaving high school (first year students) where the instructor is the center of attention and students are passive recipients. Second, we believe team-based learning may not be the appropriate tool for teaching some of the heavy-technical courses in engineering and sciences. Heavy reliance on self learning in such courses would lead to frustration, discouragement, and likely to fire back. As a result, we proposed a methodology to teach CS1 using a modified team-based learning to overcome both problems above and make a smooth transition from the traditional model to the new one. The course still has two parts: lectures and laboratories. The first change we made was to the lab format. The lab instructor now spends the first 10-15 minutes describing the algorithms required (not the code) to solve the assigned problems (usually two problems) and then the students are giving the rest of the time to write, compile, and run the programs (currently we teach C++). At completion time, the grades are immediately provided to the students by the instructor. A similar method to the one used in ACM National Programming Competition is used to evaluate each student's work. The instructor and the lab assistance have a data set that they use to test each submitted program to ensure the correctness of the submitted algorithms. By the end of the semester the students will have completed between 12 and 13 lab sessions which carry 15-20% of the semester grade. Further, there is a final lab exam at the end of the semester which carries between 10-15% of the final grade. The remaining semester grade is divided between the course work and the theoretical final exam. We have eliminated homework from the course since almost all the problems we assign have their solutions available on the Internet. In the past, lab time was unstructured; the students were giving written description of the lab's assignment and then the instructor and lab assistance would answer questions and inquiries from individual students. Their task was simply to make sure that the students don't copy from each other and to submit their assignments prior to leaving the laboratory. The second and the major change we made to the course was during the formal lecture time, which we describe in the next section.

### 2.2 Methodology

Each formal class begins by the instructor describing today's topic and assignment. Based on his/her feeling of the students' comprehension of the assigned topic, he/she may either spend 10-15 minutes describing the topic or let the group discussion begin. Similar to the laboratory format, the instructor monitors the various groups and intervene when necessary either to explain a certain point the students are having a problem understanding or to probe the groups with a question. After about 15-20 minutes, the instructor stops the discussion and begins a quiz. Therefore, LTBL requires the instructor to (i) divide the students into teams (takes place at the beginning of the semester), (ii) briefly explain the concept of today's class, (iii) allocate time for the groups to discuss and explain the new concept to each other, and finally (iv) examine the students by giving a short quiz on today's topic only, and (v) give them immediate feedback. Hence, the class time is divided into activities which are mainly carried out by the students. Beside the recommended textbook, which the students are required to purchase, the university Blackboard is used to provide the students with the materials in the form of powerpoint files. These files, along with other useful materials, are made available on weekly bases to the students. Further, the online syllabus describes in details the topics to be covered each week, the grading scheme, and the dates for the various exams. We don't make the laboratory assignments available ahead of time because of our concerns that the students may copy the solutions from the Internet. However, they may access the Internet during the laboratory time but because of the presence of the instructor and the lab assistance, their continuous monitoring of the students' progress in each session, and their familiarity with each student's ability, which they become familiar with after couple of weeks, there is very little chance of copying the whole C++ code.

## 2.3 Team formation

Teaching with small groups is not an uncommon practice. However, it is different from TBL groups. Teams are a special type of groups that are more effective and productive. Groups are formed at an early stage of the semester (first week) with a core objective of turning them into teams in few weeks. This is achieved when group members start to gain confidence in each other and build up loyalty to the welfare of the group. Over time, teams become cohesive. Teammates will soon realize that a team can accomplish far more than an individual team members or even a newly-formed group. Therefore, it is important to appropriately form the teams while guaranteeing that they will have the required resources to complete assignments and participate effectively in active learning. In accordance with team formation policies, we use three basic principles to guide the team formation process, which are create teams in the first week of the term, use transparent selection criteria, and diversify teams. We developed a survey to help forming the teams taking into account two important parameters which lead to successful teams formation. One important criterion is the human resources. We distribute students across the teams based on their knowledge of the subject, GPA, and performance in similar subjects. Such factors are likely to predict students' performance in this course. The second main criterion is to avoid self-selected teams. We collect information on students' majors and level in cohort (freshmen, sophomore, junior, and senior). Research has indicated that self-assigned teams are less effective in the course performance when compared to instructor-assigned teams. Diversity in teams is a positive sign. When students are asked to form teams, it is expected to find homogeneous teams that lack diversity. On the other hand, when instructors assign teams taking into account students' skills, assets, and liabilities, we will get diversified teams which will lead to more effective and productive results [2]. Research shows that showed that instructor-selected teams outperform student-selected teams. In addition, the selection process should be a transparent one in order to assure fair distribution of resources. Otherwise, this could hinder the whole process. As for the size of the teams, we keep it between 5 and 6 students. This is in line with recommendations reported in the literature, [13].

## 2.4 Student assessment

In the traditional curriculum, the assessment criteria included two tests (30%), lab exercises (10%), homework assignments (10%), final practice lab test (10%), and final

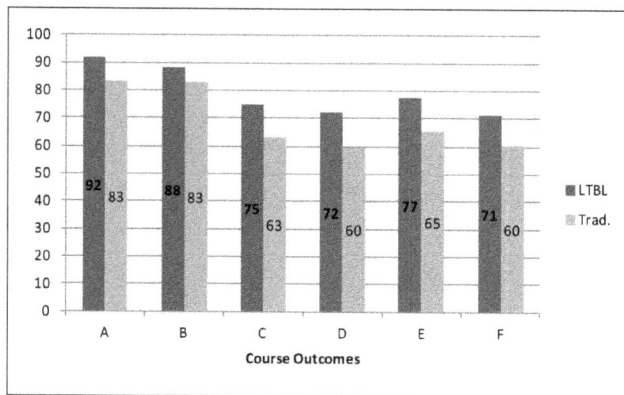

Figure 1: Comparison of students performance in terms of course outcomes achievement in Spring 2012.

exam which accounted for the remaining 40%. In the modified TBL curriculum, the assessment scheme was changed to include one midterm test (20%), lab exercises, including TBL activities, (30%), TBL activities (i.e., individual and group quizzes, in-class activity exercise (15%), final practice lab test (10%), and a final exam with 35%. Peer evaluation was conducted as part of a survey distributed to all students on LTBL. We did not include it in the assessment criteria but rather it was used for analyzing the results. As expected, students who received low scores from their peers ended up with a low grade in the course. Similarly, students who received highest scores from their peers were at the top of the individual class grades.

## 3. ANALYSIS AND RESULTS

In order to properly evaluate the possible effect of LTBL on student performance, we compared the final results between two groups of Programming 1 multi-sections over four semesters (from Fall 2010 to Spring 2012). While we subscribe to the LTBL paradigm, other instructors still employ the traditional lecture model. Our study covers 603 students over two years with enrolment between 131 and 198 students. The course is offered in multi-sections and taught by several instructors. It has a course coordinator to set up the general policies and observe the implementation of common exams. Therefore, all instructors follow the same marking scheme with the exception of replacing LTBL assessment tools with other tools such as quizzes and homework assignments. All students took the same common exams and lab exercises. The comparison of the performance of the two sets of students is based on their final grades as well as their achievement of the course outcomes. Data were collected in Microsoft Excel and transformed into two data sets (LTBL vs. traditional) for analysis. The course has six learning outcomes (numbered A-F; see Appendix A).

## 3.1 Students' Performance

Figure 1 depicts the comparison results between the traditional and LTBL methodologies which was reported recently in Spring 2012. It is clear that LTBL has outperformed the traditional method on each of the outcomes. The overall performance of LTBL sections is 79.3 whereas it is 69.2 for the remaining sections. This is quite a noteworthy improvement.

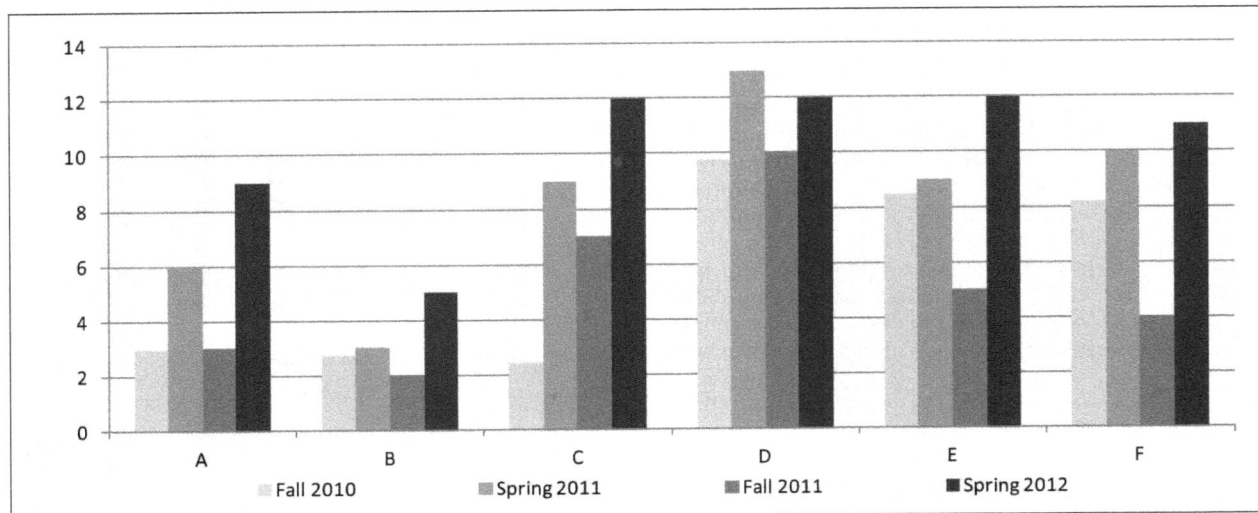

**Figure 3: The overall improvement of LTBL over the traditional methodology on course outcomes achievement over 4 terms.**

Table 1: Achievement of Course Outcomes

| Term | Mode | A | B | C | D | E | F |
|------|------|---|---|---|---|---|---|
| Fall 2010 | LTBL | 75 | 73 | 73 | 71 | 75 | **66** |
| Fall 2010 | Traditional | 72 | 70 | 71 | **61** | **66** | **57** |
| Spring 2011 | LTBL | 90 | 83 | 83 | 73 | 74 | 71 |
| Spring 2011 | Traditional | 84 | 80 | 74 | **60** | 65 | 61 |
| Fall 2011 | LTBL | 87 | 85 | 74 | 71 | 79 | 72 |
| Fall 2011 | Traditional | 84 | 83 | **67** | **61** | 74 | **68** |
| Spring 2012 | LTBL | 92 | 88 | 75 | 72 | 77 | 71 |
| Spring 2012 | Traditional | 83 | 83 | **63** | **60** | 65 | **60** |

The summary of how both groups as a whole performed in terms of final grades is shown in Figure 2. The figure illustrates the percentage of students who scored all grades ranging from "A" ($\geq 90$)to "F" ($< 60$). Notice that the percentages of students who scored "A" to "C" grades in the LTBL sections are higher than its counterpart in the other sections. On the other hand, the percentages of students who scored "D" and "F" grades in the traditional methodology based sections are higher than its counterpart in the LTBL sections. The results of (Spring 2012) are in line with the results of the three preceding terms as shown in Table 1, which summarizes the final average score for each of the course outcomes between the two sets of sections. The numbers in the table fluctuate from one semester to another because of a number of variable parameters such as type of students, instructors, and most important the assessment tools. For example, over the past several years, we have noticed that the quality of the student body that takes the course in the Spring semesters is usually higher than those who take it in Fall semesters. Numbers that are shown in bold font indicate boarder-line performance. We present Figure 3 to show the improvement trend, for each of the course outcomes, over the last four semesters between LTBL and the traditional methodologies based on Table 1.

## 3.2 Evaluation of LTBL

Student's narrative comments elicited both positive and

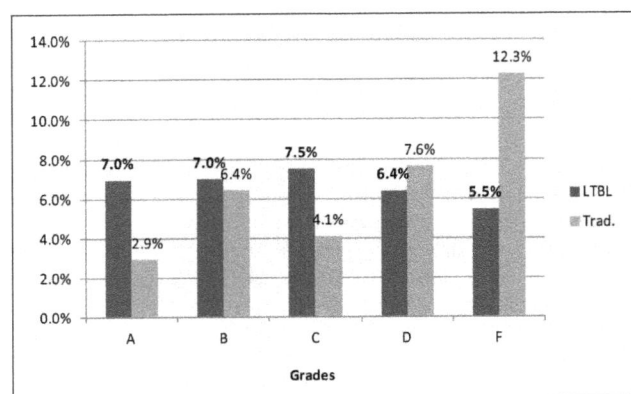

**Figure 2: Comparison of students overall performance in terms of final grades in Spring 2012.**

negative feedback on LTBL. Positive attributes included the ability to cover a vast amount of material in a short time; retention of concepts was aided and stimulated by team discussion, and course coordinators during team discussions helped to immediately clarify misconceptions. Negative attributes of our initial LTBL offering included the notion that some team assignments were too long to complete; more practice clinical application questions would have been helpful, and more time for team discussion was needed to ensure correction of mistakes and proper understanding of the tested concepts. Faculty from our department who attended the LTBL sessions were impressed by the students' cognitive engagement during the team discussions and showed interest in adopting the LTBL concept for more information technology courses. In order to elicit students thoughts and suggestions for improving the delivery of the course, we conducted a comprehensive survey (developed based on [17]) about their experiences with LTBL. The survey includes 26 statements covering three major categories: LTBL effectiveness, teamwork skills, and potential drawbacks of LTBL. The statements of the first category probed student's prepa-

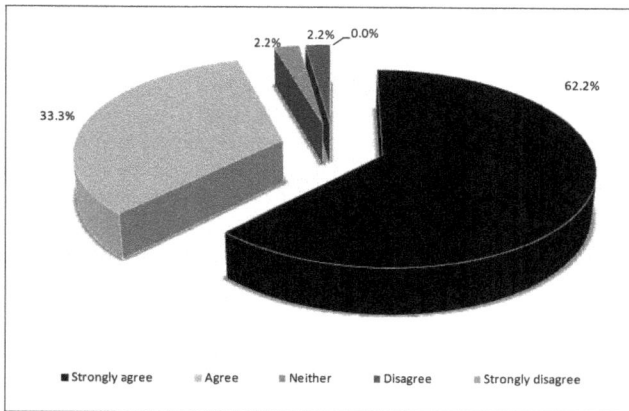

**Figure 4: Students' evaluation of the modified TBL methodology.**

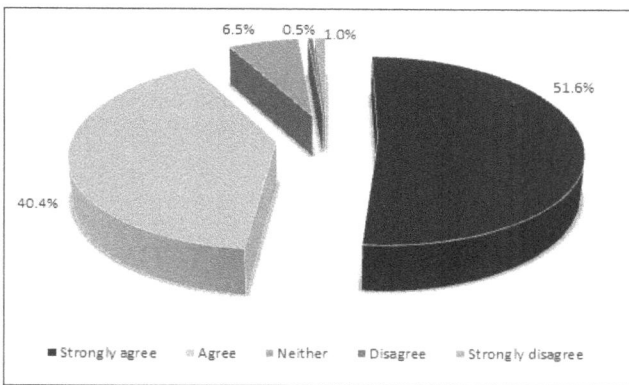

**Figure 5: Students' feedback on the effectiveness of LTBL.**

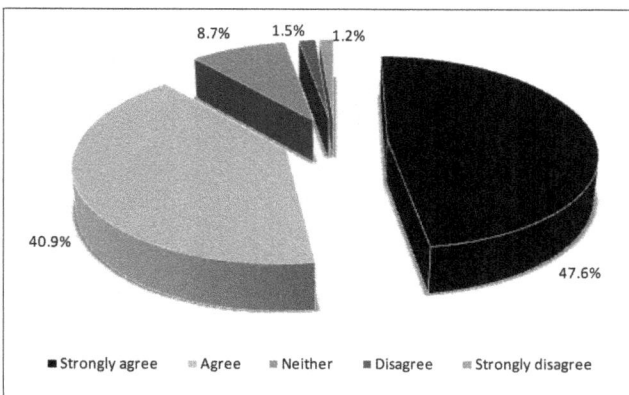

**Figure 6: Students' feedback on the team-work skills.**

ration for team discussions, usefulness of LTBL for acquiring knowledge, importance of peers discussion for deeper understanding, and preparation for exams. The second category examines the attitudes about working with peers, collaboration skills, and mutual respect during team discussions. The last part of the survey sheds the light on potential drawbacks such as getting a way without doing much, frustration from team work, and socializing instead of working. The response of the students indicates the extent to which there is agreement with each statement in the survey. The questionnaire was administered at the end of the course before the final examination, and was computer analyzed from students responses, which remained confidential. Out of 75 respondents, 12 were not used due to missing data or incomplete survey. As a result, the final sample size included (84%) respondents. The analysis lead to three main findings summarizing the students' opinions on LTBL effectiveness, teamwork skills, and potential risks. Each of these three categories is comprised of a number of statements (specifically, 13, 9, and 4 statements, respectively). Each statement is scored as 1, 2, 3, 4, or 5; a higher score represents a favorable view. We have included one statement related to students' perceptions of LTBL methodology, which says "Both lecture presentations and TBL complement each other". Figure 4 depicts the response of all respondents which summarizes the overall positive ratings (95.5% agreement) of their perception of the modified TBL when compared to traditional or even TBL paradigms. Only 2.2% indicated disagreement with this statement. Figure 5 summarizes the overall constructive scores of the students view on the degree of LTBL effectiveness with a total agreement of 92.0%. Similarly the results were encouraging on the positive contribution of LTBL to teamwork skills. Figure 6 shows an agreement of 88.3% and a disagreement of 10.6%. There are some potential drawbacks as a result of using LTBL such as getting a free-ride, socializing instead of doing the work, and frustration while working as a team. Students' perception is in line with instructors' perceptions too. The results show a disagreement of 45.5% vs. an agreement of 41.1%. This means there is a conflict on whether LTBL has a negative side. This is not surprising as the above shortcomings are controversial issues, [9].

## 4. CONCLUSION

We presented in this paper the results of using a modified version of the pedagogy TBL, which is a method of teaching that departs from the classical passive learning method, where the instructor is the center of attention in the class, to making the student the center of attention. LTBL, Lecture and Team-Based Learning is a modification to the classical TBL methodology which is better suited for programming courses and possibly other IT courses. The results from our three semester experiments show that students who are serious about learning have benefited well from this shift in the teaching methodology, which also reflected well on the course outcomes. Our intention is to continue teaching programming 1 using LTBL and will continue to refine the method so that improvements continue in the students' success rate and achieving higher percentage of course outcomes. The results are very encouraging and will be recommended to our CS department to consider LTBL as a possible pedagogy for teaching the majority, if not all, the courses in CS department.

## 5. ACKNOWLEDGMENTS

The authors would like to thank instructors of the Department of Computer Science who evaluated the LTBL methodology. Special thanks are due to Mohammed Lataifeh who helped in producing the figures .We would like to extend our thanks to Programming 1 students who provided excellent feedback on improving some of the processes over the past 2 years.

## 6. REFERENCES

[1] T. Barnes, E. Powell, A. Chaffin, and A. Godwin. Game2learn: Building cs1 learning games for retention. In *ITiCSE'07*, pages 500–504, 2007.

[2] J. Brickell, D. Porter, M. Reynolds, and D. Richard. Assigning students to groups for engineering design projects: A comparison of five methods. *Journal of Engineering Education*, 83(3):259–262, 1994.

[3] M. Clark, H. Nguyen, C. Bray, and R. Levine. Team-based learning in an undergraduate nursing course. *Journal of Nursing Education*, 47(3):111–117, 2008.

[4] N. Dale. Most difficult topics in cs1: Results of an online survey of educators. *SIGCSE Bull.*, 38(2):49–53, 2006.

[5] M. Eagle and T. Barnets. Wu's castle: Teaching arrays and loops in a game. In *Proc. of the 13th Annual Conference on Innovation and Technology in Computer Science Education*, pages 245–249, 2008.

[6] C. Feingold, M. Cobb, R. Givens, J. Arnold, and J. Keller. Student perceptions of team based learning in nursing education. *J. Nurse Educ*, 47:214–222, 2008.

[7] T. Howles. Preliminary results of longitudinal study of computer science student trends, behaviours and preferences. *J. Computing for Small Colleges*, 22(6):18–27, 2007.

[8] P. Kinnunen and L. Malmi. Why students drop out of cs1 course? In *ICER 06*, pages 97–108, September 2006.

[9] S. Kouznetsova. No more freeloading: using individual assignments to improve team-based learning outcomes. *Journal of Computing Sciences in Colleges archive*, 24(5):30–36, 2009.

[10] P. Lasserre. Adaptation of team-based learning on a first term programming class. In *ITiCSE 09 Conference*, pages 186–190, July 2009.

[11] P. Lasserre and C. Azostak. Effects on team-based learning on a cs1 course. In *ITiCS 11 Conference*, pages 133–137, June 2011.

[12] N. Letassy, M. Medina, J. Stroup, S. Fugate, and M. Britton. The impact of team-based learning (tbl) on student and course outcomes compared to lecture methods. In *Annual Meeting of the American Association of Colleges of Pharmacy*, 2007.

[13] L. Michaelsen and M. Sweet. Fundamental principles and practices of teambased learning. In *In: Michaelsen LK, Parmelee DX, McMahon KK, Levine RE (Editors). Team-Based Learning for Health Professions Education: A Guide to Using Small Groups for Improving Learning*, pages 9–34, 2007.

[14] D. Parsons and P. Haden. Parson's programming puzzles: a fun and effective learning tool for first programming courses. In *Proc. of the 8th Australian Conf. on Computing Education*, pages 157–162, 2006.

[15] B. Thompson, P. Schneider, R. Levine, K. McMahon, I. Perkowski, and B. Richard. Team-based learning at ten medical schools: Two years later. *J. Med Educ*, 41(3):250–257, 2007.

[16] N. Vasan, D. DeFouw, and S. Compton. Modified use of team-based learning for effective delivery of medical gross anatomy and embryology. *Anatomical Sciences Educ.*, 1:3–9, 2008.

[17] N. Vasan, D. DeFouw, and S. Compton. Survey of student perceptions of team-based learning in anatomy curriculum: Favorable views unrelated to grades. *Anatomical Sciences Educ.*, 2:150 Ű 155, 2009.

[18] K. Whittington. Understanding the tbl divide; examining similarities and differences between writing and programming. In *TBL Conference*, June 2007.

[19] N. Zgheib, J. Simaan, and R. Sabra. Using team-based learning to teach pharmacology to second year medical students improves student performance. *Medical Teacher*, 32:130–135, 2010.

## APPENDIX

## A. COURSE LEARNING OUTCOMES

The following are the course learning outcomes:

**A.** Identify the different phases of problem solving.

**B .** Analyze simple problems, design algorithms and write them in pseudo-code or flowcharts.

**C.** Develop, test, and debug computer programs.

**D.** Apply the concepts of variables, data types, input, output, expressions, assignment, the processes of decision-making and repetition.

**E.** Apply the concepts of modular programming using pre-defined and user-defined functions.

**F.** Use the concept of arrays and apply them to practical and real problems.

# IT Problem Solving: An Implementation of Computational Thinking in Information Technology

Jaime L'Heureux
Bunker Hill Community College
250 New Rutherford Avenue
Boston, MA 02129
617-228-3229
jllheure@bhcc.mass.edu

Deborah Boisvert
University of Massachusetts Boston
100 Morrissey Boulevard
Boston, Massachusetts 02125
617-287-7295
deborah.boisvert@umb.edu

Robert Cohen
Wellesley High School
50 Rice Street
Wellesley, MA 02481
781-446-6290
robert_cohen@wellesley.k12.ma.us

Kamaljeet Sanghera
George Mason University
4400 University Drive
Fairfax, VA 22030
703-993-1547
ksangher@gmu.edu

## ABSTRACT

This paper describes the implementation of information technology problem-solving constructs and scenarios designed to cultivate computational thinking in information technology education at the college level via a course entitled "IT Problem Solving." A project of Broadening Advanced Technological Connections (BATEC), these scenarios were developed by a team of researchers under the auspices of an NSF CPATH grant focusing on adapting Computational Thinking as defined by Jeanette Wing into a more applied framework in partnership with and validated by a broad set of Information Technology (IT) professionals. The methodologies used within this highly successful course at Bunker Hill Community College may be of interest to other departments with existing IT programs that would like to take advantage of the strengths of the problem solving approach.

## Categories and Subject Descriptors

K.3.2 [**Computers and Education**]: Computer & Information Science Education – *information technology education.*

## General Terms

Experimentation, Design

## Keywords

Information Technology (IT), Problem Solving, Computational Thinking, CPATH, Education, Curriculum Development.

## 1. INTRODUCTION

Jeanette Wing, Jan Cuny and Larry Snyder have defined Computational Thinking as "the thought processes involved in formulating problems and their solutions so that the solutions are represented in a form that can be effectively carried out by an information-processing agent." [1] Computational thinking has been defined in a very traditional computer science centric way,

using terms such as recursion, abstraction, algorithms and the like. While many of our IT-centric industry partners are in fact formally trained in Computer Science, when we discussed these concepts with them, they considered this to be "education-speak". They did not use these terms to describe similar capabilities in their typical daily routine nor did they feel that the terms reflected the broader skill set needed as an IT Professional.

We decided to work with our business partners to adapt Jeanette Wing's framework [2] to a more information technology-oriented and business-friendly format. To accomplish this, we looked at a common business scenario and broke it down into its relevant parts from needs assessment, to process and design specifications, to implementation activities, to quality control, and finally to project evaluation. We then looked at the capabilities that were needed to achieve the outcomes desired, which resulted in the following framework of computational thinking, which we believe to be more applied and broad-based so that it can be used across computing and other disciplines.

IT Problem Solving that develops analogous computational thinking capabilities involves:

- **Logical Thinking** – Creatively develop, select and test relevant hypotheses
  - Asks probing questions to uncover details of the problem
  - Clearly defines the problem
  - Defines clear success criteria for the project including measurable objectives

- **Strategizing** – Ability to anticipate and evaluate potential outcomes
  - Anticipates and evaluates the effects of various design options
  - Makes design decisions based on rational criteria

- **Abstract Thinking** – Ability to find appropriate level of detail to define and solve a problem
  - Decomposes a problem into component parts
  - Understands the relationships between components

- **Procedural Thinking** – Ability to select and execute appropriate steps to solve a problem

- o Identifies the steps and processes required to solve a problem
- o Identifies the sequence of steps including possible decisions and branching
- o Understands normal and exceptional behaviors of a solution
- **Optimizing** – Ability to analyze processes for optimal efficiency and use of resources
  - o Understands available resources
  - o Develops a solution that uses only available resources
  - o Measures and adapts the solution to optimize resource utilization
- **Iterative Refinement** – Process refinement with the goal of improving quality or precision.
  - o Measures and evaluates solutions against the success criteria
  - o Adjusts the design and implementation as needed

We have used this definition in the design of a problem-based course; it informs both the problems that we have developed and the problem-solving methodology we teach. In addition, it is these definitional constructs that are used at the end of the projects via a computational thinking survey to measure, through self-reporting, how students are building computational thinking skills while they are solving a particular problem in the course.

Further, we believe that our course can be an alternative IT-focused way to deliver the AP CS Principles course that is under development. In section 4, we present a mapping of the projects that make up our course to the learning objectives of CS Principles.

## 2. COURSE DESCRIPTION

### 2.1 Course Overview

The course is offered specifically to Computer Information Technology majors as an alternative to an existing required introductory class. The course meets in two 75-minute sessions per week during a 15-week semester. The time devoted to each topic is measured in weeks consisting of two 75-minute classes and the associated time students spend working outside of the class meetings.

Specifically, this course gives students hands-on experience in the world of modern information technology (IT). Several IT concepts are introduced that provide a basis for further study in information technology. Students work on a number of problems that will give perspectives on areas of IT including but not limited to: visual programming, mobile device programming, and desktop security. Students leave the course with an understanding of PBL, the components of modern IT systems, basic programming concepts, and the scope of knowledge needed to become an IT professional. The benefit to students is that PBL enhances employability through the development of skills such as critical and analytical thinking, problem solving, communication and teamwork. These are necessary skills for the ever-changing technology driven, data-saturated world we live in.

### 2.2 Course Objectives

The major goal of the course is to have students acquire a technical overview of modern information technology. Students who successfully complete this course should be able to:

- Understand many aspects of Information Technology and their role in modern Information Technology implementations
- Understand Problem Based Learning (PBL) and the PBL Lifecycle
- Work in teams to produce solutions.
- Research and learn about technology.
- Present solutions in writing and spoken presentations
- Demonstrate knowledge of key IT foundational skills
- Demonstrate programming concepts through program execution

### 2.3 Methods of Instruction

PBL is a student-centered pedagogy in which they learn about a subject in the context of complex and realistic problems. Students identify what they already know, what they need to know, and how and where to access new information that may lead to resolution of the problem. Students "learn how to analyze, criticize and select from alternative sources of information and courses of action; how to think about problems that may have more than one viable solution; how to work together with those of differing views; and how to confront and act upon problems and situations in constructive and creative ways." [3] As such, the instructor acts as a facilitator of learning who provides appropriate scaffolding of that process and measures student success via outcome based assessments. This methodology is highly transferable and builds the cognitive ability to apply knowledge gained to any situation a student might encounter. Such knowledge is highly valuable because it demonstrates more than rote memorization of an application's functions.

Problems are the main focus of all course activities, including discussions and labs. There are 7 problems introduced during the semester, including a final project. A typical week includes:

- A warm up problem solving exercise
- A follow-up discussion analyzing what problem solving method steps were needed or used to solve the warm up problem
- A short discussion that introduces a problem and some brief tutorial on how to approach this sort of problem
- Lab time where students work on the problem
- A wrap-up discussion where students address their own and each others' solutions

Grades are based on performance in the group and individual problems, and on deliverables generated during the problem.

### 2.4 Problem Solving Methodology

A general and widely accepted definition of problem solving is: *Problem solving is (goal directed) thinking and action in situations for which no routine solution procedure is available. The problem solver has a more or less well-defined goal, but does not immediately know how to reach it. The incongruence of goals and admissible operators constitutes a problem. The understanding of the problem situation and its step-by-step transformation based on planning and reasoning, constitute the process of problem solving.* [4]

Students are presented with the STAIR methodology [5] for solving problems as a guide to help them understand the steps needed to deconstruct problems. Specifically STAIR represents the following steps, S- State the problem; T- Tools; A - Approach or Algorithm; I – Implementation; and R – Refinement.

## 2.5 Problem 1: Eportfolio Creation (1 Week)

During the course each student is asked to create a personal electronic portfolio using a tool called Digication. After some basic introduction and instruction in Digication, students create their portfolio by making choices in the setting up, layout, and design of their personal Digication page. Student Digication pages must include student names on their home pages, several photos/graphics, several text modules, and at least one video.

Further, students also read and discuss a book called "The Last Lecture" by Randy Pausch. For this project students read the first two sections: I. The Last Lecture and II. Really Achieving Your Childhood Dreams. As they read each chapter they are asked to consider each chapter's lessons and how to apply them to their own life. Their reflections need to include thoughtful personal insight as it relates to Randy's story. They are also asked to consider topics such as:

- *Why has this lecture/book struck a chord with so many people?*
- *Where is the speaker/author "coming from"?*
- *What are my childhood dreams? How might I achieve them?*
- *What were the dreams my parents had and how did they fulfill them?*
- *Who are mentors I can turn to? What lessons have they taught me?*
- *And what wisdom would I choose to impart to the world if it was my last chance? What are the lessons of my own life?*

## 2.6 Problem 2: Mobile Application Development (3 Weeks)

In this project, students use the mobile application development tool App Inventor (www.appinventor.mit.edu) to make an application that helps solve a problem that either performs a calculation function or teaches someone something in an interactive way. Students are instructed to imagine a mobile application idea and to develop and create at least one PowerPoint slide to demonstrate their idea. Students then present the idea to their classmates and the class votes to select the best ideas for creation. The students with the selected ideas choose the classmates they would like to work to develop the application.

To encourage students to explore App Inventor's features, the apps must meet or exceed the following technical requirements. Apps must include at a minimum…

- three objects that you place in the App
- three interactive items
- object motion and/or color change

Each individual in the group assesses themselves and the other members of the group. Grades are issued by the professor using the assessments. Deliverables for the project include:

- A Mobile Application Idea as one PowerPoint slide
- A developed prototype of a Mobile App
- A journal entry that describes their experience. In particular, answer the following questions:
  - What problem are you solving with your App?
  - What did you learn working on this project?
  - What was difficult working with App Inventor? How did you overcome these difficulties?

## 2.7 Problem 3: Animated Storytelling with Programming (2.5 Weeks)

Students are asked to use Alice (www.alice.org) to make an animation that completes the following story:

> "*Alice is shocked to find Bob doing something completely unexpected…*"

Their animation should tell a story of two or more characters (at least Alice and Bob). There needs to be recognizable plot elements:

- *Exposition* – telling of the history and motivations of the characters
- *Conflict* – a problem that one or more of the characters must solve
- *Climax* - what happens when the conflict is resolved
- *Resolution* – the end of the story

To encourage students to explore Alice features, their project must meet or exceed the following technical requirements. Their world must include at a minimum…

- three objects that they place in the world
- three loops, two of them different types of loops
- camera and object motion
- run at least 60 seconds long

Deliverables for this problem include:

- A Storyboard for their animation.
- Their Alice world (the .a2w file)
- A journal entry that describes their experience. In particular, answer the following questions:
  a. What story are you telling with your animation?
  b. What are the actors? How do they interact?
  c. What did you learn working on this project?
  d. What was difficult working with Alice? How did you overcome these difficulties?

## 2.8 Problem 4: Green IT Research (3 Weeks)

The Green IT project has four parts. Firstly, students discuss what they know about sustainability and Green IT to establish a beginning point for student understanding of the topic. Then the students are shown a video and presented materials which seek to define Green IT for them, including introducing cloud computing.

Next, students complete a laboratory experiment in which they use watt power meters to measure the amount of energy that is being consumed by computers, monitors, printers, and other electronic devices and appliances throughout the college and their homes. This data is entered into an Excel spreadsheet from which students calculate the cost of supplying energy to these various devices on an annual basis, and generate an informative chart. In addition, students analyze the data, report their findings and provide recommendations indicating how the college might save money and decrease energy consumption, thereby increasing the college's commitment to become more sustainable.

In addition, students visit a local electronics recycling facility to learn about challenges and procedures specific to electronic waste, the cost and benefits to sustainability of recycling, and the impact to the earth of failing to recycle these items. After this visit, students are assigned a reflective writing piece about their experience at the recycling center. Further students are given an assignment to create a Word document recommending a policy for the disposal of outdated computer equipment for the college.

## 2.9 Problem 5: IT Career Exploration (1 Week)

Though students are just beginning their college career, they are reminded that each class they take and experience they have all contributes to a bigger picture. Like Randy Pausch says, they should be working toward achieving their childhood dreams. So, students are charged with finding a job posting in the Boston Area that they are interested in as a future career. They are to research the education, experience, and certifications necessary for success in this position. They need to use websites such as Monster.com, hotjobs.com, indeed.com, etc. to locate the job posting. Students are also challenged to research the company, its business sector and the job forecast for that position.

Students are then asked to complete the "Do What You Are" which can be found at: www.collegescope.com/bhcc. Students then look at the analysis combined with the job search they had just performed and consider whether they still want to pursue the same career opportunities or if their mind has been changed. Students are then encouraged to write in their journal about what they discovered about themselves and their career path as a result of the "Do What You Are" analysis and career research. Students are then told to be sure that they tie their writing to both items specifically to be successful with this writing assignment.

Working with their Success Coach, students are instructed to write an educational plan that will meet the job requirements of their selected career and then work in partnership to register for the next semester's classes. In parallel, students continue to read and complete "The Last Lecture" by Randy Pausch: III. Adventures….and Lessons Learned; IV. Enabling the Dreams of Others; V. It's About How to Live Your Life; and VI. Final Remarks. Students then reflect and journal on their reading and include a thoughtful personal insight as it relates to Randy's story.

## 2.10 Problem 6: Desktop Security Investigation (3.5 Weeks)

In this project students are asked by the College's IT Department to design best practice procedures for the securing of information on each student's computer and to ensure that each student's computer's resources are at the correct security level to access the college's network. The project contains four parts.

In the first part of the project, students must consider what they know about security already, what they don't know, what they need to know, and how to fill the gaps. Students must do this by brainstorming ideas as a consulting team and use Wordle (www.wordle.net) as an analysis tool. Students must then organize and categorize those ideas into a concise, coherent document. This deliverable must be submitted to the client within the client's timeline and delivery method, for their review and approval.

The second part of the project asks students to provide the client with a written proposal for further research and exploration in one of four categories:

- Access Control
- Protecting against Attacks
- Protecting against Data Loss
- Versioning, Patches and Updates

The class then breaks into four subgroups and aligns themselves with one of the four categories. Students develop and deliver a proposal for further research into the four categories, specifically identifying security threats in the category with prioritization of the likelihood of those threats occurring.

The third part of the project asks students to propose three viable solutions that work within constraints of the resources (time, money, personnel, network bandwidth, etc). They are then asked to propose three solutions that the client will review.

Further, the students are informed that the client would like to see written proof of testing that shows their solution in action. The document that they will provide to the client will contain step-by-step instructions along with screenshots demonstrating that the solution is effective.

Students must also reflect on what they have learned from this task by discussing a series of questions with their team and also writing about it in their journal. These questions included aspects regarding working in teams including team dynamics and interpersonal relationships, progress and process management, decision-making, prioritization, testing and documentation.

In part four, the last and final step, students are instructed to use the vulnerability identification and testing and analysis they have done already to develop a handbook for computer security procedures. This will serve as a guide that will help students and campus IT services stay safer. Most colleges use a student handbook to inform students about appropriate behaviors on campus, to alert students to important college policies or procedures and to protect both students and the college IT systems from potentially dangerous or illegal activities. The areas that were identified earlier serve as the four sections in the handbook:

- Access Control
- Protecting against Attacks
- Protecting against Data Loss
- Versioning, Patches and Updates

Each student group takes ownership of a section. Students need to develop the content for that section and make sure that it complies with the handbook requirements.

## 3. LESSONS LEARNED

### 3.1 Computational Thinking (CT) Survey

During the course, computational thinking was measured by using a survey generated from research under an NSF grant entitled *Advancing the Successful IT Student through Enhanced Computational Thinking* (ASSECT - CCF 0939089). This project brought together a consortium of community colleges and associated 4-year universities spanning five states (Massachusetts, represented by Bunker Hill Community College and University of Massachusetts Boston; Virginia, represented by Northern Virginia Community College and George Mason University; Indiana, represented by Ivy Tech Community College and Purdue University Calumet; Colorado, represented by Cameron University and California, represented by City College of San Francisco) to explore an innovative process that adapts the IT Body of Knowledge outcomes developed by the Special Interest Group for Information Technology Education (SIGITE) of the Association for Computing Machinery to Wing's Computational Thinking taxonomy. The project team took the underlying research on computational thinking and worked with industry partners to describe behaviors that demonstrate computational thinking in the context of information technology and develop 20 scenarios that can used to build these capabilities.

Outcomes measurement was tied to Principled Assessment Designs for Inquiry (PADI) (funded previously by NSF) which produced a body of statistically valid, evidence-centered data. Instructor training on PADI assessment was used to support or disprove the hypothesis that the treatment produces reliable improvements in computational thinking over conventional instruction. At the beginning of each term, students will be given a pretest with cognitive and computational thinking elements. At the end of instruction, students will complete a posttest and randomly selected students will also participate in a think-aloud exercise. Quantitative analyses will be conducted using exploratory factor analysis and analyses of covariance (ANCOVA) comparing teaching students on each posttest using the respective pretest as the covariate.

Further, the inability to have control and treatment groups, required utilizing a quasi-experimental design. "With quasi-experimental studies, it may not be possible to convincingly demonstrate a causal link between the treatment condition and observed outcomes. This is particularly true if there are confounding variables that cannot be controlled or accounted for." [6] Thus, the computational thinking survey was an anonymous self report study used by students to measure computational thinking behavior. Using the descriptions of these behaviors, the project created a survey to correlate computational thinking attributes with student learning.

The computational thinking survey asked students whether or not they engaged in the behavior and to explain how this was exemplified through their work. Questions included:

1. I asked probing questions and uncovered details to better understand the problem.
3. I clearly defined the problem.
5. I clearly defined what I needed to do and how my objectives would be measured.
7. I anticipated and evaluated the effects of various solution options.
9. I made decisions about possible solutions based on relevant criteria.
11. One technique of solving problems is to identify and write down the key parts of the problem (deconstruction) and then propose actions to address those parts. I deconstructed the problem into component parts.
13. I diagrammed or otherwise recorded the relationships between the parts (from above).
15. I recorded possible strategies for addressing the parts (from above).
17. I identified and recorded the steps required to solve the problem.
19. I identified typical and exceptional (or different) solutions to the problem. I measured and evaluated my solution against the success criteria.
21. I identified available and potential resources to address the problem.
23. I developed a solution that uses feasible resources.
25. I analyzed solutions to determine the optimal resources needed.
27. I measured and evaluated my solution against the success criteria.
29. I adjusted the solution and modified the implementation as needed.

## 3.2 Survey Results

For each question we analyzed whether students reported strongly agreeing with or agreeing with the statements with regard to computational thinking skills employed in the problems measured (Problems 2 and 3). Please note that Problem 6 will be measured also, but that data was not available at the time of the submission deadline for this paper.

Every question asked averaged at least a 50% response rating for strongly agreed or agreed. Therefore, it is reasonable to conclude that students feel that they are using the computational thinking skills in solving the problems presented in the course. Further, Questions 3, 17, 21, and 29 received an average response for strongly agree and agree by students of over 80%. This seems to indicate that students feel the computational thinking skills of defining the problem, identifying a sequence of steps including possible decisions and branching, understanding available resources, and being given the opportunity to adjust the solution and implementation as needed are successfully being learned and employed to solve the problems presented in the course.

For Problem 2, Questions 3 and 27 also ranked remarkably high with close to 90% of students reporting that they strongly agreed or agreed with the questions. It appears that the Mobile App Development problem pushed students to clearly define what they needed to do and understand how success of their objectives would be measured, and that they felt they were given the ability to measure and evaluate their solution against the success criteria.

However, in Problem 3, these questions only achieved a result of 75% and 62% respectively. Thus, Problem 2 seemed to allow students to achieve a depth of understanding in several computational thinking skills. Whereas, it seems as if Problem 3 had a wider reach across the computational thinking skills. Specifically, in Problem 3, 11 out of the 15 questions received a strongly agreed or agreed response by more than 2/3 of the class.

## 4. CONNECTION TO CS PRINCIPLES

As we have demonstrated, students experience a strong foundation in computational thinking through IT Problem Solving. We also have found a strong connection between IT Problem Solving and the proposed new AP CS Principles course [7]. The aim of that course is to provide a general education introduction to the "Big Ideas" in Computing. The Big Ideas are:

I. Computing is a creative human activity that engenders innovation and promotes exploration.
II. Abstraction reduces information and detail to focus on concepts relevant to understanding and solving problems.
III. Data and information facilitate the creation of knowledge.
IV. Algorithms are tools for developing and expressing solutions to computational problems.
V. Programming is a creative process that produces computational artifacts.
VI. Digital devices, systems, and the networks that interconnect them enable and foster computational approaches to solving problems.
VII. Computing enables innovation in other fields including mathematics, science, social science, humanities, arts, medicine, engineering, and business.

While numerous variations of CS Principles courses have been created and offered as pilots across the country, all have been developed using traditional computer science constructs. There is a significant need to expand that process to a more broad-based

**Figure 1. Coverage of CS Principles Learning Objectives**

| IT Problem Solving Projects | CS Principles Big Ideas and Learning Objectives | | | | | | | | | | | | | | | | | | | | | | | | | | | | | | |
|---|---|---|---|---|---|---|---|---|---|---|---|---|---|---|---|---|---|---|---|---|---|---|---|---|---|---|---|---|---|---|---|
| | I | | | | II | | | | | III | | | | | IV | | | | V | | | | | VI | | | | VII | | | |
| | 1 | 2 | 3 | 4 | 5 | 6 | 7 | 8 | 9 | 10 | 11 | 12 | 13 | 14 | 15 | 16 | 17 | 18 | 19 | 20 | 21 | 22 | 23 | 24 | 25 | 26 | 27 | 28 | 29 | 30 | 31 |
| Eportfolio | | | | | | | | | | | | | | | | | | | | | | | | | | | | | | | |
| Mobile Apps | | | | | | | | | | | | | | | | | | | | | | | | | | | | | | | |
| Animated Story Telling | | | | | | | | | | | | | | | | | | | | | | | | | | | | | | | |
| Green IT | | | | | | | | | | | | | | | | | | | | | | | | | | | | | | | |
| Career Exploration/Reflection | | | | | | | | | | | | | | | | | | | | | | | | | | | | | | | |
| Desktop Security Integration | | | | | | | | | | | | | | | | | | | | | | | | | | | | | | | |
| Final Project | | | | | | | | | | | | | | | | | | | | | | | | | | | | | | | |

computing approach while maintaining the integrity of the underlying constructs. IT Problem Solving takes a more novel and applied approach to achieve a comparable outcome. This course stresses the typical types of problems that IT professionals deal with on a routine basis – ones that are contextual, adaptable, involve inter-relationships, and are both systematic and strategic in nature.

Each of the Big Ideas is accompanied by learning objectives that provide guidance for how the "Big Ideas" can be conveyed. Figure 3 shows the coverage of the 30 learning objectives by the IT Problem Solving projects [8]. It is important to note that these learning objectives are covered multiple times throughout the IT Problem Solving course. For this reason, this course should be considered as another option for developing strong computational thinking attributes in students.

The only divergence from the current CS Principles pilots is a weaker coverage of the Big Idea IV, algorithms. This is not surprising, since the focus of information technology is on the application, integration and optimization of, rather than the development of software. In order to extend CS Principles to additional audiences of students studying IT, further research is indicated to determine a balance that will achieve the necessary skill sets that will enable them to be successful in their pursuit of more broad-based computing careers.

# 5. CONCLUSIONS

Information Technology Problem Solving was developed to implement problem solving as pedagogy and to employ some of the scenarios developed for the cultivation of computational thinking in informational technology done through an NSF CPATH grant. This was done to begin to ascertain whether computational thinking and the computer science principles could be conveyed to, and fashioned in, information technology students. We assert that this course has served to demonstrate that these can in fact be implemented in information technology curriculum and the implementation has proven to enhance computational thinking skills as reported by the students, as well as having the added benefits of increased student engagement and connection to the material.

Further research is indicated to determine whether development of computational thinking attributes is contingent on either pedagogical or content approaches, or whether a combination of the two, in IT Problem Solving.

# 6. REFERENCES

[1] Jan Cuny, Larry Snyder, and Jeannette M. Wing. "Demystifying Computational Thinking for Non-Computer Scientists," work in progress, 2010

[2] Wing, Jeanette. *Computational Thinking*, Communications of the ACM, March 2006, Vol.49, No. 3, p. 34 and *Computational Thinking,* PowerPoint presentation, http://www.imageofcomputing.com/pdf/Computational_Thin king.pdf

[3] Sally Glen and Kay Wilkie (eds). *Problem-Based Learning in Nursing: A New Model for a New Context?*, Basingstoke, Macmillan, 2000, p.12

[4] Reeff, J. P. (ed.), *New Assessment Tools for Cross-Curricular Competencies in the Domain of Problem Solving*, 1999, http://www.ppsw.rug.nl/~peschar/TSE.pdf

[5] Harris, A, *The STAIR Process and Searching the WWW*, http://cs.iupui.edu/~aharris/mmcc/mod2/abwww6.html

[6] Rossi, Peter Henry; Mark W. Lipsey, Howard E. Freeman (2004). *Evaluation: A Systematic Approach, 7th Ed.*. SAGE. pp. 237. ISBN 978-0-7619-0894-4.

[7] The College Board. *Computer Science: Principles:* Computational Thinking Practices, Big Ideas, Key Concepts, and Supporting Concepts, 2011, http://www.collegeboard.com/prod_downloads/computerscie nce/ComputationalThinkingCS_Principles.pdf

[8] The College Board. *Computer Science: Principles:* Computational Thinking Practices, Big Ideas and Key Concepts, Learning Objectives and Evidence Statements, 2011,http://www.collegeboard.com/prod_downloads/comput erscience/Learning_CSPrinciples.pdf

# The Pedagogical Value of "Eduployment": Information Technology Internships in Rural Areas

Joseph Elarde
Heartlanding Consulting
Hoffman Estates, IL 60192
jelarde@acm.org

Chong Fatt-Fei
Segi College
Malaysia
ffchong@segi.edu.my

## ABSTRACT

Providing internships for Information Technology students represents a significant issue to institutions of higher education located in rural areas where few if any organizations exist with sufficient resources to support such programs within a manageable transportation distance. This paper documents our experiences with an approach we refer to as "Eduployment" a program designed to address in part the rural internship problem.

In this paper we describe the planning, development, structure, implementation, and experiences with a faculty/student managed, University aligned, grant supported, Information Technology consulting firm's first two years of operation, evaluating effectiveness from the educator and student perspectives.

This program contributed to changes in our Information Technology internship program, provided employment for students, and positively influenced many projects and assignments in the Information Technology program's courseware.

With the changes we have observed, that students are better prepared for employment, understand the importance of customer service, meeting deadlines, time management, and working in teams. Thus far, all student graduates involved in the program have secured employment; moreover, 90% of the students stated that the Eduployment program was of value and prepared them for employment.

## Categories and Subject Descriptors

K 3.2 [Computer and Information Science Education]: Industry-Education Relationships, Student Research/Capstones/Internships, and Education – Experience Report

## General Terms

Management, Experimentation

## Keywords

Information Technology Internships, Information Technology Consulting, Startups, Survey

## 1. INTRODUCTION

Internships offer Information Technology students valuable practical work experience, insight into IT operations, team and reporting relationships, and important career networking opportunities.

However, facilitating internships for Information Technology students represents a significant issue to institutions of higher education located in rural areas where few if any organizations exist with sufficient resources to support such programs within a manageable transportation distance. For example, in cases where the college/university is located in a rural agricultural area, there may be little opportunity outside of the college/university itself to provide internships. In addition, as the practice of off-shoring expands, sending more Information Technology jobs overseas, it is reasonable to conclude that there will be less interest in providing internships by companies and other organizations that have the resources. Why support a robust domestic internship program, if the Information Technology jobs are to be developed overseas.

Internships provide students with practical work experience that cannot be fully simulated in the classroom, students gain an understanding of employment in the discipline, preparing them for the rigors of a daily work environment, and allowing them to become acquainted with reporting relationships in an organization.

The ACM SIGITE group, in their ground breaking Information Technology Computing Curricula Guide [4], stresses the importance and pervasiveness of industry-based and classroom based experiential learning. Moreover, research [1] suggests that student internships are a means of developing a feeling of self-efficacy within the student which can lead to a more productive career.

For businesses, internships are often a major part of their recruitment process, a way to market their organization to prospective labor force, and perhaps most importantly internships are an example of "try before you buy" form of prospective employee evaluation. In addition, the feedback a student receives from the partnering business or organization can help students secure employment after graduation and improve their effectiveness as employees. This type of feedback combined with the use of a skills inventory can help students, mentors, and faculty assess the capabilities of the intern and guide further instruction and certification learning [3].

Prior to 2007, the only computer related program our University offered was a Management Information Systems (MIS) major in the portfolio of programs provided by the Business Division. Our assignment was to construct, build, and grow an Information Technology program derived from the ACM's Information Technology 2005 curriculum guidelines. Since we were a startup program, no relationships with external organizations had been established, thus, we were on our own to explore establishing relationships and/or other alternatives.

Although there are realistically several potential approaches to addressing this issue, after exploring the development of the traditional business relationship approach, it became clear that the feasible opportunities were limited in the area. The rural location, miles from an organization needing and capable of supporting paid internships presented a significant challenge.

As a result, our solution was to establish and operate a project based not-for-profit Information Technology consulting firm primarily to employ, as a substitute for external internships, Information Technology, Management, and Marketing majors; however, other disciplines were also considered potential candidates for Eduployment positions. To augment our academic instruction, whenever possible, we leveraged the training and experience derived from the Eduployment enterprise, including these experiences in our Information Technology classroom discussions.

Creating the organization required the development of an entrepreneurial organic corporation, independent yet aligned with the University, an effective management structure, and well defined business processes that utilize faculty, students and some graduates as the management and labor force. However, unlike the predominately student controlled business model proposed in [5] a combination of faculty, graduates, and experienced senior students would assume C level officer and Chief Architect roles.

The strategic plan for the organization targeted IT services within the University as well as focused on local and potentially regional market segments underserved by existing IT services.

Since students gain valuable industry experience as a tradeoff for higher wages, the lower labor costs, supplemented by potential grant funds, enable the Eduployment firm to target small rural businesses and other not-for-profit organizations, which could neither afford to establish their own IT organizations nor web sites. Paper [6] in its discussion of the benefits to industry, discusses how "little or no capital investment" is needed. Thus the focus is servicing a market untouched by professional IT consulting firms. Moreover, if firms are employing outsourced services to access a lower cost labor market, the Eduployment firm can compete based on price on a limited scale in this market space. Brian Janz, et.al., [1] discuss using student labor for "onshoring" with an external consulting firm in contrast to our internal firm.

Section 2 describes the business plan, strategy, and organizational structure. Section 3 reviews faculty experiences, learning outcomes and value assessments. Section 4 presents and evaluates the student survey and feedback. And finally, section 5 provides our summary and conclusions.

# 2. BUSINESS PLAN AND STRUCTURE

Since this is an experience paper, we outline our approach to constructing and organizing this enterprise. In order to sell the Eduployment concept to others, a business plan was developed to describe the concept, nature, vision, mission, objectives, services, market, organization structure, strategy, and financials. From the business plan document, a presentation was created to describe the concepts to the University administration, local political leaders, other faculty, and students.

To sell the plan, we adapted the base presentation to the interests of each constituency. For example, administration officials are interested in the overall benefits to the University and community, marketing benefits, and costs; political leaders value community benefits to local businesses and the labor force; faculty are focused on the pedagogical value and faculty involvement requirements; and finally, students are interested in how Eduployment could help them with their careers.

The business plan needs to clearly state, why the proposed organization is of value, how it will be implemented, and how much it will cost.

## 2.1 MISSION OBJECTIVES AND GOALS

The mission statement communicates who we are, what we intend to do, and summarizes of our operating guidelines. We used the following mission statement:

*To provide quality Information Technology business information solutions, reliable and professional Technical Support, and unparalleled Customer Service through the application of ITIL best practices and principles of Quality Service Management, to provide our customers with rates that are competitive with off-shoring using student labor, and to embrace sound and ethical business practices.*

The organizational objectives we used are as follows:

- The Eduployment organization is created as an extension to Information Technology educational program designed to enhance the learning outcomes and employability of our students.
- The organization must provide a benefit to the University and community by further developing a skilled labor force that is capable of providing information technology services to select University, business, and not-for-profit clients.
- The organization should offer an alternative to outsourcing overseas or "off-shoring" by offering competitive labor costs, enabling increased usage of Information Technology in the local economy, and reducing "brain drain" by developing and retaining skilled information technologists in the area, an important issue for many rural communities.

Goals describe specific measurements to be accomplished within an identified time horizon. We selected the following initial goals:

- Complete a minimum of 6 information technology projects in our first year of operation.
- Develop and execute a marketing plan to communicate the nature of the Eduployment organization and the value of e-commerce to local and regional business.
- Complete a minimum of two grant applications to help fund pro-bono work.
- Return a minimum of 5% of generated revenue to the IT scholarship fund.

## 2.2 INITIAL SERVICES

We proposed the following initial services: web site development, legacy system migration and conversion, information technology infrastructure implementation and project management, information technology research, training, and PC repair. See Table 1 below for the list of services and classifications based upon complexity.

**Table 1: List of Services**

| Service | Class A | Class B |
|---|---|---|
| Web Development Services | Create, test, deploy, and turnover to the client. | Create, test, deploy, host, and maintain the site. |
| Legacy System Migration and Application Conversion | Migrate an application from an existing platform to a more modern and cost effective platform. | Convert existing application source code from a legacy language such as Cobol to Java, or C++. |
| Information Technology Infrastructure Implementation and project management | Plan, manage, and implement a project to setup a network infrastructure. | Use ITIL best practices to establish infrastructure. |
| Information Technology Research | Plan and manage a research project to identify IT solutions for a client. | Complete research and implementation project. |
| Information Technology Training | Provide one time training courses to clients for common office applications. | Provide ongoing training courses to clients for common office applications |
| PC Repair | Hardware software installations. | Malware removal. |

## 2.3 MARKET ANALYSIS

The market analysis describes the targeted area and customers. We specifically targeted rural small businesses and not-for-profit organizations without resources and expertise to exploit information technology. In addition, we made services available to university students such as PC repair and malware removal.

As far as being an alternative to off-shoring, our capabilities limited us to small web development and programming projects. Off-shoring, while beneficial in some cases [2], has resulted in the loss of thousands of American jobs to overseas outsourcers as companies seek to lower labor costs. Our concern is that the benefits will diminish over time, as living standards improve overseas. When the inevitable cost increases occur, businesses will have no choice, but to continue with the off-shore provider since it may take years for the American technology labor force to recover sufficiently to compete.

Beyond the issue raised above, community leaders in rural areas are acutely aware of the problems caused by "brain-drain" and the resultant job loss to the area. Due to the lack of technology jobs in rural areas, frequently the best students relocate to the cities to pursue their careers. Nevertheless, life in rural areas does have its benefits; rural areas can provide a low stress quality of life and a lower cost of living. The strategy is therefore to combine the lower cost of living, the not-for-profit status of the organization, and reduced student labor costs to be price competitive.

To highlight and summarize this concept, promoting in-shoring support for American workers and assisting our nation's students, we developed a tagline and included it in our marketing materials to help motivate our students and generate support for the initiative. The tagline we used is as follows:

*For America and its students, don't off-shore, heartland.*

The message is simple – businesses help America, help students, don't go overseas with your business, and keep your business here in the heartland of America.

## 2.4 ORGANIZATIONAL STRUCTURE

We designed the organization to be relatively flat, functioning with four distinct levels: Chief Executive Officer/Chief Information Officer (CEO/CIO), Chief Operations Officer (COO), Chief Architects, and Consultants, operating as an independent subsidiary of the University, reporting to the Vice President of External Affairs (VPEA). The CEO/CIO position was staffed by faculty while students and/or graduates filled the lower three levels. We cannot over emphasize the importance of the COO position and hiring the correct person for the position. The COO is responsible for operations, marketing, human resources, time accounting, and overall project management and is the only position paid hourly; the other consultants and architects earn compensation by project. We recommend a student majoring in Information Technology with a minor in Business Management for the COO position. We were fortunate to recruit a non-traditional student for this role who had business management experience.

Faculty members, functioning as the CEO/CIO, were required to, in collaboration with the COO, design, develop, and document the organizational structure, education plan, policies, standards, and processes. We required daily updates on project status, weekly face-to-face meetings, and monthly employee recognition meetings. It is important to emphasize the consistent use of properly documented, client engagement processes, project plans, meeting project deadlines, quality standards, and project change management processes. Students need to learn the value of controlling the change, testing, and deployment process, without which, failure is almost assured. Unless properly instructed, students will generally apply changes directly to production systems. Assigning faculty members with business experience to leadership roles, allowed us to leverage this experience to educate students on the nature of work life in the Information Technology field, stressing the importance of team work, being on time, having a strong work ethic, developing quality solutions, following development guidelines/standards, meeting deadlines, professionalism, dress codes, and the importance of customer service. For compensation, faculty can draw from project overhead expenses, or receive overload pay.

Another key to success is student recruitment. Upper division students with the majority of their information technology courseware completed are better positioned to contribute to and benefit from the organization. Each consultant, upon hire, receives an educational plan / skills inventory that is used as a guide to schedule the consultant for specific projects. For example, if the student has completed course work in Web Development, the student consultant can be scheduled for a web development project; students that have completed course work in project management are eligible for project management assignments, etc. Consultants were encouraged to complete self-study courses to improve their skill levels and thereby become eligible for a larger set of projects; however, they were not paid for self-study, although this form of learning was strongly encouraged.

Each consultant was given a polo shirt with the company logo, a set of business cards, and instructed as far as organizational processes and policies during orientation. The business cards and polo shirt served to provide a certain distinction to students in the organization, recognizing them as part of the team and encouraging others to aspire to join the organization. The small investment in business cards, impressed many students, enhancing their self image and professionalism.

As the organization evolved, student consultants were required to maintain a B average their courseware. In the event a student's GPA fell below 3.00 for a term, they became ineligible to work on projects for the following term or until the minimum grade performance target was equaled or exceeded.

## 3. FACULTY EXPERIENCE

To sell the plan, we first received input from our department chair and approval to proceed to communicate the plan to the administration. In addition, we worked with our grant writing department to seek some startup funding. Since our computing department consisted of two faculty members, it was a fairly straight forward to develop the business plan, grant proposal, and presentation. We next scheduled a meeting with our Vice President of External Affairs (VPEA) to obtain his input (both positive and negative) regarding the plan and incorporated the VPEA's thoughts into the presentation and plan. This sequence was followed by a presentation to the president of the University. Be prepared to show a detail budget, a projected income statement over 3-5 years with and without external grant funding, and list space and utility requirements for the organization if the plan is to locate the organization with in the University. We were fortunate that our Eduployment initiative was aligned with a separate University program to assist local businesses so the VPEA and president readily approved the initiative. We were also fortunate to receive external grant funding enabling us to begin operations sooner and with a larger number of consultants on board; however, in our opinion, external is not an absolute requirement.

**Marketing services:** Upon receiving approval, a web site and document describing the mission and services provided by the Eduployment organization was developed from information included in the business plan. Our initial announcements consisted of a campus wide internal communication, and an externally directed University press release, describing the existence of the organization and services provided. We also joined local commerce groups and provided presentations when requested to their meeting attendees. We compiled a listing of local small businesses and not-for-profit organizations, prioritized some top candidate customers, and arranged a visit to start developing a potential relationship. Our goal was to complete 6 projects in the first year; however, by the end of the first year there were 39 major projects either complete or in process.

**Operations:** Working with student consultants presents several interesting challenges. Since most students are unfamiliar with how effective businesses operate, CIO/COO mentoring, process definition, and guidelines documentation are important tools used to convert raw student labor to an effective, organized, reliable, professional labor force – a significant challenge!

**Contracts and waivers:** It is highly recommended to develop customer contracts for web site development projects, web site maintenance, PC repairs, and other consulting work to document requirements and help avoid scope creep.

**Organization-Communications:** CIO/COO communications took place as needed, however, we found that at a minimum a weekly status/planning meeting was necessary to keep projects on track, prioritize work, and address issues. We scheduled monthly "all staff" meetings for announcing strategies, discussing progress, motivating employees, and recognizing achievements. Consultants that distinguished themselves, by meeting quality standards, project deadlines, and/or received positive customer feedback were awarded the "Jedi Knight" award for the month.

Documenting and communicating processes and guidelines is of critical importance, as the organization matured, the goal was to eventually document every repeating process. We documented and used the following processes and support information:

- Customer Engagement Process
- Marketing Process
- Hiring and other Human Resource processes
- Change management process
- Time accounting process
- PC repair process
- Web site development and implementation
- Server configurations

**Deadlines and Scope**: Not surprisingly, one of the greatest issues we faced concerned meeting project deadlines. The student experience involves many competing demands upon time, such that, many students find it difficult to effectively balance and prioritize their education, social, family, extracurricular, and work time. We of course emphasize that their education (classroom and study time) was to have priority over work; however, our students were required to choose Eduployment work over other obligations or not be eligible for project assignments. Moreover, students will often feel obligated to help customers without regard to project scope, and therefore, are hesitant to decline additional work requests beyond what was agreed by contract.

## 3.1 CUSTOMER EXPERIENCES

Comparing external and internal customers, internal campus customers were the most reasonable and forgiving of missed deadlines. Students that used the Eduployment organization services for PC repairs and malware removal seemed very relieved that an on campus service was available at a cost significantly below what they would find in their local consumer electronics store, typically less than $15/hr labor plus parts. PC repair and malware removal was very popular with our consultants due to the short turnaround time (in general) of the work effort, direct realization that you have helped a customer, and the satisfaction of working through and resolving a problem.

Although there were several internal web development projects, creating club web sites and personal sites for faculty and administrators proved to be the most suitable projects for the organization since they involve smaller less complex sites, are appropriate for template use, and more often than not, the content is readily available. However, the most significant internal project completed, combined Eduployment and capstone course work to research, plan, and implement a Help Center for the University.

We encountered far more problematic issues with external customer projects, but ultimately these issues resulted in valuable student learning experiences. While many small businesses and not-for-profits are interested in web sites supporting online transactions, few have the time, knowledge, financial resources, and the desire to commit to the development and maintenance of the site after is deployed regardless of the potential value. Consequently, the Eduployment organization needs to encourage and be prepared to manage the site for the customer, as well as, provide training to improve the likelihood of success. In our experience, pro-bono customers will attempt to take advantage of student consultants and the organization by assuming all work after the deployment is free in perpetuity.

The students and organization encountered unethical customers and other issues, and in the final analysis, even though the customer may violate terms of the development contract they are aware that the Eduployment organization will most likely not use a legal recourse to enforce the terms of the agreement. Nevertheless, problematic customer encounters are of tremendous value to the Eduployment organization and the academic program. Given these issues, students learn the negative impact of scope creep and why it is never appropriate to deliver code until at least 90% of the contract fees are paid, regardless the relationship.

# 4. STUDENT FEEDBACK

After our first year of operation we surveyed our student consultants and management regarding the value of the experience with the objective being to improve the organization for current and future students. The survey consisted of 31 information gathering questions; the following summarizes the 6 most important questions.

**Question 1:** How valuable do you believe working for our Eduployment organization will be to you when you seek employment after graduation?

**Fig. 1 Value of Eduployment**

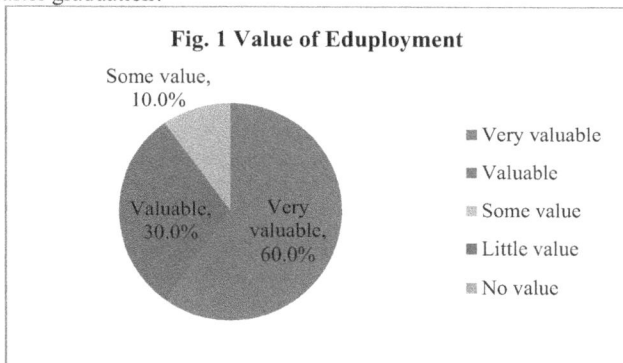

With regard to seeking employment, 60% of the surveyed consultants rated the experience very valuable. The ability to develop a resume of project involvements, position, and recognitions was deemed valuable by a majority of student consultants.

**Question 2:** How significant have the learning experiences been?

**Fig. 2 Value of Learning Experiences**

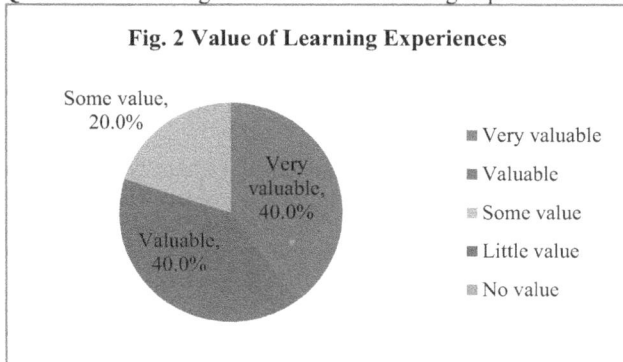

Of the surveyed consultants 40% rated their learning experiences as being very valuable. Beyond learning how an organization functions, how teams work, and working with customers, a common issue identified is that the organization's focus was limited to web development, PC repair, and project management when students were interested in other aspects of Information Technology specializations. To address this issue, we planned to create additional services to manage our own hosting environment, video productions, and training.

**Question 3:** To what significance level have you been able to identify areas where you need to improve your knowledge level?

**Fig. 3 Identifying Knowledge Deficiencies**

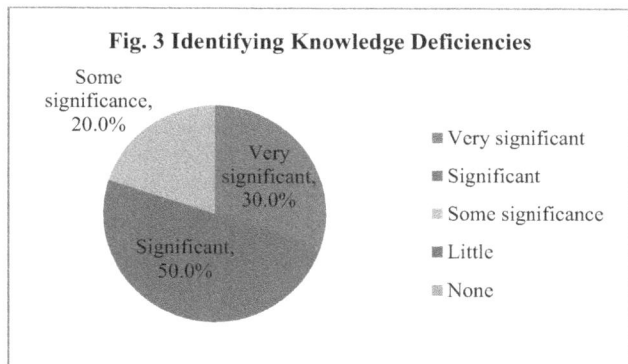

With regard to identifying knowledge deficiencies, only 30%, rated Eduployment as helping at the very significant level. As indicated, each consultant was given and required to maintain a personal skills inventory matrix enabling them to assess their knowledge level with regard to the organization's services. To address this issue, we planned a special presentation to cover the purpose and usage of the skills inventory matrix.

**Question 4:** To what significance level have you learned about customer service?

**Fig. 4 Customer Service Learning Outcomes**

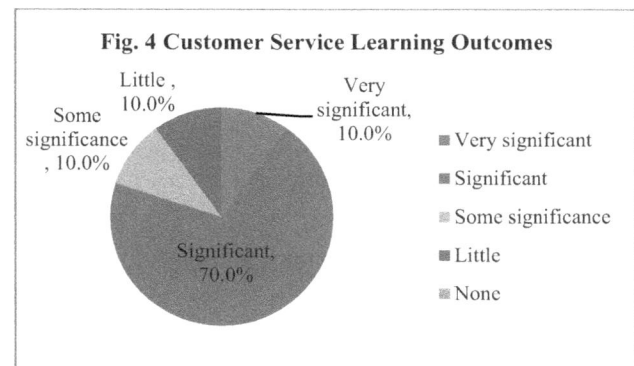

One of our most important objectives with regard to Eduployment is to educate our consultants about the importance of customer service. While 80% indicate an above average rating or better, this area can be improved. To address this issue, we planned a special presentation to show a customer service training video.

**Question 5:** To what level has Eduployment helped you better understand the importance of business etiquette and professionalism i.e., showing up, responding to emails on a timely basis, and conducting oneself in a professional manner?

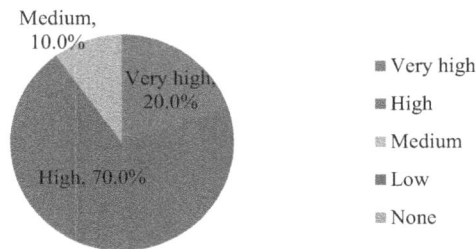
**Fig. 5 Business Etiquette & Professionalism**

Another important objective is to educate our consultants about the importance of business etiquette and professionalism. While 90% indicate an above average rating or better, this area can be improved through additional education at our all-staff meetings or implementing a program similar to one described in paper [7].

**Question 6:** To what level has Eduployment helped you better understand the importance of delivering quality products, on time, and within budget?

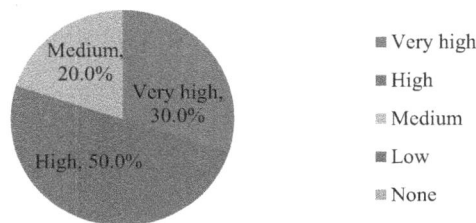
**Fig. 6 Project Quality Timeliness & Budget**

Question 6 assesses our employee's view of learning outcomes with regard to business operations and project management issues of time (deadlines), budget, and quality. While only 30% indicate they have an improved understanding of the importance of deadlines, budgets, and quality – key project management metrics. This is understandable, since not all employees have functioned as a project manager.

## 5. SUMMARY AND CONCLUSIONS

Our objective in writing this paper is to share our experiences with regard to a student internship program we refer to as Eduployment.

1. Internships offer Information Technology students valuable practical work experience, insight into IT operations, team and reporting relationships, and important career networking opportunities.
2. However, facilitating internships for Information Technology students represents a significant issue to institutions of higher education located in rural areas where few if any organizations exist with sufficient resources to support such programs within a manageable transportation distance.
3. In order to address this issue, we formed a not-for-profit IT consulting firm, operated by faculty and students, designed to focus on providing IT services to small businesses, other not-for-profit organizations, to the campus faculty and students, and businesses considering off-shoring.
4. Overall, the implementation model used has been successful; however, in our experience the Eduployment approach increases faculty workload by as much 15-20%. Although we recommend, some form of overload compensation, additional compensation was not introduced in our program.
5. From a student perspective, over 60% gave the program the highest evaluation rating, and an additional 30% rated the Eduployment experience as above average value. Areas that need improvement include enhancing our education program with regard to the use of the skills matrix, customer service, and business etiquette.

In the final analysis, overall our experiences were positive and we believe the organization is working toward achieving its goals. Although Eduployment significantly increases the workload for the faculty involved in the program, it proved to be an excellent opportunity to help students better prepare for their careers.

## 6. REFERENCES

[1] Brian D. Janz and Ernest L. Nichols. 2010. Meeting the demand for IT employees: can career choice be managed?. In Proceedings of the 2010 Special Interest Group on Management Information System's 48th annual conference on Computer personnel research on Computer personnel research (SIGMIS-CPR '10). ACM, New York, NY, USA, 8-14.

[2] Kakuma, P. and A. Portanova. Outsourcing: Its benefits, drawbacks, and other related issues. Journal of Academy of Business, Cambridge, 9 (2), 2006, pp. 1-7.

[3] Jeffrey C. Cepull. 1999. Technology training partnerships - University of Pittsburgh, Pittsburgh city schools and community college of Allegheny county. In Proceedings of the 27th annual ACM SIGUCCS conference on User services: Mile high expectations (SIGUCCS '99). ACM, New York, NY, USA, 26-30.

[4] Ekstrom, J., Gorka, S., Kamali, R., Lawson, E., Lunt, B., Miller, J. & Reichgelt, H. (October 2005). Computing Curricula, Information Technology Volume [online]. http://www.acm.org/education/curric_vols/IT_October_2005.pdf

[5] Ron Fulbright and Richard L. Routh. 2005. IPC incorporated: a student-run IT services company for experiential learning. In Proceedings of the 6th conference on Information technology education (SIGITE '05). ACM, New York, NY, USA, 211-216.

[6] Sandra Gorka, Jacob R. Miller, and Brandon J. Howe. 2007. Developing realistic capstone projects in conjunction with industry. In Proceedings of the 8th ACM SIGITE conference on Information technology education (SIGITE '07). ACM, New York, NY, USA, 27-32.

[7] Jennifer McIntosh-Elkins and Rebecca Klein. 2008. Creating pathways to develop student professionalism: a new direction. In Proceedings of the 36th annual ACM SIGUCCS fall conference: moving mountains, blazing trails (SIGUCCS '08). ACM, New York, NY, USA, 43-48.

# The Geographic Information Science and Technology and Information Technology Bodies of Knowledge: An Ontological Alignment

Brian Tomaszewski, Ph.D.
Department of Information Sciences and Technologies
Rochester Institute of Technology
Rochester, NY 14623
+1 585-475-2859
bmtski@rit.edu

Edward Holden
Department of Information Sciences and Technologies
Rochester Institute of Technology
Rochester, NY 14623
+1 585-475-5361
edward.holden@rit.edu

## ABSTRACT
In this paper, we present a philosophical discussion of ontological alignments between the fields of Geographic Information Science and Technology (GIS & T) and Information Technology (IT) based on existing bodies of knowledge (BOKs). We argue that tighter integration of concepts from GIS & T into IT curriculum can provide three specific opportunities for IT education - enhanced spatial thinking, new interdisciplinary and innovative application areas, and student employment opportunities. We also discuss specific ideas for curricular integration based on the alignments and provide a list of free and open source GIS & T software, data and learning resources for IT educators interested in incorporating GIS & T concepts and technologies into their teaching.

## Categories and Subject Descriptors
K.3.2 [**Computer and Information Science Education**]: Curriculum, Information systems education

## General Terms
Management, Documentation, Design, Theory

## Keywords
Curriculum, Geographic Information Science and Technology.

## 1. INTRODUCTION
Information Technology (IT), as both a formal academic discipline and industrial sector, has seen substantial development in the past 20+ years. Geographic Information Science and Technology (GIS & T), which shares many conceptual and technological alignments with IT, has also seen formal development as an academic discipline and industrial sector in the past 20 years. Despite having a heavy computing focus, the GIS & T field still very much unknown within IT circles. In this paper, we present a philosophical discussion of ontological alignments between GIS & T and IT based on existing bodies of knowledge (BOKs). We argue that tighter curricular integration of concepts from GIS & T into IT curriculum can provide three specific opportunities for IT education - enhanced spatial thinking, new interdisciplinary and innovative applications, and student

employment opportunities. We use a student success vignette from the Rochester Institute of Technology (RIT) as evidence of the opportunities that GIS & T and IT integration can provide.

The structure of the paper is as follows. We first provide background on the GIS & T and IT bodies of knowledge as a context for their ontological alignments. Next, we discuss specific ontological alignments between the BOKs. This discussion is followed by a conceptual discussion of the three specific opportunities for IT education that GIS & T offers as demonstrated with a student success vignette. The paper concludes with a summary and ideas for future curricular integration work. We also provide a list of free and open source GIS & T software, data and learning resources for IT educators interested in incorporating GIS & T concepts and technologies into their teaching.

## 2. BACKGROUND
In this section we discuss the GIS & T and IT BOKs separately to provide context for subsequent discussion of their alignment.

### 2.1 The Geographic Information Science and Technology Body of Knowledge

#### 2.1.1 *What is GIS & T?*
For millennia, societal needs have necessitated the creation, storage and representation of geographic information about processes and activities related to human and natural interactions at the Earth's surface – most often, but not exclusively, in the form of maps. GIS & T has emerged as an interdisciplinary field to investigate science and technology issues related to geographic information. GIS & T has been formally defined based on the intersections of three sub-domains [1]. The first is Geographic Information Science (GIScience). GIScience is a basic research domain with a focus on the underlying theoretical elements of geospatial technologies such as geographic information visualization, representation, interaction, and sense making, spatiotemporal reasoning, the impacts of geospatial technologies on society and individuals, the impacts of society and individuals on geospatial technologies and spatially-oriented themes from fields such as geography, geodesy, and cartography [2]. Furthermore, GIScience is fundamentally interdisciplinary through integration of theory and concepts from the fields of geography, information science, cognitive science, computer science, psychology, mathematics, philosophy, statistics, and anthropology. The second sub-domain is geospatial technology, which has been defined as "the specialized set of information technologies that handle georeferenced data" [1:5]. Well-known

geospatial technologies include Global Positioning System (GPS), Google Earth, and web-based mapping tools such as Bing or Google Maps. The third sub-domain is GIS & T applications. Countless examples of GIS & T applications exist such as community planning, disaster response, public safety and utilities (see [3] for a discussion of an overview of numerous GIS & T applications and the GIS & T industry).

### 2.1.2 A brief history and overview of the GIS & T Body of Knowledge (BOK)

The Association of American Geographers (AAG) published the GIS & T BOK in 2006[1]. It was an outcome of an initiative by the University Consortium for Geographic Information Science (UCGIS)[2] to consolidate over 10 years of previous efforts at formally defining an ontology for the GIS & T domain. The broader goal for developing the GIS & T BOK was to provide curricular guidelines to meet emerging and growing Geospatial Technology industry and research needs. The GIS & T BOK was modeled after the ACM Computing Curricula 2001 [1]. Thus, the GIS & T BOK shares many commonalities in terms of structure with other computing bodies of knowledge. A full discussion of intellectual evolution of the GIS & T BOK is beyond the scope of this paper, for more information on its evolution see: [1].

The GIS & T BOK consists of ten knowledge areas the cover the GIS & T domain. Each knowledge area contains units which in turn, contain topic sets that provide specific concepts, techniques, applications and methods [1]. Further discussion of specific GIS & T BOK knowledge areas, units and topics are provided in section 3.

## 2.2 The ACM Information Technology Curriculum

### 2.2.1 A Brief history of IT as a formal discipline

As the field of computing has evolved over the last fifty years, there have been several sub disciplines that have matured. One of these is Information Technology (IT). IT has been formally defined as follows: "Information Technology (IT) in its broadest sense encompasses all aspects of computing technology. IT, as an academic discipline, is concerned with issues related to advocating for users and meeting their needs within an organizational and societal context through the selection, creation, application, integration and administration of computing technologies" [4:9].

### 2.2.2 The ACM Information Technology Curriculum

In the Fall, 2001, IT faculty from a small number of colleges and universities began to meet to discuss curriculum for the IT discipline. In July, 2003, the Special Interest Group for IT Education (SIGITE) was formed as part of ACM. In addition to conferences, a subcommittee of SIGITE developed the curriculum guidelines that are in use today [4]. This curriculum contain the IT Body of Knowledge (IT BOK) that was developed by the committee. The IT BOK specifies content in thirteen high level knowledge areas. Of interest to this paper, the IT BOK does include a brief reference to **spatial databases** as its own topic under *IM. Special Purpose Databases*. "Mobile databases" and "Scientific (e.g. genomic) databases" are included as sub-topics under the spatial databases topic [4].

## 3. Ontological Alignments the GIS & T and IT BOKs

In this section we outline specific areas where the two BOKs have ontological alignments. We first briefly discuss the methodology used for aligning the two BOKs.

## 3.1 Alignment Methodology

The two BOKs are ontologies in the philosophical sense in that they attempt to define the language of concepts that exists in each respective domain [5]. Furthermore, they are not represented in an ontology syntax like Web Ontology Language (OWL) used in sematic web applications (see [6] for a discussion of OWL). Development of each BOK into formal ontology syntax was beyond the scope of the work reported in this paper. Thus, their alignments cannot be automatically computed using ontology matching tools such as *Agreement Maker* [7]. Based on these circumstances, the two BOKs were manually aligned by the authors using semantic similarity between terms and definitions in each BOK, a simple yet effective technique that is the basis for overcoming semantic heterogeneity [8]. Wherever possible, we have matched respective concepts based on exact word matches or interpretations of terms based on our combined experiences as computing professionals - Tomaszewski has a Ph.D. in Geography/GIS & T, Holden has forty years of IT industry experience. We acknowledge that this is a subjective process. However, we believe the semantic closeness of many of the concepts mitigates any unintended bias or misalignments.

## 3.2 Alignments between the GIS & T and IT BOKs

As discussed previously, each BOK uses a hierarchal structure of concepts. Table 1 outlines the hierarchical levels between each BOK to demonstrate how a given level in one BOK relates to the corresponding level in the other BOK.

**Table 1 – BOK Hierarchical Levels**

| GIS & T BOK | IT BOK |
|---|---|
| 1st Level– "Knowledge Area" – example: *Analytical Methods (AM)* | 1st Level– "Knowledge Area" – example: *Information Management (IM)* |
| 2nd Level – "Unit", a sub part of a knowledge area – example: *Unit AM3 Geometric measures* | 2nd Level – "Unit", a sub part of a knowledge area – example: *IM. Data Modeling* |
| 3rd level – "Topic" – sub part of Unit – example: *Topic AM3-1 Distances and lengths* | 3rd level – "Topic" – sub part of Unit – example: *Conceptual Models* (topics not given alpha-numeric designation) |

Table 2 lists the ontological alignments between the two BOKs. We report each alignment at the Unit and Topic levels as these levels were found to have the greatest alignment semantic power. Alignments are listed based on alphabetical ordering of GIS & T BOK units. Ordering does not imply priority of an alignment. Specific alignments are referred to by their ID value in the text following Table 2.

---

[1] http://www.aag.org/ (last retrieved 25 May 2012)

[2] http://www.ucgis.org/ (last retrieved 25 May 2012)

| ID | GIS & T BOK | IT BOK |
|---|---|---|
| 1 | Unit: AM1 Academic and analytical origins<br><br>Topic AM1-2 Analytical approaches | Unit: PF. Algorithms and problem solving<br><br>Topic: Problem solving strategies<br><br>Topic: Implementation approaches<br><br>Topic: The concepts and properties of algorithms |
| 2 | Unit: AM2 Query operations and query languages<br><br>Topic AM2-1 Set theory | Unit: MS. Math and statistics<br><br>Topic: Functions, relations and sets |
| 3 | Unit: AM2 Query operations and query languages<br><br>Topic AM2-2 Structured Query Language | Unit: IM. Database Query Languages<br><br>Topic: SQL data manipulation<br><br>Topic: SQL data definition |
| 4 | Unit: AM11 Network analysis<br><br>Topic AM11-2 Graph theoretic (descriptive) measures of networks | Unit: MS. Graphs and Trees<br><br>Topic: Trees<br><br>Topic: Undirected graphs<br><br>Topic: Directed graphs<br><br>Topic: Spanning trees<br><br>Topic: Traversal strategies |
| 5 | Unit: CF2 Cognitive and social foundations<br><br>Topic Perception and cognition of geographic phenomena | Unit: HCI Human computer interaction<br><br>Topic: Human factors |
| 6 | Unit: CF5 Relationships<br><br>Topic CF5-3 Genealogical relationships: lineage, inheritance | Unit: IPT Integrative coding<br><br>Topic: Design patterns<br><br>Topic: Interfaces<br><br>Topic: Inheritance |

Table 2 (continued)

| ID | GIS & T BOK | IT BOK |
|---|---|---|
| 7 | Unit: DA2 Project definition<br><br>Topic DA2-1: Problem definition<br><br>Topic DA2-2: Planning for design<br><br>Topic DA2-3: Application/user assessment<br><br>Topic DA2-4: Requirements analysis | Unit: SIA. Requirements<br><br>Topic: Requirements elicitation, documentation, and maintenance<br><br>Topic: Modeling requirements<br><br>Topic: Use case model<br><br>Topic: Modeling tools and methodologies<br><br>Topic: Testing<br><br>Topic: Project lifecycle phases |
| 8 | Unit: DA4 Database design<br><br>Topic DA4-1 Modeling tools<br><br>Topic DA4-2 Conceptual model<br><br>Topic DA4-3 Logical models | Unit: IM. Data Modeling<br><br>Topic: Conceptual Models<br><br>Topic: Logical models<br><br>Topic: Physical models |
| 9 | Unit: DA6 Application design<br><br>Topic DA6-1 Workflow analysis and design | Unit: SIA. Organizational Context<br><br>Topic: Business Process |
| 10 | Unit: DA6 Application design<br><br>Topic DA6-2 User interfaces | Unit: HCI. Developing Effective Interfaces (p72)<br><br>Topic: Graphical user interfaces |
| 11 | Unit: DA7 System implementation<br><br>Topic DA7-3 System testing<br><br>Topic DA7-4 System deployment | Unit: SIA. Integration and Deployment<br><br>Topic: Testing/evaluation/benchmarking<br><br>Topic: Enterprise integration approaches, standards, and best practices |

Table 2 (continued)

| ID | GIS & T BOK | IT BOK |
|----|-------------|--------|
| 12 | Unit: DM1 Basic storage and retrieval structures<br><br>Topic DM1-1 Basic data structures | Unit PF Fundamental data structures<br><br>Topic: Arrays<br><br>Topic: Records<br><br>Topic: Linked structures<br><br>Topic: Knowledge of hashing function<br><br>Topic: Use of stacks, queues<br><br>Topic: Use of graphs and trees<br><br>Topic: Strategies for choosing the right data structure |
| 13 | Unit: DM2 Database management systems<br><br>Topic: DM2-2 Relational DBMS<br><br>Topic DM2-3 Object-oriented DBMS | Unit: IM. Data Organization Architecture<br><br>Topic: Data models (includes object-relational databases) |
| 14 | Unit: DN1 Representation transformation<br><br>Topic: DN1-2 Data model and format conversion | Unit: IM Data modeling<br><br>Topic: Conceptual models<br><br>Topic: Standardized modeling in IDEF1, UML |
| 15 | Unit: GD12 Metadata, standards, and infrastructures<br><br>Topic: GD12-1 Metadata | Unit: IPT. Data Mapping and Exchange<br><br>Topic: Metadata |
| 16 | Unit: GS1 Legal aspects<br><br>Topic: GS1-3 Liability<br><br>Topic GS1-4 Privacy | Unit: SP. Legal Issues in Computing<br><br>Topic: Accountability, responsibility, liability<br><br>Unit: SP. Privacy and Civil Liberties |
| 17 | Unit: GS6 Ethical aspects of geospatial information and technology<br><br>Topic: GS6-2 Codes of ethics for geospatial professionals | Unit: SP. Professional and Ethical Issues & Responsibilities<br><br>Topic: Codes of professional conduct, such as IEEE, ACM, BCS, ITAA, AITP |

Table 2 (continued)

| ID | GIS & T BOK | IT BOK |
|----|-------------|--------|
| 18 | Unit: O2 Managing GIS operations and infrastructure<br><br>Topic: OI2-6 User support | Unit: SA. Administrative Activities<br><br>Topic: User support and education<br><br>Topic: Resource management |
| 19 | Unit: OI3 Organizational structures and procedures<br><br>Topic: OI3-1 Organizational models for GIS management | Unit: SIA. Organizational Context<br><br>Topic: Organizational culture |

## 3.3 Alignment Discussion

The following are three general observations made from the alignments. The first is that the strongest connections between the two BOKs lie in areas related to data and databases. By "strongest connection", we mean (1) where exact words were found in each BOK, and (2) our understanding of the respective topics based on our computing experience. For example, alignments 2, 3, 8, 12, and 13 all deal specifically with database topics. In the GIS & T BOK, data is the focus of two knowledge areas - Data Modeling (DM) and Data Manipulation (DN). In the IT BOK, data-related topics tend to fall under the Information Management (IM) knowledge area. The second observation is that many alignments are semantically similar, but in the GIS & T BOK, have a spatial orientation. For example, in alignment 15, Metadata in the GIS&T BOK is focused a metadata related to geospatial data assets, whereas in the IT BOK, metadata is agnostic of any particular domain and is related to XML. In alignment 16, the GIS&T BOK discusses spatial aspects of privacy (i.e., data aggregation), whereas the IT BOK discusses specific privacy laws such as HIPPA and FERPA and other privacy issues. For alignment 17, both areas are similar but are related to organizations germane to each industry. For example, the American Society for Photogrammetry and Remote Sensing (ASPRS) for GIS & T and ACM/IEEE for IT. Alignments 18 and 19 deal with topics such as user support and organizational structure that also have a spatial distinction in the GIS & T BOK. The third observation is that there are several alignments related to end-user application development. Of particular note in this regard is that the entire application development process is generally represented - from requirements analysis and definition (alignment 7), to application development (alignment 9) and user interface design (alignment 10) to system implementation (alignment 11). Furthermore, it was interesting to note that Human Computer Interaction (HCI) was not explicitly listed as a knowledge area, unit or topic in the GIS & T, despite many GIScientists drawing upon HCI literature for Geovisualization technology development [9]. Although not explicit, many HCI-related issues however are in alignment 5.

Application development alignments between the BOKs could also be a reflection of IT's focus on applications and integration [4]. Furthermore, it could be anticipated, although not investigated here, that alignments exist with other informatics disciplines, such as Bioinformatics and Medical Informatics. If that is the case then it may be an opportunity to find the commonality among the informatics disciplines. Ultimately, this could potentially lead to a movement to add informatics as a pillar of IT. This would further link IT more closely with the domain/technology integration for which it is known. We at RIT have already begun to look at informatics as a component of future program redesign.

## 4. Specific opportunities for IT education

In the following sections, we outline three opportunities for IT education based on the alignments.

### 4.1 Enhanced Spatial Thinking

Spatial thinking is the idea that the concepts of space, representation tools and reasoning processes can be used to find answers to problems [10]. A simple example of spatial thinking would be navigating to a destination by making observations of landmarks and using a map. Spatial thinking is a critical component in science and technology for addressing pressing societal issues and is useful in everyday life. For example, problems such as large scale disasters are inherently spatially when the geographic scale and inter-relationships between affected entities are considered (see: [11, 12] for specific examples of how spatial thinking can be used to solve disaster management problems) . We argue that bringing a spatial thinking perspective into IT educational practice can (a) help develop the next generation of applied science and technology innovators to address spatially-oriented problems, and (b) develop higher levels of reasoning and problem solving skills in IT students. Spatial thinking has been explicitly identified as a priority area by the US National Science Foundation (NSF) within broader STEM innovation advocacy [13].

### 4.2 Interdisciplinary and innovative applications– examples from the Rochester Institute of Technology

The Information Sciences and Technologies (IST) Department at the Rochester Institute of Technology (RIT) in Rochester, NY, USA has been making one of the first efforts to formally integrate GIS & T concepts into existing IT curricula as opposed to the more common situation of GIS & T curricula being taught in a Geography department. These integrations have led to exciting new application areas at the intersections of IT and GIS & T. The following is a short description of one interdisciplinary application area.

Faculty from the RIT IST department have been engaged in a National Science Foundation (NSF) funded Science Master's degree Program (SMP) titled "Decision Support Technologies for Environmental Forecasting and Disaster Response " (NSF DGE-1011458)[3]. The broad goal of the SMP is to train students from different disciplines to create a STEM (Science, Technology, Engineering, and Mathematics) workforce for disaster response. In the 2011-2012 academic year, an IT Master's Student was included in the SMP student cohort. This student had completed an undergraduate IT degree from RIT and was in the second year of the IT MS program when selected for the SMP cohort. Before being selected for the cohort, the student had never taken any GIS & T related courses or been exposed to GIS & T concepts. The student did, however, have a strong background in IT areas such as web development and databases. Within the timeframe of one academic year, the student took three GIS & T classes. The student was able to quickly grasp GIS & T concepts and utilize spatial thinking for developing new technologies to create map-

based representations of disaster area extents from text-based disaster descriptions [14]. The combination of underlying IT concepts (programming and web systems) when mixed with GIS & T concepts (spatial data, cartography) created an intellectual and innovation synergy for this student and led to the student having job and internship offers with government and industry organizations not typically considered by IT graduates.

### 4.3 Student employment opportunities

Although job prospects for IT graduates remains strong, we believe it is our prime responsibility as academics to be advocates for our students by helping them secure employment once they graduate. GIS & T has been identified as a key job growth area in the United States [15]. The US Bureau of Labor statistics within the last few years been releasing statistics on GIS & T related employment. Although labeled "Surveying and Mapping Technicians" and thus not directly representative of job opportunities available to IT/GIS & T graduates, the US Bureau of Labor statistics estimates a 16% employment rate in this category [16]. A particularly exciting recent development in terms of formally defining pathways and outlining competencies for student employment opportunities at the intersection of IT and GIS & T has been the geospatial technology competency model (GTCM). Specially, the GTCM has Software and Application Development as one of three, high level, industry-specific technical competencies for which there is great demand [3]. For example, an informal inspection of the GIS Jobs clearinghouse website[4] revealed strong GIS & T industry demand for application developers and database administrators.

## 5. FUTURE WORK

The philosophical perspectives presented in this paper are the basis for modifications we plan to do to existing IT courses to further and rigorously evaluate the three IT education opportunities outlined in section 4. Specifically, we plan to modify an undergraduate course focused on databases to include laboratory exercises related spatial databases and spatial query operators. We are particularly interested to see if making such modifications improves spatial thinking skills as measured by spatially-oriented problem solving tasks. We also plan to informally track new application areas students become interested in and document internship, employment or co-op opportunities students obtain that are GIS & T focused.

In addition, examining other informatics disciplines could lead to the expansion of the IT discipline to include an informatics focus.

## 6. SUMMARY AND CONCLUSIONS

In this paper, we have presented a philosophical discussion of the ontological alignments between two disciplines – GIS & T and IT based on their respective bodies of knowledge (BOKs). We demonstrated that IT and GIS & T share many specific commonalities. In particular, data and databases, application development and myriad areas that are conceptually close but differ in the spatial distinction that GIS & T makes in these areas. We also outlined three IT education opportunities these alignments make – spatial thinking, new innovative and interdisciplinary application areas and student employment opportunities. We also sketched out ideas for future educational research based on the alignments.

---

[3] http://www.cis.rit.edu/EnvironmentalForecasting (last retrieved 24 May 2011)

[4] http://www.gjc.org/gjc-cgi/listjobs.pl (last retrieved 24 May 2011)

Our hope is that the work reported in this paper will give IT educators new, innovative areas and ideas to consider in terms of curriculum development and STEM education. Ultimately, tighter integration between GIS & T and IT education can lead to improved education within both disciplines and problem solving for complex, interdisciplinary societal issues.

## 6.1 Recommended Resources

Table 3 is a non- exhaustive resource list for IT educators new to GIS & T and interested in incorporating GIS & T perspectives and tools into their educational practice. We have made of point to include only free-open source resources except in the case of Esri given their importance to the GIS & T industry.

**Table 3: GIS & T resource list – All URLs listed are active as of August 2012**

| Item | Description | URL |
|------|-------------|-----|
| Commercial GIS software | Esri – the primary commercial GIS & T company. Esri also provides free tools, data and offers open APIs | http://www.esri.com/ |
| Open Source Software | Directory of Open Source GIS & T projects | http://www.osgeo.org/ |
| Open Source Spatial Database | postGIS – an extension to postgreSQL | http://postgis.refractions.net/ |
| Open Source Geo-data web server | Geoserver | http://geoserver.org/display/GEOS/Welcome |
| Open source web client | OpenLayers – similar to Google Maps API | http://openlayers.org/ |
| Standards | Open Geospatial Consortium (OGC) | http://www.opengeospatial.org/ |
| Data | Open Street Map – A free world-wide map with downloadable data | http://www.openstreetmap.org/ |
| Data | Geonames – Free world gazetteer data | http://www.geonames.org/ |
| Educational Materials | *The Nature of Geographic Information* – open GIS & T book | https://www.e-education.psu.edu/natureofgeoinfo/ |

## 7. REFERENCES

[1] Dibiase, D., DeMers, M., Johnson, A., Kemp, K., Luck, A. T., Plewe, B. and Wentz, E. *Geographic information science and technology body of knowledge.* 0892912677, Association of American Geographers, Washington, DC, 2006.

[2] Mark, D. Geographic information science: Defining the field. *Foundations of geographic information science* (2000), 3-18.

[3] DiBiase, D., Corbin, T., Fox, T., Francica, J., Green, K., Jackson, J., Jeffress, G., Jones, B. and Mennis, J. The new geospatial technology competency model: Bringing workforce needs into focus. *URISA Journal*, 22, 2 (2010), 55.

[4] Lunt, B. M., Ekstrom, J., Gorka, S., Hislop, G., Kamali, R., Lawson, E., LeBlanc, R., Miller, J. and Reichgelt, H. *Information Technology 2008: Curriculum Guidelines for Undergraduate Degree Programs in Information Technology.* Association for Computing Machinery (ACM) IEEE Computer Society, 2008.

[5] Sowa, J. F. *Signs, Processes, and Language Games: Foundations for Ontology.* <http://www.jfsowa.com/pubs/signproc.htm>, last retrieved: 1 June 2012

[6] Bechhofer, S., van Harmelen, F., Hendler, J., Horrocks, I., McGuinness, D., Patel-Schneider, P. and Stein, L. *OWL Web Ontology Language Reference.* <http://www.w3.org/TR/owl-guide/>, last retrieved: 21 May 2012

[7] Cruz, I. F., Antonelli, F. P. and Stroe, C. AgreementMaker: efficient matching for large real-world schemas and ontologies. *Proceedings of the VLDB Endowment*, 2, 2 (2009), 1586-1589.

[8] Pavel, S. and Euzenat, J. Ontology matching: state of the art and future challenges. *IEEE Transactions on Knowledge and Data Engineering*, 99 (2011), 1-1.

[9] Robinson, A., Chen, J., Lengerich, E., Meyer, H. and MacEachren, A. Combining usability techniques to design geovisualization tools for epidemiology. *Cartography and Geographic Information Science*, 32, 4 (2005), 243-255.

[10] National Research Council *Learning to Think Spatially: GIS as a Support System in the K-12 cirriculum.* The National Academies Press, Washington, DC, 2006.

[11] National Research Council *Successful Response Starts With a Map: Improving Geospatial Support for Disaster Management.* National Academies Press, Washington, D.C., 2007.

[12] Harvard Humanitarian Initiative. *Disaster Relief 2.0: The Future of Information Sharing in Humanitarian Emergencies.* Washington, D.C. and Berkshire, UK, 2011.

[13] National Sciene Board. *Preparing the Next Generation of STEM Innovators: Identifying and Developing our Nation's Human Capital.* National Sciene Foundation, Washington, DC, 2010.

[14] Bouchard, B. and Tomaszewski, B. Automated GLIDE Number Resource Consolidation for Rapid Disaster Location Identification. In *Proceedings of the 9th International Conference of the International Association For The Study Of Information Systems For Crisis Response And Management (ISCRAM)* (Vancouver, Canada), 2012.

[15] Gewin, V. Mapping opportunities. *Nature*, 427, 6972 (2004), 376-377.

[16] Bureau of Labor Statistics *Surveying and Mapping Technicians.* < http://www.bls.gov/ooh/architecture-and-engineering/surveying-and-mapping-technicians.htm>, last retrieved: 24 May 2012

# Interactive Learning Online: Challenges and Opportunities

Mihaela Sabin (moderator)
University of New Hampshire
Manchester, NH 03101

mihaela.sabin@unh.edu

Amber Settle
DePaul University
Chicago, IL 60604

asettle@cdm.depaul.edu

Becky Rutherfoord
Southern Polytechnic State University
Marietta, GA 30060

brutherf@spsu.edu

## SUMMARY

Higher education is a labor-intensive sector. Smaller classes, more faculty-student direct interactions, prompt and individualized feedback, and more hands-on and collaborative learning with peers raise the quality of student education. Valuable person-to-person interactions, on the other hand, are costly and, to complicate matters, indicative of the Baumol's cost disease [1]. Labor-intensive sectors that are dominated by personal services, such as education and health care, do not have rising productivity through technological innovations. These "stagnant sectors", says William Baumol, keep up with salaries in sectors where more is produced with less, like in manufacturing, by raising costs.

Since the early 1990s online education and online learning systems have held the promise of increasing instructional productivity and reducing costs without sacrificing educational quality. There is no evidence to date that such promise has materialized. The impetus of the newest developments with free online courses offered by Ivy League research universities to hundreds of thousands of students might drastically transform how we teach more and better with less. The innovation that prompted this panel is called Interactive Learning Online (ILO), and has the distinctive feature of highly interactive, machine-guided instruction that can be scaled to accommodate a large number of students who benefit from targeted and personalized learning [2].

A generic software platform that would permit faculty at diverse institutions to develop ILO content with customized feedback loops and machine-guided interactivity does not exist. Bacow et al. [2] observe that it would be "foolishly inefficient to rely on a 'hundred flowers' approach". They recommend that we collectively investigate how to: (1) design, develop, and maintain

## Categories and Subject Descriptors

K.3.2 [**Computer and Information Science Education**]: Computer science education

## General Terms

Design, Experimentation, Human Factors, Management

## Keywords

Online learning, online learning platforms, personalized learning

ILO content; (2) share student performance data tracked with ILO tools to research how students learn and how technology can facilitate teaching; and (3) participate in the creation of sustainable and customizable ILO platforms. This is a compelling IT problem, for which IT educators have the technical and educational expertise.

The panelists have experimented with online learning in different ways. Their perspectives underline the challenges with improving student learning outcomes in an online environment and the difficulties with current technologies and selection of more advanced online learning tools. The panelists' institutions, at the time the panel proposal was submitted, did not have access to platforms such as Coursera (coursera.org) and EdX (edxonline.org), to see first-hand how ILO content is developed and learning analytics managed. Like the vast majority of educators who have taught online courses, the panelists have used course management systems (CMS) where ILO activities are limited to discussion boards and student breakout groups. They have enhanced their online teaching with video content and synchronous online activities through live web conferencing. Social media and cloud computing services have also been used to make the online learning environment affordable and learner-centered.

## 1. Amber Settle

When online learning was introduced in the College of Computing and Digital Media (CDM) at DePaul in a broad way in 2001, the goal was to provide a large variety of online courses while minimizing the impact on the faculty and the regular sections of courses [4]. Hundreds of courses are recorded each quarter using an in-house hardware and software system called Course Online (COL), and many of these classes have an associated online section where the students substitute class attendance with asynchronous viewing of the recordings. More recently a number of online-only classes tailored to that population have been developed. As a fulltime instructor at CDM since 1996, I have taught 17 COL-enabled online courses and developed two distinct online-only courses, which I taught a total of 13 times. The development and modification of the online-only courses has shown me that interactive learning is crucial for online student success and satisfaction.

When developing the online-only Java course, I followed these principles to facilitate student success and satisfaction:

- Create very short recordings and focus on solving relevant problems. The longest recording was 30 minutes, and many were less than 10.
- Include exercises with immediate feedback. I used the CodeLab system, but many other equivalent systems are available.

- Require students to make regular postings in a discussion forum to share tips and frustration with one another.
- Create new (very short) recordings each week in response to student questions and difficulties to ensure a more robust faculty-student dialog.

As an unexpected consequence of the course structure, the recordings became a "pull" resource, with some students only accessing the recordings to reinforce concepts not easily understood from the textbook or lecture notes. Interestingly, some students watched all the recordings, sometimes repeatedly, demonstrating that approaches to learning vary, and the course structure needs to be flexible enough to accommodate individualized learning. Course evaluations from the online Java class were significantly higher than evaluations from similar COL online courses.

## 2. Becky Rutherfoord

As we think about the future of IT online education, we need to examine ways in which we can use our own knowledge of the IT field to allow for innovative and exciting new ways of developing online content. Most of our traditional institutions do not have the monetary resources to compete with well-endowed institutions. MIT's OpenCourseWare (OCW) spends $10,000 to $15,000 and requires 100 staff-hours to publish a single course: collect and compile course materials from faculty, ensure proper licensing for sharing, and format materials for the OCW site. Courses with video content cost twice as much. Carnegie Mellon University's Open Learning Initiative is often cited for the sticker price of $1 million per state-of-the-art, rigorous course with interactive videos that embed intelligent tutoring tools [4]. This up-front, one-time cost gets amortized over time when the course reaches an equilibrium state and is reused with no or minimal changes.

Using traditional course management systems has been the standard for most of our creation of online courses and modules. To improve student learning and direct engagement with the teaching material, IT education departments should take an active role in evaluating, selecting, and integrating tools and services that emphasize more teaching and learning interactions. Some newer technologies include the Echo 360 lecture capture system (echo360.com), which allows for full video and audio capture (including student responses to questions) of the teacher's live delivery of instructional modules. The video/audio recordings can then be stored into the CMS for easy access and use. This product can cost upwards of $20,000-25,000 per classroom installation if all new equipment is purchased and the storage is hosted off-campus. If used with existing computing infrastructure (equipment, projectors, and microphones) costs are significantly lowered. Echo 360 can be enhanced with Wimba Live classrooms that allow remote students to use live, real-time web conferencing and interact with peers and instructor.

After teaching online now for several years and seeing the improvements of CMSs and other online tools over the last few years, I am confident that the availability of more sophisticated online learning products will allow us to create online content in a much more efficient and cost-effective manner.

## 3. Mihaela Sabin

An alternative to prohibitively expensive plug-and-play, monolithic CMS's is to disaggregate the development and delivery of ILO content through the use of open source and/or free software. Online Q&A, student online portfolios, or project wikis are examples of ILO content that I have developed and curated with social media tools and cloud services such as Piazza (piazza.com), Google Sites (sites.google.com), MediaWiki (mediawiki.org), and Google Code (code.google.com) [5].

I have used Piazza for the online Q&A content of my courses in the past two years. My role is to structure and prompt weekly conversations with 2-3 questions. Besides the Q&A standard activities, student participation in Piazza includes commenting, editing of peers' contributions, and "thumb-up" endorsements of useful tips and explanations. Piazza software has effective analytics that I easily tie into assessing student engagement in online activities. Students use Google Sites to create online portfolios in which they assemble learning artifacts for formative and summative assessment: solutions to assigned homework and projects, self-evaluations, status reports, and self-reflections. The wiki revision history controls in Google Sites help students with an iterative submission approach and informs me about how progress was made. For team projects, students use a MediaWiki installation on a server in the lab to document and keep track of their work openly and collaboratively. For the source code, we use Google Code project hosting service and its version control and issue tracking tools.

Replacing an instructor-controlled CMS with a suite of tools and services that are under student control is analogous to trading "one-size-fits-all" with a personalized learning environment that is a step closer to an ILO platform. My use of ILO-like tools did not increase productivity as measured by student-to-teacher ratio. Instead, student self-directed experiences became more productive when students personalize learning from a dynamic, social network of resources. This shift from top-down, CMS-centralized teaching to student-pull online learning has freed up time in my classes for interactions that do not yet have (and might never have) an online counterpart.

## 4. REFERENCES

[1] Baumol, W.M. and Bowen, W.G. 1966. *Performing arts: the economic dilemma*, New York: The Twentieth Century Fund.

[2] Bacow, L. et al. 2012. Barriers to adoption of online learning systems in U.S. higher education. New York, NY: Ithaka S+R.

[3] Knight, L., Steinbach, T., and White J. 2002. An alternative approach to Web-based education: technology-intensive, not labor-intensive. In the *Proceedings of the Information Systems Education Conference*, San Antonio, Texas.

[4] Krakovsky, M. 2010. Degrees, Distance, and Dollars. *Communications of the ACM*, 53, 9, (Sep 2010) 18-19.

[5] Sabin, M. 2012. Student-pull instead of instructor-push: in preparation for a student learning dashboard. *Journal of Computing Sciences in Colleges*, 27, 6, (June 2012) 70-72.

# Transforming Programming-Intensive Courses with Course-Embedded Research

Evelyn Brannock
Georgia Gwinnett College
1000 University Center Lane
Lawrenceville, Georgia 30043
678-939-9007
ebrannoc@ggc.edu

Nannette Napier
Georgia Gwinnett College
1000 University Center Lane
Lawrenceville, Georgia 30043
678-524-1511
nnapier@ggc.edu

Kristine Nagel
Georgia Gwinnett College
1000 University Center Lane
Lawrenceville, Georgia 30043
678-407-5872
knagel@ggc.edu

## ABSTRACT

In this paper, we discuss the Software Engineering Research Project (SERP) initiated at Georgia Gwinnett College (GGC), a public four-year institution in southeastern United States. The long-term goal of SERP involves motivating students to pursue graduate degrees, research careers, or challenging industry work. Before students can engage in software engineering research, they need to develop a deeper appreciation for professional practice, scholarly literature, and research paradigms. To that end, we have identified activities to embed in two junior-level programming-intensive courses: Software Development I and Advanced Programming. Our three-pronged approach includes attendance at professional events, participation in a research project, and exposure to computing research at a leading research university. In this paper, we detail our goals and objectives for the SERP program, illustrate a course redesign for two of the courses, and provide initial results from a pilot study.

## Categories and Subject Descriptors

K.3.2 [**Computers and Information Science Education**]: Computer science education – *curriculum*

## General Terms

Experimentation

## Keywords

Undergraduate research, software engineering course, curriculum innovation

## 1. INTRODUCTION

In Spring 2012, we initiated the Software Engineering Research Project (SERP) at GGC (Georgia Gwinnett College), a public four-year institution in southeastern United States. The long-term goal of SERP involves motivating students to pursue graduate degrees, research careers, or challenging industry work. The immediate goal involves filling knowledge gaps to prepare students for other undergraduate research opportunities and motivating students to seek additional research opportunities.

Benefits to student participation in undergraduate research have been proposed and supported in the literature including increased interest in the discipline, gains in critical thinking, and enhanced

readiness for challenging research and industry careers [1, 2]. Seymour and colleagues [1] describe four models of conducting undergraduate research: retention programs held during the summer for juniors; career promotion programs also held during the summer for juniors and designed to build confidence; research apprenticeships which are year round or summer programs with small group mentoring; and research-based learning experiences which incorporate research-like experiences into the classroom.

Although there is evidence that summer undergraduate research can have a beneficial effect on students who participate [3], such intensive programs can only impact a few students. Furthermore, program participants must be motivated enough to submit a competitive application and fortunate enough to be selected. In designing SERP, we chose to follow the research-based learning approach. A primary benefit is that embedding research into an existing course would provide research exposure to all students taking a course.

We reviewed other undergraduate research experiences in computing courses. For example, semester-long courses have been described which guide students on the formulation of a research proposal [4] or the creation of a research conference paper [5]. Others have incorporated research projects as part of a capstone experience for students [6]. Our approach is different in that we decided to integrate a focus on software engineering research into existing courses, which were very programming-intensive. A course-embedded research project, tailored to the subject area of each course, would be incorporated into the curriculum and outcomes assessment throughout the semester.

We identified two key courses to begin embedding research activities for students in our information technology (IT) program: Software Development I (SD I) and Advanced Programming (AP). During our pilot study, there was one section of SD I and two sections of Advanced Programming taught by the first and second authors. These two courses were targeted as they are complementary, at the junior level, and are required from all IT Software Development concentration majors. Although there are trade-offs to be made when deciding to insert new material into a course, we strived to keep the bulk of the traditional content. For example, Advanced Programming still contains the same material taught in previous semesters, such as advanced data structures, complex algorithms and Big-Oh analysis, and SD I still covers concepts such as the SDLC and its components, quality assurance tools and techniques and a team development project implementation.

In this paper, we detail our goals and objectives for the SERP program, describe our three-pronged approach to transforming courses, illustrate a course redesign for two of the courses, and provide initial results from a pilot study. For students, we show that the program provided an exposure to new experiences in research and industry and complemented what was being learned in the classroom.

# 2. Software Engineering Research Project (SERP)

In designing SERP, we considered the strengths, weaknesses, and typical background of students who enroll in these courses. First, we needed to address the myth that building software solutions requires primarily technical programming skills. Having a deeper understanding of professional practice would provide a necessary foundation for helping students engage in software engineering (SE) research. In the past, field trips to companies have been instructive and rated highly with students on end-of-course evaluations; therefore, we decided to include corporate site visits as a component.

Second, we needed to address students' unfamiliarity with scholarly literature in computing. Historically, our students have not been challenged to read, summarize, and synthesize peer-reviewed SE literature. This is important because we need software professionals that cannot only learn from their own experiences but also from the experiences of others.

Finally, students need exposure to SE research approaches. SE research results involve improved procedures or techniques, descriptive models, development of new methodologies or tools, and experience reports of integrating existing technologies or tools [7].

## 2.1 Goals and Objectives

The specific SERP goals and related objectives follow:

1. Improve students' understanding of the SE profession. Students will be able to:

   a. Identify and summarize a current issue being debated in the field of software engineering
   b. Describe the different phases and tools in the systems development life cycle (SDLC)
   c. Evaluate technical solutions and identify appropriate guidelines for decision-making
   d. Investigate algorithms used in real-world software applications (e.g., determining routing used for Yahoo Maps; and sorting, searching, and categorizing such as Google)

2. Improve students' ability to read, summarize, and synthesize peer-reviewed literature on software development and engineering. Students will develop the following skills:

   a. Read primary literature and extract needed information
   b. Use the library to obtain GGC in-house materials or request out-of-house material
   c. Create a bibliography for specific topic or research area
   d. Cite references using standard formats
   e. Create an extended abstract for submission at a student-friendly research conference

3. Increase student understanding of and interest in conducting SE research at the undergraduate or graduate level. As a result of this experience, more students will

   a. Express confidence in their ability to conduct research
   b. Express interest in participating in other undergraduate research opportunities in IT

   c. Express interest in attending graduate school in computing fields
   d. Be able to more comprehensively answer: "What is software engineering research"?

## 2.2 Course-Embedded Research Components

To meet these goals, three new activities were incorporated into the target courses: a corporate visit to improve understanding of professional practice, participation in a research project, and exposure to research at a local research university, Georgia Tech. The students were required to meet deliverables from each of the three goals. The combined goals also had a graded component in each of the courses. In both SD I and Advanced Programming, 20% of the grade was determined from SERP.

In each section below, we describe these components in more detail.

### 2.2.1 Corporate Visit

We required all students to participate in a corporate visit to enrich understanding of professional practice (related objectives 1a, 1b, 1c and 1d). The students could choose from two local corporate site visits organized by course faculty. The first company is a large provider of accounting and payroll software and services, in existence for over 30 years with more than 6 million customers globally. The subsidiary that extended the invitation produces accounting software targeting small businesses. The agenda included speakers from Support, User Experience, Product Management, Automation, and a questions and answers session. The second is a relatively new software vendor that provides a revenue management/optimization system that incorporates complex mathematics, analysis and trend prediction. The agenda included demonstrations of the software, and presentations from the Science Team, Development and Quality Assurance, Implementation/Support and IT. During each of these site visits, the processes, practices, tools, techniques, and skills were shared, so students were exposed to the experience from accomplished professionals, giving context to the material in the textbook. Students in Advanced Programming crafted a thank you note that served as a synopsis of the visit, and was directed to a specific staff member. These notes on detailed highlights were approved and evaluated by the professor. In SD I, each student was required to summarize the experience in one page as a graded submission.

### 2.2.2 Research Project

All students participated in a research project (related objectives 2a, 2b, 2c, and 2d). The vast majority of the students have never completed a research project in an IT class. Therefore, students selected from a set of papers chosen by the professor as applicable in the course, and with developmentally appropriate research content. In Advanced Programming, the students worked in groups of three or four; in SD I students produced individual projects.

After attending a scheduled library and research skills presentation tailored to IT areas, students were required to produce a graded annotated bibliography according to guidelines/rubric provided. Each Advanced Programming group and each individual SD I student had to locate and read four to six papers of merit on their topic, then summarize, assess and reflect on them as a body of knowledge. These were to be used as citations for their papers.

The final deliverable in Advanced Programming was a 2 to 4 page paper and an accompanying poster suitable for submission to a regional conference. SD I students delivered an individual summary, supplemented by group presentations. The papers were to be written in a scholarly fashion, complete with citations.

### 2.2.3 Research Event

All students were required to attend a research event at Georgia Tech (related objectives 3a, 3b, 3c, 3d). The students chose from two research offerings, depending on their inclination and schedule. Students observed how a research lab at Georgia Tech operates and learned about graduate school opportunities. The first was a field trip to a weekly lunch at Georgia Tech, offering guest speakers on a variety of research topics. The featured speaker was a Principal Researcher and manager of the Visual User Experience group at Microsoft Research, who spoke about organizing large amounts of digital content for easy searching and retrieval. The second was a tour of an interdisciplinary research endeavor aimed at addressing the fundamental technical, design, and social challenges for people in a home setting, as the home plays a key role in our health, lifestyle, and well-being. Students attending the tour also visited the College of Computing, where the Assistant Dean for Academic Administration spoke about the graduate school admission process, including insights on how to prepare them. All students were required to write a one page graded summary and reflection of the event they attended.

## 3. SERP IMPLEMENTATION AT GGC

SERP was implemented as a pilot at GGC College, that according to the American Council on Education is the first public four-year liberal arts college to be founded in the United States in the 21st century, and the first four-year public institution created in this state in more than 100 years. GGC opened its doors to 118 juniors in 2006, and historically has had an open-access admissions policy. As of 2011-12 academic year, GGC had grown to more than 8,000 students and has 12 degree programs with more than 40 concentrations and seven minors. In the School of Science and Technology, more than 500 students have declared their major in Information Technology, as of May 2012. Because the school is so new, it is difficult to measure the career success or the number of students that aspire to attend graduate school.

### 3.1 Undergraduate Research Experience Initiative

The School of Science and Technology (SST) has initiated an innovative four-year Undergraduate Research Experience (URE). SST challenged faculty to develop and implement a transformative STEM education model that embeds research modules in courses, through all four years of study. The goals that this continuous exposure to research will promote include critical thinking skills; utilize actively contested questions, empirical observations, and state of the art technologies; promote a sense of excitement and engagement in all our students; enhance STEM instruction and STEM education; and promote success in college and lead to careers in STEM fields.

### 3.2 Challenges of Undergraduate Research

While GGC College growth may be unique, the student population mirrors the current minority-majority demographics of many other campuses, especially those with open-access admissions policy. Since GGC population represents the changing face of the college population, our challenges to course-embedded research may apply more universally.

First, we introduce students to research in their junior year, to expand their vision of IT research and to develop their research skills. While student opinions and judgments have already been formed, this is a first step to earlier intervention in overcoming undervaluation and misinformation about IT research.

Second, students are more focused on getting a job right after graduation rather than going to graduate school. Therefore, they place a premium on obtaining skills that they consider to be directly marketable like learning a new language or working on an internship with a company. They do not readily see the connection between undergraduate research and obtaining a job. They also do not stop to think about the long term gains a graduate degree will bring, both financial and expanded opportunities.

Third, we have a large number of first-generation college students who are not familiar with graduate school admissions or the benefits of obtaining a graduate degree. For instance, students may not be aware that there are scholarships and fellowships that will pay them to be in school as opposed to them having to pay themselves.

Fourth, some students who have some interest in graduate school plan to work for a while first to get some industry experience and then return to graduate school later. There is certainly some value in doing this. However, students may not participate in the necessary steps while they are in school that would set themselves up to be successful for graduate school admissions and to be competitive for fellowships (e.g., taking the GRE, participating in a summer REU, working on a research project with a faculty member, attending an academic conference, visiting graduate schools, etc.). They also may not set firm deadlines for transitioning back to school, getting caught up in working and not return.

Finally, some of our students lack the soft skills and professional etiquette necessary to interact positively in a professional environment (e.g., using cell phone to take notes during speaker's presentation was misconstrued; not having proper business casual attire; given effective presentations).

Overall, our students present an intriguing set of challenges as we strive to integrate research into SD I and Advanced Programming courses.

## 4. Course-Embedded SERP Assessment

Fourteen students in Advanced Programming, seven students from SD I, and three faculty members successfully completed the experience, including all assessments. Some students withdrew from the courses, or did not obtain a passing grade.

### 4.1 Corporate Visit

To attain Goal 1, improve students' understanding of the Software Engineering (SE) profession, students attended one of two professional corporation visits. The visits stressed the importance of non-technical skills, in combination with technical skills. They also learned about SE practice, building partnerships for internships/careers, and the relevance of topics covered in class.

To measure Goal 1, a survey was conducted in the SD I course to poll the students' perceptions. One hundred percent of the SD I students who attended the corporate visits recommend repeating the trip for future classes. The students were also asked to briefly describe three memorable lessons from the trip. Students described benefits such as having a better understanding of their career path trajectory, the skills needed to be a successful software developer, and the importance of testing, in these sample quotes:

"What major I have selected in college may not be what I end up doing in the work force."

"The most important skills they are looking for as a software developer are having good logic (not a particular programming language) and people/communication soft skills."

"I learned that during the hiring process they don't exactly look at the interviewee's ability to solve the problems given to them but rather look at their thought process and what they are attempting to do to solve the problem."

"Being able to learn new things and adapt is ...important."

"I learned about the complexity of the programs that [the Corporation] creates and that they rely on testing."

## 4.2 Research Project

Goal 2 was to improve students' ability to read, summarize, and synthesize peer-reviewed literature on software development and engineering, and produce a research project. Students selected a significant SE topic, for their final embedded deliverable. Advanced Programming wrote a paper and created a poster, while SD I students wrote individual summaries, responded to short essay questions synthesizing the papers, and did group presentations.

In addition to the course deliverables, we used pre- and post-surveys to assess student confidence and understanding of SE professional practice, skill in use of primary literature, and interest and confidence in research practices. One survey was given to all URE participants at GGC, and the other was adapted by the authors from a research paper on perceptions of STEM research skills by undergraduates participating in a summer research experience for undergraduates (REU) [3]. The surveys included both quantitative responses and open-ended questions. In the Advanced Programming self-assessment of research skills, the average score was more favorable across all skills in the post-survey, including research poster creation, presenting technical work, explaining to non-scientists, and retrieving information effectively. In both Advanced Programming and SD courses the self-reported skill in research projects increased by the end of course, including literature review, design and carry out experiments, plan and conduct a research project (see Figures 1 and 2). However, the interest in graduate school and perception of success did not change from the initial assessment in Advanced Programming, and was lower in SD course students.

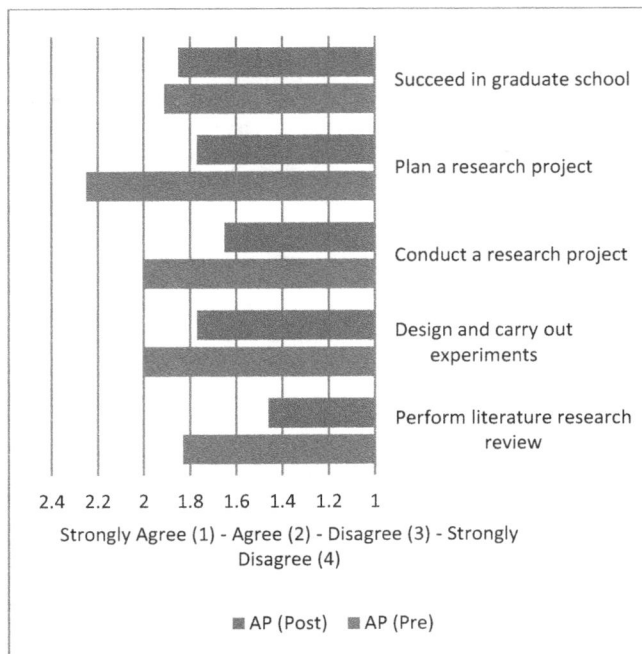

**Figure 1: Perception of Research Skills (AP students)**

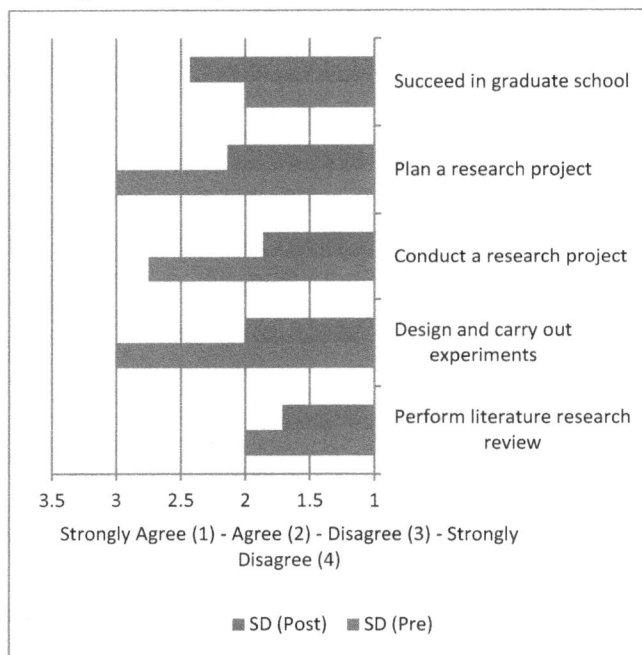

**Figure 2: Perception of Research Skills (SD students)**

All of the free form responses were reviewed for the questions "What benefit do you see in conducting research as a graduate? What challenges or drawbacks do you see in conducting research as an undergraduate?" Categories were derived from common themes that appeared in the student's response and some answers expressed more than one category in their written response. Students identified benefits in three categories: employability, "learning to learn" and teamwork (see Figure 3).

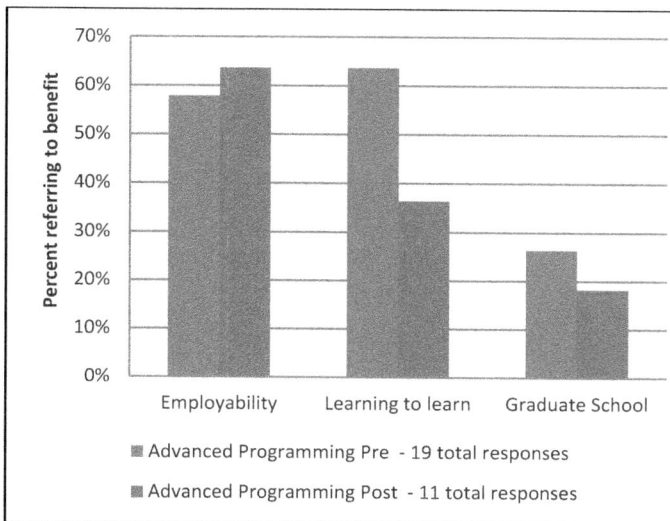

**Figure 3: Perceived Benefits of Research**

Students recognized that research could be pivotal for employability and for attending graduate school in both the pre and post surveys with comments such as "I find it useful for employability and acceptance into graduate school" (post). Employability was the most cited benefit mentioned. However, many students recognized that research could help them "learning to learn", and honing their analytical and problem solving skills with the statements "broaden my knowledge in a given subject" (pre), "...by doing research I was able to improve my organization and problem solving skills" (post) and "once I am in the workforce I will be constantly conducting research, if only to keep up with current innovations" (pre).

Two students mentioned the benefit of teamwork in "...learn how to create interpersonal relationships" (pre) and "communication with other people" (post).

Students also recognized that undergraduate research could pose challenges. The most often stated challenge was time: "Adding research to the equation (balancing schoolwork with your life at home) poses a major challenge when you have to juggle everything else" (pre) and "the class workload .... puts a burden on conducting research" (post). Relevancy is also an issue for students: "The research performed as an undergraduate can often seem to be pointless... or (an) unrealistic problem is being analyzed" (post) and "the research does not feel 'real'...everything seems to be just another school project" (post).

## 4.3  Research Event

For Goal 3, increase understanding of and interest in conducting SE research, students were required to attend one of two scheduled events. To evaluate this goal, a one page required summary provided the data, which supports that the student evaluation of the research event was very positive. The only negative comments were about the food, the directions given to

the event because the students were unfamiliar with the area, and one student contended that the presentation topic was "just a bit boring" (Advanced Programming, male, junior). The following are a collection of positive comments from the students:

Advanced Programming, female, senior: "I really enjoyed listening and learning how larger corporations research creative ideas ...The trip was refreshing."

Advanced Programming, male, senior: "I have learned something new about technology... (from) strategy to design to implementation".

Advanced Programming, male, senior: "It shows potentials for expanding on an ITEC education and the potential for moving toward a graduate degree and research."

SD I, male, junior: "The most valuable about this experience was that I now know what it takes to get into a good graduate school. With this knowledge I will be better at planning my future ambitions."

SD I, male, senior: "I thoroughly enjoyed the tour (of a research university) and have learned quite a bit.  Thank you for the opportunity to learn more about what is happening outside in the world."

## 5.  Discussion

Because the initial number of students is few, but promising, and enrollment in the ITEC program for these courses is increasing to almost triple, additional data collection should be performed. Initial analysis of post-assessment surveys showed an increase in understanding of how to do and present research. Success was achieved, evidenced by the fact that students performed well on final projects because of the skills they attained during this experience. Initial analysis of post-assessment surveys showed an increase in understanding of how to do and present research. Student feedback also showed that the corporate and research visits were extremely valuable in linking their coursework to future job skills. Students exhibited a broader understanding of SE research and reported more confidence in their ability to complete research projects.

## 5.1  Faculty Perceptions

There were also numerous challenges facing the instructor for course-embedded research. Paperwork for field trips is cumbersome. The students must be dressed appropriately, behave professionally and represent GGC well. There are timing issues related to scheduling off-campus visits. These challenges can be addressed, as the faculty members learn to streamline the paperwork, coordinate schedules well-ahead of events, and establish well-defined student expectations for each event and deliverable. To address the soft skills, we also propose inviting a speaker into the class for a presentation on professionalism.

The required activities and evaluation rubrics need to be woven into the course from day one, in multiple ways to provide students sufficient opportunities. It must be made clear from the beginning of the semester in the syllabus that the three deliverables are required, not optional activities. To motivate students to actively participate and thoughtfully complete assignments, each of the components should be worth a significant among of the student's grade. Most important, research activities must begin early in the semester, as the students need the entire semester to produce a poster and paper/presentation. The assessment of the program should be standardized amongst all instructors, such as using the same survey instruments after corporate visits and research events to make program evaluation easier and consistent for students.

Lastly, faculty members need to manage student expectations: they are not going to do "real research" right away. Students need to understand that developing research skills is a progression. Faculty can recall their initial research efforts; we didn't start doing research right away in our PhD programs. There were classes and background necessary before doing something "cool". Course-embedded research provides faculty the challenge and the opportunity to develop undergraduate understanding of research and skills.

## 5.2 Future Work

Eventually, as the 4-year URE model develops, freshmen and sophomore level IT students could be integrated into more embedded research courses at the lower division. The initial number of students in this is small, but results are promising.

The surveys will be supplemented with interviews of selected students to gain insight into what is and is not engaging students in changing their perception of SE research and how students can improve their research skills. We will employ one student assistant to support developing the assessment and interview questions, conducting interviews for objectivity, and coding results, including use of a qualitative data analysis tool, such as NVivo.

We will create a student-focused SE profile using rubrics integrated into the required course assignments. The profile encompasses the three SE research goals, with multiple skills within each goal. Each specific skill has a scale describing the expected student actions for each ability level, ranging from novice activities to professional. This profile facilitates faculty engagement with the student, providing incremental steps to develop along each dimension of the SE research profile, charting progress and setting clear expectations for the student. We will assess both individual students and the aggregate change in research competencies over the semester. When refined, the SE profile and rubrics will be made shared on a project web site (http://wiki.ggc.usg.edu/wiki/SERP).

## 6. ACKNOWLEDGMENTS

This program is made possible by funding from the Board of Regents' USG STEM Initiative II, designed to increase the success of STEM majors in college, produce better prepared STEM teachers, and promote STEM interest among K-12 students.

## 7. REFERENCES

[1] Barker, L. (2009). "Student and Faculty Perceptions of Undergraduate Research Experiences in Computing." Trans. Comput. Educ. 9(1): 1-28.

[2] Cox, M. F. and A. Andriot (2009). "Mentor and Undergraduate Student Comparisons of Students' Research Skills." Journal of STEM Education 10(1 & 2): 31-39.

[3] Jonas, M. (2011). Capstone experience: lessons from an undergraduate research group in speech at UNH Manchester. Proceedings of the 2011 conference on Information technology education. West Point, New York, USA, ACM: 275-280.

[4] Koppelman, H., B. v. Dijk, et al. (2011). Undergraduate research: a case study. Proceedings of the 16th annual joint conference on Innovation and technology in computer science education. Darmstadt, Germany, ACM: 288-292.

[5] Seymour, E., A. B. Hunter, et al. (2004). "Establishing the benefits of research experiences for undergraduates: First findings from a three-year study." Science Education 88: 493-594.

[6] Shaw, M. (2003). Writing good software engineering research papers: minitutorial. International Conference on Software Engineering, IEEE Computer Society.

[7] Ward, K. (2004). "The Fifty-four day thesis proposal: first experiences with a research course." Journal of Computing Sciences in Colleges 20(2).

# Three Years of Design-based Research to Reform a Software Engineering Curriculum

Matti Luukkainen, Arto Vihavainen, Thomas Vikberg
University of Helsinki
Department of Computer Science
P.O. Box 68 (Gustaf Hällströmin katu 2b)
Fi-00014 University of Helsinki
{ mluukkai, avihavai, tvikberg }@cs.helsinki.fi

## ABSTRACT

Most of the research-oriented computer science departments provide software engineering education. Providing up-to-date software engineering education can be problematic, as practises used in modern software development companies have been developed in the industry and as such do not often reach teachers in university contexts. The danger, and often the unfortunate reality, is that institutions giving education in software engineering end up teaching the subject using outdated practices with technologies no longer in use. In this article we describe a three-year design-based research where the goal has been to design and reform a software engineering subtrack within our bachelor curriculum that would make it possible for the students to have strong up-to-date theoretical and practical skills in software engineering without a need to remove any of the existing theoretical aspects.

## Categories and Subject Descriptors

K.3.2 [**Computers and Education**]: Computer and Information Science Education *Computer Science Education*

## General Terms

Design, Experimentation, Management

## Keywords

instructional design, modern software engineering practises, computer science curriculum

## 1. INTRODUCTION

Bachelor level computer science (CS) education has many goals. A CS curriculum should offer students a solid theoretical foundation in CS as well as convey enough practical skills and knowledge on current technologies. Although the focus of many CS departments in research universities lies in theoretical fields, such as algorithmics and computational complexity, most universities embed software engineering (SE) studies in their curriculum. This poses a great challenge for SE educators as they need to keep up with the rapid development of the IT industry. The danger, and often the unfortunate reality, is that institutions giving SE education end up teaching SE using outdated practices with technologies no longer in use [1].

According to IEEE Software Engineering is *(1) The application of a systematic, disciplined, quantifiable approach to the development, operation, and maintenance of software; that is, the application of engineering to software. (2) The study of approaches as in (1)* [3]. In contrast to more established fields of CS, the field of SE is still rather immature and has seen a radical paradigmatic change in the past decade with the emergence of agile methodologies [7, 8, 34]. In contrast to traditional plan-based methods (e.g. the so-called Waterfall method [32]), agile methodologies emphasize working software, customer collaboration, human interaction and best technological practices [8].

It has lately been recognized that SE is more a craft than a science [30, 31] and as such it is to be treated differently than the more theory-based topics. The up-to-date industrial best practices and tools should be taken into account when teaching SE. It has been noticed that with a traditional university instruction students even need to unlearn working methods acquired in formal education when entering the industry [9, 23].

One of the major problems is that most university teachers lack recent industrial experience or direct contact to industry, and as such are not aware of the emergent modern SE practises such as agile methods [1]. As teachers have not used them, they are not truly capable of conveying agile methodologies in teaching as agile methodologies can often only be learned through practicing them [34].

These issues have led to a situation where the SE-related bachelor level education is heavily out of synch with reality. Teaching yesterday's theories poses problems for the credibility of the education and leads to a lack of motivation amongst students with existing industrial experience.

The main SE learning objective of a graduating bachelor at our department is that the student should be able to perform efficiently in a modern software development project. In this paper we describe a three-year design-based research where the goal has been to design a SE subtrack within our CS bachelor curriculum that would make it possible to have strong up-to-date theoretical and practical skills in SE.

## 2. INITIAL PROBLEM ANALYSIS

The aim of design-based research [35, 10] is to construct an educational artefact [12, 26], in this case a reformed SE subtrack within our CS curriculum. The artefact is an intervention into current practices [11] and thus the process of developing the artefact begins by initial problem analysis [22]. The development of the artifact is then continued in an iterative manner where the evaluation process is undertaken repeatedly at the beginning of each iteration as well as during iterations [13, 26]. This should lead to an improved artefact and improved understanding of the process that led to the improvement [16, 33]. Next we describe the situation of the SE subtrack of the Department of Computer Science at the University of Helsinki at the beginning of the first iteration that was started in fall 2009.

The SE subtrack was based on the courses displayed in Figure 1. During the first semester the students undertake the courses Introduction to programming, Advanced Programming (together forming CS1) and Software Modeling. In the second semester they take the course Data Structures (CS2), Programming Project, and Introduction to Databases. In their second year they carry out the Database Application Project and our SE course. During the third year the students undertake what could be seen as the culmination of their SE studies so far: SE Project, a 14-week capstone project done in groups of 4-6 students. The capstone project requires roughly 200 working hours for each participant. On top of the SE subtrack the students take other courses with focus on algorithmics and networking, as well as minor-subject studies.

Evaluation of the effectiveness of SE subtrack was done by observing (1) the capability of students to work in the Software Engineering Project (2) the progress they made during the SE Project (3) their readiness to start working

as a "junior software developer" in the software engineering industry after the project was finished.

Observations for (1) and (2) were made during the SE Project course by project instructors. Observations for (3) was done in the Software Factory, a new master's level advanced software project [2]. Those of the students who are continuing beyond bachelor and are majoring in SE take part in the Software Factory which is a seven-week, five days a week project. It is done for a real client within self-organizing teams which are assumed to follow all the best practices of agile software development.

Students participation in Software Factory gave us a fine opportunity for evaluating their performance as junior software developers. The evaluation was done by the coordinator of the Software Factory project, who is an expert in industrial practices, and by a senior faculty member, both members of the curriculum design team.

Several problems were identified during the observations:

**(P1)** the programming skills and routine of most of the students were not at an adequate level

**(P2)** good programming practices [30, 25] were missing leading to lack of maintainability of the written code

**(P3)** no knowledge of theories or practices of testing

**(P4)** no practical knowledge of software design and architectures

**(P5)** lack of experience in designing and programming web applications

**(P6)** outdated knowledge of software development processes

**(P7)** lack of elementary SE tool skills and knowledge such as version control, integrated development environments (IDEs), shell scripting and system administration

**(P8)** complete unawareness of agile SE practices such as user-story-based requirements engineering, planning and estimation [17] and more technical practices such as test-driven development [6], continuous integration [21] and behavior-driven development [15]

**(P9)** lack of team working skills and practises

## 3. THE REFORM STRATEGY

The goal of the reform was to raise the standard of the SE Project and to tackle the identified problems listed in the previous section within some of the courses without damaging the course passing rates. The key course for preparing students for the SE Project was the SE course that is typically taken at the later part of the 2nd year, just before attending the SE Project. However, the design team felt that reforming a six-week 4 ECTS[1] course would not be enough to root the required theoretical and practical background in students. Thus, it was decided that each of the courses leading to the SE course had to be reformed.

When this goal was set, a typical implementation strategy would have been to reform the course structure within the curriculum. This approach is both bureaucratic and time consuming, as the changes have to be ratified by different instances, after which they can only be put into action after a certain time[2]. This approach is also inefficient as it often leads to introduction of courses into specific knowledge

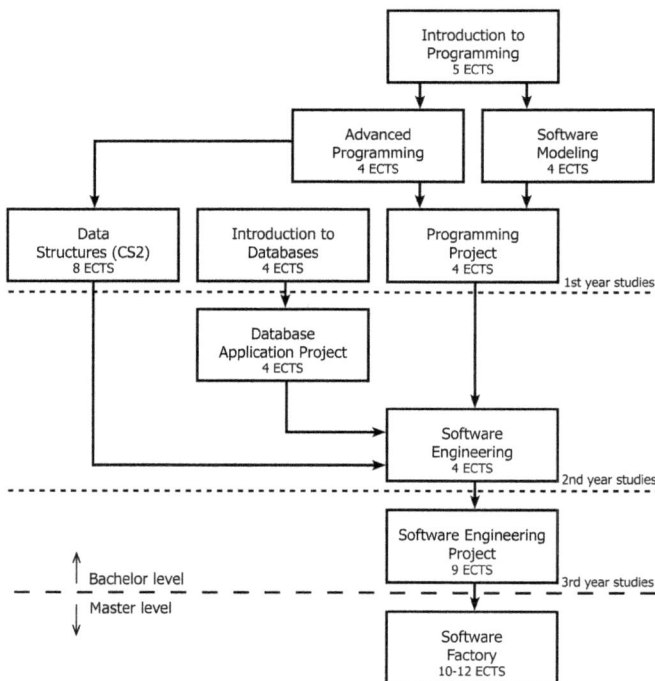

**Figure 1: SE subtrack at University of Helsinki.**

---

[1]European Credit Transfer and Accumulation System credits where one academic year corresponds to 60 ECTS.

[2]The course structure of the curriculum can be changed at the University of Helsinki in two-year intervals.

areas, which in turn would not affect other courses. For example creating a course in software testing would not force good testing practices into other courses.

Instead of introducing new courses the reform strategy chosen was to completely rethink the contents, structures and pedagogical practices of the existing courses. It was decided that up-to-date industrial best practices should be introduced from day one and emphasized even in more theory-oriented courses such as CS2. This emphasis on practical undertakings is a major shift from the typical approach taken before at our department where the goal was to teach the *idea* of software development on a high level.

The departmental competencies lie in the theory of SE and not in the industry practices. This forced the design team to employ an unusual strategy for a research university for laying out the reformed curriculum. The main responsible faculty member of the reform – tenured assoc. prof. – went on to participate in the Software Factory as a normal student to find out the problems himself and to engage in a real industry project. The development team also recruited students within the department with strong industry backgrounds as developers and teachers for the reformed courses.

## 4. DESIGN ITERATIONS

The first design iteration took place in fall 2009 and has since progressed into a completely reformed SE subtrack in spring 2012. During the three-year period one or two courses in each iteration were restructured. Each iteration lasted one academic term when the courses reformed were given. In each iteration, courses already reformed were further refined according to experiences and data gathered from the students' performance in subsequent courses. Next, we will present an overview of the iterations.

### Fall 2009

The reform took a rather cautious start. The first step was to integrate the Software Modeling course to progress lockstep with the Advanced Programming course which was taken at the same time by the same set of students. The content of the course (UML class and sequence diagrams and introduction to object design) remained much the same as it had been before. The course was set to emphasize iterative and agile software processes in contrast to the more traditional approaches emphasized before. Also, the UML-modeling was done in a less rigorous manner than before with the aim to introduce agile modeling principles [5], where UML is used as a help for communication and design during the program development phase, not as a comprehensive documentation tool. Thus, during the first term only item (P3) from the problems listed in Section 2 was addressed.

### Spring 2010

The design team felt that the main problem was item (P1): the lack of adequate programming skills that the students possessed even after several years of study. The team decided that the old lecture-based programming instruction had to be replaced by a more pragmatic approach with a heavy emphasis on actual programming under guidance of more experienced programmers.

As a result a new pedagogical model was developed for introductory programming courses, the *Extreme Apprenticeship* method (XA) that is based on principles of Cognitive Apprenticeship [19, 18] as well as modern SE practises.

XA was highly successful from the point of view of learning outcomes and was also well received by the students [36]. The new method of programming instruction boosted the programming skills of our students considerably. Programming used to be a disliked topic among a remarkably large portion of the student population. This made the further development of our SE subtrack much easier.

### Summer 2010

As a continuation to XA the Programming Project course was arranged in a completely new form. The project consists of students designing and implementing a program on their own: typically a game such as Tetris or a simple data organizing application.

The project used to be organized to imitate the Waterfall-development model: the first three weeks contained analysis and design, which was followed by two weeks of programming ending in a single week of testing. Heavy documentation was required at the end of the project. Usually the students' working process was reduced to a "code and fix"-type of programming effort where design and testing were almost completely ignored, and the resulting documentation was a mix of initial plans and a final document that was often reverse engineered from the actual implementation.

In order to work on the problem items (P3), (P6) and (P8), the course was reformed into an agile, iterative project, where each iteration lasted a week during which a small increment of the program was to be completed. After six iterations the program should be completed. Along the implementation the students were required to build automated unit tests using the JUnit-testing framework [6], and also to have up-to-date UML-based implementation documentation sketches at all times.

### Fall 2010

The XA-model of programming instruction was further elaborated and scaled to a much larger audience than the first instance [37]. More emphasis was put on code quality (P2), and not just the correct behavior of the code.

The Software Modeling course was aligned with the XA type of programming instruction. As automated tests were added as a mandatory part of the Programming Project, there was a need to incorporate them into the learning objectives of at least one of the previous courses as well. Automated unit testing was incorporated as a part of the software modeling course, leading to further work on the problem item (P3).

### Spring 2011

XA-based programming instruction was further elaborated by completely removing the lectures altogether (lectures had previously been decreased from four weekly hours to two) and focusing even more on the students' active problem solving [28].

In order to work on the problem item (P7), the Programming Project was iterated to enforce basic use of a version control system (VCS), that had not previously been emphasized. This led to an extremely inefficient workflow in the SE Project. Since the programming project is a one-person project, the students had a relaxed environment for learning the basics of a VCS workflow without more challenging VCS-related issues such as merge conflicts.

Problem items (P1) and (P2) were focused on in a significant change within the Data Structures course [29]. The

Data Structures course is a typical CS2-course covering basic data structures (stack, binary search tree, balanced binary search tree, heap, graph) and the related algorithms. The old approach was based on mathematical analysis and pseudo-code, no real programming was done in the course. The course had a rather high drop-out rate and most of the students passing the course were not particularly good in applying the theory to practical problem solving.

The design team decided to refocus the CS2 course to contain more practical problem solving tasks that were implemented using a real programming language instead of pseudocode. A total of sixty new programming tasks were included into the course, some of which were quite challenging. All theoretical aspects were also kept in the course, which led to an increase in the workload of students in contrast to the old CS2 course.

Part of the lectures were restructured to contain worked example-style [14] problem solving, and best programming practices were emphasized throughout the course. Increased retention rate, observed learning outcomes, and positive student feedback showed clearly that the restructuring of the course was a success [29].

### Fall 2011

The Software Modeling course saw its third refinement in fall 2011[3]. The new course put even more emphasis on agile processes and agile modeling principles that center around maximal enhancement of communication among software developers and other stakeholders.

The course introduced communication and team-related aspects in the form of design and modeling sessions. In the sessions students worked in teams of 4-6 people around a large whiteboard designing and modeling larger tasks that would have been very challenging for most of the students to be done on their own. Whiteboards were used to emphasize that designs can always be changed and improved. The amount of lectures was also reduced, which allowed focusing more on active problem solving during the course. These modifications addressed items (P4), (P6), (P8) and (P9).

### Spring 2012

In spring 2012, major changes were made to improve the SE curriculum. A new course focusing on web application development was introduced and the first implementation of a totally reformed SE course took place.

Some web application development had been done as part of the curriculum already before the new course. The Database Application Project that had been in the SE curriculum for more than a decade had slowly evolved to a project where the students designed and implemented a web application that was backed by a database. Most students learned some PHP or Java Servlet techniques on their own in order to implement the application. Before XA-style programming instruction, programming skills were poor and there was a total disrespect for code quality and structure. The web applications that students created during their project did not usually follow any of the best practices of web programming, such as separation of representation, structure and behavior or layered architecture [4, 27].

To remedy this problem (P5), the design team set up the Web Application Development course, where students were guided to do web programming *the right way*. Strong emphasis was put especially on the maintainability of written code, further addressing the problem item (P2). The course was scheduled to be taken in the second term of the second year, just before the SE course. In contrast to the rest of the SE subtrack, Web Application Development was not compulsory. However, roughly half of the students took the course.

The design team completely restructured the SE course for the first time in the later part of spring 2012, just after the new Web Application Development course. The previous SE course was a theoretical walkthrough of phases found in any software development methodology: requirements analysis, design, testing and software maintenance. The course focus was on the Waterfall model and its interpretation of the role of the phases in the development process. This view was far too theoretical, abstract and outdated from the point of view of current industrial practises that rely heavily on agile development [8, 34, 7].

The reforms made to earlier courses in the study path had given a partial remedy to many of the problems listed in Section 2. The rest needed to be taken care of in the SE course. The learning objectives of the course were set high in order to provide students with the capability of working productively in the SE Project that was arranged as an intensive Scrum-like agile project. The specific learning objectives were:

- learn the basics of Scrum
  - iterative and incremental development
  - roles: Scrum Master, Product Owner, Developer
  - meetings: sprint planning, daily scrum, review, retrospective
  - artifacts: product and sprint backlog
- agile planning, requirements engineering and execution of an iteration
  - user stories, their estimation and prioritization
  - product backlog grooming
  - planning game to maximize the customer value of the developed product
  - splitting stories to tasks in sprint backlog
  - reporting the progress within an iteration
- concepts of program testing and practical techniques in automatic testing
  - test-driven development
  - story level testing, behavior-driven development
  - continuous integration
- support for program design
  - layered architecture and domain-driven design
  - object-oriented principles: encapsulation, cohesion, low coupling, testability, maintainability
  - design patterns
- efficient use of Git version control system in group work
- use of static analysis tools to give diagnostics on developed programs

The new course implementation consisted of three components. Twenty hours of lectures contained a broad introduction to the covered topics. Weekly task sets aimed at building routine in the use of the Git version control system, design patterns [24] and the use of the Spring framework [38]. Both the lectures and the tasks set the stage for the third component: a SE mini-project. The mini-project was a simulation of an agile SE project done in three iterations, each taking one week. The mini-project was done in groups of 3-5 students. Each group (22 altogether) was given the same

---

[3]Because of the shifts in content the course was renamed to "Methods for Software Engineering" starting from fall 2012.

topic and the course instructors acted as customer, product owner and scrum master. The developed program was not particularly large, and the focus was on gaining more in-depth knowledge of agile principles and practices that were introduced to students in the lectures.

The working hours for each student within an iteration were limited to four hours. This was an important aspect since one of the most critical skills in agile development is the capability to commit to a workload (e.g. a set of *user stories*) that the team believes can be implemented in high quality (including automated tests) within one iteration [8, 34]. Committing to implement a certain set of user stories in an iteration also motivates students to estimate the work that is required for implementing each user story. The user story management was done with *product* and *sprint backlogs* as the current industry best practices recommend [17]. The project groups were encouraged to have proper sprint planning sessions and retrospectives during the mini-project.

Students found the mini-project a beneficial experience. Most of the groups struggled during first iteration but thanks to the inspect-and-adapt nature of iterative development and coaching given by the course instructors, all groups matured substantially during the three iterations. During the mini-project, students saw an immediate benefit of the theories from the lectures and various tools and techniques practised in the normal exercises.

The design team evidenced a similar phenomenon in the SE course as in the CS2 course a year earlier: when compared to the traditional lecture-based course the students learned the theoretical topics at a deeper level when the course consisted of active student participation and practical tasks.

## 5. ANALYSIS AND FURTHER WORK

After three years of iterations the SE curriculum has almost been renewed. The quality and the working process in the currently ongoing SE Project course shows that the students have progressed towards the goal set for their SE subtrack. They are much more prepared to participate in software projects using modern agile practices and use up-to-date methods and tools when compared to the students that took the pre-reform SE subtrack.

One of the main objectives was to gradually introduce various practices and theoretical ideas to the courses. This has resulted in strong inter-course links, introducing a concept in one course and the development of the same theme further in another course. E.g. the idea of automated testing together with some practical tasks are introduced in the course Software Modeling. When students take part in the Programming Project, they are required to have a rather comprehensive unit testing harness. Finally, in the SE course, the theories and concepts behind testing are covered more thoroughly and agile practises such as TDD and BDD are introduced to students within a realistic setting. This is a big difference to the old model where one concept was taught mostly only within a single course and the connections between courses were rather weak.

During the new course Web Application Development we made an important finding: despite the much increased programming routine, a considerable amount of students struggled in sysadmin-like issues such as working in command line, shell scripting, and server installations. These issues are important in web application development since a web application also involves the server components. The weak sysadmin skills were surprising. It had been assumed for a long time that sysadmin-related skills are easily learned by each student on their own and having those as part of university courses would not be necessary or even wise. However, it has been recognized that nowadays the clear separation of software developers and administrators is no longer valid in the software industry, at least in smaller companies [20]. Thus some level of sysadmin skills must be included in the SE curriculum.

We have embedded some sysadmin skills already in the new SE course (more emphasis on working with command line with VCS and Build management systems such as Maven). In the future the introduction of sysadmin concepts and skills should be embedded in several courses, as is currently done with testing. Suitable courses where the existing theory could easily be enriched with these topics are Operating Systems (working with command line, shell scripting), Introduction to Databases (installation and operation of a database server), Introduction to Computer Networks (internet-related command line tools such as telnet, traceroute and curl, installation and operation of a web server).

The courses Introduction to Databases and Database Application Project are currently in a rather old-fashioned state. The courses have remained almost intact for more than 10 years and are heavily based on relational algebra and relational database model. A reform is clearly needed: active student participation should be increased, the old dust should be wiped out. Also, strong connections to the programming courses should be established. Currently the courses do not at all mention the important concept of object relational mapping, i.e, how objects in a program implemented e.g. in Java could be persisted to a relational database. Further, the emergence of nosql-databases should be taken into account in the curriculum. These improvements are in focus in the next iterations of the curriculum reform.

## 6. CONCLUSIONS

In this article we have presented three years of design-based research to reform our software engineering curriculum. During the reform we have made no compromises. None of the core CS topics have been dropped, while relevant content and new approaches have been introduced.

The renewed versions of CS2 and SE courses contain all the old theoretical elements as well as a substantial amount of practical problem solving. The average student workload has increased considerably. Although the average workload has increased heavily, the student feedback has been overwhelmingly positive. The students seem to enjoy working more as the connections to the reality of the software industry are made clear.

How is this possible? We have a strong feeling that the reform would not have been possible without XA-based programming instruction that has raised the programming routine of our students to a completely new level as well as introduced them to working hard starting from day one. The reformed CS2 and SE can be seen as a direct continuation of active learning-based education, which boosts student motivation and confidence and by that helps students to grasp also the more theoretical topics more easily.

The reform process has been research driven [22] with publications linking current scientific research to various design iterations. Our work has not only produced a renewed SE curriculum, but also new student-centered teaching methods [36, 37], renewed ways of presenting old content [29] and new ways of organizing administration [28].

# 7. REFERENCES

[1] P. Abrahamsson. Inaugural lecture: The new era of software quality (in Finnish). http://www.cs.helsinki.fi/kolumni/ohjelmistojen-laadun-uusi-aikakausi, December 2009.

[2] P. Abrahamsson, P. Kettunen, and F. Fagerholm. The set-up of a valuable software engineering research infrastructure of the 2010s. In *Workshop on Valuable Software Products*, 2010.

[3] A. Abram, J. W. More, B. Pierre, and D. Robert, editors. *Guide to the Software Engineering Body of Knownledge*. IEEE Computer Society, 2004.

[4] D. Alur, D. Malkis, and J. Crupi. *Core J2EE Patterns: Best Practices and Design Strategies*. Prentice Hall, 2 edition, 2003.

[5] S. W. Ambler and R. Jeffries. *Agile Modeling: Effective Practices for Extreme Programming and the Unified Process*. Wiley, 2002.

[6] K. Beck. *Test Driven Development: By Example*. Addison-Wesley, 2002.

[7] K. Beck and C. Andres. *Extreme Programming Explained: Embrace Change (2nd Edition)*. Addison-Wesley Professional, 2004.

[8] K. Beck, M. Beedle, A. van Bennekum, A. Cockburn, W. Cunningham, M. Fowler, J. Grenning, J. Highsmith, A. Hunt, R. Jeffries, J. Kern, B. Marick, R. C. Martin, S. Mallor, K. Shwaber, and J. Sutherland. The Agile Manifesto. Technical report, The Agile Alliance, 2001.

[9] A. Begel and B. Simon. Struggles of new college graduates in their first software development job. In *Proceedings of the SIGCSE '08*. ACM, 2008.

[10] P. Bell. On the theoretical breadth of design-based research in education. *Educational Psychologist*, 39(4), 2004.

[11] C. Bereiter. Design research for sustained innovation. *Cognitive Studies Bulletin of the Japanese Cognitive Science Society*, 9(3):321–327, 2002.

[12] A. L. Brown. Design experiments: Theoretical and methodological challenges in creating complex interventions in classroom settings. *The Journal of the Learning Sciences*, 2(2):141–178, 1992.

[13] H. Burkhardt and A. H. Schoenfeld. Improving educational research: Toward a more useful, more influential, and better-funded enterprise. *Educational Researcher*, 32(9):3–14, 2003.

[14] M. E. Caspersen and J. Bennedsen. Instructional design of a programming course: a learning theoretic approach. In *ICER '07: Proc. of the 3rd international workshop on Computing education research*, 2007.

[15] D. Chelimsky, D. Astels, B. Helmkamp, D. North, Z. Dennis, and A. Hellesoy. *The RSpec Book*. Pragmatic Bookshelf, 2010.

[16] P. Cobb, J. Confrey, A. diSessa, R. Lehrer, and L. Schauble. Design experiments in educational research. *Educational Researcher*, 32(1):9–13, 2003.

[17] M. Cohn. *Agile Estimating and Planning*. Prentice Hall, 2005.

[18] A. Collins, J. Brown, and A. Holum. Cognitive apprenticeship: Making thinking visible. *American Educator*, 15(3):6–46, 1991.

[19] A. Collins, J. Brown, and S. Newman. Cognitive apprenticeship: Teaching the crafts of reading, writing, and mathematics. In L. Resnick, editor, *Knowing learning and instruction Essays in honor of Robert Glaser*, volume Knowing, l of *Psychology of Education and Instruction Series*, pages 453–494. Lawrence Erlbaum Associates, 1989.

[20] Devops: A software revolution in the making? *Cutter IT Journal*, 24(8), 2011. Special issue.

[21] P. Duval, S. Matyas, and A. Glower. *Continuous Integration: Improving Software Quality and Reducing Risk*. Addison-Wesley, 2007.

[22] D. C. Edelson. Design research: What we learn when we engage in design. *The Journal of the Learning Sciences*, 11(1):105–121, 2002.

[23] A. Fox and D. Patterson. Crossing the software education chasm. *Communications of ACM*, 55(5):44–49, May 2012.

[24] E. Gamma, R. Helm, R. Johnson, and J. Vlissides. *Design Patterns: Elements of Reusable Object-Oriented Software*. Addison-Wesley, 1994.

[25] A. Hunt and D. Thomas. *The Pragmatic Programmer: From Journeyman to Master*. Addison-Wesley, 1999.

[26] K. Juuti and J. Lavonen. Design-based research in science education: One step towards methodology. *NorDiNa*, 4:54–68, 2006.

[27] J. Keith. *DOM Scripting: Web Design with JavaScript and the Document Object Model*. friends of ED, 2005.

[28] J. Kurhila and A. Vihavainen. Management, structures and tools to scale up personal advising in large programming courses. In *Proceedings of the SIGITE '11*. ACM, 2011.

[29] M. Luukkainen, A. Vihavainen, and T. Vikberg. A software craftsman's approach to data structures. In *Proceedings of the SIGCSE '12*. ACM, 2012.

[30] R. C. Martin. *Clean Code: A Handbook of Agile Software Craftsmanship*. Prentice Hall, 2008.

[31] P. McBreen. *Software Craftsmanship: The New Imperative*. Prentice Hall, 2001.

[32] W. Royce. Managing the development of large software systems. In *Proceedings of IEEE WESCON 26*. TeX Users Group, August 1970.

[33] A. H. Schoenfeld. Bridging the cultures of educational research and design. *Educational Designer*, 1(2), 2009.

[34] K. Schwaber and M. Beedle. *Agile Software Development with SCRUM*. Prentice Hall, 2002.

[35] The Design-Based Research Collective. Design-based research: An emerging paradigm for educational inquiry. *Educational Researcher*, 32(1):5–8, 2003.

[36] A. Vihavainen, M. Paksula, and M. Luukkainen. Extreme apprenticeship method in teaching programming for beginners. In *Proceedings of the SIGCSE '11*. ACM, 2011.

[37] A. Vihavainen, M. Paksula, M. Luukkainen, and J. Kurhila. Extreme apprenticeship method: key practices and upward scalability. In *Proceedings of the ITiCSE '11*. ACM, 2011.

[38] C. Walls. *Spring in Action*. Manning Publ., 2011.

# Supporting the Review of Student Proposal Drafts in Information Technologies

Samuel González López and Aurelio López-López
Instituto Nacional de Astrofísica, Óptica y Electrónica
Luis Enrique Erro No. 1, Tonantzintla, Puebla México
52 + (222) 2663100 Ext: 8314
{sgonzalez,allopez}@inaoep.mx

## ABSTRACT

In many cases, academic programs or courses conclude with a thesis or research proposal text, elaborated by students. The review of such texts is a heavy load, especially at initial stages of drafting. This paper proposes a model that allows linguistic and structural review of some essential elements in proposal drafts of undergraduate students. The model aims to support the review from vocabulary to the argumentation in the draft, and is part of an intelligent tutor to monitor student progress. This work presents the initial results in terms of lexical and global coherence analysis of proposal drafts of students. Lexical analysis is done in terms of lexical density, lexical diversity, and sophistication. Global coherence is evaluated using the Latent Semantic Analysis technique. Our results show that the level reached so far by the analyzer is adequate to support the review, taking into account for one section the level of agreement with human reviewers.

## Categories and Subject Descriptors

K.3.2 [**Computers and Education**]: Computer and Information Science Education – *Computer Science Education.*

## General Terms

Measurement, Experimentation, Languages, Verification.

## Keywords

Student drafts, lexical density, lexical variety, sophistication, coherence, evaluation, intelligent tutor, language models.

## 1. INTRODUCTION

Academic programs or courses conclude often with a thesis or research proposal text, elaborated by students. The usual process that students follow is to write a first draft and then improve the document with the iterated recommendations of the adviser. Some educational institutions have a guide that supports students in structuring the proposal document, however in many cases this is insufficient. It was observed that students often need help on how to structure all aspects of their draft. This requires that the academic adviser or instructor spends extra time in the review process. This paper focuses on developing a computational model

that helps undergraduate students of computing and information technologies area, to improve their draft during the writing process, especially in the early stages. Also we intend that this model implemented in a system helps the academic adviser by reducing the time dedicated to the draft review, focusing on the content. The results reported here on lexical analysis and global coherence, are part of a larger project that may help students to evaluate early their drafts, and facilitate the review process of the academic advisor.

The proposed model consists of four levels; where the first focuses on the lexicon used by the student in his/her draft, the second level seeks to identify and assess the level of coherence, the third level considers language models intended to identify the particular structure of each element of the proposal, and the last one focuses on identifying answers to methodological questions that characterize certain elements of a proposal document, for example: What will you do?, How are you going to do it? These levels of evaluation will be managed by an intelligent tutor that will provide feedback to the student. We selected eight essentials elements of a research proposal: title, problem statement, justification, objective, research questions, hypothesis, methodology, and conclusions.

We report in this paper some initial results about evaluating global coherence and the lexical analysis in proposal drafts. Our initial results show that our analyzer provides adequate review, considering the level of agreement with human reviewers.

## 2. LEXICAL AND COHERENCE ANALYSIS

This section reviews the main work in the area of natural language processing (NLP) techniques related to lexical analysis including some measures employed, and for coherence assessment.

### 2.1 Lexical analysis

There are a variety of methods to evaluate the use of vocabulary (lexicon) in text, all with different goals. To measure the sophistication of some papers using a text word lists, in [1], they used a list of 3000 easy words. For Spanish, some studies use the list provided by the SRA[1] (Spanish Royal Academy) of 1000, 5000 and 15000 most frequent words. In [2], 32 lexical measures were used to predict demographic attributes, such as age or gender regardless of the domain. Those measures were grouped in lexical diversity, lexical density, and sophistication.

---

[1] Most frequent word list available at http://corpus.rae.es/

Others works have used Yule's K to measure the richness in texts [3], where this kind of measures focus on the word repetitions and is considered a measure of lexical diversity. In our work this assessment is on the basis of the evaluation process of a proposal draft. We are looking for lexical analysis to identify frequent deficiencies in student writings such as too much use of empty words, abuse of certain terms, or low knowledge of technical terminology. Once identified these common errors, the tutor can provide feedback.

## 2.2 Coherence analysis

A formal definition given in [4] establishes that coherence is the connection of all parts of a text into a whole: the interrelationship of the various elements of the text. Also coherence is classified based on its scope: local and global. The global coherence means that a document is related to a main topic, i.e. it is not consistent when its elements have no such main topic. And local coherence is defined within small textual units [5]. Therefore, coherence within proposal draft is important because if it does not have each of the elements related into a whole or sections are not close to a topic, the document would not exhibit coherence. Different techniques such as Latent Semantic Analysis (LSA) and Grid Entity have been used to assess coherence. The first focuses on the semantic aspect and the second in syntactic features.

In [6], their work assessed automatically the coherence of police news, that is, given police news reports written by a columnist, the evaluation system provided the degree of coherence in the reports. This research used the technique of Latent Semantic Analysis, first compiling a police news corpus, which served to train the system. From this set of texts, the system evaluator measured the coherence of the news. The expected result was that the software evaluator will approach the results of evaluations obtained by a columnist and a Spanish language expert.

In our work, we also applied the LSA technique to assess the global coherence of the sections in proposal drafts, to provide a measure of coherence to the student about his/her writing.

A representation of discourse called Entity Grid is presented in [7], which is constructed in a two-dimensional array that captures the distribution of entities in the discourse across sentences, where rows correspond to the sentences and the columns represent the entities of discourse. The cells can have values, such as: subject, object or neither. The main idea of this representation is that, while the object and subject are present in the sentences, the assessed coherence is stronger. They assume that certain types of transition of subject and object are likely to appear in locally coherent discourse. The Entity Grid technique is intended to reveal local coherence and compared to LSA in terms of correlation [8], both techniques showed low correlation, so they capture different aspects of coherence.

A combination of algorithm BL08 (nouns and pronouns) for entity grid with writing quality features, such as grammar, word usage, and mechanics errors, showed improvements in the review of the coherence of student's essays on three different populations [9].The experiments used a corpus of 800 essays related to Test of English as a Foreign Language (TOEFL) and the Graduate Record Admissions Test (GRE). After performing the experiments, only two out of three populations obtained acceptable Kappa values, between humans and system.

## 3. INTELLIGENT TUTORS

A system called AutoTutor is presented in [10], an intelligent tutorial, which simulates the pattern of discourse and the teaching strategies of a human tutor. AutoTutor modules have a set of processors and storage units that keep the content dynamic with qualitative and quantitative parameters. The aim of AutoTutor is to build an intelligent agent that can produce effective conversational dialogues pedagogically, using natural language conversations to help students actively to construct knowledge.

The tutor is designed to teach Newtonian physics to students, and starts with an introduction and an overview of the subject of two minutes, and then moves to the learning session. After the introduction, the conversation begins by establishing a problem and asking the student for an answer. From this point, it starts a conversation between the student and the tutor. The goal is that students using the intelligent tutor can answer the questions correctly. The outputs of AutoTutor are stored and updated during the process of mentoring, in this way it creates and updates the tutor for each student, by the history of their dialogue. This tool uses the Latent Semantic Analysis (LSA) technique to represent semantic knowledge of physics, and allows a comparison of the contributions of the student to the expected responses. This type of work focuses on creating an environment similar or close to what the student would have with a teacher who provides help.

One of the artificial intelligence techniques to model the student in intelligent tutoring is Bayesian networks. Similar to our proposal, the paper [11] presents the modeling of the students, integrating the Bayesian networks and the tools of the relational database model. In modeling the student, the cognitive state is inferred from two parts: the data prior to the student and the behavior during the interaction with the system.

A tutor that allowed the student to solve thermodynamic problems is reported in [12]. The student can select a problem and solve it in the workspace. Solving such problems involves two main phases: drawing the diagram, and later calculating unknowns, the solution can be sent to the tutor for evaluation and feedback. This selection feature will be incorporated into our intelligent tutor for the student to evaluate their partial or global proposal and receive feedback.

## 4. ANALYZER MODEL

Our model incorporates a module for linguistic and structural review, both will be integrated into an intelligent tutor, which allows students to get feedback and adapt the information displayed depending on their performance.

Currently, we have a corpus of 50 thesis proposal documents stored in database, these research projects are in Spanish and mainly from the Computing and Information Technologies domain. The topics included in the corpus are diverse, some documents are in the area of computer architecture, intelligent tutoring, machine learning, information retrieval, communication networks, and software engineering. The coherence and lexical analyzer is embedded in an intelligent tutor using Bayesian network technology to build the student model.

The intelligent tutor generates a model for each student and the model is updated each time the student uses the analyzer, the aim is that the tutor can monitor student performance and send feedback about their proposal draft. The analyzer model consists of the following modules.

*Reached level identifier:* This identifies the level of student when he/she enters the intelligent tutor, accessing a repository of previous levels achieved by the student to extract the most recent. This level lets the tutor to establish a scenario according to the student's progress, for instance suggestions, material or recommendations that the tutor displayed while the student uses the analyzer. When the user utilizes the tutor for the first time, he/she starts with a low level and a basic scenario with definitions, for example, of concepts of coherence, lexical diversity, lexical density, or sophistication. In Figure 1, we illustrate this module.

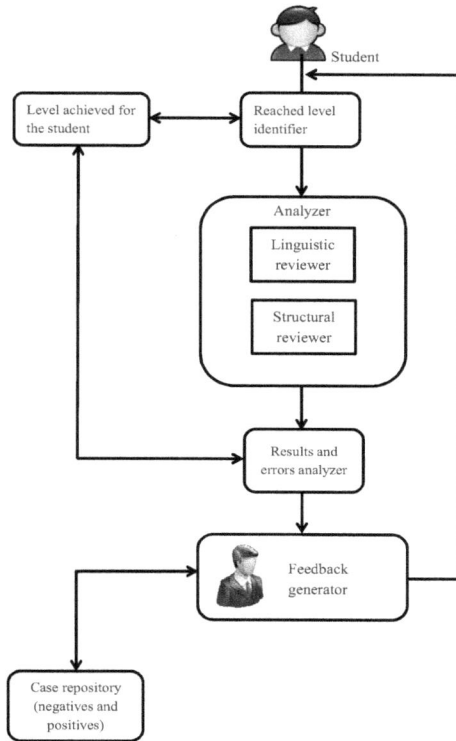

**Figure 1. Analyzer Model**

*Achieved levels:* It is a repository for saving the student reached level and updating each time the student makes an assessment of the elements of his/her proposal draft.

*Analyzer:* This module contains two types of reviewers. The first, the Linguistic reviewer, has the purpose of analyzing the different elements considered as essentials in a proposal draft. The aim is to evaluate linguistic characteristics of each element. The second, the Structural reviewer, seeks the coherence of the different elements and the relation that there has to exist between them. The aim is to give a result of a global analysis of the elements of a research project proposal document.

*Results and errors analyzer:* This module focuses on adapting the tutor to the student, i.e., in taking into account the student actions and the results produced by the reviewers to generate the level of achievement. For this module, the frequencies of mistakes are considered.

*Feedback generator:* This component will provide different recommendations to the student, based on the performance achieved. The goal is that the intelligent tutor can supply positive or negative example to illustrate something wrong, this decision will depend on the results that the student is generating using the

tutor. For instance, when a student receives a low evaluation of overall coherence in the objectives section of the proposal, the tutor sends two examples and these let students identify how an appropriate objective has to be written, and also sends a negative example for comparing them and see the differences. For instance, a positive example of global coherence[2] *"Explore the requirements for sharing information through a search and retrieval system among interoperable digital libraries with the open archives initiative, using mobile agent"*. A negative example of global coherence *"Inquire what is the role of school cooperatives in the government of national schools, analyzing the scope and limits of family involvement in schools and the educational system"*.

It also displays a brief explanation of both examples, negative and positive, with the aim of distinguishing the errors and good decisions of each.

*Case repository:* This contains positive and negative examples of each section in proposal drafts, grouped by each aspect that is evaluated. The examples were taken from thesis of research institutes and universities with computing and information technologies programs. The repository will be updated with the same elements evaluated, once they obtain high measures and the approval of academic adviser.

*Linguistic and Structural reviewers* will be based on a four levels assessment. This module starts with a basic assessment and goes to a more complex level.

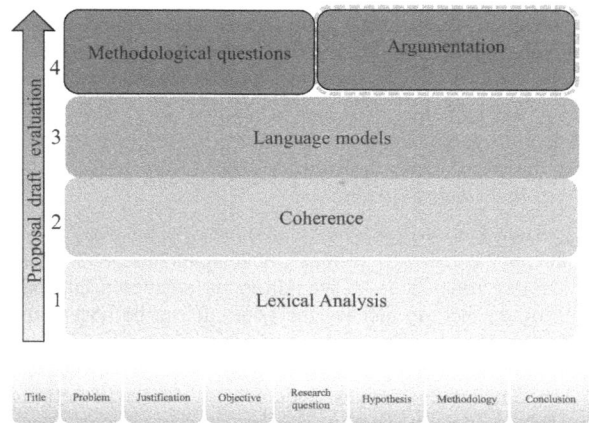

**Figure 2: Four-level evaluation**

The eight elements of project proposals to evaluate are illustrated at the bottom of Figure 2, the first level is a lexical analysis. For a full assessment at this level, there are three dimensions, the first is the lexical diversity which seeks to measure student ability to write their ideas with a varied vocabulary, the second dimension refers to the lexical density whose goal is to reflect the proportion of content words after removing empty words, finally the sophistication reveals the knowledge of the technical subject and is the proportion of "advanced" or "sophisticated" words employed. Together, the three dimensions will identify the lexical level of the student writing. The sophistication would be a plus for the undergraduate student. In section 4, we describe the initial experiments and preliminary results about lexical analysis.

---

[2] Examples are translations of actual Spanish texts in our corpus

At the second level, an evaluation of coherence for the essentials elements of the document written by the student is done. This level incorporates the LSA and Entity Grid techniques to capture the global and local coherence. Currently, we have developed a coherence analyzer with LSA technique only, this analyzer performs an assessment of global coherence of each section horizontally, i.e. where each element is compared to a specific corpus for that element. We want to know if the item is coherent with respect to a latent semantic space previously generated as reference. In section 4, we describe the initial experiments and preliminary results for global coherence.

After the second level, we consider the creation of language models for each element of the proposal drafts. The language models are intended to consider a syntactic view, whose aim is to identify syntactic patterns independent of content but proper to the specific element (section). For instance, a general objective most often begins with a verb in infinitive, subsequently displaying a noun with some additional clause. This type of characteristics would be revealed by the language models. In summary, the idea is to capture the particular syntax used in each element of proposal drafts.

In the fourth level, we propose to develop a method to identify the existence of answers to methodological questions. This question receives as answer a word sequence that makes sense to what is asked, for example, a methodological question to formulate the objective is *What will you do?*. The answer requires the use of a verb expressing an action and an object of the verb that indicates the context on which execute the action. This context is diverse and involves a variety of words to use. Using the following example, we illustrate the answers to methodological questions:

*Develop an inductive learning algorithm for solving binary classification problems from unbalanced data sets, where the results obtained take appropriate reach consensus between accuracy and comprehensibility.*

The question *What will you do?* would have the answer: "Develop an inductive learning algorithm". The methodological question *How are you going to do it?* would require an appropriate answer specifying the way to achieve the goal. It can be observed that the answers consist of a sequence of terms. Identifying this type of answers is a challenge, since current studies have focused on very specific answers such as dates, places, people, or definitions [13]. Methodological questions are characteristic of elements such as objective and justification.

Also in the fourth level we have identified the argumentation as a feature that in the future could be assessed. The argumentation in a project proposal is relevant since it allows determining the resources used to argue on a position or idea expressed in the proposal draft by the student. Some works have studied how knowledge can build collaborative argumentation in online discussions [14]. Once achieved the four levels of evaluation, the intelligent tutor can send the student a score or a set of scores along suggestions of ways to improve the draft.

# 5. INITIAL RESULTS

We gathered a corpus of the different elements in proposal documents in Spanish. We distinguished in this corpus two kinds of student texts: graduate proposal documents, and undergraduate drafts. The first kind of texts includes documents already reviewed and approved by faculty, so they are considered as reference or training examples. The second kind of documents are used as test

examples. The whole corpus consists of a total of 380 collected training samples and 80 test samples, as detailed in Table 1. The corpus domain is computing and information technologies.

**Table 1. Training and Test Corpus**

| Section | Training | Test |
|---|---|---|
| Problem statement | 40 | 10 |
| Justification | 40 | 10 |
| Research Questions | 40 | 10 |
| Hypothesis | 40 | 10 |
| Objectives | 60 | 20 |
| Methodology | 40 | 10 |
| Conclusions | 40 | 10 |

## 5.1 Lexical Analysis

We are already evaluating student drafts at lexical level, i.e. the lexical analysis at the bottom of our 4-level evaluation. This analysis was performed along the three dimensions detailed in previous section, each in the range of 0 (worst) to 1 (best). Lexical diversity measures the number of types or different words used in the text. Density is computed as the proportion of lexical items and the total number of words in the text. Sophistication is computed as the percentage of word out of a list of common words (in our case in the 1000 common words according to SRA). Using the collected corpus, examples of undergraduate level were assessed in the three dimensions and compared against the values obtained for the graduate corpus. Figure 3 depicts the average of the three measures for the different elements, obtained for both subsets of the corpus. As expected, one can notice that graduate documents produced higher averages than undergrad drafts for the different elements.

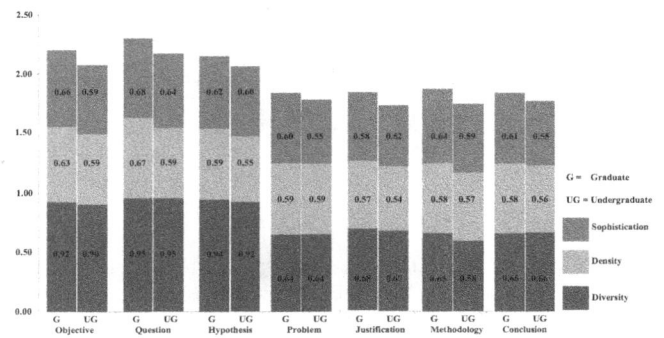

**Figure 3. Lexical Analysis Results**

We also used the ranges of values produced by the graduate subset to define a scale to assess new drafts in this aspect. The scale was defined on three levels: High, Medium and Low. So, High level is defined as one standard deviation (Sigma) above average, Low as one standard deviation below average, and Medium, in between.

In consequence, we obtained different ranges that define the scale for the eight sections of a draft. Applying the scale, we obtained the following examples of objectives with High and Low marks in the lexical analysis:

Objective (High level): *Implement an algorithm based on hierarchical structures with volume enveloping of spheres for collision detection.*

Objective (Low level): *Create an information management system for franchises with relevant data of each establishment and personnel data of each franchise, as well as references of franchisees and personal of trust that manage the franchises.*

One can notice that the first example is succinct and concrete, whereas the second example is quite verbose, with scarce technical terms, and abusing of the term *franchise*, lowering its lexical diversity.

## 5.2 Coherence

To assess global coherence using Latent Semantic Analysis in drafts, we set an experiment to validate our process. First, we asked three instructors to evaluate our whole collection of objectives (training and test subsets), eighty in total, see Table 1. We evaluate the level of agreement among evaluators. Then, we computed the semantic spaces for the different sections of our training subset and then evaluating automatically the objectives in the test subset. Finally, we evaluate the level of agreement between the grade assigned by the system and by instructors.

All the collection of objectives was sent for evaluation to three instructors serving as reviewers, that have experience in advising students in the preparation of their drafts in computing and information technologies. The reviewers did not know beforehand the level (graduate or undergraduate) of each sample. Each reviewer was requested to assign a level to each sample, using the scale: High, Medium and Low coherence, where the highest level meant that the text has a strong coherence or relationship to the domain of computing, and the low level means that the relationship is weak relative to the domain. An example of high coherence is: *Analyze problems that arise in the system development of software architectures of Enterprise type.* We can observe that the word "systems", and "software" are very close to the domain, including the term "architecture" surrounded by the above terms fit within the domain of computing. Likewise, words with less thematic load such as "development" or "analyze" are close to the domain. We find low coherence in this example: *Identify the effect of feedback on the learning of the business leader, to allow to be more effective.* Notice that even though terms like "learning" or "feedback" may have some proximity to the domain, the words or phrases "business", "leader" or "be more effective", are the central topic and do not match the domain of interest.

The assessments provided by our reviewers allowed to exclude those examples in our training set considered low by at least two, or those where they did not agree, since they will bias the construction of the semantic spaces. On the other hand, the assessments on the test set allow comparing the automatic evaluation of coherence.

The Fleiss Kappa[3] coefficient of agreement was computed for the three reviewers considering the test corpus. Table 2 shows the Fleiss Kappa results for each level, for the objective section.

**Table 2. Kappa for test corpus**

| Kappa | Fleiss | Cohen |
|---|---|---|
| | Reviewers | Coherence analyzer |
| High | 0,6862 | 0,0000 |
| Medium | -0,0378 | 0,2609 |
| Low | 0,7353 | 0,4218 |
| Overall | 0,5458 | 0,2237 |

The reviewers had a Substantial agreement for the Low and High grading, and a Poor agreement in the Medium. For the results obtained, we conclude that reviewers clearly identified High and Low levels. The overall level achieved between evaluators was 0.54, this giving Moderate confidence of agreement for the experiment.

We built the latent semantic space using the LSA technique with training samples of the whole collection, and in particular of objectives. The texts were processed by removing stop words and applying lemmatization using Freeling[4].

Similarly as for the lexical analysis, we obtained the scale for automatically assessing coherence in each section, but here we used cross-validation, obtaining the levels High, Medium and Low, according to ranges of values produced by LSA. These levels allow to automate the evaluation of the coherence analyzer. In particular, for the objective section, we got an average of 0.49 with a standard deviation of 0.17, resulting in the highest threshold of 0.64 and the lowest threshold at 0.28.

Once the scale is defined, we evaluated the test samples with the aim to compare the results produced by human evaluators. In this case, Cohen's Kappa is pertinent to compare the level of agreement between human and our coherence analyzer results. Table 2 shows the Cohen's Kappa results for the human versus coherence analyzer.

We observed that the levels of agreement in the Low case is Moderate and Medium level is Fair, the overall level of agreement between humans and the analyzer was Fair. We conclude that the analyzer would have an acceptable support for the student and academic advisor in the process of preparing the proposal draft.

After comparing the statistical results, in terms of the Kappa coefficient of agreement, we also performed a qualitative analysis between the results of coherence analyzer and the process of reviewing a proposal draft, i.e. the advisor would expect that the analyzer was a first filter so that when the drafts reach him, at least have a Medium or High Level. Under this premise, the results of our analyzer match the concept of a strict filtering reviewer, because it provided low and medium values in most test objectives.

We can observe that if our system does not achieve at this time a higher level of agreement in the high level, this is not a problem since the analyzer is being stricter to assign the high level. In the experiment, the analyzer evaluated as Medium the few highest levels assigned by the reviewers. If the analyzer behaves more flexible and allows high level to objectives that have to be of a medium or low level, this could cause a burden to the academic advisor, failing to support in review.

Finally we note that between the coherence analyzer and human evaluators, the agreement is Moderate for low levels, bringing confidence that the analyzer is identifying those objectives that were classified as Low level for evaluators.

After assessing coherence, the analyzer sends feedback to the student for the seven selected sections in the draft, and updates the parameters of performance in the intelligent tutor. The analyzer can send recommendations, managed by the intelligent tutor. For example if the analyzer identifies a low level, the

---

[3] Kappa(Landis y Koch, 1977)

[4] This software is available at http://nlp.lsi.upc.edu/.

recommendation could be *"It's suggested to restructure your objectives, making explicit the technical details of the computing and information technologies domain"*.

These recommendations are handled by the intelligent tutor, being part of the student profile, with the aim to improve student writing.

# 6. CONCLUSIONS

In this paper, we have presented a model that combines natural language techniques and intelligent tutors. The model considers important features of writing at different level.

In terms of vocabulary usage, we already can provide feedback when the draft is poor in terms of content words (i.e. excessive use of empty words), use of certain terms (many repetitions), or knowledge of technical terms. Also, we validate that graduate student showed a higher level in writing than undergraduate, in our corpus, regarding these three dimensions.

The LSA technique allowed evaluating the global coherence of objective section in proposal drafts, reaching an acceptable result of the percentage of agreement respect to human reviewers. It was crucial to have a gold standard to compare our results.

We will continue increasing the size of the corpus, so that the analyzer has a higher coverage, since the computing and information technologies domain is quiet extensive and growing.

In these initial experiments, the evaluation of coherence and lexical analysis was important to identify the student level, but could be improved by using all the four levels proposed for the evaluation. This will help students to improve their writing, and academic adviser would have more time to review the contents of the proposal documents. This model assumes that students have prior knowledge to write general documents, so it is not our interest to consider a grammar reviewer.

We expect that this computational tool generates in students a motivation to develop their proposal drafts and this analyzer will contribute to the advance in their proposal drafts. We currently have a web interface for the student to evaluate the draft in the first two levels, coherence and lexical analysis.

Bringing our model to a different domain does not seem too challenging, neither moving it to a different language, assuming similar language processing resources and corpus are available.

Currently, we are working on integrating the Entity Grid technique to evaluate the local coherence. We are also exploring the language models based on n-grams for characterizing each element. Also we are in the process of developing a method to identify answers to methodological questions within the elements and objective justification of a proposal draft.

We foresee an experiment that includes a pilot test with a control and experimental group of students. This test will provide an insight on whether there are improvements in students in the process of proposal drafting when helped by the intelligent tutor.

# 7. ACKNOWLEDGMENTS

We thank the three objective evaluators: Rene Castro Morales, Claudia I. Esquivel López, and J. Miguel García Gorrostieta. This research was supported by CONACYT, México, through the scholarship 1124002 for the first author. The second author was partially supported by SNI, México.

# 8. REFERENCES

[1] Schwarm, S. and Ostendorf, M. 2005. Reading level assessment using support vector machines and statistical language models. In Procs of the 43rd Annual Meeting on Association for Computational Linguistics (ACL '05), pp. 523-530.

[2] Roberto, A., Martí, M. and Salamó, M. 2012. Análisis de la riqueza léxica en el contexto de la clasificación de atributos demográficos latentes, Procesamiento de Lenguaje Natural, No. 48, pp. 97-104. ISSN:1135-5948.

[3] Miranda, A. and Calle, J. 2006. Yule's Characteristic K Revisited. Language Resources and Evaluation, 39, 4, pp. 287-294, DOI: 10.1007/s10579-005-8622-8.

[4] Vilarnovo, A. 1990. Coherencia textual: ¿coherencia interna o coherencia externa?. ELUA Estudios de Lingüística, ISSN 0212-7636, pp. 229-239.

[5] Louwerse, M. M. 2004. A concise model of cohesion in text and coherence in comprehension. Revista Signos, 37, 56, pp. 41-58. DOI: 10.4067/S0718-09342004005600004.

[6] Hernández, S. and Ferreira, A. A. 2010. Evaluación automática de Coherencia textual en noticias policiales utilizando Análisis Semántico Latente. Revista de Lingüística Teórica y Aplicada, 48(2): pp. 115-139.

[7] Barzilay, R. and Lapata, M. 2008. Modeling local coherence: An entity-based approach. Comput. Linguist. 34, 1 (March 2008), pp. 1-34. DOI: 10.1162/coli.2008.34.1.1

[8] Lapata, M. and Barzilay, R. 2005. Automatic evaluation of text coherence: models and representations. In Procs of the 19th International Joint Conference on Artificial Intelligence (IJCAI'05). Morgan Kaufmann Publishers Inc., San Francisco, CA, USA, pp. 1085-1090.

[9] Burstein J., Tetreault J., Andreyev S. 2010. Using entity-based features to model coherence in student essays. In HLT'10. Association for Computational Linguistics, Stroudsburg, PA, USA, pp. 681-684.

[10] Jackson, T. and Graesser, A. 2006. Applications of human tutorial dialog in AutoTutor, an intelligent tutoring system. Revista Signos, 39, 60, pp. 31-48.

[11] Noguez, J. and Sucar, E. 2005. A Probabilistic Relational Student Model for Virtual Laboratories. In Procs of the 6th Mexican International Conference on Computer Science (ENC '05). IEEE Computer Society, Washington, DC, USA, pp. 2-9.

[12] Williamson, C., Bebbington, A., Mathews, M., Suraweera, P., Martin, B., Thomson, D. and Holland, J. 2011. Thermo-Tutor: An Intelligent Tutoring System for Thermodynamic. In Global Engineering Education Conference (EDUCON): pp. 378–385. DOI: 10.1109/EDUCON.2011.5773164

[13] Montes, G. M., Villaseñor, P. L., López, L. A. 2008. Mexican Experience in Spanish Question Answering. Computación y Sistemas, 12,1, pp. 40-64. ISSN 1405-5546

[14] Donmez, P., Rosé, C., Stegmann, K., Weinberger, A. and Fischer, F. 2005. Supporting CSCL with automatic corpus analysis technology. CSCL '05. International Society of the Learning Sciences pp.125-134.

# Dwindling Numbers of Female Computer Students: What are We Missing?

Donna Saulsberry
New Mexico State University
PO Box 30001 MSC 3DA
Las Cruces, NM 88003
1-575-528-7215
dsaulsbe@nmsu.edu

## ABSTRACT

There is a common agreement among researchers that women are under-represented in both 2-year and 4-year collegiate computer study programs. In spite of twenty years of research, the number of women graduating with computer degrees continues to decline, suggesting that perhaps there are causal factors that have not been identified. This paper describes an alternate approach; asking a group of female students who are pursuing a computer technology degree at a community college to describe experiences which have affected their academic success. A significant finding was that the women struggled to understand the [deductive] problem solving method used by the instructors and the pace of the classes made it difficult for them to work out their own problem solving approach. (This paper is taken from a broader dissertation which explored other facets of the women's experiences as well.)

## Categories and Subject Descriptors

K.3.2 [**Computers & Education**]: Computer & Information Science Technology – *Computer Science Education.*

## General Terms

Human Factors

## Keywords

females, community college, phenomenology, inductive reasoning

## 1. INTRODUCTION

It is the first day of the new semester. I walk into the Introduction to Computer Networking class I teach and look around the room at the group of new faces, eager to get started with another semester. Even though the faces are new, the fact that they are mostly males is not. That has been the case with every networking class I have taught. Even though this class is required for everyone seeking an associate's degree in computer technology at Southwest Community College, the class averaged only 23% female students over the last five years.

Southwest Community College is not alone in the statistic. The percent of women pursuing computer degrees nationwide is much lower than the percent of males and despite twenty years of research and intervention, the percent of females receiving associate degrees in the computer field has actually decreased from 40% in 2000-2001 to 26% in 2008-2009. The percent of computer field bachelor's degree recipients who are female is even lower: having fallen from 28% in 2000 to 17.7% in 2008 [13]. U.S. Department of Labor statistics show a similar pattern. In 2008, only 25% of those employed by computer companies were women. That percent has decreased from 36% in 1991 [19] [2].

Over the last ten years, Southwest Community College has awarded an average of 37% of the associate degrees in computer technology to females. The ratio declined from 53% in 2000-2001 to 21% in 2009-2010. Over the same time period, the National Center for Education Statistics reported a decline in associate degrees being awarded to female computer majors from 40% in 2000-2001 to 26% in 2008-2009, the last year for which national statistics are available [12].

National Center for Education Statistics data is important when assessing progress in increasing the number of females receiving computer degrees because NCES is the only source that compiles data from all colleges and universities in the United States with students who are receiving federal financial aid [12]. NCES completion data is reported by gender and CIP code (Classification of Instruction Program) which makes it possible to track the number of females receiving computer degrees. CIP code 11 is the general classification for computers.

NCES data is the most accurate method of measuring national progress; however the CIP codes may not present an accurate picture especially when assessing community college programs. For example, Southwest Community College proposes CIP codes for new degree programs at the time they are created; the codes are then approved by the state's higher education department. There is additional paperwork the college can submit if it is necessary to change CIP codes after a degree program is created. Southwest Community College changed the CIP code under which it reported its computer technology graduates in 2007. Prior to 2007, the college reported its computer technology majors under CIP code 30.999 which is a generic Multi-Interdisciplinary category. Since 2007, Southwest Community College has reported its computer technology graduates under CIP code 11.03 which is one of the Computer and Information Sciences and Support Services categories. Sanders and Tescione [16] reported a wide-spread practice of community colleges including women who are receiving degrees which prepared them for word processing and other data entry jobs in the computer or information technology degree statistics.

This particular study is unique because of its focus on community college students and its methodological approach. This is a phenomenological study which asked female students to describe their own experiences as they related to com pleting a degree in computer technology. Most of the studies described in the literature have asked wom en to respond to pre-defined research questions rather than asking th em to choose the experiences which they think have impacted their com puter studies. This research aims to explore the experiences which the women feel are significant. Undertaking this phenomenological approach is important since two decades of studying what researchers identify as being important has not had a significant impact on the percent of women students who are earning a degree in computers.

## 2. SITUATING THIS STUDY IN THE LITERATURE

Very little detailed research has been published on women who are studying computers at the community college level; and no phenomenological research has b een published about this group. Most of the major research has been done on bachelor degree programs. Three foundational books which explore the low number of females who are study ing computers and other related technical fields in Am erica's colleges and universities are Unlocking the Clubhouse: Carnegie Mellon [10] , Educated in Romance [8], and Talk About Leaving: Why Undergraduates Leave the Sciences [17] . Unlocking the Clubhouse: Carnegie Mellon, is entirely focused on women majoring in computers. The second book, Educated in Romance, is focused on women who were studying the broader fields of math and science. Talk About Leaving: Why Undergraduate Leave the S ciences, focuses on both men and women who began thei r collegiate studies in math, science, or technology but then decided to change majors

Many of the issues which Margolis and Fisher [10] and others have identified as being obstacles to women at the bachelor's level may not be present at the community college level but to date there is not enough published research about community college programs to make a determination. These issues include large class sizes at the fresh man and sophomore level, more emphasis on the theoretical than the practical, and a larger number of required math and programming classes.

Community colleges typically emphasize skills more than theory. Classes at Southwest Community College are taught in hands-on computer labs where students learn the skills by actually performing them. Distance education clas ses use software-based simulators to provide the hands- on component. In contrast, many four-y ear programs consist of what Tonso [18] describes as abstract, generalized knowledge that is represented mathematically. Another major difference between com munity college computer technology program and ty pical four-year computer programs is the lack of emphasis on math and programming classes which are often problematic for women. For instance, an associate degree at S outhwest Community College only requires one math class and one programming class in contrast to four-y ear programs which usually require 8-10 math classes and 15-20 programming cl asses. Community college student-to-instructor ratios are ty pically lower than those found in freshman and sophomore level classes in four-y ear programs. Southwest Community College's stude nt-to-instructor ratio is 18

to 1. Margolis and Fisher [10] noted that large classes and the lack of example driven ins truction were cited as obstacles by the females at Carnegie Melon.

## 3. STUDY METHODOLGY

This phenomenological study was designed to answer the research question: What experiences affect wom en's academic success in computer studies at a com munity college? The research design involved three types of data coll ection. Eleven female students who were sophomores between 2009 and 2011 were interviewed in depth, the female students who were sophomores in spring 2011 participated in a focus group, and both the freshman and sophomore students who were enrolled in spring 2011 participated in an Internet-bas ed survey which m easured the extent to which their experiences aligned with those described in the literature. All of the participants had declared com puter technology as a major. Six of the 2009 sophomores were not interviewed due to a health issue in my family. All of the 2011 females who were willing to partic ipate were interviewed. (One declined.) Two of the 2011 females had a time conflict and did not participate in the focus gr oup. Pseudonyms were assigned to protect the women's anonymity.

The goal of phenomenological research is to describe the lived experiences of a group of individuals in relation to a phenomenon. It focuses on the commonality of the experience among a group of people. Phenomenology can be divided into two ty pes: (1) hermeneutic phenomenology which focuses on the researcher's interpretation of the research pa rticipants' descriptions and (2) psychological phenomenology which emphasizes the participants' descriptions than the res earcher's interpretations [4] . This research uses the psychological approach. Phenomenology is part of the larger dom ain of qualitative research. When conducting qualitative research it is im portant to identify the researcher's assumptions, worldview, and theoretical lens.

My assumption is that the human-kind would be better served if there were m ore women in the com puter fields, especially in research and development as we ll as management. This would facilitate future development being targeted at areas that wom en are typically more interested in [10]. Facebook, who's Chief Operating Officer is a woman, is a good example of computers being used to facilitate relations hips. Kristin Tolle, a research director at Microsoft, is a good example of women researching ways to use computers to improve health care in impoverished nations [14]. This research us es a constructivist worldview; meaning it focuses on subjective meanings of experience. Researchers who have a social constructivist worldview look for the complexities of views rather than narrowly classifying them into a few categories or ideas [4] . A fem inist perspective is the theoretical lens used in this research. This perspective views women's situations and the ins titutions that fram e them as problematic. This research is an attem pt to discover which institutions frame women's lack of participation in computers and identify specifically which parts of those institutions are problematic.

### 3.1 Research Setting

Southwest Community College was established 35 y ears ago as a vocational-trade school under the auspices of a large land-grant institution. It is within 45 m iles of the Mexican border, in an area which was dominantly agricultural until World War II. During the war, the federal government established three large military bases in the area which have continued to expand, bringing in a host of aerospace and defense contractors.

Southwest Community College's computer technology program was established 26 years ago to provide skilled technicians to local government and businesses. Historically, computer technology graduates have been hired in minimum-wage, entry level positions with the more lucrative positions being filled by 4-year graduates of the land-grant institution's engineering and computer science programs. However, under the leadership of a new department chair, within the last six years, the computer technology department has strengthened its curriculum and is now targeting the placement of its students directly into network administration type positions along with providing them adequate preparation to complete their bachelor's degree in business, engineering technology, or computer science within two or three years after receiving their associate degree.

To help protect the anonymity of the females who participated in this research, their demographics were not collected; but, college wide: 63% of the student body selected Hispanic on the ethnicity portion of their college admission form, 22% selected White, 2% selected Native American, 2% selected Black, and 11% selected other. Eighty-two percent of the students at Southwest Community College receive financial aid. The demographics of students in the computer technology department are consistent with those of the college as a whole.

## 3.2    Data Collection and Reduction

The research data collected was from individual interviews, a focus group discussion, and an Internet survey. Using three different sources to collect the information is known as methodological triangulation. The purpose of triangulation is to give a more detailed and balanced picture of the situation [1]. Cohen, Manion, and Morrison [3] also say that triangulation is an "attempt to map out, or explain more fully, the richness and complexity of human behavior by studying it from more than one standpoint" (p. 254).

### 3.2.1    Interviews

Eleven women were interviewed by either me or a former female student who assisted me in collecting the data. (To avoid a potential conflict of interest, New Mexico State University's research policies prevented me from collecting data from students who were currently enrolled in classes I was teaching.) Each of the participants was given a written explanation of the purpose of the research and signed a consent form before being asked the broad opening question: "What have you experienced in your studies at Southwest Community College?" and the follow up question: "What conditions or situations have influenced or affected your college experience?" Additional prompt questions were used to assist the participants in exhausting the description of their experience. Each 30-60 minute interview was digitally recorded and transcribed verbatim.

After reading each woman's interview transcript several times, I isolated the individual experiences she described and sorted them into themes. Isolating the individual experiences was necessary because in many cases the women rambled in disjointed phrases until they congealed their memory of an experience enough to describe it. After I went through all of the interview transcripts in this manner and isolated the experiences, I identified them es

which appeared in more than one interview and used a color coding scheme to classify them.

### 3.2.2    Focus Group

At the end of the spring 2011 semester, after the individual interviews had been conducted, the women who had participated in the interviews were brought together as a focus group to discuss their experiences at Southwest Community College. The purpose of the focus group, which was moderated by the former student who had conducted the interviews, was to validate and further explore what the women had said in their individual interviews. I wanted to explore their socially constructed knowledge and see if it provided richer, detailed descriptions than the individual interviews. One topic I asked the moderator to explore was any academic difficulties the women had experienced and if they had experienced and any difficulties with the male students. Academic difficulties were an area that the women had not elaborated on during their individual interviews even though one mentioned that she had failed a class. Having taught the female students and assisted them with their academic advising, I knew there had been others who had repeated courses or feared they were going to have to repeat a course and that those had appeared to be significant experiences to them at the time.

Using a process similar to what I had used with the individual interviews, I identified the individual experiences that were described by the women and sorted them into the themes I had identified in the interviews; in the process I verified that no new themes were suggested. I then matched the experiences described in the focus group with those described in the interviews and added any experiences that were not already recorded in the data.

### 3.2.3    Internet-based survey

A third source of information, in addition to the individual interviews and the focus group, was an Internet survey. All 21 of the female computer technology students who were freshman and sophomores during the spring 2011 semester, were asked to respond to the Internet-based survey which was conducted using Survey Monkey. The goal of the survey was to assess the extent to which the opinions of the survey group, some of whom had taken less classes so had less experience in the computer technology department, matched those reported in the literature and those described by the interview group.

The women were invited to participate in the survey via two different emails which included a description of the purpose of the research. The survey stayed open for two months. During that time, 12 women completed the survey. The Likert-type survey, which I designed and pretested on a group of six former students, consisted of 18 statements which summarized what has been documented as the experiences of female students at other institutions.

After the survey period ended, I downloaded both the raw data (how many respondents chose each possible answer for each of the 18 questions) and the Survey Monkey analysis of the data. Since I had not delivered a survey using Survey Monkey before, I also analyzed the raw data using a spreadsheet. My results confirmed the accuracy of Survey Monkey's analysis tool. The results were then compared to the experiences reported in the research and those described by the interview group.

# 4. RESULTS AND DISCUSSION

To make the data more useful to both Southwest Community College and institutional research at large, I divided the experiences the women had described into two groups: ones that had contributed to the their success and ones that had caused them to struggle. This process was complicated by some of the women seeing the same experience as contributing to both their success and their struggles. For example, if they had a professor who did not stay on topic, that caused them to struggle; but having to learn to research and understand the topic on their own ultimately contributed to their success. I related those incidents in the section on experiences that contributed to the women's struggles because even though these particular women compensated for the negative experiences, other women may not and they may be an obstacle to other female computer students.

## 4.1 Experiences that contributed to success

Over 80% of the women who responded to the Internet survey agreed with the statement, "I have a close relationship with a computer faculty member who mentors me." Three of the women who were interviewed had worked in the Computer Technology department office as paid student employees. Three others had completed their required 180 hours of cooperative education experience as unpaid lab assistants in the Computer Technology department. Karla, one of the women interviewed, felt that working in the department definitely contributed to her success. She said, "I think that the great advantage I have is I'm working here because I think I have an opportunity no other student has; like for example, I can just go work at the labs anytime and no others will be able to do that. I think I have the experience that almost no one else has that's because I'm here with all of you guys. I get to do so many things—I'm very privileged." Other women talked about how much a specific male faculty member had helped them. Sandra said, "Ted is my advisor. He is the one who has taken me through all of these courses. He's my guy. He's the one who does all my stuff. He makes sure I'm doing ok in classes. He assures me of everything so I'm very happy with that." Referring to Ted and another male faculty member, Arial said laughingly, "They dealt with the blond one who was confused. They helped me though all of my problems. You know, one year it was my daughter, another my health, and now my teeth." She added, "Kevin even took us to his house to build computers. When I had trouble with my computer he took it to his class and they fixed it in just a few seconds."

Seventy-five percent of the women who responded to the survey agreed with the statement "The male students in the computer department respect and treat me as an equal." One commented, "I think they all respect me as a computer technology student. In some cases I think I might intimidate them but that happens in most of my life not just here." The survey respondents were divided in their responses to the statement "I am in regular contact with other female computer students who provide me with support and companionship." One half of the women said they agreed. One fourth said they disagreed. The remaining quarter did not express an opinion.

Sandra said, "Most of them [fellow students] seem surprised that they see a girl in the classroom but they don't mind it. If you are here for a learning experience it's probably why. We're all here for the same thing." Caroline talked about becoming "really good friends" with some of the male students; explaining that they "treat me like I am one of them." However, she said the men in her network security class were "way above her knowledge." She said, "They are really nice and everything but they are on a level I'm not!" Alice related her experience of being mentored by one of the male students. She said: "He is someone I go to when I don't understand. I don't let him brush me off." She explained that he gets frustrated and says, "I sit there and show you and then you do it completely different and you find your way. You just need me to tell you this is how you can do it but for you to go at a completely different angle and come up with the right answers." She explained to him, "This is how it works for me—you know I need to hear yours for it to click and open a door somewhere else so I can do it." She said he sometimes thinks working with her is a waste of time.

Rachel, who spent two summers participating in a community college research program at a nearby university, says she was strongly influenced by the people she met there. One of the mentors talked to Rachel about her experience of becoming a mother while she was still in college. Rachel said the mentor told her, "She kept going to school. She didn't drop out or anything. She seems content and happy." Rachel, who was the single parent of an infant daughter at the time, explained, "I have my daughter and I want her to have a life I didn't have. Economically that's what I want." Mary, who recently completed a tour of duty with the Army, described being mentored by the men she served with in her military unit. She said they were a large part of the reason she decided to pursue a degree in computer technology.

Several of the Internet survey questions measured the extent to which the Southwest Community College women agreed with statements describing academic practices which have been identified in the literature as being helpful to women at other colleges. All of the survey respondents except one agreed with the statement, "My computer classes are small enough that I get the personalized attention I need." Eighty percent of the women also agreed that "My computer instructors call on male and female students equally." The majority of the respondents (75%) agreed with the statement, "I prefer having a computer instructor explain the 'big picture' before they go into the individual steps." This is identified in the literature as helping women succeed in computer classes [15] [20]. Two thirds of the survey respondents did not agree with the statement, "My computer instructors encourage competition by encouraging students to show that they are smarter than their peers." Instructors encouraging competition by allowing students to show they are smarter than their peers is identified in the literature as being discouraging to women [5].

In the interviews, the women did not discuss academic practices which enhanced their success, for the most part. However, referring to the Introduction to Networking class, Mary said, "It's new to me. I'm a little worried as far as a grade but learning stuff–like this past test we had I was really studying. I would read it and then try to Google the other perspectives of it but the teacher has been really informative. She said she was thinking about taking the second networking course but that she wanted to understand the "whole concept first before I go up higher."

## 4.2 Experiences that caused women to struggle

Arial, who described having been sexually molested by her father, talked about how much the instructor of her android programming class discouraged her. She said, "I asked the instructor to slow down three times but he just wouldn't. I got so discouraged I just quit. You know once I'm lost, I'm lost. Then the bad self-esteem kicks in. You know the same s*** my dad would tell me, 'Just smile and look pretty.'"

Sally was discouraged by her first operating systems class instructor. She said, "We didn't talk about the coursework very much but the book itself was very thorough and the course was laid out in a way that if you followed the coursework you got the work out of it." She said, "I didn't think the instructor really had much to offer. I think he knew his job [well enough] to do his own work but not to teach it…" Later in the interviews he said, "There is so much material out there and in a program like computer and information technology it encompasses so much that you can find yourself getting a little lost within it." After thinking it over, she concluded, "Most of the instructors I had were very helpful and supportive. They kind of reminded us that you aren't expected to know it all. That's why you are in school."

Most of the women who were interviewed did not view the male students in the computer technology program as a discouraging factor but Mary did. She said, "As far as the guys, it's been kind of weird. I'm used to being around guys being in the military but in class it's been different. They aren't really [pause] I just need to get the grade." She continued, "Besides being around the guys, maybe they feel kind of uncomfortable." The example she gave was, "In the [network] lab, I actually asked one of the guys if he wanted to pair up [as lab partners] but he just looked at me like...So it was me and Jon [who did become her lab partner]. I have him in several other classes so we get along pretty good."

Referring to the second networking course, Alice said it was especially hard because she had not gotten the information that she needed in the prerequisite Introduction to Networking class. She said the students could not get any information "above a kinder level" out of the instructor of the first class because she "didn't have it." She says that even though the second networking class was hard, "Once I fell into it, I enjoyed it—I love it--I like the challenge. I like the fact that I have to think really hard to get things to fall into place. There's so much more information that's coming in that I need to organize into my little boxes. Make everything fall into a pattern."

Most of the other information about academic practices which made it more difficult for the women to succeed came from the focus group. One woman in the focus group said she did not like the PC Maintenance course because the instructor always presented troubleshooting as a series of "boring" steps, rather than looking it as a problem with symptoms to be solved. Another woman said the instructor did not utilize the book. Referring to another course, the women commented that they were "brushed off" by two different instructors when they tried to ask questions. The instructors responded to their questions by saying "We will go back to that" (but they never did), "we need to move on," or "we're on a schedule." When asked by the facilitator if they gave the same responses when male students asked similar questions, the women all said they did. One woman said, the instructors "do not have any patience." The facilitator then asked the women if they had tried going to the professor's office to ask questions or get help. Two women said they had gone to one of the instructor's office and that he was very patient and answered all of their questions when they were in his office.

## 5. FINDINGS

The interview participants were bothered by the fast pace of the courses leaving their questions unanswered. In both the individual interviews and the focus group, the women described several classroom experiences in which they asked instructors to "slow down" but the instructors would not. For example, Arial described her negative experience with a programming instructor who refused to slow down, even though she asked him to three times. The instructors either ignored them or responded by saying "We will go back to that" (but they never did), "we need to move on," or "we're on a schedule." Most of the women just became frustrated but one actually dropped a required programming class. However, two of the women in the focus group said they went to the office of one of the instructors who would not answer their questions in class and in his office he answered all of their questions and worked with them patiently until they understood the material.

After reading the women's comments, in an informal discussion with computer technology faculty at Southwest Community College I asked if any one recalled being asked to slow down or answer student questions and refusing to do so. Two of the male faculty members participating in the discussion said they would "never get anywhere" if they slowed down enough to make everyone happy or spent class time answering all of their questions. They said they are always available to work with students who need extra time or help in their offices but that in order to cover all the material and keep the rest of the class from getting bored they have to keep moving.

Another woman in the focus group commented that she was totally lost in a programming class. When the facilitator inquired about whether she asked questions or asked for help, she said she tried but that the instructor had already moved on to another topic and would not back up. She said that at the time he was initially covering the topic, she could not even get enough of a grasp of it to figure out what to ask.

Alice's description of her experience being tutored by the male student may provide additional insight. Alice said that he would become frustrated after he spent time showing her exactly how to work a problem and she would not accept his solution method but would instead go work out another method of solving the problem on her own. She said he thought "it was a waste of time."

Perhaps this is indicative of the difference between how males and females learn to solve problems. Maybe the females feel the pace is too fast because they need time to work it out in "their" logic. Mary talked about using an Internet search engine to see if there was another perspective (other than her instructor's) that would help her understand the material better.

Authors like Gurian [6] contend that females learn math, science, and technology differently than males. He says this is partially based on biological differences. In his book, Boys and Girls Learn Differently: A Guide for Teachers and Parents, he describes an encounter with a recent college graduate who had struggled with physics in high school. The graduate described watching her male teacher and the male students at the blackboard. She said, "They were going so fast figuring things out, and I couldn't quite get it" (p. 298). Gurian advocates sex-segregated education; believing that girls learn best when they are in classes with other girls and are taught by women. He contends that girls learn concepts better when they can work with them hands-on. They have trouble with concepts being rapidly presented on the blackboard. Gurian also postulates that teachers tend to teach in their own preferred learning styles, meaning that male teachers tend to optimize learning for other males and female teachers tend to optimize learning for other females.

Hodgins [7] also contends that differences in the anatomy of typical male and typical female brains affect their respective learning styles. He asserts that males are visual learners (indicates that seeing things on the blackboard would improves learning); females are verbal learners meaning they need detailed verbal explanations. It is possible that male teachers and students are showing (visual) without verbally explaining what they are doing. This needs more research.

Hodgins [7] and Gurian [6] agree that males tend to use deductive reasoning and females tend to use inductive reasoning. Gurian says, "Males tend to be deductive in their conceptualizations, sharing their reasoning process frequently from general principle and applying it, to individual cases." He says females on the other hand, "tend to favor inductive thinking, adding more and more to their based of conceptualization. They tend to begin with concrete examples." (p.7).

This is another possible factor contributing to the women's struggles. Males can look at the new material presented in a lesson and quickly accept that it supports a general principle they have already learned; females, on the other hand, need to take time to assemble all of the material relative to the topic before they decide if it supports the principle.

This needs more research but it may be one of the keys to increasing the success rate of female computer students. Some possible solutions which Southwest Community College is implementing are: using female lab assistants, using Cmap (a cognitive mapping program) as an instructional tool [9], and using muddiest point activities [11] to ensure that all questions get answered.

# 6. REFERENCES

[1] Altrichter, H., Feldman, A., Posch, P. and Somekh, B. 2008. *Teachers investigate their work; An introduction to action research across the professions (2nd ed.)*. London: Routledge

[2] Ashcraft, C. and Blithe, S. 2010. Women in IT: the Facts. http://www.ncwit.org/pdf/NCWIT_The Facts_rev2010.pdf.

[3] Cohen, L., Manion, L. and Morrison, K. 2000. *Research Methods in Education* (5th ed.) London: Routledge.

[4] Creswell, J. 2007. *Qualitative Inquiry and Research Design: Choosing Among Five Approaches* (2nd ed.) Thousand Oaks: Sage Publications.

[5] Garvin-Doxas, K., and Barker, L. 2004. Communication in computer science classrooms: Understanding defensive climates as a means of creating supportive behaviors. *ACM Journal of Educational Resources in Computing*, 4 (1), 1-18.

[6] Gurian, M. 2011. *Boys and Girls Learn Differently! A guide for Teachers and Parents*. San Francisco: Jossey-Bass.

[7] Hodgins, D. 2011. Male and Female Differences. http://languagelog.ldc.upenn.edu/myl/llog/Hodgins1.pdf

[8] Holland, D. and Eisenhart, M. 1990. *Educated in Romance: Women Achievement and College Culture*. Chicago: University of Chicago Press

[9] Institute for Human and Machine Cognition 2010. IHMC Cmap Tools. http://cmap.ihmc.us

[10] Margolis, J. and Fisher, A. 2002 *Unlocking the clubhouse: Women in computing*. Cambridge: MIT Press.

[11] Mosteller, F. 1989. "The muddiest point in the lecture" as a feedback device. http://isites.harvard.edu/fs/docs/icb.topic771890.files/OTL3-Mosteller-Muddiest.pdf

[12] National Center for Education Statistics. 2010. http://nces.ed.gov/ipeds/cipcode/wizard/report.aspx

[13] National Science Foundation. 2010. Women, minorities, and persons with disabilities in science and engineering. http://www.nsf.gov/statistics/wmpd/degrees.cfm

[14] Robertson, J., DeHart, D., Tolle, K., and Heckerman, D. 2009. Healthcare delivery in developing countries: Challenges and potential solutions. http://research.microsoft.com/en-us/collaboration/fourthparadigm/4th_paradigm_book_part2_robertson_heckerman.pdf

[15] Rosser, S. 1989. Teaching techniques to attract women to science: Application of feminist theory and methodologies. *Women's Studies International Forum*, 12 (3), 263-277.

[16] Sanders, J. and Tescione, S. 2002. Gender equity and technology. In J. Koch & B. Irvy (Eds.) *Defining and redefining gender equity in education*. Greenwich, CT: Information Age Publishing.

[17] Seymour, E., and Hewitt, N. 1997. *Talking about leaving: Why undergraduates leave the sciences*. Boulder: Westview Press.

[18] Tonso, K. 2003. *Designing gender equity into engineering and science cultures: Have we met the enemy and is he us?* http://equity.tamu.edu/past_events/dsgn'g_eqty_paper.doc

[19] United States Department of Labor Women's Bureau. 2009. Nontraditional occupations for women in 2008. www.dol.gov/wb/factsheets/nontrad2009.pdf

[20] Volman, M. and Van Eck, E. 2001. Gender equity and information technology in education: The second decade. *Review of Educational Research*, 71 (4), 613-634.

# Engaging Students by Intertwining Puzzle-Based and Problem-Based Learning

Jalal Kawash
University of Calgary
2500 University Dr. NW
Calgary, Alberta, Canada
+1 (403) 220 6619
jalal.kawash@ucalgary.ca

## ABSTRACT

In this paper, we describe our experience in a first-year computer science course on problem solving that is aimed at non-majors. The majority of the target audience of this course is from management and social science faculties. The course is unique in the sense that it covers proper problem solving skills that are typically only covered in a course directed at computer science or engineering students. We describe how puzzles are used as bait that lures the target audience to subjects such as logic, algorithms, and graph theory. That is, we discuss how we intertwine puzzle-based and problem-based learning in order to engage, an often unmotivated, crowd. Our initial assessment of the approach shows that the use of puzzles is perceived by students as helpful to learn the course material. Furthermore, it is contributing to their interest in computing.

## Categories and Subject Descriptors

K.3.2 [**Computers and Education**]: Computer and Information Science Education – *Computer science education, Curriculum, literacy.*

## Keywords

Computer Science education, problem-solving, first-year curriculum, computer literacy, puzzles

## 1. INTRODUCTION

"There are three buckets. One is labeled with *oranges*, the second with *apples*, and the third with *oranges & apples*. The labels are guaranteed to be wrong. You can draw one fruit at a time from a single bucket. What is the minimum number of draws you can make in order to determine which bucket contains what?" This is one of many similar interview questions tabled to potential software developers at Microsoft. Other IT companies, such as Google, present similar questions to their interviewees.

Developers' Web sites are full of such puzzles compiled by interviewees (for example, see Glassdoor[1]).

The choice of such IT giants to use puzzles as interview questions is not surprising. Poundstone addressed this trend in interview questions [1]. It is believed that there is correlation between the ability to solve such puzzles and the ability to solve problems in general. Falkner *et al.* [2] clearly frame it: "*There is a strong connection between the ability to solve puzzles and the ability to solve industry and business problems.*"

Therefore, it is natural to employ and exploit puzzles in teaching problem-solving and critical thinking. This has been the case for a long time in elementary and secondary education. Puzzle-based learning has recently found its way to post-secondary education. Universities like the University of California, Santa Barbra [3], Carnegie Mellon University [2], and Adelaide University [2] introduced puzzle-based courses, typically at the freshman level, aimed at engineering and computer science students.

Puzzles are attractive because they illustrate problem-solving rules in a simple setting. At the same time, many conclusions are applicable to real-world problems. Due to their entertaining and provoking natures they engage students.

However, the full power and the benefits of this approach in post-secondary education is not yet completely understood. It is still a work in progress. Recently, Falkner *et al.* [2] described their experience at Carnegie Mellon and Adelaide universities with puzzle-based courses. The motivations for Falkner *et al.* is to address two issues: (1) teaching thinking skill rather than simply content and (2) the decline in math skills among students.

Falkner *et al.* describe learning as a continuum (their illustration is reproduced in Figure 1) with three areas: puzzle-based, problem-based, and project-based. Puzzle-based learning is domain independent, but the other two areas are domain-specific. Puzzle-based learning fosters critical thinking, logical and abstract reasoning. In problem-based learning, students acquire domain-specific knowledge and use this knowledge for reasoning when solving specific problems. Finally, in project-based learning, the learners work in teams to identify the questions, and these questions are answered while dealing with uncertainty and changing conditions.

---

[1]http://www.glassdoor.com/Interview/Microsoft-Interview-Questions-E1651.htm

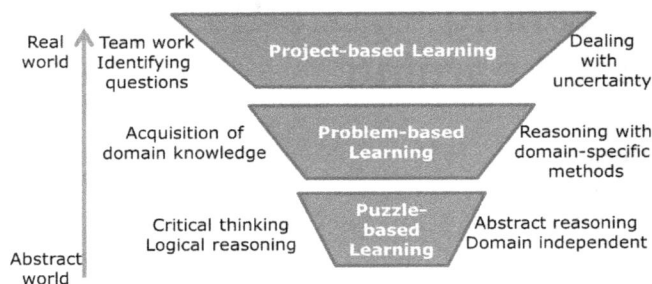

**Figure 1. A reproduction of Falkner et al.'s learning continuum [2]**

There are other papers that deal with the use of puzzles in the classroom with varying objectives. Parahami's [3] concern is retention of engineering and computer science students. Levitin and Papalaskari [4] and Shilov and Yi [5] use puzzles in the context of teaching the design and analysis of algorithms and model checking respectively. Michalewicz and Michalewicz use puzzle-based learning for engineering students [6]. A major objective of their work is to break the ice barriers that students typically have with mathematics. Rao studies the use of puzzles and storytelling in a software engineering course [7]. Rao finds that this approach improves the quality of end-term projects, slightly improves final marks, and reduces team friction. Xu and Mayer [8] present their experience with using puzzles to teach critical thinking in an on-line course. Cha *et al.* [9] design an experiment that the shows the use of *physical* puzzles (with tangible objects) improves students' strategies for problem-solving and enhances their grasp of abstraction and generalization.

In this paper, we describe our experience with using puzzles in a course on problem-solving. What is unique about this experience is that our course is not aimed at computer science or engineering students, unlike all the papers cited earlier. The course is a service to students from different disciplines, but they are mainly from management and social sciences. Hence, its design is not concerned with preparing future software developers, computer scientists, or engineers. A common goal with other research, though, is to foster critical thinking and problem-solving methods and techniques in real-life scenarios.

The course is unique in its design. To the best of our knowledge, no other course has its breadth and depth in computer science topics and is, at the same time, targeted to students outside the computer science or engineering disciplines, namely students in management, social sciences, and the arts [10].

Unlike Falkner *et al.*'s courses, we use puzzle-based learning to support problem-based learning. That is, in the lectures, we move through their learning continuum from puzzle-based learning to problem-based learning. Hence, the use of puzzles serves as bait. A typical lecture starts with puzzle-based learning, transitions to the domain-specific problem-based learning, comes back and forth as needed. We also touch on project-based learning in the course, but this is conducted outside the lectures and is outside the scope of this paper. Unlike Xu and Mayer, we use puzzles to engage students in a classroom rather than on-line.

The rest of this paper is organized as follows. Section 2 gives a brief overview of the course in order to contextualize the following sections. Section 3 provides our approach to the use of puzzles and a detailed example. A preliminary assessment of the students' perception of this design is presented in Section 4. Finally Section 5 concludes the paper.

## 2. THE COURSE

CPSC 203 is titled "Introduction to Problem Solving Using Application Software". It is a first year computer literacy course for non-majors. The big ideas [11] of the course are in Table 1. These big ideas are of a long-lasting nature in a constantly changing field.

The bulk of our students are from the management and social sciences schools. Yet, students from natural sciences, communications, and other disciplines also register in the course. Hence, there is a wide variety of students who take the course. It is a required course for students taking 3$^{rd}$ year information systems management courses, and is an elective course for other disciplines.

**Table 1. Big Ideas and Understandings of the course**

| | Big Ideas | Understandings | Essential Questions |
|---|---|---|---|
| 1 | Abstraction | Abstract thinking; hiding irrelevant details; focusing on relevant details; use of discrete structures | How and when is abstraction advantageous? What abstract structure is most appropriate, why and when? |
| 2 | Generalization | Abstract models can lead to generalized conclusions; when is it a good idea to generalize and when not to | How and when is generalization advantageous? When is it not? |
| 3 | Problem Modelling | Abstract thinking; use of appropriate discrete structures | What abstract structure is most appropriate, why and when? What ready-to-use (canned) models can be readily employed? What if the model is inappropriate? |
| 4 | Problem Solution Development | Algorithmic thinking; think like a machine; following an algorithm; developing an algorithm | Would I be able to start thinking "from scratch" (free from what we take for granted? When is an algorithm correct? Is an algorithm the best way to solve the given problem? |

## 2.1 Course Format

The course is a 3-credit hour course delivered in a combination of lectures and tutorials: 150 minute lectures and 100 minute tutorials every week in a 13-week semester. The course's intake of students is at least 600 per semester, with lectures ranging from 100 to 175 students in a regular 13-week term (and about 60 students in a condensed 6-week term), with a cap of 25 students for each tutorial. Staffing requirements are from 2-4 instructors and at least 14 teaching assistants (TAs) per semester.

## 2.2 Course Content

The course's objectives are achieved via a set of concepts and a set of skills. While these are not completely independent, the concepts are covered in the lectures and the skills are covered in the tutorials. The scheduling takes into consideration the relationships between the concepts and skills so that they are run in parallel between lectures and tutorials. The concept topics include:

### FUNDAMENTALS

- **Logic, naïve set theory, and algorithms:** propositional logic, truth tables, quantifiers, sets, relations, and functions, algorithms, correctness and efficiency of algorithms.

- **Graphs and trees:** graphs (undirected, directed, and labeled), Euler paths, example graph algorithms such as graph coloring, applications to scheduling, trees, binary trees, coding, Huffman's coding algorithm, finite state machines.

### ARCHITECTURE

- **Computer Organization:** modern computer components, memory hierarchy, multi-core machines, magnetic and optical disk operation.

### APPLIED PROBLEM SOLVING

- **Databases:** Entity-Relationship (ER) modeling and ER diagrams, database schema, translating an ER diagram to database schema, first, second, and third normal forms, Query By Example (QBE), SQL, set operations in SQL, natural joins in SQL, aggregate functions in SQL.

- **Programming:** Alice programming, object-oriented concepts, variables, functions, conditionals, lists, loops, event-based programming, searching and sorting, top-down and bottom-up designs.

The fundamentals provide a basic framework of concepts in which problem solving skills can be developed through clear logical reasoning and the construction of simple graph-based models. The fundamentals are often illustrated with "classic" examples from computer science. These fundamentals are then augmented with an understanding of modern systems. Finally, we focus on solving real-world problems taken from various domains (business, sciences, and arts) first through developing database applications, and finally via developing simple programs. In the last section, we repeatedly emphasize the use of fundamentals to design an appropriate solution.

The resulting lectures cover a smaller set of concepts than typical of many survey courses – but cover them in greater depth than most survey courses. Students are introduced to fundamental concepts in computer science with sufficient grounding that they could pursue higher level (2$^{nd}$ or 3$^{rd}$ year) courses in the same subjects. Judicious choice of problems and examples is used to appeal to the diverse backgrounds of the students.

The tutorials cover lower-level, hands-on skills, such as using spreadsheets and database management systems. We will not discuss tutorials further since what we discuss in this paper is based on the lecture design.

## 3. THE USE OF PUZZLES

The puzzles and problems used in the classroom are of three types, categorized by their objectives. The first category constitutes domain-independent puzzles and is aimed at igniting students' curiosity and interest. Such puzzles are used at the beginning of a lecture before a certain subject is introduced. However, these puzzles are chosen carefully to serve as a bridge to the lecture material. The second category's objective is re-enforcement. It belongs to problem-based learning. These are used in order to allow students to directly or indirectly apply the concepts learnt in a lecture. The third category is used as a reflection mechanism, which permits students to entertain the limitations, extensions, and approximations of learnt concepts. This can be either in the puzzle-based or problem-based arena.

## 3.1 Detailed Example

We present an example lecture in the context of the fundamentals module, discussing Euler paths in graph theory. An objective of this lecture is to see how graphs can be used to abstractly represent real-life problems and how it can lead to generalized conclusions and universal applications.

**Pre-lecture puzzle:** The class is challenged with tracing shapes, such as the ones depicted in Figure 2. The shapes are chosen such that one shape is not traceable, the second is traceable as long tracing starts and ends at different points, and the third is traceable as long as tracing starts and ends in the same point. The students are given a few minutes to try to trace these shapes, working in teams. Then, they are asked to try to reflect with their team mates on why shapes are or are not traceable, and if they are, they should try to see if all shapes are traceable in the same way. More specifically, if a shape is traceable, can it be traced starting at any point in the shape or not? If not, where does tracing start and where does it end? No answers are given at this stage to these fundamental graph theory questions. Yet, the students are told that the answers will be given later in the lecture.

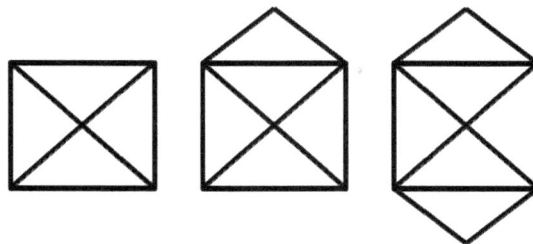

**Figure 2. Traceable and non-traceable shapes**

**Lecture:** The lecture is started by the Konigsberg story leading to a graph representation of the town's layout. The question of taking the famous town tour, crossing each bridge exactly once should lead the students to make the connection to tracing shapes. Is the Konigsberg graph traceable, and if not, why? The lecture proceeds to exploring Euler's theorems regarding an Euler cycle and an Euler non-cycle path. Once these fundamentals have been thoroughly explained, the Konigsberg graph is revisited as well as the shapes used in the pre-lecture puzzle. Students now get the chance to see how these shapes can be represented as graphs and how Euler's theorems hold the answers to what is traceable and what is not. The lecture continues with Euler's algorithm for finding a tour (alternatively tracing a shape).

**Post-lecture reflection:** The pre-lecture puzzle and the lecture in the form that was explained earlier do indeed capture students' attention. At this stage, we used to expect students to pose the question "so what?" or "how does this benefit me in real-life?" However, students are quite submerged, engaged, and having fun with tracing shapes to the extent that we have not yet faced any question of this form! Hence, we are the ones who pose this question.

So, one remaining piece of the puzzle is how this relates to real-life problems. Here, one example is to use a scheduling problem from real-life, such as scheduling equipment when paving streets. The students are given a map of a small section of downtown Calgary (Streets in certain areas of downtown Calgary are straight, forming a nice grid of lines to work with). The objective of the problem is to schedule paving equipment so that all the streets in the area are paved, and it is not desirable to have the equipment driven on newly paved streets. It will take students a few minutes of discussion in teams to realize that this can be represented as graph problem and that an optimal solution would an Euler path for this graph. We have also used other take-home reflection problems, where students need to design a courier delivery schedule.

The second remaining piece of the puzzle is what to do when an Euler path is impossible due to the characteristics of the given graph. This serves as a bridge to the topic of approximating a solution. That is, if an Euler path cannot be found, then it is required that the number of edges to be re-traversed should be minimized. Students are then asked to brain-storm identifying real-life problems with Euler tours can be used as part of their solution.

**Take-home problems:** Students leave with some graph examples where Euler paths are impossible. They are asked to find an approximate path that minimizes edge re-traversal. Often, they are also asked to modify (or at least think about modifying) the presented algorithms in the lecture so that it minimizes edge re-traversal, when an Euler path is impossible.

## 3.2 Other Examples

In this section, we give a few other puzzle examples that we have used and the context in which they are used. We do no intend this to be a comprehensive treatment of all the puzzles we use.

**Set theory:** The course includes a week-worth of material on naïve set theory. One puzzle that we have used is the following counting problem (from [12]):

An examination in three subjects, Algebra, Biology, and Chemistry, was taken by 41 students. The following table shows how many students failed in each single subject and in their various combinations.

| Subjects: | A | B | C | AB | AC | BC | ABC |
|---|---|---|---|---|---|---|---|
| Failed: | 12 | 5 | 8 | 2 | 6 | 3 | 1 |

How many students passed all three subjects?

In the context of this course, students are expected to solve this counting problem using Venn diagrams.

**Graph coloring:** Graph coloring often spans a 75 minute lecture. An example puzzle used is:

A framer has a canoe that can fit a single object in addition to him. He wants to transport three objects using his canoe from one bank of the river to the other. These objects are a sheep, wolf, and a bundle of hay. The farmer cannot leave some of these objects unattended; he cannot leave the wolf with sheep unattended and he cannot leave the sheep with the hay bundle, otherwise, one will eat the other. How should he safely transport these objects?

This puzzle serves as a good bridge to constrained scheduling. While the puzzle is simple, we see benefits in modeling it as a graph of objects, where adjacent vertices are the ones in conflict (cannot be left unattended). The use of graph coloring on this graph can give valuable hints on where to start and how to formulate the schedule.

We have often constructed more complex versions of this puzzle, by adding more objects and increasing the size of the canoe to justify the use of graphs and graph coloring.

A reflection problem on the subject of graph coloring follows. This example is an application of the graph coloring algorithm, yet it illustrates additional constraints that must be met in order to get an optimal solution. Any legitimate coloring of the resulting graph is not necessarily an acceptable solution. This creates some rich reflective discussion. The problem is:

You are managing a team of 15 workers: Alice, Bob, Chuck, Dianne, Elise, Frank, George, Hasan, Isabel, Jacky, Kip, Lora, Mike, Norman, and Olga (A to O). You're to come up with a schedule for your staff for 3 time slots, but you have the following restrictions:

- Couples should not put them in the same slot; couples are:
  - Alice and Bob
  - Kip and Jackie
  - Norman and Olga
  - George and Dianne
  - Isabel and Hasan

- People with the same specialty should not work in the same slot, if possible. The specialty groups are:
  - Elise, Bob, and Chuck
  - Alice, Dianne, and Hasan
  - Lora, Norman, and Mike

- People who had friction working together in the past, should not work in the same lot if possible. These are:
  - George and Kip
  - Lora and Chuck
  - Olga and Hasan
  - Alice and Chuck
  - Mike and Jackie
  - Elise and Isabel
  - Frank and Isabel
  - Frank and Bob
  - Frank and Elise

**Algorithmic thinking and efficiency:** One puzzle that promotes algorithmic thinking is (this also seems to be an interview question; see My Tech Interviews[2]):

You've got someone working for you for seven days and a gold bar to pay them. The gold bar is segmented into seven connected pieces. You must give them a piece of gold at the end of every day. If you are only allowed to make two breaks in the gold bar, how do you pay your worker?

Another puzzle that touches on efficiency of algorithms is:

A merchant learnt that one of his 4096 golden coins is fake. All coins look exactly the same (including the fake one). The only difference between a fake and a real coin is in the weight; a fake coin is lighter. Find an efficient algorithm to locate the fake coin.

This puzzle allows the students to see the benefits of logarithmic time algorithms over linear-time algorithms without having the background to analyze the complexity of algorithms. The students see the benefits of finding the fake coin in 12 steps (weighing operations) rather than 2048. This is further re-enforced by asking the students to double the total number of coins and re-do the calculations. Doubling the number of coins adds one more step to the logarithmic approach, while it adds 2048 to the linear approach.

One reflection problem asks the students to formulate an algorithm that works for any number of coins, not necessarily a power of two.

Another asks the students to improve on the logarithmic time. In the context of a first year course, we have formulated this as a fixed puzzle:

The merchant has 8 coins, one of which is a fake and is lighter. The logarithmic approached discussed earlier yields the fake coin in three steps. Find another algorithm that can achieve this in 2 steps only. Then, we can move to more complex instances in order to generalize the algorithm.

Efficiency of algorithms in the context of our course is a topic that we do not dare to wonder to had not it been discussed in the context of puzzles.

**Logical inference:**

We finally give a puzzle that promotes logical inference:

A basket contains 5 hats (3 black and 2 white). A person randomly chooses three hats from the basket, and puts them on 3 blindfolded people. Let's call these 3 people A, B, and C. Then, these people are lined up so that A can see the hats of B and C, B can only see that hat of C, and C can see no hats. When the blindfolds are removed, A says "I do not know the color of my hat"; B says "Neither do I"; C quickly says "My hat is black". C is right; explain her logic

## 4. ASSESSMENT

Our assessment is still work in progress. In a recent on-line survey of a 6-week condensed term, we asked students if puzzle-based learning helps them *better learn* the material. The survey also asked them if puzzle-based learning *got them interested* in the course material. There were 56 students registered in the course, and roughly 30 students constantly attended the lectures. Attendance is not mandatory. We received 16 valid instruments

(53% of the attending population and 28.5% of the whole class population). The student's perceptions are summarized in Figure 3. This is the second and most recent offering of the course under this format.

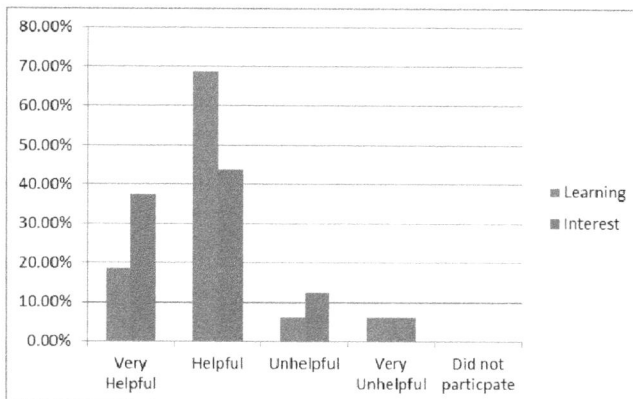

**Figure 3. Summary of students' feedback in a condensed 6-week semester.**

Our first offering of this course was in a regular 13-week semester, with 150 enrolled students. Only 27 valid (on-line) instruments were received. A different survey was used, but the assessment of the effect of the use of puzzles on "learning" was common between the surveys used in both semesters. Figure 4 shows a summary of the feedback for both offerings (for comparison).

The feedback shows a vast majority (Especially in the second offering) rating the approach as helpful in learning the material and getting interested in the subject. Written positive feedback includes comments like: "puzzles keep me awake", "puzzles are provoking", and "it is fun to talk to and work with people on these brain teasers". Negative comments include: "I would be more happy learning the required material" and "I do not feel comfortable talking to others in the classroom; working alone is frustrating".

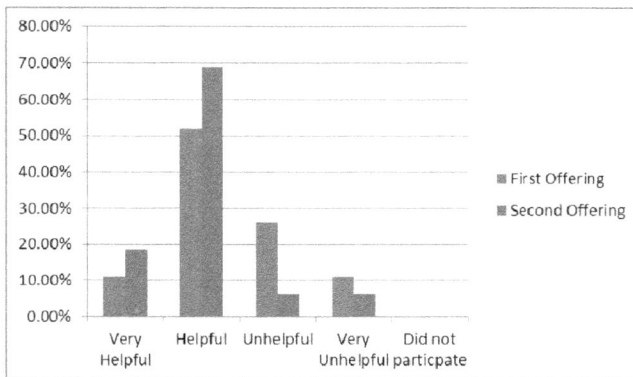

**Figure 4. Summary of students' feedback on "how helpful are puzzles in *learning* the course material.**

## 5. CONCLUSIONS

Puzzles are fun and engaging. They can teach some universal problem-solving skills in a simple context. Technology giants, such as Microsoft and Google, have shifted their interviewing paradigms to look for and hire problem-solvers. Their interview questions typically consist of puzzles. Some universities have designed "all-puzzle" freshman courses in order to retain students

---

[2] http://www.mytechinterviews.com/gold-for-7-days-of-work

and counter the problem of declining math skills in students. We have benefited from such previous work and implemented a course design that uses puzzles as bait to catch students' interest in problem solving. One challenging aspect in this course is that students are not from engineering or computer science. This is a service course and our students are largely from management and social sciences.

Our students used to find that computer science is "dry" and often too abstract to relate with. Motivating and engaging students have been an ongoing challenge in this course. The introduction of puzzles has started to break the ice. The feedback we are getting from students indicate that they are more engaged and more interested in learning the subject. Yet, more data needs to be collected in order to have more thorough analysis, especially to address the negative feedback.

# 6. ACKNOWLEDGMENTS

My thanks to project Engage and its staff at the University of Calgary, who gave me the necessary theoretical and logistical help for this redesign and its execution.

I am also thankful to Mishtu Banarjee for his feedback on an earlier draft of this work.

# 7. REFERENCES

[1]  W. Poundstone (2000). "How Would You Move Mount Fuji?" *Microsoft's Cult of the Puzzle—How the World's Smartest Companies Select the Most Creative Thinkers*, Little Brown and Company.

[2]  N. Falkner, R. Sooriamurthi, and Z. Michalewicz (2010). Puzzle-Based Learning for Engineering and Computer Science. *Computer*, April, pp. 21-28.

[3]  B. Parhami (2009). Puzzling Problems in Computer Engineering. *Computer*, March, pp. 26-29.

[4]  A. Levitin and M.A. Papalaskari (2002). Using puzzles in teaching algorithms. *Proceedings of ACM SIGCSE*, pp. 292-296.

[5]  N. V. Shilov, and K. Yi (2001) .Puzzles for Learning Model Checking, Model Checking for Programming Puzzles, Puzzles for Testing Model Checkers. *Electronic. Notes on Theoretical Computer Science*, 43: 34-49.

[6]  Z. Michalewicz and M. Michalewicz (2007). Puzzle Based Learning. *Proceedings of the 2007 AaeE Conference*, pp. 1-8.

[7]  M.R.K. Krishna Rao (2006). Storytelling and Puzzles in a Software Engineering Course. *Proceedings of ACM SIGCSE*, pp. 418-422

[8]  Zhiguang Xu and Joe Mayer (2007). Teaching Critical Thinking and Problem Solving Skills Through Online Puzzles and Games. *7th International Conference on Distance Learning and Web Engineering*, pp. 321-325.

[9]  S. Cha, D. Kown, and W. Lee (2007). Using Puzzles: Problem-Solving and Abstraction. *Proceedings ACM of SIGITE*, pp. 135-140.

[10] S. Banarjee and J. Kawash (2009). Re-thinking Computer Literacy in Post-Secondary Education. *Proceedings of the 14th Western Canadian Conference on Computing Education*, pp. 17-21.

[11] G. Wiggins and J. McTighe (2005). *Understanding by Design 2nd ed.* Association for Supervision & Curriculum Development.

[12] Thomas Scott Blyth, T. S. Blyth, and E. F. Robertson (1984). *Algebra Through Practice: Sets, Relations, and Mappings*. Cambridge University Press.

# Comprehensive Design of Cyber Physical Systems

Richard Helps, Francis Mensah
BYU Information Technology
265 CTB
Provo UT, 84602, USA
801-422-6305
richard_helps@byu.edu, fnmensah@gmail.com

## ABSTRACT

In recent years there has been a confluence between different fields addressing the broad field of embedded computer systems (cyber-physical systems). Traditional 8-bit microcontroller-based systems have become more capable and frequently feature 32-bit processors with networking capabilities, thus overlapping larger OS-based systems. Single-board OS-based computers have shrunk to credit-card size and prices on the low end have dropped substantially to overlap the application domain of microcontroller systems and, thirdly, mobile platforms (smartphones, tablets, e-readers etc.) also share many characteristics of these systems and overlap their design and application domains. These systems each have their own design communities, tools and standard approaches. However their commonality and overlapping application domains indicate that they share common design problems. The evolution into newer application areas also brings new problems. The situation becomes more complex when these systems are integrated into larger diverse systems.

Design approaches and design problems for these different types of embedded system are reviewed. Overlapping and non-overlapping characteristics and design issues are analyzed. A comprehensive design approach tailored to these cyber-physical systems is proposed. The comprehensive approach addresses design issues for all three of the overlapping fields. It also includes factors sometimes neglected when systems are developed within their own narrower design domains.

One of the findings of this investigation is that design in this domain requires a diverse set of skills, usually only found in multi-disciplinary teams. One discipline that is needed but has not traditionally contributed much in this domain is Information Technology. Another finding is that designers trained in the IT discipline with a systems-oriented approach have design skills that are necessary for successful design of these diverse systems.

## Categories and Subject Descriptors

J.7 [**Computers in Other Systems**]: Real time, Industrial Control

## Keywords

Embedded Systems, Design, Cyber-Physical Systems, Information Technology, Project Management.

## 1. INTRODUCTION

Embedded computer systems have evolved in recent years from several different sub-domains or communities of design. Three of the most prominent include designs based on microcontrollers (µC); small single-board computers (SBC); and commercial mobile platforms. Commercial Mobile Platforms (CMP) is a term used to describe the emerging family of small systems that are mobile and include a variety of sensors and interfaces. Typical examples include devices such as smartphones, PDAs, tablets and e-readers. A previous paper has discussed the convergence of these three sub-disciplines [1]. Since there is no universal definition of embedded systems as a design domain, identifying characteristics from the literature will be presented for each of these classes of embedded system. These characteristics show the three different sub-domains share many common characteristics, which also differentiate them from conventional computing systems.

Since these types of computer system share many common characteristics it is not surprising that these systems also share common design factors. Not only do they share design factors as separate classes of system but these systems are also frequently combined together to create larger, complex, heterogeneous but integrated systems. The characteristics that distinguish these sub-domains from conventional computing, both in terms of application and design, point to the need for a design approach different from that used for conventional computing. Their overlapping characteristics point further to the need for a comprehensive design approach which will allow designers to develop any of these systems or combinations of these systems with awareness of the design factors.

The embedded system literature discuss the need for integrated design [2, 3] and various formal models aimed at this diverse design environment [4-6], but there remains a need for a comprehensive design/project approach. The paper offers such an approach.

### 1.1 Cyber-Physical Systems

In more recent publications embedded systems are being referred to as Cyber-Physical Systems (CPS). Lee defines Cyber-Physical Systems as, "integrations of computation and physical systems." [7] He argues, with some merit, that the term encompasses all of what we now call embedded systems and somewhat more. He further suggests that this is a very large growth area for computing. In another definition Marwedel describes CPS as computer systems embedded in a physical environment [8].

The term "cyber-physical" is intended to emphasize the interaction between these computer systems and the real-world, which is one of their key distinguishing characteristics. It also suggests the impact of physics on the design of these systems, in other words not only do these systems measure and control the real-world but the dynamism, or real-time response of the systems is also a significant factor. This is a pointer to some of the design issues of such systems. The term is finding traction with the emergence of conferences (EG ICCPS sponsored by IEEE/ACM), symposia (EG CSL Symposium in 2011 sponsored by U. Illinois) and journals (EG IJSCCPS). Several educational institutions are also offering course-work using this term.

Since CPS effectively incorporates embedded systems and emphasizes some of the key issues in their design this is a useful descriptive name, and will be adopted for this analysis.

The remainder of this article will characterize CPS and the related design factors and propose a model for designing systems.

## 2. CHARACTERISTICS OF CPS

The different domains of CPS systems are defined relative to conventional computer systems (CCS). Conventional computer systems are considered to be those which include one of the well-known operating systems (Windows and Unix-derivatives), are intended for a wide range of computing services by running multiple application programs, include 802.nn network connections and interface primarily through a keyboard, monitor and mouse. In contrast to this the three categories of CPS are shown in Table 1 below with their distinguishing characteristics.

### 2.1 CPS Defined by Characteristics

It must be stated that characteristics are being identified, not defining properties. Exceptions to any of the listed characteristics can easily be found; nevertheless these characteristics do describe recognized sub-domains each with their own design communities and bodies of literature.

As Table 1 shows there are a number of factors that characterize CPS, but some of the leading ones are:

- Separate development and target systems: This leads to a variety of design issues, in particular what Wolf describes as "limited observability and controllability" [9]. This characteristic is shared by all three sub-domains of CPS
- Narrowly focused: A key characteristic of embedded systems is that they are not general-purpose computers. Modern tablets and smartphones (CMP) are stretching this limitation with the availability of many thousands of "apps", however these systems share many other characteristics of CPS.
- HCI standards: HCI standards and guidelines are well defined and available for conventional computer systems but most CPS require custom design.
- Use of sensors and actuators: This is common in CPS, rare in conventional systems. For microcontrollers sensors and actuators are often the primary or sole user- and world-interface.

Other characteristics shared by CPS could be mentioned such as reliability (discussed, for example, by Lee and by Henzinger and Sifakis [7, 10]), low-power concerns, low-cost concerns (especially μC), low processing power and so on, but these are all adequately addressed elsewhere.

**Table 1. Characteristics of Different Types of System**

| Factor | CCS | SBC | μC | CMP |
|---|---|---|---|---|
| Separate dev. sys. | no | yes | yes | yes |
| Narrowly focused | no | yes | yes | Limited range of purposes |
| UI (HCI) Standards & guidelines | Yes | custom | custom | Competing stds & custom. Few cross-platfm standards. |
| Sensors/ actuators | v. limited | yes | Extensive | multiple |
| UI (HCI) Stds & guidelines . | Yes | custom | custom | Competing standards |
| Human Interface | Kbd, Monitor mouse | Custom displays & kbd. | Custom & sensor/ actuator-based | (multi-) touch-scrns, soft kbds, sensors & actuators |
| Network | IEEE 802.n std. | IEEE 802.n avail. | rare | Wifi common, others N/A |
| Other communication protocols | USB, BT, etc. *Serial ports rare.* | USB, BT, RS232 avail. | Serial Others poss. (daughter-board) | Bluetooth common. USB rare, Others rare |
| Cell-phone link | - | - | - | common |
| Storage | HDD, SDD & others | SD Card, USB memory | Primarily flash memory | Primarily on-board flash |
| Storage size | 100's GB+ | 100's MB | KB to low MB | Low GB typical |
| Mobile energy capability (if mobile) | Laptops: Watts to 10's of watts | Varies if mobile | 10's-100's of mW | Mobile by definition. 100's of mW |
| Real-time | no | Yes—with limitations | yes | no |

Although the sub-domains do not share all characteristics, there is strong commonality between them and clear differences between them and conventional computer systems, which defines them as a design entity and in need of special design considerations.

### 2.2 Common Design Factors

The shared characteristics of CPS sub-domains lead to a set of shared design factors. These shared factors are listed in Table 2. Once again conventional computer systems (CCS) are listed to emphasize the distinction between the CPS and CCS systems.

**Table 2. Design Factors for Different Types of System**

| Design Factor | CCP | SBC | µC | CMP |
|---|---|---|---|---|
| Modern software design | yes | yes | yes—mostly | yes |
| IAS | yes | yes | yes—mostly | yes |
| Hardware design | no | yes | yes | rarely |
| Custom HCI design | no | yes | yes | Provider defined. Some emerging standards |
| Single-Application focus | no | yes | yes | Mostly, but many general-purpose apps emerging on popular devices |
| Limited SDK availability | no | yes | yes | yes |
| Separate dev sys & target | no | yes | yes | yes |
| Limited processing power | yes | yes | yes | yes |
| Limited memory (RAM or permanent) | no | Some-what | yes | yes |
| Power-consumption | no | yes | yes | yes |
| Real-time design | no | some | yes | no |

Two notable factors shared between CCS and CPS are software design and Information Assurance and Security (IAS) concerns. Modern software design in the above table refers to the availability of modern languages (OO etc.) and techniques. IAS has been neglected in the CPS domain, because traditionally the systems were isolated and the CPS design communities were not deeply involved in IAS issues. That isolation is much less true as many CPS systems acquire networking capabilities. The problem with designer familiarity with IAS remains, and will be addressed later in this paper.

The table makes it clear that there are a host of concerns faced by CPS designers as well as the usual software design concerns. A clear design approach is needed that addresses the characteristics of CPS.

## 3. ANALYSIS

The problem with CPS design is that it incorporates a number of critical factors that are less significant in conventional systems design. For example software design and software design models have been extensively analyzed, but software design only represents a sub-set of the issues faced by CPS designers. In this regard Lee comments that, "it will not be sufficient to improve design processes, raise the level of abstraction, or verify (formally or otherwise) designs that are built on today's abstractions. To realize the full potential of CPS, we will have to rebuild computing and networking abstractions. These abstractions will have to embrace physical dynamics and computation in a unified way." [7] Other researchers have addressed the need for CPS design such as formal models for

Another key issue is the HCI factor. Both µC and SBC systems need to interact with humans and there are no well-established HCI design standards and guidelines in this area. Guidelines are emerging for CMP but standardization is still under development. HCI for conventional computer systems can be designed with guidelines such as those from SIGCHI [11] and many others but these do not apply well to a device that communicates through sensors and actuators, rather than through a screen and keyboard. With the diversity of applications of CPS it may be that no single standard is possible but that HCI designs will have to depend on basic HCI principles.

Another serious consideration is that of Information assurance and Security (IAS). With the widespread deployment of networking on CPS and more extensive storage of user data on CPS IAS issues are becoming much more prominent in a field where they have not previously been a major factor. Mobile platforms are starting to address these issues but they are still in their infancy in both µC and SBC design fields. There have been some notable failures in this area in the past [12, 13], and more attention needs to be paid to this area.

### 3.1 Complexity of CPS Systems

There is a further problem that designers in each of the separate sub-domains of CPS have focused in their own area, but with the progression of Moore's law the systems are evolving to acquire capabilities in larger domains. For example microcontroller designers have focused strongly on the needs and capabilities of microcontroller performance and real-time responsiveness, but now that microcontrollers have evolved to include 32-bit capability and network connectivity they too need professional software and information technology approaches to be combined with the hardware and real-time concerns.

The different sub-domains are also evolving and impinging upon each other. For example, there are multiple low-cost, low-power, small SBC systems such as the Gumstix unit (www.gumsix.org), the recent Raspberry Pi unit (www.raspberrypi.org) and others. These systems compete in size, power consumption and price with microcontroller systems but run a modified Linux OS. The OS both expands their capabilities and limits them with respect to real-time performance and flexibility of IO connections. Similarly microcontrollers with 32-bit CPUs and network connectivity, overlap with SBC applications. In the CMP domain modern smartphones and tablets often include accelerometers, GPS, gyroscopes, vibration actuators, proximity sensors and others, which have been used by creative designers to apply these devices in application domains that overlap both SBC and µC.

In addition to overlapping sub-domains some designs use combinations of systems including both conventional and various types of CPS. These diverse systems inherit all the design factors of the three sub-domains plus additional complexity.

## 3.2 Multi-disciplinary Design Needs

These factors in CPS design indicate that we are rapidly approaching the point where design requires a multi-disciplinary approach. Hardware design and low-level design skills, such as those commonly taught in EE and CompE programs are necessary, as are software design skills, such as those taught in CS programs. A discipline that has not been heavily involved in CPS design is that of Information technology, however IT has core skills in system integration, HCI and IAS design. These are detailed in the IT Body of knowledge and ABET accreditation requirements. [14, 15]. Whether these skills come from multiple designers or from a multi-skilled designer the nature of the design task now requires more than a single focus.

## 4. DESIGN MODEL PROPOSAL

A design model is proposed for cyber-physical systems. Standard software life-cycle and design models do not take the distinguishing characteristics of cyber-physical systems into account. The proposed design model adapts and extends existing approaches to address the specific needs of CPS. The approach is currently being used for a small on-going project.

The proposed CPS design model consists of four main phases namely Creativity, Specification, Prototyping and Deployment.

## 4.1 Design Model: Creativity Phase

The design process begins with the Creativity phase. See Figure 1. An essential aspect of this phase is understanding users and their real needs. The disciplines of HCI and user-centered design strongly influence design at this stage. Understanding the users and their needs ensures that the design is focused on the correct problem, outlines the UI design and the framework of the technical design that follows. These design concepts have been extensively discussed and validated in the literature, for example, [16-22]. During this phase, a design concept is created to either meet an existing need or to create new opportunities. The idea is validated and evaluated as part of the creativity process. After each evaluation, the process may be repeated until a consensus is reached to proceed. The result at the end of this phase is a document containing a conceptual design specification of the final product (also known as the user requirements document).

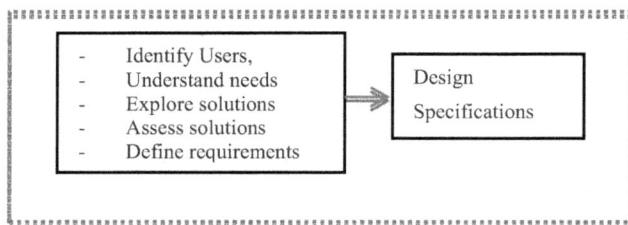

**Figure 1. Creativity Phase**

## 4.2 Design Model: Specification Phase

The technical specification phase makes use of the user requirements document and develops a detailed prototype specification. See Figure 2. The design of this phase reflects some of the parallel development ideas discussed by Marwedel [8], but with a much broader viewpoint of the diverse systems contributing to the overall design and at a higher level of abstraction. This is the primary phase for ensuring that the diverse nature of CPS design is addressed. The different parallel stages designed here will be evaluated in the later phases, but must be included in the structure at this point. Issues omitted at this phase may have serious consequences later.

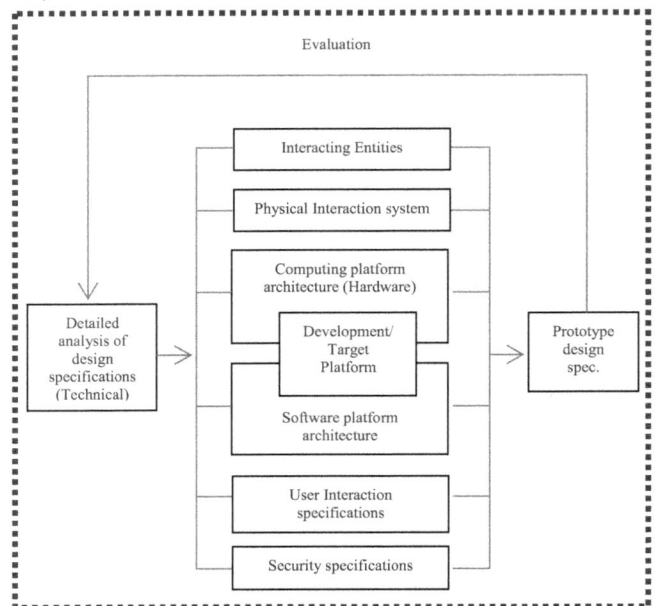

**Figure 2. Specification Phase**

The following requirements are considered during this phase:

- Physical world interaction: This specifies the requirements for the actuators, sensors and real-time requirements for the system.

- Computing system hardware specification: Unlike conventional systems the hardware selection is an essential part of the design process CPS have issues with size, computational power, memory, real time requirements and power consumption. All these must be considered when specifying the hardware.

- Software specification: Specific issues to be considered in this phase include hardware compatibility, need for—or omission of—operating systems, available software libraries and suitability for real time applications.

- Development and Target Systems: Overlapping the Hardware and software selections are considerations of both the development and target environment. Since there are limited selections of each they should be considered early in the design process.

- User Interaction/HCI specification: CPS are distinguished by their non-standard user interfaces. Systems often fail because of their inability to interact effectively with the user. It is therefore necessary to consider the user interface early in the design process to avoid having to do a major design change later in the process.

- IAS: Technologies such as networking and storage, among others, have introduced security and privacy concerns that need to be addressed early in the design process.

- Interacting Entities: Cyber-physical systems do not work in isolation and are most likely either going to depend on services provided by other entities or provide services to them. These entities may include legal institutions, financial institutions, and communication networks. It is crucial to include consideration of these entities early in the design process

The output of this phase is a prototype specification document. The complete phase may be included in the iterative design loop as necessary. The overall relative risk at the end of this phase is reduced because many of the risk factors that have a major impact on the success of the project have now been addressed.

## 4.3 Design Model: Prototyping Phase

The prototyping phase (Figure 3) takes the output from the specification phase and based on the recommended specifications a preliminary design is produced. This design includes all the hardware that will be used, as well as the software that will be responsible for all the application logic. The design is then decomposed into several smaller portions each of which may be considered as a mini project. The preliminary design is then implemented in incremental stages over multiple iterations.

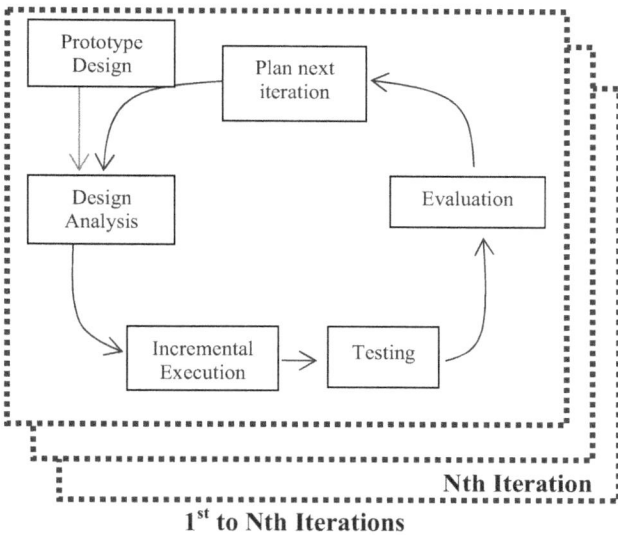

**Figure 3. Prototyping Phase**

Each iteration implements one of the smaller design loops and the result is evaluated. Depending on the result of the evaluation, either the next incremental portion will be implemented in the next iteration or the same iteration will be repeated. It may even be necessary to review the technical specifications phase following the discovery of a problem during iteration. This phase is similar in concept to other iterative models such as Boehm's spiral model or the Rational Unified Process [23, 24]

This approach enables bottom-up-build in CPS. It also allows flexibility to go back and forth within the design process. This is important especially for cyber-physical system design where some problems only become visible during implementation.

The iterations in this phase include the following steps

- Design analysis: The design is analyzed; outputs and test requirements (expectations) for this cycle are determined.
- Execution: The design step is implemented. This step may include integration of previous design stages or components.
- Testing: To what extent are expectations met?

- Evaluation: the accomplishments of this phase are evaluated with respect to diverse CPS factors
  - o Physical interaction correctness
  - o Hardware performance (power, real time, memory performance, CPU performance)
  - o Software correctness
  - o Information assurance and security
  - o User experience

One or more of the iterations may include developing a manufacturable prototype. The final product of this phase is the final manufacturable product ready to be deployed.

By the end of the prototyping iterative design phase most of the risks have been identified and resolved.

## 4.4 Design Model: Deployment Phase

At this phase of the design process, the final product is fully defined, and evaluated (figure 4). The activities in the deployment phase mainly deal with manufacturing the product/system and distributing it to the final user. The phase begins with a final customer pass-off. The product now meets customer and user expectations and the risk of failure is very low.

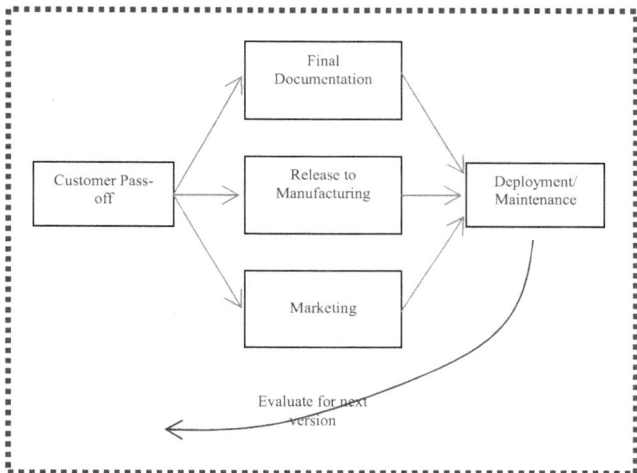

**Figure 4. Deployment Phase**

The next activities include preparation of the final documentation (note: each phase also produces its own documentation), release of the final design to manufacturing, and marketing (for a commercial product). The product is then finally deployed into its application environment. As time goes on, its performance is reviewed and evaluated and if necessary a re-design or new version is proposed. The design process then begins again.

## 4.5 Risk Management

One of the important benefits of iterative development models is risk management [24]. By moving riskier design aspects earlier in the process probability of success is significantly improved. This model uses that approach to an enhanced degree.

Figure 5 compares the risk profiles for the traditional waterfall, iterative and the proposed cyber-physical design models with respect to cyber-physical systems. One of the known weaknesses of the waterfall model is that risk mitigation only begins when the project is well advanced.

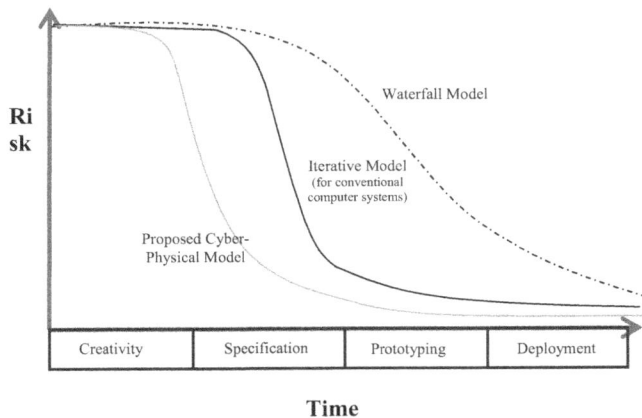

**Time**

**Figure 5. Risk Reduction Graph**

Iterative design models, as used in standard computing systems, improve the situation by discovering and mitigating risks earlier in the design process. However, CPS systems have a much wider range of risk factors. The proposed model takes into account these factors and addresses them early in the design process. The anticipated result is the much improved risk profile as seen in the figure.

## 5. CONCLUSIONS

Cyber-physical systems in various sub-domains will continue to evolve and overlap. CPS will continue to grow as an important part of the broad computing discipline. A comprehensive design approach, as proposed here, is required to address the complex needs of CPS design.

The comprehensive model proposed here is derived from existing, validated models and has been expanded to incorporate the characteristics of CPS design. The model is currently being applied in a trial project and further development is planned.

The complexity of CPS design requires a multi-disciplinary approach, particularly to include factors such as HCI design, IAS concerns and system integration, in addition to the more traditional skills in hardware and software. Information Technology, although not traditionally heavily invested in this growth area, is well positioned to provide some of these missing skills.

Further detailed expansion of this model to address various aspects in depth and to validate it will follow.

## 6. REFERENCES

[1] Helps, C. R. G. *Blurring the lines: The Intersection of Mobile and Embedded Systems and Information Technology*. ASEE, City, 2012.

[2] Lewis, B. Need for Architecture Description Language with Standardized Well Defined Meaning for Architecture Centric Engineering of Cyber-Physical Systems. In *Proceedings of the Analytic Virtual Integration of Cyber-Physical Systems Workshop (AVICPS)* (San Diego, November 30, 2010).

[3] Sha, L. and Meseguer, J. Analytical System Composition. In *Proceedings of the Analytic Virtual Integration of Cyber-Physical Systems Workshop (AVICPS)* (San Diego, November 30, 2010).

[4] Bhatia , G., Lakshmanan, K. and Rajkumar, R. R. An End-to-End Integration Framework for Automotive Cyber-Physical Systems Using SysWeaver. In *Proceedings of the Analytic Virtual Integration of Cyber-Physical Systems Workshop (AVICPS)* (San Diego, November 30, 2010).

[5] Bhave, A., Krogh, B., Garlan, D. and Schmerl, B. Multi-domain Modeling of Cyber-Physical Systems Using Architectural Views. In *Proceedings of the Analytic Virtual Integration of Cyber-Physical Systems Workshop (AVICPS)* (San Diego, November 30, 2010).

[6] Redman, D., Ward, D., Chilenski, J. and Pollari, G. Virtual Integration for Improved System Design. In *Proceedings of the Analytic Virtual Integration of Cyber-Physical Systems Workshop (AVICPS)* (San Diego, November 30, 2010).

[7] Lee, E. A. *Cyber Physical Systems: Design Challenges*. City, 2008.

[8] Marwedel, P. *Embedded System Design: Embedded Systems Foundations of Cyber-Physical Systems*. Springer, 2010.

[9] Wolf, W. *Computers as Components: Principles of Embedded Computer System Design*. Morgan Kauffman, 2005.

[10] Henzinger, T. and Sifakis, J. The Discipline of Embedded Systems Design. *IEEE Computer*, 40, 10 (Oct. 2007 2007)

[11] Hewett, T. T., Baecker, R., Card, S., Carey, T., Gasen, J., Mantei, M., Strong, G. and Verplank, W. *Curricula for Human-Computer Interaction ACM-SIGCHI*, 2007.

[12] Bright, P. *Cars hacked through wireless tire sensors*. Ars Technica, City, 2010.

[13] Zetter, K. *How Digital Detectives Deciphered Stuxnet, the Most Menacing Malware in History*. Wired, City, 2011.

[14] ABET *Criteria for Accrediting Computing Programs: Effective for Evaluations During the 2011-2012 Accreditation Cycle* ABET Inc. , City, 2010.

[15] Lunt , B. M., Ekstrom, J. J., Gorka, S., Hislop, G., Kamali, R., Lawson, E. A., LeBlanc, R., Miller, J. and Reichgelt, H. *Information Technology 2008: Curriculum Guidelines for Undergraduate Degree Programs in Information Technology*. ACM, IEEE-CS, 2008.

[16] Garret, J. J. The Elements of User Experience: User-Centered Design for the Web2002).

[17] McCracken, D. D. and Wolfe, R. J. *User-centered Website Development : A Human Computer Interaction Approach*. Prentice Hall, Upper Saddle River, NJ, 2004.

[18] Rogers, Y., Sharp, H. and Preece, J. *Interaction Design: Beyond Human-Computer Interaction*. J. Wiley, 2011.

[19] Shneiderman, B. A Grander Goal: A Thousand-Fold Increase in Human Capabilities(November/ December 1997 1997).

[20] Shneiderman, B. *Designing the User Interface: Strategies for Effective Human-Computer Interaction*.

[21] Kelley, T. and Littman, J. *The Ten Faces of Innovation*. Doubleday, Random House, New York, 2005.

[22] Kelley, T. and Littman, J. *The Art of Innovation: Lessons in Creativity from IDEO, America's Leading Design Firm*. Doubleday, New York, 2001.

[23] Boehm, B. W. A spiral model of software development and enhancement. *Computer*, 21, 5 1988), 61-72.

[24] Kruchten, P. *The Rational Unified Process: An Introduction*. Addison-Wesley/Pearson education, 2004.

# Teaching Mobile Web Application Development: Challenges Faced And Lessons Learned

Peter Alston
Department of Computing
Edge Hill University
Ormskirk, UK
alstonp@edgehill.ac.uk

## ABSTRACT

Given the increasing popularity of smartphones and their accompanying applications, a number of Higher Education (HE) institutions in the UK are offering a mobile applications development module as part of their undergraduate degrees. Each institution has their own method of implementing such a module and will also have certain restrictions to work within.

This paper reports on the author's experiences of delivering a Mobile Application Development module to 3rd year undergraduate Web Systems Development (WSD) students and the challenges faced in developing an alternative curriculum for a module originally intended for Computing students with experience using the Java programming language. Module evaluations indicate that the alternative curriculum provided to WSD students was well received and the practical hands-on tutorials used in the delivery of the module give students a sense of empowerment and the confidence they need to succeed.

## Categories and Subject Descriptors

K.3.2 [**Computer and Information Science Education**]: Computer Science Education.

## General Terms

Design, Experimentation, Human Factors

## Keywords

Mobile Web Design, Curriculum and Delivery, Best Practices, Smartphones, Implementation

## 1. INTRODUCTION

In 2010, smartphones outsold PCs 101 millions to 92 million thus making the smartphone market much larger than the PC market [1]. We live in a world today were the mobile device is seen as the primary mechanism for people to access the Internet [2] as people require access to information on the move, rather than being confined to a chair and a monitor. It is also suggested that over a period of seven days, 60% of the population who own a mobile device will have used their device to access the World Wide Web. [3]. With this, it is no surprise that demand has increased for highly skilled developers to craft applications for a variety of mobile devices to enable businesses to reach customers in all

corners of the world. For the most part, many mobile applications that are developed are considered to be 'native' applications, in that they are developed for a specific platform and have access to the hardware of a device through the use of Application Programming Interfaces (APIs). Whilst this is considered to be the norm with a number of marketplaces available today in which to market these applications, it becomes much more challenging when trying to develop an application for multiple platforms.

Condor and Darcy [4] argue that the mobile development community is at a tipping point in that mobile users demand more choice, more functionality and more opportunities for customization whilst mobile developers want the freedom to develop powerful mobile applications with minimal roadblocks. It seems that the idea of developing just for one platform is no longer enough.

Recent advances in Web technologies (including HTML5, CSS3 and JavaScript) [5][6][7] have enabled the development of mobile applications, which are created using Hypertext Markup Language (HTML), Cascading Style Sheets (CSS) and JavaScript. These applications, known as mobile Web applications, can then be deployed to multiple platforms including Android, iOS, Blackberry and Windows Phone and even the desktop PC, through a Web browser. More recently, the developments of HTML5 now enable Web developers to access the native hardware of a device and thus allowing mobile Web applications to function just as well as their native counterparts.

## 2. MODULE OVERVIEW

The Mobile Applications Development module is a 12-week, one semester module offered as part of the final year BSc (Hons) Computing and BSc (Hons) Web Systems Development (WSD) programmes at Edge Hill University. Students who study Computing can choose the module as an elective for their final year studies whilst for final year WSD students it is a core requirement.

The module runs for 12 weeks (1 semester) and consists of a 1-hour lecture to discuss associated theory and a 2-hour practical lab session, where students can put into practice the theory they have learnt. Pre-requisites for the module require students to have an understanding of HTML and Object Oriented (OO) programming principles, which are covered during 1st and 2nd year studies for Computing and WSD students.

Students are required to complete two assignments during the module; CW1 involves the students producing a 4-page academic paper on a topic related to mobile application development whilst CW2 asks the student to plan, design and develop a mobile application intended for the Android platform based on a given scenario.

## 2.1 Previous Implementations

In previous years, the module has only been available to final year Computing students. During the module, students developed mobile applications using the Java programming language. Students were introduced to J2ME and the Eclipse IDE to design and develop their mobile applications, which would be deployed via the Symbian (Nokia) platform. These applications were then tested on a limited number of mobile devices that were available within the department.

For this year's implementation of the module, as well as delivering the module to both Computing and WSD students, it was decided that students would develop applications for the Android platform. To facilitate this, the department purchased a number of devices (both tablet and mobile) to allow students to develop using the Eclipse IDE, the Java programing language and the Android SDK.

## 2.2 Fundamental Issues

When discussing the logistics of the current module delivery, a number of issues were raised regarding the content, and application of knowledge.

Firstly, the pre-requisite knowledge of WSD students was considered and how appropriate it was to developing mobile applications in the Java programming language. Currently, WSD students are taught OO programming principles in the second year of their studies using ActionScript 3 and the Adobe Flash environment. Here, students are required to develop an object oriented 'Web-site', which demonstrates an understanding of the principles they have learnt throughout the module. This is very different to their Computing counterparts, who develop applications in Java using the Eclipse IDE as part of their 2$^{nd}$ year OO programming module, thus giving them a good insight to the language before they embark on their third year studies.

Secondly, since both sets of students were studying the same module, they also had to complete the same pieces of work and achieve the same set of learning outcomes. Whilst CW1 (academic paper) would not present many problems, CW2 asks the students them to develop a mobile application for the Android platform based on a given scenario.

A number of options were discussed as to how to proceed. One option was to carry on as planned, running the module from a purely programming aspect and asking the students to develop mobile applications using Java and the Android SDK. This presents an issue in that whilst the programming principles taught to the two groups of students in previous years are the same, the methods of implementation are very different. WSD students are not exposed to the Java programming language in any great detail (beyond a six week block in 1$^{st}$ year studies) and thus may be hindered in their ability to achieve high marks on the module if developing applications in the same way as Computing colleagues.

Another option discussed was to create a new module to allow the WSD students to study an alternative to Mobile Application Development and utilise the skills they had developed over the first two years of their course. However, due to time constraints, this option was not feasible and thus not considered.

A final option was presented by the author which would allow the Computing and WSD students to study the same module, but develop mobile Web applications based on the skills and knowledge they had acquired, using HTML, CSS and JavaScript.

## 2.3 A Viable Alternative

By allowing WSD students to develop mobile Web applications, it meant that both Computing and WSD students could 'study' on the same module, complete the same assignments and still achieve the same learning outcomes. There would be no need to develop an alternative module and the learning outcomes allowed for some movement in what students would create for the mobile application. What was needed now was a curriculum for the WSD students, which would allow them to write a conference paper and also allow them to develop a functional Mobile Web Application, comparable to what the Computing students would produce.

## 3. DEVLOPING A MOBILE WEB APPLICATIONS CURRICULUM

When deciding on the curriculum content, it was important to consider the learning outcomes and assessment requirements of the module. An emphasis was made on using similar content within the Computing and WSD sessions to ensure that both sets of students were able to complete the required assessment and that they would not be disadvantaged in any way.

One of the main reasons for this was due to the first assignment - the academic paper. Students needed to conduct research first, in order to have the necessary information in which to produce their paper. Regardless of whether students were approaching this from a 'native' mobile application (Computing students) or a 'web' mobile application (WSD students) aspect, they would be faced with some of the same issues regarding security, bandwidth (if making use of any Web services) and device constraints to name but a few. Thus it would be conceivable to imagine a Computing student and a WSD student producing an academic paper, which talked about the same issues.

Another aspect to consider was to ensure that discussion of the relevant technologies and frameworks were included within sessions to allow WSD students to create their application. A curriculum covering aspects of Web design for mobile devices was of great importance, along with examples on how they could potentially access the native hardware of the device being used to provide a true mobile experience.

## 3.1 Curriculum For WSD Students

Taking into account all the factors discussed previously, it was decided that the topics listed below would form the basis of the curriculum for WSD students:

- Overview and Challenges of Mobile Computing
- HTML5 Features (Storage, Connectivity, Offline, etc.)
- CSS3 (Styling, Transitions, Transforms & Animations)
- Strategies for Web Design
  - Graceful Degradation [8]
  - Progressive Enhancement [9]
  - Hardboiled Design [10]
  - Responsive Design [11]
  - Mobile First [12]
- JavaScript Libraries and Frameworks
  - jQuery, jQuery Mobile, Sencha Touch, PhoneGap, Appcelerator Titanium, ExtJS, Mobilize.js, etc.
- Cross Platform Deployment and Marketing

Material used as part of the sessions on HTML5 and JavaScript were developed based on the case studies and tutorials available at HTML5 Rocks Community (http://www.html5rocks.com). Other theoretical concepts covered during the module included the challenges faced in the development of mobile applications, security, accessibility and usability. The topics were covered over the first ten weeks of the module as part of a series of lectures and practical lab/tutorial sessions, allowing time during the final weeks to work on their assignments with guidance from the tutor.

## 4. MODULE DELIVERY

For the first part of the module, students were exposed to the theoretical nature of the module through a series of lectures and directed seminar activities. The purpose of the activities was to aid students in the development of their academic paper by exposing them to previously published papers and current technological issues being discussed in relation to mobile application development.

The seminar activities required students to pick one paper each week from a series of published conference papers (four were provided each week) on areas related to mobile application development and the use of Web technologies to create mobile applications. Students were then asked to write a half page (A4) précis of the paper and then present it the following week as part of a discussion with the rest of the group. Each student was asked to read their summary to the group and provide a unique point about the paper that had not already been discussed (since there were only four papers presented each week, the same paper was talked about on more than one occasion each week).

During the later part of the module, the focus was shifted to the second assignment; the development of a mobile Web application. Development. Over a period of five weeks, students participated in a series of tutor led practical sessions in which they were introduced to a number of features that they could utilise in the development of their mobile application, including Geolocation, Application Cache, Local Storage, Responsive Design and the use of jQuery Mobile as a framework in which to guide their development. During these sessions, the tutor and students would work on examples together, developing code in a step-by-step process. The tutor would begin to write the code (which students could follow along with), explaining the functionality of the early parts of the code, and then asking questions about what the next steps would be. These questions typically lead to the development of pseudo code first, before the production of functional code after further discussion with the group.

## 4.1 Developing A Scenario For The Mobile Web Application

It is estimated that worldwide mobile payment transactions will surpass $171 billion in 2012; a rise of 62% from $106 million in 2011 [13]. It has also been reported that mobile coupon redemption is ten times bigger than traditional coupons [14]. With this, a scenario was devised for the WSD students for the mobile application build in that they were required to develop a 'voucher code' style application and produce documentation, which detailed this process (designs and a narrative discussing the frameworks and design strategy they adopted). The scenario and requirements for the application are detailed below.

'Pete and Dave's Discount Codes' is a fictitious business which supplies customers with a list of vouchers from a variety of retailers, offering discounts on products and services. They have

requested a mobile application to be developed to allow them to share these vouchers with a larger customer base. In regards to functionality of the application, users should be able to select one of these vouchers and redeem it against a product or service. Depending on the device they were using to access the application, the voucher code would be displayed in one of two formats. If the user accessed the application from a mobile device, a Quick Response (QR) code (mobile devices) would be displayed which the user could then present in store to be scanned. If the user was viewing the application on a tablet device, then a text code should be displayed which could also be used in store.

Other requirements for the mobile application included the use of a number of HTML5 and CSS3 related features including:

- Geolocation (e.g. to allow the user to find the nearest store)

- Local Storage (e.g. to save a voucher to the device)

- Application Cache (to allow for offline viewing of the application)

- Responsive Design (i.e. the application should make use of available screen estate on both mobile and tablet devices and as such, the layout of elements should be appropriate to the device e.g. through Media Queries)

- CSS Transitions

- An application icon and start screen (for iOS devices)

- An ability for the user to filter the vouchers either by 'Eat', 'Stay' or 'Shop'

- An .apk file to allow the application to be installed natively on Android devices.

In order to proceed with the assignment, a number of supporting files and resources were made available to the students to aid them in the development of their mobile Web application. These included:

- A MySQL database containing a list of vouchers (along with associated details e.g. vendor name, voucher title, description, code, start date, end date, etc.)

- A PHP connection file to allow the students to access the database to retrieve the vouchers, and a PHP file which queried the database to return in JavaScript Object Notation (JSON) format a list of vouchers which could be viewed on mobile devices (and another for tablet devices)

- A series of images containing the QR codes to be used in the application (these were linked to file paths held in the database)

- A series of images to depict each of the retailers in the database (should the students wish to use them).

One of the primary reasons to output the database content in JSON format was so that students could avoid using PHP files to create their applications. PhoneGap (the framework which would be used by the students to create the .apk file) does not parse PHP and by exporting the data to JSON format, it meant that they could use JavaScript and HTML in which to format the content, thus allowing PhoneGap to create a native Android application file.

## 4.2 Building A Mobile Web Application

Students were engaged in the development of the application from the very beginning and seemed to benefit from the practical tutorial sessions provided as part of the module delivery. Whilst the majority of the students opted to use the jQuery Mobile framework in which to develop their application, a number of students chose to develop purely in HTML5, CSS3 and JavaScript, which was pleasing to see. Many of the students adopted an 'agile' approach to the development of the application, starting with designs for the mobile (Fig 1) and tablet (Fig 2) versions of the application, whilst also considering the structure that their 'pages' would have (Fig 3).

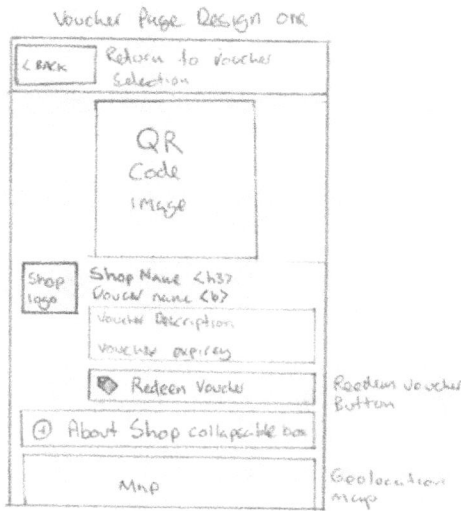

**Figure 1. A design submitted for the mobile version of the application**

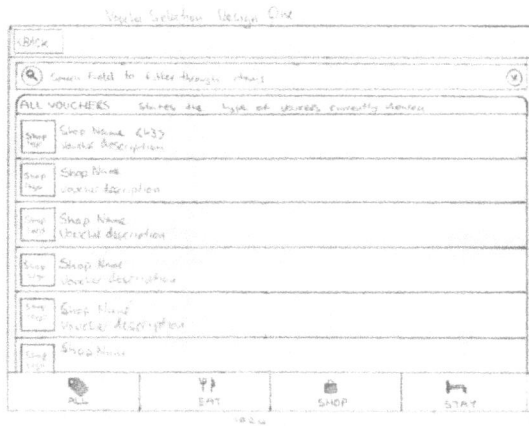

**Figure 2. A design submitted for the tablet version of the application**

Armed with their designs, the students set about the development of their applications using their chosen languages/framework. Whilst some students had issues during the development stages, all who submitted their application managed to produce an application which included an application icon, allowed users to view QR codes and also provide some form of Geolocation (most were limited to just finding the current location of the user.) Students who were able to implement the features indicated above

achieved the minimum pass mark required for the practical aspect of the assignment.

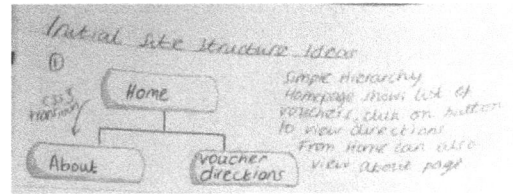

**Figure 3. A consideration of page structure for the application**

It was also interesting to see how students worked with the requirements for the application and the range in terms of the design and functionality of the applications submitted was pleasing to see. A number of students managed to embrace some of the more technical elements of the assignment (Application Cache, Local Storage) to craft successful mobile applications (Fig 4 and 5) which worked extremely well when tested on mobile and tablet devices.

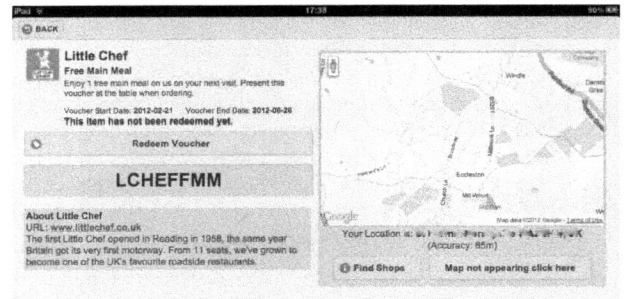

**Figure 4. Tablet view of a submitted application**

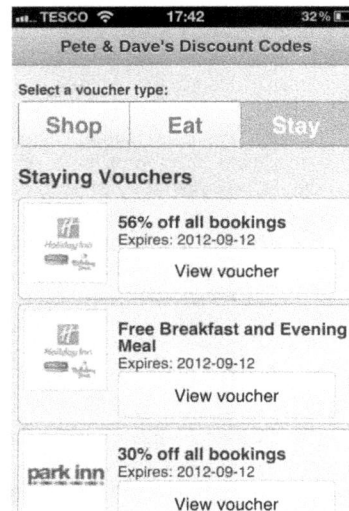

**Figure 5. Mobile view of a submitted application**

## 4.3 Feedback From Students

Upon completion of the module, students were asked to complete a short evaluation of the module, indicating their experiences of the work they completed. Of the 31 students registered on the module, a total of 26 students responded to the evaluation representing an 84% completion rate.

The evaluation was split into two parts; the first listed five closed questions to obtain quantitative data, whilst the second included four open questions in which to elicit qualitative data. The responses to the quantitative questions were limited and aligned to a 5-point Likert scale of "Strongly Agree", "Agree", "Neither Agree or Disagree", "Disagree" and "Strongly Disagree". For the qualitative questions, students were allowed to write their own responses.

When analysing the quantitative data, answers to each of the questions were reduced a numeric value according to the responses on the Likert scale. Answers of "Strongly Agree" were awarded a 5; "Agree" answers were awarded 4, and so on with "Strongly Disagree" answers being awarded a value of 1. Scores were then aggregated across the 26 submitted evaluations to provide an average mark for each question. For each question in the qualitative section, answers were grouped together based on common themes/categories in which an answer would only fit into one.

## 4.3.1 Quantitative Evaluation

The first question asked whether the module was useful in helping them understand the concepts of Mobile Application Development. A score of 4.50 (highest – 5, lowest – 3) indicates that students agreed with statement this felt that they material that they had learnt during the module had been extremely useful to them. The next question asked whether the students believed the content and delivery of the module aided the development of their mobile application. Students responded with a score of 4.41 (highest – 5, lowest – 3) suggesting that the practical sessions provided during the course were extremely useful to the students. Students were then asked about their confidence in developing other mobile applications after completion of this module. A score of 4.27 (highest – 5, lowest – 3) indicates that the students believe they have the necessary skills and knowledge to develop mobile applications in the future.

In regards to whether students felt that the module was intellectually challenging for them, a score of 4.50 (highest – 5, lowest – 3) suggests that the content was at an appropriate level to both simulate their interest in the subject and required them to demonstrate the higher order learning skills required of a 3rd year undergraduate student. The final question in this section asked the students about whether they felt the work they completed for CW1 (academic paper) helped them to complete CW2 (mobile application build). A score of 3.86 (highest – 5, lowest – 2) suggests that students were undecided on this with most suggesting that it did, but there were a number of students (3) who felt that the academic paper did not help prepare them for the build.

Given the range of topics discussed as part of CW1, the author questions whether the students who scored this question with a score of 2/3, chose a topic that was not related to mobile Web application development. This is evident in a small number of papers submitted which focused on specific aspects of Mobile Application development, such as Geolocation, security and the Wireless Application Protocol (WAP), whilst the majority focused on mobile Web applications, the differences between Web and native applications and a small minority also discussed the notion of 'hybrid' applications; those which take advantage of the benefits of both Web and native applications. Perhaps those students who discussed these topics were appreciative of the process required to create mobile Web applications, along with the frameworks and technologies needed to develop.

## 4.3.2 Qualitative Evaluation

The first two questions were based around eliciting student experiences of the module and focused on their perceived level of difficulty of the module, how much they enjoyed studying on the module. The last two questions focused on what the delivery on the module, asking students what they think worked well and should be implemented next time and what did not work and should be discontinued.

For the first two questions, the answers provided can be grouped into three distinct but related categories, loosely linked to Blooms Taxonomy of learning [15]. The three categories identified are detailed below along with some student feedback.

*a) Acquiring new knowledge (Comprehension)* – here the students highlighted their experiences around their learning during the module.

The hardest thing for me on this module was:

> *"Learning responsive design" (#13)*
>
> *"Learning to adapt design from desktop to smaller space" (#8)*

I enjoyed doing the following the most:

> *"Learning jQuery Mobile" (#10)*
>
> *"Practical tutorial sessions" (#8 & #13)*

*b) Development of the Mobile Web Application (Application)* – here the students highlighted their experiences around the development of their mobile Web application.

The hardest thing for me on this module was:

> *"Trying to implement jQuery Mobile" (#17)*
>
> *"Using the PHP files within the build" (#11)*

I enjoyed doing the following the most:

> *"Creating a cross platform application" (#15)*
>
> *"Using the Google Maps API" (#2)*

*c) Expressing theoretical knowledge (Analysis & Synthesis)* – here the students highlighted their experiences about expressing the theoretical content that they had acquired in the module, mainly through the academic paper.

The hardest thing for me on this module was:

> *"Writing the IEEE paper" (#1)*
>
> *"Developing my writing style to match the IEEE format" (#4)*

I enjoyed doing the following the most:

> *"The academic paper" (#9)*
>
> *"Writing the paper" (#17)*

When asked what aspects of the module they think work well and should be continued, out of the 13 responses to the question, the students were mostly unanimous in their response in that the practical tutorial sessions in which the tutor talked them through the code they were writing and developed sample applications together should be kept. It was clear from the sessions in question that the students felt a sense of empowerment from having instant validation of the code they were producing from the tutor with one student stating *"the seminars following lecturer writing code was a good method of learning "* (#4). Students also appreciated the distribution of the published academic papers during the early stages of the module, which helped them with their first assignment.

Finally, when asked what they think should be changed for next year, only ten students made a suggestion. The majority of these were related to the scenario used in the application build, with some suggesting that it was *"Too complex and too big"* (#4) whilst one suggested *"Let the app subject be the student's choice"* (#8). When deciding on the scenario for the assignment, the author considered this last suggestion, but the choice was made to implement this 'voucher code' scenario to aid the students who would struggle to develop their own ideas for applications. In addition, the scenario also allowed a minimum specification for functionality to be developed to ensure that students were exposed to a number of different aspects of mobile application development. This may not have happened had students chosen their own idea and the required functionality also ensured that students knew what they needed to do to achieve a pass mark on the practical element of the assignment. The development of the supporting files which were given to help the students should have ensured that the application build should not have been too complex, but from the applications submitted, it appears that a number of students chose to modify/amend these files to suit their own programming style.

Other suggestions from the students indicated that they would like to have had more practical tutorial sessions in which they could follow the tutor as they were coding, a refresher on using JavaScript and the Document Object Model (DOM) and running the module over two semesters instead of one. Whilst these are all valid suggestions, time restrictions both in-module and on the course as a whole mean that none could feasibly be implemented. As mentioned previously, five weeks were set-aside for practical tutorials during the module and the students study a module on JavaScript during their 2nd year.

## 5. CONCLUSIONS

This paper has reported on the experiences of the author in providing an alternative curriculum to be run as part of Mobile Application Development module, allowing WSD students to create cross platform mobile applications, utilising the skills and knowledge they have acquired during their first two years of studies. The results of the evaluation indicate that this has been well received by students and it is believed that the content, delivery and assessment strategy in place works well to allow students to achieve a high mark in the module.

Given that the lower order skills of knowledge, comprehension and application are typically showcased in 1st and 2nd year studies, it is no surprise that students had some difficulty in analysing and synthesising information for their academic paper, since these are skills which are tested during 3rd year studies. One important point to note is that this was the first and only point in their undergraduate degree that these students were required to write an academic paper as if they were submitting to a conference. The author believes that this is a skill that students should be exposed to in other modules on the programme, since a number of students do progress on Masters and PhD level study. In addition, perhaps more time should be devoted during the module to allow students to practice articulating the theoretical knowledge they have acquired, since this is just as important as the practical aspect.

The increase in the number of mobile devices available on the market today, it appears that teaching students how to develop applications for one particular platform in 'a one size fits all' method is no longer a viable solution. Businesses want applications

that can be deployed 'cross-platform' and by teaching students to develop application in this way can only serve to improve their employment prospects when they finish their degree.

The curriculum and delivery method outlined earlier in this paper has proved to be a success and received well by students and the author strongly recommends that anyone wishing to implement a similar course should consider adopting a similar strategy for delivery.

## 6. REFERENCES

[1] Menn, J, 2011. *Smartphone shipment surpasses PCs.* Retrieved January 24th, 2012 from http://www.ft.com/cms/s/2/d96e3bd8-33ca-11e0-b1ed-00144feabdc0.html#axzz1DQNdT4kR

[2] Oehlman, D. and Blanc, S. 2011. *Pro Android Web Apps – Develop for Android Using HTML5, CSS3 & JavaScript.* APress, New York.

[3] Levey, R.H. 2011. *Consumers, Marketers Adapt to Mobile At Different Speeds: Survey.* Retrieved January 25th, 2012 from http://sip-trunking.tmcnet.com/news/2011/06/28/5603614.htm

[4] Conder, S. and Darcey, L. 2011. *Android Wireless Application Development.* 2nd ed. Addison Wesley, Michigan.

[5] Hogan, B.P. 2010. *HTML5 and CSS3: Develop with Tomorrow's Standards Today.* Pragmatic Programmers, LLC., Raleigh, N.C.

[6] Sneath, T. 2010. *HTML5: A Specification or a Platform?* Retrieved January 12, 2012. http://blogs.msdn.com/b/tims/archive/2010/10/03/html5-a-specification-or-a-platform.aspx

[7] Lawson, B. and Sharp, R. 2011. *Introducing HTML5.* New Riders, Berkeley, CA.

[8] Heilmann, C. 2009. *51: Graceful degradation vs. Progressive Enhancement.* Retrieved January 18th, 2012 from http://dev.opera.com/articles/view/graceful-degradation-progressive-enhancement/

[9] Champeon, S. and Finck, N. 2003. *Inclusive Web Design for the Future.* Retrieved January 18th, 2012 from http://hesketh.com/thought-leadership/our-publications/inclusive-web-design-future

[10] Clarke, A. 2010. *Hardboiled Web Design.* Five Simple Steps, Penarth.

[11] Marcotte, E. 2011. *Responsive Web Design.* A Book Apart, New York.

[12] Wroblewski, L. 2011. *Mobile First.* A Book Apart, New York.

[13] Walsh, M. 2012. *Global Payments To Hit $171 Billion This Year.* Retrieved May 30th, 2012 from http://www.mediapost.com/publications/article/175693/global-mobile-payments-to-hit-171-billion-this-ye.html?edition=47405

[14] Loechner, N. 2010. *Mobile Marketing Emerges With Couponing.* Retrieved January 18th, 2012 from http://www.mediapost.com/publications/article/126351/

[15] Krathwohl, D. R. 2002. *A revision of bloom's taxonomy: An overview.* Theory into Practice, 41 (4), 212-218.

# App Inventor for Android in a Healthcare IT Course

Bonnie MacKellar
Division of Computer Science, Math,
and Science
St John's University
Queens, NY 11439
mackellb@stjohns.edu

## ABSTRACT

App Inventor for Android is a new programming environment that allows novice programmers to build applications for Android mobile devices. In this paper, we describe a healthcare IT course in which students with little or no programming background built healthcare related mobile applications. The course was designed based on the principles of studio-based learning, with students completing and sharing projects of their own choosing. Mobile applications were used to illustrate the role of IT applications in healthcare and teach design and user interface principles. In this paper, we discuss our experiences with this augmented course, describing the rationale, the process of introducing the new material, the student-designed applications, and the results from the course evaluation.

## Categories and Subject Descriptors

K.3.2 [**COMPUTERS AND EDUCATION**]: Computer and Information Science – *Information Systems Education.*

## General Terms

Experimentation, Human Factors, Languages,

## Keywords

Healthcare informatics, education, studio-based learning, mobile applications

## 1. INTRODUCTION

Healthcare IT (HIT) is a field attracting a great deal of interest within the computer science and information technology community. There is currently a push to expand HIT education in the United States, in part due to the American Recovery and Reinvestment Act of 2009, which mandates that healthcare providers adopt certified electronic medical record systems by 2015 or face reduced Medicare reimbursement. As a result, hospitals need to hire many additional HIT specialists. A report by the Computing Community Consortium on Information Technology Challenges for Healthcare, mentions the need to train "fledgling" computer scientists in the biomedical domain as a critical need [6]. For this reason, educational institutions are ramping up their offerings in this area.

At St John's University, we have established a HIT undergraduate major. This degree is housed within the computer science department but has been developed in conjunction with our healthcare administration department. Students take coursework in healthcare administration, computer science and information technology, and in a set of specialized HIT courses. Students who graduate from this program may end up specifying, purchasing, designing, and even implementing healthcare-related software systems. Thus, it is important that students learn about the system design process as it relates to the healthcare setting.

Like many other IT fields, there is currently a lot of interest in mobile applications in the HIT world. Mobile devices, such as smartphones and tablets, are uniquely suited to the healthcare setting because of their portability and ubiquity. Healthcare professionals are on their feet, moving around constantly, in the course of their work. Computer applications that require physicians and nurses to enter data into a stationary computer have long been a source of complaint, since it is often difficult to locate computers right at the site of patient care.

One issue for HIT education is that programming mobile devices is relatively difficult. Developing for the Android or the iOS platforms requires a strong knowledge of object-oriented concepts and multithreading. HIT majors in our program, however, only take two computer programming courses and thus do not have the background to tackle mobile device development in the traditional fashion. However, the introduction of a new Android development environment aimed at novice programmers, App Inventor [15], has changed all of this. Even students who have never programmed before can develop full-fledged mobile applications using this environment. It has been used in a number of computer science courses to teach computational thinking. In our program, however, we are using it to teach the process of designing applications for the healthcare setting.

We decided to focus on mobile applications for the healthcare setting in one of the core HIT courses in our sequence. This course is the second semester in the sequence, and focuses on data and information in the healthcare setting, the role of electronic applications in healthcare, and the systems lifecycle. We used mobile applications as a means of discussing these topics, and added material on building applications in App Inventor, case studies of mobile applications in healthcare, and material on design of user interfaces for healthcare. The course was designed based on the principles of studio-based learning [8], with students completing and sharing projects of their own choosing. In this paper, we discuss our experiences with this augmented course, describing the rationale, the process of introducing the new material, the student-designed applications, and the results from the course evaluation.

## 2. BACKGROUND

### 2.1 Mobile applications in healthcare

Applications for mobile devices may be designed for patients or for providers. Patient oriented applications often are intended to reinforce healthy behaviors, educate about a health related topic, or allow a patient to record treatment and symptom data. According to Klasnja and Pratt [10], key drivers of adoption by patients of mobile technology include the fact that these devices are pervasive – everyone seems to own one, and they are carried around everywhere – and they have the capability of interacting with the user's environment through technologies such as GPS, cameras, and the ability to communicate with external software services. A recent survey by the Pew Internet and American Life Project found that nearly 3 in 10 Americans have accessed medical information on their phones. In addition, about 10% use health-related applications on their phones [3].

Similar reasons are driving provider adoption. An amazing 84% of physicians use smartphones [7]. In addition, needed infrastructure such as networking is in place at most hospitals. Hospitals are finding it cheaper and faster to develop mobile applications in-house [5]. And finally, the portability of these devices makes a lot of sense in the hospital setting, where it is often difficult to locate computer terminals right at the point of care. Mobile applications allow providers to enter and access patient information, to write orders, and to capture charges for billing purposes in real time [1].

### 2.2 Mobile technology in IT education

Currently, there seems to be little or no published research in teaching the design and implementation of mobile applications in healthcare IT courses. Standards such as the IMIA draft recommendations do not explicitly mention mobile technology, although the recommendations do contain categories that would likely encompass mobile technology [13].

There are published papers on teaching mobile development in the computer science education literature. Examples include [16], [9], [18] and [2]. Most of these are upper division courses that focus strictly on learning advanced programming technologies such as the Android SDK or Objective C for iOS. Massey, et al, [14] however, describe an approach that is closer to our approach. They created a problem-based environment within a IT graduate course in which students with diverse backgrounds, including non-programmers, collaborated to explore the both the use and the design and development of mobile technologies in specific environments.

The closest effort to ours was a studio-based computer science course that used App Inventor [4]. This was an introductory computer science course that taught fundamental programming concepts such as iteration and procedures. The course was organized using studio-based principles; students learned through projects of their own design and shared their projects with each other. The course differed from ours, however, in a significant way; since their course was a programming course, it focused on correct use of the programming concepts rather than user interface design or the role of the application being designed in an organization. Their course also was completely devoted to App Inventor. In our course, however, we use App Inventor as a means to another end: to learn about the role of mobile apps in healthcare and to explore how design choices affect the user experience.

### 2.3 App Inventor

App Inventor [15] is a new technology that was developed to allow nonprogrammers to build Android applications. App Inventor was initially hosted at Google but now is hosted by MIT as part of its Center for Mobile Learning. It draws on the lessons of earlier programming environments for beginners, especially Scratch [17] and Lego Mindstorms [11], sharing their visual approach to programming. What makes App Inventor an especially good platform for students to explore the world of design with computers is that it is relatively easy to create an application that looks and behaves like other mobile phone applications. Unlike earlier programming environments for beginners, applications created with App Inventor can interact with the outside world. This means that creators of these applications can assess their creation with respect to the world at large and ask questions about the impacts of their design choices and the effects of their application on real people.

App Inventor is similar to Scratch in that it uses a blocks metaphor for specifying the logic of an application. Users are freed from learning the intricacies of a programming language syntax, and instead choose from a menu of behavior blocks to build the program. App Inventor differs from Scratch, however, in that there is a first phase in application development in which the design and layout of the user interface is specified. This forces the developer to think about interface design very early in the process of building an application. The App Inventor environment includes a realistic phone emulator which shows changes to the user interface in realtime; in addition, students were able to test on a set of inexpensive Android phones. Figure 1 shows the blocks editor and the emulator running a very simple program in App Inventor. This program simply switches colors based on a random number.

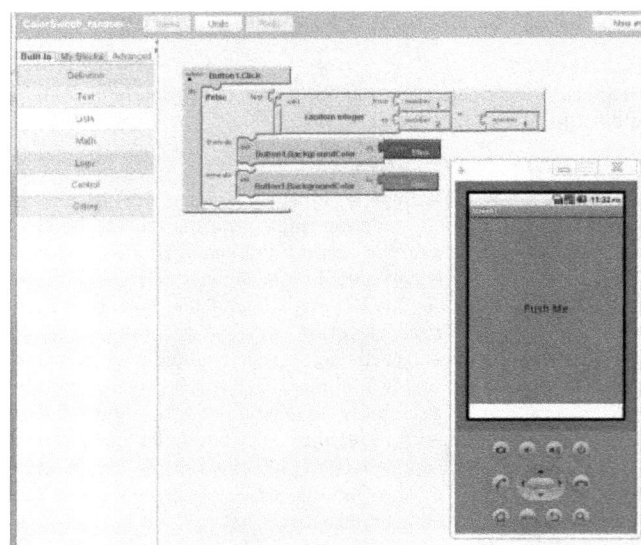

**Figure 1 App Inventor Blocks Editor**

## 3. COURSE DESCRIPTION

The course that is described in this paper, HCI1002, "Healthcare Information Flow and Data Management", is the second semester course in the HIT sequence. Most of the students who take it are HIT majors; however, computer science majors also take it either as part of an HIT minor or simply as an elective. During the semester when the augmented course was offered, ten students finished the course. Most of the students were HIT majors; three had never taken a programming course, two were taking the first programming course concurrently, and two had taken over a year of programming. Thus, there was wide variation among the students in programming knowledge.

The course was run as a hybrid class, which meant there was a significant online component, as well as one class meeting a week. Since the mobile application development component of the class was intended to be hands-on, we focused on that during the class meeting each week, and the chapter readings on healthcare applications and systems lifecycle formed the online component. The course was designed to use studio-based learning principles. One of the key components of the studio-based approach is that students should share their thought processes as they design their projects, as well as sharing the finished projects. To that end, students were asked to create and maintain a course portfolio, using Google Sites. One of the roles of the portfolio pages was to contain student reflections on their projects.

## 3.1 App Inventor labs

During the first half of the course, in-class sessions were devoted to guided labs designed to teach various aspects of mobile application development. For students who had never programmed before, it was their first encounter with constructs such as conditional and iterative logic. Even for students who had taken a programming course before, there were many concepts to be learned since none had ever seen event-driven programming before or worked so closely with a graphical user interface. We made use of the educational materials maintained on the Center For Mobile Learning's educator website, as well as the tutorials in [20], but modified a number of them to make them more specific to healthcare applications.

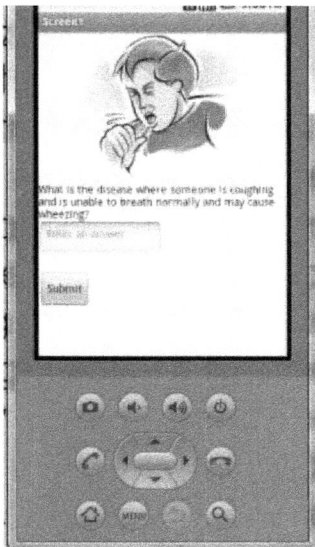

I target the asthma population because I noticed that with my friends and family, patients with asthma rarely realize that they can avoid getting asthma attacks by avoiding triggers. Also, patients sometimes don't know how to use the metered dose inhaler properly. If the patient knows how to use the MDI in the proper way, they would get faster resolution of the attack. Also, if patients recognize the triggers to an asthma attack, they can avoid these triggers and would reduce the frequency of their attacks. Asthma is one of the most common diseases for children. I developed the app to quiz children on the definition of asthma and the basic steps to using their inhaler. I also quizzed them on

**Figure 2: Lab Page in Student Portfolio**

Students were asked to create a page for each lab on their class portfolios. Many of the labs included discussion questions in which students were asked to relate the concept in the lab to healthcare applications. Students placed their answers to these questions, screenshots of their applications, and screenshots of the blocks that they used on their lab page in their portfolio. **Figure 2** shows an example of such a page.

Labs started with topics such as setting up the portfolio page and writing a simple app, and progressed through topics such as using the drawing canvas, adding sound, simple games and animations, and basic programming concepts such as variables, loops and conditionals. Later labs were more complex and more focused on healthcare and design issues. Here are some of the later labs:

- Lab4: OrderDroid is an application described in [19] that takes user-input orders and sends email. Once students completed this app, they were asked to come up with a healthcare application that uses the same idea of reading a collection of user input and sending a message based on that input. They then designed and implemented it.
- Lab5: Students completed a quiz app described in [20], and then were asked to identify a health education need and a target audience (children, the elderly, etc) and design a similar quiz application, addressing the health education topic they had chosen. This was done in order to get them thinking about designing for particular audiences before getting to the final project.
- Lab6: Students built a application that lets a user enter patient vitals and then uses Google Charts, a web-based service, to build a chart showing temperature over time.

Once students had completed these labs, they had acquired a toolbox of techniques for building applications and were ready for the next phase of the course: researching, designing, and building a more complex healthcare application.

## 3.2 Project organization

In preparation for the final project, students were asked to read several papers describing types of mobile applications in healthcare, as well as a paper that described in detail the process of designing and evaluating a mobile user interface for elderly patients [12]. We also spent one class period looking at healthcare related mobile applications and discussing their purpose, target users, and design. Then, the students, grouped into pairs for the purposes of the project, were given the project assignment. There were several phases to the project.

First, the students were asked to choose a general healthcare need for their project. Students chose areas related to their personal experiences for the most part, such as asthma control, diabetes education, and nutrition. One student worked for a care facility for developmentally disabled adults, and chose to focus on daily record logging in that facility. After choosing the healthcare need, they were asked to write a short paper surveying other software applications, including desktop, web-based, and mobile systems, addressing the same need. This familiarized them with the range of applications in the chosen area.

The next step was to submit a design on their portfolio site. The design had to be specified as a series of screen mockups, showing clearly how interaction with the app would proceed. In addition, they were asked to answer the following questions as part of the design submission:

- What need does the project address and why is this an important need?
- Who are the target users?
- How does your design meet the special needs of your target users?

Once the designs were posted, the next step was for the students to critique each others' designs. Students were required to comment on every design, keeping in mind aspects such as target users and visual design. Critiques were posted as comments on the design sites so that students could respond to each other. Most of the comments were essentially just agreement with a design. But a number of student comments were more insightful, and led to real changes in the applications. Here are some sample comments:

*"I like this app a lot it looks very organized and well set up. I suggest maybe adding a chart or page that shows a schedule that displays the times the user has to take his medicine. You can make it so that the user enters the times and this can be connected to the alarm that you are trying to incorporate into the app. Then you can make it so that at the end of the application it displays if the user took all his medications."*

*"Your app looks very clear and right to the point. I suggest maybe adding pictures or more color to the app so that it won't look too plain and more user friendly. You can also include an age input box because from what I have read I know that asthma attacks are more frequent at a younger age, and I think that maybe should be included for record. "*

*"Its a very good idea. You should add a pop of color or some other type of graphic so it can engage the user a bit more. Also it could be cool if that data could somehow be transmitted into a cloud of some sort with the user's medical history"*

Students were expected to respond to the critiques and incorporate them as changes in their projects. The pair that designed the daily log app for the care facility was advised by other students that their design was too busy for a small smartphone. That group realized that the busy interface had to do with the care facility's requirements for the app, and decided to design for a tablet interface instead, even managing to get a tablet as a loaner from the care facility.

The final step was to implement the project. The students had 3 weeks in which to accomplish this. For the most part, the students were careful to base their projects on App Inventor constructs that they already knew. The one problem that several groups encountered was the lack of support within App Inventor for multiple screens. One student, however, found a workaround on a discussion board, and showed the other project groups how to do it. In addition, another group had included Twitter posts in their original design, but was unable to make that functionality work.

During the final week, the students gave presentations and demos of their projects to the rest of the class. They also created final project pages on their portfolios. The instructions for creating the final page stated: *"you should put another page on your portfolio with screenshots of the final app, a description of how it works, a description of changes you made and why, and reasons why you incorporated or did not incorporate suggestions made by the other students. Your final project page should "sell your system" a little bit – it should be attractive and make readers want to try your app."*. Students were also directed to put screenshots of their blocks on the page, as well as a downloadable version of the app so that others, including the instructor, could try it out.

## 3.3 The projects

There were five projects submitted in the class. Here is a list:

- Diabetes app. This app consists of two parts. The first part is educational, consisting of a step by step guide on using a glucometer. The second part allows the user to record blood sugar readings and medications and chart them over time. Figures 3 and 4 are illustrations of the app from the students' final presentations.
- Keep Breathing. The Keep Breathing application is designed to help asthma patients record their asthma attacks and their peak flow readings. Users of the application can record the date and time of a peak flow reading. Later, they can view this data on a chart. The app also allows patients to record the details of their asthma attack, details such as date, time, location, trigger, symptoms and treatment.
- Care Chart. One of the members of the pair working on this project works in a care facility for developmentally disabled adults. He observed that the workers record myriad pieces of information throughout the day, such as medication times, food intake, seizures, and other observations, on paper. He thought that a mobile application would ease the burden. The application was designed for a tablet rather than a phone, and designed to be as easy to use as possible: many data points are entered simply by touching a circle. The students were able to get feedback from the caregivers at the care facility in order to improve the application, and there is interest in finishing it for use by the caregivers.
- Healthy Choices. This is a game aimed at children, to help teach healthy food choices. The game presents pairs of food choices and asks the player to choose the healthier one. Figure 5 shows the project page for this app, and Figure 6 shows the AppInventor blocks used to create the app.
- Another app aimed at children is designed to encourage them to exercise. This app, which is started as the user begins to exercise, shows how close the user is to meeting recommended daily exercise targets, using an hourglass metaphor. This app also has a mechanism for submitting the data to Twitter, although this is not fully functional.

The following figures show illustrations from some of the student project pages. These give the reader an idea of the student work.

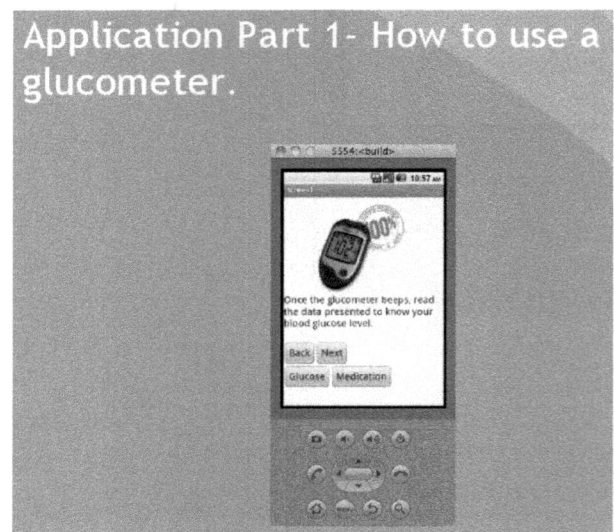

**Figure 3: Diabetes app**

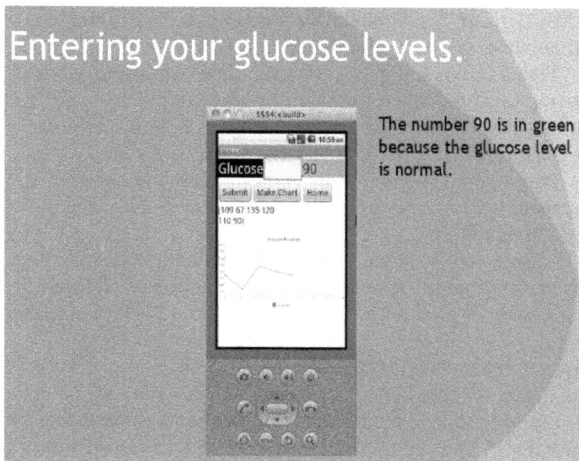

**Figure 4: Diabetes app**

Entering your glucose levels.

The number 90 is in green because the glucose level is normal.

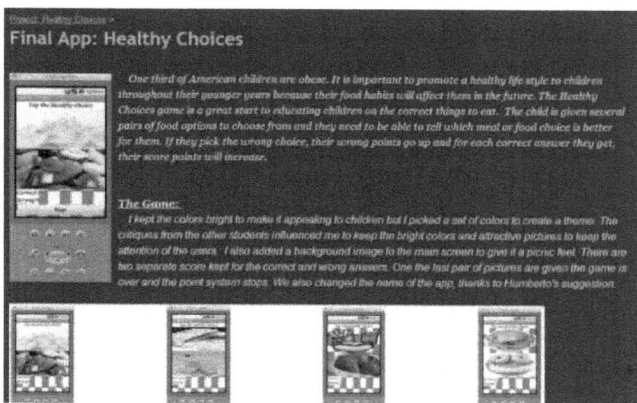

**Figure 5: Final Project Page for Healthy Choices**

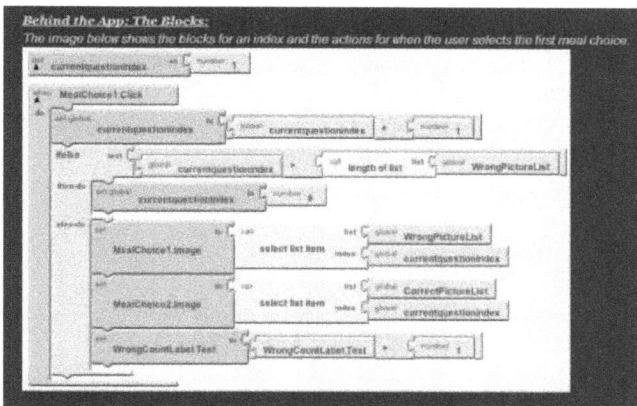

**Figure 6: Portion of final project page for HealthyChoices**

## 4. EVALUATION

In order to measure student perspectives on what they had learned in the course, a 3 part survey was developed and administered at the end of the semester. The first part of the survey consisted of 7 questions on student background before taking the course. We found that 7 students were majoring in HIT, 3 in CS, and 1 in security. Only 2 of the students had worked at a healthcare related job or internship, and 6 had used a healthcare related smartphone app. All 10 owned smartphones, either Android or iOS.

The second part of the survey asked 3 questions about their experience with App Inventor. Students were asked to rate the difficulty of working with App Inventor, using a scale of Easy, Somewhat Easy, Medium, Somewhat Difficult, and Difficult. The most common response was Medium, chosen by 7 students; Somewhat Difficult was chosen by 3 students. All 10 students responded with Yes to the question "Do you think that learning to develop mobile applications will be useful to you in the future"? Students were also asked to list the aspects of App Inventor that they found most difficult. By far, implementing multi-screen applications was chosen as the most difficult aspect, with 8 students mentioning this. App Inventor does not have explicit support for multi-screen applications, so this result was not surprising.

In the third part of the survey, 6 class topics were listed. Students were asked to list the ones they had learned the best, the ones that they felt were most important to their future career, and the ones that they felt were least important to their future career. The questions were also more open ended and allowed them to insert comments. The topics were

1. Understanding how data is used in the healthcare setting
2. Understanding how electronic medical records are implemented
3. Understanding how the Internet has impacted healthcare information systems
4. Understanding how mobile applications are designed and built
5. User interface design and its impact on user acceptance
6. Group communication and working in a team

Table 1 lists the numbers of students choosing each response:

**Table 1: Survey responses**

| topic | Most important | Least important | Learned it the best |
|-------|----------------|-----------------|---------------------|
| 1 | 5 | 3 | 2 |
| 2 | 4 | 1 | 2 |
| 3 | 4 | 2 | 0 |
| 4 | 6 | 0 | 4 |
| 5 | 6 | 1 | 4 |
| 6 | 6 | 0 | 1 |

The responses do not add up to the number of students in the class because students could choose more than one option; in addition, 2 students chose "None" in response to the question about least important topic. Also, 2 students did not answer the question about the topic that was learned the best. While the numbers are too small to be significant, it is noticeable that more students chose the mobile development, user interface design, and group communication topics as most important, and the fewest students chose those as least important.

## 5. DISCUSSION AND SUMMARY

The survey results showed that the App Inventor programming environment was well suited to the students' backgrounds, with most choosing Medium or Somewhat Difficult as the level of difficulty. In addition, all of the students agreed that learning about mobile applications in the healthcare world would be important to their futures, with some students adding comments such as "*yes, very*", and "*extremely useful*". Thus, we believe that adding the focus on mobile applications and App Inventor was engaging and educational for the students, and we plan to offer the course in the same fashion next year. We are also exploring partnerships with area healthcare agencies so that the students can work on applications for real clients, adding another level of critique.

In sum, App Inventor seems to be a promising technology for quickly bootstrapping students with little programming experience into mobile application design, while powerful enough at the same time to engage more experienced students. Applications built in App Inventor are full-fledged mobile applications that harness the capability of mobile devices to interact with the external world through messaging, GPS, cameras, and other features of the platform. This allows students in fields such as HIT to explore design issues for mobile devices without having to spend years learning advanced programming techniques.

## 6. ACKNOWLEDGMENTS

This project has been supported by a grant from the St John's University Teaching and Technology Fellows program.

## 7. REFERENCES

[1] P. Adkison, "Revolutionizing the coding and billing cycle with intelligent mobile technology.," *Health Management Technology*, vol. 32, no. 5, pp. 8, 11, May 2011.

[2] R. England, "A software development course featuring iPad app construction," *Journal of Computing Sciences in Colleges*, vol. 27, no. 5, pp. 93-100, May, 2012.

[3] S. Fox, "The Power of Mobile," *The Pew Internet and American Life Project*, 2010. [Online]. http://www.pewinternet.org/Commentary/2010/September/The-Power-of-Mobile.aspx . [Accessed: 30-May-2012].

[4] P. Gestwicki, "App Inventor for Android with studio-based learning," *Journal of Computing Sciences in Colleges*, vol. 27, no. 1, pp. 55-63, October 2011.

[5] G. Gillespie, "Making the most of mobile IT," *Health Data Management*, 2010.

[6] S. Graham and D. Estrin, "Information technology research challenges for healthcare," *SIGHIT Record*, vol. 1, no. 1, pp. 4-9.

[7] Healthcare IT News Staff, "iPhone to dominate U.S. physician smartphone market," *Healthcare IT*, 2011.

[Online]. http://www.healthcareitnews.com/news/iphone-dominate-us-physician-smartphone-market.

[8] C. Hundhausen and N. Narayanan, "Exploring studio-based instructional models for computing education," in *Proceedings of the 39th Technical Sympsium on Computer Science Education SIGCSE08)*, 2008, pp. 392–396.

[9] L. Ivanov, "The i-Phone/i-Pad course: a small college perspective," *Journal of Computing Sciences in Colleges*, vol. 26, no. 6, pp. 142-148, 2011.

[10] P. Klasnja and W. Pratt, "Healthcare in the pocket: mapping the space of mobile-phone health interventions.," *Journal of Biomedical Informatics*, vol. 45, no. 1, pp. 184-98, February 2012.

[11] "Lego Mindstorms," 2012. [Online]. http://mindstorms.lego.com. [Accessed: 30-May-2012].

[12] A. Lorenz and R. Oppermann, "Mobile health monitoring for the elderly: Designing for diversity," *Pervasive and Mobile Computing*, vol. 5, no. 5, pp. 478-495, October 2009.

[13] J. Mantas et al., "Recommendations of the International Medical Informatics Association (IMIA) on Education in Biomedical and Health Informatics. First Revision.," *Methods of Information in Medicine*, vol. 49, no. 2, pp. 105-120, Jan. 2010.

[14] A. P. Massey, V. Ramesh, and V. Khatri, "Design, development, and assessment of mobile applications: the case for problem-based learning," *IEEE Transactions on Education*, vol. 49, no. 2, pp. 183-192, 2006.

[15] MIT, "MIT App Inventor," 2012. [Online]. http://www.appinventor.mit.edu/. [Accessed: 30-May-2012].

[16] V. Matos, "Building applications for the Android OS mobile platform: a primer and course materials," *Journal of Computing Sciences in Colleges*, vol. 26, no. 1 pp. 23-29, October 2010.

[17] M. Resnick et al., "Scratch: Programming for all," *Communications of the ACM*, vol. 52, pp. 60–67, Nov. 2009.

[18] D. Riley, "Using mobile phone programming to teach Java and advanced programming to computer scientists," in *Proceedings of the 43rd ACM Technical Symposium on Computer Science Education - SIGCSE '12*, 2012, p. 541.

[19] J. Tyler, *App Inventor for Android.* Wiley & Sons, 2011.

[20] D. Wolber, H. Abelson, E. Spertus, and L. Looney, *App Inventor: Create Your Own Android Apps.* O'Reilly Media, Inc., 2011.

# CS/IT Outreach from a Canadian Perspective

## [Panel]

Daryl H. Hepting
(moderator)
University of Regina
Regina, CANADA
hepting@cs.uregina.ca

Gerry Donaldson
University of Calgary
Calgary, CANADA
gddonald@ucalgary.ca

Peter R. King
University of Manitoba
Winnipeg, CANADA
prking@cs.umanitoba.ca

Danny Silver
Acadia University
Wolfville, CANADA
danny.silver@acadiau.ca

## SUMMARY

Computer Science Education Week (a.k.a. CSEdWeek) [3], officially recognized in the United States, has also helped to raise the profile of Computer Science Education in Canada and to start many conversations about computer science education that typically find receptive audiences across many sectors. Yet, the focus does not need to be computer science alone. The Association for Computing Machinery has two special interest groups explicitly dedicated to education: SIGCSE for computer science and SIGITE for information technology. Looking at the CC2005 document [5], one also finds mention of computer engineering, information systems, and software engineering. Still more areas, such as bioinformatics, may be included in future computing curricula surveys.

Programming can be identified as a common thread within these areas. As educators, we do not expect that all students who take programming will pursue computer science or information technology in post-secondary education. However, we do want students to choose programming over being programmed [7]. In a 2009 Conference Board of Canada survey of young people, most could not identify an ICT (Information and Communication Technology) job. However, ICT jobs are everywhere with only about half inside the traditional information technology sector. Students, parents, teachers, guidance councillors, and school administrators need to see computing as "fun, cool, creative, and social" [8] and a great choice for a rewarding career.

Computing curriculum is not standardized across provinces, where it exists in various stages of renewal. Ideally, students will be exposed to CS/IT at an age when they are interested in exploring the possibilities that it presents. K-12 teachers, both pre-service and in-service, need support and resources to help them encourage students in computational thinking and CS/IT. Although it may be too late attract students new to CS/IT in Grade 12 as potential post-secondary majors, post-secondary education should provide pathways for these students to incorporate CS/IT into their programs of study.

The panel will give a representation of very encouraging CS/IT outreach efforts in Canada offered by various organizations working in this space. These include (in alphabetical order): the Canadian Association of Computer Science/Association d'Informatique Canadienne (CACS/AIC), comprising post-secondary institutions offering Computer Science degrees; the Canadian Information Processing Society (CIPS), known as Canada's Association of I.T. Professionals; the Canadian Coalition for Tomorrow's ICT Skills (CCICT), an industry-led coalition of employers, universities and industry organizations with the aim of ensuring availability of ICT professionals for Canadian organizations; and the Computer Science Teachers Association (CSTA - international, with chapters forming across Canada), a membership organization that supports and promotes the teaching of computer science and other computing disciplines.

## Categories and Subject Descriptors

K.3.2 [**Computers and Education**]: Computer and Information Science Education—*Accreditation, Computer science education, Curriculum, Information systems education*; K.7.1 [**The Computing Profession**]: Occupations

## General Terms

Human Factors, Standardization

## Keywords

Community Outreach, K-12 Education, Curriculum, Collaboration Initiatives, Industry-Education Relationships, Non-Traditional Students

## 1. POSITION STATEMENT: HEPTING

Events during CSEdWeek in Regina have been successful so far (in 2010 and 2011) because the dates fell during the week between the end of classes and the start of final exams. In 2012, CSEdWeek occurs later so our events must be held earlier. There is an opportunity to find a more friendly Canadian date for these activities and to honour Canadian computing pioneers in the process. It may also be that this celebration could be scheduled differently in each province and territory.

A luncheon co-organized with CIPS has provided a great opportunity to interact with local professionals. The 2011 events included a very successful professional development day for teachers in Grades 6-12. In 2012, a follow-up is being planned for Regina and 2 other communities with help from Google's CS4HS program. For teachers who teach CS in Grades 11 and 12, we plan to use *The Beauty and Joy of Computing* [4] as a foundation. *Exploring Computer Science* [2] is a curriculum designed to address equity issues and we will work with teachers of Grades 6-10 to adapt it to our own equity concerns: increasing the participation of women and First Nations, Métis, and Inuit.

Throughout the year, we are working to increase our contact with potential future students, either on our campus or at their schools. We have found the CCICT CareerMash video and website [1] to be a great tool to get students thinking about careers in ICT. Local alumni serve as examples of achievable pathways to exciting careers.

## 2. POSITION STATEMENT: DONALDSON

I have always believed Computer Science to be cool and I have always encouraged my students to follow what they love and to believe that the money will follow. Money is always welcomed, but passion is a far greater motivator. For many students now, computing can be part of their passions. How do we communicate this message?

With limited resources in high schools, is it possible to offer different streams for different computing disciplines? Can schools offer CS as well as IT? Is programming the best entry point for all students interested in CS/IT?

How do we prepare teachers to teach computing and computational thinking? Computer Science is unique in its approach to teacher training. Is it time to develop instructional methods courses for Computer Science and require them in addition to academic background in the area?

Today MIT and Harvard, and many others, are delivering courses online. Most popular for K-12 topics is the freely available Khan Academy [6]. How should teachers integrate these publicly available resources into their facilitation of learning among their students?

## 3. POSITION STATEMENT: KING

One of the central goals of successful outreach at the K-12 level should be to attract more students into college and university programs in IT and Computer Science, and ultimately into careers in these fields. What do we tell students about the differences between the various fields comprising IT and Computing? In our outreach, do we tell students about the differences Information Technology versus Computer Science versus Software Engineering versus Business Technology Management (BTM) versus Computer Engineering versus ...? We probably do not and maybe we should not, but then how do students make the correct choice of program? The picture in Canada is complicated, due to the organizational separation of these programs. IT is usually available only as a college, 2 year diploma subject: no university programs in IT currently exist. And while a number of College-University articulation agreements do exist, they are spotty and are generally not well known or widely used. In many universities, Computer Engineering, Computer Science, and BTM are in different faculties with difficult, or no, articulation between them. My own view

is that the post-secondary education sector in this country should work to remove as many of these artificial barriers as possible. These areas all have considerable overlap in their curricula and we should aim to give students increased flexibility in selecting these programs so that their best interests are being served.

## 4. POSITION STATEMENT: SILVER

There are many barriers to the entry of CS Education in the Canadian school system. Some are straightforward to identify: a focus on technical education that doesn't place CS as a science course; lack of human resources - few teachers with content and pedagogical knowledge about computing; lack of computing curriculum in most provinces; and poor math skills - students opt out of math in Grade 9 because it is not needed for other high paying professions. There are also softer, more challenging barriers that will take time to resolve:

- Misunderstanding: parents and teachers think that our children know about building digital technology because they are knowledgeable about using digital technology

- Culture: many Canadians are not predisposed to high tech jobs and many do not feel that we are able to build high tech companies

- Computing $\neq$ computer literacy: we are great in using ICT as a learning technology; good in using ICT in application domains; terrible at building ICT

- Peer pressure: computing is not seen as being cool

- Women and IT special challenges: culture, greater peer pressure to conform

## 5. ACKNOWLEDGMENTS

The panelists thank the Canadian Association of Computer Science/Association d'Informatique Canadienne (CACS/AIC) for financial support.

## 6. REFERENCES

[1] CCICT. CareerMash. http://careermash.ca/, 2011.
[2] J. Goode, G. Chapman, and J. Margolis. Exploring Computer Science. http://www.exploringcs.org/curriculum, 2009.
[3] S. Greengard. CSEdWeek takes hold. *Communications of the ACM*, 54(12):20, December 2011.
[4] B. Harvey, T. Barnes, and L. Segars. AP CS principles and the 'Beauty and Joy of Computing' curriculum. In *Proceeding SIGCSE '12: Proceedings of the 43rd ACM technical symposium on Computer Science Education*, page 677, 2012.
[5] Joint Task Force for Computing Curricula. Computing Curricula 2005. www.acm.org/education/curric_vols/CC2005-March06Final.pdf.
[6] S. Khan. KhanAcademy. http://www.khanacademy.org/, 2008.
[7] D. Rushkoff. *Program or be Programmed: Ten Commands for a Digital Age*. Soft Skull Press, 2011.
[8] D. Ticoll. Winning the jobs war. *National Post*, October 3 2011.

# Author Index

www.ingramcontent.com/pod-product-compliance
Lightning Source LLC
Chambersburg PA
CBHW061358210326
41598CB00035B/6028